Witch-Hunting and Darwinism

Andreanne Rohan

Contents

Introduction 9

1. Foundations 19
1.1 History and the "hard" natural sciences 19
1.2 History and the "soft" natural sciences 25
1.3 Human nature 31
1.4 Gene-culture coevolution 38
1.5 Culture as a semi-autonomous force 45

2. Functions 53
2.1 The riddles of functionality 53
2.2 The origins of biological functions 59
2.3 The origins of cultural functions 68
2.4 The purposes of biological functions 74
2.5 The purposes of cultural functions 85

3. The theory 97
3.1 Darwinian cultural evolution 97
3.2 Darwinian origins of cultural functions 104
3.3 Intermezzo: Epistemic relativism 113
3.4 Darwinian purposes of cultural functions 124

4. Witch-hunts 137
4.1 Witch-hunts as a case study 137
4.2 The early modern environment 141
4.3 The cumulative concept of witchcraft 150
4.4 The dynamics of witch-hunting 161

5. Explanations 173
5.1 An explanatory problem 173
5.2 Explanatory attempts 184
5.3 Explanatory failures? 190
5.4 The state of the art 198
5.5 Darwinian attempts 204

6. Cases 215
6.1 Wiesensteig 1562 215
6.2 Trier 1582 230
6.3 Ellwangen 1611 246
6.4 Culture's struggle for life 259

7. Reflections 277
7.1 Multifunctional instrumentalization? 277
7.2 What proponents said 292
7.3 What opponents said 310
7.4 "Viral" hunts? 330
7.5 The end of witch-hunting 344

Introduction

As a young boy, the renowned philosopher Daniel Dennett contemplated on the possibility of inventing a "universal acid".[1] With some of his schoolboy friends he fantasized about a liquid so corrosive that it would eat through anything it encountered. Keeping the substance in a glass bottle or a stainless steel canister would be useless for the acid would dissolve its container as readily as a paper bag. What would happen if a liquid like this were invented? Surely, it would transform everything in its path, or so Dennett and his schoolboy friends thought, but would it eventually destroy everything? And what would it leave behind?

An acid like this has never been invented and remained the topic of Dennett's childhood fantasy. But the tale itself has become a classic story of science history, as Dennett believes to have come across a scientific idea that resembles this universal acid. As he professed in 1996, this scientific idea would penetrate anything it encounters. Attempting to put it on hold or restrict it to a certain domain would lead to nothing: "It eats through just about every traditional concept, and leaves in its wake a revolutionized world-view, with most of the old landmarks still recognizable, but transformed in fundamental ways."[2] The idea that Dennett was speaking of is Darwin's theory of evolution by means of natural selection. The theory's key insight is that a mindless process of the selection and accumulation of accidentally adaptive variants can produce adaptations to specific environments. While the process as such has neither intentions nor goals, its outcomes look as if they were intelligently and purposefully designed; it concerns design without designer.[3] In biology, this core idea has found wide acknowledgement. But in his *Darwin's dangerous idea* (1996) Dennett proclaimed that Darwinism reached beyond living nature.[4] To him, the theory was also about the cosmos, the human mind, language, culture, morality, and even the deepest questions about the meaning of existence. The far-reaching implications of the "universal acid" had not yet been fully thought out.

Dennett deserves credit for his predictive abilities. Over the past decades, Darwinian approaches have indeed experienced a significant growth outside biology itself.[5] Evolutionary perspectives on the biological foundations of human behavior have garnered ever more attention in cognitive science and evolutionary psychology.[6] An approach named gene-culture coevolution has shed new light on many human traits.[7] Dennett also saw much potential for Darwinian views on cultural change: "The open question is not whether there will be a Darwinian theory of culture but what shape such a Darwinian theory will take."[8] And indeed, a new and interdisciplinary field

---

[1] Dennett, *Darwin's Dangerous Idea*, 63.
[2] Dennett, 63.
[3] Dennett, *Darwin's Dangerous Idea*; Ayala, "Darwin's Greatest Discovery."
[4] Dennett, *Darwin's Dangerous Idea*.
[5] Buskes, *Evolutionair denken*; Wilson, *Evolution for Everyone*; Stewart-Williams, *The Ape That Understood the Universe*; Bergh, *Human Evolution beyond Biology and Culture*; Frank, *The Darwin Economy*; Ridley, *The Evolution of Everything*.
[6] Buss, *Evolutionary Psychology*; Stewart-Williams, *The Ape That Understood the Universe*.
[7] Henrich, *The Secret of Our Success*; Laland, *Darwin's Unfinished Symphony*.
[8] Dennett, "Foreword," ix.

of cultural evolution is emerging, which aims to analyze cultural change through a Darwinian lens, focusing on processes of variation, selection, and transmission, resulting in adaptations.[9] Through various applications, Darwinian tools and methods are entering disciplines like psychology, linguistics, sociology, anthropology, archeology, and economics. Eventually, or so it is assumed by some proponents, the impact of Darwinian theory on the humanities and social sciences will be similar to the impact it once had on biology.[10]

At the same time, and despite Dennett's claims, much research into cultural phenomena has hardly been affected by the "universal acid". Trained as a qualitative historian myself, I have seldom encountered colleagues who took much notice of the new Darwinian developments, let alone apply them to their own research. There have been some calls amongst historians for more integration, but these have largely fallen on deaf ears.[11] But it is not just in qualitative history that the new Darwinians fail to have much impact. Their influence has remained similarly negligible in other disciplines oriented towards qualitative research. Scholars familiar with the world of cultural symbols, and specialized in interpreting their complex and multilayered meaning have traditionally been wary of science-oriented approaches.[12] The emphasis in these domains is normally on hermeneutics, that is, the interpretation of texts within their historical context. The models from the "hard" natural sciences are thought to be too coarse to do justice to the intricacies and subtleties of human history and socio-cultural life. This assessment puts the new Darwinism at a disadvantage from the start. Moreover, existing reservations are strengthened by the fact that the field of cultural evolution has taken a clear quantitative direction, paying little attention to qualitative methodologies. The response from the 'soft' socio-cultural disciplines has thus mostly been skeptical, or even hostile.[13] "Evolution – is one kind of change, history is another", one current critic puts it.[14] The novel evolutionary approaches are thought either to misrepresent and simplify human history and culture, or to merely rephrase what social scientists and scholars of the humanities knew all along. "Old wine, new bottles", the sociologist Ted Benton remarked.[15]

So, has the "universal acid" reached an impenetrable barrier after all? Is qualitative history, or even qualitative scholarship in general, a domain where Darwinism will fail to make a lasting impact? Or is this verdict premature, and has it not yet been properly assessed how

---

[9] Blute, *Darwinian Sociocultural Evolution*; Mesoudi, *Cultural Evolution*, 2011; Henrich, *The Secret of Our Success*; Wilson, *This View of Life*; Henrich, *The WEIRDest People in the World*.
[10] Hodgson and Knudsen, *Darwin's Conjecture*, x; Mesoudi, *Cultural Evolution*, 2011.
[11] Ferguson, *The Ascent of Money*; Smail, *On Deep History and the Brain*; Mokyr, *A Culture of Growth*.
[12] Collingwood, *The Idea of History*; Geertz, *The Interpretation of Cultures*; Dussen, *Filosofie van de geschiedenis*; Beiser, *The German Historicist Tradition*; Kleinberg, "Just the Facts"; Howell and Prevenier, *From Reliable Sources*, 94.
[13] Kleinberg, "Just the Facts," 98; Howell and Prevenier, *From Reliable Sources*, 133–34; Kuper, "If Memes Are the Answer, What Is the Question?"; Benton, "Social Causes and Natural Relations"; Ingold, "The Trouble with 'Evolutionary Biology'"; Goodheart, *Darwinian Misadventures in the Humanities*; Bloch, "A Well-Disposed Social Anthropologist's Problems with Memes"; Fracchia and Lewontin, "Does Culture Evolve?"; Wilterdink, "Te veel darwinisme, te weinig sociologie"; Kronfeldner, *Darwinian Creativity and Memetics*.
[14] Bryant, "An Evolutionary Social Science?," 489.
[15] Benton, "Social Causes and Natural Relations," 216.

Darwinian theory may actually change and revitalize these domains of academic scholarship? This question will take center stage in this dissertation, which, for this reason, is called *Qualitative Darwinism*. The key question will be as follows: **Can Darwinian theory, and most particularly the idea of Darwinian cultural evolution, renew qualitative historical research?** Does this approach allow us to pose novel questions? Does it have new insights in store for us? The potential integration of Darwinian theory and qualitative historical scholarship deserves consideration since it has hardly been examined. This is a loss, since cultural evolution offers exciting new avenues for historical investigation. Two key ideas will be explored in detail in the chapters that follow.

The first is the idea that culture and society follow a process of Darwinian cultural evolution, resulting in socio-cultural forms of "design without designer".[16] Even in the cultural evolutionary field it is of course widely accepted that human intentions play an important role in how socio-cultural functions, or adaptations, come about. Nevertheless, human intentional design in itself is thought to be an insufficient explanation for all cultural functionalities. In many cases human actors do not recognize how and why certain cultural variants spread, or do not intend them to do so. Similar to genetic mutations, some cultural variants may be accidentally adapted to their environment, without any conscious forethought, intention of recognition. As soon as such chance hits are then cumulatively preserved, they may gradually evolve into cultural adaptations that are neither intended by the actors involved, nor recognized by them as something they had wished for.

The second key idea concerns the question of what cultural adaptations are built *for*. Who or what benefits from them? Scholars of socio-cultural disciplines are traditionally much interested in this question. Do socio-cultural phenomena serve those in power, the needs of individuals, or perhaps social systems? Drawing inspiration from selfish gene theory in evolutionary biology, authors like Daniel Dennett, Richard Dawkins and Susan Blackmore have pointed to possible beneficiaries thus far overlooked: the socio-cultural phenomena themselves.[17] They argue that cultural items may be adapted to serve no ends other than their own "selfish" reproduction. Cultural phenomena can evolve like harmful viruses or other pathogens that spread at the expense of their human hosts.

The methodology
Qualitative historical investigation is indispensable in the examination of these hypotheses. If the latter are to be proven correct, the historical record should offer examples of cultural phenomena with adaptive features that evolved outside of people's intentions and recognition. To examine the issue empirically, we need to compare the apparently adaptive or functional traits of cultural

---

[16] Wilson, *Darwin's Cathedral*, 2002; Dennett, *Breaking the Spell*; Henrich, *The Secret of Our Success*.
[17] Dawkins, "Viruses of the Mind"; Blackmore, *The Meme Machine*; Dennett, *From Bacteria to Bach and Back*; Dennett, *Breaking the Spell*; Dawkins, *The Selfish Gene*, 189–201.

items to the way actors themselves view the functionality of those items. The study of what historical actors did or did not understand requires the kind of tools qualitative hermeneutical historians are traditionally familiar with. We need to comprehend people's intentions, recreate their thoughts in our own minds, and interpret the rich symbolic worlds they were living in.

The claim that cultural phenomena can spread "selfishly", while harming the interests of their hosts, also raises the question of whether the historical record provides convincing examples. The Darwinian proposal that cultural phenomena can resemble pathogens is highly contested even in the field of cultural evolution itself, mostly for theoretical reasons.[18] But why not simply examine it? The hypothesis contains many components that demand qualitative answers. How are we to understand and define 'benefits' or 'harm', and in what way should we relate that to the understanding of the actors involved?

To concretely address such theoretical and empirical issues, this dissertation will delve into one case study: early modern European witch persecutions. These notorious trials mostly occurred between 1430 and 1750 and constituted a complex phenomenon rife with interpretative difficulties.[19] Since the rich symbolic worldview underlying the early-modern hunts may appear alien today, understanding it requires applying the tools that qualitative history has to offer. Witchcraft scholarship traditionally combines empirical precision with theoretical sophistication. Yet, despite lavish academic attention, certain dimensions of the persecutions remain mysterious. One is that beliefs and practices regarding witchcraft, as they developed from the fifteenth to the early seventeenth centuries, were remarkably well adapted to creating ever larger witch trials. We might think of the idea of the witches' sabbath, the witches' nightly flight, the idea of child witches, or the practice of using torture to uncover witches' hidden identities. In the past, historians thus often assumed that witchcraft concepts and trials were intelligently designed for ulterior purposes. They pointed to such things as financial gain, the strengthening of clerical power, the oppression of women, or the destruction of traditional peasant culture.[20] More recently, however, many experts have concluded that the people responsible for the persecutions were genuinely afraid of witches, while the trials occurred in a rather unplanned and haphazard manner.[21] Moreover, the effects of witch persecutions often appear to have been dysfunctional. But if this is so, how did the witch-hunting phenomenon become so well adapted to its environment, and why did it recur so often over such a long time? In what follows, I will explore the Darwinian possibility that the witch-hunt system itself was a culturally evolved "design without designer", that spread in a virus-like manner to the detriment of its human hosts.

---

[18] Lewens, *Cultural Evolution*, 2015.
[19] Levack, *The Witch-Hunt in Early Modern Europe*; Dillinger, *Hexen und Magie*, 2018; Briggs, *Witches & Neighbours*; Rummel and Voltmer, *Hexen und Hexenverfolgung*.
[20] Hansen, *Zauberwahn, Inquisition und Hexenproceß im Mittelalter*; Muchembled, *Sorcières*; Barstow, *Witchcraze*; Currie, "Crimes without Criminals"; Heinsohn and Steiger, *Die Vernichtung der weisen Frauen*.
[21] Dillinger, *Hexen und Magie*, 2018; Behringer, *Hexenverfolgung in Bayern*; Goodare, *The European Witch-Hunt*; Briggs, *Witches & Neighbours*; Scarre, *Witchcraft and Magic*; Beliën and Eerden, *Satans trawanten*.

By integrating Darwinian insights with qualitative historical scholarship, this dissertation draws heavily on different disciplines, above all history and biology. Interdisciplinary ventures such as this are known to come with risks.[22] Researchers from different fields often lack understanding of each other's concepts, use terms differently, or work within paradigms that can be mutually exclusive. Moreover, the boundaries between disciplines are often vehemently defended as soon as the respective practitioners feel they are under threat. Such responses certainly apply to efforts of taking Darwinism beyond biology. But at the same time, interdisciplinary endeavors are worth the effort. "We are not students of some subject matter, but students of problems. And problems may cut right across the boundaries of any subject matter or discipline", Karl Popper maintained.[23] Disciplines normally have their own methodological precision and investigatory depths, but black spots are inevitable. A look beyond disciplinary boundaries may thus offer crucial inspiration; it is no coincidence that Charles Darwin gained insights from geology, demography, physics, linguistics and political economy in developing his groundbreaking theory of evolution.[24] As many interdisciplinary scholars have stressed, we should not think of interdisciplinary research as a one way street. When disciplines take stock of each other's understandings, and find common ground that allows for greater integration, all of them reap the benefits. This is exactly what this dissertation aims at; not only will qualitative history gain new insights, but so will the field of cultural evolution.

Outline of the dissertation
The unusual, interdisciplinary character of this project has some consequences for how the dissertation is organized. Historians have often been wary of theory; the illustrious Dutch historian Johan Huizinga once cautioned his colleagues not to use more than a teaspoon of it.[25] For my thesis, however, theoretical considerations are crucial. The first three of the seven chapters are therefore entirely devoted to general theory. This theoretical groundwork is necessary to subsequently apply Darwinism to the witch-hunt case study in a comprehensible way. Many of the terms central to the analysis, like culture, adaptation, or function, can mean different things to different people. So, the definitions must be clear. Moreover, while this is primarily a historical dissertation – written by a historian, for historians – it also has an multidisciplinary audience in mind, especially including scholars from the field of cultural evolution. As a consequence, the text may sometimes dwell on things that will seem overly obvious to historians, like the history and peculiarities of the profession, the need for qualitative research, or a basic understanding of the early modern period. On the other hand, since many historians are largely unaware of Darwinian insights, some necessary elaborations on that topic

---

[22] Rutting et al., *An Introduction to Interdisciplinary Research*; Repko, *Interdisciplinary Research*.
[23] Quoted in: Rutting et al., *An Introduction to Interdisciplinary Research*, 13.
[24] Depew and Weber, *Darwinism Evolving*, 31–166; Bowler, *Evolution*, 141–76.
[25] Otterspeer, *Orde en trouw*, 167.

will appear superfluous to experts in evolution. Hopefully, the reading will not require too much perseverance on either side of the disciplinary divide.

The first chapter, "Foundations", dissects some of the first difficulties that any Darwinian approach to history will find on its path. At the start I grapple with the long standing division between history and 'hard' science. What grounds do historians have to have been traditionally so dismissive towards approaches that draw inspiration from the natural sciences? We will see that many past concerns may well have been legitimate, but that current insights from the natural sciences, especially evolutionary biology, are no longer as unfitting for history as they perhaps once were. Things that historians traditionally hold dear, like complexity, contingency, and irregularity, are now much more appreciated *within* the natural sciences. In the same chapter I will address the various ways in which Darwinian theory encroaches on the human and socio-cultural disciplines. I shall review the manner in which scientists have studied our evolved human nature, and processes of gene-culture coevolution. The analysis of our biological predispositions, and how they interact with culture, is the most obvious way of applying Darwinian theory outside of biology. These approaches also provide building blocks for the framework as it will be adopted here. The key topic in this dissertation, however, is cultural evolution as a semi-autonomous process. I will thus address on what grounds culture can be considered a semi-independent phenomenon that also deserves to be studied in its own right.

The second chapter then delves into a concept of essential importance here: functions. The observation that cultural phenomena can be functional, or adaptive, is a precondition for the key hypotheses mentioned above. So, what are functions? How do they come into being? And what are they for? Scholars of cultural evolution have been accused of too often ignoring established insights, and to operate as if they were the first to study the socio-cultural world.[26] This objection is not entirely unjustified, so this chapter will thoroughly engage itself with the insights already available. How have social scientists and scholars of the humanities analyzed the functionality of socio-cultural phenomena so far? Questions regarding functions, and especially the relation between functions and human meaning-making, have been addressed most explicitly by sociologists and anthropologists. Their theories will thus receive the lion's share of attention. Established views on the origin and purposes of socio-cultural functions will be compared with the way biologists have dealt with similar questions regarding functions in living nature.

These comparisons lay the groundwork for chapter three, which introduces the theory of Darwinian cultural evolution. It will be argued that insights from Darwinian evolutionary biology can indeed offer breakthroughs in long-standing, unresolved issues. Many older approaches, like Durkheimian functionalism or Marxism, have already assumed that socio-cultural phenomena possess unintended and unrecognized functions – that is, they exist due to effects that the actors involved did not observe as such. Cultural Darwinian theory can now provide an explanation for

---

[26] Ingold, "The Trouble with 'Evolutionary Biology'"; Benton, "Social Causes and Natural Relations."

the manner in which such functions arise. Moreover, the idea of cultural phenomena spreading "selfishly" opens up a fundamentally new investigatory dimension. Importantly, the explanatory models that are proposed make a distinction between the unreal effects of cultural phenomena, which are perceived as real by involved actors, and their real effects, which are perceived as such by scientists. This distinction, however, is bound to raise eyebrows among socio-cultural scholars today with a relativist orientation; they are likely to consider it epistemologically unwarranted. An intermediate section in chapter three will address these objections.

Chapters four to seven then thoroughly explore the witch-hunt case study. Chapter four introduces witch-hunting itself. In what kind of an environment did these persecutions flourish? What did beliefs about witchcraft look like, and how did those beliefs affect the course of witchcraft trials? Chapter five addresses the innumerable approaches that have been taken to make sense of, or explain, witchcraft persecutions. The chapter culminates in the proposal of witch-hunting as an evolved 'design without designer' that spread 'contagiously'. This scenario assumes that cultural variants that *accidentally* created larger witch-hunts cumulatively survived because of that enhancing effect. Chapter six examines how this purported selection process may have operated concretely, mainly by looking at interactions between beliefs and trials in Germany from 1560 to 1630. This was the time and place where witch-hunting experienced its greatest surge. After a pioneering study from 1972 by Erik Midelfort on persecutions in southwest Germany, these trials have been studied minutely, which provided helpful guidance for this investigation.[27] Lastly, chapter seven offers some critical reflections on the application of cultural evolution to witch-hunting. It begins with the most challenging alternative model, developed by various German historians. The latter postulate that witchcraft accusations and trials were instrumentalized for multifunctional ulterior purposes. In subsequent sections I then scrutinize a range of primary sources to see for which of the interpretations those sources provide the best clues. I then consider the comparison between witch-hunts and contagious disease, and the dissertation ends with the question of why the persecutions eventually ceased.

The chapters dealing with the case study mostly rely on secondary literature on witch trials, especially publications in English and German. But there is also a thorough engagement with primary sources, mostly in German, often in French, and occasionally in English and Dutch. Many important sources from the time period were written in Latin, but fortunately I was able to rely on early-modern and modern translations into English, German or French. This dissertation does not break new ground with respect to primary sources. Many historians of witch trials have studied original material in archives, but that has not been the case here. The originality of the empirical component lies in new questions and theoretical re-interpretations, using sources already familiar to the field.

---

[27] Midelfort, *Witch Hunting in Southwestern Germany*. For further studies, see especially the series *Reihe Hexenforschung* and *Trierer Hexenprozesse: Quellen und Darstellungen*.

The hazards of social-Darwinism

Before we start, some words on a thorny issue are in order. That applications of Darwinism outside biology so often face skepticism is partly the consequence of important moral and political considerations. Often lumped together under the label "social-Darwinism", earlier attempts at extending Darwinian insights to humans and their societies have been associated with horrific ideological derailments.[28] "One general law, leading to the advancement of all organic beings, namely, multiply, vary, let the strongest live and the weakest die", was Darwin's vision in his *On the Origin of Species* from 1859.[29] He spoke of a "struggle for existence" and a "war of nature", interpreting competition and death in a rather positive light.[30] Darwin presented struggle as the creative force behind the evolution of the "most exalted object which we are capable of conceiving, namely, the production of the higher animals".[31] Certain scholars who oppose application of the theory to the socio-cultural domain argue that Darwin's ideas have provided inspiration to organize human societies along harsh ideological lines.[32] Darwinian theory has been linked to the eugenic movement, starvation of the poor, ruthless capitalism, colonialism, Nazism and imaginations of racial superiority. In her book on race science, Angela Saini does not seek its roots only in Darwinism, but she does consider the theory to be a significant factor.[33] The American historian Richard Weikart devoted much of his career to demonstrating how Darwinian thought helped to give shape to Nazi ideology. *From Darwin to Hitler* is the telling title of one of his books, and Weikart maintains that Darwinism offers an essential key for understanding why the Nazis acted so evilly.[34]

Conversely, some proponents of broader applications of Darwinian theory play down such past harmful ideological consequences.[35] In Kevin Laland's and Gillian Brown's view, past ideologies have used "crude distortions of Darwin's theory, which derive more from the work of other 19th-century intellectuals such as Jean Lamarck and Herbert Spencer, although it is Darwin's name that is often unfairly linked to these views."[36] David Sloan Wilson speaks of "the myth of social Darwinism", stating that it dishonestly smears the theory and hinders scientific understanding.[37] Indeed, there are good arguments for this line of defense.[38] Darwin had little to

---

[28] Hawkins, *Social Darwinism in European and American Thought 1860-1945*; Hermans, *De dwaaltocht van het sociaal-darwinisme*; Browne, "Charles Darwin and ideology."
[29] Darwin, *The Origin of Species*, 263.
[30] Darwin, 114, 459.
[31] Darwin, 459.
[32] Weikart, "The Role of Darwinism in Nazi Racial Thought"; Hofstadter, *Social Darwinism in American Thought, 1860-1915*; Weikart, *Hitler's Ethic*; Pichot, *La société pure*; Yahya, *The Evolution Deceit*.
[33] Saini, *Superior*.
[34] Weikart, *From Darwin to Hitler*.
[35] Wilson, *This View of Life*; Laland and Brown, *Sense and Nonsense*; Richards, *The Tragic Sense of Life*; Richards, *Was Hitler a Darwinian?*
[36] Laland and Brown, *Sense and Nonsense*, 19.
[37] Wilson, *This View of Life*, 16–34.
[38] Theunissen, "Sociaal-darwinisme"; Allen Orr, "Darwin and Darwinism"; O'Connell and Ruse, *Social Darwinism*.

say on politics, but one political topic that *did* greatly motivate him was the abolition of slavery.[39] Moreover, the ideologies mentioned also drew inspiration from countless other sources. Darwinism has provided guidance for all sorts of persuasions, not all of them callous or evil. This suggests that it was not necessarily the theory that brought people to certain ideas, but that the theory was also used as a pretext for convictions that people already held for other reasons. Importantly, key Nazis like Hitler or Himmler did not explicitly refer to Darwin at all; Himmler's worldview, for instance, was highly spiritualist.[40]

At the same time, however, this defensive response is a little too facile, as there are certainly links between Darwin's work and crude political programs. Darwin's personal friends, like his nephew Francis Galton and his colleague Ernst Haeckel, did use elements of his theory to legitimize political proposals that aimed to remove the weak from society.[41] Leading German Darwinists, like again Haeckel, or Friedrich Ratzel, also popularized terms such as "Lebenswerth" (life worth) and "Lebensraum" (living space) that would later influence Nazi thought.[42] In his role as a Darwin enthusiast, Daniel Dennett is therefore right in being somewhat more self-critical: "It is important to recognize that Darwinism has always had an unfortunate power to attract the most unwelcome enthusiasts – demagogues and psychopaths and misanthropes and other abusers of Darwin's dangerous idea."[43]

How then to deal with this tainted history? Let us first remind ourselves that we should not succumb to the moralistic fallacy, which holds that normative claims can justify factual claims – something is supposed to be a particular way because it morally ought to be that way.[44] Yet, whether something is true or false does not in any way depend on what we like to be true on moral grounds. Still, academic scholars have a responsibility to treat delicate topics with care, and to be aware of the moral hazards that their scientific ideas might bring. At various points this dissertation will thus reflect on the possibly harmful ideological ramifications of current Darwinian ideas, for instance, in the case of gene-culture coevolution, or with regard to the viral analogy. But reassuringly, the reader will find out that this dissertation mostly elaborates on ideas that differ greatly from the old social Darwinism. In fact, the ideas may even carry the promise of enhancing human welfare.[45]

It is now time to develop an argument that aims to expand our comprehension of sociocultural processes. Hopefully it will become apparent that the approach advanced here is neither about reducing cultural complexity to some lower-level explanation, or about making qualitative history subservient to "hard" science. On the contrary, the aim is to give qualitative

---

[39] Desmond and Moore, *Darwin's Sacred Cause*.
[40] Richards, *Was Hitler a Darwinian?*, 192–243; Kurlander, *Hitler's Monsters*.
[41] Hermans, *De dwaaltocht van het sociaal-darwinisme*, 331–59, 449–90; Haeckel, *Die Welträtsel*; Hawkins, *Social Darwinism in European and American Thought 1860-1945*, 216–48.
[42] Haeckel, *Die Welträtsel*, 442-72."Lebenswerth"; Ratzel, *Der Lebensraum*.
[43] Dennett, *Darwin's Dangerous Idea*, 264.
[44] Stewart-Williams, *The Ape That Understood the Universe*, 164, 284.
[45] Norman, *Mental Immunity*.

methodologies a new relevance, and to make our understanding of humanity's meaningful and symbolic worlds more multifaceted and sophisticated. In his recent book with the appealing title *Darwin's Unfinished Symphony*, Kevin Laland stated, concerning the Darwinian prospects, that: "Far from destroying culture, our understanding of the underlying science feeds back to make the historical analysis richer and less mysterious."[46] I could not agree more.

---

[46] Laland, *Darwin's Unfinished Symphony*, 320.

Chapter 1: Foundations

1.1 History and the "hard" natural sciences

In a speech at the university of Strasbourg on 1 May 1894, the German philosopher Wilhelm Windelband presented a distinction that he believed marked the essential difference between history and the natural sciences.[1] At the time, Windelband was not the only one seeking a philosophical foundation undergirding the separation of scientific domains.[2] His colleague and compatriot Wilhelm Dilthey had already introduced a division between the so called *Geisteswissenschaften*, the sciences of the spirit or the mind, and *Naturwissenschaften*, the sciences of the natural world. Windelband found this division unsatisfying, as some of the disciplines that studied the human mind, like psychology, used methods that were more akin to the natural sciences. His proposal was thus not to make a distinction in the kinds of objects that were studied, but, rather, in the method of studying them. While the natural sciences searched for general laws, history focused on individual and unique events. Windelband described it as a distinction between *nomothetic* inquiry versus *idiographic* inquiry, and his conceptual pairing would become a lasting success; it continues to be used to this day.[3]

During the lecture Windelband painted a cold picture of the natural sciences. It was a world of abstractions, timeless immutability, mathematical formulations, and deterministic necessity. Natural scientists had no interest in anything transient, and a single object was only relevant to them insofar as it served the formulation of a general law. Historical scholars, on the other hand, cared about "the loving expression of the particular", aiming to evoke rich images of humankind in all its peculiar forms and individual liveliness.[4] The German philosopher painted a warm picture of how historians studied people's past languages, faiths, values, poetry, thought, and struggles for power and freedom. The gap between the two domains of knowledge was deep and irreconcilable. It brought him to the conclusion that "the law and the event will remain the last incommensurable entities of our worldview."[5] His philosophical colleague Heinrich Rickert soon elaborated upon the distinction, maintaining that historical scholars neither could, nor *wanted*, to generalize along the lines of the natural sciences.[6]

The two philosophers were defending one of the most significant intellectual achievements of the nineteenth century, which often goes under the name of historicism.[7] This academic movement mostly took shape in Germany and brought historical scholarship to

---

[1] Windelband, *Geschichte Und Naturwissenschaft*; Jaeger and Rüsen, *Geschichte des Historismus*, 151–56.
[2] Jaeger and Rüsen, *Geschichte des Historismus*, 146–51.
[3] Kleinberg, "Just the Facts"; Vries, "Changing the Narrative," 322.
[4] Windelband, *Geschichte Und Naturwissenschaft*, 16. "der liebevollen Ausprägung des Besonderen."
[5] Windelband, 27. "Das Gesetz und das Ereignis bleiben als letzte, incommensurable Grössen unserer Weltvorstellung nebeneinander bestehen."
[6] Rickert, *Kulturwissenschaft und Naturwissenschaft*, 54.
[7] Jaeger and Rüsen, *Geschichte des Historismus*; Collingwood, *The Idea of History*; Iggers, *Historiography*, 23–30; Tollebeek, "Het Duitse debat"; Beiser, *The German Historicist Tradition*.

unprecedented levels of professionalization and sophistication. Obviously, the historicists were not the first to study the past.[8] What had made them different though, was that they no longer understood historical people, institutions or events against a rather ahistorical background, but tried to comprehend how all human creations undergo historical change. A desire to distinguish oneself from the natural sciences was not there from the beginning; some of the early exponents of the movement, like Johann Gottfried Herder and Friedrich Carl von Savigny, drew inspiration from the organic, irregular development of plants or animals.[9] Nations, religions, languages, or systems of law were thought to have no immutable essences, but to be fundamentally malleable and always connected to a particular historical context. In the hands of the historicists, the eternal categories that had been taken for granted before, dissolved into continuous flux. Apart from being an intellectual revolution, it was also an institutional revolution, as history, for the first time, established itself as a separate discipline at universities with professional historians studying the past for its own sake.

The best known representative of the movement that Windelband and Rickert were defending was the Berlin professor of history Leopold von Ranke, often considered the founding father of the discipline.[10] In Ranke's view, history ranked amongst the sciences, as its first demand was the "pure love of truth" and its final aim "to show how, essentially, things happened."[11] Yet, it was a distinct form of science at the same time, as it turned sympathetically to the particular. Ranke distanced himself from grand philosophical theories that painted history in broad strokes and along generalizing lines. Instead, he wanted to stay as close as possible to the subjects that he studied. Historical epochs were to be understood within their own terms. Through the critical and meticulous examination of historical sources, preferably in archives, Ranke aimed to reconstruct the concrete intentions and thoughts of individual human beings. Since history was a messy affair, it was up to the historian to get an intuitive understanding of things and to turn events into a coherent chronological story. History was to be told as a narrative, making it not only a science, but an art at the same time. Ranke called for attention to be paid to various aspects of society, but in the end it was political and diplomatic history, and the unique development of individual nation states, that interested him the most. In an age of emerging nation states, this model of history proved to be in tune with its own historical context, as it was copied by universities throughout the western world.

However, by the late nineteenth century philosophers like Dilthey, Windelband and Rickert felt a need to defend this tradition, as it was increasingly under pressure from another model of doing history. The nineteenth century had also witnessed a continuing ascent of natural science, which achieved new triumphs in its ability to predict and control nature. The

---

[8] Wiersing, *Geschichte des historischen Denkens*, 36–313.
[9] Beiser, *The German Historicist Tradition*, 105, 136, 151, 250.
[10] Ranke, *The Theory and Practice of History*; Jaeger and Rüsen, *Geschichte des Historismus*, 81–86, 92–95; Iggers, *Historiography*, 1–3, 23–27; Bentley, *Modern Historiography*, 36–43; Tollebeek, "Het Duitse debat," 17–21.
[11] Ranke, *The Theory and Practice of History*, 39, xix, xx.

development made a growing number of scholars eager to extend those successes into the domain of human society.[12] The hero of the "hard" natural sciences, Isaac Newton, once expressed some skepticism in this regard when stating that he could "calculate the motions of the heavenly bodies, but not the madness of people."[13] Many nineteenth-century thinkers were growing more confident though. Take Karl Marx, who proclaimed to have uncovered history's ultimate laws of how material conditions and class struggle determined the inevitable collapse of capitalism and the establishment of socialism.[14] In France, Auguste Comte had created a positivist science of society, sociology, which aimed to find the general causal explanations for social processes. Herbert Spencer and Emile Durkheim soon followed in Comte's footsteps, making derogatory comments about the work of their historical colleagues.[15] According to the sociologists, historians only focused on "series of accidents", like "court intrigues, plots, usurpations, or the like", and their highest relevance lay in furnishing the materials for a comparative sociology.[16] Durkheim warned that if historians failed to learn sociological lessons, they would "fall into idle erudition".[17] Some historians decided to jump on the bandwagon of a more scientific history, like Hippolyte Taine, who claimed that "vices and virtues are products like vitriol and sugar", or Thomas Buckle, who was after nothing less than "fixed and universal laws".[18]

Around 1890 the situation came to a head when a history professor in Germany broke the historicist consensus in his country.[19] Karl Lamprecht aimed to unveil the social and material collective forces, and "biogenetic fundamental laws", that underlay the allegedly superficial events that his colleagues were studying.[20] The response of the German historical establishment was vitriolic, triggering one of the most bitter conflicts in the history of the profession. This so called *Methodenstreit*, "the methods dispute", provided the context in which Windelband and Dilthey came to the historians' defense. Their dichotomy between disciplines was only one amongst many attempts to demarcate history's terrain. Another famous distinction assumed that the natural sciences aimed at *erklären* (explaining), meaning the search for causal connections between facts, whereas historians focused on *verstehen* (understanding), referring to the interpretation of people's meaningful intentions within a historical context. While early historicists had drawn inspiration from the natural sciences, over the course of the nineteenth century historicism came to see itself in opposition to "hard" natural science.[21] Looking back on

---

[12] Bentley, *Modern Historiography*, 43–52; Tollebeek, "Het Duitse debat."
[13] Kaul, *Easy Money*, 87.
[14] Wiersing, *Geschichte des historischen Denkens*, 395–413.
[15] Durkheim, *Cours de science sociale. Leçon d'ouverture*, 5–6, 20; Spencer, *Herbert Spencer on Social Evolution*, 83–96; Burke, *History and Social Theory*, 6–9.
[16] Durkheim, *Cours de science sociale. Leçon d'ouverture*, 6."une suite d'accidents"; Spencer, *Herbert Spencer on Social Evolution*, 36.
[17] Durkheim, *Cours de science sociale. Leçon d'ouverture*, 20.' "il tombe dans la vain érudition."
[18] Tollebeek, "Het Duitse debat," 27."Le vice et la vertu sont des produits comme le vitriol et le sucre."
[19] Jaeger and Rüsen, *Geschichte des Historismus*, 141–46; Iggers, *Historiography*, 31–34; Tollebeek, "Het Duitse debat"; Wiersing, *Geschichte des historischen Denkens*, 459–79.
[20] Jaeger and Rüsen, *Geschichte des Historismus*, 145."biogenetischen Grundgesetzen."
[21] Beiser, *The German Historicist Tradition*.

these efforts with sympathy, the twentieth-century philosopher Robin Collingwood later described it as history's effort of "liberating itself from the tyranny of natural science."[22]

The outcome of the *Methodenstreit* was that the historical establishment in Germany largely kept their discipline clean from nomothetic approaches. The model of a more scientific history turned out to be a formidable opponent though. Social sciences like economics, psychology and sociology, established themselves at universities, sometimes combining a "hard" scientific orientation with an interest in history. Beyond Germany, history departments also offered room for new approaches.[23] The most influential movement of the twentieth century, the Annales-school, took shape in France and aimed to move beyond Rankean history.[24] Fernand Braudel, one of its leading figures, somewhat disdainfully described the work of his nineteenth-century colleague as "l'histoire evenementielle" (the history of events). In his view it only focused on political oscillations and superficial excitements.[25] Instead, Braudel explored the "abysmal depths" of history, like the deep patterns of civilizations, the immobile structures of geographical and climatic constraints, the slow rhythms of economic conjunctures, or the regularities of social and mental processes.[26] He aimed to uncover the interconnections of *all* human activities, and in that spirit Braudel argued for a constructive rapprochement to the social sciences. It would not only make history more scientific, but the social sciences more historical.

There were more twentieth-century schools that sought to model history more closely after the "hard" scientific model.[27] Marxist history gained widespread traction with its claim that economic conditions determined social, political and cultural developments. Mid-twentieth-century philosophers of history became interested in a so called "covering law model", which was developed by the philosopher Carl Hempel. It focused on deduction from predictive laws of history.[28] By the 1960s some nomothetically oriented historians even managed to breach the walls of historicist dominance in Germany, like Ulrich Wehler, who called for a "historical social science" that studied the transformation and modernization of social structures.[29] There was a new thirst for quantitative methods – "history that is not quantifiable cannot claim to be scientific" stated the Annales historian Emmanuel Le Roy Ladurie – and the new opportunities afforded by computers attracted lively interest.[30] Overall, the era was characterized by a widespread confidence that major problems of historical explanation would soon be resolved.

But the relationship between the nomothetic and the idiographic bears some resemblance to the tides; just as the structural models reached an unprecedented peak in the

---

[22] Collingwood, *The Idea of History*, 193.
[23] Iggers, *Historiography*, 33–47; Bentley, *Modern Historiography*, 81–101.
[24] Jaeger and Rüsen, *Geschichte des Historismus*, 173–80; Iggers, *Historiography*, 51–64; Burke, *The French Historical Revolution*; Braudel, *Ecrits sur l'histoire*.
[25] Braudel, *Ecrits sur l'histoire*, 22–23.
[26] Braudel, 24."Dans leurs profondeurs abyssales."
[27] Iggers, *Historiography*, 3–5, 65–96; Vries, "Changing the Narrative," 313.
[28] Lorenz, *De constructie van het verleden*, 61–68; Nickles, "Covering Law Explanation."
[29] Jaeger and Rüsen, *Geschichte des Historismus*, 181–85; Iggers, *Historiography*, 65–77.
[30] Iggers, *Historiography*, 44.

1970s, a counter-movement was already in the making.[31] In 1979 the historian Lawrence Stone captured a new mood when publishing a landmark article named "The Revival of Narrative".[32] For quite some time Stone had been working on quantitative social history himself, but by now he expressed a widely shared feeling that the grand theories had failed to deliver. Many historians were fed up with what Stone called "turgid and excruciatingly dull tomes full of tables of figures, abstruse algebraic equations and percentages given to two decimal places."[33] What followed was "a return of the event", "a return of the actor", and a new focus on the discontinuities, contingency, diversity, and otherness of the past. Historians wanted to tell stories again, and give history a more human face. It was no longer the material conditions that mattered, but how people experienced those conditions. Some Italian historians received wide acclaim with their method of *Microstoria*, which studied specific people and events from a "microscopic" perspective.[34]

The model of scientific history was dismissed as naïve, or even as a myth, and the word "science" came to be used in an ironic tone of voice.[35] A problem of the generalizing theoretical models, at least according to opponents, was that they were either too vague, or too false on many details.[36] As soon as general theories made information-rich predictions about specific processes, it always turned out that historical reality was more complex and that there were too many exceptions for a general rule to work. However, if the theories were then re-designed to account for those complexities, they became so very abstract and meaningless that they evaporated into thin air. In 1884 the philosopher Friedrich Nietzsche already described the search for general principles of history as "a neat balancing act between falsehood and tautology."[37] By the late 1970s this problem seemed more apparent than ever before.

The revival of narrative did not imply a return to Rankean political and diplomatic history. Most of all it was cultural history that won the day, with its interest in the interpretation of language, rituals, and symbolic meaning.[38] New inspiration was drawn from highly idiographic and qualitative forms of cultural anthropology, like the methodology of "thick description", as developed by Clifford Geertz.[39] In contrast to "thin description", which only describes human behavior, "thick description" aims to interpret the complex layers of meaning of human behavior within its socio-cultural contexts. It inspired a plethora of qualitative historical studies, focusing on idiosyncratic topics like the symbolic meaning of cat-slapping in an eighteenth-century Parisian neighborhood, or the disappearance and reappearance of a certain sixteenth-century

---

[31] Vries, "Changing the Narrative," 314–22; Iggers, *Historiography*, 10–16, 97–140; Jonker, *Historie*, 30–31, 116–18.
[32] Stone, "The Revival of Narrative."
[33] Stone, 12.
[34] Ginzburg, "Microhistory."
[35] Stone, "The Revival of Narrative"; Vries, "Changing the Narrative," 315.
[36] Berlin, "History and Theory."
[37] Nietzsche, *Die Geburt der Tragödie ; Unzeitgemässe Betrachtungen*, 287."zwischen Tautologie und Widersinn künstlich schwebende."
[38] Stone, "The Revival of Narrative," 17; Burke, *What Is Cultural History?*, 32–51.
[39] Geertz, *The Interpretation of Cultures*.

French peasant.[40] Some historians took their rejection of science even further and relativized the idea of historians studying history as it really happened.[41] Take the English historian Keith Jenkins, who wrote that "when we study history we are not studying the past but what historians have constructed about the past."[42] His American colleague Hayden White – who is often labelled as belonging to the postmodern movement – went to lengths to compare the works of historians to the writings of novelists, also maintaining that there are no theoretical grounds on which one can judge one narrative as more realistic than the others. Hence, "the best grounds for choosing one perspective on history rather than another are ultimately aesthetic or moral rather than epistemological".[43] This relativist move went too far to the taste of many other historians, who still remain committed to the idea that their stories need to be based in factual reality.[44] But the popularity of postmodernism illustrates how deep the schism between "history" and "science" had become.

But, as I said, the changing relationship between the nomothetic and the idiographic bears some resemblance to the tides, and there are indications that the tide is turning again.[45] The economic historian Jan de Vries observes how historians "are emerging from the comfortable refuge that their predecessors occupied nearly forty years ago." He sees them move away from narrative, micro, and subjectivist histories, towards a "coherent, causal explanation of societal change." De Vries senses a re-appreciation for "the value of theory-informed, systematic, comparative historical study."[46] In a similar vein, a *History Manifesto* by David Armitage and Jo Guldi calls for a renewed focus on big data and long-term processes, referring positively to Fernand Braudel. The historian Ethan Kleinberg, on the other hand, criticizes the new turn towards the sciences, warning his colleagues not to subordinate or sublimate "the practice of history to a fantasy of 'scientific method'."[47] After all, historical inquiry has rendered general laws problematic, which is why historians should stick to their idiographic and interpretative methods.[48] If not, they will run the risk of erasing themselves in an unconditional surrender.[49] The days of the *Methodenstreit* are long gone, and much has happened since then. But if we look at some of today's arguments it still looks pretty much like 1894.

Hence, as we watch the tides of nomothetic and idiographic orientations move back and forth, the gap between the two forms of history may seem unbridgeable. It raises questions about the prospects of this project. After all, the aim here is to integrate the scientifically oriented

---

[40] Darnton, *The Great Cat Massacre*; Davis, *The Return of Martin Guerre*.
[41] Iggers, *Historiography*, 10–14; Thompson, *Postmodernism and History*; Jenkins, *Re-Thinking History*.
[42] Jenkins, *Re-Thinking History*, 56.
[43] White, *Metahistory*, xii.
[44] Iggers, *Historiography*, 15, 133–40; Elton, *Return to Essentials*; Evans, *In Defense of History*; Appleby, Hunt, and Jacob, *Telling the Truth about History*.
[45] Vries, "Changing the Narrative."
[46] Vries, 330, 32, 33.
[47] Kleinberg, "Just the Facts," 99.
[48] Kleinberg, "Just the Facts."
[49] Kleinberg, 100.

field of cultural evolution with qualitative historical scholarship. Considering the depth and age of the divide, the universal acid of Darwinism is confronted with a formidable barrier indeed. Yet, there might still be an opening. It does not lie in finally making one model dominant over the other. Rather, it is a more critical look at this old distinction between the nomothetic and the idiographic that may help us bridge the gap. Because interestingly, through all the skirmishes, this division itself has remained largely uncontested. Scholars disagree about the methodological course that history should take, but not necessarily about what the underlying landscape of possibilities looks like.

It almost goes without saying that on one side of the spectrum we find the model of the "hard" natural sciences, with its universal laws, macro perspectives, structures, determinism, quantification and abstraction. On the other side we find the "soft" hermeneutic model of qualitative interpretation, meaning, events, intentionality, contingency, irregularity and complexity. Auguste Comte once classified the sciences as a ladder, from mathematics, astronomy, physics, chemistry, biology, to sociology, and it is not by accident that the philosopher Isaiah Berlin, who belonged to the opposing idiographic camp, gave him some credit for that.[50] Berlin characterized it as "rungs in a descending order of comprehensiveness and precision, and in an ascending order of concreteness and detail."[51] Being the richest and most elastic of the disciplines, it was natural for Berlin to place history at the most distant position from the natural sciences. Within this paradigm it also makes sense to place the social sciences somewhere in between.[52] The historical sociologist Max Weber, for instance, saw sociology as a mixed discipline that combined the methods of *verstehen* and *erklären*. Weber was interested in the meaningful and irrational aspects of human behavior, but tried to make his approach more scientific by capturing those aspects in ideal types, structures, and regularities.[53]

But do these dichotomies from the nineteenth century still make sense in 2022? Should a further integration of history and the sciences inevitably depend on models that turn history into something more abstract, inflexible, and deterministic? Fortunately, things do not have to be like that at all, as the natural sciences have developed a much "softer" side. This side has been disregarded by historians for far too long, so we will now explore what it looks like.

1.2 History and the "soft" natural sciences

When Windelband and Rickert created their distinction in the late nineteenth century, they already admitted that it was actually somewhat outdated.[54] Geologists like James Hutton and Charles Lyell had already shown long before that Earth's surface undergoes slow and continuing processes of upheaval, erosion, and sedimentation, or, in other words, change. Since 1859,

---
[50] Berlin, "History and Theory."
[51] Berlin, 16.
[52] Jonker, *Historie*, 16–18.
[53] Weber, *Wirtschaft Und Gesellschaft*; Jaeger and Rüsen, *Geschichte des Historismus*, 156–60; Iggers, *Historiography*, 39, 44.
[54] Windelband, *Geschichte Und Naturwissenschaft*, 12–13; Rickert, *Kulturwissenschaft und Naturwissenschaft*, 7, 107–11.

Darwin's biological theory of descent by modification had also made science's view of living nature more malleable. Darwin assumed that all the branches of life on Earth took their own divergent and unique course in an ongoing struggle for survival.[55] This caused Rickert to complain that biology's new hybridity "caused some confusion" to the dichotomy between the idiographic and the nomothetic.[56] But still, the two philosophers saved their distinction by simply admitting that some of the natural sciences used idiographic methods too, and for the rest, they focused on scientific theories that fitted more nicely into their model, such as the fixed laws of planetary orbits, of embryological processes, or the mechanics of electrons. Overall, Rickert still saw the natural sciences as "a solid tradition", with a common goal, representing "unity and connectedness", and Windelband spoke of a "world of atoms, colorless and soundless, without all the qualities of sensory experience."[57]

But not long after Windelband made this statement, the eternal world of atoms also began to show some cracks.[58] In 1896 the French physicist Henri Becquerel accidentally discovered that uranium salts in his cabinet emitted a mysterious form of radiation. Shortly thereafter Marie and Pierre Curie saw the same kind of energy coming from thorium, and coined it as radioactivity. Early twentieth-century science soon found out that this radiation was caused by the disintegration of atoms, implying that atoms were not as "colorless and soundless" as Windelband had assumed, but that they were subject to change. The destabilization of the natural world was taken even further when an assistant examiner at a patent office in Bern, Albert Einstein, put time and space on more shaky grounds.[59] Newtonian physics had always assumed an immutable universe in which motion and time could be measured according to some fixed and unchanging point in a fixed and unchanging space. Yet, Einstein's theories of relativity showed that time and space itself are not absolute, but relative to speed. The 1920s and 1930s had even more surprises in store for the Newtonian worldview. The new science of quantum mechanics found that subatomic particles do not obey the predictable laws of Newtonian mechanics.[60] These particles could be at different places simultaneously, acquiring a definite location only when they were interfered with by measuring instruments. Thus, without interference, what was "out there" was undetermined and could only be talked about in terms of probabilities.

There was a prominent historian who noticed it all.[61] Not long before he was killed as a member of the French resistance movement against the Nazis, Marc Bloch observed that the

---

[55] Hutton, *Theory of the Earth*; Lyell, *Principles of Geology*; Darwin, *The Origin of Species*.
[56] Rickert, *Kulturwissenschaft und Naturwissenschaft*, 7."einige Verwirrung angerichtet hat."
[57] Windelband, *Geschichte Und Naturwissenschaft*, 18."eine Welt von Atomen, farblos und klanglos, ohne allen Erdgeruch der Sinnequalitäten"; Rickert, *Kulturwissenschaft und Naturwissenschaft*, 7."einder festen Tradition", "Einheit und Zusammenhang."
[58] Bauer, *The Story of Science*, 136–39; Vermij, *Kleine geschiedenis van de wetenschap*, 245–47.
[59] Einstein, *Über die spezielle und die algemeine Relativitätstheorie (gemeinverständlich)*; Bauer, *The Story of Science*, 215–24.
[60] Bauer, *The Story of Science*, 225–37; Vermij, *Kleine geschiedenis van de wetenschap*, 250–52.
[61] Bloch, *Apologie pour l'histoire ou Métier d'historien*, xv–xvii, 5–23.

natural sciences were moving in the direction of historians. In his book *The Historian's Craft*, Bloch stated that historians, when placing themselves amongst the sciences, no longer had anything to be ashamed of. Due to his early death, Bloch would not experience how these developments would continue even further. Over the next decades, Big Bang cosmology won the day with its claims that the universe was not a fixed and ahistorical place, but that it had a beginning, the Big Bang, and that all the atoms, molecules, stars, and galaxies had appeared at some point in time and have been subject to change since that point.[62] What is more, in the 1950s and 1960s conclusive evidence appeared for a hypothesis that had already been proposed by Alfred Wegener in 1912, namely that the apparently fixed and solid continents are continually on the move.[63] The theory had initially been rejected for want of a convincing explanation for how it happens, but plate tectonics finally resolved the problem: convection currents in deep layers of the earth make continents slide over the mantle.

Again, there was an important historian who noticed these developments. In his short book *What is History?* (1961), Edward H. Carr proclaimed that the "historian has some excuse for feeling himself more at home in the world of science today."[64] The new developments made Carr realize that the old distinction between the generalizing natural sciences and the singularizing historical sciences was becoming increasingly obsolete.[65] He remarked that many natural scientists, such as paleontologists or geologists, could not test their hypotheses in laboratories, but relied on traces of past processes that were often ambiguous and contradictory.[66] Moreover, in the natural world "no two geological formations, no two animals of the same species, and no two atoms are identical."[67] But the uniqueness of every object did not prevent natural scientists from searching for more general patterns and principles, and Carr reflected on the paralyzing effects of an overly idiographic focus. It leads, as he put it, towards "a philosophical *nirvana*, in which nothing that matters can be said about anything."[68]

After Carr made his remarks, the softening of the natural sciences would be taken even further. An important development of the latter part of the twentieth century was the rise of so called chaos theory, and the importance it ascribes to contingent events.[69] When contemplating the contingency of history, historians traditionally liked to refer to the example of Cleopatra's nose – had it been somewhat smaller, Caesar and Anthony might not have fallen under her spell, thereby drastically altering history's course.[70] But since 1972 the natural sciences have found their own equivalent in the so called "butterfly effect". In the late 1960s the American

---

[62] Bauer, *The Story of Science*, 238–51; Vermij, *Kleine geschiedenis van de wetenschap*, 214–20.
[63] Bauer, *The Story of Science*, 141–48; Vermij, *Kleine geschiedenis van de wetenschap*, 213–14.
[64] Carr, *What Is History?*, 51.
[65] Carr, *What Is History?*
[66] Carr, 41–44.
[67] Carr, 57; The argument had already been made by Herbert Spencer, see: Spencer, *Herbert Spencer on Social Evolution*, 92.
[68] Carr, *What Is History?*, 57.
[69] Gleick, *Chaos Making a New Science*; Bauer, *The Story of Science*, 252–56.
[70] Carr, *What Is History?*, 92–95; Gaddis, *The Landscape of History*, 71–89; Liveley, "Cleopatra's Nose."

meteorologist Edward Norton Lorenz made computer simulations of weather conditions, and found that minor perturbations could have enormous consequences. He eloquently summarized his argument by stating that the flapping of a butterfly's wings in Brazil could set off a tornado in Texas.[71] Chaos theory, of which Lorenz was a key exponent, highlights how big events, as well as very tiny events, could generate endless cascades of changing conditions, resulting in drastically different outcomes. Closely related is "complex systems theory". It describes how systems in the natural world can consist of innumerable components that interact with each other in infinitely intricate ways, disallowing predictions in a precise Newtonian sense.[72]

One of the domains in which this trend towards increased complexity, contingency and irregularity has become apparent is evolutionary biology.[73] Darwin himself was already much of a complexity thinker who stressed the irregular and undirected aspects of evolution. He emphasized that species have no fixed essences, but continually adapt to particular environments, which gives his theory a rather idiographic twist. For a long time such assumptions were not mainstream amongst his colleagues.[74] A contemporary expert described evolution as a process "from the simple to the complex, from the lower to the higher, from evil to good."[75] In Germany, Ernst Haeckel visually depicted biological evolution as a tree of life that meanders a little, but overall grows in a fairly straight line towards humans at the top.[76] During much of the twentieth century, the ascent of complex life was often seen as a rather ladder-like phenomenon. It started with an "age of invertebrates", followed by an "age of fishes", then ages of amphibians, reptiles, birds, and finally leading to our own present "age of mammals". Even though they are not completely incorrect, such notions have begun to feel increasingly uncomfortable to biologists, as the trajectories of life on earth turned out to be far more messy, full of conflicting trends and counter trends.[77] Moreover, newly discovered mechanisms of symbiosis and lateral gene transfer demonstrated that various evolutionary branches had merged again, making the metaphor of a splitting "tree of life" problematic. Some biologists thus suggest we might speak of a "bush", "mangrove" or cluttered "net" of life.[78]

Evolutionary biology also learned to appreciate the significance of events. In the late twentieth century much evidence appeared to suggest that the extinction of the dinosaurs was caused by an asteroid impact around sixty-six million years ago.[79] This chance event had dramatic consequences, as it created opportunities for mammal species to develop into much larger forms. In a thought experiment that he called "rewinding the tape of life", the paleontologist Stephen

---

[71] Erdi, *Complexity Explained*, 16.
[72] Holland, *Complexity*; Thurner, Klimek, and Hanel, *Introduction to the Theory of Complex Systems*.
[73] Zimmer, *Evolution*; Gould, *Wonderful Life*; Ward and Kirschvink, *A New History of Life*; Gould, *Full House*; Rose, *Lifelines*.
[74] Bowler, *Evolution*.
[75] Moore, *The Post-Darwinian Controversies*, 151.
[76] Richards, *The Tragic Sense of Life*, 141.
[77] Ward and Kirschvink, *A New History of Life*.
[78] Gould, *Full House*, 61–69; Zimmer, *Evolution*, 119–35; Doolittle, "Uprooting the Tree of Life"; Kunin et al., "The Net of Life."
[79] Alvarez, *T. Rex and the Crater of Doom.*; Dawkins, *The Ancestor's Tale*, 597–629.

Jay Gould also contemplated the impact of very small events: "alter any event, ever so slightly and without apparent importance at the time, and evolution cascades into a radically different channel."[80] Not everyone is convinced by Gould's radical contingency. Colleagues like Richard Dawkins and Edward O. Wilson suggest that a rewinding of the tape of life would still produce remarkably similar patterns.[81] To back their argument, they refer to separate evolutionary processes on different continents that often led to eerily similar species, such as the Australian marsupial moles and mice that are very much like their Eurasian placental counterparts. The positions in this debate are nuanced, and surely far removed from the straight and simple determinism of a "nomothetic" model. Current biology highlights how living nature is a world of incredible richness, in which organisms continually interact in infinitely complex ecosystems. The evolutionary theorists Peter Richerson and Robert Boyd rightly state: "the evolutionary biologist knows complexity and diversity as intimately as the historian."[82]

Again, there are important historical scholars who noticed these fascinating developments.[83] The American world historian William McNeill speaks of a "grand convergence" of history and science, in which history is no longer the "hopelessly inexact laggard" that it once was.[84] In France, Paul Ricoeur in 1992 argued for a "return of the event", but stressed that it does not necessarily put history further away from the natural sciences. In fact, it may bring them closer together.[85] The Scottish historian Niall Ferguson draws inspiration from Stephen Jay Gould and chaos theory, arguing for what he calls "chaostory", which reconciles causation and contingency.[86] These developments also bear upon the relationship between history and the social sciences. The historian John Lewis Gaddis maintains that the social sciences are no longer the bridge between "hard" and "soft" methodologies that they used to be.[87] Many economists, for instance, still strive for abstract and parsimonious models in which rational agents interact in systems that move towards equilibrium. Notably, natural scientists today often level criticisms against such models that historians have expressed for ages.[88]

Critics of an alleged "grand convergence" might retort that the fixed law of gravity, Newton's three laws of motion, or the laws of electromagnetic forces, are still generally applicable. But even here the situation might be more nuanced. It is still a speculative theory, but many cosmologists now assume that our universe might be a part of a multiverse, in which various universes have their own physical laws and constants.[89] So, even at this point we may be moving towards greater diversity and less inevitability. Step by step many of the old distinctions

---

[80] Gould, *Wonderful Life*, 51, 283.
[81] Wilson, *The Diversity of Life*, 120–28; Dawkins, *The Ancestor's Tale*, 230–37.
[82] Richerson and Boyd, *Not By Genes Alone*, 95; A similar point is made by: Haig, *From Darwin to Derrida*, 362.
[83] McNeill, "History and the Scientific Worldview"; Berry, "The Laws of History."
[84] McNeill, "History and the Scientific Worldview," 1.
[85] Ricœur, "Le retour de l'Événement."
[86] Ferguson, "Virtual History," 79.
[87] Gaddis, *The Landscape of History*, 71.
[88] This point is also nicely illustrated in: Beinhocker, *The Origin of Wealth*, 46–75; Wilson, *Consilience*, 218.
[89] Gribbin, *In Search of the Multiverse*.

between science and history have evaporated, making a further integration of the sciences ever more palpable. Illustratively, the historian David Christian and the anthropologist Fred Spier came to the wonderful idea of turning the history of physical nature, living nature, and human history, into one continuing narrative. They call it *Big History*, and it tells the story of everything from the Big Bang until now.[90]

One might expect that this "softening" of the natural sciences has pleased and fascinated innumerable historians, eagerly contemplating the consequences for their own work. But surprisingly, scholars like Carr, McNeill, Ricoeur and Gaddis are very much the exceptions. Over the past decades, the stereotypes from the days of Windelband have proved remarkably resilient.[91] When reflecting on the essential differences between history and science, the Italian micro-historian Carlo Ginzburg did not compare his own method to that of a contemporary natural scientist, but to that of Galileo Galilei from the seventeenth century![92] The philosopher of history Frank Ankersmit calls any notion of a unity of the sciences "a dumb dogma", as history will never live up to science's generalizing and exact standards.[93] The theorist of history Chris Lorenz states that the natural sciences normally deal with closed systems, making them fundamentally different from history, which always deals with open and undetermined systems.[94] Or in the words of Hayden White:

> To be sure, history is the last of the disciplines of the human sciences to presume that society is radically other than the rest of the natural world; that it is a product of human work, labor, and creativity; and that the understanding of any of its processes must always be directed at the search for its origins, its relations to its time and space and socially specific contexts, and the employment of its transformations over time.[95]

Hayden White, as we saw, blurred the distinction between fact and fiction, which may help explain his rather fictional account of the natural sciences. But even key historians who defend history against relativism fail to mention how history and science converged.[96]

In 1959 the English scientist and novelist C.P. Snow spoke of "two cultures" – the sciences and the humanities – that are often painstakingly unaware of each other's insights.[97] Regrettably, many of his observations still stand today. This raises the question of why the softening of the natural sciences has failed to penetrate mainstream historical consciousness. Perhaps the

---

[90] Christian, *Maps of Time*; Spier, *Big History and the Future of Humanity*; Christian, *Origin Story*.
[91] See, for instance: Martin, "The Essential Difference between History and Science"; Howell and Prevenier, *From Reliable Sources*; Dussen, *Filosofie van de geschiedenis*.
[92] Ginzburg, "Clues Roots of a Scientific Paradigm."
[93] Ankersmit, "Representatie Als Cognitief Instrument," 261.
[94] Lorenz, *De constructie van het verleden*, 240.
[95] White, "Afterword," 318.
[96] Appleby, Hunt, and Jacob, *Telling the Truth about History*; Evans, *In Defense of History*; Hunt, *History: Why It Matters*.
[97] Snow, *The Two Cultures*.

bogeyman of the "hard" sciences is too convenient an enemy to say goodbye to. Or perhaps historians fear the shifting borders and destabilization that a new integration of insights might trigger. Whatever the causes may be, from a methodological point of view it is a loss. Past idiographic historians were right that nomothetic models provide us with an overly tight straitjacket that will never fit history's irregular shapes. But now that the natural sciences have become so much softer we might give "scientific history" a new chance. Not only on grand macroscopic levels, as happens in Big History, but also on small and more idiographic scales.

In this context we will now begin exploring the methodological potential of Darwinian theory. Some prominent historical scholars have already scouted the territory. Niall Ferguson draws comparisons between the evolution of species and the evolution of financial markets.[98] Daniel Lord Smail keenly observes how Darwinism dovetails with historians' traditional skepticism of essentialist and ahistorical categories.[99] The economic historian Joël Mokyr, who has studied the topic most extensively, maintains that Darwinian theory can help us find a middle ground between "the extremes of a materialist analysis that regards historical outcomes as inexorable and foreordained and a nihilist approach that sees nothing but randomness everywhere."[100] But how exactly can the universal acid of Darwinism be put to use in concrete historical research? We will first have a look at its most well-known application: the idea of an evolved human nature.

1.3 Human nature

In 1978 the normally rather calm annual meeting of the *American Association for the Advancement of Science* was suddenly disrupted.[101] The seminar was devoted to a new scientific field, sociobiology, and the audience was getting ready for a lecture by the famous sociobiologist Edward O. Wilson. This professor in entomology from Harvard University had shifted his attention from the social life of insects to that of humans, and was about to present his research into the biological basis of human social behavior. But when Wilson started his talk a group of activists from the *Committee Against Racism* rushed forward, carrying placards with crossed-out swastikas, and they shouted, "Racist Wilson, you can't hide, we charge you with genocide!" Two of them poured a jug of water over his neck, yelling triumphantly: "Wilson, you are all wet!"[102] After much commotion the activists left again, and the lecture was continued. But when Wilson finished his talk he was still dripping water.

The incident marks the atmosphere in which Darwinism made its comeback in the human sciences. In the late nineteenth century, it had been quite common to understand human behavior and societies in Darwinian biological terms, but over the course of the twentieth century

---

[98] Ferguson, *The Ascent of Money*, 370–408.
[99] Smail, *On Deep History and the Brain*, 124–25.
[100] Mokyr, *A Culture of Growth*, 32.
[101] Wilson, *Naturalist*, 247–50; Pinker, *The Blank Slate*, 110–11.
[102] Wilson, *Naturalist*, 247–50.

such approaches were increasingly resisted.[103] The academic debate over "nature versus nurture" came to a head in the nineteenth century, and after 1945 the horrors of the Nazi regime rendered the nature perspective on human behavior and human differences largely taboo. A broad consensus took shape that human behavior is largely determined by socio-cultural factors, and not by biological predispositions. Behavioral patterns like sleeping, eating, or feeling pain obviously had biological roots, but for the rest, socio-cultural influences were thought to be crucial. However, by the late 1970s this model was under pressure. Ethologists and evolutionary biologists had made much progress in the study of animal behavior, and now claimed that not only the physical traits of animals had a genetic evolutionary basis, but also many of their specific behavioral patterns. An example was the mechanism of imprinting, whereby species such as geese or ducks become attached to the first large object that they see after birth, normally their mother.[104] Around the same time it became apparent that many of the preceding socialist and idealist experiments to reform society had degenerated into nightmares. This raised the question of why they had failed.[105] Was it perhaps due to something as old and immutable as an evolved human nature, that limited the possibilities of utopian human malleability?

In this context Edward O. Wilson developed his research program of human sociobiology.[106] In animal sociobiology it was assumed that behavior was shaped by natural selection and eventually served the reproduction of the organisms' genes. It resulted in adaptations like parental care, altruism between siblings, or specific mating patterns.[107] Wilson's key claim from the mid-1970s was that the same applies to much of human behavior. During our long evolutionary past, natural selection had endowed our species with hereditary behavioral mechanisms that enhance the reproduction of our genes. Examples include aggression, dominance, ethics, tribalism, altruism, or differences between the sexes. In addition, Wilson maintained that such universal biological propensities continue to shape behavior today. As he wrote about gender disparities: "even with identical education and equal access to all professions, men are likely to continue to play a disproportionate role in political life, business and science."[108] Wilson did not deny the impact of socio-cultural factors, but believed that their scope was limited: "the genes hold culture on a leash. The leash is very long, but inevitably values will be constrained in accordance with their effects on the human gene pool."[109]

Wilson's proposals triggered a new and heated round in the old "nature versus nurture" debate.[110] The Darwinian take on humans encountered fierce resistance from a broad alliance of

---

[103] Pinker, *The Blank Slate*, 1–136; Fracchia and Lewontin, "Does Culture Evolve?," 54–55.
[104] Buss, *Evolutionary Psychology*, 10–17, 28–31.
[105] Pinker, *The Blank Slate*, 154–58.
[106] Wilson, *Sociobiology*, 271–304; Wilson, *On Human Nature*.; Segerstråle, *Defenders of the Truth*.
[107] Wilson, *Sociobiology*, 1–270.
[108] Wilson, "Human Decency Is Animal."
[109] Wilson, *On Human Nature.*, 167.
[110] Segerstråle, *Defenders of the Truth*.

academics, ranging from social scientists, scholars of the humanities, to biologists.[111] Wilson was accused of biological imperialism, genetic determinism, reductionism, and it was said that his approach was built upon speculative reconstructions of prehistoric selection pressures, and equally speculative claims about the links between genes and behavior. His Harvard colleague Stephan Jay Gould described Wilson's accounts as "Just so stories" – explanations that may sound plausible, but are not supported by rigorous evidence.[112] Sociobiology treated categories like dominance, tribalism, or aggression as natural objects, whereas it actually concerned historically and ideologically conditioned constructs. By claiming that aggression or sex differences had biological roots, Wilson was not just explaining them, he legitimized them. Some critics summarized the sociobiological position as follows: "What we are is natural and therefore fixed. We may struggle, pass laws, even make revolutions, but we do so in vain."[113] It reminded people of the biological underpinnings of eugenics and Nazism.

In their turn, Wilson and his supporters accused the critics of an ideological attack on the spirit of free inquiry.[114] The charge of condoning and corroborating social injustices was dismissed, because explaining and legitimizing is not the same thing. From their point of view, it was the nurture camp that clung to an unscientific and ideologically motivated belief in the all-powerful force of learning and culture. While resistance against sociobiology limited much of its academic outreach, the genie was out of the bottle. From the 1970s onwards, the study of the biological causes of human behavior developed into an impressive interdisciplinary research program, ranging from human genetics, neurology, biochemistry, psychological testing, to cross-cultural comparison.[115] A field of study that particularly continued to offer support is animal behavior. Careful observational studies, as well as biochemical evidence, further indicated that many of the emotions and cognitive mechanisms that were traditionally deemed uniquely human, can also be found in certain animal species. Some biologists claim that rodents, elephants, horses, or apes also, to varying degrees, feel sorrow, love, fear, or a sense of fairness. This suggests that our emotional repertoire has deep biological roots.[116]

Evolutionary psychology
The name sociobiology is heard less often because the research program mostly lives on under the name of "evolutionary psychology".[117] Much of its groundwork has been laid by John Tooby and Leda Cosmides, who, in contrast to sociobiologists, not so much focus on what genes make

---
[111] Lewontin, Rose, and Kamin, *Not in Our Genes*; Eriksen and Nielsen, *A History of Anthropology*, 246–50; Harris, *Cultural Materialism*, 119–40; Schreier et al., "Against 'Sociobiology.'"
[112] Gould, "Sociobiology: The Art of Storytelling"; Lewontin, Rose, and Kamin, *Not in Our Genes*, 258–64.
[113] Lewontin, Rose, and Kamin, *Not in Our Genes*, 18.
[114] Wilson, "For Sociobiology"; Segerstråle, *Defenders of the Truth*.
[115] Schmitt and Pilcher, "Evaluating Evidence of Psychological Adaptation"; Buss, *Evolutionary Psychology*.
[116] Waal, *Mama's Last Hug*.
[117] Lewens, *Darwin*, 146–58; Tooby and Cosmides, "The Psychological Foundations of Culture"; Cosmides, Tooby, and Barkow, "Introduction"; Pinker, *The Blank Slate*; Buss, *Evolutionary Psychology*; Stewart-Williams, *The Ape That Understood the Universe*.

humans do, but, rather, on what our brains are *designed* to do. As they write: "Evolutionary processes are the 'architect' that assembled, detail by detail, our evolved psychological and physiological architecture."[118] But since biological evolution is a slow process, they assume that our brains and bodies are not adapted to our current environments, but to the environment in which our species mostly evolved, the African savannah. We still house, as Tooby and Cosmides put it, a "stone age mind", largely built for survival within our former "Environment of Evolutionary Adaptedness".[119] Why, for instance, are children in New York City more afraid of spiders and snakes than of cars and cigarettes, although the latter are more likely to kill them? Evolutionary psychology's answer is that the fear of spiders and snakes is an innate mental module that evolved as an adaptation to our former environment in which those animals were still a serious threat.[120] Or why do modern people eat unhealthy amounts of sugar and fat? Again, it is supposed to be our stone age constitution that plays a trick on us. Sweet fruits and fatty food were in short supply on the savannah, making us still crave sweet and fatty tastes, even when there is no shortage.[121]

Like sociobiology, evolutionary psychology takes a keen interest in sex differences. It assumes that men and women faced dissimilar survival problems during their evolutionary past. Men more often participated in hunting and warfare, while women did more of the gathering and child rearing.[122] Consequently, men on average evolved better abilities of conceptualizing large distances and spatial reasoning, as well as specific bodily machinery for fighting, like superior muscular powers and psychological propensities for physical aggression.[123] This would explain why men have been significantly overrepresented in acts of physical violence throughout human history. Women on the other hand, evolved enhanced abilities of language acquisition and spatial location memory, which was of more help in their specific niches. Another area of interest is alleged average differences in mating preferences.[124] The evolutionary psychologist David Buss presented cross-cultural data which supposedly show that men have stronger preferences for mating quickly with young and healthy-looking partners, whereas women are more selective and eager to look for partners with resources. Buss relates this to the fact that men have nearly limitless amounts of sperm cells and are free to look for more mates when fertilization is complete. Women on the other hand, have limited numbers of egg cells, and need to make more of an investment – just think of gestation and breast feeding. This would explain

---

[118] Tooby and Cosmides, "The Psychological Foundations of Culture," 50.
[119] Cosmides and Tooby, "Evolutionary Psychology: A Primer"; Tooby and Cosmides, "The Psychological Foundations of Culture"; Buss, *Evolutionary Psychology*, 88–90.
[120] Buss, *Evolutionary Psychology*, 90–97.
[121] King, "The Brain, the Environment, and Human Obesity."
[122] Pinker, *The Blank Slate*, 337–71; Buss, *Evolutionary Psychology*, 80–87.
[123] McDonald, Navarrete, and Van Vugt, "Evolution and the Psychology of Intergroup Conflict"; Buss, *Evolutionary Psychology*, 299–330.
[124] Buss, *Evolutionary Psychology*, 105–204, 359–92; Buss, *The Evolution of Desire*.

why women on average are instinctively more careful when choosing a partner, and look for optimal genes as well as prospects of continued support.

The proponents of sociobiology and evolutionary psychology have expressed high expectations of putting the human sciences on this new Darwinian footing.[125] Tooby and Cosmides call for a "vertical integration" and a "unity of science" that will make the various disciplines of the social sciences and the humanities more consistent with the biological level, as well as with each other.[126] A key hindrance is something they call the "Standard Social Science Model", which dominates many of the socio-cultural disciplines. It treats the mind as an empty vessel that can be filled with socio-cultural processes in almost any direction. Allegedly, this model fails to understand how human culture and behavior are continually shaped by our evolutionary makeup. Everywhere we go, Tooby and Cosmides argue, we find people with the same evolved modules who "desire, plan, deceive, love, gaze, envy, get ill, have sex, play, can be injured, are satiated; and on and on."[127] Of course there is much cultural variation, but Tooby and Cosmides maintain that it does not suggest that humans have fewer instincts than animals, but a lot more. Human behavioral flexibility is only possible because humans possess a plethora of highly specialized mental modules built for the purpose.[128] The recognition of those modules, or so this psychological duo promises, will revitalize the human and socio-cultural disciplines.

Fortunately, the fury of the late 1970s debates calmed down a bit over subsequent decades, as ever more scholars became open-minded about interactions between nature and nurture factors. Newly found mechanisms like neuroplasticity and epigenetics further indicate how biological and environmental explanations complement each other.[129] Still, resistance against the biological take on human behavior remains paramount, and even seems to have been gaining new strength in recent years.[130] In many ways, the criticisms of evolutionary psychology reiterate earlier criticisms of sociobiology, such as accusations of "just so stories", underlying ideological agendas, and a neglect of behavioral flexibility. This resistance can sometimes take on radical forms, for instance when gender theorists maintain that categories like 'men' and 'women' are almost entirely socially constructed.[131] Evolutionary psychologists rightly complain about gross misrepresentations of their field, and a disregard for their vast and fruitful body of interdisciplinary research.[132] In general, it looks implausible indeed that natural selection would have shaped our bodies in the minutest details, but left our psychological and behavioral makeup

---

[125] Pinker, *The Blank Slate*; Slingerland, *What Science Offers the Humanities*; Barkow, "Missing the Revolution"; Wilson, *Consilience*.
[126] Cosmides, Tooby, and Barkow, "Introduction," 13; Tooby and Cosmides, "The Psychological Foundations of Culture," 14,.
[127] Tooby and Cosmides, "The Psychological Foundations of Culture," 89.
[128] Tooby and Cosmides, 38–39, 93.
[129] Paul, *Mixed Messages*; Harper, "The Sentimental Family"; Rose, "The Human Sciences in a Biological Age"; Ridley, *Nature via Nurture*.
[130] Prinz, *Beyond Human Nature*; Rippon, *Gender and Our Brains*; Rose and Rose, *Alas Poor Darwin*; Buller, *Adapting Minds*.
[131] Butler, *Undoing Gender*.
[132] Segerstråle, *Defenders of the Truth*; Pinker, *The Blank Slate*; Flock, "What Good Is Evolutionary Psychology?"; Perry and Mace, "The Lack of Acceptance."

almost entirely unaffected.[133] As Steven Stewart-Williams writes about male aggression: "why would natural selection give men the physical equipment needed for violence but not the psychological machinery to operate it? This would make about as much sense as giving us teeth and a digestive system, but not a desire to eat."[134]

However, this is not to say that evolutionary psychology is without problems. Critics are right to point to issues regarding evidence. This becomes apparent in Buss's claim about women being more eager to mate with financially secure partners.[135] Buss offers cross-cultural data on the widespread occurrence of this preference, like those collected through psychological questionnaires, but such findings do not yet prove a biological origin. A complementary if not alternative explanation might consist of a mixture of economic disparities, cultural learning, and stereotyping. Moreover, it is questionable whether ancestral women on the African savannah were as economically dependent on men as Buss's model seems to suggest. In that respect, the current ascent of women in many highly ranked professions also makes Edward O. Wilsons earlier comments on disparity look increasingly time bound. Evolutionary psychology often faces such problems. Nature and nurture factors can lead to similar results, making it hard to determine what exactly causes what. The nature camp thereby finds itself in a disadvantaged position. Cultural causes can often be proven convincingly, for instance when a behavioral pattern changes within one or a few generations, while biological causes are more difficult to substantiate. Even when a behavioral pattern is present across all human societies, it still offers no conclusive proof for an innate module. Alternatively, the trait's universality may result from an early introduction and common environmental pressures.[136]

The relevance for history
So, to what extent can evolutionary psychology renew and revitalize historical research?[137] Long before Darwin, the notion of a universal human nature attracted much attention amongst historians. Take the eighteenth-century historian and philosopher David Hume: "Mankind is so much the same, in all times and places, that history informs us of nothing new or strange in this particular. Its chief use is only to discover the constant and universal principles of human nature."[138] Yet, it was one of the key breakthroughs of historicism that it problematized such notions.[139] The movement made clear how deeply human thought and behavior are shaped by particular historical contexts. Robin Collingwood typically contended that any science of the

---

[133] Scheidel, "Evolutionary Psychology and the Historian," 1565.
[134] Stewart-Williams, *The Ape That Understood the Universe*, 107.
[135] Lewens, *Darwin*, 226–32; Smail, *On Deep History and the Brain*, 138–49; Buller, *Adapting Minds*; Wilterdink, "Darwinisme in de Sociale Wetenschappen," 448–49.
[136] Brown, "Human Nature and History," 148; Lewontin, Rose, and Kamin, *Not in Our Genes*, 255–58; Stewart-Williams, *The Ape That Understood the Universe*, 190.
[137] Brown, "Human Nature and History"; Scheidel, "Evolutionary Psychology and the Historian"; Harper, "The Sentimental Family"; Smail, *On Deep History and the Brain*, 138–49.
[138] Brown, *Hierarchy, History and Human Nature*; Hume, *An Enquiry Concerning Human Understanding*, 78.
[139] Iggers, *Historiography*, 28–29; Carr, *What Is History?*, 27; Collingwood, *The Idea of History*, 205–31.

permanent and unchanging laws of human nature "mistakes the transient conditions of a certain historical age for the permanent conditions of human life." What primarily came to interest historians is change and difference, which may help explain why evolutionary psychology failed to gain much traction.

It can be argued, though, that this lack of attention is a loss. Evolutionary psychology tries to map what the biological universals look like, and historians have invaluable information at their disposal on the range of behavioral diversity.[140] As the evolutionary anthropologist Donald Brown laments: "It is thus a shame to think of all that information in the historical records not being put to scientific use." Moreover, historical scholars often pride themselves on their ability to comprehend historical people through the re-enactment of past human thought in their own minds. But such abilities only result from the fact that humans in all times and places have so many traits in common.[141] Without a broad intercultural range of emotional and cognitive repertoires the whole method of *verstehen* would have been impossible in the first place. Hence, evolutionary psychology can help protect historians against overly naïve beliefs in human variation and malleability.[142] In addition, the approach can produce new empirical questions. Martin Daly and Margo Wilson for example looked into historical data on violence and homicide, and discovered that stepparents are significantly more likely to kill or harm their children than biological parents – exactly what a Darwinian perspective leads us to expect.[143] Donald Brown also reflected on how inborn traits helped to shape historical events, like tendencies towards in- and out-group biases that trigger violence between groups. He referred to the Balkans as a case in point.[144]

But it is in the latter example of the Balkans that a stark limitation of this evolutionary model comes to the surface. Let us take the Yugoslav wars of the 1990s as an illustration.[145] Donald Brown may surely be right that biological propensities for in-group and out-group biases were activated during these events, and that we are unlikely to find historical societies where such biases were absent. Yet, when a historian wants to understand how and why the Yugoslav wars occurred at that particular time and place, an appeal to universal mental modules remains rather hollow. What exactly would they explain? In this case it seems more fruitful to consider things like the death of President Tito, the worldwide decline of socialism, the resurgence of religion and nationalism in the region, some political decisions of the Serbian leader Slobodan Milošević, and the inability of external powers to intervene. In other words, this is just history as we already know it. The example illustrates that a nomothetic human nature cannot fully explain idiographic and highly complex historical events. Daniel Lord Smail comments: "Evolutionary

---

[140] Barkow, "Missing the Revolution," 41; Harper, "The Sentimental Family," 1549; Brown, "Human Nature and History."
[141] Tooby and Cosmides, "The Psychological Foundations of Culture," 92.; Slingerland, *What Science Offers the Humanities*.
[142] Brown, "Human Nature and History"; Scheidel, "Evolutionary Psychology and the Historian."
[143] Daly and Wilson, *Homicide*.
[144] Brown, "Human Nature and History," 142–43.
[145] Berry, "The Laws of History," 164.

psychology is naturally ahistorical and would resist the best efforts of even a sympathetically minded historian."[146]

But do the limitations of evolutionary psychology also limit the explanatory powers of evolutionary theory per se? When arguing for Darwinism's wide applicability, sociobiologists and evolutionary psychologists tend to stress the importance of biological factors, while downplaying the cultural ones.[147] John Tooby even rendered the terms "learning" and "culture" ready for retirement.[148] When opponents of Darwinism on the other hand try to curtail the theory's scope, they stress culture's diversity, power, and prevalence. But such moves and counter-moves are increasingly out of date. A growing number of evolutionary theorists recognizes that culture needs to be taken more seriously than has happened so far. Culture *itself* is becoming a subject of Darwinian attention. We will now see why culture is so very important if we aim to understand humans and their societies.

1.4 Gene-culture coevolution

An evolutionary biologist who tries to look at *Homo sapiens* as objectively as possible will encounter mysterious features.[149] Some oddities already become apparent at the moment we are born.[150] For many animal species, giving birth is a relatively smooth operation. Chimpanzees, for instance, can do it on their own and are finished within two hours on average. The risks are also relatively marginal. Human females, in contrast, need nine hours on average, and are crucially dependent on help from others in most cases. The hazards are also significant, as the death of the mother and the child was a serious risk before the rise of modern medicine. Once a human child is born, new problems immediately occur. Many animals are quickly able to function on their own – reptiles can take care of themselves from their first day onwards, and a giraffe cub already walks around within a few hours. Conversely, human babies are unable to perform even the simplest tasks for months, and will remain almost entirely dependent on help from others for many years to come.[151] Later in life, biological peculiarities continue to accumulate. People do not develop into physically strong beings like our close relatives, the chimpanzees and gorillas. Physically, we are remarkably weak; we would probably lose a fight with a baboon less than half our size.[152] Human weaknesses also extend to our capabilities for food processing, because human mouths are small and our teeth feeble.[153] These deficiencies are not compensated in the digestive tract, as our colons and stomachs are short. This is surprising,

---

[146] Smail, *On Deep History and the Brain*, 148; Wilterdink, "Darwinisme in de Sociale Wetenschappen."
[147] See, for instance: Wilson, *On Human Nature.*, 78; Barkow, *Darwin, Sex, and Status*, 142.
[148] Tooby, "What Scientific Idea Is Ready for Retirement?"
[149] Henrich, *The Secret of Our Success*, 1–7.
[150] Rosenberg and Trevathan, "Birth, Obstetrics and Human Evolution"; Rosenberg and Trevathan, *Costly and Cute Helpless Infants and Human Evolution*.
[151] Henrich, *The Secret of Our Success*, 61–65.
[152] Henrich, 69–71; Pagel, *Wired for Culture*, 233.
[153] Henrich, *The Secret of Our Success*, 65–69.

because humans need much energy for the nutrition of an energy-absorbing, disproportionally large head. Hence, from a purely biological point of view, we may seem unlikely candidates for an evolutionary success story.

But we did become an evolutionary success story, and one without parallel. Humans have become an ecologically dominant species that spread over all the continents of the planet, and uses a hundred times more biomass than any species before us. Together with our domesticated animals we make up 98% of all terrestrial vertebrate biomass, and we are on the brink of causing the sixth mass extinction in the history of life on Earth.[154] Any scientific model that attempts to explain these developments from our biotic traits alone will remain painfully incomplete. Apparently, we need to look beyond our purely biological makeup, and this is precisely what many evolutionary theorists today are doing. Over the past decades, our cultural skills have turned into a focal point of evolutionary research. Innovative perspectives are shedding new light on humanity's reproductive success, as well as on the aforementioned mysterious traits.[155]

What exactly is culture? In exploring this question evolutionary theorists are not entering uncharted waters. The social sciences and the humanities have been thinking about this for a long time, and in 1952 the anthropologists Alfred Kroeber and Clyde Kluckhohn already collected 164 scientific definitions.[156] Some people interpret culture in a rather narrow and normative way, like the nineteenth-century poet Matthew Arnold who famously called culture "The best which has been thought and said in the world."[157] Anthropological approaches are broader, such as Edward Tylor's well-known designation from 1871, framing culture as "that complex whole which includes knowledge, belief, art, morals, law, custom, and any other capabilities and habits acquired by man as a member of society."[158] Interestingly, current evolutionary definitions often come close to Tylor.[159] Peter Richerson and Robert Boyd describe culture as: "Information capable of affecting individuals' behaviors that they acquire from other members of their species through teaching, imitation, and other forms of social transmission."[160] Here, too, culture is seen as all information that humans acquire beyond their biological heredity, and this is also the definition that will be adopted throughout this dissertation.

One of the key insights of current evolutionary research is that culture, in this broad inclusive sense, is not uniquely human. It can also be found to varying degrees amongst certain animal species.[161] Recent research has produced an avalanche of studies demonstrating that behavioral patterns that were once interpreted as genetic, are likely products of social copying.

---

[154] Laland, *Darwin's Unfinished Symphony*, 6–7; Stewart-Williams, *The Ape That Understood the Universe*, 231–43; Henrich, *The Secret of Our Success*, 8; Kolbert, *The Sixth Extinction*.
[155] Richerson and Boyd, *Not By Genes Alone*; Henrich, *The Secret of Our Success*; Laland, *Darwin's Unfinished Symphony*.
[156] Kroeber and Kluckhohn, *Culture*.
[157] Arnold, *Culture and Anarchy*, 6.
[158] Tylor, *Primitive Culture 1. 1.*, 1.
[159] See, for instance: Henrich, *The Secret of Our Success*, 3; Mesoudi, *Cultural Evolution*, 2011, 2,3.
[160] Richerson and Boyd, *Not By Genes Alone*, 5.
[161] Jablonka, Lamb, and Zeligowski, *Evolution in Four Dimensions*, 153–88; Laland, *Darwin's Unfinished Symphony*, 31–50; Deacon, *The Symbolic Species*; Mesoudi, *Cultural Evolution*, 2011, 189–204.

Apes can imitate each other's techniques for using stones to crack nuts, or sticks for catching insects. Dolphin pods develop their own culturally transmitted hunting styles, and some whale and bird species copy each other's songs. Long-term studies of Japanese macaques even provide clues for a certain accumulation of cultural innovations. Yet, when considering such cases, it remains clear that human culture is different.[162] Animal traditions do not even come close to writing novels, holding religious festivals, or sending satellites to outer space. Human culture is more robust, cumulative and complex, and evolutionary researchers try to figure out what makes the difference. Various possible factors are brought forward, but experts today especially focus on our capacity for composite symbolic communication.[163] Some animal species have signals for communication, such as primates who use alarm calls to warn each other of snakes. But what animals cannot do is communicate about snakes when there are no snakes around, let alone integrate the concept of "snake" into complex and meaningful stories. Through our proficiency in the use of open-ended language with syntax, humans transfer information about things that are elsewhere, that happened in the past, or that will happen in an envisioned future. We are able to create a parallel world of the imagination, which greatly expands our capacities for the transmission and accumulation of cultural information.

How humans developed these capacities is difficult to reconstruct, because all of it happened in a distant evolutionary past that left few traces behind. But evolutionary theorists are working on scenarios for how it *could* have happened, and often rely on a key concept from evolutionary biology: coevolution. This term concerns processes in which species reciprocally adapt to each other's evolutionary advances.[164] Lions are well adapted to run after gazelles, but gazelles, in their turn, are well adapted to stay out of the lion's claws. Nuts have evolved hard shells to prevent birds from cracking them, but this stimulated the evolution of birds to develop stronger beaks. Coevolution does not necessarily lead to hostile arms races, as living nature also teems with examples of harmonious coevolutionary cooperation. Just think of flower species which provide bees with nectar, and bees who carry the pollen that fertilizes the flowers. As they became entangled in a coevolutionary dance, bees and flowers adapted to each other in shapes, smells and colors. Tens of millions of years ago their ancestors lived independently from each other, but after gradual evolutionary interactions they came to depend on each other for their mere survival. This opened up new evolutionary vistas for both of them.

What many current evolutionary theorists propose, is that the human species has entered a coevolutionary dance with a product of its own making: its culture.[165] According to this scenario it all started modestly with ancestors who used simple forms of cultural transmission,

---

[162] Laland, *Darwin's Unfinished Symphony*, 9–12; Pagel, *Wired for Culture*; Richerson and Boyd, *Not By Genes Alone*, 103–11.
[163] Laland, *Darwin's Unfinished Symphony*, 22–23, 175–207; Jablonka, Lamb, and Zeligowski, *Evolution in Four Dimensions*, 189–228.
[164] Durham, *Coevolution*; Richerson and Boyd, *Not By Genes Alone*, 191–236; Henrich, *The Secret of Our Success*; Lumsden and Wilson, *Genes, Mind, and Culture*; Ridley, *Evolution*, 613–42.
[165] Lumsden and Wilson, *Genes, Mind, and Culture*; Deacon, *The Symbolic Species*; Durham, *Coevolution*; Richerson and Boyd, *Not By Genes Alone*, 191–236; Henrich, *The Secret of Our Success*.

comparable to animal culture today. But incremental changes, such as the culturally acquired use of slightly more complex tools, gradually changed the environment our hominid ancestors were living in. When some individuals became better at using those tools, it created competitive advantages and new selection pressures on the mastery of culture. Subsequently, this stimulated even more complex forms of culture, which triggered new selection pressures, and vice versa. Somewhere in this process, ancestral humans must have crossed the Rubicon that created an escalating and self-enforcing process of gene-culture interactions. The current archeological record indicates that the first stone tools appeared from 2.6 million years ago, and from around 1.8 million years ago the pace of change seems to have intensified.[166]

New light on old traits
From this perspective, some of the mysterious biological traits that we started with begin to make more sense. One of the most important cultural innovations was the control of fire, which probably dates from around 1 to 1.5 million years ago. A key effect of domesticated fire was that its heat could be used to soften food, making it easier to digest. A significant part of the digestive work that was done by large teeth and long gastrointestinal tracts could thus be transferred to the cooking process. This created the evolutionary opportunity of letting our teeth and tracts become smaller.[167] Furthermore, the development of cultural assets such as spears, bows and arrows changed the conditions of hunting and warfare. Success in those domains became less dependent on muscular strength and more so on cultural skills, causing evolution to dispose us of much of our physical prowess.[168]

One organ proved to be an exception to this trend of energy cutbacks. The explosion of our culture was both the cause and the effect of an expansion of our heads.[169] The size of the human brain has nearly quadrupled over the last three million years, as it became ever more important for the acquisition and preservation of cultural information.[170] Some scholars argue that its growth happened so quickly that the rest of our primate body hardly managed to keep up. The size of the brain pushed the boundaries of the birth canal, which may help explain why human childbirth is so difficult.[171] The coevolutionary perspective might also shed new light on our helplessness during the formative years. Animal species acquire most of their information through genetic transmission, which implies that the transfer of information is largely finished when they are born. By contrast, humans obtain much of their essential information only *after* they are born. Most of the inner connections of the human brain still need to take shape, allowing us to obtain the cultural information necessary for survival. Hence, the unusual long-term

---
[166] Henrich, *The Secret of Our Success*, 280–95.
[167] Henrich, 65–69; Wrangham, *Catching Fire: How Cooking Made Us Human*.
[168] Henrich, 57–71.
[169] Henrich, 61–65; Laland, *Darwin's Unfinished Symphony*, 235.
[170] Laland, *Darwin's Unfinished Symphony*, 26, 57.
[171] Many aspects of the hypothesis are contested. See, for instance: Rosenberg and Trevathan, "Birth, Obstetrics and Human Evolution"; Rosenberg and Trevathan, *Costly and Cute Helpless Infants and Human Evolution*.

dependency on adults might be explained as a by-product of our elaborate cultural learning skills.[172]

Humankind came to inhabit a world of growing socio-cultural complexity, and we physically adapted to it. We now even depend on our culture for our mere survival.[173] Edward Wilson stated that genes hold culture on a leash, but this scenario shows that the leash tugs both ways.[174] The psychologist and anthropologist Joseph Henrich – a key proponent of the coevolutionary field – states that "trying to understand the evolution of human anatomy, physiology, and psychology without considering culture-gene coevolution would be like studying the evolution of fish while ignoring the fact that fish live, and evolved, underwater."[175] The newly acquired capability of cultural transmission worked out remarkably well for us, as it offered humans the possibility to adapt to new ecosystems more quickly than would have been possible through genetic evolution alone. It sparked a spectacular spread over the globe within an evolutionary blink of the eye.

However, as was discussed in the introduction, this dissertation is about the implications of Darwinian theory for history, and these coevolutionary interactions all happened in a distant prehistoric past. Their relevance for historians is not immediately apparent. Biological adaptive change is often thought of as a slow process that requires much longer time spans than historical periods .[176] As Stephen Jay Gould stated: "There's no biological change in humans in 40,000 or 50,000 years. Everything we call culture and civilization we have built with the same body and brain."[177] But the effects of gene-culture coevolution may in fact extend into the historical period, as Gould's claim is being contested.[178] There are indications that the coevolutionary dance between nature and culture continued, or even accelerated, in the last millennia.[179] An example is the ability of some humans to digest milk throughout adulthood. All humans are able to break down lactose milk sugars as infants, since they need to drink their mother's breast milk. But amongst various populations this trait extends into adulthood, and there is compelling evidence that it evolved as a response to the culturally acquired practice of cattle farming; milk is highly nutritious, so this cultural innovation stimulated new selection pressures on the ability to digest animal milk.[180] Another example is the "Asian flush" – an unpleasant response to the consumption of alcohol that is particularly prevalent amongst East Asians. According to some scholars the trait evolved as a coevolutionary response to the early adoption of alcoholic

---

[172] Henrich, *The Secret of Our Success*, 61–65.
[173] Henrich, 22–33.
[174] Laland, *Darwin's Unfinished Symphony*, 229; It has to be noted here that Wilson was amongst the first to explore the co-evolutionary approach: Lumsden and Wilson, *Genes, Mind, and Culture*.
[175] Henrich, *The Secret of Our Success*, 317.
[176] Cochran and Harpending, *The 10,000 Year Explosion*, 1–24.
[177] Cochran and Harpending, 1; This is also one of the few issues where Gould and Tooby and Cosmides were on the same page: Tooby and Cosmides, "The Psychological Foundations of Culture."
[178] Wade 110-4
[179] Akey, "Constructing Genomic Maps of Positive Selection in Humans"; Laland, *Darwin's Unfinished Symphony*, 209–33.
[180] Durham, *Coevolution*, 226–85; Henrich, *The Secret of Our Success*, 88–92.

beverages amongst these populations, offering protection against the temptations of drinking too much.[181]

A thorny twist

Some authors argue that gene-culture co-evolution also affected cognitive and behavioral traits over the past millennia, or even centuries. Yet, at this point the approach suddenly takes a tricky and thorny twist.[182] Joseph Henrich backs down here, but other scholars move forward.[183] It is argued that coevolution resulted in noteworthy genetic differences between human populations. Proponents of this idea refer to cognitive and behavioral changes that happened to domesticated species within relatively short time spans.[184] The Soviet scientist Dmitriy Belyaev, for instance, conducted a long-term experiment with domesticated silver foxes, selecting them for tameness. Within eight generations he had achieved significant results. Unexpectedly, the foxes also evolved patches of white hair, thinner skulls, and floppy ears. So why would rapid biological change be impossible in humans?

A well-known and highly incendiary case study is the "Ashkenazi Intelligence Hypothesis", put forward by the anthropologists Gregory Cochran and Henry Harpending.[185] Nicolas Wade, a former science reporter for the *New York Times,* more recently elaborated upon it.[186] As they point out, Ashkenazi Jews on average score exceptionally high on IQ-tests, and are significantly overrepresented amongst Nobel prize winners and chess champions. The authors propose that the Ashkenazi Jews evolved biological propensities for high intelligence as a response to their millennium-long European sojourn in a niche of cognitively demanding jobs. Genetic research indicates that this group remained relatively isolated from around 900 to 1800, and more so than other ethnic groups the Ashkenazi worked in professions like trade and money-lending. Allegedly, survival in this cultural niche, and the ability to generate offspring, strongly depended on innate propensities for high intelligence. This made genes for brainpower spread throughout the population. In the modern period, when the Ashkenazi abandoned their ghettos and competed with non-Jews in the educational system and the job market, these advantages suddenly became apparent. Ashkenazi intellectual and economic success would thus be related to their biological pre-adaptation for the cognitive demands of the modern world.

In his widely read book *A Farewell to Alms*, the historian Gregory Clark developed a similar scenario for the unusual advances of the English during the Industrial Revolution.[187] Clark looked at medieval and early modern datasets on the reproductive success of various groups within

---

[181] Henrich, *The Secret of Our Success*, 86–88.
[182] Clark, *A Farewell to Alms*; Cochran and Harpending, *The 10,000 Year Explosion*; Wade, *A Troublesome Inheritance*.
[183] Henrich, *The Secret of Our Success*, 94–96.
[184] Cochran and Harpending, *The 10,000 Year Explosion*, 1–23; Wade, *A Troublesome Inheritance*, 159, 166–67.
[185] Cochran, Hardy, and Harpending, "Natural History of Ashkenazi Intelligence"; Cochran and Harpending, *The 10,000 Year Explosion*, 187–224.
[186] Wade, *A Troublesome Inheritance*, 197–213.
[187] Clark, *A Farewell to Alms*.

English society and he maintains that it demonstrates a "survival of the richest"; the wealthy had more surviving offspring than the poor.[188] In addition Clark argues that being rich was often related to biological dispositions for thrift, patience, negotiation, prudence, and hard work. Hence, Darwinian selection pressures affected the English people, and "middle-class culture spread throughout the society through biological mechanisms."[189] Supposedly, these processes were stronger in England than elsewhere, providing us with one of the explanations for why the industrial revolution happened in England.

In this form, Darwinian theory begins to look more idiographic, and if these scenarios are correct it would indeed shed new light on some of human history's trajectories. A problem, though, is that the evidence is largely speculative.[190] What stands out in these texts is that they are full of sentences about genetic differences that "may play a part", "may well have operated", but have "yet to be identified" and, "if valid", "perhaps" or "maybe" explain particular differential outcomes.[191] The claims are also thoroughly contested by colleague experts.[192] In other words, the evidence for these theories is not by a long stretch strong enough for historians to rely on. A thorny additional problem is that these authors endow particular ethnic groups with traits that are usually interpreted in a positive light, like intelligence and hard work. But obviously there is another side to this coin, as it also implies that other groups are *less* well endowed with such qualities. These gene-culture enthusiasts have few inhibitions about moving in that direction. According to Cochran and Harpending agricultural societies selected for hard work, while in hunter-gatherer societies "being lazy made biological sense."[193] Purportedly, this biological heritage still bears upon their descendants today.[194] Clark states that foragers may be genetically "more violent", and Nicolas Wade postulates that sub-Saharan Africans are biologically adapted to their tribal socio-cultural environment.[195] It may even be one of the reasons why African countries suffer from socio-economic problems.[196] Wade refers to "variations in their nature, such as time preference, work ethic and propensity to violence."[197] Again, the evidence is largely speculative.

What should we make of this? This is an illustration of the dilemma of the moralistic fallacy. Whether something is scientifically true or false is independent of our prescriptions for

---

[188] Clark, 113.
[189] Clark, 259.
[190] Pinker, *The Better Angels of Our Nature*, 619–21.
[191] Cochran and Harpending, *The 10,000 Year Explosion*, 112,117, 220; Wade, *A Troublesome Inheritance*, 9,12,64,181; Clark, *A Farewell to Alms*, 11.
[192] Bowles, "Genetically Capitalist?"; Allen, "A Review of Gregory Clark's "A Farewell to Alms"; Hunley, "The 10,000 Year Explosion"; Allen Orr, "A Troublesome Inheritance"; Brooke and Larsen, "The Nurture of Nature"; Reich, *Who We Are and How We Got Here*, 247–74.
[193] Cochran and Harpending, *The 10,000 Year Explosion*, 115.
[194] Cochran and Harpending, 85–128.
[195] Clark, *A Farewell to Alms*, 121.
[196] Wade, *A Troublesome Inheritance*, 181–88.
[197] Wade, 182.

moral decency.[198] It is also difficult to rule out completely that human populations underwent some behavioral and cognitive changes since they diverged. Stronger evidence may appear in the near future.[199] But as I also said, scientists have an obligation to handle delicate topics with care. The social activists who once disturbed Edward O. Wilson's lecture in 1978 feared that a resurgence of Darwinism in the human sciences would stimulate racism. The aforementioned publications show that this concern is not necessarily unwarranted. Claims about biological differences between ethnic groups have an excessive potential for arousing harmful stereotypes and political abuse.[200] It makes the speculative claims of these coevolutionary enthusiasts worrisome, irritating and deplorable – racist stereotypes are being revoked. Then there is a further scientific problem. The authors repeatedly suggest that we somehow *need* biological factors to explain puzzling phenomena like varying IQ-scores, wealth differences, or the Industrial Revolution. But this is unconvincing, since the non-biological causes could be multiple. These gene-culture enthusiasts regularly pay lip service to socio-cultural factors, but do not seem to grasp their full explanatory potential.[201] Hence, it is high time to discuss what those socio-cultural factors look like, and to begin exploring the complex dynamics of the socio-cultural world.

1.5 Culture as a semi-autonomous force

In the previous section we encountered some traits of humans' physical constitution that appeared mysterious, from a purely biological point of view. But when we look at some of our behavioral patterns, things get even stranger. The ultimate goal of an organism's existence in the Darwinian world is the reproduction of its hereditary material through procreation. Admittedly, there are some animals who lost their breeding capacities, like sterile worker ants and worker bees. But this is compensated by the enhanced reproductive success of close genetic kin, like the queen ant or queen bee.[202] The historical record of humans, however, teems with examples of societies that fostered traditions of celibacy where no direct genetic benefit seems involved.[203] Think of the vestal virgins of Ancient Rome, the monks of Buddhism, or the clergy of the Roman Catholic church. Some communities even banned the generation of offspring altogether. The American sect of the *United Society of Believers in Christ's Second Appearing*, better known as the "Shakers", required its members to remain sexually continent, marking off the purity of believers in an impure world.[204] The eighteenth-century Native American Mbaya people, living in what is today Paraguay, also forbade pregnancy, and transgressions were severely punished. Expectant women ran the risk of being abandoned by their husbands, while the newborns were

---

[198] Pinker, *The Better Angels of Our Nature*, 614.
[199] Reich, *Who We Are and How We Got Here*, 247–73.
[200] Saini, *Superior*.
[201] Wade, *A Troublesome Inheritance*, 66; Clark, *A Farewell to Alms*, 14.
[202] Queller and Strassmann, "Kin Selection and Inclusive Fitness"; Kay, Lehmann, and Keller, "Kin Selection and Altruism."
[203] Sobo and Bell, *Celibacy, Culture, and Society*.
[204] Sobo and Bell, 115.

given to shamans who buried them alive or left them in the jungle, if they had not already been handed over to women who twisted their necks.[205]

"Natural selection will never produce in a being anything injurious to itself" wrote Darwin, as organisms who cause pain or injury to themselves will be removed from the population.[206] True, some animals take hazardous risks to save others, yet again, such cases directly serve the survival of close genetic kin.[207] Human history, however, offers countless examples of people tattooing, flagellating, scarring, blood-letting, or piercing themselves, often at the expense of their own health, while genetic advantages are not at all obvious.[208] Such practices are even encoded in carefully transmitted cultural traditions, like Christian hermits depriving themselves of food, Shia Muslims flagellating themselves to commemorate the lost battle of Karbala, or Buddhists who set themselves on fire to symbolize their willingness to abandon the body.[209] Particularly notorious in this respect are traditional funerals of Australian aboriginals. Participants wounded themselves with fiery sticks, knives, or tomahawks, often until their heads and bodies were burned or dripping of blood, with fatal injuries being a risk.[210]

Death is sought even more eagerly in traditions of martyrdom, in which people are encouraged to kill themselves, or let themselves be killed. A Roman governor of Asia named Arrius Antoninus was once caught by surprise when numerous Christians gave themselves up to the authorities, showing remarkable appetite for the death penalty. After the governor had some of them executed, those left urged him to consign them to death as well, bringing Arrius Antoninus to the exasperating comment: "You wretches, if you want to die, you have cliffs to leap from and ropes to hang by."[211] Other examples include the Japanese suicide practice of "seppuku" through disembowelment, the willingness of soldiers to fight for their national armies, or Islamist terrorists blowing themselves up in airplanes, subways, or busses.[212] Underlying genetic explanations will not do in these cases, as the moral entities that these "martyrs" are doing it for, like their honor, nation, or religion, often far extend genetic relatives, or do not overlap with genetic kin at all, as can be seen in cases of Islamist terrorists who converted to Islam only individually.[213]

In other words, an evolutionary biologist confronted with *Homo sapiens* is almost like a physicist confronted with a tree full of upward falling apples. The examples seem to fly in the face of evolutionary theory, so we need to, and will, grapple with them in this dissertation. Overall, evolutionary psychology and gene-culture coevolution deserve credit for their

---

[205] Ricky, *Native Peoples A to Z*, 1409–12; Saeger, *The Chaco Mission Frontier*, 84–86; Paul, *Mixed Messages*, 50–53.
[206] Darwin, *The Origin of Species*, 229.
[207] Kay, Lehmann, and Keller, "Kin Selection and Altruism."
[208] Stein and Stein, *The Anthropology of Religion, Magic, and Witchcraft.*, 92–94, 104–8.
[209] Wilson, "Starvation and Self-Mutilation in Religious Traditions."
[210] Durkheim, *Les formes élémentaires*, 556–92; Stein and Stein, *The Anthropology of Religion, Magic, and Witchcraft.*, 177–78.
[211] Bowersock, *Martyrdom and Rome*, 1.
[212] Carrasco, "Sacrifice/Human Sacrifice in Religious Traditions"; Wilson, "Starvation and Self-Mutilation in Religious Traditions"; Cook, "Martyrdom in Islam."
[213] Schuurman, Grol, and Flower, "Converts and Islamist Terrorism."

elucidation of many human traits, but as these examples indicate, human behavior can be overtaken by forces that lie beyond the genetic framework. As Ernst Mayr, one of the most prominent evolutionary biologists of the twentieth century, was willing to admit: "To be sure, man is, zoologically speaking, an animal. Yet, he is a unique animal, differing from all others in so many fundamental ways that a separate science for man is well-justified."[214] Social scientists and scholars of the humanities will not beg to differ. In the decades around 1900, when new disciplines like sociology and cultural anthropology were institutionalized, the insufficiency of psycho-biological models was also eagerly brought forward to mark off the new disciplines' distinctive territory.

Classics of social science: Durkheim and the Boasians
Presenting himself as an example, the sociologist Emile Durkheim stated that as an individual he *could* decide not to speak French anymore, cease using the *Franc*, decline to honor his contracts, and stop fulfilling his obligations as a husband or a citizen.[215] However, in all of these cases his attempts would fail miserably. The present institutions would quickly compel him to obey and an optional struggle would most likely be lost. As Durkheim argued, from the moment that he or she is born, every human being is confronted with "social facts" of their particular society that they did not themselves create, that they will subsequently acquire and transmit, and that will often persist long after he or she has passed away. Social facts have an external and coercive character, implying that traits of individuals, such as biological instincts or psychological processes, can never fully explain them. A social fact always involves something that takes place *between* individuals, and this observation was Durkheim's foundation of sociology as an autonomous science.

Durkheim did not render other levels of knowledge irrelevant for sociology. On the contrary, his approaches had a nomothetic orientation and he drew much inspiration from biology – a topic that will be addressed later on. But the French sociologist still argued that the laws of human societies, as they had yet to be discovered, needed to be elucidated and applied within their own specific domain.[216] Durkheim pointed out that social facts hardly overlap with racial categories, and change more quickly than biological explanations can account for.[217] He, for instance, referred to the history of art styles and the rapid switch around 1800 from a rationalistic to a romantic mindset. Society had to be to be understood as a reality *sui generis*, in which social facts are to be explained from other social facts.[218] The Aboriginal funerals were amongst Durkheim's favorite examples, as their harmful practices seem incomprehensible from a biological point of view. Instead, it is society that imposes the behavior on its individual

---
[214] Mayr, *The Growth of Biological Thought*, 438.
[215] Durkheim, *Les Règles de La Méthode Sociologique*, 3–14.
[216] Durkheim, *Cours de science sociale. Leçon d'ouverture*.
[217] Durkheim, *Les Règles de La Méthode Sociologique*, 106–9.
[218] Durkheim, 9, 109.

members, showing how society is something real and separate, that needs to be studied as such.[219]

A similar role in cultural anthropology was played by the German-American ethnologist Franz Boas.[220] As a student, Boas had been trained in the natural sciences, but from his German homeland he absorbed many lessons of historicism. This gave his anthropological work an idiographic twist. Yet, while differing from Durkheim in that regard, Boas's rejection of biologically reductionist models was similar. In his time, it was still widely thought amongst scientists that cultural differences reflected biological differences, and some races were thought to be more advanced than others. Boas made it his life work to disconnect the two categories. He stressed how the diversity and changeability of cultural forms hardly matches racial types.[221] In 1878 a German colleague had explained Japan's inertia as a result of biological dispositions, but as Boas commented in 1911: "how weak appear his conclusions, in view of the modern economic, political and scientific development of Japan which has adopted to the fullest extent all the best and worst traits of western civilization."[222] Further proof of culture's power was found in his newly adopted homeland, the USA. Migrant communities like the Irish, Italians, or Jews, had markedly different cultural heritages, which at the time were often explained racially. By contrast, Boas highlighted how the English that new generations of migrants spoke, the kind of gestures that they used, or the prevalence in crime rates that they had, changed so very quickly that it made biological explanations evaporate.[223] The evidence for socio-cultural effects on behavioral differences was overwhelming, while the evidence for racial factors remained flimsy at best.

Boas would have a lasting impact on American cultural anthropology, giving rise to what is often called the Boasian school of anthropology.[224] His many pupils turned the diversity, changeability, and autonomy of culture into the trademark of their profession.[225] The concept of "culture" was preferred over that of Durkheim's "social facts", as it was argued that it is not so much our sociality that sets us apart – many animals also live socially – but the transmission of complex cultural forms.[226] Referring to the biological principle of *Omnis cellula e cellula* (every cell is derived from some other cell) the Boasian Robert Lowie formulated the similar cultural principle of *Omnis cultura ex cultura* (all culture is derived from other culture).[227] Since racial as well as general psychological explanations had failed to solve the problems of culture, Lowie

---

[219] Durkheim, *Les formes élémentaires*, 556–92.
[220] Harris, *The Rise of Anthropological Theory*, 250–89; Pöhl and Tilg, *Franz Boas - Kultur, Sprache, Rasse*; Moore, *Visions of Culture*, 30–41.
[221] Boas, *The Mind of Primitive Man*.
[222] Boas, 139.
[223] Boas, 30–75.
[224] Harris, *The Rise of Anthropological Theory*, 290–372; Adams, *The Boasians*; Moore, *Visions of Culture*, 59–106; King, *The Reinvention of Humanity*.
[225] Kroeber, *The Nature of Culture*; Lowie, *Culture and Ethnology*; Benedict, *Patterns of Culture*.
[226] Kroeber, *The Nature of Culture*, 22–23.
[227] Lowie, *Culture and Ethnology*, 66.

argued that it was now up to culture to solve the problems of culture.[228] Another Boasian, Alfred Kroeber, framed it as the domain of "the superorganic", which was not just "a link in a chain, not a step in a path, but a leap to another plane."[229]

In the accounts of sociobiologists and evolutionary psychologists, Durkheim and the Boasians are often staged as the bogeymen of the Standard Social Science Model.[230] Purportedly, they were the ones who disconnected human behavior from its biological basis, which led us towards dualism, irrationalism and relapses into unscientific thinking. Tooby and Cosmides even compare the distinction between biology and culture to the outdated premodern opposition of the terrestrial versus the celestial sphere.[231] The supporters of the envisaged "vertical integration" of culture and biology thus emphasize that "human nature is necessarily involved in everything that humans do", and that "nothing fundamental separates the course of human history from the course of physical history, whether in the stars or in organic diversity."[232] To some extent such criticisms are warranted. Durkheim and the Boasians did take their rejection of biological explanations too far.[233] Durkheim claimed that even sexual jealousy, familial piety and parental love are not innate, but products of collective organization.[234] Boasian anthropology led to excesses, like Boas's famous pupil Margaret Mead who painted a rosy picture of a stress-free sex life on pacific Samoa that seemed to defy all biological constraints.[235] But later on it was found out that her ethnographic data – as was the case with more anthropological works at the time – were meager and overly gullible. Mead had stayed only shortly on the island, did not fully master the language, and conclusions were based on possibly fanciful accounts of adolescents.[236]

However, we should be careful not to dismiss the legacy of Durkheim and the Boasians altogether. These founding fathers of the social sciences – including Mead – did make essential observations that still stand today. Culture may not be fully autonomous, as the traits of our evolved brains both shape and constrain what culture looks like. But culture surely *is* semi-autonomous. It has much of a dynamics of its own that cannot be reduced to the biological traits of individual people. True, after the advent of postmodern relativism in the 1970s, segments of the social sciences and humanities fell victim to forms of irrationalism and obscurantism, but more about that later. But Durkheim and the Boasians were not yet part of that problem. They still endorsed scientific principles, and disallowed socio-cultural theories that contravene

---

[228] Lowie, 46, 90–95.
[229] Kroeber, *The Nature of Culture*, 22, 49.
[230] Tooby and Cosmides, "The Psychological Foundations of Culture"; Pinker, *The Blank Slate*, 22–26; Slingerland, *What Science Offers the Humanities*, 82–83.
[231] Tooby and Cosmides, "The Psychological Foundations of Culture," 19.
[232] Brown, "Human Nature and History," 138; Wilson, *Consilience*, 9.
[233] Mesoudi, *Cultural Evolution*, 2011, 51–53.
[234] Durkheim, *Les Règles de La Méthode Sociologique*, 106.
[235] Mead, *Coming of Age in Samoa*.
[236] Freeman, *Margaret Mead and Samoa*; King, *The Reinvention of Humanity*, 161–67.

physical, biological or psychological facts.[237] It was just that they thought to have good *scientific* reasons for their non-reductionist outlook. As Lowie put it: "culture cannot construct houses contrary to the laws of gravitation nor produce bread out of stones. But the principles of psychology are as incapable of accounting for the phenomena of culture as is gravitation to account for architectural styles."[238]

Emergence

What Durkheim and the Boasians referred to is an essential scientific principle known as "emergence".[239] It is often summarized as "the whole is more than the sum of its parts", or as "more is different". Its principle is not unique to the relationship between biology and culture, but can be found throughout scientific domains. When experts in fluid mechanics want to explain how water flows, they understand that water only consists of molecules made of hydrogen and oxygen atoms. Yet, at the same time they understand that the traits of individual atoms and molecules cannot explain all of it. This is why they refer to higher level "emergent" properties of water that only occur when many water molecules combine, like wetness, vorticity, or turbulence.[240] Or take the example of a frog jumping away from an approaching snake.[241] Modern biology accepts that the jump happens in accordance with physical and chemical laws. But it also accepts that when we want to understand how and why the frog jumps, we need to look beyond those laws. Biologists thus delve into higher level phenomena, like the complex interactions of the various organs at the moment of the jump, the development of the individual frog, or interactions between ancestral frogs and snakes in their evolutionary history. In other words, biology cannot be reduced to physics or chemistry.[242] And neither can culture be reduced to biology.

Now that evolutionary theorists are beginning to study culture more closely, its emergent properties are increasingly appreciated.[243] In his defense of evolutionary psychology, Steven Pinker levelled some harsh criticisms against Durkheim and the Boasians.[244] But in a later book, in which he responds to the racial theories of the current gene-culture coevolutionists, his argument suddenly turns Boasian:

> Between 1788 and 1868, 168,000 British convicts were sent to penal colonies in Australia, and one might have expected that Australians today would have inherited the

---

[237] Durkheim, *Les Règles de La Méthode Sociologique*, 10, 100–110; Durkheim, *Les formes élémentaires*, 25; Kroeber, *The Nature of Culture*, 4, 10, 50; Lowie, *Culture and Ethnology*, 17, 25–26, 66.
[238] Lowie, *Culture and Ethnology*, 25–26.
[239] Holland, *Complexity*, 1–5; Rees, "Explaining the Universe," 42; Corning, "The Re-Emergence of 'Emergence.'"
[240] Rees, "Explaining the Universe," 42; Holland, *Complexity*, 4.
[241] Rose, *Lifelines*, 10–14.
[242] Dawkins, *The Blind Watchmaker*, 10–11.
[243] Turchin, *Ultrasociety*, 220; Dawkins, *The Selfish Gene*, 164.
[244] Pinker, *The Blank Slate*.

obstreperous traits of their founding population. But Australia's homicide rate is lower than that of the mother country; in fact, it is one of the lowest in the world. Before 1945 the Germans had a reputation as the most militaristic people on earth; today they may be the most pacifistic.[245]

Pinker maintains that the profound impact of socio-cultural factors on human behavior, as well as the rapid changeability of those factors, should make us wary of racial biological explanations.[246] Similarly, Alex Mesoudi in his book on cultural evolution highlights how deeply children are socialized within their societies and how quickly migrants can adopt cultural traits of their newly adopted homelands. It brings him to the conclusion that "any explanation of human behavior that ignores culture, or treats it in an unsatisfactory manner, will almost certainly be incomplete."[247] Such statements would surely have met with Durkheim's and Boas's approval.

In the previous sections we noted that Darwinism in the form of evolutionary psychology, or of gene-culture coevolution, still remains tied to the biological level. But when Darwinism is applied at the level of culture as an emergent semi-autonomous force, whole new explanatory vistas may be opened up. As many current evolutionary experts argue, culture gradually came into being through the processes of gene-culture coevolution. But when it had arisen, and when cultural information came to be transmitted from person to person, new variants continually appeared, and only the variants best adapted to their environments survived. Hence, the three key ingredients of Darwinism, variation, selection and reproduction, made their appearance and a new evolutionary process was set in motion.[248] Cultural phenomena grew into other cultural phenomena through lineages of descent, and began to take adaptive directions of their own. When Daniel Dennett called Darwinism "a universal acid", it was especially this idea of a semi-autonomous cultural Darwinian process that he thought of, not least because it might shed new light on mysterious cultural practices like celibacy or martyrdom.[249]

We should move carefully here though. As mentioned in the introduction, most scholars of the socio-cultural disciplines, as well as many biologists, remain skeptical of the theory's added value. "What constitutes an evolutionary process as opposed to a 'merely' historical one? What explanatory work is done by claiming that culture has evolved?", historian Joseph Fracchia and geneticist Richard Lewontin wonder in a critical review.[250] As skeptics argue, the field of Darwinian cultural evolution grossly distorts and simplifies the workings of cultural processes. It allegedly fails to understand the importance of human agency as well as culture's contextual

---

[245] Pinker, *The Better Angels of Our Nature*, 619.
[246] Pinker, 618–22.
[247] Mesoudi, *Cultural Evolution*, 2011, i–24, 1.
[248] Dawkins, *The Selfish Gene*, 189–201; Blackmore, *The Meme Machine*; Richerson and Boyd, *Not By Genes Alone*; Henrich, *The Secret of Our Success*; Paul, *Mixed Messages*; Mesoudi, *Cultural Evolution*, 2011.
[249] Dennett, *Darwin's Dangerous Idea*; Dennett, *Breaking the Spell*.
[250] Fracchia and Lewontin, "Does Culture Evolve?," 57.

embeddedness. [251] Fracchia and Lewontin write that "this formulaic treatment is fully inappropriate to the labyrinthine pathways, the contingent complexity, the many nuances, and general messiness of history."[252] Moreover, as far as critics accept that the theory of Darwinian cultural evolution is not mistaken, they think it merely restates the obvious. Allegedly, the model just rephrases common insights, parasitizes existing knowledge, or pointlessly re-describes "ordinary cause-and-effect sequences using the verbiage of natural selection."[253] Hence, if many experts consider the theory a non-starter, does it even warrant the attention that it will here receive?

As announced, this dissertation will indeed support the theory's innovative power: Darwinian cultural evolution can both integrate, renew, and enhance our understanding of human culture and history. But considering all the skepticism we need to move prudently. What exactly is it about socio-cultural phenomena that the theory wants to explain? Did established approaches fail to explain it, and in what way does Darwinism provide us with a better alternative? It is with this first question about what the theory may explain, or its explanandum, that we begin. This requires a little detour though, as we neither start with socio-cultural phenomena, nor even with biological ones. Instead, we first briefly immerse ourselves in the world of physical nature and ask ourselves an important question about it: Do physical phenomena have functions?

---

[251] Ingold, "The Trouble with 'Evolutionary Biology'"; Kuper, "If Memes Are the Answer, What Is the Question?"; Bloch, "A Well-Disposed Social Anthropologist's Problems with Memes"; Bryant, "An Evolutionary Social Science?"; Lewens, *Cultural Evolution*, 2015.
[252] Fracchia and Lewontin, "Does Culture Evolve?," 77–78.
[253] Lewens, "Cultural Evolution," 2012, 468; Pinker, "The False Allure of Group Selection."

Chapter 2: Functions
2.1 The riddles of functionality

I have had the pleasure of working for a few years at an institute for interdisciplinary studies, which gave me the opportunity to discuss a wide range of scientific topics with students. There were ample subjects that stimulated lively debates, like the biological underpinnings of gender, the pitfalls of cognitive relativism, and the alleged merits of free market capitalism. But interestingly, none of the topics stimulated discussions as lively as the question of whether physical phenomena can be functional. What for instance, I asked them in an interdisciplinary course on evolutionary theory, about the Sun? Does the Sun have a function, and if so, what is it? Or what about mountains? Are they in any way purposeful, and what would their purpose be? Or the tectonic movement of the Indian continent? The eruptions of volcanos? The existence of black holes? Or the connecting of hydrogen atoms to oxygen atoms?

Whenever I asked these questions the students were thoroughly divided. To some it seemed obvious that such phenomena were purposeful. The Sun serves the functions of making planets orbit, burning protons in its inner core, making plants grow, and tanning skins on warm sunny days. If the Sun had not been doing these things, we would not even be here discussing it. Mountains can serve the purposes of stopping winds, letting rivers flow down, or giving us the pleasures of winter sport. Volcanic eruptions release tensions in the earth's crust, black holes clean up stars, hydrogen and oxygen atoms make up water molecules, and the movement of the Indian plate creates the Himalaya mountain range. Other students were willing to admit that the Sun has the *effect* of making planets orbit or letting plants grow, while mountains, indeed, stop winds and volcanos release tensions. Yet, this is not what such physical phenomena are *for*. It is not their *purpose*. After all, the Sun already existed before it made plants grow, and will continue to exist long after all plants on Earth have disappeared into evolutionary oblivion. Neither is the existence of black holes in any way dependent on the consumption of stars, nor do continental plates move because of their effects on mountain ranges. These things do not fulfill functions – they are just *there*.

The students who did take a functionalist stance on the existence of physical things were tapping into a pervasive tendency of human thought, often labelled as "teleology". It assumes that things have goals.[1] Amongst cognitive scientists today it is argued that teleological thinking may even be an inborn trait of the human mind.[2] Religions are traditionally saturated with notions of supernatural agents infusing nature with purposes, and teleological interpretations of physical nature have also been embraced in science for many centuries, not least by the great Greek philosopher Aristotle – the students who adopted the teleological stance could be assured

---

[1] Perlman, "The Modern Philosophical Resurrection of Teleology"; Leroi, *The Lagoon*, 84.
[2] Banerjee and Bloom, "Why Did This Happen to Me?"

that they were in good company.[3] "Nature does nothing in vain", Aristotle wrote, as "everything by nature is for the sake of something."[4] In his many works, the ancient philosopher assumed that things have various levels of causes.[5] There are "material causes" – what things are made of, "formal causes" – what design things have, and "efficient causes" – what sets things in motion. But on top of that Aristotle added a so called "final cause", referring to what things are eventually *for*. In Aristotle's world all natural phenomena possess an internal drive towards completion with respect to their capacities.[6] The celestial bodies, for instance, have an inner potential of orbiting in perfect circles around the earth, while the motions of the Moon and the Sun also drive the seasons on our planet.[7] This is not just what these bodies do, it is also their function to do it. The Aristotle expert Armand Leroi expresses the philosopher's viewpoint: "the celestial bodies are *perfectly* designed to do what they do."[8]

However, the anti-teleological students could also be assured they were in good company, or arguably even better company, as they have modern science on their side. The rejection of teleological explanations in physical nature is often considered a key breakthrough of the scientific revolution of the seventeenth century.[9] The English philosopher Francis Bacon, one of this revolution's heralds, accepted Aristotle's material and efficient causes, but wanted to have none of the final causes: "The inquisition of Final Causes is barren, and like a virgin consecrated to God produces nothing."[10] In the new worldview that gradually took shape in the works of Descartes, Galilei and Newton, it would no longer be accepted that physical bodies move because of an internal drive towards completion or a final goal. Instead, objects like planets or stones are inert and undirected. As Newton's first law postulates, they only keep doing what they were already doing unless an external force acts upon them. The rejection of teleology should not be placed too abruptly in time, as some critiques of it preceded the scientific revolution, while many goal-oriented notions continued to linger on long after it.[11] But the break with Aristotle in the physical sciences was still profound, and has made teleology one of physical science's ultimate sins: things have to be explained from their causes, and not from allegedly functional effects.

Functions in living nature

---

[3] Leroi, *The Lagoon*; Johnson, *Aristotle on Teleology*; Leunissen, *Explanation and Teleology in Aristotle's Science of Nature*; Broadie, "The Ancient Greeks." This is not to say that Aristotle would have endorsed all the aforementioned teleological explanations. He thought that the purpose of physical phenomena mostly lay in their own self-fulfillment, and not necessarily in the effects that they had on other phenomena. .
[4] Johnson, *Aristotle on Teleology*, 80.
[5] Johnson, 42–55.
[6] Johnson, 85–90; Broadie, "The Ancient Greeks."
[7] Leroi, *The Lagoon*, 305–41; Johnson, *Aristotle on Teleology*, 131–58.
[8] Leroi, *The Lagoon*, 332.
[9] Johnson, *Aristotle on Teleology*, 23–30; Depew and Weber, *Darwinism Evolving*, 88–89; Vermij, *Kleine geschiedenis van de wetenschap*, 31–106; Haig, *From Darwin to Derrida*, xxiii–xxviii, 1–5.
[10] Bacon, *The Works of Francis Bacon*, 4: Translations of the Philosophical Works 1:365.
[11] Johnson, *Aristotle on Teleology*, 25–30; Broadie, "The Ancient Greeks," 23.

Yet, during the discussions with the students I did not restrict the conversation to physical nature, as I then moved on to living nature. What about the long neck of the giraffe? Does it have a function, and if so, what is it? Or what about the whiteness of the polar bear's fur? The sting of a bee? Or the pumping of a human heart? Do these things serve a purpose? While the question regarding physical functions triggered debates, this time students moved towards consensus quickly. They widely accepted that these things have functions. The long neck of the giraffe is for reaching high hanging leaves, the polar bear's white coat makes the animal invisible to prey on the Nordic ice, while the sting of a bee is for stinging, and the heart for circulating blood. Unlike physical phenomena, these things not only have effects, they are also predisposed and adapted *in order to* have those effects. Not just some isolated parts of living organisms are functional, as their whole bodies, from the eyes, veins, leaves, bones, roots, legs, to toes are organized in complex ways to achieve certain ends. The persistence of organisms even depends on their effects.

It will not come as a surprise that this is also how Aristotle saw things.[12] The prose of the ancient philosopher was often restrained, but when discussing the functions in living nature his style could turn more ecstatic. Aristotle was passionate about the plants and animals that he studied, "whose works", he said "are everywhere full of purposeness and beauty."[13] "Every instrument is for the sake of something", he wrote, and amongst his concrete examples were wings for flying, lungs for breathing, and flowers for attracting insects.[14] In addition, Aristotle observed that certain instruments fulfilled several functions at the same time, and an organ that made a particular impression on him in that regard was the elephant's trunk.[15] "The elephant's nose is unique among animals because of its length and extraordinary versatility", he claimed.[16] The philosopher discerned functions of grabbing food, snorkeling, defense, trumpeting, as well as the uprooting of trees. Aristotle experts sometimes argue that living nature was the philosopher's greatest passion, and crucially shaped his teleological outlook. He saw that functions in organisms are ubiquitous and subsequently assumed that physical nature works in similar ways.[17]

Yet, while Aristotle's physics has been superseded in almost every respect, significant parts of his biology still stand. The life sciences today are still infused with functional analyses and purposeful language. When reading current scientific literature one is likely to find sentences about somatic cell divisions being "used to make mortal tissues", photosynthetic membranes having "an ingenious structure to fulfill all its functions", or an exploration of the "reason why nature developed macromolecules".[18] Such purposeful language has often been contested in

---

[12] Leroi, *The Lagoon*; Johnson, *Aristotle on Teleology*, 159–210.
[13] Depew and Weber, *Darwinism Evolving*, 4.
[14] Johnson, *Aristotle on Teleology*, 172.
[15] Leroi, *The Lagoon*, 137–40.
[16] Leroi, 137.
[17] Broadie, "The Ancient Greeks," 30–31.
[18] Hanke, "Teleology," 143–44.

biology.[19] Francis Bacon's attack on final causes also included what we would now call the life sciences, where he rendered final causes "remoras and hindrances to stay and slug the ship from further sailing." [20] Criticism continues to this day, like a current botanist who dismisses teleological accounts as "fundamentally unscientific modes of thought."[21] Nevertheless, goal-oriented reasoning has remained pervasive in the life sciences. As the early twentieth-century Austrian biologist Ernst Theodor von Brücke said: "Teleology is a lady without whom no biologist can live. Yet he is ashamed to show himself with her in public."[22] Today's biological teleology might differ from Aristotle's views, but the embracement of the concept as such is still widespread and has even experienced a revival.[23]

It is widely recognized that living nature is simply different.[24] In contrast to physical phenomena, living organisms are full of functional complexity, making teleological reasoning an indispensable tool. As the renowned cosmologist and astrophysicist Martin Rees admits: "A star is simpler than an insect, which embodies layer upon layer of structure. Biologists, tackling the intricacies of butterflies and brains, face tougher challenges than astronomers." [25] When reflecting on the difference, the biologist David Sloan Wilson maintains that physical things require a "physical reasoning mode", while organic traits demand a "functional reasoning mode."[26] Likewise, Daniel Dennett argues that the physical sciences can be satisfied with "how come" questions, asking for the process narrative of how things causally came about, whereas biology needs "what for" questions on top of that.[27] Many philosophers dealing with issues regarding functions have also developed a workable model for what a function is: when a phenomena's existence has depended, or depends, on the effects that it has, it may count as functional.[28] Francis Bacon and kindred spirits thus failed to drive the demon of Aristotle's final causes out. Armand Leroi rightly comments on the Baconian position in biology that it "is to betray a remarkable incuriosity about the point of one's own body."[29]

Socio-cultural functions

---

[19] Leroi, *The Lagoon*, 345–78.
[20] Bacon, *The Advancement of Learning and the New Atlantis*, 105.
[21] Hanke, "Teleology," 143.
[22] Haig, *From Darwin to Derrida*, 359.
[23] Perlman, "The Modern Philosophical Resurrection of Teleology"; Perlman, "Changing the Mission of Theories of Teleology"; Haig, *From Darwin to Derrida*, 5–16.
[24] Dawkins, *The Blind Watchmaker*, 1–10; Godfrey-Smith, *Philosophy of Biology*, 50–65.
[25] Rees, "Explaining the Universe," 44.
[26] Wilson, *This View of Life*, 38–40.
[27] Dennett, *From Bacteria to Bach and Back*, 33–54.
[28] Godfrey-Smith, *Philosophy of Biology*, 62; Perlman, "The Modern Philosophical Resurrection of Teleology"; There are also alternative theories that focus on how things functionally contribute to complexly achieved capacities of their systems. See for instance: Wouters, "Biology's Functional Perspective" However, because of its non-historical angle this orientation will not be pursued in this historical dissertation.
[29] Leroi, *The Lagoon*, 372.

After finishing the discussion with students about biological functions, I still had one domain to go: the world of the socio-cultural. What about a hammer? Does it have a function, and if so, what is its function? This time consensus followed and the question sometimes even stimulated some amusement. Because of course a hammer has a function, and it is banging nails! Other artefacts like clocks, combs or teapots triggered similarly prompt responses. A little more discussion ensued when complex socio-cultural institutions were discussed, like the police force, or money. Now answers diverged somewhat. Is the function of the police to uphold the law, as most students maintained, or is it a vehicle for oppression, as a few others suggested? The proposed functions of money diverged from the exchange of goods, getting rich, to the preservation of resources. But whether such phenomena fulfill any functions at all was not even up for debate. Socio-cultural phenomena are well adapted *in order to* have certain effects, and their persistence depends on their effects. In other words, they fit the function ascription that was mentioned above perfectly.

Unsurprisingly, Aristotle also interpreted socio-cultural phenomena from a teleological angle. He, for instance, wrote about coats: "there is an excellence that belongs to a coat, for a coat has a particular function and use." Amongst his further examples were ships, houses and statues.[30] Aristotle also reflected on the functions of more complex socio-cultural phenomena, like the institution of the state, which, in his view, not only has an origin and a development, but also a purpose, an optimal size, and mechanisms for self-maintenance.[31] Furthermore, cities were for ensuring the good life, popular gods were a useful invention for the multitude, and, more notoriously, he considered slavery to be a suitable part of the organic whole of society.[32]

No scholar today would endorse Aristotle's affirmative take on slavery, but the idea that socio-cultural phenomena can be functional has remained paramount in the socio-cultural disciplines. One of the most influential theoretical movements in sociology and anthropology even labeled itself as "functionalism".[33] Emile Durkheim, who laid much of the groundwork for this approach, specified that the "social facts" that he analyzed not only have effects, but that these effects also ensure the persistence of those facts: "without a doubt, the effect cannot exist without its cause, but this, in its turn, needs its effect."[34] In a similar vein, history books are full of military battles being fought for the purpose of winning a war, taxes being raised for the increase of the state's revenues, and palaces being built for the glorification of a ruler. Admittedly, certain forms of purposeful reasoning have attracted criticisms in the social sciences and the humanities. Functionalism has become contested as a school of thought – more about that later – and the word teleology even suffers from a bad reputation. It is often associated with

---

[30] Johnson, *Aristotle on Teleology*, 318.
[31] Leroi, *The Lagoon*, 314–15.
[32] Leroi, 337; Johnson, *Aristotle on Teleology*, 237–46.
[33] Wallace and Wolf, *Contemporary Sociological Theory*, 15–66; Kincaid, *Philosophical Foundations of the Social Sciences*, 101–14.
[34] Durkheim, *Les Règles de La Méthode Sociologique*, 95."Sans doute, l'effet ne peut pas exister sans sa cause, mais celle-ci, a son tour, a besoin de son effet."

the idea that history *as a whole* is moving towards a predetermined goal, like Judgement Day, Western Civilization, the self-realization of the World Spirit, or the communist worker's paradise.[35] Historical scholars are right to have become wary of such narratives. However, no school of thought would reject the existence of functions in the socio-cultural realm tout court.

Hence, the world of living nature and the world of the socio-cultural have something essential in common. In contrast to physical nature, things in both domains are purposefully organized. This observation was not lost on Auguste Comte, the founder of sociology as a discipline. In the nineteenth century he already distinguished the "sciences of the raw bodies", which included the disciplines of physical nature, from the "sciences of the organized bodies", which concerned biology and sociology.[36] His sociological colleague Herbert Spencer made similar remarks about human societies that "ally themselves with the organic world and substantially distinguish themselves from the inorganic world."[37] The insight now reappears in new guises in the work of David Sloan Wilson and Daniel Dennett. They point out that "functional reasoning modes" and "what for" questions bring the biological and socio-cultural sciences together, while setting them apart from the physical sciences.[38]

This observation has scientific relevance. It implies that both domains of science face similar questions, and may possibly benefit from each other's answers. A first question that both domains need to address is how functions come about. After all, the existence of functions cannot be taken for granted, as the physical realm does not provide them. Aristotle already justifiably stressed that functional complexity cannot result from mere luck or chance. So, we are confronted with a problem that needs a special explanation.[39] Section 2.2 will discuss how biologists have struggled with the origin of functions, and in what way Darwinian theory offered a breakthrough. The mechanism of natural selection has been mentioned above, but its explanatory character will here be addressed in greater detail. Section 2.3 subsequently explores how the socio-cultural disciplines struggled with the origin of functions, and what some of their answers have looked like.

The existence of functions also raises a second, and arguably even deeper question. What function do functions actually fulfill? The example of the long neck of the giraffe may help to illustrate what is meant here. As we saw, the purpose of the neck is reaching high hanging leaves. But what then would the function of reaching those leaves be? The answer is obvious: eating the leaves. Yet, this is only the beginning of a chain of questions that will become progressively complex, as the next question would be what function eating has. Here the answer still remains feasible: ensuring the survival of the individual giraffe. But what is the function of the giraffe's survival? An answer might be that it serves reproduction, but even this does not resolve the

---

[35] Trüper, Chakrabarty, and Subrahmanyam, *Historical Teleologies in the Modern World*.
[36] Heerikhuizen, "Sociaal evolutionisme in de vormende jaren van de sociologie, in het bijzonder in Nederland," 85–86.
[37] Spencer, *Herbert Spencer on Social Evolution*, 135–36.
[38] Wilson, *This View of Life*, 38–40; Dennett, *From Bacteria to Bach and Back*, 33–54; Wilson, *Darwin's Cathedral*, 2002, 6.
[39] Johnson, *Aristotle on Teleology*, 100.

explanatory chain, because what purpose would reproduction serve? The problem had also dawned on Aristotle, and to him the end of all functional explanations was that "being is better than not being, and living is better than not living. For this reason, there is the reproduction of animals."[40] But even this should not satisfy us, because why would being be better than not being, and what precisely is being reproduced? In section 2.4 we will see how this has been, and to some extent still is, a major point of contention in evolutionary biology. It will especially be considered how selfish gene theory claims to have an answer for us.

Questions regarding the purpose of purposes have also bedeviled scholars of the socio-cultural disciplines. Hammers fulfill the function of banging nails, but what would the function of banging nails be? The answer seems obvious: turning elements into a larger artifact. But here things also get tricky when we ask ourselves what the function of artifacts is. A possible answer might be the insurance of our biological survival. Yet, many artifacts seem rather superfluous from that point of view, so we are tempted to look for additional explanations. Is the function of artifacts to provide us with pleasure? To enhance individual people's status? To stimulate consumerism? Or to make society function as a whole? If so, what would the functions of pleasure, status, consumerism, or operative societies be? In section 2.5 we will discuss some of the answers that the socio-cultural disciplines have formulated regarding the question of the purpose of socio-cultural purposes. Eventually, this will clear the ground for the comparison of the theory of Darwinian cultural evolution and its non-Darwinian counterparts.

2.2 The origins of biological functions

The German thinker Immanuel Kant has a reputation as one of the greatest philosophers who ever lived – a well-deserved reputation, as he possessed the remarkable ability of synthesizing and renewing some of western philosophy's most troublesome issues. Yet, there was also a major problem that he failed to resolve satisfactorily. It was the question of how biological functions come about.[41] The topic had attracted Kant's attention in the first place because he astutely understood the difference between organic and inorganic phenomena discussed above. In his book *The Critique of Judgement* (1790) Kant pointed out that rivers connect people in the interior of countries, and that mountains preserve snow during summer. However, the existence of rivers and mountains is not in any way causally or purposefully connected to such effects. What Kant realized was that living nature is different. Trees produce leaves, but this is not only an effect of the tree, as it is simultaneously the cause of the tree's existence. Trees without leaves do not survive, which is also what trees are producing leaves *for*. The purposeful organization of living organisms reminded Kant of things created by humans. The construction of a house, for instance, has the effect of the new residents paying rent, and this anticipated effect is also the cause of

---

[40] Johnson, 175.
[41] Kant, *Kritik Der Urteilskraft*, 305–458; Depew and Weber, *Darwinism Evolving*, 102–4; Theunissen and Visser, *De wetten van het leven*, 54–56.

the house being built.[42] It brought Kant to the conclusion that living organisms need to be understood *as if* they had been purposefully created. It was "an indispensable need" and "a necessary maxim" to understand living things in teleological terms.[43]

Kant was assuredly not the first person to recognize that living organisms show a semblance of intentional design. Traditionally, this observation served as one of the essential proofs for the existence of a divine creator.[44] When pondering on the eyelids Socrates noticed that we can close them when we want to fall asleep, but re-open them when waking up. This indicated "a wise artificer full of love for all living things."[45] This line of reasoning was later adopted as the "argument from design" by the Christian tradition, and the ascent of modern science initially strengthened rather than weakened the argument.[46] The invention of the microscope offered new opportunities for studying organisms in great detail, and researchers encountered new worlds of incredible functional complexity. The entomologist Jan Swammerdam in 1678 claimed to show "the almighty finger of God in the anatomy of a louse."[47] Well into the nineteenth century many naturalists continued to work within the tradition of "natural theology", which both examined and celebrated nature's functions as proof of the benevolence and intelligence of our creator.[48] One of its exponents, the English clergyman William Paley, typically pointed out that the complicated design of a watch shows the existence of a designer – the watchmaker – as "there cannot be design without a designer".[49] So in a similar fashion the marvelous designs of organisms proved the existence of a designer, God. One of Paley's followers, John Shute Duncan, happily referred to the giraffe's "lofty neck [which] enables him to feed on branches eighteen or twenty feet above the ground."[50]

However, Immanuel Kant struggled with the problem of living nature's purposes because he rejected this explanation.[51] Kant was not the first to do so, as Aristotle had thought that nature's functionality resulted from principles intrinsic to nature, and later thinkers like Hume and Voltaire remarked that an appeal to an intentional designer only shifted the explanatory problem.[52] How had the designer itself come about, and in what way exactly did it do the designing? This position was reaffirmed by Kant: the argument from design brought us from the domain of empirical science into the domain of metaphysics. Yet, if living nature's purposes were not created by an intentional designer, then how was science to account for them? Kant knew

---

[42] Kant, *Kritik Der Urteilskraft*, 318–27.
[43] Kant, 349-50."unentbehrlich nötig", "eine notwendige Maxime."
[44] Sober, *The Design Argument*.
[45] Leroi, *The Lagoon*, 85; Johnson, *Aristotle on Teleology*, 116.
[46] Jorink, *Het boeck der natuere*.
[47] Jorink, 80."den almaghtigen vinger Gods, in de anatomie van een luijs."
[48] Bowler, *Evolution*, 38–41; Paley, *Natural Theology*.
[49] Paley, *Natural Theology*, 10.
[50] Duncan, *Botanical Theology*, 67.
[51] Kant, *Kritik Der Urteilskraft*, 322–32, 51.
[52] Johnson, *Aristotle on Teleology*, 4–6; Leroi, *The Lagoon*, 87; Hume, *Dialogues Concerning Natural Religion*, 63–66; Voltaire, *Oeuvres completes de Voltaire*, 19–33.

that modern science disallowed teleological explanations in physical nature, but still, organisms were teleologically organized. So how was one to resolve this explanatory gap? Kant failed to provide his readers with a solution, and asked them to accept that our minds inescapably interpret livings organisms as purposeful, but that we would always remain ignorant of how non-intentional purposes are scientifically possible.[53] In a rather defeatist fashion he projected the following:

> It is quite certain that in terms of merely mechanical principles of nature we cannot even adequately become familiar with, much less explain, organized beings and how they are internally possible. So certain is this that we may boldly state that it is absurd for human beings even to attempt it, or to hope that perhaps someday another Newton might arise who would explain to us, in terms of natural laws unordered by any intention, how even a mere blade of grass is produced.[54]

Fortunately, not all scientists have been willing to settle with Kant's self-imposed defeatism. Around the same time naturalists increasingly began to flirt with the idea of species undergoing processes of fundamental change over many generations, which provided new explanatory openings. Speculations on the change of species can be traced back to ancient Greece at least, but around 1800 the French naturalist Jean-Baptiste de Lamarck was the first to work the issue out in greater scientific detail.[55] Importantly, his account also included a materialistic explanation of how biological functions arise. Lamarck noticed that organisms are functionally organized to survive within their environments, and thought that such adaptations resulted from what he called "the influence of circumstances".[56] In his view, organisms change their habits in response to environments, and the acquired habits are then transmitted to the descendants. After many generations, this mechanism would lead to complex adaptations. The ancestors of giraffes, for instance, had continually been striving for higher hanging leaves, and thus "it has resulted from this habit, which has long been maintained in all individuals of his race, that his front legs have become longer (…), and that his neck has grown so long that the head, without standing on the hind legs, reaches six meters in height."[57] Amongst his other examples

---

[53] Kant, *Kritik Der Urteilskraft*, 351–68.
[54] Kant, 352."Es ist nämlich ganz gewiß, daß wir die organisierten Wesen und deren innere Möglichkeit nach bloß mechanischen Prinzipien der Natur nicht einmal zureichend kennen lernen, viel weniger erklären können; und zwar so gewiß, daß man dreist sagen kann, es ist für Menschen ungereimt, auch nur einen solchen Anschlag zu fassen, oder zu hoffen, das noch etwa dereinst ein Newton aufstehen könne, der auch nur die Erzeugung eines Grashalms nach Naturgesetzen, die keine Absicht geordnet hat, begreiflich machen werde: sondern man muß diese Einsicht den Menschen schlechterdings absprechen."; The translation is derived from: Kant, *Critique of Judgment*, 282–83.
[55] Godfrey-Smith, *Philosophy of Biology*, 6; Stott, *Darwin's Ghosts*; Bowler, *Evolution*, 48–95; Pietro Corsi, "Jean-Baptiste Lamarck."
[56] Lamarck, *Philosophie zoologique*, 1:218–68.
[57] Lamarck, 1:256."Il est résulté de cette habitude, soutenue, depuis longtemps, dans tous les individus de sa race, que ses jambes de devant sont devenues plus longues (…), et que son col s'est tellement allongé, que la girafe, sans se dresser sur les jambes de derrière, élève sa tête et atteint à six mètres de hauteur."

were plants that gradually adapt to environments of drought, and snakes who lost their limbs as a result of not using them for many generations. Lamarck's proposal has brought him much fame, as this mechanism of change is still known as "Lamarckism".

However, while Lamarck's proposal was significant, it should also be put into perspective. First of all, it was not the only mechanism of change that he conjectured, and arguably not his most important one. He also postulated an internal force, "the power of life", which supposedly drove the change of species towards greater complexity.[58] In contrast to the "influence of circumstances" Lamarck does not seem to have thought of this mechanism as an adaptive response to environments, but, rather, as something that caused changes irrespective of conditions of existence. It is worth mentioning that Lamarck was not the only naturalist who played down the importance of adaptedness to environments.[59] In contrast to functionalists like Aristotle or Paley, some researchers stressed that internal structures of organisms often seemed unrelated to circumstances. All mammals for instance, ranging from whales to bats to horses, have similar vertebrate body plans, despite their radically different environments. Such internal unities of type suggested that adaptations were mere epiphenomena.

Another reason for putting Lamarck's explanation for nature's functions into perspective was that he provided little evidence for it. His account of the transformation of species was largely speculative, which was at least one of the reasons why much of the scientific establishment remained committed to the idea of species being fixed in time.[60] In retrospect, it can also be questioned how plausible Lamarck's explanation for adaptive change really was.[61] While the length of the giraffe's neck or the disappearance of the snake's limbs look like credible candidates, other adaptations are less likely outcomes of any such principle. Just think of the intricate internal organization of cells, or the camouflage making animals invisible to predators or prey. How, for instance, did stick insects acquire their stick-like colors, or how did ancestral polar bears whiten their coats in response to the arctic environment? Lamarck's mechanism also faces the problem of many acquired characters not being improvements at all. If broken legs and smallpox scars are also transmitted, Lamarckian inheritance might easily become a mechanism of deterioration rather than of adaptation. Hence, Kant's explanatory problem of how purposes in living nature come about had hardly yet been resolved.

Darwin's solution
For a genuinely new proposal the world had to wait until 1859, when Charles Darwin published his *On the Origin of Species by Means of Natural Selection*.[62] Unlike Lamarck, Darwin provided a plethora of empirical evidence for the transformation of species, ranging from biogeographical

---

[58] Lamarck, 1:133; Pietro Corsi, "Jean-Baptiste Lamarck," 13–14.
[59] Depew and Weber, *Darwinism Evolving*, 48; Bowler, *Evolution*, 121–24.
[60] Lamarck, *Philosophie zoologique*, 1:87–95, 108–20.
[61] Dawkins, *The Blind Watchmaker*, 290–303.
[62] Darwin, *The Origin of Species*.

data, fossils, animals' mutual affinities, to rudimentary organs. This time the scientific establishment largely gave in. What Darwin described as "descent by modification" became known as "evolution", and the idea turned into an established scientific fact.[63] In addition, Darwin delved more deeply into the question of *how* change occurs, and he had no time for Lamarck's internal "force of life" for which no convincing evidence existed. Instead, he entirely focused on the transformative effects of environments, allowing some room for Lamarck's adaptive mechanism of inherited acquired traits.[64] However, Darwin thought this mechanism insufficient as an explanation for all of nature's adaptations, so he looked for something else. The conundrum would absorb him for many years, and his thinking process eventually resulted in a breakthrough that Daniel Dennett has described as "the single *best idea* anyone has *ever* had."[65]

Darwin would draw some of his key inspiration from the work of pigeon fanciers.[66] He noticed that pigeon breeders transformed the animals through artificial selection in various directions after multiple generations. When new and desired characteristics appeared, like certain wing lengths or colors of plumage, the fanciers preserved the traits by fostering the offspring of the animals carrying the traits. Darwin's suspicion was that a similar selective force operates in living nature, cumulatively preserving chance variants that are adapted to environments. But what Darwin could initially not figure out was what kind of force this was.[67] Eventually, the work of the political economist Thomas Malthus gave him a start. Malthus stressed how a discrepancy between high population growth and insufficient food production could result in mass starvation. As Darwin later recollected in his autobiography:

> I happened to read for amusement Malthus on *Population,* and being well prepared to appreciate the struggle for existence which everywhere goes on from long-continued observation of the habits of animals and plants, it at once struck me that under these circumstances favourable variations would tend to be preserved, and unfavourable ones to be destroyed. The result of this would be the formation of a new species. Here, then, I had at last got a theory by which to work.[68]

Darwin came up with a potent core idea: the selection and accumulation of chance hits. According to his scenario, giraffes did not develop the traits of somewhat longer necks because the trees were high in the first place.[69] The variation, Darwin argued, is random. So, giraffes were born with slight variations of neck types in all directions. This was an insufficient explanation for adaptation as such, because undirected variants are mostly non-adaptive – they bring about

---

[63] Bowler, *Evolution*, 141–223; Depew and Weber, *Darwinism Evolving*, 57–160.
[64] Darwin, *The Origin of Species*, 175–79.
[65] Dennett, *Darwin's Dangerous Idea*, 21.
[66] Bowler, *Evolution*, 160–61; Darwin, *The Origin of Species*, 71–100.
[67] Bowler, *Evolution*, 141–72; Zimmer, *Evolution*, 3–31.
[68] Depew and Weber, *Darwinism Evolving*, 71.
[69] Darwin, *On the Origin of Species*; Cameron and du Toit, "Winning by a Neck."

chaos rather than functions. However, what was not random was which of these giraffes eventually survived. In the on-going Malthusian "struggle for existence" it was the giraffes that *accidentally* possessed longer necks that could eat more leaves and subsequently had better chances of survival, also resulting in the survival of the hereditary traits of the longer neck itself. If these accidental hits were then cumulatively preserved in reiterated rounds of selection, the process would lead to the adaptation that we know so well. Hence, it was no longer mysterious internal forces, or actively changed habits, that drove the transformation of species, but the external selective force of scarcity in the environment. Paraphrasing the concept of artificial selection, Darwin described it as "natural selection". This process, he wrote, was "daily and hourly scrutinizing throughout the world, every variation, even the slightest; rejecting which is bad, preserving and adding up all that is good; silently and insensibly working, whenever and wherever opportunity offers, at the improvement of each organic being."[70]

"How extremely stupid not to have thought of that", is how Darwin's colleague Thomas Huxley responded when learning about Darwin's idea.[71] Indeed, the theory is so very simple that it can be explained in a single paragraph.[72] But it is a deceiving simplicity, as it is not by accident that it took so long before anyone figured it out. The three key ingredients of the process – variation, selection and reproduction – had already been widely recognized long before Darwin. Naturalists knew that organisms continually vary, that vast numbers of them die in a relentless struggle for life, and that traits are passed on from parents to offspring. But the variations amongst organisms were traditionally understood as oscillations from the normal state, while the massive natural culling was seen as a conservative force that ensured organisms did not diverge from the mean.[73] Darwin's essential insight was to recognize that reiterated selection is not a only *stabilizing* force, but also life's essential *creative* force. Everyday small-scale variation provided the raw material for a process of selection, that, given vast stretches of time, could build its own adaptive complexity from it.

Darwin's theory is so very logical that it is sometimes misinterpreted for being tautological. As the American author Charles Fort wrote in 1919: "The fittest survive. What is meant by the fittest? Not the strongest; not the cleverest – weakness and stupidity everywhere survive. There is no way of determining fitness except in that a thing does survive. (...) Darwinism: that survivors survive."[74] This objection is flawed because there actually is a way to determine fitness other than that a thing survives. The long neck of the giraffe does not count as "the fittest" simply because it survived, but because it is *adapted to its specific environment*: a savannah with high hanging leaves.[75] As soon as we would find giraffes with costly necks that are longer than

---

[70] Darwin, *The Origin of Species*, 133.
[71] Huxley and Huxley, *Life and Letters of Thomas Henry Huxley*, I:246.
[72] Wilson, *This View of Life*, 233.
[73] Depew and Weber, *Darwinism Evolving*, 37; Bowler, *Evolution*, 67.
[74] Fort, *The Book of the Damned*, 18.
[75] Cameron and du Toit, "Winning by a Neck."

trees are high, while no other function appears to be involved, the theory would face a problem.[76] After all, if the struggle for life is as relentless as Darwin presupposed, such energy-costing non-adaptive characteristics should have been removed from the population. Darwin's theory thus predicts a superabundance of adaptive traits, as well as innumerable less adaptive variants that disappear into evolutionary oblivion.[77] Other potentially falsifiable elements of the model are the vast stretches of time that it requires, as well as the non-directedness of new variation – the latter continues to be a topic of debate today.[78]

Darwinism after Darwin
The non-tautological character of the theory also becomes apparent from the fact that it took quite a while before the scientific community accepted it.[79] Darwin's evidence for evolution was overwhelming, but his mechanism still contained loose ends. There were doubts whether the earth was old enough to account for his slow and gradual scenario. People further wondered why adaptive traits would not blend out in a larger population. The exact mechanisms of heredity were still shrouded in mystery, and what critics found particularly hard to swallow was the idea that undirected variants provided sufficient raw material for something as diverse, complex, and creative as living nature. Well into the twentieth century biologists thus continued to look for alternatives.[80] For some time, natural theology re-appeared as "theological evolutionism", assuming that the process was guided by the hand of God. Lamarckian notions of an internal life force revived under the name "orthogenesis", and his hereditary mechanism of adaptation became central to the movement of "neo-Lamarckism". The early twentieth century also witnessed the rise of a new movement, "mutationism", which was inspired by the rediscovery of Mendel's genetic laws. Many of the first geneticists assumed that living nature's transformative power did not so much lie in the selection of small-scale continuous variation, as Darwin had assumed, but in the robust appearance of discontinuous, large genetic "mutations", which were not necessarily adaptive. In the decades around 1900 the various theories of evolution turned biology into a scientific battlefield, with Darwinism being just one of the candidate explanations.

It was only in the 1930s and 1940s, after other competitors had lost much of their scientific appeal, that Darwinism and genetics merged into a new paradigm, named the "Modern Synthesis".[81] What this model adopted from genetics is the assumption that hereditary traits are located on genes, and that characteristics are often inherited in a particulate and discontinuous manner. This would help explain why adaptive variants did not blend out in a wider population.

---

[76] An additional explanation for the evolution of the long neck might be sexual selection: Simmons and Scheepers, "Winning by a Neck."
[77] Darwin, *The Origin of Species*, 227–30; Cordingley, *Viruses*, 287.
[78] Wagner, *Arrival of the Fittest*.
[79] Bowler, *Evolution*, 177–324; Depew and Weber, *Darwinism Evolving*, 167–242.
[80] Bowler, *The Eclipse of Darwinism*.
[81] Bowler, *Evolution*, 325–46; Depew and Weber, *Darwinism Evolving*, 243–329; Theunissen and Visser, *De wetten van het leven*, 221–66.

Yet, what made the Synthesis thoroughly Darwinian was that new variation was thought to result from random small-scale genetic mutation and recombination, subsequently being steered towards adaptation by natural selection. So, it was the *combination* of mutation and selection that gave life its adaptive creativity.[82] Some of the architects of the Synthesis, such as Ronald Fisher, John Haldane, and Sewell Wright, had built their assumptions upon mathematical models, showing how selection could plausibly make chance variants spread throughout a population of interbreeding organisms. At one point the Synthesis even out-Darwinized Darwin, as Lamarckian inheritance was excluded. Genes were thought to affect the organism's make-up, the so called 'phenotypes', but information was never supposed to travel the other way around. Adaptive phenotypical changes had no ability of altering genes during an organism's lifetime. Only selection over many generations possessed robust adaptive power.

The Modern Synthesis was one of the triumphs of twentieth century science. Around 1900 the many fields of biology, like paleontology, field biology, and genetics, had been working past one another, often endorsing mutually inconsistent claims. By the mid-twentieth century the various branches of biology increasingly began to work within an overarching and more consistent Darwinian framework. In 1973, Theodosius Dobzhansky, one of the Synthesis's architects, happily proclaimed that "nothing in biology makes sense except in the light of evolution."[83] One of the things that helped make the Synthesis a success was the clear research agenda it set.[84] When confronted with complex and apparently functional traits, biologists are supposed to look for the traits' effects within the environment that ensure their continuation. The theory thus nicely combines the nomothetic and the idiographic. Organisms adapt to their environments *in general*, but since adaptedness is always context-dependent and different in each instance, the theory also looks for the particular.[85] Evolutionary biologists are well aware that single traits can also fulfill multiple functions at the same time. The various functions of the elephant's trunk, as they were discerned by Aristotle, are translated into various "selection pressures", or effects that trunks have within their environments, that have caused, and still cause, the organ's survival.[86]

The adaptive research agenda should not, however, be taken too far into assuming that everything in living nature is adaptive.[87] One of the strengths of the model is that, unlike natural theology, it can explain why certain traits are non-adaptive. Darwin already referred to rudimentary organs, like the snake's limbs, that had lost their former function but had not yet entirely disappeared.[88] The idea of common descent also provides a plausible scenario for the

---

[82] Godfrey-Smith, *Philosophy of Biology*, 40–41.
[83] Dobzhansky, "Nothing in Biology Makes Sense except in the Light of Evolution."
[84] Mayr, *What Evolution Is*; Ridley, *Evolution*.
[85] Godfrey-Smith, *Philosophy of Biology*, 52.
[86] Shoshani, "Understanding Proboscidean Evolution."
[87] Wilson, *This View of Life*, 42.
[88] Darwin, *The Origin of Species*, 428–32.

mysterious similarities between organisms' internal structures.[89] The various types of mammal, for instance, adapted to various environments after they diverged, but maintained much of their internal composition. Natural selection is a tinkering small-scale process, so it cannot drastically rearrange organisms, implying that things are not optimally adapted to current environments; they also carry the heritage of past environments.[90] Additionally, there is the option of things being a by-product of something else. Bones are white, but it would be a mistake to call this an adaptation, as it has no known effects that ensure its survival. Instead, the color is a by-product of the fact that bones are made of calcium salts which just happen to be white.[91] Lastly, Darwin speculated on the existence of "variations neither useful nor injurious [that] would not be affected by natural selection." Current evolutionary biology accepts that something like that occurs at the genetic molecular level.[92] Many mutations have no phenotypic consequences visible to natural selection, and so continue to exist as "genetic drift".

The role of randomness in the model is also something that requires careful consideration. A common misinterpretation of the theory states that organisms just resulted from chance. Richard Dawkins responds: "Mutation is random; natural selection is the very opposite of random."[93] But even the randomness of mutations deserves closer attention.[94] In quantum mechanics, randomness implies that things have no causes, but in evolutionary biology the term has a different meaning. The discovery of DNA in the 1950s showed that genetic information is encoded on DNA-molecules, which are normally copied with high accuracy. But every now and then copying errors occur, and it is in these "mutations" that modern biology recognizes the origin of new variation. But such mutations to DNA are non-random in the sense that they have specific causes like UV-radiation, and certain types of mutations are also more likely to occur than others at the molecular level (for chemical reasons that will not deter us here).[95] So, the randomness that the model refers to only concerns randomness regarding fitness outcome – the mutations giving rise to longer giraffe necks were random in the sense that they were unrelated to high trees on the savannah. *That* was a chance hit.

Science and teleology united
It is at this point that mechanistic explanation of physical science meets teleological explanation of biology.[96] The Newtonian model assumes that inert and undirected objects are steered by external forces, and in an important respect Darwin's model is much like that – undirected

---

[89] Darwin, 233.
[90] Dawkins, *The Greatest Show on Earth*, 337–72.
[91] Weiner, *Handbook of Psychology, History of Psychology*, 50.
[92] Darwin, *The Origin of Species*, 131; Ridley, *Evolution*, 155–93.
[93] Dawkins, *The Blind Watchmaker*, 41.
[94] Depew and Weber, *Darwinism Evolving*, 113–14; Baer, "Mutation."
[95] Dawkins, *The Blind Watchmaker*, 307–12; Baer, "Mutation"; Maderspacher, "Epigenetics," 426.
[96] Leroi, *The Lagoon*, 300; Haeckel, *Die Welträtsel*, 121; Godfrey-Smith, *Philosophy of Biology*, 60.

variation is being steered by the external force of a selective environment.[97] Yet, while the Darwinian process itself is mechanistic and entirely purposeless, its outcome looks radically different: purposeful complexity. In 1790 Kant claimed that a reconciliation between mechanical science and teleology was a chimera. Yet, as Ernst Haeckel commented in 1899: "seventy years later, this impossible 'Newton of organic nature' made its appearance with Darwin, who brilliantly resolved the daunting task which Kant had declared to be entirely insoluble."[98] According to Daniel Dennett, Darwin has turned the world upside down.[99] Older forms of thought assumed that functional complexity is created "from above" by even higher forms of complexity. Or in Paley's words: "there cannot be design without a designer". But Darwin demonstrated that design without designer is actually a real possibility: functional complexity can arise "from below", without the involvement of any intentional actor.

The impact of Darwin's insight for biology has been profound and its added value is undisputed. But should it remain restricted to biology? Richard Dawkins thinks that Darwinism is "too big a theory" to keep it confined to the domain of living nature. Like Dennett he wants to take it into the socio-cultural realm.[100] But can the theory here again express its "universal acid"-like abilities of transforming traditional concepts in fundamental ways? For instance, by offering an explanation for socio-cultural "design without designer"? This first raises the question of whether such an explanandum even exists in the socio-cultural world. We saw that Paley and Kant referred to watches and houses as obvious examples of intentional human design. But can we safely assume that *all* purposes in the socio-cultural world are deliberately created by human actors? This is not as obvious as it might first appear; the origin of functions has also puzzled scholars of the socio-cultural disciplines. To understand what their debates look like we now begin with a classic case study from sociology and anthropology: the Hopi rain dance.

2.3. The origins of cultural functions

In 1957, the American sociologist Robert King Merton decided to make a plea for the significance of the Hopi rain dance.[101] According to many of his contemporaries the ritual was hardly more than a relic of the past, outdated by modern knowledge. The Hopi Indians believed that their dances could help to create rain, but as modern meteorology demonstrated, rain has rather different causes. The ritual could therefore be considered to be a relic without any function at all. Robert Merton, however, believed that things were not necessarily as simple as that. The avowed purpose of the dance was indeed to evoke rain, but hidden underneath, unintended and unrecognized by the Hopi themselves, these dances had other effects of greater importance. The

---

[97] Depew and Weber, *Darwinism Evolving*, 6–9, 110.
[98] Haeckel, *Die Welträtsel*, 119."Siebenzig Jahre später ist dieser unmögliche „Newton der organischen Natur" in Darwin wirklich erschienen und hat die große Aufgabe glänzend gelöst, die Kant für ganz unlösbar erklärt hatte.".
[99] Dennett, *Darwin's Dangerous Idea*, 25,65.
[100] Dawkins, *The Selfish Gene*, 191.
[101] Merton, *Social Theory and Social Structure*, 73–138.

ceremony, as Merton stated, "may fulfill the latent function of reinforcing the group identity by providing a periodic occasion on which the scattered members of the group assemble to engage in a common activity."[102] As a form of collective expression, the rain dance provided the foundation for group unity. The ritual was not simply a relic from the past; it still had a function in the present.

The Hopi rain dance became such a famous case study because it was emblematic for the school of thought to which Merton belonged: functionalism.[103] What makes Merton's account of the rain dance so very characteristic of this school is that he assumed that a socio-cultural phenomenon can have a function beyond the understanding of the actors involved. As the functionalist anthropologist Radcliffe-Brown stated: "The reasons given by the members of a community for any custom they observe are important data for the anthropologist. But it is to fall into grievous error to suppose that they give a valid explanation of the custom."[104] Emile Durkheim even claimed that we humans are "the victims of an illusion which leads us to believe that we have ourselves produced what has been imposed upon us externally."[105] The functionalists acknowledged that many functions *are* intended and recognized – Merton defined these as "manifest functions" – but the latent functions interested them most. Merton even stated that uncovering the latent functions was his primary task as a social scientist.[106]

In the functionalists' explanations of specific socio-cultural phenomena, relatively little attention is paid to the avowed purposes of the actors. For instance, people believe that they punish criminals as a form of retribution, but a latent function, Durkheim claimed, was the enhancement of collective sentiments through the emotional solidarity that results from commonly expressed aggression.[107] Similarly, the function of magic, as argued by Bronislaw Malinowski, was not to be found in the intended effects "on the soil and spirits, on the spider and the full moon. This is a native belief which, important as it is, does not directly bind us." Rather, it was "the indirect effects of the words upon the psychology and physiology of the native organism, and hence upon social organization, which probably gives us the best clue to the nature of magical thinking."[108] And whereas religious believers may be convinced that their worship of gods serves a higher purpose, many functionalists have argued that a hidden function is more tangible because religion reinforces the integration and preservation of society.[109]

The notion that cultural practices fulfill unintended and unrecognized functions was not only confined to functionalism. During the 1970s, the cultural materialist anthropologist Marvin

---

[102] Merton, 118–19.
[103] Moore, *Visions of Culture*, 42–58, 122–46; Wallace and Wolf, *Contemporary Sociological Theory*, 15–66; Ritzer, *Contemporary Sociological Theory*, 13–18, 64–84.
[104] Radcliffe-Brown, *Structure and Function*, 142.
[105] Durkheim, *Les Règles de La Méthode Sociologique*, 7."Nous sommes alors dupes d'une illusion qui nous fait croire que nous avons élaboré nous-meme ce qui s'est imposé a nous du dehors."
[106] Merton, *Social Theory and Social Structure*, 114–35.
[107] Durkheim, *Les Règles de La Méthode Sociologique*, 69–72, 95–97.
[108] Malinowski, *Coral Hardens and Their Magic*, 241.
[109] Durkheim, *Les formes élémentaires*; Radcliffe-Brown, *Structure and Function*, 153–77.

Harris garnered much attention with his argument that apparently irrational beliefs actually form hidden adaptations to material-ecological environments.[110] The Hindus may believe that they refrain from eating cows to protect their karma, but an underlying explanation, as argued by Harris, was the preservation of an indispensable draught animal and source of manure.[111] The Aztec Indians may have been genuinely convinced that their sacrifice and consumption of humans ensured the rise of the Sun, but a hidden function of these rituals was again, different. Due to the lack of domesticated animals as a source of food, the Aztecs suffered from protein deficiencies, and this was made up by human flesh.[112]

Table 1: The functionalist explanatory model

Practice	Intention	Function
Rain dance	Making rain	Social cohesion
Punishment	Retribution	Enhancement of collective sentiments
Holy cow	Karma	Preservation of indispensable animal
Human sacrifice	Rising of the Sun	Protein intake

The former popularity of the functionalist explanatory model (see Table 1) should not come as a surprise. Many socio-cultural practices do indeed appear to be adaptive in ways that the actors did not intend or recognize as such. What is particularly striking is that the avowed purposes very often do not coincide with apparently functional consequences. However, Merton articulated these views over half a century ago, and the privilege of hindsight now allows us to conclude that the social sciences have taken an ironic turn since that point. Later on, it was Merton's analysis *itself* that became a relic of the past. The functionalist school lost its dominant position in social theory long ago. While the functionalists claimed to uncover all kinds of latent functions around the middle of the twentieth century, in the course of the last sixty years this form of reasoning became unpopular and the influence of functionalism waned. Many other schools of thought, ranging from practice theory, social constructivism, symbolic anthropology, to rational choice theory, won the day. While these movements had all sorts of mutual disagreements, an aversion to functionalism tied them all together.[113] The functionalists have been accused of many things – more about that later – but it was this idea of unintended and unrecognized functions that vexed opponents in particular.[114]

---

[110] Harris, *Cows, Pigs, Wars, & Witches*; Harris, *Cannibals and Kings*, 1991.
[111] Harris, *Cows, Pigs, Wars, & Witches*, 11–34.
[112] Harris, *Cannibals and Kings*, 1991, 127–69.
[113] See, for example; Dahrendorf, "Out of Utopia"; Homans, *Bringing Men Back In*; Berger and Luckmann, *The Social Construction of Reality*; Gouldner, *The Coming Crisis of Western Sociology*; Giddens, *The Constitution of Society*.
[114] Moore, *Visions of Culture*, 146–47, 205–7; Hamilton, *The Sociology of Religion*, 103–8; Stark, "Micro Foundations of Religion," 272.

The criticisms of functionalism

To understand why functionalist theory came to be seen as deficient, let us first return to the Hopi rain dance, and we shall especially focus on the critiques as formulated by the school of practice theory. As we saw, the avowed purpose of the ritual was to make rain, and the latent function of social cohesion, Robert Merton argued, was unintended and remained unrecognized by the Hopi themselves. But as critics asked, would it really be true that making rain, for the Hopi, was the only thing this ritual was about? A young Hopi man on his way to the rain dance was possibly also eager to marry and therefore curious about the possible candidates he might encounter that day. Similarly, he might urgently need to talk about a little bridge over the creek that needed repairing. Perhaps the relationship with a neighboring tribe was under serious pressure; hence, he was looking forward to the communal ceremony that always provided a sense of common strength. If the Hopi had been asked directly what this dance was for, his answer may well have been the making of rain. However, underneath, it is likely that he did have a certain knowledge that this dance was about more than just that.

If the arguments of practice theorists such as Pierre Bourdieu and Anthony Giddens are to be considered, these forms of tacit knowledge play a crucial role in human social life.[115] Apart from the directly conscious and avowed purposes of our behavior, we also possess, as Bourdieu defined it, a *sens pratique* – a sense of practice – or, as formulated by Giddens: a practical consciousness.[116] In our daily routines, from labor, ceremony and leisure to the way we dress, talk, or move our bodies, we are supposed to possess a profound level of practical knowledge. If asked about this practical knowledge directly, we will not be able to translate it into discursive expression. However, the role of this *sens pratique* in the day-to-day construction and reproduction of the structures of society is seen as crucial. According to this view, Merton's assumption that the rain dance was about more than just rain could have been correct. His mistake, however, was to conclude that these functions existed beyond Hopi knowledge. The social functions of the rain dance may not have been unintended and unrecognized after all.[117]

Bourdieu and Giddens highlighted a crucial weakness in the functionalist argument. After reading these social theorists, the clear boundary between manifest and latent functions appears to be simplistic and too clear cut. To understand the functional character of social phenomena, these unexpressed levels of knowledge must be taken into account as well. Research on the Hopi has also shown that from these Indians' own perspective the practical and the spiritual are inextricably interrelated.[118] What provides Bourdieu's and Giddens' argument with additional strength is that their ideas correspond to, or are at least not contradicted by, the evidence provided by scientists in other fields. Psychologists and cognitive neuroscientists also claim that

---

[115] Bourdieu, *Esquisse de théorie de la pratique*; Bourdieu, *Le Sens Pratique*; Giddens, *The Constitution of Society*; Jenkins, *Pierre Bourdieu*.
[116] Giddens, *The Constitution of Society*, xxii.
[117] Giddens and Pierson, *Conversation with Anthony Giddens*, 92.
[118] Loftin, *Religion and Hopi Life in the Twentieth Century*.

the human mind makes decisions of which people are not consciously aware, let alone are able to express discursively.[119] This claim means that an ultimate scientific explanation for the origin of unexpressed functions, as Bourdieu and Giddens envisioned them, appears possible.

What if we ask the same question about the origin of latent functions as Merton defined them, if latent knowledge was not the cause? Merton remained unclear about this issue and did not offer an explanation beyond a rather vague appeal to unintended consequences.[120] This appeal is hardly convincing, however, because it remains unclear why unintended consequences should lead to functions. Given the undirected nature of unintended consequences, chaos would be a more likely outcome than functions. The functionalists ultimately explained social phenomena by referring to their effects, which critics found unsatisfactory because science is supposed to explain things from their causes – the "functionalist fallacy" it is called.[121] In other words, the functionalists presented us with an explanandum but failed to provide a convincing explanans.[122] As Anthony Giddens concluded in regard to Merton's account of the Hopi rain dance:

> This treats the Hopi as ignorant of what they are up to. Participants in most ceremonials, after all, have some sense of the various ends they might serve. Moreover, showing that the rain dance fosters social solidarity *cannot possibly* be an explanation of the actions of the Hopi unless at least some of them sense this is so and act accordingly.[123]

This weakness made the functionalists an easy target for their critics. By talking about social institutions that contain functions beyond people's knowledge or social systems that have needs, they could be accused of treating society as if it possessed a mind or consciousness of its own, while only people possess such capabilities. The cultural materialist Marvin Harris spoke of culture that adapted to the environment, whereas again, culture should be considered a means through which *individuals* adapt to their environment.[124] The functionalists were blamed for reification.[125] Abstract concepts such as "social systems" or "culture" appeared to live a life of their own. Sometimes this reification appeared almost mystical. During his lifetime, Durkheim was accused of mysticism and platonic idealism, and some even argued that he had remained stuck in the metaphysical stage of thought.[126] Marvin Harris faced similar ridicule. If the rational ecological adaptations that he believed to have uncovered were not created by knowledgeable

---

[119] Dijksterhuis and Nordgren, "A Theory of Unconscious Thought"; Haggard P, "Human Volition."
[120] Merton, *Social Theory and Social Structure*, 73–138.
[121] Callinicos, *Making History*, 61.
[122] Elster, *Explaining Technical Change*; Pettit, "Functional Explanation and Virtual Selection"; Stein and Stein, *The Anthropology of Religion, Magic, and Witchcraft.*, 20.
[123] Giddens and Pierson, *Conversation with Anthony Giddens*, 92. Emphasis added.
[124] Giddens, *The Constitution of Society*; Keesing and Strathern, *Cultural Anthropology*, 128; Sanderson, *The Evolution of Human Sociality*, 152; Salisbury, "Non-Equilibrium Models in New Guinea Ecology."
[125] Stein and Stein, *The Anthropology of Religion, Magic, and Witchcraft.*, 20.
[126] Lukes, *Emile Durkheim*, 296–319.

actors, then who or what had created them? The "Big Ecologist in the Sky" perhaps?[127] This critique was painful because Durkheim and Harris presented their approach as scientific par excellence. Yet, a satisfactory counter-argument remained elusive.

The diverse opponents of functionalism did not deny that society or culture could be a coercive force, acting on individuals. The social constructivist Peter Berger stated that we produce society, but that society also produces us.[128] The symbolic anthropologist Clifford Geertz described culture as "a set of control mechanisms (…) for the governing of behavior."[129] The crucial distinction between functionalism and many of its critics, however, remained the umbilical cord between socio-cultural functions and the knowledge that actors have of them. Several quotes from prominent social scientists illustrate this point. "Man is an animal suspended in webs of significance he *himself* has spun", Clifford Geertz wrote.[130] The anthropologists Roger Keesing and Andrew Strathern commented that "rationality is in the eye of the cultural actor, not the Big Ecologist in the Sky." Or as Peter Berger expressed it: "society is a product of man. It has no other being except that which is bestowed upon it by human activity and consciousness."[131]

The strengths of functionalism
However, though such critiques of functionalism are legitimate in many ways, the arguments of their opponents contain unsatisfactory elements as well. The functionalists did not offer a convincing explanans, but does this necessarily imply that their explanandum is invalid? Despite all of these criticisms, socio-cultural phenomena do indeed appear to possess a functional integration and adaptive ability that transcends the conscious and subconscious knowledge of human actors. From state structures and economic systems to religions or languages, socio-cultural structures often appear more functionally organized than would have been possible had they been designed by human hand. In the words of the economists Geoffrey Hodgson and Thorbjorn Knudsen: "Many complex and efficacious human institutions such as language and common law are not the outcome of an overall plan."[132] The role of individual actors in the formation of functional systems may often seem marginal at best and hardly inspired by knowledge of the eventual consequences of their actions. What remains particularly striking, as I stated earlier, is that the avowed purposes and seemingly functional consequences very often do not coincide.

The belief of the Hopi was most likely sincere, just as Hindus genuinely believe in the importance of cows for personal karma. The authenticity of the beliefs in fact seems crucial, because otherwise these traditions would lose much of their prowess – if Hindus no longer

---

[127] Keesing and Strathern, *Cultural Anthropology*, 128.
[128] Hamilton, *The Sociology of Religion.*, IV:50.
[129] Geertz, *The Interpretation of Cultures*, 43.
[130] Geertz, 5. Emphasis added.
[131] Hamilton, *The Sociology of Religion.*, IV:50; Keesing and Strathern, *Cultural Anthropology*, 128.
[132] Hodgson and Knudsen, *Darwin's Conjecture*, 6.

believed that eating their cows *really* affects their karma, there would be less of a barrier to eating them. However, how do people so often develop convictions that are factually false, yet apparently functional in their results? A possible explanation is that some Hopi were well aware that common dancing does not actually create rain, but grasped the social function of others sharing the belief that it does. What if they then purposely encouraged the ritual for that reason? In other words, was the rain dance a product of socio-cultural intelligent design? Though this option should not be rejected out of hand, it is questionable whether human actors possess that much sociological ingenuity in deceiving their companions.

It is also questionable whether an appeal to the *sens pratique* will always provide a sufficient explanation in such cases. As we discussed, it is possible that the Hopi, at the back of their minds, did have a certain knowledge that their dance was about more than just rain. Yet, whether the Hopi in their *sens pratique* also realized that it was functional for them to have a *genuine* belief in the magical powers of their dance, and whether this belief was ingeniously introduced and transmitted from the *sens pratique* for that reason, is something rather different. The capabilities of our practical consciousness could be easily overestimated this way. This explanatory route is also unsatisfactorily complex. Even if one would consider the scenarios of deliberate intelligent design or design through the *sens pratique* to be plausible ones, we would still face problems regarding evidence. How can we examine empirically what the Hopi were consciously or subconsciously aware of when creating their practice? We have no sources that would allow for such an investigation.

In other words, the counter-functionalist argument appears to contain its own unsolved mysteries as well, which is most likely why the functionalist reasoning turned out to be harder to eradicate than expected. Some social scientists continued working within the tradition, and as the anthropologists Jon McGee and Richard Warms wrote about their colleagues: "Functionalism continues to be a powerful idea, and most anthropologists are probably more functionalist than they generally acknowledge."[133] The weaknesses in the counter functionalist argument beg the question of whether the evolution of socio-cultural functions could nonetheless be guided by adaptive forces beyond our knowledge. But before we move on to the discussion of what these forces could be, we need to address the arguably even more complicated aforementioned issue of what the ultimate purposes of biological, and also cultural, adaptations are like.

2.4 The purposes of biological functions

"Cui bono?" is a question that Daniel Dennett does not get tired of asking. Who benefits? It is a stock Latin phrase often used by lawyers, but for Dennett the question is of great importance when examining characteristics in the biological and socio-cultural worlds. When we are confronted with traits that seem functional, it is crucial to ask ourselves what they are ultimately

---

[133] McGee and Warms, *Anthropological Theory*, 154; Wallace and Wolf, *Contemporary Sociological Theory*, 57–66.

functional for. But as Dennett warns us, the ultimate beneficiaries of functions can be elusive, so we need to cast our nets widely.[134] One of the reasons for Dennett for embracing Darwinian theory so enthusiastically, is that he believes that it helps uncover some of the less obvious beneficiaries. Selfish gene theory in particular made a lasting impression on him, and he is eager to extend its insights into the sociocultural domain. In the next chapter we will discuss Dennett's proposals in that regard. But first, let us explore how evolutionary biology has addressed the *cui bono* question, and in what way selfish gene theory claims to have offered a breakthrough.

What adaptations in living nature are essentially functional for, was a question that already occupied Darwin. Overall, he was inclined to think that the struggle for life was most intense between individuals of the same species, for instance when they competed for food within the same area.[135] Traits that survive, like camouflage, claws, leaves, or fur, are normally for the benefit of the individual organism. Yet, Darwin realized that this model runs into some trouble.[136] What, for instance, about the sting of a bee? The trait seems to offer protection to the bee's community, but for the individual bee it is an outright disaster, as using the sting often kills it. Many bees are even sterile, and apparently devote their entire lives to the well-being of the community. Such traits look like evolutionary dead-ends. So why did natural selection not remove them from the population? The solution, Darwin presumed, lay in applying natural selection beyond the individual. He wrote: "in social animals it [natural selection] will adapt the structure of each individual for the benefit of the community; if each in consequence profits by the selected change."[137] Darwin hinted that the sacrifices of some members are compensated by the enhanced survival of other members of the community, who subsequently produce offspring with similar altruistic traits. Nevertheless, he admitted that such altruistic traits were his theory's "most serious special difficulty."[138]

Darwin was right to recognize this as a challenge.[139] Current evolutionary biology shares his main focus on individual selection, since the bulk of adaptations indeed seem to benefit individual organisms.[140] However, the examples of organisms who make altruistic sacrifices for others are numerous, indicating that individual selection cannot be the whole story. Importantly, altruism here does not equal cooperation, as the latter is even far more widespread in nature, like flocking birds, penguins huddling together, or mammals that hunt or herd in packs.[141] Unlike altruism, cooperation is not much of an evolutionary mystery because all the participating individuals can benefit from the interactions; huddling preserves heat, while flocking and herding offers protection against predation. The explanatory problem of altruism only begins where

---

[134] Dennett, *Breaking the Spell*, 62–63.
[135] Darwin, *The Origin of Species*, 126; Depew and Weber, *Darwinism Evolving*, 75.
[136] Darwin, *The Origin of Species*, 258–63; Darwin, *The Descent of Man*, 149–57.
[137] Darwin, *The Origin of Species*, 135.
[138] Darwin, 262.
[139] Godfrey-Smith, *Philosophy of Biology*, 120; Wilson, *This View of Life*, 75; Dawkins, *The Selfish Gene*, 4.
[140] Okasha, "Units and Levels of Selection," 203.
[141] Dawkins, *The Selfish Gene*, 166; Strassmann and Queller, "Cooperation and Conflict," 671–72.

organisms help others, while apparently harming their *own* chances of survival. Some forms of altruism are still relatively easy to explain, like reciprocal altruism, where animals do each other small favors in return.[142] Think of apes who groom each other or vampire bats that exchange blood. In relatively stable groups, where animals can recognize and remember each other, such practices may benefit all the individuals involved – we might even wonder whether this is altruism at all.

A point where things become more difficult is when animals take significant risks for others. A classic example is prey animals who send alarm calls when predators are in sight.[143] The trait looks adaptive because it helps others look for shelter, but not so much from the caller's point of view: the alarm might divert the predator's attention to the caller. Another example, and one that is so very obvious that it sometimes escapes attention, is parental care: many organisms make sacrifices for their offspring.[144] Darwin was right to regard social species of bees, but also termites, ants, or wasps, as the most serious challenge.[145] Such species are characterized by a division of labor in which some individuals specialize in reproduction, most notably the queens, while many others, the "workers", fulfil cooperative tasks such as food collection, building the nest, rearing the young, or protecting the colony. Examples can be beguiling, like ants who developed thickened and enlarged heads to block the nest's entrance, or so called "kamikaze termites" that explode in order to glue enemies of the colony in poisonous secretions.

It is not only *between* organisms that altruism can take self-destructive forms – it also occurs *within* organisms. One of the essential discoveries of nineteenth-century biology was that large organisms are made up of vast collections of cells that all descended from other cells. Most organisms are unicellular, but in the evolution of life large assemblages of cooperating cells have evolved, the multicellular organisms, which are also characterized by an internal division of labor.[146] Some germ cells reproduce into a far future, while the overwhelming majority of somatic cells function as evolutionary dead-ends. The somatic cells all specialize, as skin, brain, or liver cells, and their existence is entirely devoted to the well-being of the whole. Like the kamikaze termites, somatic cells can also kill themselves in "programmed cell death", which occurs as soon as their existence burdens the organism.[147] These mechanisms are not perfect, because every now and then some cells start reproducing for their own, which we call cancer.[148] But cancer is unusual, since individual cells normally work harmoniously together for the higher-level benefit of the organism.

The explanatory problem of altruism is as follows: alarm sounding animals, kamikaze termites, and somatic cells hinder their own survival, so that their traits should be doomed. If

---

[142] Dawkins, *The Selfish Gene*, 183–88, 202–33.
[143] Dawkins, 168–69; Kay, Lehmann, and Keller, "Kin Selection and Altruism."
[144] Dawkins, *The Selfish Gene*, 6.
[145] Keller, Chapuisat, and Losos, "Evolution of Eusociality"; Queller and Strassmann, "Kin Selection and Inclusive Fitness."
[146] Dawkins, *The Selfish Gene*, 258–59; Smith and Szathmary, *The Major Transitions in Evolution*, 201–16.
[147] Wilson, *This View of Life*, 80.
[148] Yong, *I Contain Multitudes*, 87; Okasha, "Units and Levels of Selection," 200; Wilson, *This View of Life*, 79–84.

evolution is as relentless a competitive process as Darwin assumed, selfishness should reign everywhere. Earlier on we saw that the key debates of evolution long focused on the mechanism of change, but when the dominant position of Darwinism was established, this problem of altruism came prominently to the surface. A new round of debate was triggered in the 1960s when the Scottish zoologist Vero Wynne-Edwards argued that animals altruistically regulate individual reproduction, in order not to overexploit the carrying capacity of the environment.[149] His explanation was that groups of altruists outcompeted groups of non-altruists, as the latter overexploited their resources and thus sealed their own fate. A somewhat similar argument was made by the Austrian ethologist Konrad Lorenz, who highlighted that animals from the same species hardly go all the way in mutual combats, as gestures of surrender are often accepted by the victor.[150] Lorenz interpreted this as an adaptation for the benefit of the species, that prevented costly conflicts.

The gene-centered view of evolution

However, many biologists were no longer willing to buy such explanations.[151] People like George C. Williams and William D. Hamilton pointed out that group selection, or species selection, suffer from the problem of internal subversion.[152] Groups of altruists can be invaded by free riders who reap the benefits of the group without contributing to it themselves – think of an animal that profits from alarm calls, but never raises alarms. Through mathematical modelling it was argued that selection between individuals is fast and continuing, while selection between groups is weak and slow. So even when free riders make the group go downhill, there is still plenty of time for them to prosper at the expense of altruistic fellows. Groups are simply thought of as too instable an entity to become a target of selection.[153] Yet, if group selection is deficient, then how to explain higher level altruism? Williams's and Hamilton's key innovation was not to look at the higher level of groups or species, but rather, and quite counterintuitively, to move a few levels down; they descended to the level of the gene.

What this generation of evolutionary biologists realized, building on insights from the Modern Synthesis, was that Darwinian selection is essentially about things being transmitted or not being transmitted. While individuals, groups, or species are not transmitted, ultimately it is the survival of *genes* that counts – genes here often being defined as segments of DNA that survive the shuffle of sexual recombination.[154] So to answer the *cui bono* question these biologists looked at adaptations from the perspective of the genes' reproduction. Hamilton made the argument even "more vivid by attributing to the genes, temporarily, intelligence and a certain

---

[149] Wynne-Edwards, *Animal Dispersion in Relation to Social Behaviour*; Dawkins, *The Selfish Gene*, 7–10; Okasha, "Units and Levels of Selection," 200–201.
[150] Lorenz, *Das sogenannte Böse*; Okasha, "Units and Levels of Selection," 201.
[151] Godfrey-Smith, *Philosophy of Biology*, 42–45, 120–28; Depew and Weber, *Darwinism Evolving*, 368–74.
[152] Williams, *Adaptation and Natural Selection*; Hamilton, "The Genetical Evolution of Social Behaviour. I."
[153] Dawkins, *The Selfish Gene*, 7–8.
[154] Depew and Weber, *Darwinism Evolving*, 369–70.

freedom of choice."[155] Suddenly a whole lot of things began to make more sense. Genes reside inside organisms, so normally genes "want" their organism to flourish – this would explain why most adaptations benefit individuals. However, since organisms are only temporary carriers, genes must ensure that copies of them will live on in other organisms. The most obvious way of doing so is to create new organisms that carry the same genes, and to make the parents care about their offspring – this would explain parental altruism.[156] But as was realized by Hamilton in particular, the same genes not only reside in offspring, but also in other close relatives, like brothers and sisters, or nephews and nieces. So, if altruism aids close relatives, there is a certain likelihood that the recipient of the altruistic action will itself be an altruist. When relatives are saved, copies of the genes are saved, and altruism might spread.[157]

The theory is known as "kin selection" or "inclusive fitness", and it makes a clear prediction: non-reciprocal altruism should focus on close relatives. What helped make the theory a lasting success is that empirical research has provided abundant confirmation. Alarm calls predominantly focus on kin, and the underlying rationale would be that one carrier of the involved genes is put at risk in order to save the lives of a few other carriers.[158] The most startling evidence was found in social insects – the colonies of which are in fact huge families with an unusual genetic system named haplodiploidy.[159] The genetic details of this system need not detain us here, but its crucial consequence is that individual females are normally more closely related to full sisters than to their own offspring. From the reproductive perspective of the genes, it is thus not a good strategy to let these females have offspring themselves. Rather, the females should devote their lives to the reproduction of the mother, the queen, and protect her life at all costs. This would explain kamikaze-like actions: the deed kills the organism, but enhances the reproductive chances of the genes involved. Further proof for kin selection was provided by multicellular organisms, as cells belonging to the same organism are genetic clones.[160] The somatic cells are like the "workers" who make the organism function as a whole, to ensure the continuation of the genetically identical germline.

This gene-centered perspective reached its culmination in 1976, when Richard Dawkins encapsulated the theory into his famous metaphor of "the selfish gene".[161] In Dawkins's view, genes are the "replicators" of evolution, who's true purpose "is to survive, no more no less."[162] In a mutual struggle for survival, genes have evolved ever more complex ways of making copies

---

[155] Hamilton, "Altruism and Related Phenomena, Mainly in Social Insects," 195.
[156] Dawkins, *The Selfish Gene*, 89–93, 105.
[157] Dawkins, 88–107; Okasha, "Units and Levels of Selection," 202.
[158] Dawkins, *The Selfish Gene*, 168–69; Strassmann and Queller, "Cooperation and Conflict"; Kay, Lehmann, and Keller, "Kin Selection and Altruism."
[159] Hamilton, "The Genetical Evolution of Social Behaviour. I"; Hamilton, "Altruism and Related Phenomena, Mainly in Social Insects"; Depew and Weber, *Darwinism Evolving*, 371; Dawkins, *The Selfish Gene*, 71–75; Queller and Strassmann, "Kin Selection and Inclusive Fitness," 217.
[160] Okasha, "Units and Levels of Selection," 205.
[161] Dawkins, *The Selfish Gene*; Dawkins, *The Blind Watchmaker*.
[162] Dawkins, *The Selfish Gene*, 15, 45.

of themselves, and Dawkins considers organisms as just a way of achieving that goal. Organisms are the "vehicles", or "survival machines" of genes, and their whole performance is in aid "of one thing and one thing only, the spreading of DNA."[163] Normally, the interests of genes and organisms coincide: genes that program gazelles to run away from lions enhance their own survival as well as the gazelle's. But when the reproductive interests of genes and organisms do *not* coincide, ruthless selfishness comes to the fore. In that case, genes make organisms do things that are not good for organisms, but for the good of the genes' own survival. Dawkins wrote about the "selfish replicators".

> Now they swarm in huge colonies, safe inside gigantic lumbering robots, sealed off from the outside world, communicating with it by tortuous indirect routes, manipulating it by remote control. They are in you and in me; they created us, body and mind; and their preservation is the ultimate rationale for our existence.[164]

Selfish gene theory makes logical sense, because after all, genes that instruct organisms to make more copies of genes will be most successful at exactly that.[165] Despite its clarity the theory keeps giving rise to two common misconceptions. The first states that Dawkins argues that *organisms* are selfish. The philosopher Mary Midgley: "He [Dawkins] is an uncritical philosophic egoist in the first place, and merely feeds the egoist assumption into his a priori biological speculation", for instance when claiming, as Midgley summarizes it, that "the emotional nature of man is exclusively self-interested."[166] To some extent Dawkins himself is to blame for this misconception, as one sentence from *The Selfish Gene* states that "we are born selfish."[167] But this claim contradicts much of the rest of his book, because it is by placing selfishness at the level of genes that Dawkins wants to explain why organisms, under certain conditions, are altruistic.[168] In a later edition he also asks his readers to "mentally delete that rogue sentence."[169]

A second misconception is that Dawkins argues that genes are *literally* selfish. The biologist Steven Rose laments in a critique that "genes cannot be selfish; it is people, not neurons nor yet brains or minds, who think, remember, and who show emotion."[170] But obviously that is not what Dawkins meant.[171] Time and again he emphasized that genes are molecules without any literal intentions, emotions or intelligence at all: "they did not know they were struggling, or

---

[163] Dawkins, *The Blind Watchmaker*, 111; Dawkins, *The Selfish Gene*, xxi.
[164] Dawkins, *The Selfish Gene*, 19.
[165] Haig, *From Darwin to Derrida*, 17–27.
[166] Midgley, "Gene-Juggling," 439.
[167] Dawkins, *The Selfish Gene*, 3.
[168] Dawkins, 88, 202–33, 267.
[169] Dawkins, ix.
[170] Rose, "The Biology of the Future and the Future of Biology," 141.
[171] See for instance: Dawkins, *The Selfish Gene*, 89, 139, 151, 184, 208; Dennett, *Darwin's Dangerous Idea*, 328.

worry about it: the struggle was conducted without any hard feelings, indeed without feelings of any kind."[172] The reason for writing about genes *as if* they possess the emotion of selfishness is that it makes it easier for us to comprehend what is happening. It is the key insight of Darwinism: something can look and behave *as if* there is an intelligent agency involved, while actually there is not. As the chemist Lesly Orgel put it, "evolution is cleverer than you are".[173] Had genes literally been shrewd selfish agents, they would probably roughly be doing what they are already doing.

The fruitfulness of Dawkins's metaphor is further illustrated when we consider interactions between organisms and other life forms that reside within them.[174] Multicellular organisms not only host their own genes, but also a whole ecosystem of bacteria, fungi, protists and viruses, known as the microbiome. Dawkins argues that the relationship between organisms and such creatures is somewhat similar to the relationship between organisms and selfish genes. Normally, the survival of microbes or viruses depends on the survival of their hosts, so they do not "want" their hosts to be harmed. We often think of viruses and bacteria as harmful, but life scientists have increasingly come to the conclusion that most of them are actually neutral or beneficial.[175] The survival of organisms can even depend on these tiny creatures, as they fulfill a wide range of positive coevolutionary functions, like enabling the storing of fat, the creation of new blood vessels, or the fine tuning of the immune system. Human guts, for instance, are inhabited by innumerable microbes that play essential roles in the digestion of food. Squids contain a bacterium that creates light inside them, which ensures that the animals do not cast a shadow in the moonlight when seen from below.[176]

However, we should not be naïve. Eventually, it is only their own survival that the DNA (or RNA) of microbes or viruses cares about. As soon as the reproductive interests of guests and hosts diverge, ruthless selfishness comes to the fore again.[177] Especially when microbes or viruses quickly move from organism to organism, there is little hindrance to causing severe damage to their temporary hosts as a by-product of their spread. It is something we call contagious disease. Such pathogens can in certain cases even adaptively "manipulate" or "hijack" the bodies and behavior of their organisms, turning them into vehicles for their own reproduction. The rhinovirus for instance, better known as the common cold, makes our noses run, which has no function for us.[178] But it *is* very functional for the rhinovirus, because through the snot it gets on our fingers, then on objects, and when other people touch those objects the virus enters new bodies. A more frightening example is the rabies virus.[179] When it enters a dog it manipulates the

---

[172] Dawkins, *The Selfish Gene*, 19.
[173] Quoted in: Dennett, *Breaking the Spell*, 187.
[174] Dawkins, *The Selfish Gene*, 234–66; Dawkins, *The Extended Phenotype*, 209–27; Cordingley, *Viruses*, 16–18.
[175] Yong, *I Contain Multitudes*; Wilson, *This View of Life*, 58–65; Moelling, *Supermacht des Lebens*; Zimmer, *A Planet of Viruses*.
[176] Yong, *I Contain Multitudes*; Strassmann and Queller, "Cooperation and Conflict," 672.
[177] Dawkins, *The Selfish Gene*, 234–66; Yong, *I Contain Multitudes*, 76–83; Bailey, "Evolution of Apparently Nonadaptive Behavior," 713.
[178] Zimmer, *A Planet of Viruses*, 10.
[179] Dawkins, *The Selfish Gene*, 246–47; Yong, *I Contain Multitudes*, 76.

dog's brain, turning normally quite peaceful animals into restless wanderers with foaming mouths who aggressively look for other animals to bite. If we ask what function this behavior has for the dog we will not get anywhere. In fact, it is quite dangerous for dogs because they might be killed for it. But when we ask what function is has for rabies, it all suddenly makes sense: through the bites the virus is transmitted. Another fearsome example is *Toxoplasma gondii*.[180] This parasite has a life cycle that can depend on a phase inside mice, and a phase inside cats, so in order to survive it needs to get from mice into cats. The microbe's way of achieving that goal is by manipulating the mouse's brain and making it feel attracted to the smell of cats, thereby ending up in a cat's belly. Hence, organisms can be used as the marionettes of their invisible microbial or viral puppeteers.[181]

The relationship between organisms and their guests is an ambiguous one.[182] Complex organisms cannot survive without their microbiome, but exploitation, manipulation and abuse are perpetually lurking in the dark. Some parasites can even be good and bad at the same time. Wasps, for instance, cannot lay eggs without the Wolbachia bacteria, but whenever it serves the bacterium's own purposes, it turns male wasps into females, thereby harming the reproductive interests of wasps.[183] The science writer Ed Yong describes microbes as having evolved "a continuum of lifestyles, between 'bad' parasites and 'good' mutualism", with interactions also being flexible, as "our allies can disappoint us and our enemies can rally to our side."[184] Again, we should be mindful about the power of metaphor here. Microbes or viruses obviously do not "manipulate" or "hijack" their organisms in any literal sense. Like selfish genes they have no intentions, intelligence, or consciousness whatsoever. The anthropomorphic language is used in order to make it easier for us to understand what is going on, and to make predictions about novel phenomena.[185]

Criticisms

Yet, apart from some obvious misinterpretations, selfish gene theory is also criticized on more serious methodological and empirical grounds. To a large extent the theory is built upon the Modern Synthesis, which, as we saw, ruled out Lamarckian inheritance entirely, and privileged the gene as the ultimate unit of heredity. Selfish gene theory then radicalized this perspective by anchoring all nature's purposes into the reproductive interests of genes. However, numerous voices in biology maintain that this has taken things too far. It is claimed that we need an "expanded" or "extended synthesis" that offers a richer and more inclusive picture of

---

[180] Yong, *I Contain Multitudes*, 76; Dennett, *Breaking the Spell*, 63.
[181] Bailey, "Evolution of Apparently Nonadaptive Behavior," 713; Yong, *I Contain Multitudes*, 76.
[182] Yong, *I Contain Multitudes*; Cordingley, *Viruses*, 39–45.
[183] Yong, *I Contain Multitudes*, 78.
[184] Yong, 80–82.
[185] Cordingley, *Viruses*, 2.

evolution.[186] Many of its supporters hasten to add that it is not Darwinian theory as such that they have troubles with, but, as Eva Jablonka and Marion Lamb put it, "the prevalent gene-based unidimensional version of it."[187]

A first strand of critique maintains that *selection* takes place at more levels than genes alone. According to a counter-model named "multilevel selection theory", genes have no special status, as other entities can also become targets of selection.[188] "One of the beauties of multilevel selection theory is that it employs the same principles at all levels of the biological hierarchy", David Sloan Wilson tells us about the approach.[189] Especially group selection is finding new support. Proponents admit that earlier models of group selection were overly naive, but it is said that the gene selectionists made a statistical error in their turn.[190] Selfish organisms may indeed outcompete altruistic organisms *within* groups, but when groups with a relatively high number of altruists vastly out reproduce groups with egoists, the undermining effects can still be compensated. Especially, a mathematical paper from 2010 by some prominent biologists triggered a new round of debate.[191]

The response of mainstream biology has been mixed. According to many the whole debate may actually revolve around a false opposition, as group selection and kin selection may come down to the same thing. In some cases, it is just more practical to look at the level of groups, the level of individuals, or the level of genes.[192] Others take a far more critical stand, though. Opponents of group selection maintain that it is unclear what concrete empirical phenomena group selection would precisely help explain.[193] Its supporters have a tendency of re-describing well-known cases of inclusive fitness, like social insects and multicellularity, as resulting from group selection, sometimes without even mentioning the wide support for the alternative model of kin selection.[194] But if group selection is an effective force, we should expect to find, as the evolutionary biologist Jerry Coyne puts it, "altruistic behavior in nature between individuals who were completely unrelated. That is, individuals would often sacrifice their lives (or reproduction) to help those who don't share their genes." Yet, as Coyne adds, "that is exactly what we *don't* see."[195] A further problem is that multilevel selection blurs the essential distinction between things that are transmitted and things that are not transmitted.[196] Richard Dawkins: "there is one

---

[186] Pigliucci and Müller, *Evolution, the Extended Synthesis*; Laland et al., "The Extended Evolutionary Synthesis"; Gould, *The Structure of Evolutionary Theory*; Jablonka and Lamb, *Evolution in Four Dimensions*.
[187] Jablonka and Lamb, *Evolution in Four Dimensions*, 4.
[188] Wilson, "Multilevel Selection and Major Transitions"; Wilson, *The Social Conquest of Earth*; Wilson, *This View of Life*, 76–92.
[189] Wilson, *Darwin's Cathedral*, 2002, 141.
[190] Wilson, 12–14; Turchin, *Ultrasociety*, 82–88.
[191] Nowak, Tarnita, and Wilson, "The Evolution of Eusociality."
[192] Walsh, Lewins, and Ariew, "The Trials of Life"; Okasha, "Units and Levels of Selection"; Sterelny and Griffiths, *Sex and Death*, 151–79.
[193] Abbot et al., "Inclusive Fitness Theory and Eusociality"; Bourke, "The Validity and Value of Inclusive Fitness Theory"; Coyne, "The Demise of Group Selection."
[194] Wilson, *This View of Life*, 77–81; Wilson, *The Social Conquest of Earth*.
[195] Coyne, "Genes First."
[196] Dawkins, "The Descent of Edward Wilson"; Hodgson and Knudsen, *Darwin's Conjecture*, 158.

thing, and only one thing, that singles genes out as unique, and that is that they are the things that go on to the next generation."[197] What effective group selection would imply is that genes are transmitted that make organisms behave in group functional ways. But as we already saw in regard to the individual organism, "selfish" interests of genes do not necessarily conflict with the interests of higher levels of organization. Enhancing group-ish behavior in an environment of effective group selection may just be the selfish genes' strategy of living on to the next generation. So, even if the empirical evidence for group selection would someday grow stronger, it is still questionable to what extent selfish gene theory is undermined.[198]

There is also another strand of critique that is perhaps more challenging, as it states that *transmission* takes place at more levels than genes alone. In that regard, it is particularly the field of epigenetics that attracts attention.[199] The term epigenetics refers to everything that happens to genetic information during the development of individual cells. All cells in multicellular organisms are genetic clones, but due to mechanisms of epigenetics in which some genes are switched on or off, cells still look remarkably different. As such, the notion of epigenetics is entirely uncontested. What is currently stimulating debates is that recent studies suggest that epigenetic changes can also be transmitted to offspring. As it is claimed, events during an organism's lifetime can affect which genes are switched on or off in subsequent generations, without any changes to the genetic code. One study for instance upholds that humans who suffered from severe hunger passed on their epigenetic effects to their offspring. Another study maintains that yellow monkeyflowers grew stronger protective hair after they were damaged by insects, and that the trait was then transmitted epigenetically to descendants who had no experience with insects themselves.[200]

Proponents of the extended synthesis also look into further non-genetic mechanisms of transmission, like the aforementioned topic of animal culture, as well as a presumably neglected process described as "niche construction".[201] The latter term refers to what happens when organisms actively seek their environments and subsequently change those environments, like rabbits that dig holes, or rats that alter their diets. Such behavior is framed as the "construction" of a new environmental "niche", which generates new environmental selection pressures and thereby adaptive change. Earlier on we saw that Dawkins tends to depict genes as active "replicators", while organisms are presented as more passive robot-like "vehicles". Epigenetics and niche construction suggest that such language might be up for renewal. The new insights indicate that changes to the organismic vehicle can be transmitted without any changes to the genetic replicator, and that the active behavior of the vehicle may change which future genes will

---

[197] Rose, Richard Dawkins interviews Steven Rose.
[198] Stewart-Williams, *The Ape That Understood the Universe*, 33.
[199] Maderspacher, "Epigenetics"; Jablonka and Lamb, *Evolution in Four Dimensions*, 111–52; Laland et al., "The Extended Evolutionary Synthesis," 4.
[200] Maderspacher, "Epigenetics," 424–25.
[201] Odling-Smee, "Niche Construction"; Laland et al., "The Extended Evolutionary Synthesis," 4; Jablonka and Lamb, *Evolution in Four Dimensions*.

be selected. Instead of speaking of the selection of atomistic "genes", Jablonka and Lamb thus propose to use more flexible and inclusive terms like "heritably varying traits", "reproducers", or developmental "networks".[202] These advances have a ring of Lamarckism, and this comparison is indeed sought explicitly.[203] One author even frames the new findings as "Lamarck's revenge".[204]

Still, mainstream evolutionary biology remains skeptical about the need for this extended synthesis. Many of these arguments are rendered overblown.[205] The possible evolutionary significance of epigenetics is indeed attracting attention, but the evidence for robust adaptive effects over many generations is still flimsy. If such effects exist at all, they are either very difficult to detect, or just some interesting exceptions to the rule of genetic adaptation.[206] The mechanisms of niche construction are far more widely accepted, but according to critics this is exactly the problem: the concept hardly offers anything new. The prominent evolutionary biologist Douglas Futuyama comments: "'Niche construction' is a new label for a wide variety of well-known phenomena, many of which have been extensively studied, but (as with every topic in evolutionary biology) some aspects have been understudied. There is no reason to consider it a neglected 'process' of evolution."[207] In summary, the need for an extended synthesis has yet to be determined. Still, even if heredity would include whole developmental networks, we may again question whether it undermines the key logic of selfish gene theory, as its logic does not necessarily rely on genes as hereditary units.[208] We could also expect developmental networks to become good at reproducing themselves, making them metaphorically "selfish".

Importantly, it was Dawkins himself who highlighted that the logic of his theory does not depend on genes. In an argument named "universal Darwinism" he maintains that the mechanism of Darwinian selection is substrate neutral, and does not even automatically depend on organic molecules.[209] "Individuals and groups are like the clouds in the sky, or dust storms in the desert", he wrote, while genes "like diamonds, are forever."[210] But importantly, Dawkins added that genes are not forever in exactly the same way as diamonds. Like the clouds in the sky DNA-molecules come and go. What makes genes robust over generations is not their particular physical structures, but, rather, the *information* encoded on those structures.[211] Any form of hereditary information that undergoes processes of non-random selection of undirected variation will result in adaptive complexity. Precisely this observation helped spark Dawkins's

---

[202] Jablonka and Lamb, *Evolution in Four Dimensions*, 77, 369–70.
[203] Jablonka and Lamb, 355–56; Gissis, Gissis, and Jablonka, *Transformations of Lamarckism*; Ward, *Lamarck's Revenge*.
[204] Ward, *Lamarck's Revenge*.
[205] Futuyma, "Evolutionary Biology Today"; Charlesworth, Barton, and Charlesworth, "The Sources of Adaptive Variation"; Coyne, "Once Again."
[206] Maderspacher, "Epigenetics," 426; Futuyma, "Evolutionary Biology Today," 6–7; Charlesworth, Barton, and Charlesworth, "The Sources of Adaptive Variation."
[207] Futuyma, "Evolutionary Biology Today," 1.
[208] Hodgson and Knudsen, *Darwin's Conjecture*, 114–15.
[209] Dawkins, "Universal Darwinism"; Godfrey-Smith, *Philosophy of Biology*, 45–49.
[210] Dawkins, *The Selfish Gene*, 34–35.
[211] Dawkins, *The Blind Watchmaker*, 170.

social-cultural application of Darwinism. It is to this application, as well as to the applications of others, that we turn in chapter three. But only after we have addressed what the established academic answers to the *cui bono* question look like in the socio-cultural world.

2.5 The purposes of cultural functions

The question of who or what benefits from socio-cultural functions has been even more a point of contention in the social sciences and the humanities than the question of how those functions come about. The debate strikes right at the heart of essential disagreements, not least because of its ideological ramifications. The *cui bono* question is often closely related to what we think society should look like, and what responsibilities academics have. More so than the biological debate, the socio-cultural debate is a rather messy one, with schools and disciplines talking past each other, and answers being sought in many directions. In order to gain some overview, three major perspectives will be discerned. A first perspective explains socio-cultural phenomena as functional for the maintenance of social systems. The second looks for the maintenance of power structures, while a third focuses on the fulfillment of individual needs. This classification is somewhat arbitrary and should be understood as nothing more than an ideal type. Various schools of thought also drew inspiration from each other, and the work of major social theorists is more multifaceted than can be discussed here. Still, the threefold division helps to bring some order to the chaos.

The maintenance of social systems

The first perspective, which focuses on the maintenance of social systems, is essentially about the question of social order.[212] Why does society not fall apart? How do individuals maintain social systems that last over many generations? According to scholars working within this orientation it is humanity's socio-cultural phenomena that are doing the trick. Through their symbols, rituals, traditions, institutions, and beliefs, people learn to stick together and act as a part of a greater whole. Society is seen as a huge organism, with humans being like the cells, or the organs, all playing their part in the grander scheme of things. This view of the socio-cultural world is a very old one. Ancient Chinese and Greek philosophers already reflected on the social utility of religious rituals, and the comparison of human societies to organisms is one of the most pervasive notions of social thought.[213] Especially after the chaotic events of the French Revolution many people contemplated on the hidden cohesive effects of traditions. Like Napoleon Bonaparte, who in religion did not so much "see the mystery of the incarnation, but that of social order."[214]

---

[212] Ritzer, *Contemporary Sociological Theory*, 13–19, 64–85; Wallace and Wolf, *Contemporary Sociological Theory*, 15–65; Farganis, *Readings in Social Theory*, 55–90, 181–218.
[213] Moore, *Visions of Culture*, 107; Maclay, *The Social Organism*; Radcliffe-Brown, *Structure and Function*, 157–63.
[214] Carpentier and Lebrun, *Histoire de France*, 256. "dans la religion, je ne vois pas le mystère de l'Incarnation mais celui de l'ordre social."

The modern scientific expression of this perspective is to be found in functionalism, and most particularly in the work of Emile Durkheim.[215] We already noted that Durkheim analyzed social facts as existing externally to the individual, so it should not come as a surprise that he also sought to answer the *cui bono* question outside of the individual. In his view, it is not people's needs that socio-cultural practices fulfill, but the "general needs of the social organism."[216] Durkheim was especially interested in the veneration of collective sacred symbols, like a totem, the cross, or a national flag. In his view it creates a state of effervescence and excitement that symbolizes how the individual has no meaning or existence other than as part of something greater and more enduring, *other* than the self. This is also how he interpreted the rituals of self-mutilation at aboriginal funerals: the individuals are harmed, but society is made "more alive and more active than ever."[217] The reason why social traditions solidify society, Durkheim thought, is that "if social phenomena would generally be parasitic in character, the budget of the organism would be in deficit, and thereby social life would become impossible."[218]

One of the major functionalists of the twentieth century, the American sociologist Talcott Parsons, developed the analogy of the social organism in more detail.[219] Social systems, he argued, consist of differentiated and interrelated parts that make the system function as a whole. When a biological organism meets challenges, like a rise in temperature, the organism's internal mechanisms immediately retain the system's self-maintenance and equilibrium. Parsons thought that social systems do something similar: when individuals diverge from their roles, the social system immediately responds by putting these individuals back on track. In most cases this is not even necessary, because after people have internalized the norms and values of their society from a young age onwards, the maintenance of social cohesion is largely a matter of consensus. Of course, many societies are characterized by gross dissimilarities in wealth and power, but functionalism also developed an answer to that.[220] Parsons's colleagues Kingsley Davis and Wilbert Moore argued that social inequality is "an unconsciously evolved device by which societies ensure that the most important positions are conscientiously filled by the most qualified persons."[221]

Durkheimian functionalism also exerted influence on historians. In their analyses of Medieval European society, the French Annales historians were greatly impacted by Durkheim's ideas about structural collective sentiments.[222] But functionalism has also been used to interpret

---

[215] Durkheim, *Cours de science sociale. Leçon d'ouverture*; Durkheim, *Les Règles de La Méthode Sociologique*; Durkheim, *Les formes élémentaires*.
[216] Durkheim, *Les Règles de La Méthode Sociologique*, 95."les besoins généraux de l'organisme social."
[217] Durkheim, *Les formes élémentaires*, 574."plus vivante et plus agissante que jamais".
[218] Durkheim, *Les Règles de La Méthode Sociologique*, 96-7."Si donc la généralité des phénomènes sociaux avait ce caractère parasitaire, le budget de l'organisme serait en déficit, la vie sociale serait impossible."
[219] Parsons, *The Social System*; Wallace and Wolf, *Contemporary Sociological Theory*, 25–44; Ritzer, *Contemporary Sociological Theory*, 68–80.
[220] Ritzer, *Contemporary Sociological Theory*, 65–67; Davis and Moore, "Some Principles of Stratification."
[221] Davis and Moore, "Some Principles of Stratification," 184.
[222] Burke, *The French Historical Revolution*, 43–86; Bloch, *Les rois thaumaturges*; Bloch, *La société féodale*.

the cults of the Roman emperors, or the imperialism of the second German Reich, as contributions to the stabilization of their respective societies.[223] Or when Peter Burke reflected on the mixed and elaborate institutions of the Venetian Republic, and how these institutions ingeniously enhanced order and stability in society, he also thought them almost to have been invented to demonstrate the strengths of functionalism.[224] The outlook has generated some internal criticisms, though, not least from Robert Merton.[225] In 1949 he remarked that certain social usages or sentiments may be "functional for some groups and dysfunctional for other groups in the same society."[226] The interactions between white Americans and the black minority had his particular interest in that regard. Additionally, he highlighted how religion is not only a stabilizing force, but also a thoroughly divisive one. In Merton's view we should not automatically assume that all existing institutions are necessary, and thus by default good.

Merton's self-critiques foreshadowed the criticisms of functionalism that would unfold in the next decades. Functionalism reached its zenith in the consensus-oriented 1950s, but in the tumultuous 1960s it was branded a conservative ideology under the veneer of objective science.[227] By analyzing institutions as positively functional for the stability of society, the functionalists were accused of supporting and enhancing those institutions. The sociologist Barrington Moore cynically commented: "to maintain and transmit a value system, human beings are punished, bullied, sent to jail, thrown in concentration camps, cajoled, bribed, made into heroes, encouraged to read newspapers, stood up against a wall and shot, and sometimes even taught sociology."[228] Especially, the functionalist account of social stratification was vilified for being a legitimization of inequality and exploitation. It tells the rich and powerful that their privileges were well earned. Instead of Durkheimian functionalism, the focus around this time thus shifted to the second key perspective on the *cui bono* question: the maintenance of power structures.

The maintenance of power structures
This perspective also has old precedents. The ancient Greek philosopher Heraclitus already stated that "war is the father of all things, of all things it is the king", while Friedrich Nietzsche spoke of a "will to power" dominating all human interactions.[229] The modern academic form of this perspective is sometimes called "conflict theory", and the differences with Durkheim are vast.[230]

---

[223] Lorenz, *De constructie van het verleden*, 206.
[224] Burke, *History and Social Theory*, 127–34.
[225] Merton, *Social Theory and Social Structure*, 79–114, 484–88; Ritzer, *Contemporary Sociological Theory*, 80–85; Wallace and Wolf, *Contemporary Sociological Theory*, 48–55.
[226] Merton, *Social Theory and Social Structure*, 81.
[227] Wallace and Wolf, *Contemporary Sociological Theory*, 42–44, 64–66; Ritzer, *Contemporary Sociological Theory*, 67–68; Hamilton, *The Sociology of Religion*, 105.
[228] Quoted in: Wallace and Wolf, *Contemporary Sociological Theory*, 44.
[229] Collins, "Reassessments of Sociological History," 147–60.
[230] Turner, "Conflict Theory"; Ritzer, *Contemporary Sociological Theory*, 85–91; Wallace and Wolf, *Contemporary Sociological Theory*, 68–157.

Here society is not seen as a place where people work harmoniously together due to shared values, but as a power arena in which groups continually compete for dominance. Norms and values are the weapons that favor those in power, and as far as social order exists it largely results from coercion. But stability never lasts long. Subordinate groups will make new attempts at gaining power, thereby creating new rounds of dynamical conflicts.

This focus on power and conflict is less homogeneous an orientation than functionalism, and it is characterized – perhaps unsurprisingly – by more internal strife.[231] Roughly two main traditions can be discerned. One tradition, sometimes dubbed "analytic conflict theory", draws key inspiration from Max Weber and aims to analyze society as objectively as possible. It assumes that power is very attractive, but scarce at the same time, so conflicts of interest are permanent and inevitable. Power relations are multifaceted, and entail a wide mixture of economic, political and symbolic alliances. Or as the American sociologist Randall Collins – who aligned himself with conflict theory for some time – said it: "different orders of stratification do not line up neatly."[232] The other key tradition takes an arguably even more negative stance on current affairs, but expresses greater confidence in the future. After the mechanisms of oppression have been exposed, there is the promise of creating a far more harmonious society, in which the human potential will be fulfilled. Intellectuals bear an essential moral responsibility of critiquing society, and changing it for the better. The dividing lines between the powerful and the oppressed are drawn in much sharper lines, and all science claiming to be "objective" or "value-free" is seen as putting itself into the service of those in power.

The arch-example of the latter approach is Karl Marx.[233] "The history of all hitherto existing society is the history of class struggle" he wrote. In Antiquity this struggle involved slave-holders versus slaves, in the Middle Ages landlords versus serfs, while the modern era gave rise to the exploitation of the working class by the capitalist bourgeoisie.[234] The essence of power relations is thereby seen as a material one, essentially coming down to who own the means of production. The "higher" domains of human social life, like morality or the arts, are merely representations of material power relations. The prevailing ideas are always the ideas of the ruling classes. Hence, religion is not a glue keeping society together, but helps maintain inequality and exploitation. It is, as Marx famously put it: "the sigh of the oppressed being, the heart of a heartless world, and the soul of soulless conditions. It is the opium of the people."[235] Yet, Marx presaged that internal deterioration was about to prompt capitalism's self-destruction, leading up to a proletarian revolution and the establishment of communism.

---

[231] Wallace and Wolf, *Contemporary Sociological Theory*, 68.
[232] Quoted in: Wallace and Wolf, 141.
[233] Marx, *Das Kapital: Kritik der politischen Oekonomie*; Turner, "Conflict Theory," 134–35; Collins, "Reassessments of Sociological History," 157–68; Wiersing, *Geschichte des historischen Denkens*, 395–413.
[234] Wiersing, *Geschichte des historischen Denkens*, 404."Die Geschichte aller bisherigen Gesellschaft ist die geschichte von Klassenkämpfen."
[235] Marx, *Der junge Marx*, 109."der Seufzer der bedrängten Kreatur, das Gemüt einer herzlosen Welt, wie sie die Geist geistloser Zustände ist. Sie ist das Opium des Volkes" .

We now know that Marx's prophesies were largely mistaken, and that the modern capitalist rise of consumption has continued to entice populations worldwide. Marxist theory remained resilient though, and it has interpreted modern consumerism as an even more insidious way of deadening people's critical capacities and propensities for revolt.[236] Thinkers like Antonio Gramsci and Theodor Adorno thereby shifted Marx's focus on the material base to how structures of oppression are reproduced at symbolic levels of socio-cultural life. More loosely inspired by Marx, while also sharing tenets with the analytic tradition, is Pierre Bourdieu. He views all domains of socio-cultural life as consisting of particular "fields", such as the fields of the arts, religion, or sports, in which people continually defend their hierarchical position or try to improve it.[237] Apparently trivial things, like preferences for art styles or beverages, are in fact the battlegrounds on which positions of power are distributed. By having the ability to make the "correct" aesthetic choices, privileged groups recognize each other. So, it is through subtle and implicit means that positions of dominance are maintained.

The interest in the symbolic aspects of oppression is also central to the other key movement within this tradition of conflict theory: poststructuralism, or as it is more broadly known, postmodernism.[238] Unlike Marxism, postmodernism rejects all pretentions of doing "hard" science. Nevertheless, its view on power as the essential force governing social life, and the sharp dividing lines that it draws between collective groups of oppressors and oppressed, are often remarkably similar. Instead of the bourgeoisie versus the proletariat, it is antagonisms between straight people and sexual minorities, white people and people of color, or cisgenders and transgenders that take central stage. Instead of the "worker's paradise", now the ideals of "multiculturalism" and "diversity and inclusion" operate as history's grand destinies. Postmodernism is especially interested in how power is encoded in our use of language, or as it is often called, discourse. Through a "deconstruction" of discourse, it is believed that power structures can be dismantled.

Postmodernism has become particularly productive in feminist theory and gender theory. Authors like Luce Irigaray and Joan Scott have argued that patriarchic norms are deeply entrenched in the subconscious traditions of the west.[239] Males have always been a standard point of reference – just think of a word like "mankind" – while women were marked as "the Other". Judith Butler highlights how even a dichotomy between "men" and "women" already represents power, by excluding gender-fluidity.[240] Although he did not like the designation himself, the French historian and philosopher Michel Foucault is often considered the most influential postmodernist. His main aim has been to deconstruct standard narratives about liberal

---

[236] Ritzer, *Contemporary Sociological Theory*, 103–17; Marcuse, *One-Dimensional Man*; Farganis, *Readings in Social Theory*, 397–412.
[237] Bourdieu, *La distinction*; Ritzer, *Contemporary Sociological Theory*, 172–83.
[238] Thompson, *Postmodernism and History*; Ritzer, *Contemporary Sociological Theory*, 215–52.
[239] Irigaray, *Speculum*; Scott, "Gender."
[240] Butler, *Undoing Gender*.

modernity being a movement towards increased liberation from external constraints.[241] In Foucault's view, modernity has only made the mechanisms of control over human bodies more pervasive and exploitative. New strategies of subjugation and disciplining were developed in prisons, and subsequently entered mental asylums, schools and hospitals. Unlike Marx, Foucault did not so much assume one group of dominators versus one group of dominated, as power engulfs all relations.[242] Sometimes it almost seems as if power *itself* has become the entity benefiting from it all.

Power oriented approaches have become tremendously influential, and currently hold a stronger position in the social sciences and the humanities than Durkheimian functionalism. Yet, they also face some serious criticisms.[243] If shared values and consensus are mere illusions, then how does society stick together? Is coercion truly a sufficient explanation for the persistence of the social fabric? It is also questioned whether human interactions are as zero-sum as the conflict oriented theorists assume, and whether our personalities are indeed that cynical and power-hungry. While functionalism was accused of legitimizing the injustices of the status quo, this orientation is suspected of setting people against each other. Marxist ideology has a ghastly track record of destabilizing and damaging people as well as societies.[244] It is probably too early to evaluate the effects of postmodern ideology, but some authors warn us about its fracturing effects on current societies of the west.[245] Moreover, power and conflict oriented models often suffer from a theoretical problem similar to that of functionalism: how did the alleged oppressive structures precisely take shape?

Some conflict theorists have been accused of the functionalist fallacy, as they assumed that functional power structures came into being beyond people's intentions and recognition.[246] Karl Marx saw collective classes as the key actors of history – not individuals – and thought that oppressive mechanisms largely come into being "behind people's backs".[247] A central concept to later Marxist theory was "false consciousness", referring to people's misguided understanding of their real class interests.[248] Likewise, Michel Foucault greatly downplayed the creative role of individuals, assuming that discourses of power are constituted by invisible sets of rules.[249] And along the lines of Robert Merton, the analytic conflict theorist Ralf Dahrendorf distinguished "latent power interests" from "manifest power interests".[250] Pierre Bourdieu, on the other hand,

---

[241] Foucault, *Surveiller et Punir*; Downing, *The Cambridge Introduction to Michel Foucault.*; Ritzer, *Contemporary Sociological Theory*, 218–25.
[242] Downing, *The Cambridge Introduction to Michel Foucault.*, 5.
[243] Wallace and Wolf, *Contemporary Sociological Theory*, 155–57.
[244] Courtois and Kauffer, *Le Livre Noir Du Communisme.*
[245] Huntington, *Who Are We?*; Chua, *Political Tribes*; Pluckrose and Lindsay, *Cynical Theories*.
[246] Wallace and Wolf, *Contemporary Sociological Theory*, 423–24; Hamilton, *The Sociology of Religion*, 83, 103; Sanderson, *The Evolution of Human Sociality*, 67–68.
[247] Marx, *Das Kapital: Kritik der politischen Oekonomie*, I:6, 19,85-6, 149, 196, 378."hinter dem Rücken", "hinter ihrem Rücken".
[248] Ritzer, *Contemporary Sociological Theory*, 25; Wallace and Wolf, *Contemporary Sociological Theory*, 71.
[249] Downing, *The Cambridge Introduction to Michel Foucault.*, 6, 10, 39.
[250] Ritzer, *Contemporary Sociological Theory*, 89.

was eager to anchor the reproduction of power structures in the actions and practices of concrete individuals. He did not see strategies of oppression as consciously preplanned, but did locate them in the more tacit domains of the *sens pratique*.[251] Analytic conflict theorists like Max Weber or Randall Collins were even more pronounced in locating the exertion of power in the micro-interactions of actual people. This brings their work quite close to our third major perspective on the *cui bono* question: the fulfillment of individual needs.[252]

The fulfillment of individual needs
This last perspective is probably the most multifaceted of all. It can be found in a wide range of theoretical schools, with often highly diverging methodologies. Still, a common thread is that socio-cultural phenomena are not thought to benefit abstract entities like "systems" or "classes", but flesh and blood people.[253] Its micro-oriented focus on individuals almost automatically leads to a closer affinity with psychology, and in some cases the orientation is related to the liberal individualism of free market economics. Importantly, proponents do not deny that socio-cultural phenomena can fulfill social functions, or that culture can be used in conflicts. A key difference though, is that such functions are thought to emerge from the actions and needs of the individuals who created and maintained those phenomena in the first place. Neither is it denied that socio-cultural phenomena possess a complexity that greatly exceeds the intentions of any of the actors involved. But again, such complexity is thought to accumulate from the micro-interactions of individuals.

Interestingly, this perspective also counts one prominent functionalist in its ranks.[254] Bronislaw Malinowski was a typical functionalist in the sense that he claimed that socio-cultural phenomena hang together in functional and unintended ways. But unlike the Durkheimians he thought that "the individual, both in social theory and in the reality of cultural life, is the starting-point and the end."[255] It was not the needs of social systems that have to be fulfilled, but the biological needs of individuals. Malinowski listed a few such needs, like metabolism, bodily comforts, safety and health. He saw cultural phenomena as integrated responses, albeit in often highly indirect ways, to these requirements. For instance, when explaining rituals of magic, Malinowksi not only focused on the social function, as Merton did, but additionally addressed psychological and emotional dimensions: people live in uncertainty about things beyond their

---

[251] Bourdieu, *La distinction*; Bourdieu, *Le Sens Pratique*; Ritzer, *Contemporary Sociological Theory*, 174–78.
[252] Weber, *Wirtschaft Und Gesellschaft*, 6; Wallace and Wolf, *Contemporary Sociological Theory*, 150.
[253] Farganis, *Readings in Social Theory*, 263–368; Wallace and Wolf, *Contemporary Sociological Theory*, 197–380; Hamilton, *The Sociology of Religion*, 157–215.
[254] Malinowski, "The Group and the Individual in Functional Analysis"; Malinowski, *A Scientific Theory of Culture*; Moore, *Visions of Culture*, 126–27.
[255] Malinowski, "The Group and the Individual in Functional Analysis," 964.

control, such as rain, and a magical ritual, like a rain dance, provides a consoling sense of empowerment – it offers a ritualization of optimism.[256]

Malinowski was not the only one to stress the emotional side of magic and religion.[257] Psychoanalytic theorists like Sigmund Freud or Karl Jung assumed that humans suffer from great emotional tensions and frustrations to which religion can provide subconscious responses. Through its gratification and relief, religion fulfills almost psychotherapeutic functions. In contrast to the emotional approach, some earlier nineteenth-century scholars highlighted intellectual dimensions.[258] Authors like Edward Tylor and the philologist Max Müller emphasized how humans are continually confronted with incomprehensible events. "At first, nothing seemed less natural than nature. Nature was the greatest surprise, a terror, a marvel, a standing miracle", Müller wrote, and the explanations offered by magic and religion provided people with some logical comprehensibility.[259]

After the decline of functionalism in the 1960s, the individual-oriented approaches gained new momentum, leading to the popularity of schools like symbolic anthropology, social constructivism and symbolic interactionism.[260] In contrast to functionalism, these schools wanted to stay as close as possible to the meaning that actors themselves give to things. The anthropologist Marshall Sahlins thought that the unity of cultural order is constituted by meaning. So, it was "this meaningful system that defines all functionality."[261] When considering religion, Clifford Geertz even wanted to dispense with questions regarding functions or dysfunctions altogether. He rendered them mere chimeras. But surprisingly, and quite inconsistently, only a few sentences later Geertz launched his own functional interpretation of religion. In his view it serves as a "framework in which a wide range of experience – intellectual, emotional, moral – can be given meaningful form."[262] Geertz did not share the optimistic outlook of Malinowski though, remarking that "over its career religion has probably disturbed men as much as it has cheered them."[263] Religion, in his view, does not help us avoid suffering, but teaches us *how* to suffer and resist the meaninglessness of profound and unremovable pain.[264]

These approaches focusing on symbols and meaning have little pretentions of doing "hard" science. But over the past decades the individual-oriented perspective also gave rise to an approach that is staunchly scientific in its ambitions: rational choice theory. This school of

---

[256] Malinowski, *A Scientific Theory of Culture*, 198–99; Malinowski, *Magic, Science and Religion*, 90; However, on other occasions he does seem to place the needs of groups above the needs of individuals: Malinowski, *A Scientific Theory of Culture*, 92, 109.
[257] Hamilton, *The Sociology of Religion*, 45–70.
[258] Tylor, *Primitive Culture 1. 1.*; Müller, *The Essential Max Müller*; Hamilton, *The Sociology of Religion*, 24–29.
[259] Müller, *The Essential Max Müller*, 267.
[260] Farganis, *Readings in Social Theory*, 303–68; McGee and Warms, *Anthropological Theory*, 438–87; Wallace and Wolf, *Contemporary Sociological Theory*, 197–301.
[261] Sahlins, *Culture and Practical Reason*, 206.
[262] Geertz, *The Interpretation of Cultures*, 123.
[263] Geertz, 103.
[264] Geertz, 104–5.

thought is closely linked to economics, but also gained ground in other social sciences.[265] A key assumption is that human actors are rational profit seekers who make cost-benefit analyses based on available knowledge. Humans deliberately choose those things that seem to serve their purposes most effectively. The approach has little time for explanations that invoke "the weight of tradition", "socialized values", or "the impact of culture". Socio-cultural phenomena are only thought to persist because they appeared useful to people in each instance.[266] The approach is commonly applied to the exchange of economic goods – where it indeed makes most sense at first sight – but has also been put to use in explaining the exchange of more intangible goods, like approval, respect, or happiness. Simply anything that people can desire is phrased as a "reward" that rational agents will pursue.

From this perspective, the world of religion is understood as a marketplace where religious goods are on offer, and with consumers making calculations of utility.[267] The American economist Laurence Iannaccone puts it as follows: "subscribing to a religion is a bit like buying stock."[268] The market of religion is thereby thought of as a place of continuing competition, such as cults competing with cults in Ancient Rome, or churches competing with churches in Modern America. Some suppliers sometimes also gain a monopoly, like the Roman Catholic Church in Medieval Europe. Yet, the position of religions always remains instable. As soon as other suppliers offer better bargains, people will look for solace elsewhere. Proponents of rational choice theory pretend that their perspective highlights dimensions of religious life that other approaches failed to see, like financial motives behind religious choices, as well as social, emotional, intellectual or spiritual benefits.[269] "Scholars have scrutinized religion from every angle *except* that of rational choice", Iannoccone writes.[270]

Like the other two main perspectives, the individualistic orientation has faced criticisms. From the Durkheimian point of view it can be retorted that socio-cultural phenomena are functionally integrated in ways that extend the meaning or intentions of the involved actors.[271] A conflict theorist might remark that the impact of power is underestimated, as people do not always rationally or meaningfully *choose* what cultural forms to adopt. Very often those forms are *imposed* on them.[272] Furthermore, the symbolic approaches, as well as rational choice theory, claim to stay close to the meaning that actors themselves give to things, but this is not entirely convincing.[273] If sixteenth-century Catholics would have been confronted with the idea of their religion being a way of "giving meaning to life", or "an attractive good on the religious

---

[265] Wallace and Wolf, *Contemporary Sociological Theory*, 302–80; Farganis, *Readings in Social Theory*, 263–302; Ritzer, *Contemporary Sociological Theory*, 149–59.
[266] Wallace and Wolf, *Contemporary Sociological Theory*, 309; Sanderson, *The Evolution of Human Sociality*, 100.
[267] Iannaccone, "Voodoo Economics?"; Stark, "Micro Foundations of Religion"; Stark and Finke, *Acts of Faith*.
[268] Iannaccone, "Voodoo Economics?," 81.
[269] Iannaccone, 86; Stark, *The Rise of Christianity*.
[270] Iannaccone, "Voodoo Economics?," 86.
[271] Kincaid, *Philosophical Foundations of the Social Sciences*, 142–90.
[272] Hamilton, "Rational Choice Theory: A Critique."
[273] Stark, "Micro Foundations of Religion," 266–74; Hamilton, *The Sociology of Religion*, 157–64, 216=8.

marketplace", it probably would have sounded strange and heretical to them. They thought of Roman Catholicism as an eternal *truth* on which salvation was dependent.

Eclecticism as a solution?
So, to conclude, each of the three main perspectives have highlighted important dimensions of socio-cultural life. But when applied too generally, or too exclusively, they can lead us astray. Very often socio-cultural phenomena do not seem to fulfill the functions that they are supposed to fulfill according to one of those perspectives. The borders between the main approaches can also be porous on closer scrutiny. Analytic conflict theory, for instance, slides into Durkheimian functionalism when conflicts are seen as crucially functional for society. Ralf Dahrendorf described conflict as "the great creative force of human history", while Lewis Coser thought that that internal strife enhances a group's survival when internal discord prevents "group dissolution through the withdrawal of hostile participants."[274] On the other hand, when conflicts are analyzed as occurring between specific people who all pursue their own ends, conflict theory slides into the individualistic outlook.

This all indicates that socio-cultural phenomena are highly multifaceted, and escape any single-minded framework. So how should we deal with a reality that always seems more complex? A common response, not least amongst historians, is to opt for an eclectic approach. One just picks and chooses those elements from general frameworks that seem most fitted to the phenomenon one studies.[275] Take the example of beliefs in the afterlife. According to the Durkheimians, such beliefs fulfill the function of bolstering social behavior in individuals. When people think that bad conduct is punished after death, they will think twice before behaving asocially.[276] Marx, on the other hand, saw the afterlife as something that maintains exploitation: it makes people less likely to revolt against earthly injustices. From the individualistic perspective it has been highlighted that the belief offers emotional or intellectual support. Malinowski argued that humans cannot face the idea of complete cessation, so grasping at death they reach for "the comforting belief in spiritual continuity and in the life after death."[277] Overall, it seems that there is something to be said for all of these perspectives. They all touched upon at least one essential element of beliefs in the afterlife, so why not eclectically use a mixture of them?

Eclecticism is not without problems of its own, though. In a critique of theoretical pluralism, the Dutch sociologist Nico Wilterdink notes that "On closer scrutiny the toolkit of theories is quite a mess. The instruments are not ordered neatly next to each other, with each of them having a clear function of its own. In this higgledy-piggledy box it is often not even clear

---

[274] Quoted in: Wallace and Wolf, *Contemporary Sociological Theory*, 122, 133.
[275] Ritzer, "Sociology: A Multi Paradigm Science"; Sil and Katzenstein, "Analytic Eclecticism in the Study of World Politics."
[276] Hamilton, *The Sociology of Religion*, 117; Davis, *Human Society*, 526–31.
[277] Malinowski, *Magic, Science and Religion*, 51.

beforehand what tool can be used for what."[278] Marvin Harris once rudely commented that eclecticism abounds with hidden dangers: "in practice, it is often little more than a euphemism for confusion, the muddled acceptance of contradictory theories, the bankruptcy of creative thought, and the cloak of mediocrity."[279] We might retort here that eclecticism is probably to be preferred over Harris's own procrustean bed of "cultural materialism", but his critique is not entirely beside the point. Take for instance the question of whether latent functions exist. When examining the issue, the biologist David Sloan Wilson discovered that some social scientists take the existence of latent functions for granted while others vehemently oppose it. Wilson rightly concludes that "you know there is a problem when one man's heresy is another man's commonplace."[280] Eclecticism is not going to resolve this problem. Moreover, eclecticism borrows insights from more ambitious approaches, like functionalism or Marxism, but those approaches were only developed because its creators refused to settle with the messiness of eclecticism. They aimed for something bigger and more consistent. Eclecticism thus exploits the rich wells of grander theories, without offering much creativity in return.

Hence, ideally, we should want to work with an approach that unites valuable insights from other perspectives into a more consistent framework, while also being a source of creativity itself. Some sociologists, like Norbert Elias, Anthony Giddens, and Randall Collins later in his career, have tried to combine various perspectives into something more consistent.[281] But none of those attempts really persevered. So, might current Darwinian theory be a promising new candidate model in that regard? We shall now examine whether the theory is indeed the panacea we might hope for.

---

[278] Wilterdink, *Omstreden Wetenschap*, 11. "De gereedschapskist van theorieën is bij nader inzien nogal een warboel. De stukken gereedschap liggen niet netjes naast elkaar, elk met een duidelijke eigen functie, maar schots en scheef door elkaar heen, waarbij niet op voorhand duidelijk is welk voorwerp waarvoor te gebruiken is."
[279] Harris, *The Rise of Anthropological Theory*, 285; Harris, *Cultural Materialism*, 287–314.
[280] Wilson, *Darwin's Cathedral*, 2002, 84.
[281] Elias, *Was ist Soziologie?*; Giddens, *The Constitution of Society*; Collins, *Interaction Ritual Chains*.

Chapter 3: The theory
3.1 Darwinian cultural evolution
In the spring of 1955, a remarkable meeting took place in the American city of New Haven between scholars from two different generations.[1] With a colleague, the social scientist Donald Campbell visited an emeritus professor from Yale, Albert Galloway Keller. Like many people of his academic generation, Campbell had a progressive orientation – he adored Roosevelt's New Deal and was averse to anything conservative. Keller, on the other hand, was one of the last living of an older generation of evolutionary theorists who had used Darwinian theory to understand culture and society, and who leaned towards the political right. Keller's evolutionary ideas had once been avant-garde, but in the 1920s and 1930s they were already disregarded, and by 1955 they seemed to disappear into oblivion.[2] Yet, despite the ideological differences, Joseph Campbell and his colleague were curious to meet the old Keller. They actually found his Darwinian perspective quite stimulating, and were eager to learn more about it.

The two visitors were pleasantly surprised by Keller's hospitality. At the same time, it soon became apparent how widely their political views diverged. Campbell expressed his supposition that Keller's theory about Darwinian cultural selection offered a justification for Roosevelt's New Deal: old institutions had functioned badly and the New Deal created new and diverse institutions that stimulated innovations. But Keller would have none of it. He started an exposé on how society was currently changing for the worse, how his favorite magazine had turned into a left-wing propaganda sheet, and to Campbell's dismay he even went as far as to tell jokes about Eleanor Roosevelt's teeth. Darwinian social scientists had a reputation for conservatism, and Campbell argued that the picture was more diverse. But here he had to admit that Keller just proved the point. Nonetheless, that day these scholars came to speak extensively about their shared interest in Darwinian cultural evolution, and from the perspective of the history of science it made the visit a fascinating one: it was the bridge between an endpoint and a new beginning. Keller had been one of the last representatives of a school of thought that once looked promising but faded away over the course of the early twentieth century, while Campbell represented a revival that would gradually unfold over the next decades.[3] This meeting in 1955 thus demonstrates something important: the idea of Darwinian cultural evolution was never entirely gone.

Early applications
Darwin's theory, as proposed in *On the Origin of Species*, concerned biological evolution. But soon after his book was published in 1859, scholars began to wonder whether its explanatory

---
[1] Campbell, "Variation and Selective Retention in Socio-Cultural Evolution," 24–25.
[2] Campbell, "Variation and Selective Retention in Socio-Cultural Evolution."
[3] Carneiro, *Evolutionism in Cultural Anthropology*, 68–72, 91–95, 173–78.

power might also extend to the socio-cultural realm.[4] Amongst these people was Darwin himself. He was particularly intrigued by apparent similarities between the evolution of living nature and human languages, and in 1871 he wrote that "The formation of different languages and of distinct species, and the proofs that both have been developed through a gradual process, are curiously parallel."[5] In addition he compared the competition between words in languages to the process of natural selection, and toyed with the idea of non-intentional adaptations to languages: "no philologist now supposes that any language has been deliberately invented; it has been slowly and unconsciously developed by many steps."[6] Such remarks were relatively marginal to his work though, as Darwin remained first and foremost a biological researcher.

However, many others began to explore such similarities between living nature and socio-cultural phenomena in more detail.[7] Walter Bagehot drew comparisons between natural selection and the competitive struggle between political institutions and nations. Benjamin Kidd wrote about the selection of ethical principles. William James contemplated on the selection of ideas in the history of science, and the American ethnographer and explorer John Wesley Powell bombastically stated in 1885 that:

> He [man] transfers the struggle for existence from himself to his activities, from the subject, man, to the objects which he creates. Arts compete with one another, and progress in art is by the survival of the fittest in the struggle for existence. In like manner, institutions compete with institutions, languages with languages, opinions with opinions, and reasoning with reasoning; and in each case we have the survival of the fittest in the struggle for existence. Man by his inventions has transferred the brutal struggle for existence from himself to the works of his hand.[8]

These avenues of research looked promising, but it often remained somewhat unclear what precisely was being selected. Applications of Darwinism to the socio-cultural realm tended to result in confusing mixtures of the alleged selection of individuals, groups, nations, races, institutions, and ideas. What often remained particularly unclear was the distinction between the selection of biological variants and cultural variants.[9] Many Darwinian theories from this time were ultimately concerned with the former.[10] The emergent properties of socio-cultural processes, as would later be explored by Durkheim and the Boasians, were still poorly understood.

---

[4] Carneiro, 68–72; Hodgson and Knudsen, *Darwin's Conjecture*, 8–11.
[5] Darwin, *The Descent of Man*, 112–13.
[6] Darwin, 108, 113.
[7] Hodgson and Knudsen, *Darwin's Conjecture the Search for General Principles of Social and Economic Evolution*, 8–11.
[8] Powell, "From Savagery to Barbarism," 193.
[9] Hodgson and Knudsen, *Darwin's Conjecture*, 5–8.
[10] See, for example: Ammon, *Die Gesellschaftsordnung und ihre natürlichen Grundlagen.*; Lapouge, *Les sélections sociales.*

This problem also became apparent in Darwin's own work. In his book *The Descent of Man* he expressed his worries about a foreseeable degeneration of the human race. Darwin quoted a social commentator named William Rathbone Greg, who wrote that "the careless, squalid, uninspiring Irish multiplies like rabbits", whereas the "frugal foreseeing, self-respecting, ambitious Scot (...) leaves few behind him."[11] Darwin agreed, and interpreted these alleged differences as a consequence of biological predispositions. An alternative view, namely that such alleged differences may reflect cultural variations if not stereotypes, does not seem to have crossed his mind. Darwin used the quote to express his concerns about modern society, which supposedly selected for the wrong biological types; people with undesirable traits were outbreeding people with desirable ones.[12] In the late nineteenth and early twentieth centuries many others shared these concerns, and it became a powerful influence of Darwinism on social thought. Today, this is what often goes under the name of social Darwinism.[13]

At the same time, some contemporaries did recognize that the selection of biological and socio-cultural units were two potentially different things.[14] The philosopher David George Ritchie sharply observed that human experiences could be transmitted quite independently from the continuity of biological traits, and that the mechanism of natural selection could thus be "applied in a new sphere."[15] As he wrote in 1896: "There is going on a natural selection of ideas, customs, institutions, irrespective of the natural selection of individuals and of races."[16] The renowned economist Thorstein Veblen would soon reach very similar conclusions, and in 1915 Albert Keller made it the key focus of attention in his book *Societal Evolution*.[17] The wisdom of hindsight now allows us to conclude that it formed a promising line of investigation that deserved closer scrutiny.

Yet, as I already mentioned, when Donald Campbell visited Keller in 1955, the old social scientist was a remnant of a bygone era. In the first half of the twentieth century the socio-cultural disciplines increasingly distanced themselves from Darwinian approaches.[18] The theory came to be associated with apologies for reactionary politics, biological reductionism, rough capitalism, and racially supremacist colonialism. Unfortunately, such associations were not entirely unwarranted.[19] It was especially concerns about the biological degradation of the race that had taken an ugly turn. We saw that Darwin shared these concerns from a scientific point of

---

[11] Darwin, *The Descent of Man*, 164.
[12] Darwin, 158–72.
[13] Hawkins, *Social Darwinism in European and American Thought 1860-1945*; Hermans, *De dwaaltocht van het sociaal-darwinisme*.
[14] Hodgson and Knudsen, *Darwin's Conjecture*, 8–13.
[15] Ritchie, *Darwin and Hegel and Other Philosophical Studies*, 2:47–49, 99–100.
[16] Ritchie, "Social Evolution," 171.
[17] Veblen, "Why Is Economics Not an Evolutionary Science?"; Keller, *Societal Evolution*.
[18] Campbell, "Variation and Selective Retention in Socio-Cultural Evolution"; Carneiro, *Evolutionism in Cultural Anthropology*, 75–98; Hodgson and Knudsen, *Darwin's Conjecture*, 13–18; Hofstadter, *Social Darwinism in American Thought, 1860-1915*.
[19] Hawkins, *Social Darwinism in European and American Thought 1860-1945*; Hermans, *De dwaaltocht van het sociaal-darwinisme*.

view, but he backtracked when it came to political measures. Darwin believed that any forced attempts to stop the "unfit" from propagation would conflict with our instinct of sympathy, which he considered "the noblest part of our nature."[20] However, others had fewer inhibitions, and in the twentieth century Darwinism became one of the key inspirations for the notorious socio-political program of eugenics. In various countries, such as the USA and Sweden, this program resulted in mass-sterilizations of the alleged unfit, and in Nazi Germany people were even killed for this reason.[21] Understandably, such crimes contaminated all socio-cultural applications of Darwinism. The nuance that a scientific theory about the selection of cultural units is different from any eugenics program easily got lost.

On top of that, cultural Darwinism became too strongly associated with a school of thought that is often labeled as "evolutionism". This perspective treats socio-cultural development as a form of progression in several stages.[22] The idea preceded Darwin, and can be traced back to the French enlightenment at least.[23] In the second half of the nineteenth century it found new scientific support in authors like Herbert Spencer, Edward Tylor and Lewis Hunt Morgan. These scholars presented human history in broad strokes as a development from savagery at the bottom, barbarism in the middle, to civilization at the top. While this approach never convinced many historians, in the first half of the twentieth century it also came to be radically rejected by many social scientists.[24] Critics like the Boasians vilified evolutionism for its conjectures, imprecisions, and racist and colonialist biases. But again, we need to highlight distinctions here. The idea of Darwinian cultural evolution is something potentially different, because it can imply more capricious and historically contingent processes.[25] Interestingly, this was recognized by Franz Boas himself, but his comments were to no avail – the bad reputations of social Darwinism and evolutionism weighed heavily on cultural Darwinism, which waned accordingly.[26] The baby was thrown out with the bathwater.

The revival

In these circumstances Campbell decided to pick up the idea in the 1950s.[27] Describing it as a model of "variation and selective retention in socio-cultural evolution", he recognized its scientific potential. In 1965 he wrote:

> Elaborate adaptive social systems, such as the priesthood dominating irrigation civilizations, could have emerged, just as termite societies, without any self-conscious

---

[20] Darwin, *The Descent of Man*, 159.
[21] Bashford and Levine, *The Oxford Handbook of the History of Eugenics*; Levine, *Eugenics. A Very Short Introduction*.
[22] Carneiro, *Evolutionism in Cultural Anthropology*; Wilterdink, "The Concept of Social Evolution."
[23] Harris, *The Rise of Anthropological Theory*, 8–53.
[24] Carneiro, *Evolutionism in Cultural Anthropology*, 75–98; Harris, *The Rise of Anthropological Theory*, 250–604.
[25] Carneiro, *Evolutionism in Cultural Anthropology*, 171–79; Mesoudi, *Cultural Evolution*, 2011, 37–40.
[26] Lewis, "Boas, Darwin, Science, and Anthropology"; Wilson, *This View of Life*, 107.
[27] Campbell, "Variation and Selective Retention in Socio-Cultural Evolution."

planning or foresightful action. It provides a plausible model for social systems that are 'wiser' than the individuals who make societies, or the rational social science of the ruling elite.[28]

In other words, Campbell proposed a possible answer to the question that was posed above: how do non-intentional cultural adaptations come about?[29] Nonetheless, few colleagues were willing to adopt his ideas. Around this time evolutionism made a comeback in the social sciences, but its key exponents, such as Leslie White and Julian Steward, remained primarily focused on the idea of development in several stages, largely disregarding Darwinian selection.[30] For the rest, resistance to Darwinism in the socio-cultural disciplines remained paramount.[31]

Despite this opposition several isolated scholars further elaborated upon the idea, and in the following decades they would take it in new and auspicious directions. One of them was Richard Dawkins.[32] In his book *The Selfish Gene* he added a bold little chapter on the cultural application of Darwinian evolution. As Dawkins claimed, there are cultural equivalents of the gene. By shortening the Greek word for imitation, *mimeme*, and by making it sound like gene, he created a new word for this cultural item: the meme. In Dawkins' view, all elements of culture that are transferred as separate units could count as memes, and amongst the examples he mentioned were "tunes, ideas, catch-phrases, clothes, fashions, ways of making pots or building arches."[33] Like the genes, Dawkins saw these memes as unconscious and blind replicators that undergo a Darwinian process of variation, selection and replication, thus evolving into things that look *as if* they were designed. So far, Dawkins's thoughts resembled Campbell's earlier observations.

What made Dawkins's little chapter special though was that he added something else: he imported the concept of "selfish replicators" from the biological into the cultural domain. In Dawkins's argument, genetic evolution had initially created bigger brains to store memes that helped human propagation. But once these new memetic replicators arose, a whole new kind of evolution was set in motion. Many of Dawkins's biological colleagues still tended to look for sociobiological answers when explaining human behavior, but Dawkins presumed that novel replicators can develop novel purposes. So, the reproductive interests of genes and memes do not necessarily coincide. "What we have not previously considered is that a cultural trait may have evolved in the way it has, simply because it is advantageous to itself."[34] Dawkins's key proposal was that memes can spread like selfish genes, or infectious parasites, while subverting

---

[28] Campbell, 28.
[29] See also: Campbell, "On the Conflicts between Biological and Social Evolution," 174.
[30] Harris, *The Rise of Anthropological Theory*, 605–89; Carneiro, *Evolutionism in Cultural Anthropology*, 99–288.
[31] Hodgson and Knudsen, *Darwin's Conjecture*, 18–23.
[32] Dawkins, *The Selfish Gene*, 189–201.
[33] Dawkins, 192.
[34] Dawkins, 200.

the interests of their human carriers. In other words, our behavior is not only controlled by selfish genes, but also by "selfish memes".

Dawkins's little chapter went largely unnoticed for quite a while, but in the 1990s it suddenly gained more traction.[35] Several people became intrigued by the idea of "selfish" cultural phenomena that were designed by natural selection and spread in a pathogen-like way at the expense of their human hosts. It was particularly in this idea that Daniel Dennett saw Darwinism's greatest potential of renewing the socio-cultural disciplines.[36] In 1997 a so called *Journal of Memetics* was launched which aimed to turn meme theory into an accepted scientific discipline, and in 1999 the English psychologist Susan Blackmore wrote a pop-science best-seller named *The Meme Machine*.[37] Moreover, Dawkins's meme turned into an enormous and lasting success in popular culture. The internet today is full of so called "internet memes" – small texts, images, or videos, often humorous in nature – that spread across the web.

However, in sharp contrast to its popular appeal the academic reception of "memetics" was a disaster. Many biologists were skeptical, and responses in the socio-cultural disciplines were almost entirely hostile.[38] According to the French anthropologist Maurice Bloch the idea of memes as body snatchers is "as intriguing, as frightening and as likely as invasion by little green men from Mars."[39] It is especially meme-theory that critics rejected as either a vacuous re-description of things we knew all along, or as a fad that completely misrepresents the workings of socio-cultural processes. The suggestion that cultural units have a selfish "will of their own" was something that critics jumped at, as it seemed to reduce human agents to passive vehicles, while reifying culture to a bizarre extent. The term "meme" itself also encountered skepticism, as hardly anyone saw the added value of chopping culture into little distinct units. These critiques were not without effects, because meme theory failed to establish itself as a scientific field. The *Journal of Memetics* was discontinued in 2005, and Daniel Dennett is amongst the few remaining advocates today.[40]

The field of cultural evolution
At the same time, however, and more quietly at first, the idea of Darwinian cultural evolution stimulated approaches that would become a more durable success.[41] In the 1980s and 1990s two academic duos, Luigi Cavalli-Sforza and Marcus Feldman on the one hand, and Peter Richerson

---

[35] Robert Aunger, *Darwinizing Culture*.
[36] Dennett, *Darwin's Dangerous Idea*, 335–69.
[37] Blackmore, *The Meme Machine*.
[38] Sperber, "An Objection to the Memetic Approach to Culture"; Bloch, "A Well-Disposed Social Anthropologist's Problems with Memes"; Millikan, *Varieties of Meaning*; Lewens, *Cultural Evolution*, 2015; Fracchia and Lewontin, "Does Culture Evolve?"; Kuper, "If Memes Are the Answer, What Is the Question?"; Wilterdink, "Darwinisme in de Sociale Wetenschappen," 451–52; Kronfeldner, *Darwinian Creativity and Memetics*.
[39] Bloch, "A Well-Disposed Social Anthropologist's Problems with Memes," 201.
[40] Dennett, *From Bacteria to Bach and Back*.
[41] Cavalli-Sforza and Feldman, *Cultural Transmission and Evolution*; Boyd and Richerson, *Culture and the Evolutionary Process*; Richerson and Boyd, *Not By Genes Alone*.

and Robert Boyd on the other hand, developed a form of cultural Darwinism that managed to succeed where memetics failed: it established itself as an academic field. These authors had mathematical backgrounds in the natural sciences, and what distinguished their approach was the elaborate use of mathematical evolutionary modelling from biology. Their quantifications of how cultural traits spread within a population reaffirmed the quite obvious insight that cultural transmission can occur semi-independently from biological transmission. Simultaneously, these authors avoided the pitfalls of memetic terminology. Instead of "memes" they used the common term "culture", and as a unit of selection Richerson and Boyd preferred the more flexible notion of "cultural variant". From around the 2000s onwards this application of Darwinian theory started to gain ground. A new field of cultural evolution is growing rapidly, and has gained its own research budgets, conferences, institutes, and major publications.[42] The claims of the field may not sound as grandiose as those from memetics, but the ambitions are still significant. One of its key exponents, the psychologist Alex Mesoudi, expressed the very prospect of "synthesizing" the balkanized socio-cultural sciences, just like Darwinian theory once synthesized the disciplines of biology.[43]

A few aspects of this growing interdisciplinary field stand out. First, its precursors have succeeded in setting a new standard of quantitative modelling.[44] The methods used are highly diverse, ranging from field studies and laboratory experiments to the collection of comparative datasets, but nearly all of them are anchored in mathematical models, often adopted from population biology. Evolutionary biologists, for instance, make use of phylogenetic models to reconstruct evolutionary relationships between species, and such models are now being applied to the reconstruction of evolutionary connections between culturally-transmitted traits such as fairy tales or languages.[45] As a result of this strongly quantitative outlook, the relationship with qualitative and interpretative approaches in socio-cultural disciplines remains largely unexplored territory.[46]

Second, while the field distances itself in some respects from the biologically reductionist programs of sociobiology and evolutionary psychology, it still seeks to build models that are based upon realistic assumptions about individual cognition.[47] The approaches of the field often presuppose the existence of innate and adaptive biological "learning biases" that result from gene-culture coevolution. Those biases make some cultural variants more likely to be adopted and transmitted than others.[48] Two examples are the so called "conformist bias", making people adopt cultural variants that are dominant within their population, and the "prestige bias", which

---

[42] Mesoudi, *Cultural Evolution*, 2011; Lewens, *Cultural Evolution*, 2015; Mesoudi, "Pursuing Darwin's Curious Parallel."
[43] Mesoudi, *Cultural Evolution*, 2011, 205–20.
[44] Mesoudi, "Cultural Evolution," 2016.
[45] Mesoudi, 488–89; Tehrani J.J, "The Phylogeny of Little Red Riding Hood"; Gray, Drummond, and Greenhill, "Language Phylogenies Reveal Expansion Pulses and Pauses in Pacific Settlement."
[46] Mesoudi, *Cultural Evolution*, 2011, 18–20.
[47] Sperber, *Explaining Culture*; Mesoudi, "Cultural Evolution," 2016.
[48] Richerson and Boyd, *Not By Genes Alone*, 119–26; Mesoudi, *Cultural Evolution*, 2011, 55–84.

makes people likely to adopt cultural variants from successful individuals. Some exponents of the field are moving even further away from evolutionary psychology, claiming that these learning biases themselves can be a product of cultural learning.[49]

Third, many key authors endorse Campbell's, as well as Dawkins's claim, about the evolution of non-intentional cultural adaptations.[50] As Joseph Henrich vividly puts it in his account of the cultural evolutionary process: "(it) is – in some crucial sense – smarter than we are. Over generations, often outside of conscious awareness, individuals' choices, learned preferences, lucky mistakes, and occasional insights aggregate to produce cultural adaptations."[51] The biologist David Sloan Wilson writes that "cultural evolution often results in practices that work without anyone knowing why they work", and he explicitly draws comparisons to sociological and anthropological functionalism.[52] However, Dawkins's claim about "selfish replicators" has not found much support.[53]

The field of cultural evolution is growing so quickly that it has already become difficult to summarize all the current trends. So, for our purposes we focus on the two key questions that we encountered above: how do cultural adaptations come into being, and what are they purposeful for? As this section shows, Darwinian cultural evolution has two potentially new answers in store for us. First, variation and selective retention in cultural evolution results in unintended and unrecognized cultural adaptations. Second, cultural adaptations are well-built to ensure their own self-reproduction, sometimes even at the expense of their human hosts. We shall now take a precise look at these answers. Do they have genuine explanatory power, and what might concrete examples of such cultural adaptations be?

3.2 Darwinian origins of cultural functions

Robert Merton provided no convincing explanation for how latent functions arise. Why would unintended consequences produce functions rather than chaos? Darwinian theory might offer an opening here. What if we assume that people introduce all sorts of cultural variants with unintended consequences, most of which die out, but that every now and then variants appear that are functional *by accident*? And what if such cultural chance hits are then cumulatively preserved in repeated rounds of selection? In the case of the Hopi rain dance this would come down to a scenario in which the newly introduced dance enhanced social cohesion only accidentally at first. But when Hopi groups performing the dance faced ecological or military challenges, the cohesion resulting from their ritual improved the group's persistence, also leading to the persistence of the dance itself. At an earlier stage we saw that a phenomenon can be seen

---

[49] Mesoudi, "Cultural Evolution," 2016, 492.
[50] Wilson, *Darwin's Cathedral*, 2010; Runciman, *The Theory of Cultural and Social Selection*; Henrich, *The Secret of Our Success*; Kincaid, "Functional Explanation and Evolutionary Social Science," 2007.
[51] Henrich, *The Secret of Our Success*, 34.
[52] Wilson, *Darwin's Cathedral*, 2010, 47–85; Wilson, *This View of Life*, 207.
[53] Lewens, *Cultural Evolution*, 2015.

as functional when its existence has depended, or depends, on the effects that it has. Within this framework, the rain dance can thus be said to have served a function of social cohesion, even if the actors themselves were incognizant of the effect.

What again did Anthony Giddens write? "Showing that the rain dance fosters social solidarity *cannot possibly* be an explanation of the actions of the Hopi unless at least some of them sense this is so and act accordingly."[54] Like a William Paley of sociology Anthony Giddens here basically argued that there cannot be design without designer. Yet, through a Darwinian process of cumulative preservation of chance hits, the evolution of socio-cultural design without designer becomes a real option. Genuine yet factually false beliefs may survive because of effects that the involved actors neither intended nor recognized as such. What this model implies is that Merton's unintended consequences provide the raw material for a process of selection that builds its own adaptations from it. In other words: the "functionalist fallacy" is not necessarily a fallacy. Anthony Giddens overlooked something crucial. Instead, we might speak of an "intentionalist fallacy", which holds that socio-cultural functions, by default, result from people's conscious or subconscious intentions.

This Darwinian scenario is quite simple, but like biological Darwinism it is deceptively so. All ingredients of the process have been recognized innumerable times before. Merton was surely not the first to highlight unintended consequences – John Locke, Georg Hegel, Max Weber, Norbert Elias and many others preceded him.[55] That cultural variants are subject to forms of competition has also been widely recognized, as analytic conflict theory or rational choice theory help to illustrate. The observation that culture is socially reproduced from person to person has often been marked as culture's very essence. What mainstream socio-cultural scholarship has failed to recognize properly, however, is the counter-intuitive outcome that these elements can have *in combination*: unintended socio-cultural functions. Hence, schools of thought like functionalism or cultural materialism may have been right after all when assuming that not everything functional is deliberately created.[56] In Dennett's words, a process behind cultural design can be that "same sort of blind, mechanical, foresightless sifting-and-duplicating process that has produced the exquisite design of organisms by natural selection."[57]

Admittedly, some earlier authors from time to time came close to something like it. Notions of selection and survival were often in the background in functionalist accounts.[58] Talcott Parsons maintained that when people do not fulfill their social roles, "society would very soon cease to exist."[59] Malinowski pointed out how beliefs and practices which "put a halo of sanctity round tradition and a supernatural stamp upon it, will have a "survival value" for the type of

---

[54] Giddens and Pierson, *Conversation with Anthony Giddens*, 92. Emphasis added.
[55] Vernon, "Unintended Consequences."
[56] Whitehouse, "Why Is a Science of the Sociocultural so Difficult?," 422.
[57] Dennett, *Breaking the Spell*, 79–80.
[58] Kincaid, "Functional Explanation and Evolutionary Social Science," 2007, 214–19.
[59] Quoted in: Wallace and Wolf, *Contemporary Sociological Theory*, 44.

civilization in which they have been evolved."[60] Marvin Harris said things about "selection processes" and "differential survival" that have a Darwinian flavor. He even compared the cultural sanctity of the Indian cow to that of the cow's biological adaptations, seeing both as products of natural selection.[61] Yet, such isolated remarks were not developed into a consistent Darwinian framework. In the end, the functionalists were quite uninterested in processes of change, leaving the question of functions' origins largely unexplored. When Malinowski explicitly compared a Darwinian scenario of cultural selection to that of "providence directly guiding human history", he thought it "a problem of theology or metaphysics."[62] Marvin Harris eventually even backed down on his claims about hidden adaptations. Cultural adaptive change, he said in later work, results from "the thought and activities of individual men and women who respond opportunistically to cost-benefit options." Darwinian cultural evolution, in his view, was merely "a step backwards" and "a misleading analogy".[63] And so it was thus that the functionalists and Harris robbed themselves of a plausible answer to the counter-functionalist critique.

Now that the field of cultural evolution is reviving the old functionalist notions, this counter-functionalist position is also making an appearance again. In an extensive criticism of the field the historical sociologist Joseph Bryant notes that societies "have no power to 'act' or 'adapt' in any fashion", since it is human actors who reflexively and non-randomly construct and define their own social spheres.[64] The anthropologist Tim Ingold laments that the new Darwinians create a wrongheaded "topsy-turvy world" in which humans do not adapt through culture, but where culture adapts through humans.[65] Yet, what these authors seem to have missed is Darwinism's true potential. Ingold is surely right when stating that Darwinian theory turns the world upside down, but that is exactly the whole point! A Darwinian model can help us understand how socio-cultural phenomena *do* in fact have a power to "act" or "adapt" through humans. These critiques illustrate how the theory does not just parasitize existing knowledge, but offers something new and essential. The critics failed to see how the theory can finally explain how culture adapts beyond our intentions and recognition.

Queries

However, the model does raise some theoretical questions. What for instance about history's idiographic complexity? Some current versions of cultural evolution are so very abstract, mathematical, and coarse-grained that it will indeed be difficult to reconcile these versions with what Fracchia and Lewontin describe as "the labyrinthine pathways, the contingent complexity,

---

[60] Malinowski, *Magic, Science and Religion*, 40.
[61] Harris, *Cultural Materialism*, 60.
[62] Malinowski, *Magic, Science and Religion*, 62; Yet, he takes a more favorable stance in: Malinowski, *A Scientific Theory of Culture*, 144.
[63] Harris, *Cultural Materialism*, 61; Harris, *Theories of Culture in Postmodern Times*, 106–7; Harris, *Cannibals and Kings*, 1991, 291.
[64] Bryant, "An Evolutionary Social Science?," 476.
[65] Ingold, "The Trouble with 'Evolutionary Biology,'" 16.

the many nuances, and general messiness of history."[66] But as we discussed above, idiographic complexity as such does not have to be a problem for Darwinism at all.[67] The Canadian sociologist Marion Blute rightly observes that the theory has a potential of resolving the old divide between the idiographic and the nomothetic: cultural phenomena adapt to their environments *in general*, but since adaptedness is always context dependent and possibly different in each instance, the theory simultaneously looks for the particular.[68] Like the biological example used above – the multifunctional elephant's trunk – cultural phenomena can be thought of as being subject to changing and multifaceted selection pressures. Hence, we can avoid mono-causal or mono-functional explanations.

The assumption that cultural traits are "adaptive" should not be taken too far though. We must avoid the pitfall of assuming that everything cultural has a function.[69] It was already said that Darwinian theory offers room for non-functional traits. Socio-cultural phenomena may for instance contain adaptations to past environments.[70] A familiar example is the QWERTY-keyboard, designed to make typing more difficult and thus slower, in order to prevent early typewriters from jamming. Despite having lost this original function, and despite the availability of alternatives that would make typing easier, QWERTY still survives because people have become accustomed to it.[71] There is also the possibility of cultural phenomena being a by-product of something else. Looking for the function of traffic jams will probably not lead anywhere, since they are more likely by-products of car traffic. Moreover, new cultural variants might be neutral in their effects on their own survival, thus leading to cultural equivalents of genetic drift.[72]

The most pressing issue however, as already resurfaced in Bryant's and Ingold's comments, is the role of human agency. While biological evolution may indeed be a process of "design without designer", the evolution of cultural adaptations at first sight looks more like "design *with* designers" in the form of creative and reflexive human agents. In so far as Joseph Bryant accepts the notion of culture adapting to environments at all, he thinks it is "accomplished through the symbolic interaction of acculturated, minded selves."[73] Even Steven Pinker, one of Darwinism's staunchest public defenders, maintains that the theory requires "iterations of copying of random errors", which purportedly does not hold in the cultural realm. After all, cultural "mutations" are produced deliberately by our highly non-random brains in response to felt needs.[74]

---

[66] Fracchia and Lewontin, "Does Culture Evolve?"; Ingold, "The Trouble with 'Evolutionary Biology.'"
[67] Mokyr, *A Culture of Growth*, 27–31; Ritchie, *Darwin and Hegel and Other Philosophical Studies*, 2:137; Hodgson and Knudsen, *Darwin's Conjecture*, viii, 40; Richerson and Boyd, *Not By Genes Alone*, 247–48.
[68] Blute, "History versus Science," 345.
[69] Wilson, *Darwin's Cathedral*, 2002, 203; Kincaid, "Functional Explanation and Evolutionary Social Science," 2007, 225.
[70] Campbell, "On the Conflicts between Biological and Social Evolution," 169.
[71] Mesoudi, *Cultural Evolution*, 2011, 35–36; Blackmore, *The Meme Machine*, 208.
[72] Mesoudi, *Cultural Evolution*, 2011, 76–79.
[73] Bryant, "An Evolutionary Social Science?" 475.
[74] Pinker, "The False Allure of Group Selection."

What to make of this critique? First of all, we should remind ourselves that the randomness of the model does not refer to the causes of "mutations", but only to their fitness outcome. Pinker may be right that cultural variants normally do not occur randomly, but the effects that make them survive can still be accidental and unrecognized.[75] But of course, still, human intentional design *does* make a significant difference here, and any model of Darwinian cultural evolution needs to take account of that. The difference does not yet refute the Darwinian mechanism though, because intentional design and blind evolution may simply offer complementary models of explanation. Proponents of the theory already pointed out time and again that many cultural adaptations are indeed a product of human intentions and recognition – Merton called them "manifest functions" – but that (sub)conscious intentions seem insufficient to explain *all* cultural adaptations. It is here that Darwinism may provide an outcome.[76] We could think of it as a spectrum, with conscious intentional design at one end and blind Darwinian design at the other end. The actual evolution of adaptations might thereby often be a complex mixture of intended, subconscious, and unintended elements, with the levels of recognition also differing from person to person. The extent to which the Darwinian mechanism operates is simply something to be addressed empirically.

This empirical dimension immediately takes us to another counter-argument often used against the model, namely of it being a tautology. In Anthony Giddens's words: "it is of little value indeed to claim that those societies or types of society which have survived for a period of time, because they survived, must have survived."[77] Apart from contradicting the objection that the theory is incorrect, this fails to recognize how the model contains multiple non-tautological elements.[78] The scenario of the Hopi rain dance for instance contains several premises: (1) The Hopi introduced innumerable variants, most of which did not make it. (2) The variant of the rain dance strengthened social cohesion. (3) This social cohesion subsequently contributed to the preservation of groups performing the dance. (4) The survival of these groups helped preserve the ritual itself. (5) The effect on social cohesion was unintended and unrecognized by the Hopi involved. All these premises have a potential of being false to various degrees.

Concrete case studies
Fortunately, the current field of cultural evolution has not only delivered a hypothetical model but also presents case studies. One of the most fruitful domains is the resurgence of old functionalist theories of religion.[79] Trendsetting was David Sloan Wilson's 2002-book *Darwin's*

---

[75] Wilson, *This View of Life*, 196; Smail, *On Deep History and the Brain*, 91; Hodgson and Knudsen, *Darwin's Conjecture*, 48–51.
[76] Wilson, *Darwin's Cathedral*, 2002, 76–79; Dennett, *From Bacteria to Bach and Back*; Ridley, *The Evolution of Everything*; Henrich, *The Secret of Our Success*; Blute, *Darwinian Sociocultural Evolution*, 138–61.
[77] Giddens, *The Constitution of Society*, 235; Moore, *Visions of Culture*, 171.
[78] Kincaid, "Functional Explanation and Evolutionary Social Science," 2007, 223–26, 237; Runciman, *The Theory of Cultural and Social Selection*, 222.
[79] Wilson, *Darwin's Cathedral*, 2002; Sosis and Petersen et al., "Why Cultural Evolutionary Models"; Joseph Bulbulia et al., "The Cultural Evolution of Religion."

Cathedral, which analyses how seemingly irrational and fictional religious convictions can have this-worldly effects on the enhancement of social cohesion. Wilson for instance looked at the historical example of Calvinism, as it emerged in sixteenth-century Geneva.[80] In his view, the European Reformation was a process of many experiments, few of which survived, and Calvinism possessed certain traits that made it a durable success. Calvin's Catechism, for example, told its adherents to abandon self-will and to make sacrifices for the common good. It thereby effectively stimulated the cooperative functioning of Calvinist groups as adaptive units. A broader case study, developed by the psychologist Ara Norenzayan, explores the adaptive value of sincere belief in gods who watch us and punish immoral behavior.[81] Psychological testing shows that people who feel watched tend to behave more strongly according to pro-social norms and Norenzayan's proposal is that observant big gods, who are alleged to police people, form an adaptation that was "stumbled on" by the cultural evolutionary process.[82] It helped create larger societies in which people cooperated in unprecedented numbers.

Another study, by Joseph Henrich, Robert Boyd and Peter Richerson, looks at the gradual spread of monogamous societies at the expense of polygynous ones over the past millennia.[83] As their well substantiated argument goes, polygyny created a great surplus of unmarried men, who, due to their increased frustration, criminal behavior and violence, destabilized the societies of which they were a part. Monogamous societies on the other hand contained larger numbers of married, and thus more stable men, which gave those societies a competitive edge. The current field has looked into many more case studies of socio-cultural phenomena that allegedly enhance social cohesion, including old functionalist classics like common celebrations, dances, and rituals of self-mutilation.[84] It is thereby added that it can even be essential that the actors themselves do not understand the functional rationale of their supernatural belief systems, because it is the sincerity of beliefs that endows those systems with at least some of their effectiveness.[85]

In addition, there is a resurgence of the kind of eco-materialist explanations that were once explored by Harris and others. Joseph Henrich recalls how during field work in Fiji he came across a taboo on the consumption of eels during pregnancies. The taboo makes sense from a scientific perspective, as eels contain elements potentially toxic to fetuses. However, when Henrich asked the Fijians themselves about the function, they simply referred to "custom" and did not seem to be doing it for health reasons in any way. Henrich thus claims that the underlying adaptiveness of the taboo is, as he calls it, one of culture's "secret tricks".[86] Similarly, David Sloan Wilson delved into the complex and ingenious irrigation system on the Indonesian island of Bali.

---

[80] Wilson, *Darwin's Cathedral*, 2002, 86–124.
[81] Norenzayan, *Big Gods*.
[82] Norenzayan, 10.
[83] Henrich, Boyd, and Richerson, "The Puzzle of Monogamous Marriage"; Henrich, *The WEIRDest People in the World*.
[84] Laland, *Darwin's Unfinished Symphony*, 300–301; Joseph Bulbulia et al., "The Cultural Evolution of Religion"; Henrich, *The Secret of Our Success*; Whitehouse, "Dying for the Group."
[85] Henrich, *The Secret of Our Success*, 106, 165; Norenzayan, *Big Gods*, 54.
[86] Henrich, *The Secret of Our Success*, 100–103, 145.

Building upon the work of the anthropologist Steve Lansing, he suggests that the irrigation activities are functionally monitored by Bali's elaborate water temple religion.[87] Its design would partly be "authored" by blind evolution. This line of investigation is promising, and might also revitalize older case studies, like the Hindu holy cow or Aztec human sacrifice.[88] The effect of protein intake, for instance, may have enhanced the survival of cannibalistic sacrifices, even if the Aztecs themselves were incognizant of it. Previously we saw that Marvin Harris was caricatured for believing in the *Big Ecologist in the Sky*, who, outside of people's understanding, created cultural adaptations to ecological circumstances. So, might this mysterious figure in fact listen to the name of Darwinian cultural evolution?

The discipline that has probably toyed with Darwinian cultural evolution most endurably, is economics.[89] Since the days of Adam Smith economists have been familiar with the idea of "an invisible hand" that leads liberal economic processes towards non-designed functional outcomes. In the second half of the twentieth century the famous Austrian economist Friedrich Hayek elaborated upon that, using selectionist notions that were vaguely Darwinian in their outlook.[90] Hayek saw "the emergence of order as the result of adaptive evolution", which resulted from a "survival of the successful".[91] In addition he cautioned politicians not to interfere in this process, since the evolutionary mechanisms were far better able to lead to adaptive outcomes than deliberate design; this would help explain why capitalist economies outperformed communist ones. More recently, others have looked at the selection of firms and organizations, whereby it is claimed that businesspeople themselves often do not fully understand which institutions or routines made their companies successful, or unsuccessful.[92] Another domain where the idea is being implemented is the evolution of language.[93] Some linguists maintain that our language systems contain internal structures and a usefulness that results from unintended Darwinian selection.

A domain where blind evolution may seem rather implausible is that of human artefacts. If we want an arch-example of "design *with* designers", our technology looks much like it. No sane person would uphold that the evolution of knives was not in any way guided by an understanding of their practical use for cutting things. But even artefacts might contain blind Darwinian elements.[94] In the early days of cultural selectionist theory the French philosopher Emile-Auguste Chartier reflected on the evolution of Breton fishing boats, and in 1908 he made the following lovely comment:

---

[87] Wilson, *Darwin's Cathedral*, 2002, 126–33.
[88] Whether the alleged adaptive effects were significant enough can still be contested, as happens in: Kincaid, *Philosophical Foundations of the Social Sciences*, 122-6.
[89] Ridley, *The Evolution of Everything*, 96–117; Frank, *The Darwin Economy*; Mesoudi, *Cultural Evolution*, 2011, 177–88.
[90] Hayek, *The Constitution of Liberty*; Beck and Witt, "Austrian Economics and the Evolutionary Paradigm*."
[91] Hayek, *The Constitution of Liberty*, 57–59.
[92] Nelson and Winter, *An Evolutionary Theory of Economic Change*; Hodgson and Knudsen, *Darwin's Conjecture*, 36.
[93] Kirby, "Language as an Adaptive System."
[94] Kelly, *What Technology Wants*.

> Every boat is copied from another boat. (...) Let's reason as follows in the manner of Darwin. It is clear that a very badly made boat will end up at the bottom after one or two voyages and thus never be copied. (...) One could then say, with complete rigor, that it is the sea herself who fashions the boats, choosing those which function and destroying the others.[95]

This suggestion remained dormant for a long time, but has been revived in a recent study on the adaptiveness of Polynesian canoes.[96] Another team of researchers examined how classical violins are efficiently adapted to have much resonance power, and their internal structure even contains an underlying mathematical logic that past violin builders could hardly have been aware of.[97] The researchers thus propose a selection process in which violins that just happened to sound better, accumulated into a magnificent "hidden" design.

The need for qualitative history
These many case studies look promising, but we must note some empirical issues. Take the example of the Fijian food taboo on eels. Henrich's blind scenario sounds plausible, but it is difficult to rule out that past Fijians consciously, or subconsciously, intended and recognized the taboo's positive effect on pregnancies. Unfortunately, Fijian history has not left behind many sources that would enable a detailed investigation into how the taboo evolved, and what people themselves understood about its effects. This is a problem that also bears upon other examples, like the Hopi rain dance, Aztec cannibalism, or Polynesian canoes. Importantly, this lack of evidence is not just a problem for the blind Darwinian scenario, but also for competing scenarios of conscious or subconscious design. In many cases we simply cannot know how functions came about. This was also one of the reasons why functionalist anthropologists in their time left the issue unexplored.[98]

Historians are amongst those best able to offer solace at this point because they traditionally study processes that *did* leave a lot of sources behind. Wilson's case study of Calvinism, for instance, looks more promising, because there are ample sources that would allow a more detailed reconstruction of how Calvinist doctrines enhanced the cooperative survival of Calvinist groups, as well as to see what involved actors themselves understood about this rationale. Notably, this is something that Wilson himself has not yet done in any detail. "We can safely conclude that conscious intentional thought explains some but not all of the functionality of Calvinism", he insists. Yet, his empirical evidence is meagre.[99] Wilson consulted Calvin's

---

[95] Quoted in: Rogers and Ehrlich, "Natural Selection and Cultural Rates of Change," 3417.
[96] Rogers and Ehrlich, "Natural Selection and Cultural Rates of Change."
[97] Nia et al., "The Evolution of Air Resonance Power Efficiency in the Violin and Its Ancestors."
[98] Radcliffe-Brown, *Structure and Function*, 50; Malinowski, *Magic, Science and Religion*, 62.
[99] Wilson, *Darwin's Cathedral*, 2002, 121.

catechism and ordinances, but their implementation was still a relatively intentional and top-down affair. He furthermore highlights how Calvinists continually encouraged social behavior, and compared their communities to an organism.[100] But that actually indicates manifest functions rather than latent ones. In sum, Wilson led the way towards a research area of much importance, but hardly penetrated the terrain himself.

Another example is a recent book by Joseph Henrich which delves into how people in western Europe over the past two millennia developed a distinctive culturally induced psychological pattern of individualism, nonconformism, and trust in strangers.[101] Henrich attributes a decisive early role to the medieval Roman Catholic Church. By stimulating monogamy and by banning marriages between relatives, the Church broke the old shackles of kin-based institutions. In addition to his earlier argument about monogamy, Henrich claims that these rules strengthened pan-tribal social identities and more cooperation between strangers. The Church itself also reaped the benefits, as it became a more effective rival for people's loyalty at the expense of tribal loyalties. Monogamy furthermore made numerous powerful families die out, with their possessions falling into ecclesiastical hands. Importantly, Henrich claims that all this happened accidentally and unintentionally: the medieval Roman Catholic Church was "just the 'lucky one' that bumbled across an effective recombination of supernatural beliefs and practices."[102] This fits into Henrich's overall argument about institutions evolving through hidden processes of selection, with actors mostly being incognizant about how or why those institutions work.[103] But did medieval clergymen really have no clue whatsoever about their marriage policies breaking tribal power and enhancing the Church's own supremacy? Answering that question would require a thorough qualitative engagement with medieval sources. What did people comprehend, or not, about such matters? Henrich provides a thought provoking argument, but this essential empirical dimension remains unaddressed.

The absence of more detailed research in this direction is probably due to the field's quantitative orientation. This focus has many advantages – the value of mathematical modelling for Darwinian theory is undisputed – but if we really want to put the idea of "design without designer" to the test, the field simultaneously needs to move beyond that. The design hypothesis demands investigations into how involved actors themselves comprehended the functionality of their socio-cultural phenomena, and to compare those actors' understanding with the actual adaptive effects that helped those phenomena survive throughout particular periods of time. The examination of people's own understanding requires things like *Verstehen*, hermeneutics, thick description, and the meaningful interpretation of historical documents. However, due to the cultural evolutionary field's quantitative orientation hardly any of this research has been undertaken yet. So, what the field needs right now is a qualitative turn. In addition to its

---

[100] Wilson, 86–124; Wilson, *Evolution for Everyone*, 233–54.
[101] Henrich, *The WEIRDest People in the World*.
[102] Henrich, 161, 167, 281.
[103] Henrich, 94.

quantitative methodologies, it would benefit from developing a methodologically "softer" side. In the next chapters we shall see how European witch-hunting provides an auspicious case study in that regard.

Yet, two theoretical steps first need to be taken. Of course, we still have to look at the issue of what purposes cultural adaptations fulfil. But there is also another topic that demands attention. The cultural Darwinian model that is defended here assumes that some effects of cultural phenomena are real, like social cohesion or protein intake, while other effects are non-real, like supernaturally induced rainfall or sunrise. This assertion, in its turn, presupposes that modern science potentially has a more accurate understanding of certain aspects of reality than alternative viewpoints. However, this is something that will make many socio-cultural scholars today dig their heels in. Over the past half century various forms of epistemic relativism have gained influence, rendering distinctions between "fact" and "fiction", "science" and "non-science", or "objective" and "subjective" obsolete. If warranted, this would make the whole Darwinian model break down immediately. This relativist movement is often called "postmodernism", and although we have already touched upon it a few times, its epistemic position still needs to be addressed in more detail. We will now take a closer look at it, especially by addressing the work of the author Bruno Latour.

3.3 Intermezzo: Epistemic relativism

"We won't try to discipline you, to make you fit into our categories; we will let you deploy your own worlds, and only later will we ask you to explain how you came about settling them." This is how the French philosopher and social theorist Bruno Latour suggests social scientists approach the actors they study. "The task of defining and ordering the social should be left to the actors themselves, not taken up by the analyst", he upholds.[104] Let actors disclose their own view of things, no matter how strange this initially appears. Social scientists should not treat actors as mere "informants", while attributing to themselves a broader and more complete understanding of things.[105] Latour even renders the idea of scientists having a better understanding of a reality "out there" unjustified altogether.[106] Taken to its logical extreme, this viewpoint puts a bomb under the cultural Darwinian model. Because how, epistemologically speaking, could any academic scholar determine that the Hopi rain dance did not fulfil the function of making rain, while pointing at other effects that the Hopi themselves did not put forward as such?

Accordingly, when I present the approach of Darwinian cultural evolution to colleagues from the social sciences or the humanities, Latour is the name they mention the most when objecting to the approach. Reading Latour, as it has often been put forward to me, would clarify why academic scholars should not aim to distinguish real from illusory effects. That Latour's name

---

[104] Latour, *Reassembling the Social*, 23.
[105] Latour, 32–33.
[106] Latour and Woolgar, *Laboratory Life*, 180–83.

is mentioned so often is hardly surprising, since he belongs to the most cited scholars in the humanities.[107] The New York Times calls him "one of the most inventive and influential of contemporary philosophers", while the French magazine L'Obs says that he "inspires the planet."[108] Latour is also described as the "most illustrious champion" of the vast field of science and technology studies, which aims to examine science in its broader context.[109] Hence, considering his reputation, we surely need to contemplate whether Latour's epistemic position indeed convincingly undermines that essential distinction between real effects and non-real effects.

Latour is often labelled as one of the representatives of postmodern relativism. The question of what this movement precisely is can engender much confusion and controversy, as the meaning of the term is as slippery as the movement's academic status is contested.[110] In academic parlance, postmodern relativism normally refers to the thought of a loose amalgam of French thinkers, including Jacques Derrida, Michel Foucault, Jean-Francois Lyotard, Jacques Lacan, Julia Kristeva, Gilles Deleuze, and Bruno Latour, although some of these authors, not least Latour, reject the label themselves. From the 1960s onwards their influence on the social sciences and the humanities has been substantial. Especially in the Anglo-Saxon world their ideas gained traction, with Judith Butler, Donna Haraway, or sometimes Richard Rorty, being mentioned as influential advocates.[111] The controversies regarding the movement came to a head in the so called "science wars" of the 1990s – a series of vehement intellectual exchanges between opponents and proponents – but disagreements continue to this day.[112]

Postmodern relativism for and against
In the eyes of its supporters, postmodernism is a creative movement that has helped us understand that "reality" cannot be represented through human conceptual categories. This would imply that no account of "reality" can be epistemologically more accurate than any other account.[113] Of course, relativist notions about knowledge being historically conditioned, with no one having privileged access to the truth, are much older.[114] "Man is the measure of all things", the philosopher Protagoras already stated in ancient Greece.[115] Yet, in the late 1970s, when

---

[107] "Most Cited Authors of Books in the Humanities, 2007 | Times Higher Education (THE)."
[108] Kofman, "Bruno Latour, the Post-Truth Philosopher, Mounts a Defense of Science"; Noyon, Porte, and Aeschimann, "Comment Bruno Latour est devenu le penseur qui inspire la planète."
[109] Fuller, *The Philosophy of Science and Technology Studies*, 4; Law, "STS as Method"; Sismondo, *An Introduction to Science and Technology Studies*, 65–74.
[110] Searle, "Rationality and Realism, What Is at Stake?," For overviews of the movement, see for instance:; Gross and Levitt, *Higher Superstition*; Boghossian, *Fear of Knowledge*; Butler, *Postmodernism*; Drolet, *The Postmodernism Reader*; Wilterdink, "The Sociogenesis of Postmodernism."
[111] Wilterdink, "The Sociogenesis of Postmodernism"; Leezenberg and Vries, *History and Philosophy of the Humanities*, 293–354.
[112] Sokal, *Beyond the Hoax*; Fuller, *The Philosophy of Science and Technology Studies*.
[113] Brown, *Postmodernism for Historians*, 7–11; Thompson, *Postmodernism and History*, 91–94.
[114] Baghramian and Coliva, *Relativism*.
[115] Baghramian and Coliva, 26.

grand narratives of modernity appeared to have broken down, people's minds were ripe for a novel surge of relativist ideas. The new upcoming movement of "postmodernism" then showed skepticism towards unifying metatheories, and instead aimed to be acceptant of difference and variety.[116] Its thinkers were especially interested in language, which was seen as a system of signs that all refer to each other, rather than to an outer objective world. Language constructs "reality", implying that science is just one system of language amongst others, and that it has no privileged access to an objective world "out there".[117] In addition, postmodern theorists portrayed modern science as being inextricably linked with power, or what is more, that science is a form of oppression itself. So, by "deconstructing" science's language and its claims of objectivity, established positions of power can be challenged. This would give postmodernism an emancipatory and transformative potential. While the movement is not necessarily in itself an ideology, it surely enables ideologies, like feminism, LGBTQ+ activism, antiracism, multiculturalism or postcolonialism.[118] Postmodern theory would thereby carry the promise of creating a more accepting social environment in which oppressed groups or cultures are shielded from the charge of holding false beliefs.[119]

Opponents on the other hand describe the postmodern epistemic position as sheer folly.[120] The movement is said to have broken down standards of academic quality, so "higher superstition", "intellectual impostures", "the intellectual equivalent of crack", or "the vacuous rhetoric of mountebanks and charlatans" are some of the designations used.[121] A French critic renders it "a mixture of nihilism, relativism, dogmatism and utopianism. It holds that there is no such thing as truth, except one: that there is no such thing as truth."[122] Criticisms focus on a few key issues in particular. The language postmodernists use is said to be opaque and obscurantist; it has the pretension of being profound, but in fact comes down to a vacuous mixture of trivialities and absurdities. Noam Chomsky says that the works of postmodernists consists of "truism, error, or gibberish" with the "truism or error" being "only a fraction of the total word count."[123] Another point concerns the denial of scientific facts. Postmodern relativists are accused of dismissing scientific discoveries about the world, seeing those discoveries as mere socio-cultural constructs. But if the postmodernists really mean what they say, or so their critics

---

[116] Browning, *Lyotard and the End of Grand Narratives*.
[117] Thompson, *Postmodernism and History*, 15.
[118] Brown, *Postmodernism for Historians*, 8.
[119] Boghossian, *Fear of Knowledge*, 130; Law, "STS as Method," 46–47.
[120] Sokal and Bricmont, *Intellectual Impostures*; Sokal, *Beyond the Hoax*; Chomsky, "Noam Chomsky on Post-Modernism"; Gross and Levitt, *Higher Superstition*; Dawkins, "Postmodernism Disrobed"; Pluckrose and Lindsay, *Cynical Theories*; Aya, "Reign of Error"; Aya, "Gellner's Case against Cognitive Relativism."
[121] Gross and Levitt, *Higher Superstition*; Sokal and Bricmont, *Intellectual Impostures*; Elton, *Return to Essentials*, 41; Dawkins, "Postmodernism Disrobed," 141.
[122] Boudon and Leroux, *Y a-t-il encore une sociologie ?*, 155."Le postmodernisme est en effet un mélange de nihilisme, de relativisme, de dogmatisme et d'utopie. Il n'y aurait plus de vérité, sauf une : qu'il n'y a plus de vérité."
[123] Quote in: Aya, "Reign of Error," 33; See also: Chomsky, "Noam Chomsky on Post-Modernism."

wonder, how can they substantiate their *own* claims about the world?[124] "Fact-constructivism is such a bizarre view that it is hard to believe that anyone actually endorses it. And yet, it seems that many do", Paul Boghossian states.[125]

In the eyes of these opponents, postmodernists respond to such criticisms in unsatisfying ways. Questions about the precise meaning of their words are usually met with evasions, irritation, and denunciations. Noam Chomsky observes that instead of offering further clarification on what they exactly mean to say, "the response is cries of anger: to raise these questions shows 'elitism,' 'anti-intellectualism,' and other crimes." The counter-accusation of elitism is seen as particularly strange, since it is the postmodernists themselves who use unnecessarily complicated language that parasitizes people's intellectual insecurities. It makes their audiences think that they are not intelligent enough to understand it. Not explaining their positions in plain and concrete language fulfills a function, however: people would immediately deflate the hot air postmodernists produce. The incomprehensibility further endows key postmodernists with a guru-like status. Authors like Lacan or Butler gained a devoted following of people who were impressed by apparent profundity.[126] Another method postmodernist thinkers are accused of using – especially when confronted with their own relativist statements – is to suddenly pretend that their claims were ironic rather than absurd. Their opponents retort: if postmodernists are just joking around, why do they respond so angrily to criticisms, accept significant academic salaries, and want to be taken seriously on so many important issues?[127]

The example we will mostly stick to here is Bruno Latour, whose thought has a direct bearing on that distinction between real and non-real effects. Some critics describe the French scholar as one of the most dishonest exponents of the postmodern movement.[128] His work is said to be "vague, contradictory or simply unintelligible", consisting of "philosophical mystifications" that boil down to "a metaphysical conceit (in both senses of the word) of astounding proportions."[129] In one academic paper, Philippe Stamenkovic contemplates the question whether to consider his work mere "bullshit" or "pseudo-profound bullshit", and he eventually opts for the latter.[130] What would make Latour particularly tricky is that he masks his mysticism with a charming, seemingly science-friendly posture.[131] His work has a Janus-faced character, springing from relativism to endorsements of scientific facts and back. Latour is able to deny on

---

[124] Sokal and Bricmont, *Intellectual Impostures*, 49–96; Wallace and Wolf, *Contemporary Sociological Theory*, 421–26; Rosenau, *Post-Modernism and the Social Sciences*, 90; Evans, *In Defense of History*, 220, 231.
[125] Boghossian, *Fear of Knowledge*, 25.
[126] Mercier, *Not Born Yesterday*, 234–36.
[127] Dawkins, "Postmodernism Disrobed," 142.
[128] Stamenkovic, "The Contradictions and Dangers of Bruno Latour's Conception of Climate Science"; Malm, *The Progress of This Storm*; Sokal and Bricmont, *Intellectual Impostures*; Sokal, "Pourquoi j'ai écrit ma parodie"; Sokal, *Beyond the Hoax*; Gross and Levitt, *Higher Superstition*.
[129] Stamenkovic, "The Contradictions and Dangers of Bruno Latour's Conception of Climate Science," 4; Sokal, "Pourquoi j'ai écrit ma parodie""mystifications philosophiques"; Gross and Levitt, *Higher Superstition*, 58.
[130] Stamenkovic, "The Contradictions and Dangers of Bruno Latour's Conception of Climate Science," 10–11.
[131] Stamenkovic, 2.

one occasion what he demonstrably said on an earlier one; previous relativist statements are then suddenly transformed into banalities nobody would disagree with.[132] So what are people so upset about? For his critics Paul Gross and Norman Levitt, such a response "drives more earnest and responsible philosophers of science into paroxysms of disgust when confronted with it."[133] Although Latour gained much popularity at universities, his critics maintain that his following has the semblance of a religious cult. He has been described as a "new priest", "the chief of a religious sect", or "the pastor leading his sheep to some kind of revealed truth."[134] Yet, Latour's "animism" and "new age mysticism" is considered far from innocent as it fosters the post-truth predicament of alternative facts.[135] Behind the disguise of apparent friendliness, he replaces the ideal of truthfulness with a vulgar Machiavellianism in which might is right.[136] Latour himself has leftist political views, but his critics warn that his methods open the door to fact-free Machiavellianism in the context of any ideology. Philippe Stamenkovic considers his work dangerous, and argues that it cannot be considered as "belonging to social or human science."[137]

Unsurprisingly, Latour and the people inspired by him dismiss such charges as vindictive. "People never really understood what I was saying", Latour retorts.[138] "I was associated with that postmodern relativist stuff, I was put into that crowd by others."[139] Roger Luckhurst similarly argues that his "point is misunderstood", while the New York Times renders Latour "France's most famous and misunderstood philosopher."[140] What his critics allegedly fail to see is that Latour in fact criticized the kind of postmodern relativism that perceives scientific findings as mere human constructions of the world. Latour is celebrated for offering a nuanced approach that transcends older divisions between the human and the non-human.[141] Instead of solely focusing on nature determining science, as positivists would have it, or science constructing nature, as outright constructivists would have it, Latour has looked at human as well as non-human actors – also described as "actants" – which become connected with each other through networks. For example, we should not solely perceive a researcher like Louis Pasteur as an observer who made discoveries about microbes that already existed passively.[142] Pasteur, his instruments, the microbes, colleagues, social institutions, politicians, and other actants came to form complex networks, in which all actants changed due to their interacting with each other.

---

[132] Sokal, "Pourquoi j'ai écrit ma parodie"; Gross and Levitt, *Higher Superstition*, 59.
[133] Gross and Levitt, *Higher Superstition*, 58.
[134] Charlie, "Bruno Latour""nouveau curé"; Stamenkovic, "The Contradictions and Dangers of Bruno Latour's Conception of Climate Science," 3; Lamy, "Des disciples bien disciplinés""d'un pasteur menant ses brebis vers une sorte de vérité révélée."
[135] Stamenkovic, "The Contradictions and Dangers of Bruno Latour's Conception of Climate Science," 2, 9.
[136] Malm, *The Progress of This Storm*, 9–10, 27–29; Stamenkovic, "The Contradictions and Dangers of Bruno Latour's Conception of Climate Science," 23.
[137] Stamenkovic, "The Contradictions and Dangers of Bruno Latour's Conception of Climate Science," 29.
[138] Paulson, "The Critical Zone of Science and Politics:"
[139] Vrieze, "Bruno Latour, a Veteran of the 'Science Wars,' Has a New Mission."
[140] Luckhurst, "Bruno Latour's Scientifiction," 5–6; Kofman, "Bruno Latour, the Post-Truth Philosopher, Mounts a Defense of Science."
[141] Luckhurst, "Bruno Latour's Scientifiction"; Dijstelbloem, "De democratie anders"; Vries, *Bruno Latour*.
[142] Latour, *The Pasteurization of France*.

Latour himself maintains that he "was just arguing that humans and nonhumans are now mixing together more and more intimately."[143] The only thing he did was to provide a more scientific and honest view of how science is practiced. That Latour asserts that certain networks become more robust than other networks, would also give his work a non-relativist twist. So, in the eyes of his supporters this renowned French thinker in fact "mounts a defense of science", which we badly need in an age of post-truth politics.[144]

Bruno Latour's relativism
Considering these widely diverging viewpoints, what to make of Latour, and how to assess the validity of his work? Is it vacuous and self-contradictory relativism, or does Latour actually move subtly beyond that? Does his work make this distinction between real and non-real effects redundant? In Latour's defense, it can indeed be said that he did innovative work on the complex interactions characteristic of scientific research. Latour became particularly famous for bringing the methods of ethnography, traditionally used to study non-western peoples, into the scientific laboratory.[145] His aim was to look at scientific researchers as if they were "a foreign tribe".[146] During his sojourns in the laboratory Latour began to notice that the endurance of scientific "facts" does not simply hinge on their correspondence to the truth. To a large extent it is a wide range of social, institutional and technical factors that decide the matter, not least the competitive struggles for dominance between scientists supporting or contesting those facts. Networks of alliances can make a scientific claim stand or fall. While the sociology of science preceded Latour, his empirical work did offer a new counterweight against overly simplistic notions of scientists as objective and rational agents of truth.

However, while we may question the rudeness of his critics, a calmer look at Latour's work does show them to be correct about his epistemology.[147] "Although Latour repeatedly denies being relativist, his writings speak for themselves", Stamenkovic contends.[148] So let us have a look at some of Latour's quotes. The Routledge encyclopedia of philosophy defines epistemic relativism as the view that "everything or every truth is relative to some standards so that, when two or more people disagree about these issues, they may all be correct."[149] The Stanford encyclopedia similarly says that "Relativists argue that beliefs and values get their justification or truth only relative to specific epistemic systems or practices."[150] Unmistakably, Latour has made statements that fit these definitions. Take this quote from 1988:

---

[143] Paulson, "The Critical Zone of Science and Politics:"
[144] Kofman, "Bruno Latour, the Post-Truth Philosopher, Mounts a Defense of Science"; Vrieze, "Bruno Latour, a Veteran of the 'Science Wars,' Has a New Mission"; Paulson, "The Critical Zone of Science and Politics:"
[145] Vries, *Bruno Latour*, 21–52; Latour and Woolgar, *Laboratory Life*.
[146] Latour and Woolgar, *Laboratory Life*, 40.
[147] Baghramian and Coliva, *Relativism*, 135–39.
[148] Stamenkovic, "The Contradictions and Dangers of Bruno Latour's Conception of Climate Science," 7.
[149] Tanesini, "Epistemic Relativism."
[150] Baghramian and Carter, "Relativism."

> There is no difference between the 'real' and the 'unreal', the 'real' and the 'possible', the 'real' and the 'imaginary.' Rather, there are all the differences experienced between those that resist for long and those that do not, those that resist courageously and those that do not, those that know how to ally or isolate themselves and those that do not.[151]

Simply put, whether something is true or false is beside the point; it only matters whether it endures. Hence, if Latour's rejection of the quest for truth is not relativism, what is relativism? In a book on his actor-network approach from 2005 Latour also made striking claims about the nature of reality, typical for the field of Science and Technology Studies.[152] He argued that we live in a "pluriverse", in which things are fundamentally multiple.[153] As he specifies: "this has nothing to do with the 'interpretive flexibility' allowed by 'multiple points of views' taken on the 'same' thing. It is the thing itself that has been allowed to be deployed as multiple."[154] The notion of "alternative facts" presupposes the idea that there are not just multiple perspectives on reality, with no one knowing the full and complete truth – in itself a reasonable and defensible position – but that there are multiple versions of reality itself. That is exactly what Latour is saying here.

As mentioned, Latour purportedly takes a nuanced position regarding the debates about constructivism. But if this is so, how should we interpret this statement from 1987? "Since the settlement of a controversy is the cause of Nature's representation, not its consequence, we can never use this consequence, Nature, to explain how and why a controversy has been settled."[155] If we take seriously what Latour says here, it would imply that when scientists agreed that the Moon has craters, or that sperm cells fertilize egg cells, that this was not *in any way* a consequence of the fact that the Moon indeed has craters, and that sperm cells indeed fertilize egg cells. A closer scrutiny of his actor-network perspective leads us to further strange assertions. As Latour's argument goes, the scientific examination of entities changes those entities, or actants, to the extent that we cannot gain knowledge about them as they existed *before* they were examined. So, we cannot make claims about things beyond our own networks. In 1976, French scientists used modern tools to examine the mummy of Ramses II, and concluded that the pharaoh died of tuberculosis. Latour objected, because this bacillus was only diagnosed and examined as such by the late nineteenth century researcher Robert Koch. Its existence could therefore not be extrapolated into ancient Egypt.[156] "Before Koch, the bacillus had no real existence", Latour stated.[157] Hence, saying that Ramses II died of tuberculosis would be as anachronistic as saying that he died due to machine gun fire, or the stress of a stock market crash.

---

[151] Latour, *The Pasteurization of France*, 159.
[152] Law, "STS as Method," 43–44.
[153] Latour, *Reassembling the Social*, 116–17; The claim is reaffirmed in: Latour, *Face à Gaïa*, 50.
[154] Latour, *Reassembling the Social*, 116–17.
[155] Latour, *Science in Action*, 258.
[156] Latour, "Ramsès II est-il mort de la tuberculose ? Jusqu'où faut-il mener des découvertes scientifiques."
[157] Latour, 84."Avant Koch, le bacille n'a pas de réelle existence."

But is Latour's comparison not patently absurd? Machine guns obviously did not exist in ancient Egypt, while everything that we know about bacilli confirms that they did already exist. If Latour is serious here, he might just as well blame Koch for unleashing tuberculosis on humanity!

In his more detailed study of Koch's colleague and rival Louis Pasteur, Latour is more ambiguous on this issue. At some point he wonders: "Did the microbe *exist* before Pasteur?" His answer: "from the practical point of view – I say practical, not theoretical – it did not."[158] But this again is a bewildering claim that raises further questions. What about microbial diseases *before* Pasteur? Did these microbes already kill people from a theoretical point of view but let the people live happily ever after, practically speaking? Latour probably does mean to say something that strange, but the real meaning of his words remains shrouded in mystery. Nowhere in his book does he explain this distinction between the practical and the theoretical. We saw that Latour complains about being misunderstood, but how is one to understand him correctly if he does not explain such an apparently bizarre statement?

Since Latour's own publications, as his critics correctly point out, lack clarity on the precise epistemic purport of his words, we might look for solace elsewhere. In a television interview he was once pressed a bit on this topic. The interviewer asked him about Pluto, the celestial body.[159] At some point people observed Pluto, but that did not change the object itself, right? Latour first responded that "Pluto has been mobilized within human astronomy." This sounds typically vague, but if it means that the observation of Pluto changed something with regard to human astronomy, Latour's claim is warranted but obvious at the same time – he retreats to a banality. The interviewer was not satisfied yet, and repeated the question: what about Pluto *itself*? Latour evades the question by stating that it is "a meaningless question", but subsequently insists that the observation "does change a lot", as "every time you send a probe, if you send a satellite, Pluto will have a completely different atmosphere, will be constituted differently." Yet, in fact, no probes or satellites had been sent to Pluto at the time whatsoever. Even if a probe had been sent – as happened in 2015 – this would have changed little to the atmosphere, let alone its constitution.[160] Latour's response here is important and deserves consideration, because as far as I can tell it is the only instance where he became somewhat precise and concrete about what he means. But that he gave such an eerie answer to such an obvious question indicates that Latour's epistemic position cannot be understood correctly because he does not understand it himself.

A careful reading of more recent interviews further shows that his apparently science-friendly posture needs to be questioned. In one interview Latour dismisses the allegation of him paving the way for post-truth politics. After all, he supports the idea of "solid facts".[161] But later

---

[158] Latour, *The Pasteurization of France*, 80. Emphasis added.
[159] Latour, Noorderlicht aflevering: "Wat is wetenschap?"
[160] The first probe that approached Pluto only arrived in 2015. See: Northon, "New Horizons Spacecraft Begins First Stages of Pluto Encounter."
[161] Verschuer, "'Hoop is nu een laffe uitvlucht'""solide feiten."

on in the same interview he maintains that "I do not think it is important to be rational, as long as you are civilized."[162] Yet, how can one be scientific if rationality is not necessarily important? The interview in which Latour allegedly "mounts a defense of science", later on also recounts about him claiming that gravity was "created and made visible by the labor and expertise of scientists."[163] But that raises the question of how stars were formed and how the solar system stuck together during all those billions of years before scientists on Earth "created" gravity. In sum, it is not others who put Latour in the camp of the relativists; he did so, and keeps doing it, himself. That Latour makes incorrect statements about his own work need not surprise us. Providing correct information only matters to those who care about the distinction between true and false, but since Latour dismisses this distinction altogether, what else to expect from him?

Other authors associated with postmodern theory make similar epistemological claims. Some do write more clearly than Latour at times, like Richard Rorty and Michel Foucault. Yet, epistemologically speaking these authors also slide towards relativism. In Foucault's view, claims about reality or truth are actually disguised representations of power; "in fact power produces; it produces reality; it produces domains of objects and rituals of truth."[164] Richard Rorty proposed abandoning the aim of truth-finding as correspondence to reality altogether, and replace it with "pragmatism", which simply redefines truth as "what is good for us to believe."[165] As Rorty explained:

> We pragmatists cannot make sense of the idea that we should pursue truth for its own sake. We cannot regard truth as a goal of inquiry. The purpose of inquiry is to achieve agreement among humans about what to do, to bring about consensus on the ends to be achieved and the means to be used to achieve those ends.[166]

Relativism's critics correctly point at the problem of inconsistency and self-refutation. If Latour is serious about his claim that scientific research fundamentally changes the entities that it examines, then what about his own research? Did laboratories already exist before he began studying them? Did Bruno Latour himself already exist before others started writing about him? On what grounds can he actually make claims about laboratories, if the scientists who work there do not necessarily share those claims? Anyone who uses relativism consistently will wind up in quicksand. "Taking Latour's radicalism seriously, there is no point at which it stops", Jeroen Bouterse remarks.[167] But Latour does not use relativism consistently – he only uses it when it suits his purposes. When it concerns his *own* claims, the relativism suddenly undergoes a

---

[162] Verschuer, "ik denk niet dat je rationeel hoeft te zijn, als je maar beschaafd bent."
[163] Kofman, "Bruno Latour, the Post-Truth Philosopher, Mounts a Defense of Science."
[164] Foucault, *Surveiller et Punir*, 196. "En fait le pouvoir produit; il produit le réel; il produit des domains d'objects et des rituels de vérité."; See also, for instance: Rabinow, *The Foucault Reader*, 51–75.
[165] Rorty, *Objectivity, Relativism, and Truth*, 22.
[166] Rorty, *Philosophy and Social Hope*, xxv.
[167] Bouterse, "Nature and History," 114.

vanishing act. In some instances, he refers to insights about plate tectonics, research on primates, and especially climate change.[168] But why not use his own weapons against him? Climate change was only created when scientists examined it. Temperatures did not really exist before human and technological actants measured them, which disallows long term comparisons. In the Latourian pluriverse climate change may also be going on in some versions, but not in alternative versions. Similarly, Richard Rorty repeatedly refers to aspects of Darwinian evolution to support his "pragmatist" viewpoints; however, Darwinian evolution is built upon a Mount Everest of controllable evidence that resulted from the consistent use of scientific principles like truth finding, rationality and empirical evidence.[169] By using Darwinian insights, Rorty selectively relies on scientific evidence, while simultaneously undermining the principles that made the evidence possible in the first place.

Postmodern relativism's popularity
If epistemic relativism is self-refuting in this way, then why did it spread in the academic world? The answer to this question is multifaceted, but postmodern relativists themselves tend to focus on politics and ideology as crucial determinants of academic viewpoints. Let us therefore have a look at postmodernism's own ideological context.[170] The relationship between science and ideology has always been a problematic one. Science examines reality, and reality, to the dismay of any ideologist, has a tendency of not complying with our ideological desires. So, ideologies need to find a way around that.[171] At the time of Galileo Galilei the Roman Catholic church used a rather crude strategy: it oppressed science. But over the course of the modern era, as the prestige of science grew, this approach became increasingly untenable. So, new ways of dealing with this issue came into being. Communists, for instance, embraced science's prestige unreservedly, but often maintained that Marx and Lenin had reached ultimate scientific truths that could no longer be contested. That approach broke down in the 1970s and 1980s, and it is probably not by accident that around this time postmodern relativism won the day amongst certain branches of the left with something more maneuverable.[172] On the one hand, people like Latour endorse science; they accept its nomenclature, tap into its budgets, use its publication cultures, and rely on its authority whenever convenient. But when scientific research does not lead to the outcomes that were hoped for, a plethora of relativist tools can be used to get rid of those outcomes.[173] Latour-like relativism can thus operate as a flexible protective shield for ideological desires.[174] "The promise of power to mold the world in accordance with one's sense

---

[168] Latour, *Reassembling the Social*, 24, 116; Latour, *Face à Gaïa*.
[169] See for instance: Rorty, *Philosophy and Social Hope*, 38, 64–69, 263, 266.
[170] Gross and Levitt, *Higher Superstition*; Aya, "Reign of Error."
[171] This analysis drew inspiration from: Harari, *Sapiens: A Brief History of Humankind*, 279-83. However, Harari does not analyse postmodernism itself here.
[172] Wilterdink, "The Sociogenesis of Postmodernism," 206.
[173] Wilterdink, 197; Boudry and Hofhuis, "Het vandalisme van ideologische wetenschap."
[174] Gross and Levitt, *Higher Superstition*.

of justice is far more qualified and ambiguous than was the case with hard-line Marxism", Gross and Levitt maintain.[175] "Winning the battle that Marxism lost", is how Rod Aya describes postmodern relativism's major function.[176]

Many key relativists are quite straightforward about their underlying ideological aims. Richard Rorty, in the passage quoted above, illustrates how he makes the scientific aim of truth finding subservient to his ideologically loaded aim of bringing about consensus. In addition, he intends to "demote the quest for knowledge from the status of end-in-itself to that of one more means towards greater human happiness."[177] In a similar vein Foucault frankly admits that he has no intention of emancipating "truth from every system of power (which would be a chimera, for truth is already power)", but instead aims to detach "the power of truth from the forms of hegemony, social, economic, and cultural, within which it operates at the present time."[178] In other words: because the concept of truth is inherently political, we can simply swap the political and ideological purposes for which we use it. Latour similarly conflates the political with the scientific, and as we saw, makes rationality subservient to being civilized.[179] The moralistic fallacy is not considered a fallacy.

One of the hallmarks of good science is that it offers an invitation to everyone, at least potentially, to participate in the debate on an equal basis. As long as someone's claims are consistently rational, and supported by a sufficient amount of empirical evidence, they deserve to be taken seriously, no matter how absurd, despicable, or uncivilized those claims may at first seem to be. But in the relativist pluriverse no such obligations exist. When someone's scientific arguments do not serve the proper purposes of "bringing about consensus", or "greater human happiness", they can be rejected outright and without further ado.[180] In a detailed study, Helen Pluckrose and James Lindsay elucidate how the early generation of postmodern relativists paved the way for increasingly zealous academic ideologists who no longer tolerate counter voices.[181]

But now back to the model of Darwinian cultural evolution. We saw that epistemic relativism, if warranted, would undermine the model, and that a currently popular form of relativism can be found in the work of Bruno Latour. But as we also saw, Latour's epistemic position is too unclear and too inconsistent to be considered a valid academic argument. Yet, having said that, let us also note that there is nothing wrong with Latour's call for taking actors seriously. The importance of carefully interpreting people's own view of things is one of the major topics of this dissertation. A certain degree of epistemic relativism – or probably we should better say fallibilism – is also warranted. It can be meaningful to remind ourselves that current scientific understanding of the world is likely to be very incomplete. Other systems of thought may well

---

[175] Gross and Levitt, 42–43.
[176] Aya, "Reign of Error," 37.
[177] Rorty, *Philosophy and Social Hope*, xii.
[178] Rabinow, *The Foucault Reader*, 74–75.
[179] Latour, *Politics of Nature*.
[180] Aya, "Reign of Error," 35; Chomsky, "'Rationality/Science,'" 52.
[181] Pluckrose and Lindsay, *Cynical Theories*; Kaufmann, "Academic Freedom in Crisis."

see aspects of reality that modern science fails to see. Many of today's insights will probably, and hopefully, be overtaken by future and better insights. Moreover, all narratives suggesting that the Hopi Indians were in some sense stupid or ignorant for believing that their dance triggers rain should be painstakingly avoided. This is not about smart versus ignorant, but about having access to the results of centuries of scientific research or not. Philosophically speaking, we cannot rule out the possibility that someday new evidence will appear that validates unexpected causal links between common dancing and rain fall. Yet, because such evidence is currently unavailable, it would be unwise to let relativist contemplations distract us too much. Some questions regarding relativism will reappear in the witchcraft case study, but for now we will leave it aside and pick up where we left off. What does Darwinian cultural evolution have to say about the purposes of cultural adaptations?

3.4 Darwinian purposes of cultural functions

"Man employs the extrasomatic tradition that we call culture in order to sustain and perpetuate his existence and give it full expression." This is how the cultural evolutionist Leslie White celebrated human culture in 1959. Its function, he thought, was to make life "secure and enduring for the human species."[182] Likewise, Bronislaw Malinowski stated in his functionalist account that "any theory of culture has to start from the organic needs of man."[183] Scholars sympathetic to the idea of culture "evolving", or of it being "adaptive", have more often sought culture's functionality in this direction.[184] After all, humans are the carriers of culture, so if culture enhances our biological survival it should also thrive itself. When looking for culture's beneficiaries from a Darwinian point of view, this indeed looks like an obvious place to start.

Now that the evolutionary take on culture is gaining new momentum, culture's biological advantages are again attracting attention.[185] Current theorists of gene-culture coevolution argue that humans have evolved into culture-absorbing sponges, which strongly indicates genetic benefits. Why otherwise would culture have evolved in the first place? When looking at humans' spread over the globe it is not difficult to fathom *how* culture has enhanced human survival. When individuals adopt cultural information about their environment, it becomes much easier for them to adapt. Just think of the Inuit and how they have survived the hostile arctic setting due to culturally learned assets of building igloos, hunting seals, and making clothes. Our vast body of cumulative cultural knowledge saves us from having to reinvent the wheel each time anew. The coevolutionary waltz between humans and culture has boosted the survival of both of them, and Joseph Henrich even designates culture as "the secret of our success".[186]

---

[182] White, *The Evolution of Culture*, 8.
[183] Malinowski, *A Scientific Theory of Culture*, 72; Malinowski, *Magic, Science and Religion*, 89–90.
[184] Moore, *Visions of Culture*, 157–59.
[185] Henrich, *The Secret of Our Success*; Laland, *Darwin's Unfinished Symphony*; Stewart-Williams, *The Ape That Understood the Universe*, 231–43; Richerson and Boyd, *Not By Genes Alone*, 99–147.
[186] Henrich, *The Secret of Our Success*.

Yet, it was already mentioned above that cultural phenomena like martyrdom, celibacy, asceticism, or self-mutilation suggest that direct biological survival cannot be the whole story. Admittedly, the celibate Shakers have dissolved as a cultural unit, while Christian denominations that require their members to be "fruitful and multiply" are still amongst us.[187] But Shakerism was still reproductively successful for quite a while, because the lack of biological descendants was compensated by large numbers of converts.[188] Their celibacy may even have been advantageous in that regard, as it enhanced their reputation for moral purity. Likewise, the aforementioned infanticide of the Native American Mbaya people was an outright disaster for their genes, but not necessarily for Mbaya culture. These Indians had a mobile lifestyle of robbing and parasitizing neighboring peoples, and the absence of infants and young children enhanced their unusual flexibility. The Mbaya also persisted for a significant period of time, as their numbers were maintained through the raiding of older children elsewhere.[189] What is more, innumerable details of human culture, like art styles, fashions, or television quizzes, seem rather arbitrary and superfluous from a biological perspective alone.[190] Aztec human sacrifice possibly offered the advantage of protein intake, but these rituals were characterized by a ceremonial splendor and a meaningful complexity that indicates additional purposes.[191] "Why build a temple, when all you need is a butcher's block?", Marshall Sahlins once retorted to Harris's eco-adaptationist model.[192] This message has not been lost on the current field of cultural evolution: it recognizes that the *cui bono* question needs be addressed more broadly.[193] One name is thereby on people's lips again: Emile Durkheim.[194]

Durkheimian functionalism revisited
"The godfather of the field" he has been called. When encountering the work of this French sociologist David Sloan Wilson thought Durkheim to be speaking to him "across the chasm of time."[195] Some of the case studies mentioned already illustrated how the new proponents of cultural evolution identify the cultural group, or society, as the beneficiary of culture's hidden adaptions. Campbell took the lead in 1975 when stating that "there can be profound social system wisdom in the belief systems with which our social tradition has provided us." The current field abounds in Durkheimian talk about religion as an "organic" and "interlocking" system, a "complex adaptation that serves to support human social life", or the "glue" that holds society

---

[187] Stewart-Williams, *The Ape That Understood the Universe*, 247; Wilson, *Darwin's Cathedral*, 2002, 133.
[188] Sobo and Bell, *Celibacy, Culture, and Society*, 115.
[189] Ricky, *Native Peoples A to Z*, 1409–12; Saeger, *The Chaco Mission Frontier*, 84–86; Paul, *Mixed Messages*, 50–53.
[190] Moore, *Visions of Culture*, 205; Stewart-Williams, *The Ape That Understood the Universe*, 242.
[191] Sahlins, "Culture as Protein and Profit"; Smith, *The Aztecs*, 60–65, 218–19.
[192] Sahlins, "Culture as Protein and Profit."
[193] Stewart-Williams, *The Ape That Understood the Universe*, 219–82; Dennett, *Breaking the Spell*.
[194] Whitehouse, "Dying for the Group"; Sosis and Petersen et al., "Why Cultural Evolutionary Models"; Slingerland and Sullivan, "Durkheim with Data"; Turchin, *Ultrasociety*; Wilson, *Darwin's Cathedral*, 2002.
[195] Slingerland and Sullivan, "Durkheim with Data," 314; Wilson, *Evolution for Everyone*, 239.

together.[196] Power and oppression are thought an insufficient basis for society, so there is the perpetual need for ritual performance and social values, and the old comparison of societies to organisms is receiving scientific reconsideration.[197] Like Durkheim, Campbell warned people not to liberate themselves too eagerly from their traditions since important wisdom might be lost, and David Sloan Wilson prides himself on his relatively positive stance on religion.[198]

The theoretical pedigree of this revitalization of the organismic framework partly lies in multilevel selection theory from evolutionary biology.[199] The principles of Darwinian selection are applied at all levels of the human socio-cultural hierarchy, and especially a mechanism named "cultural group selection" is drawing attention. It assumes that culturally marked groups are entangled in continuing processes of competition, and that the ones that operate most smoothly as organismic units survive. "The costly institutions of complex societies manage to spread and propagate because the societies that possess them destroy those that don't", is how Peter Turchin frames it.[200] But the cultural group selectionists also look at less warlike mechanisms, like the differential survival of environmental challenges, the ability to attract individuals from other groups, as well as the adoption of practices and beliefs from more successful groups.[201] The current field has gathered significant databases on how and when such selection concretely occurred in human history in the form of struggles between tribes, states, and empires.

This revitalization of the Durkheimian orientation is not welcomed by everyone though. Critics find the differences between human societies and organisms too significant for this comparison to take hold.[202] Human individuals are not as loyal to social groups as cells are to bodies, and human groups also lack the clear boundaries and reproductive moments that organisms have. Steven Pinker illustrates his misgivings by highlighting how the Roman Empire differs from an organism:

> It was the Roman Empire that took over most of the ancient world, not a group that splintered off from a group that splintered off from a group that splintered off from the Roman Empire, each baby Roman Empire very much like the parent Roman Empire except for a few random alterations, and the branch of progeny empires eventually outnumbering the others.[203]

---

[196] Campbell, "On the Conflicts between Biological and Social Evolution," 202; Sosis and Petersen et al., "Why Cultural Evolutionary Models," 46, 48; Turchin, *Ultrasociety*, 207; Wilson, *Darwin's Cathedral*, 2002, 118.
[197] Wilson, *Darwin's Cathedral*, 2002, 45.
[198] Campbell, "On the Conflicts between Biological and Social Evolution," 198; Wilson, *Darwin's Cathedral*, 2002, 2.
[199] Wilson, *Darwin's Cathedral*, 2002, 5–85; Turchin, *Ultrasociety*, 67–94.
[200] Turchin, *Ultrasociety*, 20.
[201] Henrich, *The Secret of Our Success*, 166–69; Turchin, *Ultrasociety*; Turchin, *Historical Dynamics*; Richerson and Boyd, *Not By Genes Alone*, 195–236.
[202] Bryant, "An Evolutionary Social Science?," 462–63; Kincaid, "Functional Explanation and Evolutionary Social Science," 2007, 243–44; Wilterdink, "Te veel darwinisme, te weinig sociologie," 305; Kincaid, *Philosophical Foundations of the Social Sciences*, 140; Pinker, "The False Allure of Group Selection."
[203] Pinker, "The False Allure of Group Selection."

The cultural group selectionists probably do not mean to compare cultural groups to organisms as literally as Pinker here suggests, but their framework does easily trigger such misinterpretations. Like its biological counterpart, this multilevel model does not make the essential distinction between things that are transmitted and things that are not transmitted. In biology, we saw that genetic information is potentially transmitted, while groups are not. The same goes for culture: cultural information is possibly reproduced, unlike groups. When applied to cultural evolution, the multilevel framework tends to create a conceptual fog, eliciting confusing discussions about confusing mixtures of the selection of groups, genes, peoples, societies, or cultures, all operating as adaptive units.[204] So, what exactly is being selected here? And what is being reproduced?

In response to this confusion some authors render the whole idea of cultural group selection a non-starter.[205] Group selection does not even work in biology, so why bother about its socio-cultural application? But that is too hasty, because as soon as we *do* make a sharp distinction between things that are transmitted and things that are not transmitted, the idea of cultural group selection offers two fruitful lines of investigation. While cultural groups are not transmitted from person to person, as such, the biological or cultural information that makes individuals behave as part of a culturally marked group may well be subject to transmission and repeated rounds of selection. The problem in biology was that group selection is undermined by free riders in the form of egoistic mutants or invaders who bring in new genes that the group cannot get rid of. However, what the cultural group selectionists bring forward – and this is their first fruitful line of investigation – is that culture has created an evolutionary setting in which the selection of group-functional genetic predispositions has become a more effective force.[206]

For what happens when a human free rider enters a cultural group that is characterized by an unusual level of internal cooperativeness and solidarity? Humans are great cultural imitators, so the free rider might well adopt the group's culture, thus becoming a group-ish altruist himself. In case the free rider were to persist in his exploitative behavior, the cultural group might then decide to morally punish the detractor by excluding or even killing him – something that cultural groups quite often did, or do. Hence, culture might have opened up new possibilities of maintaining group cohesion, turning human groups into entities stable enough to be targeted by the natural selection for group functional genes. So, the proposal goes: gene-culture coevolution endowed humans with bio-psychological propensities for more group-ish behavior. In evolutionary biology we learned that it was unclear what animal traits group selection would precisely help explain. But our own species offers more promising examples in that regard, as studies into religion, nationalism, or football clubs amply show. Humans possess

---

[204] For an example of a confusing discussion, see debate over: Pinker.
[205] Pinker; Coyne, "Genes First"; Stewart-Williams, *The Ape That Understood the Universe*, 201–12.
[206] Koopmans, "Het mysterie van de naastenliefde," 126; Turchin, *Ultrasociety*, 67–94; Richerson and Boyd, *Not By Genes Alone*, 195–236; Haidt, *The Righteous Mind*.

notable tendencies of rallying around collective symbols, making sacrifices for the common good, and defending the group's interests against enemies, sometimes even at the price of death.[207]

The cultural group selectionists remark that such group-ish biological traits simultaneously come up against certain limits. "These new tribal social instincts were superimposed onto human psychology without eliminating those that favor friends and kin", Richerson and Boyd maintain.[208] Nepotism has remained a continuing threat to the cohesion of any group, and it is probably not by accident that within cultural systems group loyalty is often enforced through the use of kin related terms, like "mother Russia", the "German fatherland", or the "brotherhood of revolutionaries".[209] What further indicates limits to innate group loyalty is the cultural adoration of martyrs. During the Belgian revolution against The Netherlands in 1830, a Dutch naval officer named Jan van Speyk announced that he would rather blow up his ship, including himself, than let it fall into Belgian hands. He was subsequently cheered on by his men.[210] The reason that Van Speyk is still known in history books as an exceptional hero of Dutch patriotism is that he actually kept his word! It is unlikely that such actions would ever occur had group selection been an entirely non-existent force. But the extraordinary veneration of such "martyrs" also suggests that it takes much socio-cultural pressure to make people really do it.

It is at the level of such cultural pressures that the second key line of investigation of cultural group selection lies: the selection of group-functional *cultural* variants.[211] Pinker was right that the Roman Empire did not reproduce like an organism, but what may still have been subject to repeated rounds of selection and transmission is the cultural variants that made Rome flourish, like its military strategies, religious patriotism, or political institutions. We can think here of selection processes between empires as wholes, as well as the selection of subgroups within the Roman Empire, such as cities, military legions, religious cults, or patron-client networks. In this sense, cultural group selection possibly provides an explanation for how socio-cultural systems evolved their Durkheimian qualities of installing and maintaining values that make individuals behave as loyal members of cultural groups. It made social coalitions outgrow and supersede the initial networks of close relatives.[212]

However, in our earlier discussion of the socio-cultural *cui bono* question we noted that the Durkheimian orientation seems to have its limitations, as any cultural phenomena do not appear to enhance the functioning of societies as wholes. In an extensive critique of cultural adaptationism, the anthropologist Robert Edgerton filled a whole book with examples of cultural phenomena that damaged both biological survival *and* their social systems. His conclusion was that much culture is not adaptive or functional at all; it is merely pointless.[213] But that is too easy

---

[207] Whitehouse, "Dying for the Group."
[208] Richerson and Boyd, *Not By Genes Alone*, 215.
[209] Wilson, *Darwin's Cathedral*, 2002, 100; Fukuyama, *The Origins of Political Order*.
[210] Rovers, *"Dan liever de lucht in!"*
[211] Norenzayan, *Big Gods*, 10; Wilson, *Darwin's Cathedral*, 2002, 28–37.
[212] Henrich, *The Secret of Our Success*, 204.
[213] Edgerton, *Sick Societies: Challenging the Myth of Primitive Harmony*.

an inference because cultural phenomena may perhaps be adapted to benefit other entities. Let us remind ourselves of Dennett's dictum to cast our nets out widely, and in this light the conflict tradition first warrants renewed attention.

Power structures and individual needs
The role of power structures has already received some attention in the cultural Darwinian field.[214] William Durham created the term "selection by imposition", meaning that cultural variants can survive because some people forced them onto others. The focus of the cultural group selectionists on dynamic warlike competition also gives the field a conflict-oriented twist. Yet, the presumed outcome of the competitive processes still largely fits the Durkheimian mold of more cohesive societies. So it is not entirely unwarranted that the field is sometimes criticized for insufficient attention to power and oppression as key forces shaping our socio-cultural world.[215] But let us notice here that there is nothing un-Darwinian about power and exploitation per se. Living nature teems with adaptations of organisms that exploit others, like the ichneumon wasp that keeps captured caterpillars alive to eat from their living bodies – an example that once made Darwin doubt the existence of a benevolent creator.[216] The survival of cultural traits may well in many cases depend on who is in charge, creating selection pressures on variants that serve the interests of the privileged at the expense of the downtrodden. Hence, to broaden cultural evolution's scope it is worthwhile to integrate some of conflict theory's best insights.

The most natural ally of Darwinian theory is the analytic variant. Its dynamic model of everlasting power struggles over scarce resources in fact looks quite Darwinian already. That may not be accidental, as some early twentieth-century exponents, like Max Weber, seem to have drawn inspiration from the social Darwinism of their day.[217] The utopian desires underlying Marxism and postmodernism seem more difficult to reconcile with a Darwinian framework, but still, these schools of thought may also contain elements worthy of integration. We saw that Marxists and postmodernists often aimed to uncover power structures that are hidden to the actors involved. Darwinism may finally provide a more flexible and contingent explanation for how such hidden structures come about. Those in power face a permanent struggle to maintain their position, and some cultural variants enhance a ruling position more than others. One could, for instance, think of a scenario in which elites who genuinely believed themselves to have been chosen by gods, and who succeeded in convincing others of this belief, had better average chances of preserving their supremacy during particular periods of history. Such processes might

---

[214] Wilson, *Darwin's Cathedral*, 2002, 119; Wilson, *This View of Life*, 182–83; Durham, *Coevolution*, 198; Turchin, *Ultrasociety*; Blute, *Darwinian Sociocultural Evolution*, 80–130; Dennett, *Breaking the Spell*, 90.
[215] Lewontin, "The Wars Over Evolution"; Lewens, *Darwin*, 208; Bryant, "An Evolutionary Social Science?," 467.
[216] Stewart-Williams, *Darwin, God and the Meaning of Life*, 107.
[217] Weber, *Wirtschaft Und Gesellschaft*, 21; Runciman, "Was Max Weber a Selectionist in Spite of Himself?"; Hermans, *De dwaaltocht van het sociaal-darwinisme*, 509.

again be partially the accumulation of accidentally adaptive variants rather than intelligent design alone.[218]

Now that we are casting our nets out widely, the strengths of the individual-oriented approaches might also be reconsidered. Some of their elements again look vaguely Darwinian already, like the idea of micro-interactions adding up to complex phenomena, or rational choice theory's focus on competition. Daniel Dennett and David Sloan Wilson also expressed some sympathy for the latter's assumption that cultural phenomena often fulfill individuals' needs. Yet, while rational choice theory mostly focuses on the demand side – what people want – the Darwinian model can help elucidate the supply side, and how cultural phenomena become adapted to fulfill those wants.[219] We should not only think of deliberate and conscious aims here. Cultural variants may for instance survive because they only accidentally appealed to people's subconscious desires, or accidentally made sense within people's meaningful frameworks, but still survived because of such unrecognized effects. An author who has already integrated an individualist outlook with cultural evolution is Friedrich Hayek. According to his free market account, hidden cultural evolution created a civilization which "enables us constantly to profit from knowledge which we individually do not possess." Our traditions allow us to pursue our individual interests more successfully than would have been possible had our system been rationally designed by human hand.[220]

In sum, Darwinian cultural evolution can offer an open-minded view. The fact that the determinants of reproductive success are diverse and context dependent implies that the *cui bono* question might be addressed differently in each instance. The borders between various orientations can also be porous. The model thus provides us with the advantages of eclecticism, while simultaneously integrating insights of older approaches into a more consistent framework. Yet, in the historical overview of cultural Darwinism we saw that the theory, in addition, has something in store for us that looks genuinely new: the idea of selfish memes. It proposes that cultural phenomena might be well adapted to serve no other interest except their own self-reproduction. Considering the fierce resistance to this proposal, how seriously should we take it as a scientific hypothesis?

The "selfish" culture hypothesis
It has remained unnoticed that older approaches every now and then came close to something quite like it. The Boasians stressed that culture has a semi-autonomous power, and sometimes this led to talk about culture as having interests of its own. "We may know all about the distribution of a tribe's form of marriage, ritual dances, and puberty initiations and yet understand nothing of the culture as a whole which has used these elements *to its own purpose*",

---

[218] Despite the group selectionist orientation Peter Turchin comes quite close to something like this in: Turchin, *Ultrasociety*, 152, 160.
[219] Wilson, *Darwin's Cathedral*, 2002, 79–83; Dennett, *Breaking the Spell*, 182–84.
[220] Hayek, *The Constitution of Liberty*, 22, 25; Beck and Witt, "Austrian Economics and the Evolutionary Paradigm*."

the prominent Boasian Ruth Benedict wrote in 1934. Benedict treated culture as an agency which selects traits from the environment "which it can use, and discards those which it cannot." This process "need never be conscious during its whole course."[221] The idea of culture being "selfish" was also vaguely preceded by the conflict theorist Lewis Coser in his concept of "greedy institutions".[222] Coser spoke of organizations that demand total obedience and commitment from its members, and such greedy institutions isolate those members from competing appeals like family life or friendship. A telling example is the militant sectarianism of the Jesuits and the communists. At some points Coser does not only seem to place the greediness at the level of people behind those institutions, but also at the level of the institutions *themselves*. However, striking as these suggestions may have been, they lacked a Darwinian explanatory framework and failed to gain much traction.

Even within the Darwinian framework, Dawkins was not the first to propose the idea of culture developing reproductive interests of its own.[223] One year earlier the anthropologist Ted Cloak wrote that:

> A cultural instruction (…), although carried by an organism, can replicate itself interorganismically without waiting through the organism's life cycle. Indeed, it may replicate itself within minutes of being stored. So it should not be surprising to find (…) culture features that perform particular functions which are irrelevant, or even destructive, to the organisms whose organs help to make or do them.[224]

Cloak also preceded Dawkins in exploring the parallel of cultural things being "like an active parasite that controls some behavior of its host." At best, he argued, culture behaves like a symbiont, but at worst it manipulates and exploits us like its slaves.[225] Dawkins referred to Cloak, and developed the suggestion into his overall context of "selfish replicators".[226] This is a potent idea, because cultural forms that instruct people to make more copies of those cultural forms will be most successful at exactly that. If we accept that cultural phenomena adapt beyond our intentions and recognition – as mainstream cultural evolution now does – it is not a far stretch to presume that this might also lead to adaptations that do not align with our own interests, especially considering the pervasiveness of pathogens in biological evolution. So why has meme-theory found so little support?

Some of this resistance stems from the terminology of "memetics", and it might indeed be a good idea to adopt a more conventional vocabulary. We already have the word "culture",

---

[221] Benedict, *Patterns of Culture*, 33. Emphasis added.
[222] Coser, *Greedy Institutions*.
[223] Cloak, "Is a Cultural Ethology Possible?"
[224] Cloak, 172.
[225] Cloak, 172.
[226] Dawkins, *The Selfish Gene*, 190.

and it is unclear why "memes" would provide a better alternative. The term "meme" also has a connotation of discreteness, which, considering the often more fluid character of cultural items, might easily lead us astray.[227] I will here thus stick to Richerson's and Boyd's "cultural variant" as the more flexible unit of selection. Another issue that raises hackles is the ontological status of memes.[228] Genes are located in the molecular structures of DNA, but what exactly would memes be made of? This touches upon an old notion of culture being something intangible. Clifford Geertz for instance once stated about culture that "though ideational, it does not exist in someone's head; though unphysical, it is not an occult entity."[229] But this objection is easy to refute, because all culture consists of materialized information that is located in human brain cells or in artefacts like computers or books. The maintenance of culture also continually requires the extraction of energy from the environment, and this is exactly what keeps engendering the Darwinian process.[230] There is no such thing as a cultural free lunch.

Nevertheless, even after we have neutralized some terminological and ontological controversies, many queries remain. What would such "selfishly" reproducing cultural forms exactly look like? This requires careful consideration, as not all examples brought forward are convincing.[231] Instead of selfish memes, Richerson and Boyd speak of maladaptive "rogue cultural variants", and they use higher education as an example, because highly educated people on average have fewer children.[232] However, the possibly negative effect of culture on genetic fertility is already quite trivial an observation, and higher education in general helps people to live healthier, happier, and more powerful lives. A similarly questionable example is the smoking of tobacco.[233] This indeed has harmful effects on human health, but that does not yet mean that there are no human beneficiaries involved. In today's world we might think of people working for the tobacco industry who get richer by deliberately developing strategies of making consumers addicted. Susan Blackmore also seems overly inclusive in her search for selfish memes when adding language, modern communication, and notions of the self to her list.[234] So, in order to avoid vacuity, the selfish culture hypothesis needs to become specific about what a cultural "pathogen" would precisely entail. The Belgian philosopher Maarten Boudry has made the important argument that, in order for the "selfish meme" concept to gain traction, we need concrete examples of cultural phenomena that exhibit purposes of their own, but which do not

---

[227] Richerson and Boyd, *Not By Genes Alone*, 88–91.
[228] Dennett, *From Bacteria to Bach and Back*, 221–24.
[229] Geertz, *The Interpretation of Cultures*, 10.
[230] Dennett, *Breaking the Spell*, 80–81; Dennett, *Darwin's Dangerous Idea*, 348; Richerson and Boyd, *Not By Genes Alone*, 61–62.
[231] Boudry and Hofhuis, "Parasites of the Mind. Why Cultural Theorists Need the Meme's Eye View"; Boudry, "Invasion of Mind Snatchers."
[232] Richerson and Boyd, *Not By Genes Alone*, 148–90, 156.
[233] Stewart-Williams, *The Ape That Understood the Universe*, 252.
[234] Blackmore, *The Meme Machine*.

coincide or overlap with human purposes already familiar to us.[235] Ideally, we should find phenomena that contain "blindly" evolved adaptive elements that are well built for ensuring their own survival, while harming the purposes of the people transmitting them, as well as the functioning of their societies.

Luckily, the meme theorists also offer case studies that look more auspicious, like earworms, conspiracy theories, exasperating cultural arms races, woke ideology, or extreme overwork.[236] Yet, the case study that has been developed in most detail is that of religion.[237] Because what should a "selfish" religion be expected to look like? Surely, this religion would be unwelcoming if adherents move to another faith. So, we might expect the religious system to have evolved mechanisms of keeping people in, like threats of divine punishment, or incentives for its members to penalize or kill apostates. Something else that might endanger the religion's survival is criticism, or the ridicule of its sacred symbols. The faithful should thus be encouraged to stop that. All systems of ideas contain internal inconsistencies, but this might be overcome by telling adherents that questioning the doctrine is a sin, and that observance requires uncommitted faith. It would also be helpful if members are stimulated to make efforts of defending and spreading the faith through peaceful means, and to resort to violence if that does not work.

For anyone acquainted with the history of Christianity and Islam none of this will sound unfamiliar. It is probably not by accident that the two most successful religions on Earth have so often contained doctrinal elements that forcefully enhanced their own propagation.[238] "*Only Jesus can save you*", Christians often do not get tired of telling us, and the first pillar of Islam is not about serving the community or following the leaders, as it says that "there is no God but God, and Mohammed is his messenger". It is the undivided loyalty to the religion *itself* that comes first here. David Sloan Wilson's example of early modern Calvinism is also instructive in this regard. Calvinist principles may have indeed enhanced cohesion amongst the faithful, but what Wilson discusses in less detail is how the zealous doctrinal hairsplitting of Calvinists about their exclusive religious truths has often been a disruptive societal force. In countries like France, Germany and England, Calvinist minorities helped trigger civil wars that brought those societies almost to breaking point.

Or take the celibacy of Roman Catholic priests.[239] Their sexual continence is a disaster for the priests' genes, as well as for their romantic and sexual pleasures. However, for Roman Catholicism the prospects look less bleak, as devoted priests often have much cultural

---

[235] Boudry and Hofhuis, "Parasites of the Mind. Why Cultural Theorists Need the Meme's Eye View"; Boudry, "Invasion of Mind Snatchers."
[236] Saad, *The Parasitic Mind*; Haring, *For A Successful Life*.
[237] Blackmore, *The Meme Machine*; Boudry, Blancke, and Pigliucci, "What Makes Weird Beliefs Thrive?"; Dennett, *Breaking the Spell*; Stewart-Williams, *The Ape That Understood the Universe*, 219–23, 250–68; Boudry and Braeckman, "How Convenient! The Epistemic Rationale of Self-Validating Belief Systems"; Dawkins, *The God Delusion*, 222–40.
[238] Dennett, *Breaking the Spell*; Stewart-Williams, *Darwin, God and the Meaning of Life*, 50–68.
[239] Blackmore, *The Meme Machine*, 138–39; Dennett, *Darwin's Dangerous Idea*, 367.

"offspring". What about martyrdom?[240] "The more we are cut down by you, the more we grow in number; the blood of Christians is seed", the early Christian apologist Tertullian once told pagan authorities of Ancient Rome.[241] Tertullian's assumption was that the loss of some members was compensated by the conversion of others, and modern research into early Christianity to some extent confirms his suspicions.[242] In 2015 the Algerian-French brothers Cherif and Said Kouachi massacred the editorial staff of the Charlie Hebdo magazine for publishing Mohammed cartoons. The brothers then willingly paid with their own lives as well.[243] This was a catastrophe for the Kouachi brothers' own life fulfilling purposes, but not necessarily for the spread of radical Islam. Their actions may have been adaptive for protecting their interpretation of the faith from the undermining effects of public ridicule. So, while religion can stimulate extraordinary selflessness in individuals, the traits of religion *itself* can reveal ruthless egoism.

Let us remind ourselves of the kamikaze termites and the dogs suffering from rabies. If we ask what function their exploding or biting has for those animals we will not get anywhere. Yet, when we ask what function is has for the biological information residing inside them, it suddenly all makes a lot of sense. So, might religions function as rabies-like "viruses of the mind", that "hijack" and "manipulate" the behavior of their human hosts? Viruses can camouflage their real nature, evade the defenses of their carriers, inject themselves into cells, and then turn the hosts into the vehicles for their own propagation.[244] Might religions, to a certain degree, do something quite like that? This is exactly the proposal the meme theorists are making. While genes gang up in genomes, memes are supposed to work together in what Susan Blackmore calls "memeplexes", which, under certain conditions, exploit their human carriers.[245] Dennett speaks of "a finely tuned amalgam of brilliant plays and stratagems, capable of holding people enthralled and loyal for their entire lives."[246]

Of course, none of this is to suggest that religions or other cultural phenomena are literally selfish, or that they can think in any way. Again, what Darwinism potentially explains is how certain phenomena can look *as if* a shrewd selfish agent is operating behind the scenes. In a dismissal of meme theory, the English philosopher Tim Lewens wrote that:

> There are plenty of mainstream views about cognition that remind us that people make decisions all the time that are not in their best interests. We do not need memetics to

---

[240] Dennett, *Breaking the Spell*, 284–85; Stewart-Williams, *The Ape That Understood the Universe*, 302–3.
[241] Gwynn, *Christianity in the Later Roman Empire*, 7.
[242] Bowersock, *Martyrdom and Rome*, 59–74.
[243] Mickolus, *Terrorism, 2013-2015*, 308–10.
[244] Zimmer, *A Planet of Viruses*, 5; Cordingley, *Viruses*, 172–73.
[245] Blackmore, *The Meme Machine*, 19–20.
[246] Dennett, *Breaking the Spell*, 154.

expose the widespread existence of various forms of irrationality, weakness of will, self-deception, false consciousness, subconsciously motivated action, and so forth.[247]

What Lewens seems to have missed here is that the theory is not so much about explaining why people can be cognitively vulnerable to self-destructive behavior, but, rather, how culture can become well adapted to *exploit* those vulnerabilities. That meme theory has offered something genuinely new can be illustrated through our example of the afterlife.[248] Richard Dawkins expressed some admiration for how religion ingeniously uses the threat of hellfire to enforce people's commitment. He thinks that it "might almost have been planned deliberately by a Machiavellian priesthood trained in deep psychological indoctrination techniques." But Dawkins doubts whether priests were that smart. Instead, he proposes that "the idea of hell fire is, quite simply, *self perpetuating.*"[249] Dawkins here touches upon a dimension of beliefs in the afterlife that no one seems to have addressed before him.

Richard Dawkins uses meme theory largely as a device for his strident efforts to rid people of what he calls "the god delusion".[250] But it is important to reemphasize that the idea of "selfish replicators" does not exclude other beneficiaries. On the contrary, we might expect the reproductive interests of cultural information to normally coincide with purposes at higher levels of organization. Dennett writes that "we should not forget that the vast majority of memes, like the vast majority of bacterial and viral symbionts, are neutral or even helpful."[251] From this perspective Susan Blackmore and Daniel Dennett take a more ambiguous stance on religion, as they also highlight beneficial aspects, like group functions, altruism, consolation, or the magnificence of religious art.[252] We should remind ourselves that it is especially at the points where reproductive interests of culture and purposes at other levels do *not* coincide, that the essential explanatory power of the theory comes to the surface.[253]

The debate over the theory has already gone on for a long time, and paddles in theoretical circles. But as the cultural evolution expert Alex Mesoudi rightly states, the idea of "selfish" culture is something that simply needs to be addressed in empirical research.[254] Do historical and ethnological records provide examples of cultural phenomena that reproduced at the expense of their human hosts, as well as of their societies? David Sloan Wilson acknowledges that evolution does not make everything nice and considers cultural "pathogens" a possibility. But in contrast

---

[247] Lewens, *Cultural Evolution*, 2015, 31.
[248] Dennett, *Breaking the Spell*, 229.
[249] Dawkins, *The Selfish Gene*, 197–98.
[250] Dawkins, *The God Delusion*, 222–40.
[251] Dennett, *Breaking the Spell*, 184.
[252] Dennett, *Breaking the Spell*; Blackmore, *The Meme Machine*, 188–90.
[253] Stewart-Williams, *The Ape That Understood the Universe*, 293–303; Dennett, *From Bacteria to Bach and Back*, 205–47.
[254] This comment was made during the panel discussion of the conference *The generalized theory of evolution* (University of Duesseldorf 31-01-2018) and in personal communication.

to the meme-enthusiasts, he thinks them very exceptional.[255] Paraphrasing Ed Yong we might also expect to find a continuum of lifestyles between "bad" parasites and "good" mutualism, with cultural allies who disappoint us and enemies who rally to our side. The only way to find out is indeed by having an empirical look. Daniel Dennett wrote that some aspects of his theory sketch are pretty well established, but that "getting down to specifics and generating further testable hypotheses is work for the future."[256] It is in this light that we will now enter the sinister world of European witch-hunting.

---

[255] Wilson, *Darwin's Cathedral*, 2002, 156; Wilson, *This View of Life*, 157–59, 182; Henrich adopts a similar position: Henrich, *The WEIRDest People in the World*, 78–79.
[256] Dennett, *Breaking the Spell*, 310.

Chapter 4: Witch-hunts

4.1 Witch persecutions as a case study

In October 1782 a German publicist named Wilhelm Ludwig Wekhrlin uncovered a case of judicial miscarriage that was meant to have faded into the mists of history.[1] At the time, Wekhrlin had already made a name for himself as an audacious political satirist who was eager to challenge the authorities – something these authorities did not always take lightly as various rulers had already expelled him from their territories because of it. By 1782 Wekhrlin had found new refuge in a part of what is now Bavaria, ruled by Prince Kraft Ernst von Oettingen-Wallerstein. This princedom offered the publicist a newly won freedom to write a journal named *Chronologen*. As a child of the Enlightenment and devotee of Voltaire, Wekhrlin wanted his journal to address "cases of intolerance, superstition, brutalities of criminal justice, and the violation of the weak."[2] In 1782 he received reports about a legal case in Switzerland that were right up his alley. Wekhrlin learned that authorities in the remote canton of Glarus had tried and decapitated a forty-eight year old woman, named Anna Göldi. The official verdict was that she had poisoned the daughter of a prosperous family when she worked for the family as a servant. What attracted Wekhrlin's attention though, was that this allegation seemed to be a cover for something else. Apparently, Anna Göldi had been accused of aligning herself with the devil, and after her interrogators had tortured her she confessed that Satan had appeared to her as a black dog and gave her magical powers that she then used against the daughter of the family. The girl was supposed to have spat nails and to have suffered from convulsions. So, this was not just a case of poisoning, it was actually a witch trial! As Wekhrlin exclaimed in his journal: "behold the dreaded fate of those people who find themselves at the mercy of such magistrates!"[3]

The government of Glarus responded furiously to Wekhrlin's allegations, as witch-hunting had already become highly controversial. They asked the Prince of Oettingen-Wallerstein to hand him over.[4] Yet, while the Prince was somewhat dismayed about Wekhrlin's piece and invited him for a talk, he had no interest in taking things further and declined the Swiss request. This infuriated Glarus's government even further, as they thought that Wekhrlin's "vicious slander, falsehoods, insolence, and disrespect" should not go unpunished.[5] In a vindictive mood they put a price of a hundred Cronenthaler on Wekhrlin's head, burned his *Chronologen* in public, and sent round a search warrant that described the German satirist as a person with a thin face, thin legs, pale skin, and an unsightly appearance; just ugly in general.[6] But Wekhrlin did not flinch. He

---

[1] Wekhrlin, *Chronologen. Ein periodisches Werk*, 213–24; Hauser, *Der Justizmord an Anna Göldi*; Korrodi-Aebli, "historicum.net."
[2] Hauser, *Der Justizmord an Anna Göldi*, 14."Einzelfälle von Intoleranz, Aberglaube, Verrohung der Kriminaljustiz, Vergewaltigung der Schwachen."
[3] Wekhrlin, *Chronologen. Ein periodisches Werk*, 224."Wie sehr ist das Volk zu bedauern, dessen Leben in den Händen solcher Kriminalrechter steht!"
[4] Hauser, *Der Justizmord an Anna Göldi*.
[5] Hauser, 25."boshafter Verleumdung, Falschheit, Frechheit und Respektlosigkeit."
[6] Hauser, 25.

continued publishing about the affair and expressed his hopes that the freedom of the press would be like "an iron wedge around the neck of tyrants."[7] His hopes were not in vain, because the news about the witch trial in Glarus spread like wildfire throughout Germany and beyond. Additional reports from Switzerland largely confirmed Wekhrlin's version of the story, and enlightened public opinion was appalled. The trial was rendered a "Justizmord", a judicial murder against an innocent suspect, and people found it difficult to believe that something as superstitious and backwards as this could still happen in their "philosophical" century.[8] The public outcry was not without effect: Anna Göldi has gone into the history books as the last person to be tried and killed for witchcraft in Europe.[9] This single decapitation in Glarus has come to symbolize the end to one of Europe's most infamous and horrendous historical episodes.

And an infamous and horrendous episode it certainly had been. What looked like an absurdity to late Enlightenment polite society – allegations about harmful magic and meetings with the devil – had been taken extremely seriously by many for over three centuries.[10] Significant parts of European society had been willing to try, torture and burn people for such allegations. Ironically, it had all started not very far away from where it would eventually come to an end, the Alps of Switzerland.[11] In the early fifteenth century, especially in the region of the lake of Geneva at the foot of the western Alps, Europe had first been confronted with stories about a new and dangerous sect of Satan worshippers. Its adherents were supposed to ally themselves with the devil, and to receive harmful magical powers in return. They came to be known as "witches", and it was also in this region that the first hundreds of people were tried and burned for the purported crime. Initially, the rest of Europe did not take the danger very seriously, but over the course of the next century the notion of the diabolical witch gradually began to spread, and managed to overcome various strands of skepticism. The fires of witch burnings were ignited throughout Europe, and especially in the late sixteenth and early seventeenth centuries, in what we now call the early modern period, the hunt for witches reached an ominous peak. In this time witch panics even created chains of accusations, leading to the burnings of hundreds of people at the stake.[12] The exact numbers are impossible to reconstruct because much historical source material is lacking. But approximations today assume that around 50,000-60,000 people were killed on suspicion of diabolical witchcraft, with women being markedly overrepresented.[13]

---

[7] Hauser, 26. "eisernen Keil im Nacken der Tyrannen."
[8] Hauser, 140–47; Korrodi-Aebli, "historicum.net."
[9] Goodare, *The European Witch-Hunt*, 320–22.
[10] Rummel and Voltmer, *Hexen und Hexenverfolgung*; Levack, *The Witch-Hunt in Early Modern Europe*; Goodare, *The European Witch-Hunt*; Dillinger, *Hexen und Magie*, 2018.
[11] Behringer, *Witches and Witch-Hunts*, 60–70; Goodare, *The European Witch-Hunt*, 39–48.
[12] Levack, *The Witch-Hunt in Early Modern Europe*, 184–92.
[13] Rummel and Voltmer, *Hexen und Hexenverfolgung*, 74–79; Levack, *The Witch-Hunt in Early Modern Europe*, 19–22; Goodare, *The European Witch-Hunt*, 27.

Admittedly, this number is lower than has been assumed in the past. Earlier estimations amounted to nine million, and the real number is less impressive in comparison with other causes of death at the time, like religious warfare or contagious disease. It has recently been projected that out of every 28,000 deaths in early modern Europe only one resulted from a witch trial.[14] 50,000-60,000 is still a significant number though, and does not fully convey the scale of the phenomenon. It does not include the tens of thousands of people who were tried and tortured as suspected witches, but not killed. Nor does it include the people who were ostracized as witches by their local communities, but who were not officially tried, or the people who lived under fear of being accused as a witch, or those who were terrified about the harm that witchcraft might inflict on them.[15] The notion of the diabolical witch pervaded and plagued Europe for a long time, constituting one of the worst aspects of the period.

What makes witch trials particularly horrific from a modern perspective, is that we now know that witches actually did not exist. Or at least, they did not exist in the way that people at the time often thought they existed.[16] As the nineteenth-century German historian Wilhelm Soldan put it, these were "criminal proceedings without a crime."[17] This is not to say that all the accusations levelled against suspects were unwarranted. There might have been more real about early modern witchcraft than is often recognized today – this issue will be addressed later on.[18] Suffice to say for now that the witch-hunts were largely focused on an illusory threat. So, apart from making the trials increasingly grim, it also makes them increasingly intriguing from a scientific point of view. Why did Europeans persecute innocent people for so long and on such a scale? Why was there a hunt for imaginary enemies?

What is relevant for the purposes of this research is that the question of why witch-hunts occurred has attracted much theoretical attention.[19] Scholars have tried to explain them from a wide range of angles: romanticist, liberal, Marxist, functionalist, rational choice, feminist, to poststructuralist. In an overview from 1987 the historian Geoffrey Quaife collected forty major interpretations of the topic, and the number has only grown since.[20] Witchcraft scholarship has become a lively domain of pioneering approaches and interdisciplinary developments.[21] But despite all these efforts, explaining witch-hunting has remained a tough nut to crack. None of the large theoretical models has become particularly successful. As one of today's experts comments: "it is difficult to think of any historical problem over which there is more disagreement and confusion."[22] In the eyes of historians with an idiographic orientation this offers further proof

---

[14] Goodare, *The European Witch-Hunt*, 28.
[15] Levack, *The Witch-Hunt in Early Modern Europe*, 20–22.
[16] Briggs, *Witches & Neighbours*, 6; Levack, *The Witch-Hunt in Early Modern Europe*, 12–19; Hutton, *The Witch*, 2016–17; Dillinger, *Kinder im Hexenprozess*, 53; Voltmer, "Herren und Hexen," 51; Bradford Smith, "The Persecution of Witches," 53.
[17] Quoted in: Dillinger, *Hexen und Magie*, 2018, 155."Strafprozesse ohne Straftat."
[18] Bever, *The Realities of Witchcraft*.
[19] Barry and Davies, *Palgrave Advances in Witchcraft Studies*.
[20] Quaife, *Godly Zeal and Furious Rage*, 5–20.
[21] Davies and Barry, "Introduction."
[22] Levack, *The Witch-Hunt in Early Modern Europe*, 2.

that large theoretical frameworks are bound to fail. Scholars should thus interpret the witch-hunting phenomenon within its own particular and complex historical context.[23] Hence, if we want to find out whether the theory of Darwinian cultural evolution can live up to its promises, this case study poses the perfect challenge. Can the theory succeed where so many other theories have been left stranded?

Witch-hunting and cultural evolution
The topic of witch-hunting has already attracted some modest attention in debates over cultural evolution. In their argument about "rogue cultural variants" that so much resembles Dawkins's notion of "selfish memes", Peter Richerson and Robert Boyd shortly refer to outbreaks of witch panics as a possible example of a supernatural belief system that spread in a deleterious way amongst a population.[24] The philosopher Mary Midgley, on the other hand, uses witch trials as an example par excellence of why such approaches are bound to fail if taken to the socio-cultural realm.[25] Midgley concedes that witch-hunts may at first sight look like "selfish memes" that invaded communities lacking immunity to them, but she goes on to argue that such talk misses the point: "the meme story simply fails to give us any kind of explanation at all." Instead, she argued that "what we need to understand in such a case is how people could begin to think and act in this way in spite of the beliefs, customs and ideals which had prevented them from doing so earlier." It entails, as Midgley calls it, a "more awkward form of investigation" into "the habits of the heart."[26]

This disagreement bears precisely upon the questions that concern us here. Are qualitative historical scholarship and cultural evolution mutually exclusive, as Midgley seems to believe, or can they be integrated in novel and unexpected ways? Does the notion of adaptive, "selfish" cultural phenomena provide us with a fruitful line of investigation? These questions will be addressed here as follows. In chapter four I will introduce the topic of witch-hunting. What were early modern ideas about diabolical witchcraft like, and how did they lead to witch trials? Chapter five then looks at the various explanatory models that have been developed, and also at why those models failed to tackle the witch-hunting phenomenon satisfactorily. This failure helped to give shape to an idiographically oriented "state of the art" in witchcraft historiography. Yet, I will argue that this position is unsatisfying in its own turn as it leaves some striking aspects of witch beliefs and trials unexplained. After I propose a new Darwinian scenario in section 5.5, chapters six and seven will examine this Darwinian proposal that may help to bridge those explanatory gaps.

---

[23] Midelfort, *Witch Hunting in Southwestern Germany*; Scarre, *Witchcraft and Magic*; Briggs, *Witches & Neighbours*; Clark, *Thinking with Demons*; Gaskill, "The Pursuit of Reality"; Machielsen, *Martin Delrio*; Dillinger, *Hexen und Magie*, 2018.
[24] Richerson and Boyd, *Not By Genes Alone*, 167–69.
[25] Midgley, "Why Memes."
[26] Midgley, 83–84.

But before all that, it needs to be acknowledged that Mary Midgley was right in at least one important respect. If we aim to understand the witch-hunts, we need to undertake "this awkward form of investigation" into "the habits of the heart". European witch trials were driven by imaginations that can look irrational and bizarre to an audience today. Later on, we shall also see that the failure of some earlier explanatory models was at least partly due to an insufficient understanding of what contemporaries thought and believed. So, the interpretation and explanation of these events requires a deeper understanding of the intricate symbolic world that the involved actors were living in – it requires methods like *Verstehen*, hermeneutics and thick description.[27] But while motivations for witch-hunting were dauntingly complex, one element definitely played an important part: the emotion of fear.[28] The expert Lyndal Roper comments that "we cannot understand why witches were hunted unless we take the fears of those who hunted witches seriously."[29] So, arguably the best way to introduce this thought world is by looking at some of the key anxieties of the age, as it was those anxieties that helped shape the environment in which witch-hunting could flourish.

4.2 The early modern environment

In the public mind, the period from the fifteenth to the seventeenth centuries is often associated with the Renaissance, voyages of discovery, the scientific revolution, the Reformation, a new individualism, and a novel zest for life. As it left the alleged darkness of the Middle Ages behind, this era marked the beginning of the modern world. For quite some time such notions have also been cultivated by prominent historians.[30] According to the nineteenth-century scholar Jules Michelet, this period gave us two of the most important findings that we can think of, "the discovery of mankind and the discovery of the individual. The one we call Renaissance, the other Reformation."[31] In a similar vein the Swiss historian Jacob Burckhardt maintained that the Medieval mind had still laid "dreaming or half-awake beneath a common veil (...) woven out of faith, illusion and childish bias." People had only been able to see themselves as part of their race, group, party, or family.[32] But then, the culture of Renaissance Italy made this veil evaporate, and people finally learned to see themselves as individual human beings – a discovery that subsequently conquered Europe.[33] Those who adhere to such lofty views may be surprised that *this* was the time period in which most of the witch-hunts occurred, and that it was not the Middle Ages. It looks like a striking paradox, and historians have indeed been struggling with it

---

[27] Roper, *Witch Craze*, 6–12.
[28] Delumeau, *La Peur en Occident*; Kounine and Ostling, *Emotions in the History of Witchcraft*.
[29] Roper, *Witch Craze*, 9.
[30] Woolfson, *Palgrave Advances in Renaissance Historiography*.
[31] Michelet, *La Renaissance et La Réformation*, 7:662-3."les deux découvertes les plus importantes que l'homme puisse faire : la découverte du genre humain et la découverte de l'individu. L'une de ces découvertes s'appelle renaissance, l'autre réformation."
[32] Burckhardt, *Die Kultur Der Renaissance in Italien*, 131."wie unter einem gemeinsamen Schleier träumend oder halfwach", "gewoben aus Glauben, Kindesbefangenheit und Wahn."
[33] Burckhardt, *Die Kultur Der Renaissance in Italien*.

for quite some time.[34] For instance, they treated witch-hunts as a marginal phenomenon that was not characteristic of its time and place. Or they argued that the concept of diabolical witchcraft was a creation of the late Middle Ages, that just happened to linger on.[35]

However, if we truly want to resolve the paradox we need to recognize that there might not be a paradox at all. While much of the classical narrative about the period still stands – this indeed was the age of Erasmus, Montaigne and Galilei – historians have noted for quite some time that this era also had different and more sinister sides.[36] It was not only the age of Renaissance sculpture, the telescope, and the printing press, but also of fierce intolerance, religious wars, increased interest in magic, obsessions with the diabolical, and profound anxieties. We may now look at these centuries as the beginning of the modern world, but to many contemporaries it looked like the last age before an imminent apocalypse.[37] The Second Coming of Christ seemed to be near at hand, so enormous upheaval was expected. Numerous people presumed that the Anti-Christ was about to appear, followed by a resurrection of the dead, the last judgment, and the end of the world. Indications were supposed to be everywhere, in the form of strange weather, raging Turks, false prophets, monstrous births, and ominous comets. When a bishop of Vienna Frederick Nausea (*nomen est omen*) reflected on his epoch in 1532 he concluded that "the last age is near at hand, that the end of the world is indeed at the door, that the present age is utterly ruined, and that the death of it (as we might say) is indeed approaching to confirm the prodigies in every way."[38]

Many people thought to experience epic times in which their faith would be sorely tested.[39] Righteous Christian communities saw themselves as embattled fortresses in need of defense against dangers and enemies looming all around. The English historian Stuart Clark calls it an age of "cognitive extremism"; more so than in many other epochs of European history people tended to divide the world into binary pairs, or symbolic contraries, with religious values being strictly dichotomized.[40] During the decades around 1500 certain parts of the elites had embraced a somewhat more epicurean, secular, and optimistic Renaissance worldview, but over the course of the sixteenth and early seventeenth centuries the general mood seems to have darkened. The conflicts of the Reformation proved insoluble and grew increasingly bitter, stimulating a more gloomy and melancholic view of the world.[41] On both sides of the religious

---

[34] Briggs, *Witches & Neighbours*, 13.
[35] Hansen, *Zauberwahn, Inquisition und Hexenproceß im Mittelalter*, 4, 535–36.
[36] Kinsman, *The Darker Vision of the Renaissance*; Delumeau, *La Peur en Occident*; Clark, *Thinking with Demons*; Woolfson, *Palgrave Advances in Renaissance Historiography*; Kounine and Ostling, *Emotions in the History of Witchcraft*.
[37] Delumeau, *La Peur en Occident*, 197–231; Clark, *Thinking with Demons*, 335–74; Spinks and Zika, *Disaster, Death and the Emotions in the Shadow of the Apocalypse, 1400-1700*.
[38] Clark, *Thinking with Demons*, 366.
[39] Delumeau, *La Peur en Occident*; Clark, *Thinking with Demons*; Levack, *The Witch-Hunt in Early Modern Europe*, 100–121.
[40] Clark, *Thinking with Demons*, 39.
[41] Levack, *The Witch-Hunt in Early Modern Europe*, 100–121; Eire, *Reformations*; Walinski-Kiehl, "Witch-Hunting and State Building"; Behringer, "Witchcraft Studies in Austria, Germany and Switzerland," 87; Behringer, *Witches and Witch-Hunts*, 119–20; Goodare, *The European Witch-Hunt*, 155–88.

divide there were increasing demands for a morally rigorous, self-disciplined lifestyle, and a rejection of worldly pleasures. Many rulers and subjects alike embraced the ideal of the godly state, which was characterized by an imminent state of emergency, a dogmatic religious sensibility, and a zealous concern for the purification of society of all evils. As the prince-bishop of Würzburg, Julius Echter of Mespelbrun, expressed the mindset: "every thought of joy and gaiety prevents us from feeling sorrow, pain and tears for our sins."[42] This atmosphere found an eloquent expression in the art of the early Baroque. As Lyndal Roper writes about German Baroque culture of the period:

> [It] was characterized by intense emotionality, a profound religious sensibility, and a predilection for extremes and opposites. This era saw the building of churches that were overwhelming in their forthright totalizing theological vision of a supremely brilliant heavenly court and of depraved mortal man – not for nothing did these churches show skeletons, skulls and even rats eating away at corpses.[43]

Diabolical forces
The ultimate source of evil in this paranoid mindset was the devil, also known as the Prince of Darkness, Satan, the Angel of the Abyss, the Shadow of Death, the Prince of this World, Lucifer, or the Evil One.[44] His origins were believed to lie in heaven, where he had served God as one of his archangels. But this initial peace and tranquility were disturbed when Satan, as a result of his free will, started a rebellion against God and was cast out of heaven. He now continued his existence in hell and was filled with an insatiable hatred of God and humanity, and a thirst for revenge. Satan also sensed that the apocalypse was imminent and that time was running out, so his wish to harm was all the more pressing. The devil should not be understood as a real threat to divine powers, as God was omnipotent.[45] Dualistic notions about God and the devil being competing forces had even been stamped out as one of the key heresies of the Middle Ages. It was quite the contrary; God permitted diabolical evil, because it served him as a device for testing and punishing sinful humankind. The extent of the devil's powers depended on human cooperation, but because human sinfulness was ubiquitous, Satan had ample opportunities to exert his evil ways. The suffragan bishop of Trier, Peter Binsfeld, in 1589 wrote that "when the devil's temptations are withstood he becomes as weak as an ant, but when his temptations are met he will grow strong as a lion."[46]

---

[42] Walinski-Kiehl, "Witch-Hunting and State Building," 251.
[43] Roper, *Witch Craze*, 18.
[44] Delumeau, *La Peur en Occident*, 232–53; Muchembled, *A history of the devil*, 35–147; Levack, *The Witch-Hunt in Early Modern Europe*, 29–33, 103–7; Goodare, *The European Witch-Hunt*, 55–70; Weyer, *Witches, Devils, and Doctors in the Renaissance*.
[45] Dillinger, *Hexen und Magie*, 2018, 42–47.
[46] Binsfeld, *Tractat Von Bekantnuß der Zauberer unnd Hexen*, 43. "Der Teuffel / wenn jhm dapffer widerstanden wirdt / ist er schwach wie Omeiß / wirdt aber sein eyngeben auffgenommen / ist er starck wie ein Löwe."

What was additionally frightening was that the devil was assisted by legions of demons.[47] Like Satan, these beings had once lived peacefully as angels in heaven, but they had joined the devil's rebellion and were now a part of his malign campaign of tricking, seducing and punishing humankind. The angelic origin of the devil and his demons implied that they had maintained many of their former traits. What they were precisely capable of was a topic of intellectual debate in a domain of scholarship that historians now call "demonology". In general, it was assumed that the devil and demons were spiritual beings without physical bodies, and were thus unable to eat, drink, or procreate. What they were also incapable of was overriding people's free will, performing miracles, or changing substances. Yet, their angelic origin endowed them with special powers, like travelling at great speeds, having knowledge about the future, and creating illusions that almost looked like miracles. Amongst those illusions was metamorphosis; they could appear in people's lives in disguise as apparently normal humans or animals. So, when people at the time were confronted with beings they did not know, there were reasons for distrust. For instance, when Martin Luther was once confronted with an unknown dog in his bed in the Wartburg Castle, he assumed it was a demon and flung it out of the window.[48] The exact number of demons was a matter of disagreement – estimates diverged from several thousands to many billions – but their evil and pervasiveness were largely a matter of consensus.[49]

This mindset of "cognitive extremism", with demonic forces looming all around, also tainted social relations. Opposing groups of people were often not seen as just opponents, but as agents of the devil.[50] The Middle Ages had already witnessed persecutions and burnings of so called heretics, like the Cathars, Hussites, and Waldensians, who had diverged from the dominant Christian doctrines.[51] It was told about such groups that they held secretive gatherings where they did outrageous things, such as frenzied naked dancing, desecrating holy symbols, or plotting against Christianity. Similar fears existed regarding the non-Christian minority of the Jews. It was reported that they performed cannibalistic rituals with Christian children at their assemblages named Sabbaths. Medieval scholarly works about these groups had titles like *Malleus Haereticorum* (The Hammer of Heretics) or *Malleus Judaeorum* (The Hammer of Jews), and the institution of the Holy Inquisition was installed to combat them.[52] From the high Middle Ages onwards Europe had gradually developed the mental and institutional machinery to remove, or even wipe out, deviant religious communities.

In the fifteenth and sixteenth centuries, this zeal seems to have intensified. Jews were increasingly expelled, and by 1570 not many Jews were left in western Europe.[53] The religious

---

[47] Clark, *Thinking with Demons*; Levack, *The Witch-Hunt in Early Modern Europe*, 29–33; Dillinger, *Hexen und Magie*, 2018, 42–53; Eire, *Reformations*, 618–59.
[48] Eire, *Reformations*, 650.
[49] Levack, *The Witch-Hunt in Early Modern Europe*, 31.
[50] Delumeau, *La Peur en Occident*, 254–304.
[51] Moore, *The Formation of a Persecuting Society*; Oberste, *Ketzerei Und Inquisition Im Mittelalter*.
[52] Bink, *Als die Teufel fliegen lernten*, 108.
[53] Rublack, *Reformation Europe*; Kaplan, *Divided by Faith*, 294–332; Eire, *Reformations*.

splintering of the continent as a consequence of the Reformation also created new antagonisms between Catholicism and various branches of Protestantism. For the first time western Christendom was confronted with religiously divided societies, and this was considered profoundly undesirable: it endangered the unity of the "Corpus Christianum" and was bound to provoke God's wrath. [54] Catholics described Lutheranism as "the German plague", and a sixteenth-century French preacher warned that if Protestant deviants were not removed, God would "exterminate us all."[55] The hatred of Protestantism stimulated a vigorous institutional response, known today as the Counter-Reformation. Protestants in their turn stereotyped the Catholic church as "Satan's synagogue", and the Pope as "the Anti-Christ" or "the whore of Babylon".[56] At times people found ways of living peacefully together across religious dwivides, but such arrangements were always fragile and could easily give way to brutal conflicts, like the wars of religion in France, England, The Netherlands, Switzerland, and Germany. [57] The contemporary philosopher Blaise Pascal observed that "men never do so much harm so happily as when they do it through religious conviction."[58]

Women and misogyny
Another phenomenon that was distrusted within this male-dominated world was women.[59] There were positive notions about women as chaste and obedient servants and companions of their husbands, and Catholics venerated Holy Mary. But the ideal of the decent housewife, or the sublime and desexualized virtuousness of Virgin Mary, sharply contrasted with many actual women, the earthlier Eves, who were often perceived as weak of mind and character with an overall tendency towards moral transgressions.[60] Religious and secular authorities alike shared notions about women as imperfect men that were less rational or intellectual, and prone to traits like petulance, credulity, and madness. Such stereotypes had deep roots, often dating back to classical antiquity or biblical times.[61] Amongst the legitimizations for misogynous stereotypes was the widely held belief in bodily humors – a theory that assumed that four fluids in our bodies determine our temperaments. Supposedly, men had an overabundance of the fluid blood, associated with fire, which created forces within the body that moved upwards towards the heavens and the brain. This would explain men's broader shoulders and allegedly more creative and rational abilities. Women, on the other hand, had an overabundance of the fluid black bile,

---

[54] Kaplan, *Divided by Faith*, 35.
[55] Schilling, *Aufbruch und Krise: Deutschland 1517-1648*, 207; Kaplan, *Divided by Faith*, 75.
[56] Rublack, *Reformation Europe*; Kaplan, *Divided by Faith*, 35.
[57] Eire, *Reformations*, 525–61.
[58] Parker, *Global Crisis*, 90.
[59] Delumeau, *La Peur en Occident*, 305–46; Russell, *Eva/Ave*; Wunder, *Er ist die Sonn', sie ist der Mond*; Smith, *The Power of Woman*; Wiesner-Hanks, *Women and Gender in Early Modern Europe*.
[60] Roper, *Witch Craze*, 136.
[61] Wiesner-Hanks, *Women and Gender in Early Modern Europe*, 17–30.

associated with the earth, which created forces in the body that moved downwards, explaining women's wider hips and more emotional tendencies.[62]

A crucial consequence of this notion of women as more earthly and emotional creatures was that they were believed to have a stronger sex drive than men.[63] The female sexual appetite was often thought insatiable and difficult to control. This was a problem because extramarital sex was forbidden, and women's abilities of seduction gave them a means to exert power over men. An illustrative story, popular at the time, concerned Aristotle and Phyllis, a mistress of Alexander the Great.[64] As the story went, Alexander was in love with Phyllis and often forgot his duties and responsibilities as a king. His generals informed Aristotle about this, and so he decided to speak with Alexander to convince him to refocus on stately affairs. When Phyllis noticed Alexander's new coldness, and found out who was responsible, she became thirsty for revenge. She decided to seduce the old philosopher, and Aristotle indeed fell head over heels in love with her. When he proposed to have intercourse, Phyllis was then willing to meet his demands, but only under one condition: he would let her ride on his back. Aristotle accepted the prerequisite, and eventually the old and honorable philosopher walked Phyllis through the palace garden upon all fours. This remarkable story is unlikely to be true though, because it only first appeared in the High Middle Ages. Still, it became a popular trope in the literature and the arts, and probably this was because to male contemporaries it demonstrated something essential about women and men, namely that even Aristotle, a symbol of male wisdom and intellect, was unable to resist the deceitful forces of female sexuality, and found himself in this humiliating position. Hence, given a context in which such stories were told, women were easily seen as the devil's perfect tool.[65]

Popular beliefs

Another relevant set of anxieties that we need to address is popular beliefs.[66] What ordinary people living in the countryside precisely believed is notoriously difficult for historians to reconstruct, because these people were largely illiterate. So, most of our information has to be obtained from the biased accounts of educated classes. But what sources *do* suggest is that ordinary people thought to inhabit a world that was teeming with non-human spiritual beings, like nature spirits, ghosts, revenants, giants, fairies, and goblins.[67] Some of those creatures could dwell in and around the house, but mostly they were to be found beyond the villages and the cultivated lands, in the untamed and dangerous world of woods, lakes, moors, and mountains.[68] Stories were told about their gatherings in the middle of the night at remote places like hill tops

---

[62] Wiesner-Hanks, 34–39.
[63] Levack, *The Witch-Hunt in Early Modern Europe*, 132.
[64] Sarton, "Aristotle and Phyllis"; Javor Briški, "Eine Warnung vor dominanten Frauen oder Bejahung der Sinnenlust?".
[65] Delumeau, *La Peur en Occident*, 305–46.
[66] Goodare, *The European Witch-Hunt*, 121–54; Hutton, *The Witch*, 74–95, 120–46.
[67] Delumeau, *La Peur en Occident*, 75–97; Goodare, *The European Witch-Hunt*, 130–32; Dillinger, *Hexen und Magie*, 2018, 37–42; Habiger-Tuczay, *Geister, Dämonen, Phantasmen*.
[68] Wilson, *The Magical Universe*, 10; Habiger-Tuczay, *Geister, Dämonen, Phantasmen*.

or moors, and their rumbling sounds were sometimes thought to be heard over long distances.[69] Interactions between humans and such beings were a possibility. For instance, they flew into people's cellars to drink barrels of wine, or appeared as "persons" to people in need, and promised help, but when help was accepted suddenly turned into a spirit.[70] A popular folkloric trope concerned the so called "Wild Hunt" – the belief that fairies, the dead, or supernatural hunters, collectively flew around during the night under the leadership of pagan gods like Wotan, Holda or Diana. More worrisome were the aerial journeys of women known as *Strix* or *Lamia*, who transformed themselves into owls and flew out in order to suck the blood of babies.[71] The moral relationship between humans and such supernatural beings was often ambiguous – they could be beneficial, neutral, but also harmful.[72]

It was a "magical universe".[73] The world was alleged to be full of hidden spiritual forces that impacted daily life. While these forces were often hostile and unpredictable, they were not inanimate or indifferent, so there were possibilities of influencing them. People used a rich variety of magical practices, like spells, charms, amulets, or rituals, to stimulate fruitful harvests, good health, fertility, or safe journeys. There was hardly a domain of everyday life that remained unaffected. Some people were seen as experts, the so called cunning people, who were thought to have unusual abilities of influencing and contacting the supernatural world.[74] By the end of the Middle Ages the Christian religion may have penetrated deeply into the minds of ordinary people, but it had to coexist with a rich heritage of local customs and beliefs that often preserved older and unchristian elements.

Moreover, strong interest in magic could also be found amongst significant parts of the educated classes. From the twelfth century onwards many ancient and Arabic texts were translated into Latin, and they were full of theories about magic, which triggered a fascination for the occult sciences amongst Renaissance intellectuals.[75] Religious authorities often distrusted both the intellectual and ordinary views and practices regarding magic, as they appeared to diverge from official doctrines. And did those seemingly pagan rituals not require the invocation of demons?[76] But magical acts were so very widespread that attempts to stamp them out tended to misfire. Moreover, official Christianity also used practices that looked like magic, such as the ringing of church bells against storms or the use of holy water for protection.[77]

---

[69] Dillinger, *Böse Leute*, 139.
[70] Dillinger, "Hexenverfolgungen in der Grafschaft Hohenberg," 25–27; Dillinger, *Hexen und Magie*, 2018, 112–13.
[71] Lecouteux, *Chasses fantastiques et cohortes de la nuit au Moyen Age*; Levack, *The Witch-Hunt in Early Modern Europe*, 41–45; Hutton, *The Witch*, 125–43.
[72] Bever, *The Realities of Witchcraft*, 94; Dillinger, *Böse Leute*, 112–13.
[73] Wilson, *The Magical Universe*; Davies, "The World of Popular Magic"; Dillinger, *Hexen und Magie*, 2018, 27–37; Hutton, *The Witch*.
[74] Briggs, *Witches & Neighbours*, 171.
[75] Clark, *Thinking with Demons*, 214–32; Dillinger, *Hexen und Magie*, 2018, 25–27.
[76] Wilson, *The Magical Universe*, 460; Goodare, *The European Witch-Hunt*, 20; Levack, *The Witch-Hunt in Early Modern Europe*, 107–9.
[77] Briggs, *Witches & Neighbours*, 171; Wilson, *The Magical Universe*, xxii; Thomas, *Religion and the Decline of Magic*, 27–57.

What various levels of society at certain time periods where far less lenient on, however, was the use of magic in supposedly harmful ways. This normally goes under the name of "witchcraft". The fear of witchcraft did not make Europeans unique. On the contrary, historians and anthropologists have found anxieties about it throughout premodern societies in world history.[78] Yet, while belief in witchcraft was widespread, the concept becomes slippery as soon as scholars try to define it with precision.[79] Does it mean that certain people are supposed to harm others through magical means only unconsciously, or is it deliberately sought? Is the power of witchcraft believed to be acquired, which anthropologists sometimes distinguish from witchcraft as sorcery, or is the capacity innate? Does witchcraft depend on the invocation of supernatural forces, or does it only require the unlocking of purely natural secrets? Answers to such questions widely diverge, if the questions would have made sense to historical actors at all. Despite such intercultural differences the universal use of the term witchcraft is still helpful. What can be found throughout premodern societies is suspicions within communities about individuals who harm others through hidden and uncanny means.[80] What is also widespread is the belief that action can be taken to resist these witches, for instance through counter magic, or by persecuting and murdering them. Throughout world history there are examples of collective killings of alleged witches.

Premodern Europe was no exception. Already long before the age of the witch trials it was familiar with what historical scholars nowadays call "village witchcraft".[81] Within local communities there were often people who had built up reputations for maleficent magic and were dreaded for it. Magical countermeasures were continually taken against them.[82] Such fears should not immediately be dismissed as illusory, because it is not unthinkable that reputations for maleficent magic could be grounded in reality to some degree.[83] There are clues that certain individuals really did try to harm others through magical means, and that they may even have cultivated their reputations for it. After all, if others believed that their powers were real, it could make those others careful not to treat them badly.[84] Neither is it unthinkable that various psychosomatic mechanisms could make such attempts have real consequences, for instance, when the stress of being cursed had real damaging effects on people's health.[85]

The levels of witch persecution in Europe fluctuated. The laws of Ancient Rome already contained paragraphs against maleficent sorcery, and in the second century BC there were panics about women who allegedly spread disease through magical means. This led to the execution of

---

[78] Behringer, *Witches and Witch-Hunts*, 1–46, 196–248; Hutton, *The Witch*, 3–43; Stein and Stein, *The Anthropology of Religion, Magic, and Witchcraft.*, 213–29.
[79] Briggs, *Witches & Neighbours*, 7; Stein and Stein, *The Anthropology of Religion, Magic, and Witchcraft.*, 213–29; Dillinger, *Hexen und Magie*, 2018, 13–24.
[80] Hutton, *The Witch*, 10–35.
[81] Goodare, *The European Witch-Hunt*, 10–11, 88–121.
[82] Wilson, *The Magical Universe*, xxvi; Davies, "The World of Popular Magic," 170.
[83] Bever, *The Realities of Witchcraft*; Wiesner-Hanks, *Women and Gender in Early Modern Europe*, 260.
[84] Briggs, *Witches & Neighbours*, 55.
[85] Stein and Stein, *The Anthropology of Religion, Magic, and Witchcraft.*, 142.

hundreds of these women.[86] Worries about harmful magic also continued in the Middle Ages, and trials still sporadically occurred.[87] However, Medieval political and ecclesiastical authorities were in general not very interested in the persecution of witchcraft, and tended to dismiss beliefs in it as superstitious. It was only in the course of the fourteenth century that fears started to grow again, particularly in regard to alleged sorcery against political opponents. This helped set the stage for a new era of witch-hunting.[88]

Ecological hazards
Late medieval and early modern European communities were confronted with a further range of real and purported dangers. At the time Europe was experiencing the harsh effects of the so called "Little Ice Age".[89] After a relatively warm period in the Middle Ages, the average temperatures gradually began to drop from around 1300, and particularly from the 1550s onwards the effects were severe. There were strange weather conditions, like extreme winters, sudden frost in spring or autumn, or cold and wet summers. Contemporaries did not fail to notice these deviations, as they often caused the destruction of crops. Being part of a Malthusian economy of vulnerable ecologies, this was something that people could ill afford. Communities often lived close to subsistence level, so a failed harvest or loss of livestock could literally mean the end. The consequences of the Little Ice Age also added up to an already existing problem of overpopulation. After the devastations of the plague in the fourteenth century, the populations of Europe had started to grow again from around the mid-fifteenth century, and by the late sixteenth century the growth had reached the limits of what natural recourses could harness. This led to what historians now describe as "the iron century" from 1550-1660, or the "general crisis of the seventeenth century". There were rising food prices, epidemics, inflation, and famines, and by the 1590s agricultural and industrial production had reached its lowest level in three centuries.[90] This stimulated an atmosphere in which the health and fertility of people as well as of livestock were a matter of intense concern. Especially the deaths of infants and children were a cause of grave sorrow.[91]

In order to face these challenges, individuals depended on robust social bonds within their local communities. People often lived in the same place for generations, interacting on a daily basis for the exchange of services and goods. So, they knew each other well.[92] During times of scarcity such social cohesion could provide much-needed solidarity, but there was also a darker

---

[86] Goodare, *The European Witch-Hunt*, 31–32; Behringer, *Witches and Witch-Hunts*, 48–50.
[87] Behringer, *Witches and Witch-Hunts*, 52–57; Hutton, *The Witch*, 59–73, 147–79; Page, "Medieval Magic."
[88] Goodare, *The European Witch-Hunt*, 35–38.
[89] Behringer, "Climatic Change and Witch-Hunting"; Matthews and Briffa, "The 'Little Ice Age'"; Behringer, *Kulturgeschichte des Klimas*; Parker, *Global Crisis*, 3–25; Blom, *Die Welt aus den Angeln*.
[90] Kamen, *The Iron Century*; Schilling, *Die neue Zeit*, 264–82; Parker, *Global Crisis*.
[91] Delumeau, *La Peur en Occident*, 98–196.
[92] Briggs, *Witches & Neighbours*; Kamen, *Early Modern European Society*, 9–11; Voltmer, "Gott ist tot, und der Teufel jetzt Meister!"

side to all this. Enmities and suspicions were often building up within communities.[93] Unpopular individuals could become the objects of hostile gossiping, and as the English historian Robin Briggs writes about the ambiguous social atmosphere in villages and towns:

> People knew what their neighbours were up to and how they lived; they overheard conversations and spied on one another. Although this nosiness had its virtues – for example it may have protected children against the extremes of neglect and cruelty found in our own society – it was also oppressive and liable to magnify both discords and suspicions once they arose.[94]

When confronted with perceived transgressors, communities could lash out harshly against them. A "terror and solidarity society", another expert in premodern village life has called it.[95] The punishment of wrongdoers was increasingly taken out of the hands of those local communities, being monopolized by the state. But that did not necessarily soften the disciplinary measures.[96] During the sixteenth century the number of public executions by authorities grew significantly, and normally went together with much physical torment. Public punishments were almost folk festivals, attracting many visitors. The German historian Richard von Dülmen has called them the "theatre of horror".[97]

When taking all these aspects of the late medieval and early modern period into account, it is not so strange after all that this was the age of European witch-hunting. When historians nowadays place the trials in their historical context, they no longer treat them as an abnormality or a deviation that is in need of some special explanation, but rather as an integral part of European society.[98] However, petrifying as all these real or alleged dangers were in themselves, they did not yet create the witch persecutions. What created the possibility of witch-hunting was that all these anxieties, which had often existed independently from each other, gradually came together into a cluster of beliefs that made things even more frightening. Historians have labelled it "the cumulative concept of witchcraft". It is to this concept that we now turn.

4.3 The cumulative concept of witchcraft

The notion of a "cumulative concept of witchcraft" was first proposed by the German historian Joseph Hansen.[99] According to his early twentieth-century argument, a cumulative diabolical interpretation of witchcraft gradually took shape over the course of the late Middle Ages in the

---

[93] Roper, *Witch Craze*, 107; Briggs, *Witches & Neighbours*, 138–40; Goodare, *The European Witch-Hunt*, 88–120.
[94] Briggs, *Witches & Neighbours*, 231.
[95] Utz Jeggle is quoted in: Dillinger, *Böse Leute*, 189.
[96] Kamen, *Early Modern European Society*, 188–96; Levack, *The Witch-Hunt in Early Modern Europe*, 68–74.
[97] Dülmen, *Theater des Schreckens*.
[98] Briggs, *Witches & Neighbours*, 13.
[99] Hansen, *Zauberwahn, Inquisition und Hexenproceß im Mittelalter*, 35, 114."Kollektivbegriff der Hexe."

Alps, and it then spread throughout Europe, constituting the basis of the witch-hunts.[100] A moment of particular importance in his account was a papal bull against diabolical witchcraft in 1484, followed in 1486 by the publication of the *Malleus Maleficarum* (The Hammer of Witches). This extensive book was authored by the clergymen Heinrich Kramer and Jacob Sprenger – although the latter's involvement is contested – and it soon became a standard scholarly reference.[101] We will later see that many aspects of Hansen's theories about witch-hunting have become outdated, but his notion of a "cumulative concept of witchcraft" is still widely in use amongst experts today.[102] The current American historian Brian Levack describes the concept as "a composite or cumulative notion: composite because it consisted of ideas that formerly were not connected, and cumulative because the synthesis of these ideas occurred gradually, each new addition building upon or supplementing others." What ideas are precisely part of this concept is a matter of disagreement, because almost every historian of witchcraft uses a different set of elements. Yet, five key ideas are almost always on the list, so it is these elements that will now be discussed in due order.[103]

Five key elements
The first essential ingredient concerned the idea of a "diabolical pact".[104] Witches were supposed to be ordinary Christians who had allied themselves with the devil and were now serving his malicious campaign against God and humanity. Since demonic forces could not override people's free will, the pact always resulted from a person's own decision, making it a heinous and inexcusable crime that deserved severe punishment.[105] It was a deliberate form of apostasy and heresy, and if witches would not confess and repent, their souls were lost to an afterlife of eternal agony. But because the pact resulted from a free decision, Satan needed to make ingenious efforts to tempt Christians into this alliance. A Westphalian witch-hunter, Heinrich von Schultheis, compared the devil to a bird catcher who used the sweet tones of his pipe to lure birds in.[106] As a master of lies, Satan continuously looked for moral weak spots, and not surprisingly, many experts stressed, one category of people was especially likely to fall for that: women. [107] According to King James VI of Scotland, who had an ardent interest in witchcraft, female witches outnumbered male witches by twenty to one, and as he explained: "the reason is easy, for that

---

[100] Hansen, 398–538.
[101] Hansen, 467-500.; Institoris, *The Hammer of Witches*; Behringer and Jerouscheck, "'Das unheilvollste Buch der Weltliteratur'?," 33; Broedel, *The "Malleus Maleficarum" and the Construction of Witchcraft*, 19.
[102] Rummel and Voltmer, *Hexen und Hexenverfolgung*, 5; Behringer, *Witches and Witch-Hunts*, 57–59; Goodare, *The European Witch-Hunt*, 50–51; Levack, *The Witch-Hunt in Early Modern Europe*, 29; Dillinger, *Hexen und Magie*, 2018, 19–24.
[103] These are precisely the five elements that Dillinger uses for what he calls "the elaborate concept of witchcraft": Dillinger, *Hexen und Magie*, 2018, 20.
[104] Levack, *The Witch-Hunt in Early Modern Europe*, 29–37; Dillinger, *Hexen und Magie*, 2018, 42–47.
[105] Binsfeld, *Tractat Von Bekantnuß der Zauberer unnd Hexen*, 6; Bodin, *De la démonomanie des sorciers*, 123; Schultheis, *Eine Außführliche Instruction*, 24, 132; Boguet, *Discours exécrable des sorciers*, 42–44.
[106] Schultheis, *Eine Außführliche Instruction*, 442.
[107] Levack, *The Witch-Hunt in Early Modern Europe*, 135–41; Binsfeld, *Tractat Von Bekantnuß der Zauberer unnd Hexen*, 14–15, 42.

sex is frailer than man is, so it is easier to be entrapped in these gross snares of the Devil, as was overwell proved to be true by the Serpent's deceiving of Eve at the beginning, which makes him the friendlier with that sex since then."[108]

Satan was also keenly aware that a vulnerable spot was to be found in the female sex drive, which brings us to the second key element of the cumulative concept: "diabolical intercourse". The alleged diabolical lovemaking often went directly along with the pact, and a typical scenario of female initiation into witchcraft could happen as follows.[109] It all began when women were somewhere alone, at home or outside, finding themselves in a situation of emotional or economic distress. A stranger then appeared, who was kind and comforting, and interested in the causes of their troubles. He was a young and handsome man with stylish clothes, such as trousers of satin or velvet, and he wore a hat that was adorned with an imposing feather. He was also virile, sexually experienced, and willing to offer help. The stranger began to promise these women lovely things like wealth and prosperity, he brought them money and jewelry, and tried to seduce them to have intercourse with him. If not immediately successful, he returned on other occasions, kissing them, and whispering sweet things in their ears like "you know that I have always loved you."[110] However, there was a catch, because this stranger did not offer his favors for free: he demanded that they abjure God.

Obviously, this was no ordinary stranger. Hidden behind the appealing disguise was a demon or even the devil himself. But while Satan was a marvelous trickster, it always remained possible for women to recognize that something was not right, because the devil could never achieve a perfect disguise.[111] He for instance had the hoof of a goat, felt cold, smelled of sulfur, or lacked a shadow. But due to their moral weaknesses and sexual appetite women often did not pay careful attention and did not realize who they were actually dealing with. So, they accepted the stranger's gifts, had intercourse with him, and made the fatal mistake of renouncing God. Disillusionment immediately followed. The intercourse was not as pleasant as expected, as the stranger pushed them down like a dog in an animal-like way, and the sulfur smell, goat-like hoof, and coldness became apparent. The genital organ turned out to be long and hard, while the sperm and penis were as cold as ice, causing horrible pains.[112] The devil himself did not even enjoy it, because for him sex was not for pleasure but for corrupting.[113] As soon as the identity of the stranger had become apparent, his promises were retracted: the coins suddenly turned into dung or leaves, and the jewelry into trash or broken pieces. But at that point the disgraceful decision could not be reversed. Like in a marriage, Satan had effectively made these women "his".

---

[108] King James I and Tyson, *The Demonology of King James I*, 128.
[109] Dillinger, *Böse Leute*, 112–17; Roper, *Witch Craze*, 82–103; Goodare, *The European Witch-Hunt*, 298–305; Goodare, 298–303; Rémy, *Demonolatry*, 7–8, 69–70; Pohl, *Zauberglaube und Hexenangst im Kurfürstentum Mainz*, 245–58.
[110] Roper, *Witch Craze*, 87.
[111] For contemporary descriptions, see for instance: Rio en Maxwell-Stuart, *Investigations into Magic*, 83–98.Binsfeld, *Tractat Von Bekantnuß der Zauberer unnd Hexen*, 15; Lancre, *On the Inconstancy of Witches*, 21; Mirandola, *La sorcière*, 163, 200–201.
[112] Boguet, *Discours exécrable des sorciers*, 57–58.
[113] Institoris, *The Hammer of Witches*, 309; Lancre, *On the Inconstancy of Witches*, 232; Mirandola, *La sorcière*, 147.

They had become a "witch", and were now a part of the devil's hateful fight against Christianity, and intercourse was continued on a regular basis.

While women were far more likely to enter the pact, Satan also entangled men into his nets, and it could happen along somewhat similar lines.[114] For instance, when men were drunk, suddenly a young and handsome woman appeared who tried to seduce them, and asked them to renounce God. If careful enough, men could observe that the hands of this woman were rough and hairy, demonstrating the true masculine nature of the paramour. In her research of German trial records, Lyndal Roper noticed that in contrast to female witches, who usually had one diabolical lover at their disposal, male witches were more often provided with multiple partners.[115] But male initiation into witchcraft could also happen in many other ways. For instance, when Satan promised to take revenge on enemies, or when he offered them knowledge in exchange for their souls, as happened in the legendary case of the German doctor Faustus – a renowned tale that was conspired in this context.[116]

Narratives about men becoming witches were somewhat more diverse and instable, and were surely no match for the story about female initiation into witchcraft through diabolical intercourse. The topic of female overrepresentation also caught the attention of the authors of *Malleus Maleficarum*. They brought in many antique and biblical quotes to explain it. Had not the early church father Saint John Chrysostom already said that "what else is a woman but the enemy of friendship, an inescapable punishment, a necessary evil, a natural temptation, a desirable disaster, a danger in the home, a delightful detriment, an evil of nature, painted with nice color?"[117] Kramer and Sprenger maintained that women were the devil's easiest prey, as "everything is governed by carnal lusting, which is insatiable in them." They concluded that witchcraft "should be called the Heresy not of Sorcerers but of Sorceresses, to name it after the predominant element."[118]

When the pact was sealed and the intercourse had taken place, witches would then regularly attend a so called "witches' sabbath", also referred to as "the synagogue", "nocturnal assemblies", "schools", or "the dance". This constitutes the third key element of the cumulative concept of witchcraft.[119] This gathering, named after what Christians saw as the Jewish assemblage, was often imagined as a ghastly event where witches of all kinds, young, old, rich and poor, assembled to meet the devil and plot against Christianity.[120] These sabbaths occurred on a regular basis in the night, often close to the edges of the cultivated world, or in even more

---

[114] Briggs, *Witches & Neighbours*, 350; Roper, *Witch Craze*, 90; Goodare, *The European Witch-Hunt*, 301.
[115] Roper, *Witch Craze*, 91.
[116] Goodare, *The European Witch-Hunt*, 277–81; Füssel and Kreutzer, *Historia von D. Johann Fausten*.
[117] Institoris, *The Hammer of Witches*, 162.
[118] Institoris, 162, 170.
[119] Clark, *Thinking with Demons*, 3–94; Roper, *Witch Craze*, 104–24; Blécourt, "Sabbath Stories"; Goodare, *The European Witch-Hunt*, 73–75; Levack, *The Witch-Hunt in Early Modern Europe*, 37–41; Krause, *Witchcraft, Demonology, and Confession in Early Modern France*, 19; Rémy, *Demonolatry*, 57–61.
[120] For contemporary descriptions, see for instance: Rio and Maxwell-Stuart, *Investigations into Magic*, 83–98; Anonymous of Arras, "A History of the State, Case, and Condition of the Waldensian Heretics," 43; Meder, *Acht Hexenpredigten*, 69–72.

isolated places like woods, moors, or hill tops. The assembly was often thought to be chaired by the devil himself, who sat on a throne with the horrific appearance of a big goat, a dog, or a toad, while the witches paid homage to him. All the moral principles of Christianity were reversed: the witches worshipped Satan while they were standing upside down, and instead of kissing his lips they licked his anus. Demons joined in, and the sacred symbols of Christianity were mocked. The cross was trampled on, the host desecrated, the Holy Bible spat on, and the sign of the cross made with the left hand instead of the right. After the sacrilege, the time was ripe for intense feasting. The flesh of Christian children became the object of frenzied cannibalistic rituals, and demons and witches were sitting at long tables with plenty of food and drinks, which looked nice but were actually tasteless and unsatisfying.[121]

The exact events of sabbaths were a topic of serious scholarly consideration, for instance in a work from 1600 by the Jesuit scholar Martin Delrio, the *Disquisitiones Magicae* (Investigations into Magic).[122] This renowned intellectual depicted the witches' sabbath in great color and detail, and maintained that when the witches and demons had finished their meals, the following happened:

> Then they begin to dance. Sometimes they hold lighted candles in their hands, with which they worship the evil spirit, and exchange kisses in his presence. They sing very obscure songs in his honour, or jump up and down, to a drum or a pipe which is played by someone sitting in the fork of a tree. They behave ridiculously in every way, and in every way contrary to accepted custom. Then their demon-lovers copulate with them in the most repulsive fashion.[123]

The lovemaking was one of the most shocking elements. During the dance many witches were naked, and the intercourse happened between witches and demons, between witches and other witches, and in heterosexual, homosexual, and incestuous ways. A judge and witch-hunter in the Labourd region in southern France, Pierre de Lancre, commented that the couplings were "so abominable that it is horrible to have to tell about it in detail." To his dismay, De Lancre also recounted to have spoken with an alleged witch who said to have chosen witchcraft over Christianity because its masses offered more pomp than the real church.[124] And sometimes, it was thought, the rumbling sounds of these gatherings could be heard in adjacent villages.[125]

The fact that witches' sabbaths were often held at relatively remote places created a problem for the diabolical conspiracy, though. This was an age without cars, bikes, or street lighting, so attending sabbaths by travelling back and forth within a single night was a physical

---

[121] Rémy, *Demonolatry*, 57–59.
[122] Rio and Maxwell-Stuart, *Investigations into Magic*, 83–98.
[123] Rio and Maxwell-Stuart, 93.
[124] Lancre, *On the Inconstancy of Witches*, 147, 232.
[125] Dillinger, *Böse Leute*, 139.

impossibility for many witches. However, the devil offered the solution of the "nightly flight", which constitutes our fourth key element of the cumulative concept.[126] As Delrio wrote about the witches' voyages to the sabbath: "If they live nearby, they go on foot. If they live further away [...] they are transported to meetings."[127] The means of aerial transport varied greatly, as witches could use items like broomsticks, pitchforks, or pieces of wood. These tools were turned into vehicles for flight by smearing them with magical ointments, partly made of the fat of dead babies. Alternatively, witches travelled sitting backwards on goats, or other animals, or they were directly transported to the sabbath by demons. The voyages could happen alone, as well as in cohorts that somewhat resembled the "Wild Hunt". No matter how the witches exactly flew, one important implication remained: witches could know other witches who lived far away. Witchcraft thus formed a collective effort of people who consorted with each other over long distances.

If the diabolical pact, the intercourse, the sabbath, and nightly flight were not awful enough, the concept contained a fifth element which turned diabolical witchcraft into a threat in people's daily lives: the devil gave his witches the skill of performing "harmful magic".[128] A theological subtlety here, as least to the educated classes, was that witches did not possess magical power themselves. Their abilities always depended on the cooperation of demons, which, in its turn, depended on divine permission.[129] Yet, this nuance did not make its horrors any less frightening, as the harms that witches inflicted on decent Christians were terrifying.[130] They were known to cause sickness in people as well as in cattle by putting poisons in food and drinks, or by breathing or blowing on them. They threw herbs or pieces of straw on the ground that caused terrible pains when people or animals crossed them. They buried heads and skins of snakes under thresholds to create hatred in households. Witches drained people's resources, for instance by flying into cellars to drink barrels of wine, or by creating weather conditions, like frosts and hailstorms, that destroyed harvests. A particular focus of the witches' malign intents was children.[131] They dropped poison on them, suffocated them by smothering them with a mattress, or snatched children from the cradle to cut them in pieces or to suck their blood. A broadsheet from Ulm in 1590 even reported about a witch who had sacrificed her own child.[132]

Another target of the witches' assaults were the powers of male sexuality. One of their notorious magical activities was the tying of knots, mostly known by its French name "nouer

---

[126] Levack, *The Witch-Hunt in Early Modern Europe*, 41–45; Hutton, *The Witch*, 204–6; Dillinger, *Hexen und Magie*, 2018, 44–62; Bodin, *De la démonomanie des sorciers*, 226.
[127] Machielsen, *Martin Delrio*, 94.
[128] Levack, *The Witch-Hunt in Early Modern Europe*, 3–12; Dillinger, *Hexen und Magie*, 2018, 19–24.
[129] Förner, *Dämonenglaube und Zauberei im Jahre 1625*, 82; Dillinger, *Hexen und Magie*, 2018, 43; Nider, "Formicarius," 149; Bodin, *De la démonomanie des sorciers*, 278.
[130] Machielsen, *Martin Delrio*, 117–37; Lancre, *On the Inconstancy of Witches*, 546; Mirandola, *La sorcière*, 177; Rémy, *Demonolatry*, 67–68, 115–20; Schultheis, *Eine Außführliche Instruction*, 71.
[131] Rio and Maxwell-Stuart, *Investigations into Magic*, 119–20; Binsfeld, *Tractat Von Bekantnuß der Zauberer unnd Hexen*, 55.
[132] Behringer, *Hexen und Hexenprozesse in Deutschland*, 221.

l'aiguillette", which caused impotence among men.[133] The *Malleus Maleficarum* contained a report about something perhaps even more worrisome: witches removed penises.[134] The book maintained that witches "sometimes keep large numbers of these members (twenty or thirty at once) in a bird's nest or in some cabinet, where the members move as if alive or eat stalk or fodder, as many have seen." Men could retrieve their penises, as the authors also recounted the following incident:

> A certain man reported that when he had lost his member and gone to a certain sorceress to regain his well-being, she told the sick man that he should climb a certain tree and granted that he could take whichever one he wanted from the nest, in which there were very many members. When he tried to take a particular large one, the sorceress said, "You shouldn't take that one," adding that it belonged to one of the parish priests.[135]

This story was probably known at the time as a joke, but to the authors of the *Malleus Maleficarum* it was no laughing matter – they took it at face value.[136] Somewhat reassuring, perhaps, was that the penises were not literally removed, as demonic forces could only create the illusion that they had been taken away. But this did not make the experience less terrifying, and the story shows how the concept of witchcraft could tap into male anxieties about women. A woodcut from 1544, made by the German painter Hans Baldung Grien, vividly illustrates this dimension.[137] It shows how a groom is lying stretched out on the floor of a stable – a clearly visible crotch emphasizes his masculinity – after a witch has killed him with a magical torch. The hag is visible in the upper right corner of the picture, with wild hair, and breasts hanging out of her clothes. For men at the time, it must have been a frightening picture, showing male powerlessness against the treacherous forces of female witchcraft.

The witches' hidden identity
Diabolical witchcraft was extremely dangerous, but also difficult to combat. The identity of witches remained concealed and they pretended to be good neighbors.[138] So an aunt, the baker, or a friendly neighbor could already be a witch for months or years without anyone noticing anything. The magic, flights and sabbaths normally happened in secret, and the devil and his witches tried to ensure that nobody saw such things happening.[139] "Much is hidden, below the

---

[133] Wilson, *The Magical Universe*, 140; Bodin, *De la démonomanie des sorciers*, 182–83, 421; Daneau, *Les Sorciers*, 62; Boguet, *Discours exécrable des sorciers*, 148–49, 170.
[134] Stephens, *Demon Lovers*, 302–9; Goodare, *The European Witch-Hunt*, 305.
[135] Institoris, *The Hammer of Witches*, 328.
[136] Institoris, 328.
[137] Zika, *The Appearance of Witchcraft*, 32–34.
[138] Binsfeld, *Tractat Von Bekantnuß der Zauberer unnd Hexen*, 39–40; Goodare, *The European Witch-Hunt*, 14; Schultheis, *Eine Außführliche Instruction*, 308.
[139] Schultheis, *Eine Außführliche Instruction*, 4, 22.

surface, and secret", an author from the French town of Arras noted.[140] It was pointless to check whether alleged witches were sleeping in their beds at night, because demons created an illusion that made it look as if the witches decently slept at home. So even their husbands and wives could be clueless about the feasting at night.[141] There were some occasional reports about people who had seen witches flying, or who had gotten a glimpse of their gatherings, as was for instance recounted by the fifteenth-century French inquisitor Nicolas Jacquier.[142] He claimed to have spoken with trustworthy people who had come across a witches' assemblage while they were travelling at night, and immediately fell ill as soon as the witches saw them. During subsequent interrogations the suspected witches confessed that they had seen the wayfarers, and that demons had whipped them for letting themselves be discovered so easily. Such witness reports, however, were the exception.

Hence, if the witches' activities and identities were largely concealed, how was one going to find out who the witches were? A first indication for someone being a witch could be a person's bad name within a local community.[143] A reputation for maleficent magic could be an indication, but there were also other dimensions of people's daily behavior which could offer clues.[144] For instance, witches often tended to harm people with whom they had lingering, albeit somewhat unexpressed enmities. So, were there perhaps individuals with whom others did not get along very well?[145] Why had a certain person suddenly showed up in someone's house just before the cow fell ill, and had this same person not lately been heard talking with someone while they were supposed to be alone? In other words, was he or she in contact with demons? Strange and inexplicable sounds coming from someone's house in the night could be interpreted as a further hint. People who were caught up in a mountain storm and returned drenched might give occasion to gossiping about weather magic or visits to the sabbath. The suspicions about a woman named Margareth Shoe in the German city of Filzen started after uncanny events during her marriage.[146] People had noticed that her wedding procession was encircled by a hare, and what was particularly suspect was that the dogs who had followed the procession made no attempts to go after the hare. So, might the hare actually be a demon? Later on, people were warned not to chase the hare, because someone who tried to do so broke his neck in the forest. These stories eventually resulted in the burning of Margareth Shoe in 1626. Thus, bad reputations and other suspicious clues could be a starting point for an investigation. Martin Delrio wrote: "the accused must be notorious or the object of common gossip."[147]

---

[140] Anonymous of Arras, "A History of the State, Case, and Condition of the Waldensian Heretics," 28.
[141] Rio and Maxwell-Stuart, *Investigations into Magic*, 91–92; Rémy, *Demonolatry*, 43–44; Boguet, *Discours exécrable des sorciers*, 95–96.
[142] Stephens, *Demon Lovers*, 135.
[143] Institoris, *The Hammer of Witches*, 503; Schultheis, *Eine Außführliche Instruction*, 179–84; Boguet, *Discours exécrable des sorciers*, 407.
[144] Dillinger, *Böse Leute*, 186–91; Briggs, *Witches & Neighbours*, 42.
[145] Briggs, *Witches & Neighbours*, 94, 138.
[146] Dillinger, *Böse Leute*, 189.
[147] Rio and Maxwell-Stuart, *Investigations into Magic*, 191.

A few hurdles still needed to be cleared before a witches' identity could be established. Many parts of Europe at the time applied Roman Law, which required certain degrees of evidence, and rumors alone were insufficient. So, this made the hidden crime of witchcraft notoriously difficult to prove in a legal procedure.[148] However, there was an opening. Roman Law gave much credence to confessions of criminals, so what if one could make suspected witches confess to their deeds, for instance through painful questioning?[149] The use of torture during judicial procedures was not unusual at the time, and authorities often had a wide arsenal of devices at their disposal, like the rack, the ladder, thumb screws, leg screws, or head clamps. Yet, witch-hunters still faced the problem that the practice of torture was legally restricted in several ways. Law books prescribed that torture could not be applied more than three times, that leading questioning was prohibited, and that prisoners had the right to retract their confessions later on. But a crucial development of the age was that witchcraft gradually became known as a "crimen exceptum" – an extraordinary crime that required extraordinary means of investigation.[150] Most importantly, this implied that normal restrictions on torture could be discarded. Painful questioning also created the possibility of making witches confess who else they had seen at the sabbath. In an extensive book on witchcraft, the renowned French jurist Jean Bodin optimistically wrote that "only one is needed to denounce an infinite number of them."[151]

There were also some additional forms of evidence that persecutors could look for.[152] They could ascertain whether the accused were in possession of suspicious witchcraft equipment, like unguents and wax figures. There was also the belief that suspects could have a "devil's mark" somewhere on their skin, like a blemish, given by the devil after the witches had entered into the pact. Somewhat more unusual, and rejected by many persecutors, was the so called water ordeal, in which the floating of suspects in water was seen as proof of witchcraft.[153] Last but not least, one category of witnesses was potentially helpful during an investigation: children.[154] Especially from the late sixteenth century onwards it was highlighted that children could be witches too, and were taken to the sabbaths by their witch parents. This created persecutory opportunities, because in contrast to adult witches these children were less reluctant to tell inquisitors what they wanted to hear.

A robust concept

---

[148] Monter, "Witch Trials in Continental Europe 1560-1660," 8; Bodin, *De la démonomanie des sorciers*, 119.
[149] Roper, *Witch Craze*, 44–66; Rummel and Voltmer, *Hexen und Hexenverfolgung*, 48–51; Goodare, *The European Witch-Hunt*, 195, 202–9; Levack, *The Witch-Hunt in Early Modern Europe*, 68–81.
[150] Binsfeld, *Tractat Von Bekantnuß der Zauberer unnd Hexen*, 62–83; Boguet, *Discours exécrable des sorciers*, 405–6.
[151] Bodin, *De la démonomanie des sorciers*, 355."et n'en faut qu'un pour en accuser une infinité."
[152] Rummel and Voltmer, *Hexen und Hexenverfolgung*, 45–48; Goodare, *The European Witch-Hunt*, 197–202; Rémy, *Demonolatry*, 8–11; Schultheis, *Eine Außführliche Instruction*, 113.
[153] Rio and Maxwell-Stuart, *Investigations into Magic*, 188; Lancre, *On the Inconstancy of Witches*, 31; Schultheis, *Eine Außführliche Instruction*, 109–10; Boguet, *Discours exécrable des sorciers*, 413.
[154] Walinski-Kiehl, "The Devil's Children"; Dillinger, *Kinder im Hexenprozess*.

The cumulative concept of witchcraft gained more and more credence in the course of the fifteenth and sixteenth centuries, and spread through scholarly works, pamphlets, sermons, newssheets, conversations, and visual images such as woodcuts and drawings.[155] The concept also continued to face much resistance, but it increasingly developed abilities of evading those criticisms. Opponents might for instance object that innocent people could become victims of gossiping, but the *Malleus Maleficarum* assured that angels would not allow that to happen.[156] Or critics might wonder whether the use of torture stimulated false confessions and denouncements, but here witch-hunters retorted that God himself disallowed that.[157] If critics pointed out that the proof for witchcraft during an investigation was shaky, proponents could easily respond that demonic forces were continually removing all the evidence, implying that procedures needed to be continued.[158] *Any* subsequent event during a trial could then be interpreted as further proof that persecutors were on the right track. If physical torments made suspects confess quickly, it showed their guilt. But if they did not confess quickly, it probably resulted from demons who assisted the suspects in their ability to withstand torture, which also indicated guilt.[159] If the accused responded emotionally, it was thought to be very suspicious. But if they did not respond emotionally enough, it was equally suspicious, as it suggested an evil personality or demonic support.[160] Probably most suspect of all were the people who criticized witch-hunts and were unwilling to cooperate. These individuals were likely witches themselves.[161]

On top of that, the cumulative concept increasingly gained the weight of authority. There had been the papal bull of 1484, and some of the period's best minds endorsed the concept. Jean Bodin is still cherished as one of the sharpest political thinkers of the age who pioneered the concept of national sovereignty, and while Martin Delrio is somewhat forgotten today, his contemporaries considered him a genius – "the miracle of our age" Justus Lipsius called him.[162] Many eminent rulers condoned witch trials, and the increasing number of persecutions seemed to substantiate that the network was real. People were also warned not to think lightly of *not* acting against this sect.[163] Diabolical witchcraft combined some of the worst crimes imaginable, like heresy, blasphemy, murder, unnatural sex, and hatred of God. So, this was a real super-crime.[164] Martin Delrio wrote that "never have there been as many witches as there are today",

---

[155] Levack, *The Witch-Hunt in Early Modern Europe*, 47–56.
[156] Institoris, *The Hammer of Witches*, 358.
[157] Binsfeld, *Tractat Von Bekantnuß der Zauberer unnd Hexen*, 142–47; Anonymous of Arras, "A History of the State, Case, and Condition of the Waldensian Heretics," 59–61; Schultheis, *Eine Außführliche Instruction*, 57.
[158] Roper, *Witch Craze*, 76.
[159] Roper, 47; Krause, *Witchcraft, Demonology, and Confession in Early Modern France*, 26.
[160] Ostling and Kounine, "Introduction," 3–4.
[161] Rio and Maxwell-Stuart, *Investigations into Magic*, 203–6; Lancre, *On the Inconstancy of Witches*, 7; Meder, *Acht Hexenpredigten*, 15.
[162] Clark, *Thinking with Demons*, 668–82; Machielsen, *Martin Delrio*; Trevor-Roper, *The European Witch-Craze*, 80.
[163] Schultheis, *Eine Außführliche Instruction*, 502.
[164] Agricola, "Gründtlicher Bericht."

and Peter Binsfeld rhetorically asked his readers: "should we let this horrendous crime continue unpunished? Will we condone that their attacks and deeds against Holy Grace and the general good remain hidden? Shall we allow that day by day ever more people are being pulled into this diabolical congregation?"[165] Binsfeld presaged that God would not think lightly of that.[166]

It is worth pointing out that we should not interpret this idea of a "cumulative concept of witchcraft" in an overly rigid manner, as there was significant variation in what people believed. Did witches have the ability of metamorphosis?[167] Was the water ordeal any good, and did flights to the sabbath happen literally, or was this only an illusion created by demons?[168] Experts at the time disagreed about such questions. Or take the witches' sabbath.[169] To the literate classes this often mattered greatly because they were primarily focused on the demonological aspects of witchcraft. To many peasants on the other hand, notions of a sabbath do not seem to have mattered that much, at least not initially. Ordinary people were more focused on maleficent magic within their communities.[170] In addition, there was much diversity as to what people thought was going on at the sabbath. Some perceived it as a highly elaborate inversion of the Holy Mass, while others tended to think of an ordinary village festival with some grotesque elements. Beliefs about the sabbath were also characterized by much regional and temporal variation. The notion was central to late sixteenth- and early seventeenth-century imaginations about witchcraft, but far less significantly so in earlier ones, and in England and Holland it never gained much traction.[171]

In other words, it is important to keep in mind that there was no such thing as "the" cumulative concept of witchcraft. Instead, there were diverse, varying and changing concepts. This observation makes some experts today wary about using the term "cumulative concept" at all.[172] Still, there are good reasons for treating the belief in diabolical witchcraft as a somewhat unified phenomenon. First of all, because it is not anachronistic to do so. Authors like Delrio, Bodin and De Lancre at the time emphasized that witches did different things in different countries, but that they were still a part of the same diabolical sect.[173] Second, during a particular period of time the foregoing ideas about witchcraft very often *did* cluster together, and retained

---

[165] Rio and Maxwell-Stuart, *Investigations into Magic*, 27; Binsfeld, *Tractat Von Bekantnuß der Zauberer unnd Hexen*, 103. "Sollen dann ihre Laster ungestrafft durchgehen? Sollen ihre Rathschläge und Händel gegen gemeinen Nutz, unnd aller frommen Heyl angestellet also verborgen bleiben? Daß von tag zu tag, ihre länger ihe mehr Menschen verführt, unnd in die Teufflische gesellschaft eingezoge[n] werden?".
[166] Binsfeld, *Tractat Von Bekantnuß der Zauberer unnd Hexen*, 24, 26, 102.
[167] Levack, *The Witch-Hunt in Early Modern Europe*, 45–46.
[168] Clark, *Thinking with Demons*, 91.
[169] Blécourt, "Sabbath Stories"; Dillinger, *Hexen und Magie*, 2018, 62–72.
[170] Levack, *The Witch-Hunt in Early Modern Europe*, 53–55; Goodare, *The European Witch-Hunt*, 151; Closson, *L'imaginaire démoniaque en France (1550-1650)*, 38–39.
[171] Thomas, *Religion and the Decline of Magic*, 526–29; Waardt, *Toverij en samenleving*.
[172] Briggs, *Witches & Neighbours*, 7; Briggs, "Many Reasons Why," 54; Broedel, "Fifteenth-Century Witch Beliefs," 33; Blécourt, "Sabbath Stories"; Kieckhefer, "Mythologies of Witchcraft in the Fifteenth Century."
[173] Bodin, *De la démonomanie des sorciers*, 79, 385; Rio and Maxwell-Stuart, *Investigations into Magic*, 232; Lancre, *On the Inconstancy of Witches*, 146, 540.

a certain degree of coherence and stability.[174] When combined they could also have quite similar effects. This amalgam of ideas developed a striking capacity to trigger witch panics that spiraled out of control. To see how this could work, we now move to the German prince-bishopric of Bamberg in the year 1626.

4.4 The dynamics of witch-hunting

In the spring of 1626, the Catholic prince-bishopric of Bamberg seemed to be facing a relatively favorable future.[175] The small principality was located in the region of Franconia, in what is now southern Germany, and was part of the old and heterogeneous political body of the Holy Roman Empire. Like much of the empire, the prince-bishopric had recently experienced economic restraints, extreme weather conditions, and escalating religious and political tensions.[176] The region was fractured between Catholic and Protestant principalities, and while there were moderate factions on both sides of the divide, more militant forms of religious fervor were on the rise. An assertive new Catholicism following from the Counter-Reformation movement had alerted the Protestants, and in 1618 it was one of the triggers for a Protestant revolt against the Catholic emperor in the nearby kingdom of Bohemia. It would mark the beginning of the Thirty Years' War. As a devoutly Catholic territory, Bamberg had already expelled its own Protestants, and when the war broke out it supported the emperor with troops.[177] Later on, when the warfare moved into western parts of the empire, armies had also traversed Bamberg's own lands. But in the spring of 1626 the prospects were beginning to look more fortunate again. Catholic armies were making progress against their enemies, and encroached on the dominantly Protestant north. The victories triggered an atmosphere of Catholic euphoria.[178] On top of that, the winter of 1626 had been mild, so the corn was already flowering in May, promising rich harvests. A priest in the Bamberg town of Scheßlitz reported in his diary that the crops seemed to be growing richer and more plentiful than people could remember.[179]

But then, in the night of 27 May, tragedy struck. Throughout southern Germany the weather had been terrible, with hailstones the size of walnuts, and a frost that was so very heavy that it seemed mid-winter. The effects in Bamberg were dramatic. The fruits on the trees, the corn in the fields, and the wine grapes in the hills and mountains were frozen.[180] People in the region were upset, as the frost had severely damaged the harvests. Soon questions were asked and rumors spread about how this had happened. Obviously, this kind of weather at this time of year was strange and suspicious, so had it not been caused by internal enemies? Was this not the

---

[174] Levack, *The Witch-Hunt in Early Modern Europe*, 159–60; Goodare, *The European Witch-Hunt*, 26–27.
[175] Gehm, *Die Hexenverfolgung im Hochstift Bamberg*, 90–99.
[176] Wilson, *Heart of Europe*; Wilson, *The Thirty Years War*, 197–213; Münkler, *Der Dreissigjährige Krieg*, 41–380.
[177] Gehm, *Die Hexenverfolgung im Hochstift Bamberg*, 94–100.
[178] Gehm, 95.
[179] Jung, "Die Bamberger Hexenverfolgungen," 73–74.
[180] Parker, *Global Crisis*, 220; Jung, "Die Bamberger Hexenverfolgungen," 73–74; Gehm, *Die Hexenverfolgung im Hochstift Bamberg*, 100–102.

work of evil witches? In the small city of Zeil, located close to Bamberg, a farmer and city official named Johann Langhans reported the following course of events in his diary:

> Anno 1626, the 27th of May, the wine grapes in the Franconian bishoprics of Bamberg and Würzburg all got frozen as well as the dear grain, so much died (...) everything froze, it was worse than anyone could remember, causing an enormous rise in prices (...) thereupon there were many pleas and requests from the populace, asking why we were standing by while the sorcerers and witches were spoiling the fruits, so his princely highness did nothing less than start the punishment of this evil. [181]

That so many people in Bamberg thought of witches as the cause of their troubles did not come out of the blue. Fears about witchcraft had become rampant in many parts of Germany during preceding decades.[182] Newssheets, sermons, gossip, and scholarly tracts warned about the terrible harm that witches might cause, and throughout the empire people demanded and petitioned their authorities to take action. From around 1590 a new and ominous kind of witch persecution had appeared – William Monter calls it the "superhunt" – which could kill up to hundreds of people.[183] The cities and regions of places like Trier, Mainz, Eichstätt, Fulda, Würzburg, and Ellwangen had already experienced its devastating effects. For quite some time the prince-bishopric of Bamberg had remained largely unaffected by witch trials, because, amongst other things, its ruling bishop until 1609, Johann Philipp von Gebsattel, had been a Renaissance prince who was more interested in power and pleasure than religious zealotry.[184] However, his successors were influenced by the religious fervor of the Counter-Reformation, and possessed an ardent desire to turn their prince-bishopric into a godly state, without drunkenness, cursing, blaspheming, dancing at weddings, and also without witches.[185]

A first significant set of trials in Bamberg occurred in 1612 in the small town of Kronach.[186] An old woman named Lena Pantzerin had built a reputation for magical powers within her community, and after her own daughter and son-in-law officially accused her of witchcraft, the authorities started a trial against her. Pantzerin was arrested, tortured, and confessed to being a witch. She also mentioned some names of accomplices, which triggered a small chain of accusations that led to the arrest and torturing of fifteen more people, including the daughter of

---

[181] Gehm, *Die Hexenverfolgung im Hochstift Bamberg*, 100–101; Stickler, *Eine Stadt im Hexenfieber*, 74-5. "Anno 1626 den 27.May ist der weinwachs im Frankenland im Stift Bamberg vnt Würtzburg aller erfroren, wie auch das lieve korn, das allerley verblüeht (...) alles erfroren, das bei manns gedanken nit beschenen unt eine große teuerung verursacht (...) Hirauf ein großes Flehen unt bitten unter den gemeinen Pöffel, warumb man so lang zusehe das allbereit die Zauberer unt Unholden die früchten sogar verderben, wie dan ihr fürstliche Gnaden nichts weniger verursacht solches Uebel abzustrafen".
[182] Behringer, *Witches and Witch-Hunts*, 83–111; Behringer, *Hexen und Hexenprozesse in Deutschland*, 130–249.
[183] Monter, "Witch Trials in Continental Europe 1560-1660," 23.
[184] Gehm, *Die Hexenverfolgung im Hochstift Bamberg*, 36–38, 41; Dippold, "Die 'Hexenpolitik' Der Bamberg Fürstbischöfe," 46–48.
[185] Walinski-Kiehl, "Witch-Hunting and State Building," 251; Gehm, *Die Hexenverfolgung im Hochstift Bamberg*, 39–99.
[186] Gehm, *Die Hexenverfolgung im Hochstift Bamberg*, 47–56; Dippold, "Die 'Hexenpolitik' Der Bamberg Fürstbischöfe," 48.

Lena Pantzerin who had initiated the trial in the first place. Eventually, at least six people were killed. These events were still quite moderate in comparison to a set of trials that began in 1616. Around this time, the region experienced a terribly dry summer, followed by an unusually wet autumn, which damaged many crops.[187] The calamities were interpreted as witchcraft, and in the small city of Zeil a persecution of the allegedly responsible witches began.[188] In this case, the snowballing of accusations led to many more arrests, as the trials spread from Zeil to other towns and villages of the prince-bishopric. Eventually it killed probably around two hundred people. The persecution only came to an end in 1619, after the authorities of Bamberg had become divided about it.[189] A faction that was influenced by the Counter-Reformation wanted the hunt to continue, but they were resisted by another faction that had the powerful and wealthy chancellor of the bishop as its most important representative. Georg Haan was his name, and he had been appointed by the former prince-bishop Von Gebsattel. When Bamberg entered the war against the Bohemian rebels, Haan used the expenditure for troops as an excuse to cut off the trials' money supply. The end of the persecution left the opposing faction with a feeling of resentment against Haan, and a fear that the witches' network had not been fully wiped out.

The ultimate representative of the zealous mood in Bamberg was Friedrich Förner, the suffragan bishop.[190] Förner had been born in the region, and was later educated in Rome where he became an uncompromising proponent of Counter-Reformation ideas. After his return, he grew into a charismatic preacher of Bamberg's imposing cathedral. Many sermons that he gave during the years prior to 1626 have been published, so we know what they were like, and it was surely a frightening picture that he presented to his congregation.[191] Förner warned that Satan, filled with his hatred of humankind, was encircling the flock like a roaring lion, seeking whom to devour. By becoming Protestants many people had already been entangled in his nets, but to the devil's dismay Bamberg had expelled its Protestants, robbing him of one of his key tools. So, with his sharp eyes Satan was now looking for Catholics whom he could remove from the true faith by pulling them into his secret arch-heresy of evil magic and poisoning.[192] Recently, Bamberg had experienced what these people were capable of: they had made sacrifices to the devil, dug up the corpses of children, poisoned pregnant women, practiced sodomy, and performed almost every other sin imaginable.[193]

Förner presaged that the danger was not over yet. Evil sorcery was like a disease, and its rootlets were penetrating Catholic society more deeply every day. Through their sins people offered the devil an opening, for instance when they sought the protection of amulets, when they consulted old women for magical cures, or when they were lustful, gluttonous, greedy, idle,

---

[187] Parker, *Global Crisis*, 213.
[188] Gehm, *Die Hexenverfolgung im Hochstift Bamberg*, 57–89; Dippold, "Die 'Hexenpolitik' Der Bamberg Fürstbischöfe," 51.
[189] Gehm, *Die Hexenverfolgung im Hochstift Bamberg*, 41, 79–89; Renczes, *Wie löscht man eine Familie aus?*, 46–58.
[190] Gehm, *Die Hexenverfolgung im Hochstift Bamberg*, 42–47, 97–100; Jung, "Die Bamberger Hexenverfolgungen," 70–85.
[191] Förner, *Dämonenglaube und Zauberei im Jahre 1625*.
[192] Förner, 7–8, 185–86.
[193] Förner, 97–102.

or overly curious.[194] Women were particularly susceptible to lust, as "all female witches are the slaves of Venus." Förner also referred to children as a category that was vulnerable to curiosity. He described a recent case of a boy who was fascinated by the story of Dr. Faustus making a pact with the Devil, but then the boy was himself seduced by the devil into witchcraft.[195] "Put on the full armor of God, so that you can take your stand against the devil's schemes", was the biblical quote that the suffragan bishop cited the most. He urged his audience to seek the protection of the Holy Faith and all its practices and institutions.[196] But this was not yet enough, as diabolical evil would never stop by itself. The preacher reminded the divinely ordained authorities of their obligation to:

> *accuse, scold, tear out, destroy, chastise, and eliminate* this plague of the soul; destroy this fatal monstrosity within our community, tear it out by the root, tear off its poison-soaked limbs within the republic (...), to ensure that *the healthy part will not be impaired* and *the sick cattle will not infect the entire sheepfold*.[197]

Luckily for Förner, the new prince-bishop of Bamberg since 1623 was Johann Georg Fuchs von Dornheim, who ardently believed in the danger of diabolical witchcraft.[198] So when the populace in 1626 demanded their authorities take action, they found a sympathetic ear. The first serious allegations occurred in the small city of Zeil again.[199] A boy named Paul Rüghamer allegedly told stories about visits to a witches' dance, which alerted the local bailiff. The boy was arrested, and he indeed began to tell staggering stories about visits to a sabbath and the specific adults from Zeil whom he had seen there. The bailiff reported the case to Bamberg, and the prince-bishop decided to form a special *Hexenkommission*, a witch commission, that would lead an investigation in Zeil. The committee installed itself in one of the local towers, and inquiries began.

An escalating hunt
First, the commission arrested some of the people the boy had mentioned. The suspects were subjected to a standardized investigatory protocol containing questions such as: "Did you dance with the devil, and what other witches were present?", "How often did you bewitch livestock, cause tempests, hailstorms and night frosts?", and "How often did you fly on your broomstick

---

[194] Förner, 201-2. 241-62.
[195] Förner, 247–48, 306-7."und alle Zauberinnen Sklavinnen der Venus sind."
[196] Förner, 262–658.
[197] Förner, 131-2."klage an, schelte, reiße aus und verderbe, züchtige, und beseitige solcher Art Seelenpest; der Gemeinschaft der Menschen verderbenbringende Ungeheuer vernichte; rotte sie aus von den Wurzeln an; reiß ab die giftgetränkten Glieder (...), damit der gesunde Teil nicht beeinträchtigt wird und das erkrankte Vieh nicht den ganzen Schafstall ansteckt."
[198] Gehm, *Die Hexenverfolgung im Hochstift Bamberg*, 90–102.
[199] Dippold, "Die 'Hexenpolitik' Der Bamberg Fürstbischöfe," 52–53; Gehm, *Die Hexenverfolgung im Hochstift Bamberg*, 100–106; Dippold, "Hexereiprozesse Im Hochstift Bamberg," 232.

through the chimney to the devil's dance?"[200] The suspects were unwilling to confess, so the investigators took them to the torture chamber in the tower, showing them devices like thumb screws, leg screws, the wooden horse, and the strappado. When the sight of these tools still failed to make them talk, the suspects' bodies were shaven and painful questioning was started. Not surprisingly, confessions soon followed. A woman named Katharina Merckhlerin crucially admitted that she had taken part in a diabolical conspiracy that had created the recent frost.[201] To the witch commission, this confirmed they were onto the network, so investigations were intensified. More confessions followed, more names of accomplices were mentioned, and the circle of suspects and arrests began to widen. Soon the tower prisons were insufficient to house the accused, so additional prisons were built in a part of the city wall and some burgher houses. By January 1627 the commission had already imprisoned thirty people, of whom twenty confessed and were sentenced to death. The convicts were first decapitated, and then burned in public at the stake for the sake of destruction and purification.[202]

So far, the trials were restricted to Zeil and the city of Bamberg had remained unaffected. But in the spring of 1627 Bamberg itself was also confronted with voluntary confessions of a boy, named Hans Morhaupt, the son of a mayor. The witch commission took him into custody for interrogation.[203] At first the boy seemed intimidated, but after some time he apparently began to enjoy all the attention that he received. Without any torture he told astounding stories about a diabolical conspiracy in the city. For him personally, it had all started at his Jesuit school, where he read a book about Dr. Faustus, which his teachers took away from him. In order to retrieve the book, Hans made a pact with the devil, which introduced him into a marvelous world of witchcraft. He entered a sexual relationship with a female demon named "Kandel", and with his mother and her maid he flew on a pitchfork through a window in the attic to a witches' dance, where he met people from the prominent circle of his family. Whether Hans Morhaupt understood the consequences of his words is questionable, as it resulted in his own death at the stake, along with that of much of his family.

The new trials in the city created a novel sense of anger and panic, because the problem of witchcraft seemed worse than anticipated. Apparently, the satanic sect had even infiltrated the highest classes.[204] The persecution was continued with the support of much of the populace, qualified lawyers, clerics such as Förner, as well as the prince-bishop who was eager to rid his principality of this terrible "witch plague".[205] Meanwhile the weather remained awful. The summer of 1626 had been exceedingly dry, leaving very little hay in the fields, followed by a

---

[200] Stickler, *Eine Stadt im Hexenfieber*, 46."Mit dem Teufel getantzt- andere Unholden dabei?", "Wie oft Vieh verhext, Unwetter, Hagel, Nachtfrost gemacht?", "Wie oft auf dem Besen den Schlot hinaus zum Teufeltanz?" .
[201] Walinski-Kiehl, "Witch-Hunting and State Building," 258–59; Gehm, *Die Hexenverfolgung im Hochstift Bamberg*, 100–113.
[202] Dülmen, *Theater des Schreckens*, 125.
[203] Gehm, *Die Hexenverfolgung im Hochstift Bamberg*, 98–99, 116–18; Walinski-Kiehl, "The Devil's Children"; Jung, "Die Bamberger Hexenverfolgungen," 81–82.
[204] Gehm, *Die Hexenverfolgung im Hochstift Bamberg*, 107–70.
[205] Dippold, "Die 'Hexenpolitik' Der Bamberg Fürstbischöfe," 44; Dippold, "Hexereiprozesse Im Hochstift Bamberg," 230.

winter season of endless snow and a freezing cold that was again worse than people could remember. The summer and autumn of 1627 were characterized by intense rainfall, storms that destroyed people's houses, and a plague of caterpillars that ate away the trees.[206] This seemed to offer further proof that the network of witches had not been defeated yet.

The commission worked relentlessly. One of its members, Ernst Vasoldt, was obsessed by sabbath attendance, and even managed to extract 126 names of accomplices from one single suspect.[207] Ever more people were thrown into the dungeons, robbed of daylight, sufficient food, and contact with others, while the legal restrictions on the use of torture were violated. Still, many of the suspects remained unwilling to confess. But to the persecutors this only suggested that the devil was aiding his witches by making them insensitive to pain. It underlined the need to continue the case.[208] With all the new suspects in jail even the extended prisons in Zeil were no longer sufficient. So, in the summer of 1627 a new and large witch prison was built in the city of Bamberg. This so called *Malefizhaus* included twenty-six cells, as well as a room and a chapel where the witches could confess and repent. After all, while the witches' earthly existence was doomed, the persecutors still wanted to offer them the opportunity of heaven.[209]

With the new facilities at its disposal, the witch commission found a new target in Georg Haan. In 1619 Haan had been able to stop the hunt, but this time things took an unfortunate turn for the chancellor. First, his wife and daughter were arrested and killed, followed by his own arrest and that of his son. Haan's earlier resistance to the trials was now explicitly used against him. Eventually the whole family was burned at the stake, including many of their servants.[210] Now that the most powerful opponent of the trials had been crushed, the chain of accusations further exploded, with hundreds of new arrests and burnings.[211] Hardly anyone was safe from the investigations of the witch commission – women and men, seniors and children, as well as the rich and the poor were rounded up. Anyone who entered the *Malefizhaus* was almost certainly doomed. A significant part of the population in Zeil was wiped out, including almost the entire city council.[212] We can still trace the course of events in Johann Langhans's diary, who had to report about family members being killed.[213] During the trials of 1616-1619 he had already lost two aunts, who, as Langhans commented, had "turned away from God our savior and creator, forsaken the Lord, and given themselves to the Devil."[214] This time it became much worse, as an

---

[206] Parker, *Global Crisis*, 200; Jung, "Die Bamberger Hexenverfolgungen," 74.
[207] Walinski-Kiehl, "Witch-Hunting and State Building," 256; Walinski-Kiehl, "La chasse aux sorcières et le sabbat des sorcières dans les évêchés de Bamberg et Würzburg," 219.
[208] Gehm, *Die Hexenverfolgung im Hochstift Bamberg*, 26, 213; Walinski-Kiehl, "Males, 'Masculine Honor', and Witch Hunting," 258.
[209] Gehm, *Die Hexenverfolgung im Hochstift Bamberg*, 119–21; Jung, "Die Bamberger Hexenverfolgungen," 82.
[210] Renczes, *Wie löscht man eine Familie aus?*; Dippold, "Die 'Hexenpolitik' Der Bamberg Fürstbischöfe," 56–57; Gehm, *Die Hexenverfolgung im Hochstift Bamberg*, 87-8.
[211] Gehm, *Die Hexenverfolgung im Hochstift Bamberg*, 138–70.
[212] Dippold, "Die 'Hexenpolitik' Der Bamberg Fürstbischöfe," 68; Gehm, *Die Hexenverfolgung im Hochstift Bamberg*, 127–37; Stickler, *Eine Stadt im Hexenfieber*, 74.
[213] Stickler, *Eine Stadt im Hexenfieber*, 61–67.
[214] Stickler, 64."haben sich von gott den erschaffer vnt erlöser abgewent ihm verleugnet hergegen dem tepfel ergeben."

uncle was convicted, a stepsister, then his wife, his daughter, and in February 1628 the diary ends because Langhans was accused and burned as a witch himself. The effects in the city of Bamberg were not as drastic as in Zeil, but still severe. Especially for the elite the hunt was turning into a carnage.[215]

Amongst the victims was one of the mayors of Bamberg, Johannes Junius. There are no clues that Junius was an unpopular figure, or that he cultivated enemies. Still, after his wife was killed early 1628, he was imprisoned in the *Malefizhaus* in June of that year.[216] From his jail Junius wrote a letter to his daughter, which he tried to get smuggled out. His guards discovered the letter and added it to the trial records. It offers us a firsthand account of life in the *Malefizhaus*:

> Many hundred thousand good-nights, dearly beloved daughter Veronica. Innocent have I come into prison, innocent have I been tortured, innocent must I die. For whoever comes into the witch prison must become a witch or be tortured until he invents something out of his head – God pity me – bethinks him of something. I will tell you how it has gone on with me.[217]

Junius told his daughter about all the agonies that he had gone through, and excused himself for the bad handwriting – his interrogators had used thumbscrews that made the blood run out of his nails, which now made writing difficult. As he continued: "thereafter they first stripped me, bound my hands behind me, and drew me up in torture. Then I thought heaven and earth were at an end; eight times did they draw me up and let me fall again, so that I suffered terrible agony."[218] Eventually, after long resistance, the former mayor confessed almost everything that his interrogators wanted to hear, including the names of thirty accomplices. Junius urged his daughter to leave Bamberg as soon as possible, ending his letter with the words: "farewell, you will never see your father Johannes Junius again!"[219] Soon thereafter Junius was burned.

From the investigators' perspective, however, they were doing the noble work of uncovering a grotesque network of witches that was ravaging the area.[220] During the interrogations the committee learned that the witches were in continuous contact with Satan, had sex with demons, and desecrated holy symbols. Chancellor Haan, for instance, confessed that he had spat on the host and then danced upon it.[221] At night, the witches flew out to dance

---

[215] Gehm, *Die Hexenverfolgung im Hochstift Bamberg*, 148, 163; Dippold, "Die 'Hexenpolitik' Der Bamberg Fürstbischöfe," 68; Renczes, *Wie löscht man eine Familie aus?*, 142.
[216] Walinski-Kiehl, "Males, 'Masculine Honor', and Witch Hunting"; Gehm, *Die Hexenverfolgung im Hochstift Bamberg*, 152–57.
[217] Levack, *The Witchcraft Sourcebook*, 201.
[218] Walinski-Kiehl, "Males, 'Masculine Honor', and Witch Hunting," 261.
[219] Gehm, *Die Hexenverfolgung im Hochstift Bamberg*, 156."Leb wohl, Dein Vater Johannes Junius wird Dich nicht mehr wiedersehen!"
[220] Behringer, *Hexen und Hexenprozesse in Deutschland*, 261–64; Gehm, *Die Hexenverfolgung im Hochstift Bamberg*; Renczes, *Wie löscht man eine Familie aus?*; Dippold, "Die 'Hexenpolitik' Der Bamberg Fürstbischöfe," 35; Walinski-Kiehl, "Males, 'Masculine Honor', and Witch Hunting," 260.
[221] Renczes, *Wie löscht man eine Familie aus?*, 94.

together, for instance in a neighboring forest named the Hauptsmoorwald. They had even had the audacity to meet in Bamberg's council chamber. The harm that these servants of Satan were inflicting upon the population was startling: they stole milk, spoiled the wells, sickened livestock, and made people suffer from lice. A landlady from Zeil confessed that she had sold people fish, hares, and birds, while actually serving them mice, cats, and caterpillars.[222] The witches also killed children, or dug up their corpses, like a witch who had exhumed a child near a chapel while more than two hundred companions were watching.[223] It was further discovered that the recent storms, as well as the drought that ruined the hay, had been caused by the conspiracy. The witch commission had been just in time to thwart their new plans for creating a storm that was so powerful that it would destroy the cathedral.[224]

The events in Bamberg were spectacular, and the news about the hunt spread throughout the region. Newssheets told people about the terrible things that witches had done, and how they had been justly punished.[225] In nearby Schmalkalden a song was published that melodiously proclaimed why these witches deserved nothing but the fire.[226] But there were also critical voices. Citizens of Bamberg increasingly began to flee the city, telling their acquaintances elsewhere about the horrors and injustices of the trials.[227] As soon as the rich families were under attack, they began to make appeals to higher authorities elsewhere. The *Reichskammergericht* (Imperial Chamber Court) in Speyer indeed denounced many of the trials' procedures.[228] There were also some internal problems. At a certain point Ernst Vasoldt, the member of the witch commission, became drunk in a tavern in Zeil, losing his extensive list of further suspects. The document became known in Zeil, and created somewhat of an uproar in the city.[229] Vasoldt was discharged, but when the number of arrests kept growing, the initial popular support for trials in Zeil wavered. The committee faced an increasingly hostile mood, and at some point began arresting suspects at night to avoid troubles. Even the people who assisted the persecutors could not protect family members from being killed. It stimulated discussions within the witch commission about risks of harming the innocent.[230] A further problem was financial costs.[231] The procedures were so very expensive that they began to burden civic budgets, and in Zeil the committee was forced to build a witch oven to save costs of firewood. But due to the high number of rich witches executed, financial problems could be overcome: the rich witches' possessions were used for further

---

[222] Gehm, *Die Hexenverfolgung im Hochstift Bamberg*, 143.
[223] Stickler, *Eine Stadt im Hexenfieber*, 70.
[224] Behringer, *Hexen und Hexenprozesse in Deutschland*, 261–64.
[225] Behringer, 262–64; Gehm, *Die Hexenverfolgung im Hochstift Bamberg*, 143.
[226] Renczes, *Wie löscht man eine Familie aus?*, 154–57.
[227] Gehm, *Die Hexenverfolgung im Hochstift Bamberg*, 142, 148, 170.
[228] Dippold, "Hexereiprozesse Im Hochstift Bamberg," 57–58; Gehm, *Die Hexenverfolgung im Hochstift Bamberg*, 127–70.
[229] Gehm, *Die Hexenverfolgung im Hochstift Bamberg*, 108–22; Stickler, *Eine Stadt im Hexenfieber*, 63; Dippold, "Die 'Hexenpolitik' Der Bamberg Fürstbischöfe," 55.
[230] Gehm, *Die Hexenverfolgung im Hochstift Bamberg*, 164.
[231] Dippold, "Die 'Hexenpolitik' Der Bamberg Fürstbischöfe," 44–45, 55–56; Gehm, *Die Hexenverfolgung im Hochstift Bamberg*, 165–70.

funding.²³² This was in contravention of judicial rules, but Bamberg ignored those rules, just as it ignored the verdict from Speyer. The risks of self-incrimination also discouraged further internal criticisms. So, by 1630 there was still no prospect of an end.

A gradual slowdown
That the trials finally did begin to slow down was mostly due to outside forces.²³³ Citizens of Bamberg were making ever more appeals to authorities elsewhere about the "bloodthirsty, unchristian, and ruthless" policies of the witch commission, which brought "the city to the brink of ruin" and "the entire honorably citizenry to the ground." These complainants indeed found a sympathetic ear.²³⁴ In addition there was the spectacular escape of a landlady named Barbara Schwarz, who had been arrested in 1627. Despite *years* of torture and imprisonment she had not confessed, and in September 1630 she managed to file the bars of her prison. ²³⁵ After her escape Schwarz wrote an impressive letter to the emperor about everything that she had gone through, and received a safe conduct in return – her homecoming would be a disappointment though, as her husband wanted nothing to do with this "witch". In 1629 a woman from the prosperous and well-connected Flock family was arrested, and her husband moved heaven and earth to get her freed.²³⁶ His pleas to the emperor and the *Reichshofrat* – another judicial body of the empire – delivered two further condemnations of Bamberg's policies. At the Diet of Regensburg in 1630 officials from the prince-bishopric were openly criticized.²³⁷ As a defense, Bamberg relied on the concept of *crimen exceptum*, and the prince-bishop replied that he had "only lawfully conducted the trials for the sake of promoting and propagating the glory of God and for the salvation of many seduced souls, as was also done by other princes and electoral princes in our Holy Roman Empire." ²³⁸ His defense was to no avail. In 1631 the *Reichshofrat* issued a binding imperial mandate that ordered the prince-bishop to stop the trials immediately.²³⁹

The final end of the trials was due to another development, however. The odds in the Thirty Years' War had turned against the Catholic party and the war moved southwards again. In 1632 a Protestant Swedish army approached the city, and to its chagrin Bamberg found out that it was no longer able to defend itself. ²⁴⁰ The public budgets had largely been spent on witch trials, so there was not much money left for troops and fortifications. Johann Fuchs von Dornheim and

---

[232] Dippold, "Die 'Hexenpolitik' Der Bamberg Fürstbischöfe," 54.
[233] Gehm, *Die Hexenverfolgung im Hochstift Bamberg*, 171–228.
[234] Behringer, *Hexen und Hexenprozesse in Deutschland*, 389."blutgierig, unchristlich und unbarmherzig"; Bradford Smith, "The Persecution of Witches," 68.
[235] Dippold, "Die 'Hexenpolitik' Der Bamberg Fürstbischöfe," 35–36.
[236] Dippold, 58; Gehm, *Die Hexenverfolgung im Hochstift Bamberg*, 200–202.
[237] Behringer, *Hexen und Hexenprozesse in Deutschland*, 387–88; Gehm, *Die Hexenverfolgung im Hochstift Bamberg*, 171–210.
[238] Gehm, *Die Hexenverfolgung im Hochstift Bamberg*, 209; Behringer, *Hexen und Hexenprozesse in Deutschland*, 390."Solche Processe habe ich allein zur Ausbreitung und Beförderung der Ehre Gottes und zum Heile vieler verführten Seelen, wie andere Chürfürsten und Fürsten im Römischen Reiche mehr (...) rechtmässig geführt."
[239] Gehm, *Die Hexenverfolgung im Hochstift Bamberg*, 128, 160.
[240] Callow, *Embracing the Darkness*; Dippold, "Die 'Hexenpolitik' Der Bamberg Fürstbischöfe," 59; Gehm, *Die Hexenverfolgung im Hochstift Bamberg*, 224–28.

his allies saw no option but to flee the city. When the Swedes conquered Bamberg they encountered communities that had been ravaged by the preceding witch-hunt.[241] The city of Zeil was to a large extent depopulated and hardly any family had remained unharmed. In the city of Bamberg, the destruction of much of the upper class had damaged the economy. Many houses in Bamberg's most prestigious street, the Lange Gasse, were emptied, without anyone interested in buying them. The Swedes released the last ten suspects from the *Malefizhaus*, but for many others they had come too late. Around six hundred people in the prince-bishopric had been killed between 1626-1631, of whom around seventy percent were women.[242] The Nordic rule did not last long, as the Catholics soon recaptured the prince-bishopric, but not before the Swedes pillaged the lands even further. Yet, it seems that after all these horrors Bamberg did learn a lesson: apart from a few isolated burnings in the 1670s, the prince-bishopric would never experience a witch-hunt again.[243]

General traits of witch persecutions
Importantly, what happened in Bamberg was exceptional, and it was also exceptional by the standards of the time. In many cases witch trials involved the persecution of one or just a few people, and even those trials were only the tip of an iceberg of local angry exchanges and suspicions of witchcraft that did not result in criminal investigation.[244] This nuance brought some experts to the observation that focusing on large persecutions is somewhat misleading.[245] Big hunts often get much attention because they are spectacular, but they are not representative of the experience of witchcraft in early modern Europe. There is much to say for this argument, but at the same time the hunt of Bamberg was far from unique.[246] It had been preceded by somewhat similar hunts elsewhere, and a simultaneous persecution in nearby Würzburg killed around nine hundred people, while trials in the Electorate of Cologne even reached a number of around two thousand victims and possibly even more.[247] While chain-reaction hunts were only a small percentage of the total number of trials, they still seem responsible for a majority of the total number of executions.[248] The Bamberg trials also possessed many of witch-hunting's typical traits – the German expert Wolfgang Behringer even calls it "the 'ideal type' of massive witch-hunt."[249] So, if we want to understand what made the cumulative concept of witchcraft so inflammatory, Bamberg offers a fine case study for our current purposes.

---

[241] Gehm, *Die Hexenverfolgung im Hochstift Bamberg*, 139–48, 170–74.
[242] Gehm, 92-4. The sources provide explicit data about the death of at least 400 people, but considering the much higher number of arrests and the unlikelyhood of survival, the actual number probably lie around 600.
[243] Gehm, 224–31; Dippold, "Die 'Hexenpolitik' Der Bamberg Fürstbischöfe," 57–60.
[244] Briggs, *Witches & Neighbours*, 7, 75, 95; Levack, *The Witch-Hunt in Early Modern Europe*, 171–72.
[245] Briggs, *Witches & Neighbours*, 7; Midelfort, "Witch Craze?"
[246] Levack, *The Witch-Hunt in Early Modern Europe*, 172–75; Goodare, *The European Witch-Hunt*, 225–66.
[247] Behringer, *Witches and Witch-Hunts*, 130; Grawlich, "Der Hexenkommisar Heinrich von Schultheiß," 303–4.
[248] Goodare, *The European Witch-Hunt*, 118, 250.
[249] Behringer, *Witches and Witch-Hunts*, 115.

First of all, these trials illustrate how the cumulative concept could make unusual misfortune be interpreted as an act of diabolical witchcraft.[250] The frost of May 1626 was not just unusual – it was the result of the maleficent magic of satanic allies. What the trials of Bamberg further show is how two categories of potential suspects could get a trial going. First, there were the individuals who had built up reputations for harmful magic within their local communities, like Lena Pantzerin from Kronach.[251] Persecutions often began when local aggression against such people had reached intolerable levels. In some cases, communities took the initiative to kill such "village witches" themselves, but since authorities discouraged that, the more usual mechanism was that these people were reported to the local government. When the authorities then decided to grant such requests, a trial was started. The second category of suspects who got trials rolling was children. Here Paul Rüghamer and Hans Morhaupt are cases in point.[252] More so than adults, children were likely to offer their interrogators imaginative testimonies about witchcraft, making the use of torture unnecessary. They acted as star witnesses, providing the persecutors with a first list of accomplices.

When the first suspects were identified, the idea of witchcraft as a "crimen exceptum" then provided a crucial next step. Bamberg exemplifies how excessive torture enforced confessions. This was no exception. The historian Gerhard Schormann writes that "torture may not have been the cause of the witch trials, but it was an essential prerequisite for their massive implementation."[253] Without it, most of the apparently consistent confessions that kept the trials going on this scale would have been unthinkable.[254] The kind of questions that interrogators in Bamberg asked also typifies how the belief in the sabbath was essential.[255] Its key implication was that captured witches could tell who the other witches were. Julian Goodare rightly observes that it was only after elites started to believe in conspiracies that chain-reaction panics became a possibility.[256] The snowballing of accusations could also lead to the killing of people who were not associated with harmful magic at all, and who in many cases even had respectable positions within their communities, like mayor Johannes Junius. Brian Levack concludes that "without the belief in the sabbath European witch-hunting would have been much more limited in its scope and intensity."[257] Moreover, Bamberg's interrogations illustrate why nightly flight was important: it endowed witches with the opportunity to meet each other at various places in the middle of

---

[250] Levack, *The Witch-Hunt in Early Modern Europe*, 164–71; Rummel and Voltmer, *Hexen und Hexenverfolgung*, 87–88.
[251] Briggs, *Witches & Neighbours*, 95; Goodare, *The European Witch-Hunt*, 103–18; Behringer, *Hexenverfolgung in Bayern*, 184–85.
[252] Dillinger, *Kinder im Hexenprozess*; Walinski-Kiehl, "The Devil's Children"; Behringer, "Kinderhexenprozesse."
[253] Schormann, *Hexenprozesse in Deutschland*, 43, 52.
[254] Trevor-Roper, *The European Witch-Craze*, 42–45; Rummel and Voltmer, *Hexen und Hexenverfolgung*, 44–51; Dillinger, *Hexen und Magie*, 2018, 80–86.
[255] Cohn, *Europe's Inner Demons*, 252; Rummel and Voltmer, *Hexen und Hexenverfolgung*, 44–1; Levack, *The Witch-Hunt in Early Modern Europe*, 74–81.
[256] Goodare, *The European Witch-Hunt*, 225–63.
[257] Levack, *The Witch-Hunt in Early Modern Europe*, 37.

the night.[258] On top of that, the belief had the potential of making accusations spread over long distances, as witches were also supposed to know accomplices who lived far away.

Friedrich Förner's references to women as dangerous magical practitioners and "slaves of Venus" highlights a further key aspect: the predominant focus on women. Overall, the average percentage of female victims was probably even higher than in Bamberg, because estimations assume that the average percentage lay somewhere between seventy and eighty percent.[259] The local differences were significant though, as some regions almost exclusively executed women, while other regions had much higher percentages of male victims. Finally, the hunt in Bamberg was characteristic of the time and place in which it occurred. The overwhelming majority of the people executed died between 1560 and 1660, and probably more than half of them had lived within the boundaries of the Holy Roman Empire, speaking some dialect of German.[260] Central Europe was the ultimate hotbed of trials. Apart from the empire it was especially in parts of Switzerland, Poland, and the eastern border lands of France and the Southern Netherlands that burnings occurred. More peripheral pockets of intense hunting were to be found in the Basque country, Scandinavia and Scotland, while countries like England, Italy, France, the Northern Netherlands and Spain were characterized by more modest levels of persecution.

Bamberg thus gruesomely illustrates how the cumulative concept could trigger witch trials that were difficult to stop once set in motion. The underlying mechanisms of witch-hunting, and the way in which cumulative notions produced such lethal dynamics, have been analyzed by historians in detail. However, while their observations help us explain a great deal about witch-hunting, they still leave much unsolved. How could a phenomenon like this come into being? Why did it persist for such a long time? We will now begin to integrate the case study into the kind of functional and explanatory analyses that concern us in this dissertation. We explore what this case study may tell us about the origins and purposes of socio-cultural functions.

---

[258] Cohn, *Europe's Inner Demons*, 228–29, 252; Levack, *The Witch-Hunt in Early Modern Europe*, 41–42; Dillinger, Fritz, and Mährle, *Zum Feuer verdammt*, 34; Blécourt, "Sabbath Stories," 85.
[259] Levack, *The Witch-Hunt in Early Modern Europe*, 128–35; Rummel and Voltmer, *Hexen und Hexenverfolgung*, 79–80; Rowlands, "Witchcraft and Gender in Early Modern Europe," 449.
[260] Monter, "Witch Trials in Continental Europe 1560-1660," 14–16; Levack, *The Witch-Hunt in Early Modern Europe*, 184–223; Rummel and Voltmer, *Hexen und Hexenverfolgung*, 80–83.

Chapter 5: Explanations
5.1 An explanatory problem
What was the function of the witch-hunts? What was their purpose? If we would pose these questions to the historical actors who created and fostered the trials, they would probably be surprised. After all, the answer would have been obvious to them: evil minions of the devil were involved in conspiracies against Christianity, and launching magical attacks on the population. So, what would be a more functional thing to do than to halt such activities? The trials reduced the danger of diabolical witchcraft and this intended and recognized effect constituted their functionality. Henceforth, it is only to those who doubt the guilt of convicted witches, or to those who doubt the existence of diabolical witchcraft altogether, that questions about the hunts' functionality become a more challenging and theoretically interesting problem. If witch-hunts did *not* have the effect of stopping diabolical activities, what else were they for? Did persecutors use them as a device for alternative purposes? Did the trials have concealed functional causes and effects that the witch-hunters themselves were unaware of? Or is the question about their functionality wrongly asked?

These issues have been common themes throughout the history of scholarly debates about witch persecutions, and in the next sections we will look at various answers. But first we need to address the issue of diabolical witchcraft's reality, because it is the disavowal of its reality that gives rise to these questions in the first place. So, what was real about early modern witchcraft? And to what extent does it matter? These questions are more of an empirical and theoretical puzzle than one might first assume, and continue to divide scholarly opinion today. In what follows, I will provide a historical overview of the main perspectives that have been developed on the topic so far. This also offers the opportunity of introducing some of the key schools of thought in witchcraft historiography.

Contemporary skepticism
Doubts about the reality of the crime of diabolical witchcraft are not at all an invention of modernity. In fact, a certain degree of skepticism about the underlying assumptions of the persecutions is as old as those persecutions themselves. From its first beginnings proponents of witch-hunting faced resistance, and Julian Goodare even states that some skepticism remained "the default position" amongst judges throughout Europe.[1] But we should be careful about what we mean by "skepticism" in its early modern context. In many cases it did not imply that people doubted the possibility of diabolical witchcraft, let alone the main tenets of demonology. What mainstream skepticism at the time was about, was doubt about the guilt of the actual people who were burned as witches at the stake.[2] In this sense, some skepticism can even be found

---
[1] Goodare, *The European Witch-Hunt*, 354.
[2] Goodare, 79–82.

amongst zealous advocates of witch-hunting.³ Peter Binsfeld, for instance, expressed concerns about inexperienced persecutors who would proceed too quickly and ran a risk of torturing and imprisoning old women who had done nothing wrong.⁴ As discussed above, elements of cumulative witchcraft notions, such as nightly flight or metamorphosis, also remained contested all the time. Hence, there was no sharp distinction between "believers" and "skeptics", and we should rather look at those two positions as opposite ends of a wide spectrum of diverse and often ambiguous viewpoints.⁵

However, there was a contemporary strand of critique that had more pronounced misgivings about the reality of diabolical witchcraft and the validity of trials. As the French witch-hunter Henri Boguet complained in his book *Discours exécrable des sorcières* (The Wretched Discourse of Witches): "It is amazing that one can still find people today who believe that there are no witches at all."⁶ Such critics represented a view-point that today's scholarship describes as "the skeptical tradition".⁷ Amongst its most well-known exponents are the Dutch-German physician Johann Weyer, who in 1563 wrote an extensive critique named *De praestigiis daemonum* (On the Tricks of Demons), and the German Jesuit Friedrich Spee who in 1631 published his *Cautio criminalis* (Precautions for Prosecutors).⁸ Nineteenth and twentieth-century historiography has sometimes heralded such authors as precursors of a modern scientific outlook – the early rationalist voices crying out in a wilderness of irrationality and superstition.⁹ And indeed, their works contain critiques of the beliefs of their contemporaries that a modern rationalistic audience will be able to appreciate.

Johann Weyer mocked claims about the alleged powers of witches in ways that are still amusing today. He described how witches were supposed to ruin crops and pollute waters, and added that "these old women called *Lamiae,* by a single nod, will not only accomplish these things, but also smite armies, and shatter cities and regions, so that the enemy will consider themselves fortunate, if they are permitted to surrender."¹⁰ He then ironically wondered why generals do not use these marvelous powers in wars:

> What need then for expensive artillery? For quantities of that diabolical powder? For heaps of cannonballs and bullets? (...) This single "Empusa" of ours, the *Lamiae,* all by herself, will make manifest her omnipotence at this point. It will be appropriate to send

---

³ Levack, *The Witch-Hunt in Early Modern Europe*, 56.
⁴ Binsfeld, *Tractat Von Bekantnuß der Zauberer unnd Hexen* Vorrede.
⁵ Schwerhoff, "Rationalität im Wahn"; Clark, *Thinking with Demons*, 173–213.
⁶ Boguet, *Discours exécrable des sorciers*, i. "C'est merueille, que nous voyons encor' pour le iourd'huy des personnes, qui ne croyons point, qu-il y ait de sorciers".
⁷ Levack, *The Witch-Hunt in Early Modern Europe*, 56–59; Stephens, "The Skeptical Tradition"; Lehmann and Ulbricht, *Vom Unfug des Hexen-Processes*.
⁸ Weyer, *Witches, Devils, and Doctors in the Renaissance*; Spee von Langenfeld, *Cautio criminalis*.
⁹ See, for instance: White, *A History of the Warfare of Science with Theology in Christendom*, 350–63; For an overview, see: Elmer, "Science, Medicine and Witchcraft."
¹⁰ Weyer, *Witches, Devils, and Doctors in the Renaissance*, 218.

her against the Turk, so that Germany may be relieved and delivered once and for all from the burden of assembling help against the perpetual foe of Christianity! Indeed, we seem to have been going about blindly amidst the full light of day – we who have so stupidly neglected this possibility![11]

Weyer acknowledged that the use of diabolical forces in such ways would be an utterly unchristian thing to do, but many Christian princes did all sorts of disgraceful things, so why did they leave this option aside? With biting satire Weyer thus brought his readers to the conclusion that the assumed powers of witches were unlikely real.

Friedrich Spee took a similarly critical stance on his contemporaries' beliefs. As a priest he had been responsible for the pastoral needs of convicted witches, and he was horrified by what he saw.[12] His *Cautio criminalis* combined emotional observations about the suffering of the convicts with sharp critique of the inconsistencies of trials. Spee for instance noted that persecutions were built upon testimonies from alleged witches that were unreliable by definition: either the convicts were real witches, which would make their testimonies untrustworthy because the devil's allies are unlikely to tell us the truth, or they were not real witches, which would make them equally untrustworthy, as their witness statements had to be false.[13] Spee also understood how the combination of torture and leading questions triggered unreliable confessions[14] He concluded that "of all the people that I have accompanied to the fire, there is not one of whom I can confidently say, after having considered everything carefully, that they were truly guilty of the slander levelled against them."[15]

But we should be careful again, and not read such contemporary skeptics as modern rationalist companions in a different age. It is people like Weyer and Spee who can make us realize that the past is that foreign country where people do things differently. In surprising ways, these authors shared much of the world-view and polemical habits of their witch-hunting contemporaries.[16] Weyer and Spee were both profoundly Christian, and did not at all deny the active presence of demons in the world. On the contrary: they used demonic forces as an explanation for why witch-hunts occurred. Weyer maintained that demons created illusions in people's minds about witchcraft, amongst persecutors as well as amongst victims, and the ultimate diabolical goal of that was to trigger the human suffering of the trials.[17] According to Spee many of the inquisitors responsible for witch-hunting were actually likely to be witches

---

[11] Weyer, 218.
[12] Spee von Langenfeld, *Cautio criminalis*.
[13] Spee von Langenfeld, 380.
[14] See, for instance: Spee von Langenfeld, 276–77, 309–12.
[15] Spee von Langenfeld, 332."daß ich noch keine einzige zum Fewer begleiten helffen, die ich sagen könte, wann ich alles reifflich erwogen habe, das sie des Lasters in warheit schuldig gewesen wehre".
[16] Schwerhoff, "Rationalität im Wahn."
[17] Weyer, *Witches, Devils, and Doctors in the Renaissance*.

themselves!¹⁸ Eric Midelfort rightly commented that the contemporary debate was "not an issue between enlightened rationalists and fanatic obscurantists. The basic argument was really between two groups of pious men."[19]

Both "skeptics" also devoted attention to the overrepresentation of women amongst the victims in ways that were characteristic of their times. They wrote with compassion about the torments of female suspects, but at the same time used stereotypes about women that were eerily similar to those of fervent witch-hunters.[20] Weyer stated that the devil shrewdly seduced people into believing that they were real witches, and due to their overall weakness in character women were his most likely victim:

> That crafty schemer the Devil thus influences the female sex, that sex which by reason of temperament is inconsistent, credulous, wicked, uncontrolled in spirit, and (because of its feelings and affections, which it governs only with difficulty) melancholic; he especially seduces stupid, worn out, unstable old women.[21]

Spee pointed out that the testimonies about witchcraft were mostly derived from females who were tortured, which allegedly made these accounts twice as unreliable. After all, torturing men already stimulated false confessions, so what to expect from women?[22] The convicted suspects tended to be "insane, incomprehensible, reckless, talkative, jealous, deceitful, lying" women, who easily made judicial procedures run rampant.[23]

Was there no more fundamental skepticism at the time about things like the reality of demons, magic, or even divine providence itself? This is a much broader question about late Medieval and early modern European history that not only concerns scholars of witchcraft. The problem is also rife with difficulties of interpretation. [24] There are examples of outright skepticism, like the Italian Renaissance philosopher Pietro Pomponazzi, who denied the existence of hell and the immortality of the soul. But what often complicates things, is that people at the time could not speak freely about such matters. Outright skeptics were likely to be put to death. One can thus easily read too little disbelief in early modern documents, or actually too much, as speculations about hidden messages can run more freely.[25] A case in point is the sixteenth-century French skeptic Michel de Montaigne, author of a renowned collection of essays. His worldview has been interpreted as either sincerely Catholic, fideistic, crypto-Protestant, deistic,

---

[18] Spee von Langenfeld, *Cautio criminalis*, 242, 253.
[19] Midelfort, *Witch Hunting in Southwestern Germany*, 65.
[20] Clark, *Thinking with Demons*, 118.
[21] Weyer, *Witches, Devils, and Doctors in the Renaissance*, 181.
[22] Spee von Langenfeld, *Cautio criminalis*, 278.
[23] Spee von Langenfeld, 226."wahnsinnig, unverständig, leichtfertig, schwätzhafft, wanckelmüthig, betrüglich, lügenhafftig."
[24] For some contributions to the debate, see: Greenblatt, *The Swerve*; Closson, *L'imaginaire démoniaque en France (1550-1650)*, 50–62; Febvre, *Le problème de l'incroyance au 16e siècle*; Eire, *Reformations*; Schreiner, *Are You Alone Wise?*
[25] Lehmann and Ulbricht, "Motive und Argumente von Gegnern der Hexenverfolgung von Weyer bis Spee," 10.

agnostic, and even secretly atheist.[26] In an essay "On Cripples" Montaigne made some highly critical remarks on witch trials, but it is difficult to determine how far his doubts really went.[27] Montaigne thought that the evidence that persecutors used to convict people was thoroughly insufficient, adding that "it is putting a very high price on one's conjectures to have a man roasted alive because of them."[28] But to understand such remarks as indicative of a more systematic, critical stance on the existence of witchcraft, demonic powers, or religion's authority in society, is questionable.[29]

Arguably, a better place to look for clues of outright skepticism is not so much in the work of the "skeptics", but actually in the works of the witch-hunters and demonologists. In his book *Daemonolatreiae libri tres* (Demonolatry) from 1595, the Lorraine witch-hunter Nicolas Rémy spoke with horror about the epicurean school, which held that "no such things as spirits and Demons exist in the whole realm of nature, and that therefore it is idle to be afraid of such phantasms and apparitions." Rémy assured that the falseness of this doctrine had "been proved by agelong experience."[30] Such remarks were not unusual, as demonologists regularly felt the need to defend their basic assumptions – an indication that the contestation of those assumptions was conceivable.[31] The literary scholar Walter Stephens has recently delved into this topic, proposing that the inordinate interests in witchcraft theories between 1400-1700 should primarily be understood as a response to such skepticism.[32] The perceived threat not only concerned witchcraft, but also central tenets of Christianity itself. The excessive curiosity about contacts between demons and witches provided people with a means by which to gain knowledge about the spirit world, at a time when doubt had been cast on that world's mere existence. Walter Stephens: "The attitude of witchcraft theorists towards their theories was not belief but rather *resistance to skepticism*, a desperate attempt to maintain belief, and it betrays an uncommonly desperate *need to believe*."[33] Stephens offers many quotes from witchcraft theorists that seem to support his argument, but several key experts think that he has exaggerated the point.[34] True, witchcraft theorists were often on the defensive, but this does not mean that it was an inner atheist that they wanted to convince. More likely, their message was directed at their thoroughly Christian contemporaries who doubted their more extravagant claims. Later on, we will further discuss why there are good reasons to presume that witch beliefs were often real and genuine.

---

[26] Legros, "Montaigne on Faith and Religion."
[27] Montaigne, *Les Essais*, 1071–82.
[28] Montaigne, 1079. "Après tout c'est mettre ses conjectures à bien haut prix, que d'en faire cuire un homme tout vif".
[29] Brian Ribeiro, "Montaigne on Witches and the Authority of Religion in the Public Sphere"; Closson, *L'imaginaire démoniaque en France (1550-1650)*, 51–53.
[30] Rémy, *Demonolatry*, 79.
[31] Goodare, *The European Witch-Hunt*, 82; See, for instance in: Bodin, *De la démonomanie des sorciers*, 76, 79, 105, 215.
[32] Stephens, *Demon Lovers*.
[33] Stephens, 27.
[34] For critical comments, see: Behringer, "Walter Stephens. Demon Lovers"; Machielsen, "Thinking with Montaigne."

It was only over the course of the seventeenth century that fundamental doubts about demonology and concepts of witchcraft grew more common and explicit, to become unambiguous in the eighteenth century. The spirit of the Enlightenment in the latter century made significant parts of the educated classes think of witch beliefs as something outdated or even laughable.[35] The *Encyclopédie* of Diderot and D'Alembert typically described talk about sortileges and malefices as something for "countries and times of ignorance".[36] Still, we need to be careful and not place the full denial of witchcraft too early or too pervasively in time.[37] A crucial moment in Germany was the publication in 1701 of *De Crimini Magiae* by the jurist Christian Thomasius, which launched a frontal attack on all cumulative notions of witchcraft such as nightly flight and the sabbath. However, at the same time, Thomasius did not entirely distance himself from the possibility of magic, or from the ability of the devil to work through evil people.[38] Throughout much of the eighteenth century cumulative notions continued to receive influential support, and witch trials still occasionally occurred. It was only in the late eighteenth century that elites almost entirely distanced themselves from witchcraft beliefs.

Modern schools of thought
This spirit of the Enlightenment, with its embracement of modern science and rationalism, continued in the nineteenth and twentieth centuries, and gave rise to one of the key schools of thought in witchcraft historiography, "the liberal tradition".[39] Within this orientation the non-existence of diabolical witchcraft turned into the focal point of attention. Its exponents often looked back in anguish at what their ancestors had done and believed. Reflecting on the large trials of the early seventeenth century, the Scottish author Charles Mackay in 1841 found it "almost impossible to believe that mankind could ever have been so maddened and deluded."[40] It had been the domain of "the weak in reason and the strong in imagination."[41] In a book on the French trials from 1818, the rationalist author Jules Garinet described his efforts as a way of "attacking the errors of our fathers, some of which are still ours, with the arms of reason and more often with ridicule."[42] This remark indicates that the liberal tradition was not only about history, but also had contemporary aims in mind. Nineteenth- and twentieth-century liberalism contended with resilient forms of conservative religion, Roman Catholicism in particular, and the history of witch-hunts provided them with a useful rhetorical weapon. By exposing the Catholic

---

[35] Bever, "Witchcraft Prosecutions and the Decline of Magic"; Goodare, *The European Witch-Hunt*, 335–44; Closson, *L'imaginaire démoniaque en France (1550-1650)*, 53–62.
[36] "ARTFL Encyclopédie." "les pays & les tems d'ignorance."
[37] Behringer, "Späte Hexenprozesse - ein Pfahl im Fleisch der Aufklärung"; Vansycker, "Enlightenment and Witchcraft: The Dangers of Denying the Existence of the Devil."
[38] Dillinger, *Hexen und Magie*, 2018, 140–41.
[39] Tuczay, "The Nineteenth Century," 56–60; Goodare, *The European Witch-Hunt*, 363–65.
[40] Mackay, *Memoirs of Extraordinary Popular Delusions and the Madness of Crowds*, 158.
[41] Mackay, 114.
[42] Garinet, *Histoire de la magie en France,* viii." J'ai attaqué les erreurs de nos pères (dont quelques-uns sont encore les nôtres), avec les armes de la raison, et plus souvent avec le ridicule".

fanaticism, cruelty, and superstition of the "Witch Crazes", or the *Hexenwahn* (the witches delusion), they criticized what they saw as the religious superstition and stupidity of their own age.[43]

During the same period, witchcraft scholarship also gave rise to a powerful counter trend, "the romantic tradition".[44] Like the liberals, the romantics took a contemptuous stance towards the witch-hunts, but what made them different was their take on the question of what was real about witchcraft. The romantics assuredly did not revive the idea of real networks of magic-using devil worshippers. What they did contend, however, was that persecutors were after something else that was real. According to the nineteenth-century philologist Jacob Grimm, renowned for his fairy tales, many of the witches had actually been wise women who preserved precious elements of German folk culture. Witch-hunts should thus be understood as an attempt of religious and political elites to get rid of those women.[45] In France, the historian Jules Michelet similarly argued that witches had represented real networks of peasant social rebels that posed a threat to the establishment.[46] An influential twentieth-century version of the romantic viewpoint was developed by the anthropologist and Egyptologist Margaret Murray. She maintained that witch-hunts were actually a Christian fight against a lingering stone age fertility cult. This cult had worshipped a horned god, rebranded by the elites as the devil.[47] Probably the strangest phase in witchcraft historiography occurred in Nazi-Germany, where *Reichsführer* SS Heinrich Himmler conjectured that witches were pure Aryan carriers of Germanic customs that the Jews, or oriental Christianity at least, wanted to destroy. In secret, Himmler sent researchers into German archives with the remit to reconstruct this old Aryanism.[48]

The liberal and romantic perspectives are important to witchcraft historiography, as they dominated it well into the twentieth century, and continue to shape many popular notions about witch-hunts today.[49] Echoes of both traditions are also discernable in many scholarly works from the past decades. Yet, from the 1960s and 1970s onwards professional historical scholars have distanced themselves from both traditions.[50] The study of witch beliefs and trials achieved higher levels of empirical precision and interpretative sophistication, which made both schools of thought run into trouble. The key problem with the romantic approach is that meticulous examination of historical documents failed to provide convincing clues for real dissident networks.[51] Margaret Murray's hypotheses, for instance, have been dismissed as "fraudulent",

---

[43] Hansen, *Zauberwahn, Inquisition und Hexenproceß im Mittelalter*.
[44] Tuczay, "The Nineteenth Century," 52–56; Goodare, *The European Witch-Hunt*, 366–69; Dillinger, *Hexen und Magie*, 2018, 113–17.
[45] Grimm, *Deutsche mythologie*, I:836–1058.
[46] Michelet, *La Sorcière*.
[47] Murray, *The Witch-Cult in Western Europe*.
[48] Kurlander, *Hitler's Monsters*, 164–68; Dillinger, *Hexen und Magie*, 2018, 114–15.
[49] Goodare, *The European Witch-Hunt*, 361–69.
[50] Pivotal studies were for instance: Midelfort, *Witch Hunting in Southwestern Germany*; Cohn, *Europe's Inner Demons*.
[51] Cohn, *Europe's Inner Demons*; Goodare, *The European Witch-Hunt*, 366–69; Dillinger, *Hexen und Magie*, 2018, 113–36.

"highly selective", and it was said that her "grasp of historical method was non-existent."[52] It is important to note that this rejection of the romantic perspective was not a foregone conclusion. During the period of witch trials there were also persecutions of other groups, such as Waldensians or Anabaptists. While many ideas about these groups were illusory, they did really exist.[53] Something similar might have been possible regarding the witchcraft sect. However, all the contemporary evidence for their existence turned out to be second hand, thoroughly contaminated by leading questioning and torture, or unreliable for other reasons. That is not to mention other things that the witches were supposed to be doing, like weather magic or nightly flights, which are impossible deeds.[54] Modern scholarship has thus firmly established the non-existence of the diabolical witchcraft sect.

However, the dismissal of real networks of dissident people did not make current witchcraft scholarship endorse the liberal viewpoint. Enlightenment thought helped to stamp out witch trials in Europe indefinitely, for which it deserves credit. Yet, its tendency to interpret the behavior and convictions of historical actors as irrational and ridiculous no longer seemed helpful.[55] In the eyes of more recent historians, describing historical behavior as "maddened", "crazed", or "deluded", does not offer much of an explanation. In fact, it may actually hinder our understanding of what was going on, as it misapprehends how the historical actors involved saw things. Demonologists, for instance, were often part of respectable intellectual traditions, such as Aristotelianism, that prided themselves on their rationality.[56] Current scholarship thus tends to treat early modern witch beliefs as a complex paradigm in its own right, that possessed a certain degree of internal consistency that could be difficult to contest at the time. Only extravagant ideas about the sabbath, or large persecutions, were easier to dismiss within the available frameworks.[57]

This stance on the question of what was real about witchcraft, which we could summarize as "understanding denial", was explored at an earlier stage in anthropology. In 1937 the British anthropologist Edward Evans-Pritchard published his landmark book *Witchcraft, Oracles, and Magic among the Azande*, which made a profound attempt to understand beliefs of the African Azande people on their own terms.[58] Evans-Pritchard did not abandon the modern scientific position, as he stated that "witches, as Azande conceive them, cannot exist" and that "Azande do not possess sufficient knowledge to understand the real causes of things."[59] But at the same time he treated their convictions as an "intellectually coherent system" that offered an

---

[52] Goodare, *The European Witch-Hunt*, 368; The other two quotes are derives from: Purkiss, *The Witch in History*.
[53] Tremp, *Von Der Häresie Zur Hexerei*; Waite, *Eradicating the Devil's Minions*.
[54] Levack, *The Witch-Hunt in Early Modern Europe*, 12–18.
[55] Schwerhoff, "Rationalität im Wahn"; Gibson, "Thinking Witchcraft"; Robisheaux, "The German Witch Trials," 196.
[56] Trevor-Roper, *The European Witch-Craze*, 65.
[57] Schwerhoff, "Rationalität im Wahn"; Scarre, *Witchcraft and Magic*.
[58] Evans-Pritchard, *Witchcraft, Oracles and Magic among the Azande*.
[59] Evans-Pritchard, 63, 541.

explanatory framework for unfortunate events.[60] The Azande perception of natural causes was not illogical or uncritical.[61] An example that Evans-Pritchard mentioned was an unfortunate event that sometimes occurred in Azande villages, namely roofs of old granary houses that collapsed while people were sitting underneath them.[62] To the Azande, such events were a result of witchcraft. Evans-Pritchard initially thought that he knew better, because the collapse had been the obvious result of termites who had eaten away the structures of the house. But as he found out, the Azande understood this cause as well as he did. What required witchcraft as an explanation to *them* was the synchronized occurrence of the collapse and the people sitting underneath. From Evans-Pritchard's point of view this simultaneity was merely a matter of coincidence, but he realized that the Azande-perspective could neither be easily contradicted, nor confirmed, by experience.[63]

Two dissident viewpoints
The debate about what was real about witchcraft is not over yet, however, as this position of "understanding denial" fails to satisfy all current experts. It is contested from two angles. The first angle maintains that the debate about witchcraft's reality is superfluous, as the distinction between "real" and "non-real" is irrelevant. This viewpoint found its most elaborate expression in the influential book *Thinking with Demons* by the English historian Stuart Clark.[64] In Clark's view, much historical scholarship suffers from a "referential fallacy", that mistakably assumes that the language that we use can correspond to a reality that exists independently from ourselves.[65] Clark considers it a form of "naive positivism", "a piece of mystification", and he thus wants to unhook witchcraft scholarship from its realist moorings.[66] Clark writes: "Whether witchcraft beliefs did *in fact* correspond with reality becomes, therefore, a question not worth asking." It is a "non-issue".[67] Instead, historians are obliged to "take up a relativist position" that moves them "away from causes and towards meaning."[68] The new target for the historian has to be intelligibility and not reality.[69] In other words, Clark's work vividly shows that postmodern relativism has made its appearance in witchcraft scholarship.[70]

---

[60] Evans-Pritchard, 475, 63–83.
[61] Evans-Pritchard, 541.
[62] Evans-Pritchard, 69, 63–83.
[63] Evans-Pritchard, 473.
[64] Clark, *Thinking with Demons*; For other prominent examples, see for instance: Purkiss, *The Witch in History*, 59–90; Stephens, *Demon Lovers*, 10.
[65] Clark, *Thinking with Demons*, 6.
[66] Clark, 317.
[67] Clark, 6–7.
[68] Clark, 396, 402.
[69] Clark, 396.
[70] Postmodern relativism also appeared in the anthropology of witchcraft. See, for instance: Comaroff and Comaroff, *Modernity and Its Malcontents*; Bond and Ciekawy, *Witchcraft Dialogues*; Stein and Stein, *The Anthropology of Religion, Magic, and Witchcraft.*, 25.

How to react to this relativist viewpoint? It is important to note that it depends on the research question whether it is relevant to know to what extent beliefs were illusory or not. If the sole aim is to find out what people believed about witchcraft, and what meaning it had to them, then the question about what was real is not necessarily relevant.[71] Arguably, in that case it can be a helpful heuristic device to leave questions regarding the reality of witchcraft aside. It needs to be mentioned that Clark delivered what is probably the most profound and comprehensive account of the demonological worldview. But Clark is after bigger game, as he renders the question about witchcraft's reality irrelevant to witchcraft research *in general*. But at this point he fully enters the domain of postmodernist self-contradiction and confusion.[72] Inconsistencies in his work are paramount. Clark accuses others of the "referential fallacy", but interestingly his own book is full of references to reality! These references include things like countries, rulers, women, or courts, and his footnotes lead us to publishers, book titles, names of authors, and page numbers. So, his underlying assumption is that those things do exist somewhere out there, and can be referred to and checked by others accordingly. Furthermore, Clark accuses colleagues of a scientific "triumphalist reading of the past" which supposedly miscomprehends early modern Europe's intellectual history.[73] However, if Clark has the ability to determine that colleagues are wrong about something that exists independently from themselves, in this case early modern intellectual history, then why is it impossible for others to determine that early modern demonologists were wrong about things like nightly flights on broomsticks, or intercourse with the devil? In a typically postmodernist fashion Clark wants to have it both ways: others cannot refer to a reality out there, but for reasons that have yet to be clarified he does have this ability himself.

Much of Clark's argument is also built upon a false opposition of *real causes* versus *meaning*. As the work of Evans-Pritchard may help to illustrate, the one does not exclude the other. Moreover, from a broader academic perspective, it of course *is* relevant to know what was really going on. If there actually was a lingering pagan cult out there that Christians wanted to destroy, then Margaret Murray's good name duly needs to be restored. If there really were demons around who created illusions in people's minds about the existence of witches, Johann Weyer's explanatory models should be taken more seriously than is currently the case. If the beliefs of demonologists like Kramer, Binsfeld, or Bodin were correct, that would open up profoundly fascinating research agendas. How were witches able to magically kill cattle? How precisely did demonic forces create the apparent effect of moving penises in birds' nests? How exactly were broomsticks turned into tools for aerial journeys? What are the implications for the law of gravity, and are flights on broomsticks still possible today? It requires a remarkable lack of scientific curiosity to render questions about the reality of witchcraft a "non-issue". Lastly, it is

---

[71] This position is represented, for instance, in: Houdard, *Les sciences du diable*, 21–25.
[72] For critiques of the relativist viewpoint, see for instance: Goodare, *The European Witch-Hunt*, 3–6; Hutton, *The Witch*, 40–41.
[73] Clark, *Thinking with Demons*, 317.

also quite an affront to the tens of thousands of people tortured and burned as witches, to pretend that the question of their guilt or innocence is uninteresting.

Yet, there is still a second angle of critique on the position of "understanding denial" that deserves consideration. In contrast to the postmodern viewpoint, it aims to put the question of witchcraft's reality firmly back on the agenda. This position is mainly represented by the American historian Edward Bever, who aims to revive the notion of powerful underlying realities. Strikingly, he does so in a sense that is quite close to what early modern contemporaries thought was going on.[74] According to Bever, current scholarship grossly underestimates what was real about witchcraft. "As with every crime, of course, not every allegation was valid, but the belief that *maleficum* might be perpetrated and fear that it might cause harm were not irrational."[75] Much of Bever's argument is not entirely new for historians, as it has already been recognized for some time that contemporaries probably did attempt to use harmful magic against each other, and that various forms of psychosomatic mechanisms could make such attempts have real harmful consequences.[76] The merit of Bever's work, however, is that he delves much deeper into this line of reasoning, and abundantly refers to recent scientific findings, mostly from neuroscience, about the possible harmful effects of explicit and subliminal forms of communication. Bever also points out that many witchcraft accusations, such as allegations of poisoning, were feasible through natural means.

Bever's argument contains some further and quite surprising twists, though. He upholds that investigations into the "paranormal" have delivered "a substantial body of evidence suggesting that there are natural processes which are not adequately explained by current scientific understanding."[77] Bever has a keen interest in apparently unexplained phenomena like ball lightning, poltergeists, "urns crashing on the ground for no apparent reason; cloth torn up before peoples' eyes."[78] In his view this expands the possibilities of what was real about witchcraft. Bever's own historical research mostly focuses on trial records from early modern Württemberg and he argues that a substantial number of accusations that he encountered in those documents concern cases of real harm done. This also bears upon his functional analysis of persecutions, as he proposes that witch trials were actually quite effective in what they wanted to achieve: a reduction of harmful magical practices. "It seems reasonable to suggest that the persecutions declined in the later part of the [seventeenth] century in part because of their very

---

[74] Bever, "Witchcraft, Female Aggression, and Power in the Early Modern Community"; Bever, *The Realities of Witchcraft*; Bever, "Witchcraft Prosecutions and the Decline of Magic"; For another example, see: Henningsen, "The Witches' Flying and the Spanish Inquisitors, or How to Explain (Away) the Impossible."
[75] Bever, *The Realities of Witchcraft*, 63.
[76] See, for instance: Thomas, *Religion and the Decline of Magic*, 249; Briggs, *Witches & Neighbours*, 64.
[77] Bever, *The Realities of Witchcraft*, 39.
[78] Bever, 329–34, 438–39.

success."[79] Bever also turns a common narrative on its head when he states that the "dogmatic disbelief" of the Enlightenment made harmful magic an underrated problem.[80]

Much of Bever's argument is thought-provoking, but this introduction of the paranormal into witchcraft scholarship is difficult to adopt. The reality of such phenomena is not at all accepted by mainstream science today, so historians cannot rely on that as an explanatory model. At some point Bever also acknowledges that the existence of the paranormal is contested, and that early modern documents are unlikely to settle the debate. It additionally needs to be stressed that Bever's statements are mostly about village witchcraft. In regard to collective diabolical witchcraft – our key concern here – his claims remain far more modest. Bever provides us with some accounts of people who appealed to diabolical forces and he does not preclude the possibility that such appeals may have happened in collective settings every now and then.[81] But in regard to the cumulative notions of witchcraft even Bever is willing to accept that we are dealing with a fantasy: "the witch demonology patched together many disparate popular beliefs and practices, ascribing to them an intellectual coherence and organizational structure that did not exist, to create an illusory whole."[82]

This brings us back to the question we posed above. If witch-hunts did *not* have the effect of stopping a sect of magic-using devil worshippers, then what should a functional analysis of these beliefs and trials look like? As we shall see, this is a theoretical and empirical puzzle that is remarkably difficult to solve.

5.2 Explanatory attempts

"Too well designed", wrote the renowned cultural anthropologist Marvin Harris about the European witch persecutions.[83] A presumed danger that was omnipresent but difficult to detect, belief in nightly flights to collective meetings, and leading questioning through the relentless use of torture: to Harris it all had the appearance of something purposeful. Witch trials obviously did not fulfill the function of eradicating real networks of witches, so this adaptedness demonstrated that there was an alternative function involved. The system of witch-hunting had practical uses other than the stated goals of the witch-hunters. It was a means to a hidden end.[84] Harris was not the only one to think along these lines. From a wide range of theoretical perspectives modern scholars have been searching for the ulterior aims of the witch trials, for their concealed beneficiaries. Implicitly or explicitly the *cui bono* question occupies a central place in modern scholarly discussions about witch trials. What is interesting for our purposes is that the three key perspectives on the *cui bono* question discussed above have each made their appearance in the

---

[79] Bever, "Witchcraft, Female Aggression, and Power in the Early Modern Community," 974.
[80] Bever, *The Realities of Witchcraft*, 418–24.
[81] Bever, 65–92, 168–85.
[82] Bever, 414.
[83] Harris, *Cows, Pigs, Wars, & Witches*, 236.
[84] Harris, 207–40.

debate. Scholars have tried to understand witch-hunts as functional for social collectives, the maintenance of power structures, or the fulfillment of individual needs.

A tool of power

An illustrative example of a perspective that interpreted witch trials as a means to exert power, was developed by the aforementioned liberal tradition. During the nineteenth and early twentieth centuries these scholars were inclined to explain witch trials as a top-down tool, used by the Catholic church to exert power over the common people.[85] This makes the liberal viewpoint somewhat ambiguous – on the one hand witch-hunts were crazed, maddened and deluded, but on the other hand the evil clergy knew how to use them shrewdly. Jules Garinet for instance offered a cynical explanation for the extravagant tales about sexual relationships between demons and witches: "the monks, who abused people's credulity in order to detract attention from their own indolence, created ridiculous disguises in order to do all the extravagant things themselves which they attributed to devils."[86] Joseph Hansen also stressed the clergy's cleverness by pointing out that cumulative notions of the witches' sabbath and nightly flight were "the real source of the mass persecution", making trials spread over long distances.[87] In his view such cumulative notions had been "interwoven" by late Medieval inquisition in the Alps, before they were applied elsewhere.[88] "With all the means of educational and religious policing that it had at its disposal, [the Medieval church] created and upheld a strong delusion, that, despite all its internal inconsistencies, attained a significant propensity for propagation and persistence."[89]

We have seen that historical scholars have distanced themselves from the liberal tradition, but this interpretation of witch-hunting as a top-down tool of religious elites has lived on.[90] The English historian Hugh Trevor-Roper argued that trials functioned as an instrument of the late Medieval church, missionaries in particular, who wanted to "fabricate a second set of heresies." Witch-hunting had been "perfected in the course of a local struggle" in the western Alps and was then extended to other parts of Europe.[91] From this point of view, the intensification of witch-hunting in the 1560s seemed to make sense, as it was closely related to the escalation of the religious wars. In ongoing struggles between Catholics and Protestants, the hunt for witches provided a helpful tool for discrediting and combating religious opponents: "if we look at the revival of the witch craze in the 1560s in its context, we see that it is not the

---

[85] See, for instance: Soldan and Heppe, *Geschichte der Hexenprozesse*; Hansen, *Zauberwahn, Inquisition und Hexenproceß im Mittelalter*.
[86] Garinet, *Histoire de la magie en France,* lii-liii. "Les moines, qui abusaient de la crédulité publique, pour faire diversion à leur oisiveté, ont pu prendre des déguisements ridicule, et faire toute les extravagances, qu'il attribuaient aux diables."
[87] Hansen, *Zauberwahn, Inquisition und Hexenproceß im Mittelalter*, 510."die eigentliche Quelle für die Massenverfolgung" .
[88] Hansen, 1–36, 398–538, 535."geflochten."
[89] Hansen, 388-9."....von der Orthodoxie der mittelalterlichen Kirche entwickelten und mit allen ihr zur Verfügung stehenden Bildungsmitteln und glaubenspolzeilichen Maßregeln begründeten und aufrecht erhaltenen Wahns, woraus sich die trotz aller innerlichen Ungereimtheiten so bedeutende Propagationsfähigkeit und Dauerhaftigkeit desselben erklärt.".
[90] Trevor-Roper, *The European Witch-Craze*.
[91] Trevor-Roper, 113, 115.

product either of Protestantism or of Catholicism, but of both: or rather, of their conflict."[92] Trevor-Roper supported his claims by mentioning cases where religious struggles and witch-hunting seem to have been interconnected.[93]

An instrumental link between witch-hunting and the conflicts of the Reformation has been reaffirmed more recently by Peter Leeson and Jacob Russ.[94] These two economists analyzed substantial datasets on the timing of witch trials, and examined their correlation with several other variables such as bad weather, negative income shocks, weak states, and religious warfare. The correlation between witch-hunting and religious warfare came out as the strongest one. To explain the link Leeson and Russ project that witch trials "reflected non-price competition between Catholic and Protestant churches for religious market share in confessionally contested parts of Christendom."[95] Populations were often undecided about what side to choose in the religious wars, and at the same time they were afraid of satanic witchcraft. So, this combination provided an opportunity for religious competitors to make themselves popular. In their analysis that draws inspiration from both rational choice theory and Michel Foucault, these economists explain witch-hunts as a means by which prosecutors could advertise the superior powers of their religious denomination. It provided an effective strategy for winning over converts. The trials might have been expensive, but religious authorities understood how the overall cost-benefit ratio worked out well for them.

A different top-down power campaign was proposed by Marvin Harris, who was strongly influenced by Marxism.[96] In his view, the witch-hunt system represented a material power struggle between the ruling classes and the oppressed. Poor people were unsatisfied with their lot and potentially rebellious, so the governing classes created and sustained the scapegoat of the witch. By the time Kramer and Sprenger had finished their *Malleus Maleficarum*, the witch-hunting system had become "ready to be applied throughout Europe for the next two hundred years, with devastating results."[97] One of the ingenious effects of the trials was their ability to cause divisions among ordinary people. The aggression of the people could be targeted against alleged witches instead of the ruling classes, who reaffirmed their position of power. "It was the magic bullet of society's privileged and powerful classes. That was its secret", Harris explains.[98]

A poststructuralist orientation can be found in the work of the prominent French historian Robert Muchembled, who thought along the lines of Michel Foucault.[99] Echoing the romantic tradition, Muchembled upheld that persecutions were part and parcel of a cultural power struggle between traditional peasant society and the upcoming world of the modern city. Older

---

[92] Trevor-Roper, 67, 71.
[93] Trevor-Roper, 70, 118–19.
[94] Leeson and Russ, "Witch Trials."
[95] Leeson and Russ, 2066.
[96] Harris, *Cows, Pigs, Wars, & Witches*, 207–40.
[97] Harris, 217.
[98] Harris, 240.
[99] Muchembled, *La sorcière au village, XVe-XVIIIe siècle*; Muchembled, *Sorcières*.

women held a central and respected position in traditional peasant culture, and the idea of the witch was created by city elites as a reversal of this image. It told peasants that the women they had always respected so much were actually evil witches. By killing these women, the city elites destroyed something that was crucial to the peasant world, thereby making it easier to rule over them. Wealthy farmers were particularly eager to accuse their poorer neighbors of diabolical sorcery, as they were the ones who benefited most from the new order. The repression of witchcraft thus formed a visible part of a more or less conscious campaign of disciplining traditional rural society; "it constituted a form of pedagogy."[100] With a flair for the dramatic Muchembled described what an ordinary peasant must have seen while looking into the fire of a witch burning:

> What he saw being burned before his eyes, apart from the witch that he would have otherwise adored, was a grand part of his ancestral culture, of his superstitions, of his vision of the world. (...) The restructuring of the rural world was carried out over the ashes of a scapegoat that symbolized the old order of things, as well as the diabolical contestation of the new principles that came to regulate social life.[101]

The gender dimension of witch trials, and the strong overrepresentation of women amongst the victims, has been highlighted most particularly by feminist historians.[102] In an elaborate expression of the feminist viewpoint Anne Barstow interpreted witch-hunts as a powerful symbolic tool that was used by men to mark the subordinate position of women.[103] Male interrogators, judges, inquisitors, and executioners used the trials as a means by which to publicly demonstrate how lustful and dangerous women could be. This underlined the need to keep them confined. The persecutions made the role of women in European public and working life all the more circumscribed, and thus "as a didactic device, the ritual execution of witches succeeded superbly."[104] In a more moderate version of the argument Elspeth Whitney stated that the period of the witch trials gave rise to an increasingly hierarchal and rigid view of women's place in society.[105] The trials contained elements of "sexual terrorism" against women, which "suggest that the hunts were a more or less direct projection of sexual anxiety."[106] The misogynous rants of Kramer and Sprenger in the *Malleus Maleficarum* also represented a wider

---

[100] Muchembled, *Sorcières*, 23–24, 69.
[101] Muchembled, 194."Puis, devant le bûcher, il regardait brûler, en même temps que la sorcière, ce q'il avait autrefois adoré, c'est-à-dire une grande partie de sa culture ancestrale, de ses superstitions, de sa vision du monde. (...) La restructuration du monde rural s'accomplissait sur les cendres d'un bouc émissaire qui symbolisait à la fois l'ancien ordre des choses et la contestation diabolique des nouveaux principes régissant la vie sociale."
[102] See, for instance: Ehrenreich and English, *Witches, Midwives and Nurses*; Honegger, *Die Hexen der Neuzeit*; Whitney, "The Witch 'She'/the Historian 'He.'"
[103] Barstow, *Witchcraze*.
[104] Barstow, 156.
[105] Whitney, "The Witch 'She'/the Historian 'He.'"
[106] Whitney, 97.

tendency of using the trials as a means to discredit the power of female healers. Whitney complains that modern historians fail to take sufficient notice of such dimensions, illustrating how the misogynous "shadow of the hunts still lies over even its modern observers."[107]

Functionalism

Another perspective that received broad attention was the application of anthropological and sociological functionalism to European witch trials. In non-western societies anthropologists had encountered somewhat similar fights against alleged witches, and in the middle decades of the twentieth century they tended to explain such aggression from a functionalist angle.[108] Emblematic of this approach was Clyde Kluckhohn's analysis of witch killings amongst the Navaho Indians in the southwest of the United States. The underlying assumption of Kluckhohn's research was that "no cultural forms survive unless they constitute responses which are adjustive or adaptive, in some sense, for the members of the society or for the society considered as a perduring unit."[109] Subsequently, Kluckhohn presented a plethora of manifest and latent functions that Navaho witch killings fulfilled. As he argued, Navaho societies experienced significant strains and stresses as a result of contacts with white Americans, such as humiliating defeats, growing inequality, ecological problems, and the prohibition of tribal warfare. These created internal fears and hostilities that, if not expressed in a channeled outlet for displaced aggression, would make neuroticism and conflict endemic in society. The murdering of witches thus offered an institutionalized means of relieving anger and anxiety – it functioned as a socially approved form of "hate satisfaction".[110] In addition, witchcraft lore affirmed "solidarity by dramatically defining what is bad."[111] The pervasiveness of witch beliefs made individual Navaho Indians wary not to throw suspicions upon themselves, which thereby enforced socially cooperative behavior. With a minimum of social disturbance, the witch killings helped Navaho society restore and maintain social equilibrium at times of great turmoil.

In the early 1970s two English historians applied such insights to the witch trials of early modern England.[112] In his seminal *Religion and the Decline of Magic* Keith Thomas wrote that witch beliefs "discharged a function in early modern England similar to that which they perform in many primitive societies today."[113] Thomas highlighted how sixteenth-century English society also experienced severe stress. The rise of capitalism had put much pressure on the traditional mechanisms of solidarity and social control within villages. Simultaneously, the Reformation broke down protective armors of ecclesiastical magic that had offered relief in the face of danger.

---

[107] Whitney, 93.
[108] See, for instance: Kluckhohn, *Navaho Witchcraft.*; Gluckman, *Custom and Conflict in Africa*; Marwick, *Sorcery in Its Social Setting: A Study of the Northern Rhodisian Cewa.*
[109] Kluckhohn, *Navaho Witchcraft.*, 79.
[110] Kluckhohn, 89.
[111] Kluckhohn, 110.
[112] Macfarlane, *Witchcraft in Tudor and Stuart England*; Thomas, *Religion and the Decline of Magic.*
[113] Thomas, *Religion and the Decline of Magic*, 675.

In those circumstances witchcraft accusations "served both as an explanation of misfortune and as an expected means of redress."[114] Thomas was particularly interested in the social contexts in which accusations arose. For instance, poor people often asked their neighbors for help, which, as traditional customs prescribed, should have been provided to them. But in the new era richer neighbors were increasingly unwilling to respond to such demands, which often made beggars go away cursing. In order to overcome a sense of guilt, wealthier people then sought relief by convincing themselves that the beggars were actually evil witches. So, accusations helped to dissolve social relations that had become redundant.[115] In a study on witch trials in Essex, the historian Alan Macfarlane came to similar conclusions: "witchcraft prosecution may be seen as a means of effecting deep social change; a change from a "neighbourly", highly integrated and mutually interdependent village society, to a more individualistic one."[116]

An attempt to explain the entire European witch-hunt from a functionalist angle was made by Nachman Ben-Yehuda.[117] This sociologist also observed that early modern Europe suffered from severe stress. There was a breakdown of the old and clearly defined moral boundaries of the Middle Ages, aggravated by external catastrophes such as epidemics and the Little Ice Age. These developments created an era of deep confusion and anomie that called for a reestablishment and a redefinition of the old moral boundaries of society. Witch trials won extensive support for this reason, because they would help to "cleanse the world from all effects of social change and anomie."[118] As Ben-Yehuda put it: "in fact, the witch craze was a fictious deviance, created for those purposes."[119]

The notion that witch persecutions came into being in order to overcome certain anxieties was also brought forward by Walter Stephens, whom we encountered in the previous section.[120] Stephens asks the *cui bono* question in explicit terms, and provides a firm answer: "persecution of witches had tremendous positive value for everyone but the witches.'"[121] At the village level Stephens endorses the Thomas-Macfarlane model, and at the level of elites he makes his argument discussed above (5.1) about witch theories and trials helping people overcome mounting doubts about the existence of the spirit world. This anxiety would also explain why demonologists had an inordinate fondness for stories about sexual contacts between witches and demons: those stories offered the most valuable proof of the spirit world's reality. The desire for carnal knowledge, was thus "not pornographic, but metaphysical".[122] Tales about witchcraft also became increasingly grotesque over time, because "the less one believed in the verifiable

---

[114] Thomas, 652.
[115] Thomas, 677.
[116] Macfarlane, *Witchcraft in Tudor and Stuart England*, 197.
[117] Ben-Yehuda, "The European Witch Craze of the 14th to 17th Centuries."
[118] Ben-Yehuda, 22.
[119] Ben-Yehuda, 14.
[120] Stephens, *Demon Lovers*.
[121] Stephens, 14. For the Cui Bono?-question, see: 7, 104.
[122] Stephens, 26.

presence of the Devil, the more exaggerated claims one made for his being everywhere, at all times, in all forms."[123]

Other scholars have looked for more mundane individualistic aims. A common suspicion has been that trials were created for the purpose of financial gain.[124] What the persecutors were after, according to the social scientist Elliot Currie, was the money of the convicts.[125] Mechanisms for profit were "built into the structure of the trials". It was "a large and complex business" which created the "livelihoods of a sizable number of people."[126] That is not to mention other explanations that assumed that witch-hunting was a means of discouraging birth control, enforcing state formation, or indulging in sadistic impulses.[127] Hence, in short, we can observe that modern scholars have looked for the hidden aims and hidden beneficiaries of witch-hunts in all sorts of directions. Yet, no matter how diverse their explanations, what they all share is that many witchcraft experts have rejected them over the past decades. It is to these critical arguments that we now turn.

5.3 Explanatory failures?

"Les méchants faits détruisent les belles théories" – "nasty facts destroy lovely theories", is how the French historian Marc Bloch warned his colleagues.[128] The field of witchcraft scholarship provides us with a wonderful illustration of Bloch's dictum, as the facts of the witch trials have been unmerciful to the theories mentioned. When confronted with the complexities of history it turned out that these explanatory models did not work, or worked only to a limited extent. At three levels, significant problems for these theories can be discerned.

The problem at the first level is that primary sources have failed to reveal explicit evidence for a key hidden agenda or underlying function.[129] What we encounter in historical documents of supporters of witch trials is people telling each other how dangerous diabolical witchcraft could be, and how to stop it. It seems that they were genuinely afraid. What these people did not talk about was subjugating women, oppressing the poor, destroying traditional peasant culture, let alone relaxing the social system. This is not because such topics are entirely absent in the sources. Advocates of trials, for instance, surely expressed concerns about the well-being of social communities and underlined the need for social control.[130] However, they did not address this in an instrumentalist or functionalist sense – diabolical witchcraft as a *fictious* deviance that

---

[123] Stephens, 102.
[124] Robbins, *The Encyclopedia of Witchcraft and Demonology*, 273, 479–84; Currie, "Crimes without Criminals."
[125] Currie, "Crimes without Criminals," 32.
[126] Currie, 21–22.
[127] Heinsohn and Steiger, *Die Vernichtung der weisen Frauen*; Lehmann, "Hexenverfolgungen und Hexenprozesse im alten Reich"; Trethowan, "The Demonopathology of Impotence."
[128] Howell and Prevenier, *From Reliable Sources*, 96.
[129] Midelfort, *Witch Hunting in Southwestern Germany*; Dillinger, *Böse Leute*, 230; Clark, *Thinking with Demons*; Dillinger, *Hexen und Magie*, 2018, 127.
[130] Scarre, *Witchcraft and Magic*, 40–47.

was used *indirectly* for those ends – but in a way that was more straightforward: diabolical witchcraft was a *real* threat to communities and therefore social control was needed.

At first sight it may seem that a stronger case can be made for the oppression of women as an underlying aim – just think of the rampant misogyny in the *Malleus maleficarum*. A more careful interpretation of the sources suggests a different approach, however.[131] The *Malleus* contains a lot of misogyny indeed, but that made it somewhat of an outlier amongst demonological works. Many other key texts put no or little emphasis on the topic of female overrepresentation – Stuart Clark for instance refers to Bodin's *Demonomanie* or Boguet's *Discours* here. As far as such authors discussed the topic, they often only did so in passing, and in rather formulaic forms, before they moved on to things that they thought were of greater importance, such as the (im)possibilities of magic, or the threat of diabolical evil. Furthermore, the negative stereotypes about women were, as Stuart Clark put it, "entirely representative of their age and culture."[132] They can be found abundantly in contemporary sources that were unrelated to witchcraft, and we already saw that opponents used very similar stereotypes *against* witch-hunting. Claudia Opitz did retort however, that Stuart Clark goes too far in playing down the misogyny of an author like Bodin, and indeed there is some ground for this counter-argument: especially in an appendix of his book Bodin spilled quite a lot of ink on why witches were mostly females, relying on a wide arsenal of stereotypes.[133] Yet, still, it was hardly the central topic of his work, and Bodin also used one misogynous platitude about "the imbecility or fragility of the female sex" to argue that female witches should be punished *less* severely than male ones.[134]

So, if the persecutors of witches did not discuss the alleged underlying purposes or functions of the trials in print, how then did such hidden purposes come about? The key problem at level number two is that most of the scholars who developed such models are remarkably vague on this point. Muchembled stated that witch trials were used "more or less consciously" for the purpose of oppressing traditional peasant culture, but he does not further elaborate upon that.[135] Leeson and Russ offered statistical clues for a correlation between witch trials and religious warfare, but correlation does not imply causation, and their claim that trials were used deliberately for the purpose of winning over converts lacks evidence.[136] Marvin Harris called the system of witch-hunts "well designed", and a key claim of his book is that involved actors themselves did not intend or understand such alleged hidden functions. But an alternative

---

[131] Clark, *Thinking with Demons*, 106–31; Stephens, *Demon Lovers*, 32–57; Schwerhoff, "Hexerei, Geslecht und Regionalgeschichte," 331.
[132] Clark, *Thinking with Demons*, 115; Schwerhoff, "Hexerei, Geslecht und Regionalgeschichte," 331.
[133] Opitz-Belakhal, "Der Magistrat als Hexenjäger," 52–53; Opitz-Belakhal, *Das Universum des Jean Bodin: Staatsbildung, Macht und Geschlecht im 16. Jahrhundert*, 147–48; See, for instance: Bodin, *De la démonomanie des sorciers*, 261–67, 373, 419, 448–56.
[134] Bodin, *De la démonomanie des sorciers*, 419."l'imbecillité ou fragilité du sexe des femmes."
[135] Muchembled, *Sorcières*, 23–24.
[136] Leeson and Russ, "Witch Trials."

explanation of how such "designs" came into being was not forthcoming.[137] Keith Thomas's theories about hidden social and psychological functions suffer from a similar problem. In her critique of Thomas, the anthropologist Hildred Geertz rightfully commented that his "own assumptions about the workings of human societies and minds remain unexamined."[138]

The absence of explicit evidence in the sources does not as such refute these explanatory models. If the witch persecutions were deliberately used for a hidden purpose it is quite understandable that the involved actors did not openly discuss this in print.[139] Asking for such evidence creates a high burden of proof. Perhaps there *was* a hidden agenda, but the crucial documents are lost, or people remained deliberately silent about their true aims. Or perhaps they were only subconsciously driven forward by such motives, or something in between these options.[140] Another possibility might be that the alleged hidden agendas or functions came into being through mechanisms that current witchcraft scholarship has not unveiled yet. However, if one of those scenarios were true, the hidden agendas or functions should have become apparent in the course of the trials. But the key problem at the third level is that this is not borne out either. Historians have meticulously examined under what conditions witch trials occurred, who initiated them, who became the victims, and what the overall effects tended to be like. It did not happen along the lines that the aforementioned theories would lead us to expect.[141]

Highly diverse persecutions
The problem with the theory of a top-down Roman Catholic campaign is that the role of clerics in the development and propagation of persecutions was far more limited than claimed.[142] There are certainly examples of witch-hunts that crucially depended on confessional Catholic support, for instance in Counter-Reformation Germany, but in a majority of cases persecutions were carried out by local secular authorities. Very often, trial records also hardly demonstrate a significant involvement of clergy, and there is a significant number of cases where clergy were actually victims.[143] As Robin Briggs writes: "it is evident that had the clergy across Europe been committed enthusiasts for persecution, they could have mobilized local feeling to devastating effect."[144] But they did not, and there were even counter tendencies. In places where central Catholic authorities were relatively strong, such as in Spain or the Papal state, the number of trials remained modest. The Spanish inquisition, for instance, was an important and effective

---

[137] Harris, *Cows, Pigs, Wars, & Witches*.
[138] Geertz, "An Anthropology of Religion and Magic, I," 77.
[139] Dillinger, *Böse Leute*, 230; Dillinger, *Hexen und Magie*, 2018, 127.
[140] Scarre, *Witchcraft and Magic*, 46.
[141] Midelfort, *Witch Hunting in Southwestern Germany*, See, for instance:; Behringer, *Hexenverfolgung in Bayern*; Dillinger, *Böse Leute*; Briggs, *Witches & Neighbours*.
[142] Dillinger, *Hexen und Magie*, 2018, 91–94.
[143] Schwillus, *Kleriker Im Hexenprozess*; Voltmer, "Debating the Devil's Clergy. Demonology and the Media in Dialogue with Trials (14th to 17th Century)."
[144] Briggs, *Witches & Neighbours*, 199.

voice of skepticism.[145] There was also a significant involvement of Protestants; parts of Calvinist Scotland and Lutheran Germany experienced severe witch trials, and demonologists on both sides of the religious divide were eager to adopt each other's ideas.[146]

The theory that witch-hunts had an ulterior instrumental function during the wars of religion is also problematic for various reasons.[147] Witch persecutions preceded those wars, as the trials came into being over the course of the fifteenth century, and the correlation later on is far from precise. During the first phase of the Reformation there was a decrease of persecutions, and the most intense episodes of witch-hunting often occurred during intervals of peace. Between 1618 and 1648 Germany experienced the religious conflicts of the Thirty Years' War, but witch trials were already sharply on the rise in the late sixteenth century, abated during the late period of the war, and resurged somewhat when the fighting was over.[148] Furthermore, persecutions were also hardly focused on religious opponents – it was mostly Catholics versus Catholics and Protestants versus Protestants.

The theory that witch-hunting had a positive cost-benefit effect on winning over converts is also questionable. Leeson and Russ provide no evidence for their claim that this was what motivated rulers. Admittedly, there do seem to have been some cases where the desire for religious following in the competitive environment of the Reformation made rulers condone witch-hunts. But that was already noticed by historians prior to Leeson and Russ, and it does not work as a generalized explanation.[149] Moreover, there were also tendencies in the opposite direction.[150] Around 1589 the staunchly Catholic city of Trier experienced a large hunt and Protestants seized the opportunity to discredit the reputation of Catholicism. Was it not Catholic superstitions that had made the people of Trier such easy prey for the devil? Conversely, that Calvinist Geneva had experienced some significant trials was happily used by the Catholic demonologist Martin Delrio to throw further suspicion on Calvinism.[151] Such slander was not without repercussions: when the Catholic city of Innsbruck experienced trials in 1664, the civic authorities made certain not to broadcast it in order to avoid a Protestant backlash.[152]

The secular top-down aims proposed by Muchembled and Harris have also been abandoned by experts as explanatory models.[153] Robin Briggs: "one of the most misleading ideas about the witchcraft persecutions is that it was inspired and manipulated by the ruling classes for their own cynical purposes."[154] Some trials were primarily instigated from above, but usually

---

[145] Henningsen, *The Witches' Advocate*.
[146] Goodare, *The European Witch-Hunt*, 162.
[147] Monter, "Witch Trials in Continental Europe 1560-1660," 10–11; Goodare, *The European Witch-Hunt*, 162–63; Levack, *The Witch-Hunt in Early Modern Europe*, 12–16.
[148] Behringer, *Hexen und Hexenprozesse in Deutschland*.
[149] Pohl, *Zauberglaube und Hexenangst im Kurfürstentum Mainz*, 289; Rummel, *Bauern, Herren und Hexen*, 26–27.
[150] Dillinger, *Böse Leute*, 362.
[151] Rio and Maxwell-Stuart, *Investigations into Magic*, 28.
[152] Dillinger, *Böse Leute*, 362.
[153] Clark, *Thinking with Demons*, 549–59; Briggs, *Witches & Neighbours*.
[154] Briggs, *Witches & Neighbours*, 8.

it entailed complex interplays in which various levels of society were involved.[155] Without popular support the efforts of elites would also have remained rather toothless. In many cases initiative in fact came primarily from below, as a witch trial in the German village of Wehrheim may illustrate.[156] In 1651 this village experienced a fire, and people assumed that witches had been behind it. The population wanted their local authorities to take action, but initially those authorities were uninterested in doing so. The people of Wehrheim then took a drastic step: they fled into neighboring territories and were only willing to return under the condition of a witch trial. The authorities still remained reluctant, and even threatened the refugees with confiscating their possessions, but to no avail, and eventually the authorities gave in, conducting a trial that killed seventeen people.

Witch-hunting could also be quite risky for the ruling classes, as the dynamics of a panic were difficult to control.[157] Trials had a tendency to spread beyond one's own territories, endangering precarious relationships between dominions. Territorial rulers also made themselves vulnerable to external interference when large episodes of witch-hunting were based on abuses of the law and excessive torture, as we saw in Bamberg.[158] Or worse, when members of the ruling classes were targeted themselves. When popular anxieties about witchcraft mounted, elites could be suspected of using double standards. Were the ruling classes not protecting rich witches, while the poor ones were being burned?[159] Such popular sentiments could be difficult to resist, and in quite some cases resulted in members of the elite being burned at the stake. In contrast to what Harris's model would lead us to expect, relatively strong higher authorities were often a hindrance to witch-hunting. Many historians have noted that large and comparatively centralized states, such as France, England, Austria, and Saxony experienced relatively few trials, while medium-sized and small territories were more fertile grounds for panics.[160] It is argued that larger states possessed more elaborate judicial bureaucracies, with various checks and balances, which prevented witch trials from spiraling out of control. In smaller territories the panics escalated more easily because there were fewer distant supervisory authorities that could stop it. This would also be one of the explanations for the relatively high number of trials in politically fragmented Germany.

Then there is the theory of witch-hunting as "women hunting". We already mentioned the lack of direct convincing evidence in the sources, but the course of trials confronts us with

---

[155] Briggs, 338–41; Rummel and Voltmer, *Hexen und Hexenverfolgung*, 31; Goodare, *The European Witch-Hunt*, 249–53; Dillinger, *Hexen und Magie*, 2018, 95–105.
[156] Schormann, *Hexenprozesse in Deutschland*, 57.
[157] Dillinger, *Böse Leute*; Dillinger, *Hexen und Magie*, 2018, 98–105.
[158] Rowlands, *Witchcraft Narratives in Germany*, 63.
[159] Dillinger, Fritz, and Mährle, *Zum Feuer verdammt*, 81–93.
[160] Briggs, *Witches & Neighbours*, 190–91; Behringer, "Witchcraft Studies in Austria, Germany and Switzerland"; Levack, *The Witch-Hunt in Early Modern Europe*, 88–94; However, for a critique of this claim, see: Goodare, *The European Witch-Hunt*, 176–82.

further problems for this theory.[161] What this perspective would lead us to expect is that men instigated persecutions against women. However, very often trials started when women accused other women of witchcraft, and there are ample examples of male judges or juries that subsequently showed restraint. When brought to court male suspects were not treated more favorably than female suspects, as the conviction rates between the sexes did not differ much.[162] It has already been noted that the average percentage of males amongst the victims lay somewhere around twenty to twenty-five percent, which is still quite substantial and does not fit with the idea that oppressing women was the ultimate aim. Negative stereotypes about female witches and male witches tended to coexist.[163]

Of course, the strong overrepresentation of women amongst the victims still stands, but witchcraft scholars have developed more subtle explanations for that.[164] Misogyny was unmistakably a part of the picture, but negative stereotypes about women are no longer treated as a direct cause of persecutions, but, rather, as part of a context in which women were far more likely to be associated with witchcraft. We already discussed elite notions about women as morally weak and sexually rapacious creatures, but peasant beliefs also had a tendency to link women to the world of spirits, spells, poisoning, and nightly flights. In addition, the roles that women played in society possibly made them more vulnerable to accusations. More often than men, women were involved in tasks such as cooking, healing and taking care of children. So, if something went wrong in those domains, as when a child fell ill, it was more obvious to look for a female culprit. When accusations occurred, the weaker position of women in society then gave them less access to means of defending themselves – the unequal distribution of power between the sexes remains a crucial factor. Correspondingly, it has been suggested that women's lack of political and physical power also made them more likely to undertake the kind of covert strategies of attack that would be interpreted as witchcraft by contemporaries, like poisoning and causing spells.[165]

There is not much support either for the claim that persecutions were essentially driven forward by greed.[166] A significant proportion of the victims was poor, while witch-hunting was a very time consuming and expensive activity – just think of the costs of the trials. When the properties of burned witches were confiscated they often did not fall into the hands of the

---

[161] Briggs, *Witches & Neighbours*, 257–86; Sharpe, *Witchcraft in Early Modern England*, 42–44, 66–69; Goodare, *The European Witch-Hunt*, 267–316; Pohl, *Zauberglaube und Hexenangst im Kurfürstentum Mainz*, 293; Moeller, *Dass Willkür über Recht ginge*, 227; Groß, *Hexerei in Minden*, 249–57.
[162] Briggs, *Witches & Neighbours*, 261; Pohl, *Zauberglaube und Hexenangst im Kurfürstentum Mainz*, 293.
[163] Blécourt, "The Making of the Female Witch."
[164] Rowlands, "Witchcraft and Gender in Early Modern Europe"; Opitz-Belakhal, *Böse Weiber*, 9–41; Levack, *The Witch-Hunt in Early Modern Europe*, 128–35; Goodare, *The European Witch-Hunt*, 267–316; Schwerhoff, "Hexerei, Geslecht und Regionalgeschichte."
[165] Bever, "Witchcraft, Female Aggression, and Power in the Early Modern Community"; Bever, *The Realities of Witchcraft*, 47–59.
[166] Dillinger, *Böse Leute*, 300–305, 341–49; Levack, *The Witch-Hunt in Early Modern Europe*, 177–78; Goodare, *The European Witch-Hunt*, 216, 384; Pohl, *Zauberglaube und Hexenangst im Kurfürstentum Mainz*, 203; Midelfort, *Witch Hunting in Southwestern Germany*, 164–78.

persecutors. So, people with strictly financial motives would probably have found more efficient ways of getting what they wanted. There are certainly examples of people who gained money from trials, and some made a bit of a career out of it.[167] But even in those cases it remains questionable whether greed was the crucial underlying aim. Robin Briggs: "while it is possible to formulate a purely cynical and materialistic interpretation, this is not really plausible; even greedy witch-hunters probably convinced themselves that they were doing holy work, producing a typical amalgam of idealism and self-interest."[168] Moreover, such people could not have achieved much without wider support in society, making them facilitators rather than initiators.[169] Goodare concludes about the money-motive that "in origin it is probably a modern fantasy."[170]

What about the theories that presupposed social and psychological functions? Some aspects of the functionalist approach still inspire historians today. Thomas's and Macfarlane's observation that accusations could arise in contexts of refused charity has been found in continental cases as well, and at a general level witch trials indeed tended to occur at times of psychological and social stress.[171] However, a key problem with the functionalist model is that witch-hunts did not so much release those tensions as aggravate and foster them. In his study on witch trials in southwestern Germany – which pioneered many of the arguments presented here – Erik Midelfort concluded that "major panics served no valid social function. Society was not made stronger and more cohesive by such trials, but weaker and more torn by suspicion and resentment."[172] Midelfort is willing to accept that very small trials may have served a social function of restricting eccentric behavior, but the shock and fear of the larger hunts wrecked normal bonds of social trust, broke down friendships, made respected members of communities vulnerable to attack, and left behind families that were consumed with grief and self-accusation.[173] Other historians confirmed Midelfort's findings, and even the functional effects of small trials are highly questionable.[174] Witchcraft accusations and persecutions tended to draw people apart rather than to bring them together. The early moderns assuredly cared about social order, but as Johannes Dillinger remarks: "for this purpose people already had comprehensive systems of law enforcement at their disposal that did not require the support of witch beliefs."[175]

The haphazardness of trials

---

[167] Rummel and Voltmer, *Hexen und Hexenverfolgung*.
[168] Briggs, *Witches & Neighbours*, 342.
[169] Briggs, 189.
[170] Goodare, *The European Witch-Hunt*, 385.
[171] Behringer, *Witches and Witch-Hunts*; Goodare, *The European Witch-Hunt*, 95,166, 241; Dillinger, *Hexen und Magie*, 2018, 129–30.
[172] Midelfort, *Witch Hunting in Southwestern Germany*, 4.
[173] Midelfort, 93, 153, 175, 190.
[174] Hehl, "Hexenprozesse und Geschichtswissenschaft"; Sharpe, *Witchcraft in Early Modern England*, 46; Goodare, *The European Witch-Hunt*, 95, 166; Dillinger, *Hexen und Magie*, 2018, 133.
[175] Dillinger, *Böse Leute*, 230."Zu diesem Zweck stand ein ausdifferenziertes Rechts- und Strafverfolgungssystem zur Verfügung, das einer Unterstützung durch den Hexenglauben nicht bedurfte." .

As an overall observation it has to be noted that the aforementioned explanatory models presupposed one or a just a few systematic causes, needs, intentions, or functions behind the witch-hunts. But *if* this had been the case, we should expect the persecutions to display regular patterns, targeting specific classes of individuals rather than others. However, there was in fact quite a lot of variation in who took the initiative and who became the victims. Robert Thurston: "if any generalization about the European witch hunts is on solid ground, it is that they were highly erratic."[176] The persecutions could erupt quite suddenly, take lots of victims, then disappear for a long while, and erupt elsewhere later on. Again, it looks more like genuine fear that proliferated, rather than a shrewd and systematic campaign stemming from underlying motives. The haphazard way in which the trials occurred simply does not fit well with the large explanatory frameworks. If we assume for instance, as Walter Stephens did, that witch-hunts were a product of a constant anxiety about the non-existence of the spirit world, then how to explain the occurrence of outbursts followed by long periods of stasis? When looking at the Bamberg hunt of 1626-1632 it seems more likely that it was genuine panic about the existence of witches that made people do what they did, rather than a continuous metaphysical anxiety about their non-existence.

Historical experts still find general factors such as religious warfare, misogyny, or social stress important for the understanding of witch-hunts, but as preconditions and no longer as essential causes. After all, in the overwhelming majority of cases such factors did not result in any witch trials at all.[177] It has also been pointed out that large waves of persecutions were hardly a product of central coordination. Around the year 1590 there was a particularly intense outburst of witch trials in parts of Germany, and Wolfgang Behringer analyzes:

> In all territories the witch persecutions began unreflectively. Nowhere was there a plan that envisaged in advance how single trials would be extended elsewhere. Nor was there any arrangement between territories in which people agreed on how to cooperate, and not a single time were there special lawsuits or preliminary considerations (…). The 'outbreak' of persecutions around 1590 took the region by surprise. Reflections on the course of events only occurred after the extraordinary scale of the trials had become apparent.[178]

---

[176] Thurston, *The Witch Hunts*, 16.
[177] Briggs, *Witches & Neighbours*, 188.
[178] Behringer, *Hexenverfolgung in Bayern*, 122. "In allen Territorien begannen die Hexenverfolgungen unreflektiert. Nirgendwo gab es einen Plan, in dem von vornhein eine systematische Ausweitung der einzelnen Prozesse ins Auge gefaßt worden wäre. Es gab auch keine Absprache zwischen den Territorien, in denen speziell eine Zusammenarbeit bei den Verfolgungen festgelegt wäre, es gab nicht einmal eine spezielle Hexengesetzgebung oder theoretische Vorüberlegungen dazu (…). Der „Ausbruch" der Verfolgungswelle der Jahre um 1590 traf die Region unvorbereitet. Eine Reflexion der Ereignisse setzte erst ein, nachdem der außerordentliche Charakter der Ereignisse sichtbar geworden war.".

Behringer also makes a striking observation about officials who executed the trials. They were doing it, as he writes, "although the work was very time consuming and not very enjoyable. The boundless misery of the witch trials burdened most of the commissioners psychologically, which makes the assumption that the processes were carried out from 'lower' motives (enrichment, etc.) seem absurd."[179] So, what Behringer argues here is that not only the victims of trials suffered, but even many of the persecutors! If we make the effort to put ourselves in their shoes this may also appear comprehensible. When officials presumed that the danger of witchcraft was potentially real – not an outlandish assumption at the time – trials could confront them with painful dilemmas. Being too soft on the diabolical sect might give the witches further opportunities to harm innocent people, but being too tough might result in innocent suspects being burned at the stake, a ghastly predicament indeed.

Despite the problems with their hypotheses, it still needs to be mentioned that the works of people like Trevor-Roper, Thomas, Muchembled, or the feminist authors, have helped the field of witchcraft scholarship advance. It is especially these authors who put the topic of witch-hunting on historians' agenda and they also highlighted relevant aspects, such as the context of the Reformation, the social dimensions of village accusations, interactions between popular and elite cultures, and the overrepresentation of women amongst victims. Notably, the view that witch trials were "instrumentalized" for hidden purposes, or fulfilled certain underlying functions, is still in vogue among various German historians, who have developed a more refined version of the argument – we shall have an extensive look at their ideas after we have delved more deeply into several German persecutions.[180] But for now it can be observed that the international trend over the past decades has been to abandon theories that presupposed underlying functions or purposes.[181] The failure of the grand explanatory frameworks has given shape to a "state of the art" in witchcraft historiography that will now be further examined. It offers an example of the "idiographic" orientation amongst so many historians, as well as an understanding of this orientation's shortcomings.

5.4 The state of the art

Many modern scholars have searched for the rationality behind the apparently irrational. A hunt for a sect of flying, fornicating, magic-using and devil-worshipping witches appears so illogical to an audience today, that it seems obvious to look for an underlying rationale that makes more sense to us. But it turns out that this muddies the waters even further. If we assume that witch-hunting actually served the equilibrium of society, the eradication of peasant culture, or the

---

[179] Behringer, 320."... obwohl diese Arbeit sehr zeitraubend und wenig erfreulich war. Das grenzenlose Elend der Hexenprozesse belastete die meisten Kommissare psychisch, und die Annahme, die Prozesse wären aus „niederen" Motiven durchgeführt worden (Bereicherungsabsicht etc.), mutet absurd an."
[180] Walz, *Hexenglaube und magische Kommunikation im Dorf der frühen Neuzeit*; Rummel, *Bauern, Herren und Hexen*; Voltmer, "Hexenverfolgung und Herrschaftspraxis"; Rummel and Voltmer, *Hexen und Hexenverfolgung*.
[181] Briggs, *Witches & Neighbours*; Clark, *Thinking with Demons*; Goodare, *The European Witch-Hunt*; Dillinger, *Hexen und Magie*, 2018.

oppression of women, many aspects of witchcraft texts and trials become even stranger, less comprehensible, and increasingly illogical. A key lesson of witchcraft scholarship over the past decades has therefore been to no longer try to explain witch-hunting away as a social function or a means to exert power. Instead, let us take at face value what its proponents actually wrote and believed. If we assume that the initiators and executors of trials genuinely meant what they said, their actions do not look that illogical after all. In *that* case the trials happened pretty much along the lines we would expect. So, witch-hunting was not a means towards a hidden end; it was an end in itself.[182]

Historical scholars have found various ways of formulating this viewpoint. "That the ostensible motives for trying witches were real ones is a virtually inescapable conclusion from a scrutiny of the more detailed trial records", Geoffrey Scarre writes.[183] "Witch-beliefs were not a trick; the fear of witches was very real", states Johannes Dillinger.[184] Martine Ostorero highlights that "people really believed it, and without a doubt in good faith."[185] When dismissing all the alternative explanatory models Robert Thurston maintains that "sometimes fear is the key to history."[186] Or in Julian Goodare's words: "a witchcraft accusation was not 'really' about something else; it was really about witchcraft", as "most accusations were undoubtedly sincere."[187] According to Christina Larner "the prime interest of the authorities at the time was the pursuit of witches as such", and as she wonderfully summarizes this current viewpoint: "witch-hunting was actually witch-hunting."[188]

This is not to say that persecutions were unrelated to other conflicts or aims that people had. These historians are willing to accept that animosities between families, or between individuals, stimulated accusations and trials in many instances, as could other factors like greed or jealousy. James Sharpe writes that "it is possible to find an enormous range of antagonisms, personal feuds, and areas of competitiveness underlying a witchcraft accusation."[189] But it does not imply that the beliefs were not real, or that witch-hunting was used as a vehicle for a different purpose. Even when persecutors deliberately distorted evidence, which sometimes happened, it does not yet provide us with evidence for cynical motives. Julian Goodare explains: "they usually believed that the suspect was guilty, but were worried that the existing evidence would be insufficient – so they manufactured some more."[190] A particularly subtle model for how witch trials and other conflicts were interrelated has been developed by Johannes Dillinger, and he calls

---

[182] Clark, "Introduction"; Gibson, "Thinking Witchcraft"; Goodare, *The European Witch-Hunt*, 185, 230–31; Gaskill, "The Pursuit of Reality"; Machielsen, *Martin Delrio*, 212.
[183] Scarre, *Witchcraft and Magic*, 47.
[184] Dillinger, *Hexen und Magie*, 2018, 127."Der Hexenglaube war kein «Trick»; die Hexenangst war sehr real."
[185] Ostorero, *Le diable au sabbat*, 9.'des gens one réellement cru, et sans doute de bonne foi'.
[186] Thurston, *The Witch Hunts*, 204.
[187] Goodare, *The European Witch-Hunt*, 115, 384.
[188] Gibson, "Thinking Witchcraft," 169–70.
[189] Sharpe, *Witchcraft in Early Modern England*, 49.
[190] Goodare, *The European Witch-Hunt*, 221.

it the "'evil people' paradigm".[191] Dillinger observes that allegations of witchcraft often focused on people the accusers already disliked for other reasons, such as social upstarts, loudmouths, strangers, or vagabonds. The terms "witches" and "evil people" were often even used interchangeably at the time. This might seem to suggest that allegations served the purpose of harming ostensibly antisocial people, but Dillinger proposes a different causal connection: it was from people's allegedly asocial behavior that their identity as a witch was inferred. After all, Satan and his demons were trying to seduce as many people as they could, and obviously it was evil individuals who most easily succumbed to their will. So, when looking for witches, people tended to think of disagreeable people from the local community first.

Today, ironically, we see the people who initiated and executed these murderous trials as the evil ones, and we feel very sorry for those who were burned at the stake. But we should not forget that from the witch-hunters' own perspective they were doing honorable work. This observation does not imply moral relativism – even by the standards of the time many persecutions were seen as excessive, cruel and judicially irresponsible, and witch-hunters were labelled as zealots by their opponents.[192] Still, it does not alter the fact that the trying of witches could be motivated by genuine intentions. Some infamous trials took place in the German Prince-bishopric of Würzburg under the rule of prince-bishop Julius Echter von Mespelbrunn, and they have tainted his reputation ever since. But this same prince-bishop was also the man who turned Würzburg into one of the most beautiful baroque cities of Germany, who gave his name to a new hospital that was renowned for its care for orphans, pilgrims and the mentally ill, and who regularly went there himself to distribute food and to wash the pensioners' feet.[193] In the duchy of Lorraine the aforementioned magistrate Nicolas Rémy prided himself on killing a number of eight hundred witches, but he simultaneously expressed ardent concerns about saving the souls of the women that he burned.[194] It may look strikingly inconsistent to us today, but not to many of the involved actors at the time. From Mespelbrunn's and Rémy's own perspectives it consistently served the well-being and salvation of Christian communities.

So, if simply taking the witch-hunters at their word provides us with the best entry into understanding how the trials occurred, then why has there been this continuing tendency to look for other purposes? Several historians have reflected on that.[195] It has been highlighted that the beliefs about witches look so very strange to a modern audience, while at the same time it is so obvious that these beliefs were illusory, that we almost inevitably tend to think that it must have been about something else.[196] Hence, we look for more universal and less time-bound

---

[191] Dillinger, *Böse Leute*; Dillinger, *Hexen und Magie*, 2018, 133."«Böse Leute»-Paradigma."
[192] Behringer, *Witches and Witch-Hunts*, 175; Briggs, *Witches & Neighbours*, 407.
[193] Roper, *Witch Craze*, 23–24; Flurschütz da Cruz, *Hexenbrenner, Seelenretter*; For a summary of debates about Echter's reputatation, see: Voltmer, "Hexenbrenner Und Hexenbischöfe."
[194] Rémy, *Demonolatry*, 56; Roper, *Witch Craze*, 21–22; Briggs, *The Witches of Lorraine*, 78–80.
[195] Scarre, *Witchcraft and Magic*, 43, 61–63; Gibson, "Thinking Witchcraft," 169; Goodare, *The European Witch-Hunt*, 385; Briggs, *Witches & Neighbours*, 385; Durrant, *Witchcraft, Gender, and Society in Early Modern Germany*, 171.
[196] Scarre, *Witchcraft and Magic*, 43, 61–63; Gibson, "Thinking Witchcraft," 169; Goodare, *The European Witch-Hunt*, 385.

explanations that make sense to our enlightened frameworks, such as greed or power play. And thus, we impose our modern assumptions on the early modern world. Moreover, as Briggs writes, we "find it hard to accept that these horrible proceedings were carried out in good faith."[197] The rebuttal of the cynical interpretations of witch-hunting does not make the horrors of the trials any less awful, though. Geoffrey Scarre comments: "it was something even more depressing – a frightful example of how morally motivated action can lead to massive suffering, and good intentions produce the direst consequences."[198]

Idiographic contemplations
The failure of the earlier explanatory models in witchcraft historiography has also sparked some very "idiographic" reflections on the methodology of history. It is argued that the past, once again, is too messy, too complex, while there are always too many exceptions for a general rule to work. Jan Machielsen maintains that "any scholar of early modern witchcraft should be skeptical of grand narratives – and remind themselves that the devil is in the details."[199] It is emphasized that every witch trial had its own particular dynamics, resulting from its own complex interplay of innumerable factors, which were related to their own unique historical and regional context.[200] On closer scrutiny witch persecutions were not even a single phenomenon, making the search for any single set of laws pointless from the outset.[201] "Sweeping generalizations about it are either false or so banal as to lack any analytical power" comments Robin Briggs.[202] The collapse of grand explanatory models is thus not seen as a problem, but, rather, as a virtue.[203] Johannes Dillinger renders it a "big step forward in witchcraft research that mono-causal interpretations, that aim to uncover one key factor that would explain witch-hunting as a mass phenomenon, are no longer worthy of serious consideration."[204] In an essay with the illustrative title "Many Reasons Why" Robin Briggs proposes that we should look instead for "a more finely grained picture" and a "greater diversity at local level."[205] In a passage that is worth quoting at length he also explores how this bears upon the relationship between history and the natural sciences:

---

[197] Briggs, *Witches & Neighbours*, 383.
[198] Scarre, *Witchcraft and Magic*, 63.
[199] Machielsen, "Thinking with Montaigne," 452.
[200] Hehl, "Hexenprozesse und Geschichtswissenschaft"; Sharpe, *Witchcraft in Early Modern England*, 6; Levack, *The Witch-Hunt in Early Modern Europe*, 3; Blauert, *Frühe Hexenverfolgungen*, 23–24, 114.
[201] Briggs, *Witches & Neighbours*, 7; Kieckhefer, "Mythologies of Witchcraft in the Fifteenth Century," 105–7; Beliën and Eerden, *Satans trawanten*, 220–21.
[202] Briggs, *Witches & Neighbours*, 7.
[203] Sharpe, *Witchcraft in Early Modern England*, 6; Schormann, *Hexenprozesse in Deutschland*, 95; Behringer, *Hexenverfolgung in Bayern*, 400–430; Goodare, *The European Witch-Hunt*, 255; Kieckhefer, "Mythologies of Witchcraft in the Fifteenth Century," 105.
[204] Dillinger, *Hexen und Magie*, 2018, 73."Es muss vielmehr als großer Fortschritt in der Hexenforschung gelten, das monokausale Interpretationen, die versuchten, einen Schlüsselfaktor zur Erklärung des Makrophänomens Hexenverfolgung zu präsentieren, heute nicht mehr diskussionswürdig sind."
[205] Briggs, "Many Reasons Why," 51.

Although it may not be capable of formal expression, I suspect that there is an explanatory law which dictates that complex problems of this type never have simple or precisely identifiable causes. Careful analysis usually reveals overlapping levels and strands of both causation and meaning, which are extremely hard to rank against one another even in individual cases. Once we start aggregating, the variables multiply so fast that chaos theory, with its patterns of unpredictability, is the scientific model which best fits the case. This is not a counsel of despair, however; I would argue that it liberates us from the impossible demands created by a heavily mechanistic conception of human society. Too many theories resemble the work of Cartesian natural philosophers, wanting the world to cling in tight patterns sustained by a kind of cosmic Velcro, when reality is much more flexible and less tangible.[206]

Historians have restated this trope time and again, and in regard to early modern witch beliefs and trials it makes sense in many respects. Yes, we should appreciate the diversity of witch beliefs and trials, and place them within their own highly complex historical context. The interpretation of the meaningful symbolic world that the involved actors were living in also needs to be addressed carefully. Deterministic, mono-causal, Cartesian-like models look particularly ill-suited indeed. But at the same time there is something unsatisfying about this trope. The idiographic tendency to announce the end to all large explanatory frameworks is too easy, as it leaves so much unexplained. The empirical findings of historians about witch beliefs and persecutions have actually unearthed at least two intriguing theoretical puzzles, neither of which has been properly recognized yet, and which are crying out for an answer. What historians have found out about witch-hunts should not lead us towards a theoretical dead-end, but, rather, to a new beginning.

Unanswered questions
The first theoretical puzzle is the striking level of adaptedness that the cumulative concept of witchcraft contained. Even if we accept that witch-hunters did not deliberately create witch-hunts for an underlying purpose, and that they genuinely believed in it, one earlier observation about the witch-hunt system still stands: Marvin Harris was right to call it "too well-designed." Just think of the way in which some of the deepest anxieties of the time period, such as fear of the devil, anti-Christian communities, harmful magic, and uncontrollable female sexuality, were ingeniously arranged into one frightening concept. Or think of additional elements that stimulated the continuation of trials with an ever-increasing circle of suspects, such as the belief in the witches' sabbath, nightly flight, torture as a means of interrogation, or the focus on children as potential accusers. Such notions endowed the concept of witchcraft with a remarkable robustness, a resilience, and a striking capacity to trigger witch-hunts that spiraled out of control.

---

[206] Briggs, 53.

It is not by accident that earlier scholars assumed that it contained "built-in structures" that were "fabricated", "braided", "designed", and "perfected" to serve particular goals. If one of those older theories had actually been right, namely that the concept was indeed shrewdly designed by an interested party, then this party would have deserved much credit for their understanding of social dynamics, as well as for their psychological insight into the anxieties of the time. But there was no such interested group of people. So how did this apparent "design" of the concept of witchcraft come about?

Even some of the "idiographic" historians cannot help but be impressed by how ably the concept of witchcraft managed to spread within its historical contexts. As part of his "'evil people' - paradigm" Johannes Dillinger analyzes how this elastic concept attached itself to a broad spectrum of social conflicts.[207] "What made the notion of the witch so very explosive was its ability to translate almost every form of negative behavior into an indication of witchcraft. The range of behaviors that potentially triggered suspicions was entirely open-ended."[208] In a similar vein Robin Briggs maintains that "witchcraft was peculiarly malleable, available to fit any kind of discord, because the link between ill-will and physical effects did not need to be demonstrated."[209] Drawing inspiration from psychoanalytic theory, Briggs additionally argues that the notion of the witch played on people's unconsciousness by appealing to some of their profound anxieties, as well as to feelings of guilt and repressed libido. At the psychological level it "allowed fantasy to run riot."[210] Early modern societies normally had all sorts of checks and balances that prevented murderous hostilities from getting out of hand, but "the corporate fantasy of witchcraft was capable of breaking down such controls and encouraging people to act out their beliefs", making it a "brilliantly successful fiction"[211] Thomas Robisheaux states that witchcraft "lurked invisibly within almost any troubling or troubled social relationship", while Julian Goodare emphasized how it could "mobilize people's deepest fears."[212] Yet, the question staring us in the face here is: how did the concept develop these insidious capacities?

Then there is a second intriguing question that has remained unanswered. We saw that modern scholars have been searching for the beneficiaries of witch trials in every nook and cranny, but did not find them in considerable number. Meticulous empirical research has indicated that in many cases there were no interested groups of people who substantially benefited from the witch-hunts, and that communities as a whole were often ravaged by them. According to Wolfgang Behringer, as we saw, even many of the commissioners who participated in them suffered greatly. The persecution of witches was often destructive for nearly all and

---

[207] Dillinger, *Böse Leute*, 350; Dillinger, Fritz, and Mährle, *Zum Feuer verdammt*, 72–81.
[208] Dillinger, *Böse Leute*, 442."Die Brisanz der Hexenvorstellung bestand gerade auch darin, daß jedes als negativ erlebte Verhalten als ‚Indiz' für Hexerei ausgelegt werden konnte. Das Feld der Hexereiverdacht erzeugenden Verhaltensweisen war völlig offen." .
[209] Briggs, *Witches & Neighbours*, 265.
[210] Briggs, 166–67, 250, 265.
[211] Briggs, 164; Briggs, *The Witches of Lorraine*, 384.
[212] Robisheaux, "The German Witch Trials," 191; Goodare, *The European Witch-Hunt*, 305.

everyone. But if this is so, then how is it possible that the witch-hunting phenomenon survived for such a long time? Why was it so difficult to keep an outbreak of witch panic under control once it was set in motion? It seems strange that communities would tolerate such deleterious practices, if there was no tangible benefit that could offset the cost of human life. This is odd and begs for an explanation. In other words, what we observe is forms of socio-cultural "design", apparently without intentional designers, that did not significantly benefit anyone. How can Darwinian theory help us out?

5.5 Darwinian attempts

Darwin had the good fortune of developing his theory with data from colleagues who were, as Daniel Dennett calls it, "theoretically untainted".[213] Researchers always run a risk of seeing only those aspects of reality that match preconceived conceptions, and current evolutionary biology would be an unlikely exception to this rule.[214] Yet, while the works of naturalists before 1859 were surely characterized by all sorts of biases, a pro-Darwinian bias was obviously not a part of that. According to Dennett this posed an important check on Darwin's enthusiasm: the facts that he worked with had not been collected with the aim of proving his theory right. Still, many of those naturalists' findings, like the analyses of divine "design", or the morphological similarities between internal structures, provided his model with much needed support. Subsequently, the principle of evolution by natural selection did not make those earlier insights redundant. On the contrary – within their new theoretical context they took on a whole new meaning.

The relationship between Darwinian cultural evolution and the scholarship of European witch-hunting may possibly work out along similar lines. When witchcraft historians collected their data and developed their interpretations, none of them thought of substantiating a model of Darwinian cultural evolution. But instead of making their findings *less* valuable for the current evolutionary field, it arguably makes them *more* valuable. After all, regarding Darwinian theory, it was all worked out in theoretical innocence. Only unintentionally do so many of their findings offer clues for the development of a Darwinian scenario. Some historical scholars highlighted how the witch-hunt system appears to have been designed, while others retorted that sources provide no substantial evidence for shrewd designers operating behind the scenes. This looks exactly like the kind of "design without designer" phenomenon that people like Dennett and David Sloan Wilson have envisaged. Moreover, the deleterious consequences of witch trials on people as well as on societies, suggest a "selfish" cultural phenomenon that spread at the expense of its human hosts.

We should not immediately adopt a Darwinian explanation, though. As we saw, Robin Briggs thought chaos theory to be "the scientific model which best fits the case", and even scholars acquainted with cultural evolution stress that socio-cultural phenomena are not

---

[213] Dennett, *From Bacteria to Bach and Back*, 238.
[214] Dennett, *Breaking the Spell*, 30–32.

"adaptive" by default – they can be a by-product of something else, or result from processes of cultural random drift. An evolutionary experimental study of the spread of songs in a simulated music market, for instance, indicated that the reproductive success of songs can be due to contingent factors, and not to any inherent "adaptive" traits.[215] Neither should we forget that witch-hunts were characterized by much haphazardness and unpredictability. Still, the reason for adopting an adaptive research strategy in this case, is that the clustered cumulative notions of diabolical witchcraft simply appear too fine-tuned and well-disposed to have the kind of effects that they so often had within their historical context: the dynamics of a witch-hunt. It looks like something conspicuously functional, and chaos theory or randomness provide insufficient an explanation for that. Since intentional design seems unable to do the explanatory job either, Darwinism may provide an outcome.

Evolutionary psychology
The study of witchcraft is not an entirely pristine area for Darwinian theory. Especially evolutionary psychology has already been integrated to some extent, offering a welcome counterweight to some of the excesses of socio-cultural constructivism. A stark example of such excesses is Stuart Clark, who wants to ignore neuro-psychological or psycho-physiological causes of human behavior, because such causes were not yet a part of the meaningful frameworks of historical actors.[216] We also encountered the literary scholar Walter Stephens, who maintains that stories about sex between witches and demons were not of pornographic, but only of metaphysical interest to demonologists.[217] These cases show how some humanities scholars have lost touch with biological realities. Neurological processes already occurred before scientists described them as such, and since sexual encounters belong to the most essential reproductive facts of life, evolution has fine-tuned our brains and bodies to find them of far more than metaphysical importance.

It must be said that Clark and Stephens are not representative of the entire field. Several experts take the biological underpinnings of witch-hunting more seriously. Robin Briggs maintains that the pervasiveness of witchcraft beliefs worldwide indicates that evolved psychological propensities may lie at the root of it.[218] This does not automatically imply that humans are born with a witch-detection mechanism, as Briggs also suggests a scenario in which broader innate social skills, like the detection of antagonisms or deceit, helped trigger witch persecution under certain conditions. Julian Goodare states that "seventeenth-century people did not think *that* differently from us; their culture may have been different, but their brains and nervous systems were not."[219] Some neurologists, for instance, claim that fear is located in the

---

[215] Salganik, Dodds, and Watts, "Experimental Study of Inequality and Unpredictability in an Artificial Cultural Market."
[216] Clark, *Thinking with Demons*, 396–97.
[217] Stephens, *Demon Lovers*, 26.
[218] Briggs, *Witches & Neighbours*, 373–74, 392–94.
[219] Goodare, *The European Witch-Hunt*, 2.

amygdala region of the brain, so Goodare thinks it conceivable that this brain area was activated during outbreaks of witch-hunting.[220] Such historical reflections also correspond to what scientists from other disciplines have to say on the topic: certain mental modules, such as threat perception, coalitional psychology, or the punishment of defectors, were selected independently and not for the purpose of witch persecution. But when a persecution occurred, it was modules like these that were activated.[221]

The witchcraft historian who has addressed humans' psychobiological traits most extensively is Edward Bever, for instance when explaining the overrepresentation of women amongst the victims.[222] In his account, men are more likely to express aggression in interpersonal conflicts through physical means, whereas women more often resort to indirect means like gossiping, poisoning, and other forms of concealed attack. These differences, Bever presumes, stem from Paleolithic times, but could still make women more obvious targets for witchcraft accusations in an early modern context. Bever does not deny the impact of cultural expectations, but thinks that such expectations may be enhancements of older biological disparities.[223] The gender dimension of witchcraft might also trigger further interdisciplinary considerations. One striking aspect of early modern witch beliefs is that women were thought to have a stronger sexual appetite than men, which flies in the face of current evolutionary psychology. This either means that people at the time were dead wrong about that, or that evolutionary psychology has mistaken a current stereotype – women are pickier than men – for biological fact. On the other hand, Lyndal Roper's finding that male witches were thought to be provided with multiple partners instead of one diabolical lover, is more in line with the current evolutionary outlook.[224] Contemplations such as these can help illustrate how historical records can be put to good interdisciplinary use.

Yet, let us also re-emphasize limitations to evolutionary psychology. What a biological perspective *cannot* tell us is why people in this particular time period in European history had this very particular and culturally complex fear of diabolical witchcraft. After all, we have no "witches fly to the sabbath on a broomstick module", or a "the devil sometimes appears as a goat module", located in specific spots of our brain. True, people in Bamberg in 1626 were possibly walking around with activated amygdala areas, but a hundred years earlier, or later, they also had amygdalae, but no witch-hunt occurred. So, if we want to understand what happened in 1626, neurology will not help us much. One might retort that if the neurological processes in people's brains had not taken place as they did, witch-hunting would have been impossible. This is correct, but we could say the same about gravity. Had there been no gravity in Bamberg in 1626, everything and everyone would have been flying around, also making witch-hunts

---

[220] Goodare, 374.
[221] Parren, "The (Possible) Cognitive Naturalness of Witchcraft Beliefs"; Koning, "Witchcraft Beliefs and Witch Hunts."
[222] Bever, *The Realities of Witchcraft*; Bever, "Witchcraft, Female Aggression, and Power in the Early Modern Community."
[223] Bever, *The Realities of Witchcraft*, 49–55.
[224] Roper, *Witch Craze*, 91.

impossible. But obviously that does not imply that we can explain witch-hunting from gravity. And neither can we explain witch-hunting from brains. Preconditions do not equal explanations.

Cultural evolution
The cumulative concept of witchcraft was something thoroughly *cultural*, so it is also at the semi-autonomous level of cultural transmission and selection that the origin of its apparent design must be sought. But what might such a cultural Darwinian process have looked like? Some tentative efforts in this direction have already been undertaken, and one is to look at the cultural evolution of witch beliefs from a cognitive point of view.[225] We saw that the current evolutionary field assumes that gene-culture coevolution has endowed our brains with learning biases that make some cultural variants more easily adopted and transmitted than others. Hence, from this angle one might expect popular ideas about witchcraft to have been well adapted to those structures of our brains. The witchcraft scholar Bengt Ankarloo quotes one of the founders of this cognitive view on cultural evolution, Pascal Boyer, as follows: "the outcome of this selection is that certain features are recurrent because they are more likely to be entertained, acquired, and transmitted by human minds."[226] Ankarloo does not develop concrete examples in detail, but we might for instance think of the idea of female initiation into witchcraft through diabolical intercourse. Cognitive scientists highlighted that our brains eagerly adopt information about threats, sexual contacts, and rumors, so this variant's reproductive success may not come as a surprise.[227] It is also claimed that popular tropes tend to be modestly counterintuitive: stories containing only familiar elements do not attract attention, while stories containing only unfamiliar elements are too alien to be remembered. Narratives that thrive thus lie somewhere between the extremes.[228] Again, the idea of diabolical intercourse fits the cognitive bill perfectly well. It combines the familiar – emotional despair, physical attraction, moral dilemmas – with the unfamiliar, like the hoof of a goat, the icy penis, or the sulfur smell. Within this cognitive research agenda, we could subject further witch beliefs to similar scrutiny.

However, explanatory limitations still need to be emphasized. As a lecturer I often tell the story of diabolical intercourse to students, and notice that it still attracts immediate attention. So, apparently this cultural variant's ability to play on our minds has not yet abated. But unlike so many early moderns, students today tend to find the story quite amusing and none of them is prepared to burn others for it. Hence, if we want to understand how this particular story spread so well within its historical context, and what the effects of it were, we also need to look beyond universal cognition. It requires questions like: what did female sexuality at this specific period in

---

[225] Keitt, "Rethinking with Demons"; Singh, "Magic, Explanations, and Evil"; Mercier, *Not Born Yesterday*, 181–98; Parren, "The (Possible) Cognitive Naturalness of Witchcraft Beliefs."
[226] Ankarloo, "Witch Trials in Northern Europe: 1450-1700," 55.
[227] Parren, "The (Possible) Cognitive Naturalness of Witchcraft Beliefs"; Koning, "Witchcraft Beliefs and Witch Hunts"; Blackmore, *The Meme Machine*, 121.
[228] Mesoudi, *Cultural Evolution*, 2011, 145–46; Keitt, "Rethinking with Demons."

time *mean* to people? What did diabolical evil *mean* to them? One of the merits of the cognitive view on cultural evolution is that it takes an important step towards the realm of cultural complexity, but at the same time it still suffers from evolutionary psychology's problem of universality. Stuart Clark complains that cognitive approaches bleach out historical specificity, transforming "the rich color and texture of lived experience" into "the drab monotony of brain functions."[229] This time he has a point.

So where else to look? Another option, also tentatively explored by some, is to apply the idea of cultural group selection to witch-hunting. Older functionalist accounts lacked an explanatory model for how alleged social functions of witch trials came about, and this is exactly what cultural group selection may provide: beliefs in witches and practices of trying them had positive effects on the functioning of cultural groups, also resulting in the survival of these variants themselves. Accordingly, Donald Campbell maintained that "even witchcraft accusations serve a useful, social control function in simpler societies", and a recent paper by cultural group selectionists elaborated upon that.[230] They propose that witch-hunts, in some societies at least, functioned as an incentive for prosocial behavior, as it made people cautious not to be labeled as a witch. Additionally, it facilitated conflict resolution and the prevention of social and economic inequalities. If applied to the European case, we might presume that cultural groups which persecuted witches outcompeted other groups *because of that*.

The failure of older functionalist models should make us wary of this approach though. Village witchcraft may have been subject to such mechanisms, perhaps, but the elaborate notions of diabolical witchcraft, and the large trials resulting from them, look ill-suited to any such approach. Historians have already concluded that witch-hunts were often highly damaging for the social communities in which they occurred. Interestingly, anthropologists reached similar conclusions regarding non-western case studies.[231] "The widespread fear that witchcraft is running wild has shocking effects in everyday life – tearing families apart and setting people against each other", Peter Geschiere wrote about witch-hunting in post-colonial Cameroon.[232] In a study on witchcraft beliefs of the Gebusi people in New Guinea, Bruce Knauft concluded that its killings of alleged sorcerers did not so much reflect underlying conflicts, but were "produced by independent strains in the structure of belief."[233] The effects for Gebusi life were dramatic; its witch-hunts are at the root of one of the highest rates of homicide reported for any human society.[234] Another problem with this model is that the alleged underlying mechanism require repeated rounds of selection in which group functional variants are accumulated. However,

---

[229] Clark, "One-Tier History," 89.
[230] Campbell, "On the Conflicts between Biological and Social Evolution," 196; Joseph Bulbulia et al., "The Cultural Evolution of Religion."
[231] Gershman, "Witchcraft Beliefs and the Erosion of Social Capital"; Hutton, *The Witch*, 35; Walz, *Hexenglaube und magische Kommunikation im Dorf der frühen Neuzeit*, 37–39.
[232] Geschiere, *The Modernity of Witchcraft*, 21.
[233] Knauft, *Good Company and Violence*, 4.
[234] Knauft, *Good Company and Violence*.

regarding the European case study, this conflicts with another key finding of historians: witchcraft panics did not often occur at the same place more than once or twice.[235] So this would have provided any blind selective process with too little time to steer witch beliefs and persecutions into a group-functional direction.

This message has not been lost on the current field of cultural evolution.[236] Ara Norenzayan, one of group selection's outspoken proponents, accepts that "not all cultural beliefs and practices lead to prosocial behavior", and the joint paper mentioned above reaches a similar conclusion.[237] Its authors argue that the extent to which witch beliefs and persecutions had positive social effects, depends on "the relative strength of competition between religious groups versus the competition of subgroups or individuals within religious groups."[238] When the latter forces are stronger, witch-hunting may actually turn into a socially destabilizing force. As they maintain: "to evaluate such questions, a new collaborative evolutionary history is needed."[239] This makes the European case study all the more relevant. Might competition between subgroups, or between individuals, provide a more plausible model for how European witch-hunting evolved?

The remark about "competition of subgroups" hints in the direction of a power-oriented perspective, in which persecutions survived because they served the interests of one group within society at the expense of other groups. However, considering the stark limitations of older power perspectives, like the models of Harris, Muchembled, or the feminists, this line of research does not look very promising either. What about the option of "competition of individuals" as an evolutionary principle? The authors of the joint paper do not elaborate upon that, but this remark suggests a tendency to explain witch-hunting as a tool that serves individuals' interests. To a certain degree this suggestion is more in line with current scholarship of European witch-hunting, as one of its key findings has been that proponents of trials thought to have good reasons for what they were doing: reducing the dangers of harmful magic, as well as enhancing chances of salvation. What this observation does not tell us yet, however, is how people came to believe in diabolical witchcraft in the first place, especially considering its largely illusory character. What is more, the trials in fact often *subverted* people's interests. Think of the inhabitants of Zeil who called for a witch-hunt, but in many cases ended up at the stake or in the witch oven themselves. The literature provides many more examples of the witch-hunting phenomenon killing the initiators, or their families.[240] This makes it hard to see how a blind evolutionary process, operating at the level of competition between individuals, would have occurred.

---

[235] Midelfort, *Witch Hunting in Southwestern Germany*, 194; Roper, *Witch Craze*, 11, 133; Behringer, *Witches and Witch-Hunts*, 149; Goodare, *The European Witch-Hunt*, 323.
[236] Richerson and Boyd, *Not By Genes Alone*, 168.
[237] Norenzayan, *Big Gods*, 137.
[238] Joseph Bulbulia et al., "The Cultural Evolution of Religion," 395–96.
[239] Joseph Bulbulia et al., 396.
[240] Dillinger, *Kinder im Hexenprozess*, 135; Midelfort, *Witch Hunting in Southwestern Germany*, 93–94, 137; Voltmer and Irsigler, "Die Europäischen Hexenverfolgungen Der Frühen Neuzeit - Vorurteile, Faktoren Und Bilanzen," 40; Haas, *Hexen und*

The selfish culture hypothesis

It is at this point that the new explanatory power of the "selfish culture hypothesis" comes to the fore. Instead of looking at the competition between cultural groups, subgroups, or individuals, we could highlight the competition between cultural variants, and try to look at the whole witch-hunting phenomenon from *their* point of view. Perhaps beliefs and trials did not so much evolve to serve the interests of society, the powerful, or specific people, but rather to serve their *own* self-reproduction. Mary Midgley mentioned this option but immediately rejected it, whereas Richerson and Boyd take something like it more seriously.[241] But nobody has explored this possibility in more detail, let alone integrated the detailed insights of historians on the topic.[242] This is a loss, especially considering the fact that historians' meticulous examination of trials, as well as their careful interpretation of primary sources, provide so many clues for this scenario.

The underlying principles may have worked as follows: innumerable beliefs and practices regarding witchcraft appeared, but most of them did not reproduce well – they had no significant effects within their historical context that ensured their continuation. Yet, within this ocean of variants that were too poorly adapted for survival, every now and then variants appeared that *did* have significant positive effects on their own reproduction, like the beliefs in the witches' sabbath, nightly flight, or the child witch. In places where such notions were more prominent in people's minds, the variants often had the effect of triggering larger persecutions. Subsequently, the unusual scale of those trials may well have attracted much attention, leading to the adoption of those variants by other people, and thereby to similar events elsewhere. Inflammable cultural "germs" like these thus "infected" more and more brains. So, through repeated rounds of selection, notions conducive to witch-hunting accumulated into an ever more explosive cluster of beliefs. Importantly, this scenario does not require involved actors who comprehended these causes and effects. The sabbath belief, for instance, may have had the effect of chains of accusations only accidentally at first. But as soon as this effect contributed to the belief's own survival, a blind Darwinian process was set in motion that created this prodigious new cultural adaptation.

It must be noted that several historians came close to a scenario quite like this.[243] Older models often treated witch-hunting as a top-down product of demonology, but more recent studies stress that it frequently happened the other way around.[244] Contemporary publications on witchcraft were in many cases a response to, or a report of, significant outbreaks of witch-

---

Herrschaftspolitik, 114; Decker, "Die Hexenverfolgungen im Herzogtum Westfalen," 367; Rummel and Voltmer, *Hexen und Hexenverfolgung*, 103, 112.
[241] Midgley, "Why Memes," 83–84; Richerson and Boyd, *Not By Genes Alone*, 167–69.
[242] Some very short references to witch persecutions as a case study of "memes" can be found in: Bever, *The Realities of Witchcraft*, 182; Aunger, *The Electric Meme*, 1–2.
[243] Goodare, *The European Witch-Hunt*, 85; Levack, *The Witch-Hunt in Early Modern Europe*, 49; Dillinger, *Hexen und Magie*, 2018, 53; Richard Kieckhefer, "The First Wave of Trials," 166.
[244] Kieckhefer, "Mythologies of Witchcraft in the Fifteenth Century," 105–6; Richard Kieckhefer, "The First Wave of Trials," 166.

hunting. But as soon as the new demonological ideas were put in print, they helped trigger similar trials in other places. Robin Briggs describes the formation of witch beliefs as an untidy process in which incidental effects fed back into complex networks of causation.[245] For a long time, persecutions were sporadic and localized, and did not get going in earnest. However, "where it became intense, of course, there was a serious danger that it would reinforce popular fears and thus raise anxiety levels further."[246] Similarly, Trevor-Roper stated that "every spectacular episode increased the power of the myth", while Julian Goodare thinks that trials and demonologies were "mutually reinforcing".[247] Especially interrogations of suspects have been identified as possible breeding grounds for new demonological ideas. Lyndal Roper argues that the confessions of alleged witches continually fed back into works of demonology, which then enlarged the interrogators' idea of what crimes witches committed. "This process was a dialogue", she writes.[248] Or Brian Levack:

> The set of learned beliefs could become cumulative, since a new inquisitor, in trying the case, would use the information contained in the manual to formulate the questions he would direct to witnesses and the accused. At the same time, however, he might use some of the specific charges against the accused or his own imagination to give a new twist to the standard charges. The confession that he would extract to these somewhat different charges, perhaps embellished by the witch's imagination and folk beliefs, might then be included in another manual or treatise on witchcraft and thus be transmitted to other inquisitors.[249]

Such remarks are intriguing, but they remain fragmentary and disconnected from a broader theoretical framework. However, when we look at them from an evolutionary point of view, they can take on a whole new meaning. The remarks become essential ingredients for a Darwinian scenario in which new cultural variants provided the raw material for a selective process that built its own adaptations from it. This is not mere tautology. If we take the notion of the witches' sabbath as an example, the proposed model requires several assumptions that can be examined empirically. (1) Many cultural variants regarding witchcraft appeared, most of which did not reproduce well. (2) The belief in the witches' sabbath had the effect of triggering larger and more spectacular persecutions. (3) This effect contributed to the survival of the belief in the witches' sabbath itself. (4) This enhancing effect was neither intended nor recognized as such by the actors involved; it was a chance hit. Unlike the case of the Hopi rain dance, this time we have

---

[245] Briggs, *Witches & Neighbours*, 147.
[246] Briggs, 291.
[247] Trevor-Roper, *The European Witch-Craze*, 115; Goodare, *The European Witch-Hunt*, 85.
[248] Roper, *Witch Craze*, 106–7.
[249] Levack, *The Witch-Hunt in Early Modern Europe*, 49.

many sources at our disposal that allow for such investigations. These hypotheses also have the potential of being false to varying degrees.

What is more, the empirical research into these questions undertaken so far is only fragmentary. Hypothesis (1) has been addressed in the sense that historians have devoted much attention to how concepts of witchcraft were characterized by variation, but there is not much research into the question of what kind of variants lacked enhancing effects on trials and may have disappeared because of that. Hypothesis (2) is probably the one best examined, as a broad consensus has taken shape that the notion of the sabbath indeed triggered chains of accusations.[250] Especially trial records provide evidence for that, showing how sabbath beliefs made interrogators ask suspects for accomplices. Hypothesis (3) has been studied less explicitly, although there are many hints in this direction.[251] Briggs for instance writes that "ideas about the sabbat were also perpetuated through the trials themselves. It was routine practice to read out the confessions of the accused at their executions, itself a well-attended public event."[252] Lastly, hypothesis (4) has not been examined at all. Modern historians explicitly identify the sabbath as a key trigger for large trials, but did contemporaries also understand that? And did supporters of witch trials introduce the idea for that reason? We could ask similar questions about the enhancing effects of other cumulative notions, like nightly flight or the child witch. In other words, a research agenda lies ahead.

We shall now proceed as follows. In the next chapter we take a closer look at escalating interactions between witch beliefs and trials in Germany, especially from 1560 to 1630. This period saw the greatest rise in trials, providing us with a fine opportunity to see whether, and if so, how, the anticipated Darwinian mechanisms operated. We particularly look at outbreaks of witch-hunting in Wiesensteig in 1562, in the Trier region around 1590, and in the town of Ellwangen in 1611. Historians have highlighted these hunts as particularly influential ones. Like our discussion of the Bamberg trials, they also provide concrete cases with which to further examine how trials unfolded, and who or what their beneficiaries may have been.

The last chapter offers critical reflections on the proposed Darwinian model. It was already mentioned that various German historians have not given up on the idea of witch-hunts being instrumentalized for hidden goals. In contrast to earlier models, these historians do not look for just one or a few underlying aims, but maintain that witch-hunts were a *multifunctional* instrument, used for a different set of purposes in each instance. This is probably the most challenging counter-model, or complementary model, to the proposal made here. It thus deserves careful consideration, *after* we have gained more knowledge of how German witch-hunts occurred. Seen in this light, the empirical question of what contemporaries did, or did not,

---

[250] Rummel and Voltmer, *Hexen und Hexenverfolgung*, 43; Behringer, *Witches and Witch-Hunts*, 59; Dillinger, *Hexen und Magie*, 2018, 48; Goodare, *The European Witch-Hunt*, 13, 16.
[251] See, for instance: Trevor-Roper, *The European Witch-Craze*, 115; Behringer, *Hexenverfolgung in Bayern*, 224; Schormann, *Hexenprozesse in Deutschland*, 32–33; Labouvie, *Zauberei und Hexenwerk*, 125.
[252] Briggs, *Witches & Neighbours*, 43.

understand about the enhancing effects of cumulative notions of witchcraft becomes even more urgent. In subsequent sections I thus investigate apparent levels of comprehension that both proponents and opponents of trials seem to have had. Then, I address the prospects and pitfalls of the "viral" analogy, and I finish with an obvious and inescapable question: if concepts of witchcraft were so well built for creating continuing trials, then why did witch trials eventually cease? But that is of later concern, as we first move to Wiesensteig in the year 1562. It was in this southern German town that ominous events were about to initiate witch-hunting's most lethal phase.

Chapter 6: Cases

6.1 Wiesensteig 1562

We do not know exactly what happened during the witch-hunt of Wiesensteig in 1562. A fire in 1648 destroyed two-thirds of the town, probably taking the trial records with it. It robbed future historians of an invaluable source of information.[1] What we do know is that the events in this small Lutheran principality were sensational, particularly by the standards of their time.[2] The occurrence of a witch trial in that place and historical instance was not very surprising as such. After a terrifying hailstorm ravaged the region in August 1562, calls for witch-hunting were heard throughout the region. They were soon followed by trials. But while persecutors in towns nearby, like Stuttgart or Esslingen, put at most a few individuals on trial, those in Wiesensteig took things a lot further. Unlike in many other places, the persecutors here thought that witches had met at a crowded assembly, where they adored the Devil and planned their crimes. A *Flugblatt* (newssheet) from 1563 reported the witches' alleged misconducts in gruesome detail: they had blinded and lamed people, killed both young and old, harmed cattle, rejoiced in fornication, dug up buried children to make poisons, and caused the recent hailstorm.[3] What the *Flugblatt* further broadcasted was a staggering number of witches killed: no less than sixty-three.

At the time, witch-hunts had already been going on in Germany for more than a century.[4] After the diabolical witchcraft mythology had appeared in the lower parts of the western Alps around 1430, cumulative notions penetrated Germany, triggering trials in places like Heidelberg, Ravensburg, and Trier.[5] The spread of elaborate witchcraft concepts remained patchy, however, and trials occurred in a sporadic and restricted manner. This holds not only for Germany but for much of Europe. Only a small percentage of people killed as diabolical witches was executed before 1562.[6] From the 1520s onwards trials even underwent a decline. By 1532 Martin Luther remembered how there had been many witches and sorcerers in his youth, making pacts with the devil and bewitching other people, cattle, and especially children.[7] But he added: "now that the gospel is here you do not hear so much about it because the gospel drives the devil away."[8] Luther assumed that Satan now enticed people to commit "spiritual sorcery" of idolatry. So, while witchcraft was a real offense, Luther mostly thought it something of the past.

The early witch-hunts

---

[1] Midelfort, *Witch Hunting in Southwestern Germany*, 89.
[2] Midelfort, 88–90; Waite, *Eradicating the Devil's Minions*; Behringer, "Witchcraft and the Media," 223.
[3] Behringer, *Hexen und Hexenprozesse in Deutschland*, 138–40.
[4] Behringer, 72–129.
[5] Behringer, 110–12; Dillinger, *Böse Leute*, 110; Behringer, *Hexenverfolgung in Bayern*, 78–79; Schmidt, *Glaube und Skepsis*, 23–32.
[6] Levack, *The Witch-Hunt in Early Modern Europe*, 184–91; Leeson and Russ, "Witch Trials," 2081.
[7] Levack, *The Witch-Hunt in Early Modern Europe*, 118.
[8] Rampton, *European Magic and Witchcraft*, 335.

Why did the persecution of diabolical witchcraft fail to make much of an impact before 1562? This is not because crucial cumulative notions that would make later persecutions so deadly were missing.[9] When witch-hunting began in Alpine districts like Valais, Vaud, Bern, Aosta, and Dauphiné, the first reports already contained allegations about diabolical pacts, nightly gatherings, devil worship, trampling on the cross, banquets, dancing, illicit sex, the cannibalism of children, as well as magical crimes. From its inception, the concept also interacted with actual trials, based on confessions extracted through torture.[10] Stories about large numbers of witches likewise circulated. The first description of a witches' gathering stems from a chronicler of the Swiss city of Luzern, Hans Fründ. Around 1430 he wrote that the witches numbered seven hundred people "of whom more than two hundred were burned within one and a half years, while more are convicted and burned every day."[11] Medieval statistics were often vague and inflated, but fragmentary archival sources indicate that Fründ's reports on the trials' size had at least some grounding in reality.[12] It appears that hundreds of people were burned in the early Alpine period alone.[13]

Past interpretations, like the ones of Joseph Hansen or Hugh Trevor-Roper, presumed that those first cumulative notions had been fabricated "from above" by inquisitors.[14] Clerics were already experienced in persecuting Jews and Christian sects, and according to the theory they then transferred their attention to a new target. More recent research, however, offers a more differentiated picture.[15] True, the origin of witch trials was crucially related to the persecution of heretics, as these Alpine valleys had previously witnessed murderous hunts to put down the Waldensians.[16] But instead of being a deliberate "design", witchcraft concepts and trials only gradually emerged from these persecutions.[17] Older stereotypes and practices regarding heretics merged with popular and learned notions about practitioners of harmful magic. Secular rather than clerical authorities conducted many of the first trials, and extensive descriptions of the new sect only appeared afterwards. The authors of these accounts, as Martine Ostorero writes, "took up their pen to try to understand, explain and disseminate what had started to be said earlier

---

[9] Broedel, "Fifteenth-Century Witch Beliefs," 38–41; Bailey, "The Medieval Concept of the Witches' Sabbath"; Ostorero, Bagliani, and Tremp, L'imaginaire du sabbat.
[10] Richard Kieckhefer, "The First Wave of Trials"; Ostorero, Bagliani, and Tremp, L'imaginaire du sabbat.
[11] Fründ, "Rapport sur la chasse aux sorciers et aux sorcières," 43."Parmi ceux-là, plus de 200 furent brûlés, en une année et demie ; et on les juge et brûle encore chaque jour."
[12] Ammann-Doubliez, "La première chasse aux sorciers en Valais (1428-1436?)"; Ostorero, Le diable au sabbat, 27; Goodare, The European Witch-Hunt, 42.
[13] Paravy, "Claude Tholosan, Ut magorum et maleficiorum errores...(Introduction)," 360; Behringer, Witches and Witch-Hunts, 68.
[14] Hansen, Zauberwahn, Inquisition und Hexenproceß im Mittelalter; Trevor-Roper, The European Witch-Craze; Harris, Cows, Pigs, Wars, & Witches, 207–39.
[15] Blauert, Frühe Hexenverfolgungen; Ostorero, Le diable au sabbat, 23–78; Ostorero, Bagliani, and Tremp, L'imaginaire du sabbat; Dillinger, Hexen und Magie, 2007, 52–53; Richard Kieckhefer, "The First Wave of Trials."
[16] Paravy, "Commentaire: Le traité de Claude Tholosan, juge dauphinois (vers 1436)."
[17] Ostorero, Bagliani, and Tremp, L'imaginaire du sabbat, 509–24.

within the context of legal proceedings."[18] In a critique of the old top-down model, her Swiss colleague Andreas Blauert argues that:

> Witch trials were not simply 'invented' and then conducted alongside the persecution of heretics and sorcerers. Rather, it can be demonstrated that the underlying concept of witchcraft, as it was developed from the regional heresy and sorcery trials, had a tendency of absorbing and transforming its predecessors.[19]

A further characteristic of the cumulative concept of witchcraft apparent in the early days, was its propensity to be disseminated. To some extent its spread was fortuitous. Just around the time of its appearance in the Alps, major clergymen from all over Europe were gathering in the nearby city of Basel for the most important Roman Catholic event of the time: the ecumenical council of Basel 1431-1437.[20] Hundreds of abbots, priors, theologians and other clerics from every religious order travelled to this major city along the Rhine to discuss important issues, like papal supremacy and the Hussite heresy in Bohemia. No formal sessions were devoted to the new witchcraft sect, but outside the official program the topic was discussed in detail. One of the major representatives in Basel was Johannes Nider, a Dominican theology professor from Vienna. Impressed by the stories he heard from local persecutors, he included the topic in a popular book he wrote in 1436-1437, the *Formicarius* (The Ant Hill). The book warned people against spiritual hazards of any kind and encouraged a pious reform of Christian society.[21] Importantly, Nider also included a section on diabolical witchcraft, telling people about sabbaths and magical crimes. It would be the most influential text on witchcraft for many decades to come, and Nider was just one of many who took the news from Basel abroad.[22]

Through this prestigious council, as well as through other interactions, the diabolical witchcraft narrative soon spread throughout Europe.[23] Over the next hundred years, the mythology revealed its ability to generate trials. A notorious case occurred in the northern French city of Arras in 1459-1460.[24] It all started when one of Arras's inquisitors attended a witch trial in the eastern French town of Langres, where he learned that two people from his region were mentioned as accomplices. After his return to Arras, the inquisitor brought those two people to trial. The suspects were tortured, confessed, and mentioned the names of further accomplices.

---

[18] Ostorero, *Le diable au sabbat*, 49."Leurs auteurs ont pris la plume pour tenter de comprendre, expliquer et diffuser ce qui avait commencé à se dire auparavant dans le cadre de procédures judiciaires."
[19] Blauert, *Frühe Hexenverfolgungen*, 48-9."Hexenprozesse wurden hier nicht einfach „erfunden" und dann neben Ketzer- und Zaubereiprozessen geführt. Es läßt sich vielmehr zeigen, daß Hexenprozesse im selben Maße, in dem der zugrunde gelegte Hexenbegriff aus den regionalen Ketzer- und Zaubereiprozeßtraditionen entwickelt wurde, die Tendenz besaßen, ihre Vorläufer in sich aufzunehmen und zu transformieren".
[20] Bailey, *Battling Demons*, 5–28, 80; Bailey and Peters, "A Sabbat of Demonologists"; Goodare, *The European Witch-Hunt*, 45.
[21] Nider, "Formicarius"; Bailey, "The Medieval Concept of the Witches' Sabbath"; Bailey, *Battling Demons*.
[22] Bailey, "The Medieval Concept of the Witches' Sabbath," 420.
[23] Broedel, "Fifteenth-Century Witch Beliefs," 42–44; Behringer, *Witches and Witch-Hunts*, 68–72.
[24] Gow, Desjardins, and Pageau, "Introduction: The Arras Witch Treatises in Context"; Goodare, *The European Witch-Hunt*, 47.

This prompted a chain of accusations that led to twelve executions and many more arrests. The proceedings attracted widescale attention, and produced a wave of paranoia, with dramatic effects on the town. Three current experts write: "the city's business had been disrupted, its commercial networks damaged, and its reputation deeply tarnished."[25] Travelers from Arras even had difficulties in finding lodging elsewhere, as hosts feared being drawn into the web of accusations. The trials only ended when persecutors overstepped their mark by attacking wealthy and powerful individuals. Arras was only one example. The new witchcraft mythology for instance also instigated numerous trials in northern Italy.[26] Most persecutions there were limited, but in the city of Como a runaway panic seems to have resulted in at least thirty people being killed, and according to some contemporary reports even hundreds. Climaxing in the early sixteenth century, the topic of diabolical witchcraft further attracted the attention of some Italian Renaissance intellectuals, who fiercely debated the issue.[27]

The slow spread of witch-hunting
Still, as mentioned previously, cumulative witchcraft beliefs did not spread very effectively, and trials occurred seldomly in comparison with the period after 1562. Why this was the case warrants further investigation, but historians have already highlighted some plausible factors. One reason is that major cumulative notions, though already present, often failed to operate *in combination*.[28] A typical example is Nider's *Formicarius*. The idea of witches flying to sabbaths was probably one of the concept's most incendiary traits, as it provoked accusations over long distances. But interestingly, Nider did not connect flight to sabbath attendance and seems to have thought of witches' gatherings as nearby, local affairs.[29] When referring to flight on a later occasion, he even dismissed it as a diabolical delusion. This was no accident, as flight remained a rather ancillary element in witchcraft theory for some time.[30] The most essential trait of the cumulative concept was probably the link between harmful magic and the idea of a heretical sect. Yet, before 1562 that connection was often missing, as many trials either primarily focused on collective heresy or on magic.[31] Misogynous overtones were another inflammable trait of the concept, but for long these were not well developed either. Some authors, like Nider, highlighted women as plausible suspects, but many others did not, and in the early western Alpine trials, women were not yet markedly overrepresented.[32]

---

[25] Gow, Desjardins, and Pageau, "Introduction: The Arras Witch Treatises in Context," 2–3.
[26] Herzig, "Witchcraft Prosecutions in Italy," 250–52; Behringer, *Witches and Witch-Hunts*, 78–79.
[27] Duni, "Doubting Witchcraft."
[28] Broedel, "Fifteenth-Century Witch Beliefs," 42–49; Richard Kieckhefer, "The First Wave of Trials."
[29] Nider, "Formicarius," 134–35, 139; Bailey, "The Medieval Concept of the Witches' Sabbath," 433; Bailey, *Battling Demons*, 46–49.
[30] Stephens, *Demon Lovers*, 126; Bailey, "The Medieval Concept of the Witches' Sabbath," 125–26.
[31] Goodare, *The European Witch-Hunt*, 46.
[32] Bailey, *Battling Demons*, 49–51; Behringer, *Witches and Witch-Hunts*, 68.

The witchcraft mythology became particularly instable as soon as it spread beyond the Alpine heartlands. The cumulative concept tended to pare down as various elements went missing. The Alpine notions also became immersed in local paradigms about witchcraft and magic, thus losing much of their coherence.[33] This transmission resembles the game of Chinese whispers, where a message gets ever more distorted when it is passed on from one person to another. The hunt of Arras provides an example of a relatively successful transmission, but even here aspects characteristic of the Alpine paradigm were absent.[34] The records mention the killing of children, but say nothing about cannibalism. The diabolical pact only cropped up on a few accusations, and suspicions of harmful magic occurred in only one single case. When analyzing the spread of witch-hunting beyond the Alps, Richard Kieckhefer notes that it concerned "a highly fluid mythology, in which no two trials resemble each other very closely."[35] This lack of robust consistency of witchcraft doctrines hindered the occurrence of trials.

On top of that, both the cumulative notions of witchcraft, as well as the practices of trials, faced resistance wherever they appeared. As mentioned before, medieval political and religious authorities tended to reject beliefs in witchcraft as superstitious. Especially the notion of flying women was often interpreted as pagan.[36] An influential Catholic set of instructions known as the *Canon Episcopi*, which became part of the canon law in the twelfth century, spoke of "wicked women", who "perverted by the Devil, seduced by illusions and phantasms of demons (...) believe and profess to ride upon certain beasts with Diana, the goddess of pagans."[37] So, when proponents of witch-hunting warned the world about the danger, they often found their beliefs dismissed as diabolical trickery. To some extent this can even be observed in Nider's *Formicarius*: his dismissal of flight was backed by a reference to the *Canon Episcopi*.[38]

These obstacles to witchcraft beliefs and trials being reproduced also emerged when cumulative notions moved further into German speaking parts of the Alps, and beyond.[39] Here, witchcraft concepts were integrated with older, local witchcraft lore. The traditional German Alpine witch looked more like a solitary woman who, as Laura Stokes put, was "driven by anger to raise hail and smite her enemies."[40] Witches were connected to the darker side of nature. They tended to go out into the forest, perform weather magic, and ally themselves with wolves. In this context the notion of a diabolical sect lost much of its stature. Accusations and confessions in the area especially concerned women who operated alone, or in twos or threes, and met with

---

[33] Richard Kieckhefer, "The First Wave of Trials," 169–75; Broedel, "Fifteenth-Century Witch Beliefs"; Kieckhefer, "Mythologies of Witchcraft in the Fifteenth Century."
[34] Goodare, *The European Witch-Hunt*, 47; Mercier, *La vauderie d'Arras*, 61–85; Kieckhefer, "Mythologies of Witchcraft in the Fifteenth Century," 100–101.
[35] Kieckhefer, "Mythologies of Witchcraft in the Fifteenth Century," 102.
[36] Goodare, *The European Witch-Hunt*, 71–73; Levack, *The Witch-Hunt in Early Modern Europe*, 43.
[37] Levack, *The Witch-Hunt in Early Modern Europe*, 43.
[38] Nider, "Formicarius," 139.
[39] Richard Kieckhefer, "The First Wave of Trials," 172–75; Stokes, *Demons of Urban Reform*.
[40] Stokes, *Demons of Urban Reform*, 29.

personal devils.[41] The idiosyncratic course of the German witchcraft paradigm also became apparent in Heinrich Kramer's *Malleus Maleficarum*.[42] During a relatively intense wave of trials of around 1480 this Dominican friar operated as a witch hunter in the Alps and southern Germany. Kramer was familiar with learned discourse on diabolical witchcraft, but his German background manifested itself in the way he connected witchcraft to misogynous stereotypes, as well as in his many references to female village witches as likely culprits. Moreover, Kramer hardly stressed witchcraft's collective dimension: apart from a few succinct hints, the sabbath remained undiscussed.

Through the recently invented printing press, the *Malleus* found a relatively wide audience in Germany, enhancing the spread of witchcraft ideas. A monk in a monastery in the southern Eifel region for instance read the book around 1500 in combination with Nider's *Formicarius*, and noted how he had now learned that witches were more powerful and dangerous than he had previously thought.[43] Kramer's book also affected an influential preacher in Strasburg, Johann Geiler von Kaysersberg, who in the early sixteenth century warned his flock about the diabolical danger.[44] Yet, in comparison with later concepts, Geiler's interpretation of witchcraft was quite patchy. He did not treat it as a collective super crime, with witches meeting at large sabbaths, and he was ambiguous about the reality of nightly flight. Similarly, while acknowledging the diabolical pact and harmful magic, Martin Luther was skeptical or even dismissive about witches' gatherings and flight.[45] Two newssheets from this period describing cases of witchcraft – from Schiltach (1533) and Wittenberg (1540) – also presented a rather simple picture of the crime, and made no mention of a sabbath.[46]

The patchiness of early notions about witchcraft impacted the way trials in Germany unfolded. In some cases, the notion of witches forming networks helped activate a snowballing of accusations, but persecution mostly remained restricted to only a few women.[47] Furthermore, like in so many other parts of Europe, resistance to cumulative witchcraft beliefs and trials was paramount. Vibrant opposition to his efforts in Innsbruck had made Kramer write his *Malleus*, and not long after its publication a lawyer named Ulrich Molitor wrote a critique of witch-hunting that would be published in more editions than Kramer's book.[48] In her study on the reception of

---

[41] Stokes, 21.
[42] Broedel, "Fifteenth-Century Witch Beliefs," 44–49; Blauert, *Frühe Hexenverfolgungen*, 36; Richard Kieckhefer, "The First Wave of Trials," 172–75; Institoris, *The Hammer of Witches*, 1–58.
[43] Rummel, "Gutenberg, der Teufel und die Muttergottes von Eberhardklausen."
[44] Voltmer, "Preaching on Witccraft?"
[45] Haustein, "Martin Luther als Gegner des Hexenwahns."
[46] Zika, *The Appearance of Witchcraft*, 182–85; Grasmück, Lorenz, and Schmidt, *Hexen Und Hexenverfolgung Im Deutschen Südwesten*.
[47] Schmidt, *Glaube und Skepsis*, 23–32; Dillinger, *Böse Leute*, 110; Behringer, *Hexenverfolgung in Bayern*, 78–79; Behringer, *Hexen und Hexenprozesse in Deutschland*, 110–12; Waite, *Eradicating the Devil's Minions*, 66; Fritz, "Hexenverfolgungen in der Reichsstadt Reutlingen," 186; Meier, "Die Anfänge der Hexenprozesse in Lemgo," 93; Moeller, *Dass Willkür über Recht ginge*, 48–49.
[48] Behringer and Jerouscheck, "'Das unheilvollste Buch der Weltliteratur'?"; Behringer, "Witchcraft and the Media," 219–20; Kieckhefer, *Hazards of the Dark Arts*, 1–20, 93–148.

cumulative notions of witchcraft in the prosperous city of Nuremberg, Laura Stokes noted that elaborate witchcraft ideas were taken seriously by some and occasionally helped trigger trials. But eventually, civic authorities actively rejected those ideas.[49] One of the city's poets recited: "this is pagan and a mockery by those who don't believe in God."[50]

As was mentioned above, from the 1510s onwards witch persecution even went into decline.[51] In some places like the Low Countries and Northern Italy, trials do not seem to have abated much, but in most of Europe, including Germany, the trend was unmistakable. Illustratively, Kramer's book was reprinted at least fourteen times before 1521, but then waned in popularity.[52] What caused this decline is not entirely clear, but historians have pointed to some factors.[53] In comparison with the second half of the sixteenth century, the economic and environmental crises were mild. Witchcraft theory was criticized by Renaissance intellectuals like Erasmus or Andrea Alciato. There was also the distraction of astonishing developments, like the Reformation, the peasant revolts, and the rise of Anabaptism. Luther's quote about the Devil now working through "spiritual sorcery" might well be interpreted in that light; other problems than witchcraft attracted Luther's attention.

Apart from external factors, the modification of the cumulative concept of witchcraft itself warrants further consideration. Past scholarship has assumed that the concept was fully developed by the time the *Malleus* was published.[54] Trevor-Roper: "The new ideology reached its final form in the 1480s. From the publication of the *Malleus* onwards, its basic content never changed. There was no further development."[55] In fact, major developments were still about to happen.[56] Not only did cumulative notions remain instable and fragmentary, some elements that would help trigger the "super-hunts" of the seventeenth century were still largely missing, like standardized questioning, the idea of child witches and highly elaborate sabbaths. Admittedly, some early commentators already described sabbaths as huge events.[57] A poem from the early 1440s by the French humanist Martin le Franc featured an advocate of witch-hunting who said that witches do not assemble by twos or threes, "but by more than three thousand."[58] The Italian theologian Silvestro Mazzolini in 1521 spoke of a witches' gathering where "many thousands of men and women (…) were dancing in the uncertain light."[59] Some early visual depictions of sabbaths already looked somewhat crowded. A picture in le Franc's poem shows sixteen witches

---

[49] Stokes, *Demons of Urban Reform*, 50–61.
[50] Behringer, *Hexen und Hexenprozesse in Deutschland*, 123-4."Dis als ist haidnisch und ein spot, Bey den, die nicht glauben in Gott."
[51] Behringer, *Witches and Witch-Hunts*, 78–82; Levack, *The Witch-Hunt in Early Modern Europe*, 188.
[52] Levack, *The Witch-Hunt in Early Modern Europe*, 188.
[53] Behringer, *Hexenverfolgung in Bayern*, 105; Goodare, *The European Witch-Hunt*, 158–59; Voltmer, "Die hexenverfolgungen im Raum Trier," 717; Levack, *The Witch-Hunt in Early Modern Europe*, 185–89.
[54] Hansen, *Zauberwahn, Inquisition und Hexenproceß im Mittelalter*; Harris, *Cows, Pigs, Wars, & Witches*, 217.
[55] Trevor-Roper, *The European Witch-Craze*, 41.
[56] Jerouscheck, *Die Hexen und ihr Prozess*, 268.
[57] See, for instance: Mirandola, *La sorcière*, 178, 200.
[58] Franc, "Le Champion des Dames," 455."Ne vint mais plus de trois milliers."
[59] Stephens, *Demon Lovers*, 163.

assembled, and a book related to the Arras trials presents twelve people.[60] Nevertheless, such quotes and pictures were outliers. Not only did the idea of witches' gatherings remain relatively infrequent, sabbaths also tended to be imagined as being quite small.[61] When witchcraft for instance attracted the attention of some early sixteenth-century German artists, like Hans Baldung Grien or Albrecht Dürer, it was female sexuality that especially interested them, and not the perpetration of a collective super crime. As far as Baldung Grien depicted gatherings, these did not exceed a few people.[62] The social profile of alleged witches also often remained restricted, like a scholarly Italian Renaissance dialogue on witches which spoke of "women who are mostly rough and boorish."[63] Hence, by the 1550s, the concept of witchcraft had not yet evolved into a virulent form, and little indicated that the worst was still to come.

Changes of the mid-sixteenth century
Things began to change, however, around the middle of the sixteenth century. One factor was the Little Ice Age.[64] The first half of the sixteenth century had been characterized by relatively mild winters, and populations in Germany were growing. But by the 1550s the weather had started to do strange things. A climatic contraction of the number of fertile months stimulated fiercer competition over scarce resources, putting immediate pressures on people's livelihoods. Food prices rose, inequalities grew, and poverty worsened. In the Lutheran city of Esslingen, located close to Wiesensteig, a furrier named Dionysius Dreytwein kept a chronicle of his town, and from around 1550 began to report frightening events.[65] Terrifying hailstorms damaged crops, a flood swept away many houses, and winters produced more snow than people could remember. Dreytwein also told of increasing cases of witchcraft.[66] In 1559 two distinguished women in Horb were found responsible for weather making. One year later two women in Maulbron were "burned to ashes" for making storms, floods, and killing children. In 1562 a witch in Steinen was alleged to have killed her husband. "The Devil is very restless, piety has no place", Dreytwein commented on his age.[67]

Dreytwein was not the only one to see his time in a diabolical light. So called *teufelsbücher* (devil books) flooded the book market, expressing concerns about sin being rampant and the devil making preparations for the final battle.[68] The religious drama of the Reformation was utterly confusing to many people. In retrospect it may seem obvious that western Europe

---

[60] Ostorero, Bagliani, and Tremp, *L'imaginaire du sabbat* See illustrations.
[61] Zika, *The Appearance of Witchcraft*.
[62] Zika, 11–35, 70–98.
[63] Mirandola, *La sorcière*, 148. "se sont pour la plupart des femmes grossières et rustres."
[64] Weik, *Hexenwerk oder Gottes Zorn?*, 9–35; Behringer, "Climatic Change and Witch-Hunting"; Goertz, *Deutschland 1500-1648*, 12, 175–78; Schilling, *Aufbruch und Krise: Deutschland 1517-1648*, 373–74; Schmidt, *Die Reiter der Apokalypse*, 93–99.
[65] Dreytwein, *Esslingische Chronik*, 168–214.
[66] Dreytwein, 216–17, 234–35. "zu bullver verbrentt"
[67] Dreytwein, 234. "der teuffel ist gantz unruwig, fromheit hat kein platz."
[68] Midelfort, *Witch Hunting in Southwestern Germany*, 69; Waite, *Eradicating the Devil's Minions*, 58; Zika, *The Appearance of Witchcraft*, 192.

splintered into Roman Catholic, Lutheran and Calvinist blocks, but in the mid-sixteenth century the situation was less than clear. Many religious movements competed for domination, and Anabaptist Christian sects attracted many followers.[69] Their passionate believers rejected the religious authorities of other denominations, and uniquely rejected child baptism. Some Anabaptists were quite peaceful, but others tilted towards violence and apocalyptic hysteria. At some of their clandestine meetings, consecrated hosts and other sacramentals were dishonored. There were promises of miracles, like the healing of the sick and resurrection of the dead. In 1534 Anabaptists took over the city of Münster, where they authorized polygamy, and while waiting for the end of times they declared their leader Jan van Leiden the new king. In the city of Fulda a group of Anabaptists was thrown into prison and began to make animal noises. When presented to the Abbot they were "singing and laughing as if they were going to a dance."[70] Some of them experienced visions in which they thought to be flooded by an intense light, and in the midst of the night one Anabaptist awoke to proclaim that the deliverer was about to come. The Abbot reported that the prison seemed "full of devils".[71]

While there was some sympathy for these new sects, the overall response was one of revulsion and repression.[72] After the reconquest of Münster, Van Leiden and his allies were brutally tortured and burned in public. For a time, Anabaptists became the most heavily persecuted group of Europe. The bizarre stories about them helped fuel a poisonous climate of polemics against subversive groups, allegedly aided by the devil. Many princes in Germany secularized heresy trials in order to make persecution more effective, and the argument of a "crimen exceptum" was brought forward to ease the use of torture.[73] This repression forced Anabaptists to meet in even more secretive places, like barns, attics, forests or fields, which in turn stimulated further paranoia about hidden Anabaptist plots. In the near vicinity of the city of Esslingen authorities discovered that dozens of Anabaptists were meeting in a wooded ravine near a fortress.[74] When the group was captured in July 1562, people were upset to learn that some Anabaptists had travelled up to sixty kilometers to attend the meeting.

A pivotal hailstorm

Then, late morning on the third of August 1562, shortly after the discovery of the Anabaptist meeting, black clouds suddenly appeared in the sky. It almost seemed like midnight. Throughout the region of Esslingen and Wiesensteig thunder broke out, as well as an unprecedented hailstorm.[75] The destruction was horrific. There were severe floods, many windows were broken, and vineyards and harvests were destroyed. Martin Crusius, a local chronicler, reported that the

---

[69] Goertz, *Deutschland 1500-1648*, 149–56; Waite, *Eradicating the Devil's Minions*; Eire, *Reformations*, 248–85.
[70] Waite, *Eradicating the Devil's Minions*, 17.
[71] Waite, 17.
[72] Waite, *Eradicating the Devil's Minions*; Goertz, *Deutschland 1500-1648*, 149–56.
[73] Waite, *Eradicating the Devil's Minions*, 199.
[74] Waite, 144–46; Dreytwein, *Esslingische Chronik*, 233–34.
[75] Dreytwein, *Esslingische Chronik*, 327; Behringer, "Climatic Change and Witch-Hunting," 335–36.

event had the appearance of a military defeat with thousands of soldiers wounded and crushed.[76] The populace was exasperated. Such misfortune was traditionally explained as divine retribution for ubiquitous human sin, and many pastors again sent this message from their pulpits. But considering the scale of the disaster numerous people in the region no longer believed sin to be a sufficient explanation for the abnormal weather. They resorted to something else: witchcraft![77]

Stories about witches soon passed from mouth to mouth. In nearby Stuttgart it was reported that a few days before the storm several witches had been seen flying on pieces of wood towards a nearby moor, to return one hour later.[78] Some were identified by name, which resulted in their arrest and execution. In the city of Esslingen, a preacher named Thomas Naogeorgus incited the population against witchcraft, to the detriment of a woman called Berchta Schreinerin.[79] A few years earlier, Schreinerin had already been accused of witchcraft by a neighbor, but authorities at that time had refused to proceed against her.[80] The neighbor's tongue was even cut off for defamation. This time, however, the authorities were more undecided about the case.[81] Guests at a wedding feast claimed to have seen Schreinerin sleepwalking on a roof, and when a few of them went to check her out, no trace of the woman was found. Instead, a black cat suddenly jumped away. Officials warned Naogeorgus not to incite the people, but at the same time Schreinerin was arrested, along with a few other women. The suspects were tortured, but since they refused to confess the authorities remained unsure how to handle the case.

Meanwhile, in the nearby county of Wiesensteig things took a different course.[82] This small territory of around five thousand inhabitants was ruled by count Ulrich von Helfenstein, and here the authorities answered the popular calls for witch-hunting with a strident persecution. From August to December witch burnings were held on a regular basis, adding up to sixty-three killings. The loss of trial records disallows a detailed reconstruction of what made the chain of accusations spiral out of control, but an exchange of letters between officials in Wiesensteig and Esslingen shows persecutors in the former town to be unusually obsessed with the case.[83] Unlike the investigators in Esslingen, Helfenstein's persecutors believed themselves to be eliminating a network of witches who regularly held meetings at a large sabbath. As the historian Günter Jerouschek notes about the exchange: "by the 1560s, the Esslingen officials were only fragmentarily familiar with the concept of the sabbath, whereas the ones of

---

[76] Crusius, *Schwäbische Chronick*, 2:304.
[77] Behringer, "Climatic Change and Witch-Hunting," 335–36; Dreytwein, *Esslingische Chronik*, 236–39; Crusius, *Schwäbische Chronick*, 2:304.
[78] Weik, *Hexenwerk oder Gottes Zorn?*, 48; Dreytwein, *Esslingische Chronik*, 238, 244; Waite, *Eradicating the Devil's Minions*, 149–50.
[79] Jerouscheck, *Die Hexen und ihr Prozess*, 73–75; Midelfort, *Witch Hunting in Southwestern Germany*, 88–89.
[80] Dreytwein, *Esslingische Chronik*, 98–99; Jerouscheck, *Die Hexen und ihr Prozess*, 65–66.
[81] Jerouscheck, *Die Hexen und ihr Prozess*, 73–80; Midelfort, *Witch Hunting in Southwestern Germany*, 88–89.
[82] Dreytwein, *Esslingische Chronik*, 240–46; Midelfort, *Witch Hunting in Southwestern Germany*, 88–90; Eire, *Reformations*, 637; Waite, *Eradicating the Devil's Minions*, 144–53.
[83] Jerouscheck, *Die Hexen und ihr Prozess*, 80–86, 268–69.

Helfenstein presented far more detailed accounts on the topic."[84] The investigators in Wiesensteig also provided Esslingen with some essential information: one suspect confessed to have seen Schreinerin at the Wiesensteig sabbath, and she was alleged to have flown to it on a black devil's back. Esslingen was just about to free Schreinerin and the others, but the news encouraged them to continue the case. Erik Midelfort comments: "here we see the perfect illustration of why the concept of a witches' sabbath was of such grave structural importance. With information of this sort, a witch panic might spread from an original location to disturb all of the surrounding countryside."[85]

Still, even the renewal of torture practices in Esslingen failed to elicit confessions, and Barbara Schreinerin proclaimed herself to have a rock-solid confidence in God.[86] When new evidence failed to appear, family members of the convicted women requested their release, and all were freed. Wiesensteig was disgruntled by the decision, reminding Esslingen of its duty to obey "the strict and serious order of God."[87] That Esslingen still decided in the suspects' favor may well have been related to counter voices coming from the nearby Lutheran University town of Tübingen. Two distinguished preachers, Matthaeus Alber and Wilhelm Bidenbach, passionately opposed the new surge in witch-hunting.[88] In their view, people were mistaken to attribute the recent misfortune to witchcraft, as the real cause lay in divine punishment for our own sins. Hence, burning witches would not help the slightest bit, because it did not remove the underlying problem of human wickedness. Later on, authorities in Esslingen fired its preacher Thomas Naogeorgus, and his earlier incitements against witches seem to have been amongst their considerations.

Yet, while the hunt in Wiesensteig failed to directly enhance witch-hunting in these nearby towns, it was still a persecution of importance. The events in the county were considered newsworthy, reaching audiences far and wide – the *Flugblatt* that reported the sixty-three killings is a case in point.[89] During the early days of the Reformation such newssheets had already demonstrated their polarizing potential by spreading sensationalist news.[90] An essential source of information to the wider population, they were relatively cheap, broadly consumed, and often read aloud in communal settings. Topics normally included dramatic events like celestial apparitions, gruesome murders, monstrous births, military battles, and religious scandals. The

---

[84] Jerouscheck, *Die Hexen und ihr Prozess*, 268-9.'Die Esslinger Strafjustiz beispielsweise war noch in den 60er Jahren des 16 Jahrhunderts mit dem Sabbatkonzept nur fragmentarisch vertraut, wo im Helfensteinischen schon deutlich präzisere Vorstellungen anzutreffen waren'.
[85] Midelfort, *Witch Hunting in Southwestern Germany*, 89.
[86] Jerouscheck, *Die Hexen und ihr Prozess*, 81–86.
[87] Jerouscheck, 85-6."dem gestrengen und ernstlichen bevelch Gottes".
[88] Alberum and Bidenbach, *Ein Summa etlicher Predigten von Hagel und Unholden*; Midelfort, *Witch Hunting in Southwestern Germany*, 39.
[89] Behringer, "Hexenverfolgungen im Spiegel zeitgenössischer Publizistik," 356.
[90] Zika, *The Appearance of Witchcraft*, 179–209; Goertz, *Deutschland 1500-1648*, 98–100; Voltmer, "Hört an neu schrecklich abentheuer / von den unholden ungeheuer," 91; Warfield, "Witchcraft Illustrated"; Closson, *L'imaginaire démoniaque en France (1550-1650)*, 48–49.

Wiesensteig hunt thus nicely fitted the format. But the news about this persecution also spread through other means. Dionysus Dreytwein's chronicle of Esslingen displays a vivid interest in the trials, as he carefully documented its developments.[91] Archival sources from the nearby city of Reutlingen reveal that the persecution was vividly discussed in a local inn, and even as late as 1589 a *Flugblatt* from Ulm referred to Wiesensteig as the place where the eradication of the witches' sect had started.[92]

Importantly, the events attracted the attention of one of Germany's most charismatic Catholic preachers, Petrus Canisius.[93] This priest from the Low Countries was a member of the recently founded "Society of Jesus", better known as the order of Jesuits. After the Council of Trent 1545-1563, a new strident Catholicism aimed to restore the old faith after the onslaught of Protestantism, and Jesuits were the embodiment of this Tridentine religious zeal.[94] The order was especially involved in public preaching and education. As a head of its German section, Canisius attracted the crowds with dramatic exorcisms and sermons about incessant fights with the devil.[95] Well acquainted with Wiesensteig – in 1567 Canisius would play a crucial role in its reconversion to Catholicism – the witch trials of the town made a lasting impression on him.[96] In 1563 he wrote to a colleague about how the number of witches was "strangely multiplying". "We never saw people in Germany so devoted and dedicated to the devil. It is unbelievable what godlessness, fornication, and cruelty these depraved women have committed openly and secretly under Satan's guidance."[97]

A critical moment

The episode in Wiesensteig was, as the Canadian historian Gary Waite puts it, "a critical moment in the history of European witch-hunting."[98] According to Thomas Fritz it fulfilled a "role model function", and Behringer calls it "a visible sign of a *paradigm shift*."[99] The hunt helped stimulate some key changes to what people imagined witchcraft to be.[100] The transformation is nicely illustrated in Dreytwein's chronicle. Before 1562 he only reported about witchcraft as an endeavor of women who operated individually or in small numbers. After 1562 Dreytwein thought of it as a conspiracy of people who assembled by the dozen. What is relevant from our

---

[91] Dreytwein, *Esslingische Chronik*, 240–46.
[92] Fritz, "Hexenverfolgungen in der Reichsstadt Reutlingen," 190–92; Behringer, *Hexen und Hexenprozesse in Deutschland*, 219.
[93] Voltmer, "Jesuiten und Kinderhexen," 214; Behringer, *Hexenverfolgung in Bayern*, 112–13; Behringer, *Hexen und Hexenprozesse in Deutschland*, 132–33; Behringer, "Canisius, St. Peter (1521-1597)."
[94] Eire, *Reformations*, 367–465.
[95] Schilling, *Aufbruch und Krise: Deutschland 1517-1648*, 331.
[96] Midelfort, *Witch Hunting in Southwestern Germany*, 88.
[97] Behringer, *Hexen und Hexenprozesse in Deutschland*, 140"welche merwürdig sich mehren. Ihre frevel[t]haten sind entsetzlich (...) Man sah früher niemals in Deutschland die Leute so sehr dem Teufel ergeben und verschrieben. Unglublich ist die Gottlosigkeit, Unkeuschheit, Grausamkeit, welche unter Satans Anleitung diese verworfenen Weiber offen und insgeheim getrieben haben."
[98] Waite, *Eradicating the Devil's Minions*, 157.
[99] Behringer, *Witches and Witch-Hunts*, 83; Fritz, "Hexenverfolgungen in der Reichsstadt Reutlingen," 190."Vorbildfunktion."
[100] Midelfort, *Witch Hunting in Southwestern Germany*, 70–71; Behringer, "Witchcraft and the Media," 223.

Darwinian point of view is that the exceptional events of the Wiesensteig hunt hardly look preplanned. The hunt crucially depended on a mix of accidental events, like the hailstorm, the heightened sense of paranoia, and the disclosure of the Anabaptist meeting nearby. Gary Waite argues that this gathering had made people in Weisensteig more inclined to think of witchcraft in similar terms, as a substantial group of people secretly meeting each other, and travelling over long distances.[101] Waite admits that this interpretation lacks solid proof, but his scenario appears plausible. It makes the Wiesensteig hunt look like a prime example of a cultural "chance hit".

While the immediate causes of the Wiesensteig persecution were quite random, it was not at random that this particular hunt received so much attention. Dreytwein's chronicle wasted far fewer words on the trials at Maulbron, Horb or Steinen, plausibly because they were less sensational. The relatively modest persecutions of Stuttgart or Esslingen also largely faded into oblivion, as did other trials in the region, such as those in Rottweil (1561), Spalt (1562), Reutlingen (1565), and Illereichen (1563).[102] In the latter case, the persecution started after the populace had pressured the local count to kill a witch, but since the local ideas mostly concerned harmful magic, and not collective meetings or flight, a chain of accusations failed to occur.[103] When looking across Germany we can find many more examples, like Paderborn (1555 and 1556), Velturns, Villanders and Amt Neustadt (1558), Bürgel (1559), Osnabrück (1561), Rockenhausen (1561-1562), Winterberg (1562), Bayreuth and Bingen (1563), and Horn (1564).[104] These trials differed in scale – in Paderborn the suspects were released quickly, while in Osnabrück sixteen were burned – but none of them was as newsworthy as Wiesensteig. Here we see the proposed Darwinian mechanism in motion: some quite fortuitous cultural variants helped make the Wiesensteig hunt large. But it was precisely because of that effect that those particular variants achieved wide dissemination. Wiesensteig created the potential for more sizeable trials.

However, for the Wiesensteig variants to become successful more was needed than just making their appearance. We saw that notions about large sabbaths were already present in an earlier period, but had failed to stabilize. Reproductive success in a Darwinian process never solely depends on intrinsic qualities. In the end, it is the environment that counts. While the period before 1562 seems to have been suboptimal in that regard, the next decades became more auspicious. Weather disasters and economic deprivation worsened, and, according to Edward Bever, produced an "intensification of interpersonal conflicts and their manifestation as

---

[101] Waite, *Eradicating the Devil's Minions*, 145.
[102] Zeck, *Im Rauch gehn Himmel geschüggt*, 43,123; Behringer, *Hexenverfolgung in Bayern*, 99; Fritz, "Hexenverfolgungen in der Reichsstadt Reutlingen," 192–206.
[103] Behringer, *Hexen*, 46–48; Behringer, *Witches and Witch-Hunts*, 85–86.
[104] Decker, "Die Hexenverfolgung im Hochstift Paderborn," 323; Waite, *Eradicating the Devil's Minions*, 188; Moeller, *Dass Willkür über Recht ginge*, 49; Pohl, *Zauberglaube und Hexenangst im Kurfürstentum Mainz*, 51–52, 143; Rügge, *Die Hexenverfolgung in der Stadt Osnabrück*, 26; Schmidt, *Glaube und Skepsis*, 82; Grawlich, "Der Hexenkommisar Heinrich von Schultheiß," 306; Bradford Smith, *Reformation and the German Territorial State*, 167–68; Meier, "Die Anfänge der Hexenprozesse in Lemgo," 90.

suspicions and acts of *maleficium* among the common people."[105] In addition, an important religious and political change was taking shape.[106] The spiritual landscape fractured into Lutheran, Catholic, and Calvinist regional blocks, and within their own domains religious elites strived to bring the populace more strictly under religious control. Wolfgang Behringer speaks of a general "darkening" and "hardening" of mentalities and conditions.[107] Cultural life became more pious, disciplined, and polarized, and it provided new openings for the witchcraft concept to spread.

Witch trials tended to come and go in waves.[108] After the surge of the early 1560s had abated, many new trials in Germany started around 1570.[109] The new model of witch-hunting created by Wiesensteig proved influential: ideas about witchcraft progressively focused on sabbath meetings, nightly flights, and growing numbers of witches. A small treatise on witchcraft printed in Saxony in 1573 that called for more persecution, described how "the number of witches, as we have learned sufficiently from the experience of the trials, grows bigger every year."[110] Sensationalism also remained paramount. A newssheet printed in 1571 testified how a few female witches were burned in Alsatian Schlettstadt (Sélestat), while "surely some thousand people" had come to watch the "terrifying and cruel spectacle."[111] Around this time visual depictions of witches increasingly focused on somewhat larger gatherings. A German map from 1570 depicts a witches' dance near the town of Laub that was attended by fifteen witches.[112] In the Swiss city of Zurich, a Protestant pastor named Johann Jakob Wick amassed a magnificent news collection between 1560 and 1588, and his stories and pictures also reveal the typical trends.[113] The many reports on witchcraft included in the collection show that small trials received only modest attention, while a sensational persecution in Geneva from 1571 was covered widely.[114] One report from 1571 about Geneva said that twenty-one witches were executed, while thirty-six remained imprisoned. A later newssheet on the Geneva hunt spoke about "an incredible number of witches" there, and yet another presented an elaborate drawing of a sabbath that was attended by many demons and seven witches.[115]

---

[105] Weik, *Hexenwerk oder Gottes Zorn?*, 9–35; Behringer, "Climatic Change and Witch-Hunting"; Goertz, *Deutschland 1500-1648*, 12, 175–78; Schilling, *Aufbruch und Krise: Deutschland 1517-1648*, 371–96; Schmidt, *Die Reiter der Apokalypse*, 93–99; Bever, *The Realities of Witchcraft*, 386.
[106] Schilling, *Aufbruch und Krise: Deutschland 1517-1648*, 255–370.
[107] Behringer, *Hexenverfolgung in Bayern*, 112-21."Verhärtung", "verdüstern."
[108] For the early waves, see: Blauert, *Frühe Hexenverfolgungen*.
[109] Behringer, *Hexen und Hexenprozesse in Deutschland*, 149–59.
[110] Behringer, 158."dieweil die Zahl der Unholden, wie man aus den Processen genugsam in Erfahrung bringt, von Jahr zu Jahr immer größer wird und zunimmt."
[111] Lutz, *Warhafftige Zeitung von den gottlosen Hexen*"gewißlich etlich tausend Menschen diesem erschröcklichen unnd grausamen Spectacul zügesehen, das sich von vielen orten hierzu verfügt unnd versamlet hat."
[112] Haas, *Hexen und Herrschaftspolitik*, 62.
[113] Wick, *Die Wickiana*; Zika, *The Appearance of Witchcraft*, 194–209.
[114] Wick, *Die Wickiana*, 78–79, 161, 179; Zika, *The Appearance of Witchcraft*, 194–209.
[115] Wick, *Die Wickiana*, 184, 188–89, 196–98"ein ungleubliche antzal hexen'.

The revival of trials not only occurred in the German-speaking world, but also in countries like France, Scotland and England, generating a resurgence of demonological literature on the topic.[116] The *Malleus* was reprinted again, and many new texts appeared. Not all arguments were supportive, as the new wave probably helped motivate Johann Weyer publish his skeptical *De praestigiis daemonum* of 1563.[117] Weyer combined legal, theological, and medical arguments in what was the most extensive critique of witch-hunting so far. His book encountered passionate support, but equally passionate rebuttals.[118] Strange as it may sound, it was those rebuttals that were in certain ways more forward-looking. Weyer's argument was innovative, but in many ways it represented the older orthodoxies that had interpreted witch beliefs as diabolical trickery and delusion. The new defenses of witch-hunting challenged those orthodoxies.[119]

The intellectual renaissance of witchcraft writing especially manifested itself in France. For instance, in 1574 the Calvinist jurist and theologian Lambert Daneau published his influential *Les sorciers, dialogue très utile et très nécessaire pour ce temps* (The Witches, a Very Helpful and Necessary Dialogue for our Times), and translations into Latin, English and German appeared.[120] In 1580 it was superseded by Jean Bodin's *De la démonomanie des sorciers*.[121] This "great Renaissance polymath, jurist, political theorist, historiographer, religious thinker, natural philosopher, and demonologist", as Virginia Krause calls him, had become especially concerned about diabolical witchcraft after he learned of a young woman who had voluntarily confessed to being a witch.[122] In his book, Bodin incorporated new information from the trials, and made the sabbath a more important element than Kramer had done previously.[123] The book was soon translated into three languages and became the new go-to manual on witchcraft.[124] Thus, by the 1580s, ideas about witchcraft had become more conducive to the creation and spread of large trials.

However, concepts of witchcraft had not yet evolved into a form that would enable the super-hunts of the seventeenth century. The Bamberg hunt, which provided an illustrative case study of witch-hunting at its peak, crucially resulted from indictments coming from children, endless chains of accusations, a striking bureaucratic efficiency, and the targeting of people from almost all walks of life. In 1580 child witches were not yet a prominent topic, and the focus on large sabbaths was not yet as well developed. After the first Alpine period, the witches' social profile had also become quite restricted. Daneau reported that amongst witches, to his own

---

[116] Levack, *The Witch-Hunt in Early Modern Europe*, 189–90; Behringer, *Hexen und Hexenprozesse in Deutschland*, 130–37.
[117] Weyer, *Witches, Devils, and Doctors in the Renaissance*; Valente, "'Against the Devil, the Sublte and Cunning Enemy.'"
[118] Franz, "Antonius Hovaeus, Abt von Echternach, ein früher Gegner der Hexenprozesse"; Schmidt, *Glaube und Skepsis*, 138; Behringer, *Hexen und Hexenprozesse in Deutschland*, 147–49; Bodin, *De la démonomanie des sorciers*, 437–90.
[119] Schmidt, *Glaube und Skepsis*, 81.
[120] Daneau, *Les Sorciers*.
[121] Bodin, *De la démonomanie des sorciers*.
[122] Krause, *Witchcraft, Demonology, and Confession in Early Modern France*, 8; Krause, "The Will to Know and the Unknowable."
[123] See, for instance: Bodin, *De la démonomanie des sorciers*, 60–62, 72–73, 223–34.
[124] Krause, Martin, and MacPhail, "Introduction," 45–54; Krause, "The Will to Know and the Unknowable," 120.

surprise, one could even find people "of quality, like gentlemen, ladies, scholars, who are known for having studied much", and he also stressed that it could be "men and women, young and old".[125] Bodin did not exclude the idea of highly placed individuals becoming witches either, but overall, witchcraft theory, as well as witchcraft trials, remained more constricted.[126] A southern German lawyer in 1580 was quite typical when remarking about witches that "such women are normally poor".[127] It was only during a long wave of trials beginning in the 1580s that some of these elements began to shift significantly. As we shall see, the new innovations that would appear were not so much produced deliberately by persecutors who shrewdly aimed to further the spread of witch-hunting. Again, it would be a mixture of accidental and unforeseen conditions that produced new trials, which sparked innovations to persecutory practices, which then engendered shifts in emphasis in witchcraft theory. To see how that happened, we now move to the German city of Trier in the year 1582.

6.2 Trier 1582

In 1582, some worrisome rumors circulated in Trier.[128] In the duchies of Lorraine and Luxemburg, not far away to the west, witch persecutions had already been going on for some time, and more recently trials had also occurred in the nearby town of Saarburg. Trier itself was not yet affected by this new wave of persecution, although it had witnessed trials before.[129] What set off the new rumors was that some of the female suspects from Saarburg had fled to Trier, and were now hiding in the city walls. Trier had a reputation for being relatively lenient on witchcraft, which may help explain why these suspects sought shelter there. The rumors did alert the authorities though, and they arrested the suspects, sending them back to their hometown. This did not end Trier's involvement, as the proceedings in Saarburg led to two alleged visitors of the witches' sabbath from Trier being mentioned. It concerned a woman named Margarethe Braun – who already suffered from a bad reputation in the community – as well as her daughter. The accusations came at a conspicuous moment for the city, which was plagued by epidemic disease, bad weather, failed harvests, and rising food prices.[130] The indictments easily helped fuel an atmosphere in which these "evil women" seemed plausible culprits for causing at least some

---

[125] Daneau, *Les Sorciers*, 5."Entre lesquels (qui est encore plus estrange) se trouue gens de sorte & de qualité, comme gentilhommes, damoiselles, gens sauans & et qui ont bruit d'auoir bien estudié. (...) tant hommes que femmes, ieunes et vieux."
[126] Opitz-Belakhal, "Der Magistrat als Hexenjäger," 48; see, for instance: Bodin, *De la démonomanie des sorciers*, 229, 242.
[127] Behringer, *Hexen und Hexenprozesse in Deutschland*, 156; Dillinger, *Böse Leute*, 225; Dillinger, "Richter als Angeklagte," 123."Solche Weiber sind gewonnlich Arm."
[128] Voltmer, "Vom Hexenrichter zum Hexenmeister"; Voltmer, "Zwischen Herrschaftskrise, Wirtschaftsdepression und Jesuitenpropaganda," 60–67; Voltmer, "Germany's First 'Superhunt'?," 240–41.
[129] Biesel, "Les descriptions du sabbat," 189; Voltmer, "Zwischen Herrschaftskrise, Wirtschaftsdepression und Jesuitenpropaganda," 53–60.
[130] Voltmer, "Krieg, uffrohr und teufelgespenst," 23; Voltmer, "Zwischen Herrschaftskrise, Wirtschaftsdepression und Jesuitenpropaganda," 60–67.

misfortunes.[131] The authorities took the news from Saarburg in earnest, and Margarethe Braun was arrested and tried under the supervision of the town bailiff.

The name of this bailiff was Dietrich Flade. He was a man of high stature in Trier. His family had settled in the town quite recently, but Flade had quickly made an incredible fortune, becoming the wealthiest person of the city. He possessed much land, three magnificent houses on a prestigious street, and apart from that of town bailiff he served in a series of prominent posts, like electoral councilor, vice governor, professor, and later on as president of Trier's University.[132] Trier was a city with an illustrious past, and although it had already been in economic decline for some time, it still functioned as a religious and intellectual center.[133] In addition, it was the seat of the archbishop of Trier – a post taken by Johann VII von Schönenberg – who ruled as prince-archbishop over a significant electoral state. Yet, Dietrich Flade was not particularly liked.[134] It was widely thought that his incredible wealth had been assembled too quickly, and his sudden wealth gave him the appearance of an upstart. He was known for being exploitative, corrupt, and many people in Trier owed him debts. The 1580s were a time of economic stress and growing inequalities, and Flade could easily be seen as a typical representative of a corrupted elite that had enriched itself at the expense of others. What was more, in a previous conflict between the city and the prince-archbishop, Flade had taken sides with the prince.[135] Trier had made the effort of becoming a free imperial city within the Holy Roman Empire, but Von Schönenberg's predecessor had used military means to keep it confined within the electoral state. Flade's choice of alliance made him a traitor in the eyes of many.

A harsh edge to Flade's character became apparent during his trial of Margarethe Braun. He revealed himself as a severe investigator.[136] Flade made sure that many apparent witnesses were heard to testify against Braun. He also had her imprisoned, personally conducted a search of her house, and ensured she was subjected to repeated and progressively intense torture. When the torments did not produce the confessions that he hoped for, Flade had her relocated to an even worse prison cell. Eventually, Braun was freed, and her trial failed to trigger additional persecution. That further escalation was prevented was not so much due to any mildness on Flade's part, as it was to Braun's unwillingness to confess and her impressive ability to endure torture.

---

[131] Voltmer, "Zwischen Herrschaftskrise, Wirtschaftsdepression und Jesuitenpropaganda," 63."bösen Weiber."
[132] Franz, "Ein 'Dämonologischer Gang' durch Trier," 493; Dillinger, *Böse Leute*, 215–19; Voltmer, "Zwischen Herrschaftskrise, Wirtschaftsdepression und Jesuitenpropaganda," 42, 52–53, 60–66, 78–80; Zenz, *Ein Opfer des Hexenwahns*.
[133] Franz, "Hexenprozesse in Der Stadt Trier," 333; Dillinger, "The Political Aspects of the German Witch Hunts," 88; Voltmer, "Kurtrier zwischen Konsolidierung und Auflösung"; Schmid, "Die Erzbischöfe."
[134] Dillinger, *Böse Leute*, 209–12, 215–27; Voltmer, "Zwischen Herrschaftskrise, Wirtschaftsdepression und Jesuitenpropaganda," 52–53; Voltmer, "Die hexenverfolgungen im Raum Trier," 721–22.
[135] Voltmer, "Kurtrier zwischen Konsolidierung und Auflösung," 51; Voltmer, "Zwischen Herrschaftskrise, Wirtschaftsdepression und Jesuitenpropaganda," 43–45, 52–53.
[136] Voltmer, "Germany's First 'Superhunt'?," 257; Voltmer, "Zwischen Herrschaftskrise, Wirtschaftsdepression und Jesuitenpropaganda," 60–66, 78; Voltmer, "Krieg, uffrohr und teufelgespenst."

While witch trials in Trier abated for the moment, subsequent years did not bring the city much fortune.[137] The weather remained exceptionally cold and wet, so that fertile harvests became an exception rather than the rule. At some point a plague of snails ate away many crops. As a result of the Dutch revolt against the Spanish in the neighboring lands to the west, soldiers regularly marauded the area around Trier, resulting in what a contemporary chronicler described as "constant looting, mugging and theft."[138] Shortages began to be felt in nearly all domains of socio-economic life. The religious atmosphere was characterized by an ardent Catholicism, with zealots proclaiming the end of times and an imminent final judgment. In 1559, Calvinists had made a failed attempt to take control of the city, leading the prince-archbishop to invite the new order of Jesuits to restore Catholicism amongst his subjects. Through their sermons, visitations, and especially through their control over the educational system, the order increasingly began to impact the city's spiritual life.[139] Pupils in the gymnasium and students at the university were educated in an atmosphere of passionate religiosity. The Jesuits performed plays with them, carrying titles like "The Anti-Christ" and "The Last Judgement". Attacks of demons seemed incessant, and the clerics responded with exorcisms amongst their pupils. Typically, they also incited the population against diabolical witchcraft; one Jesuit warned that "through sorcery, female evil is exacerbating public scarcities."[140]

Unsurprisingly, accusations of witchcraft kept circulating in the city. The normal religious means of avoiding misfortune no longer seemed to suffice, so the angry populace increasingly called for the persecution of witches. Early 1586, an old woman suspected of bewitching milk was thrown off a bridge into the Moselle river by an infuriated mob.[141] The atmosphere made the authorities revive investigations, and under Flade's supervision it did not take long before the first woman was burned.[142] After an exceedingly wet summer in 1587 things escalated further. A remarkable development of the period was that hatred of witches merged more and more with the stereotypes about an allegedly corrupt elite.[143] Trials in the nearby countryside brought about accusations against rich people, like a woman from Trier who was alleged to have appeared at the witches' dance on a black horse, wearing expensive clothing. Later testimonies stated that *many* wealthy citizens from Trier were present at the sabbath, and that a dignitary from the city had spoken there. These rich witches allegedly conducted weather magic to take advantage of

---

[137] Zenz, Die Taten der Trierer, VII:10; Voltmer, "Krieg, uffrohr und teufelgespenst," 23; Dillinger, Böse Leute, 90, 239–40.
[138] Zenz, Die Taten der Trierer, VII:10."ständige Plünderungen, Straßenräubereien und Diebstähle."
[139] Franz, "Hexenprozesse in Der Stadt Trier," 334–38, 348; Schmid, "Die Erzbischöfe"; Fleck, "Das höhere Bildungswesen," 414; Voltmer, "Jesuiten und Kinderhexen," 215–16; Voltmer, "Zwischen Herrschaftskrise, Wirtschaftsdepression und Jesuitenpropaganda," 67–69.
[140] Zenz, Ein Opfer des Hexenwahns, 12."verhöhnte weibliche Falschheit vermittels Zauberi die öffentliche Not". ; Voltmer, "Germany's First 'Superhunt'?," 232.
[141] Voltmer, "Zwischen Herrschaftskrise, Wirtschaftsdepression und Jesuitenpropaganda," 67–70.
[142] Voltmer, 71–73.
[143] Dillinger, Böse Leute, 123–30, 223–29, 320-9.; Voltmer, "Zwischen Herrschaftskrise, Wirtschaftsdepression und Jesuitenpropaganda," 73–77; Biesel, "Les descriptions du sabbat," 189–95.

shortages by selling food for higher prices. Then, surprisingly, accusations from nearby villages found an unusual target: Dietrich Flade![144]

The attack on Flade
These extraordinary charges against a high official might have been dismissed had they not coincided with another atypical development: accusations coming from boys.[145] Already in 1585 a boy from the Jesuit college had told stories about visits to a witches' dance, where he professed to have played the timpani. Around the time of the accusations against Flade, new voluntary confessions appeared, now coming from two schoolboys, named Jeckel von Reinsfeld and Matthias von Weiskirchen. The youngsters claimed to be under the permanent supervision of demons, and through elaborate religious ritual the Jesuits tried to free them from their possessors. The possibility of children being witches was not wholly inconceivable at the time.[146] During some earlier trials, for instance in Switzerland and the Basque Country, children had already played roles both as convicts and witnesses, providing inside information about the diabolical sect. The topic garnered some attention in demonological literature, like Kramer and Bodin, who discussed how adult witches seduced their children, especially daughters, into witchcraft.[147] Likewise, Silvestro Mazzolini in 1521 claimed that certain children performed dances that they could *only* have learned at a witches' sabbath.[148] Such remarks had remained quite marginal though, and the notion of the child witch had neither gained much prominence in demonological theory, nor in actual trials. So, when Trier was confronted with confessions from boys, there was not much of an established tradition to rely on.[149]

Still, the voluntary confessions were met with serious consideration.[150] The boys' alleged impartiality made people interpret their testimonies as trustworthy, and at some point Von Reinsfeld and Von Weiskirchen were also presented to the prince-archbishop. In his presence they confirmed that rich people from Trier were involved in the diabolical sect. Additionally, they professed that one high official had even tried to poison the archbishop himself. The prelate had indeed been ill, so the stories did not fail to make an impression.[151] Soon thereafter Matthias von Weiskirchen happened to come across Flade, and exclaimed that this was the man that he had seen at the witches' dance. Meanwhile, accusations against Flade from the countryside

---

[144] Voltmer, "Zwischen Herrschaftskrise, Wirtschaftsdepression und Jesuitenpropaganda," 76–77; Zenz, *Ein Opfer des Hexenwahns*, 17–20.
[145] Dillinger, *Böse Leute*, 253–55; Voltmer, "Jesuiten und Kinderhexen," 215–17; Voltmer, "Zwischen Herrschaftskrise, Wirtschaftsdepression und Jesuitenpropaganda," 69–69, 76–77; Voltmer, "Germany's First 'Superhunt'?," 233–34.
[146] Behringer and Opitz-Belakhal, "Hexenkinder - Kinderbanden - Straßenkinder," 21–24; Voltmer, "Jesuiten und Kinderhexen," 214–16.
[147] Walinski-Kiehl, "The Devil's Children," 172–73; Behringer, "Kinderhexenprozesse," 33.
[148] Stephens, *Demon Lovers*, 166–67.
[149] Behringer, *Witches and Witch-Hunts*, 142.
[150] Voltmer, "Jesuiten und Kinderhexen," 215–17; Dillinger, *Böse Leute*, 253–55; Voltmer, "Zwischen Herrschaftskrise, Wirtschaftsdepression und Jesuitenpropaganda," 81–83; Franz, "Hexenprozesse in Der Stadt Trier," 339.
[151] Zenz, *Ein Opfer des Hexenwahns*, 15.

continued to pile up, and high officials around the prince-archbishop began to wonder in earnest whether the accusations might be grounded in reality.[152] The news about Flade spread like wildfire in the city. It seemed to offer further proof that witchcraft was ravaging the region, and that the network extended to the highest classes. While Jesuits continued to incite the public, pressure from many layers of Trier society, including the town guilds, made the authorities favor more persecution.[153]

The torture sessions in the city, as well as in the nearby countryside, presented an increasingly detailed picture of what this network was supposedly capable of.[154] Witches were meeting on neighboring moors, where they held festive dances and devoured child corpses, while dissonant music was performed on instruments made from horse skulls and cow horns. Under Satan's supervision, the witches had been responsible for weather disasters, illnesses, the snail plague, and the killing of people and livestock. The involvement of rich witches remained a prominent theme, and confessions presented loathsome images of their activities.[155] The rich did not fly to sabbaths on brooms or pieces of wood, but travelled on horseback, or arrived in carriages made of silver and gold. At the sabbath they sat on beautiful chairs, used silver cutlery, and ate the better food. Flade himself even sat on a golden chair, wearing a black cloak, silk doublet, velvet cap, and a golden necklace. Poor witches, on the other hand, sat at separate tables, drank from cow hoofs, and ate miserable food. They were mocked, humiliated, beaten, forced to perform the lowest of services, and were not allowed to participate in the feast. The weather magic was also dictated by the prosperous witches to ensure their future wealth.[156] When the poor witches protested – as it also destroyed *their* livelihoods – they were whipped. Worryingly, the members of the network were making plans for new magical attacks, like damaging the nearby woods so that no wood would be left for witch burnings. Some suspects confessed that there were even plans to destroy the city altogether.[157]

The sense of anger and panic amongst the population heightened, and church bells were rung throughout the night to protect the city against further magical attacks.[158] Flade could no longer move safely through the streets, as he was harassed by boys and students from the Jesuit colleges, some of whom also assembled outside his house.[159] Throughout his career, Flade had been a protégé of the prince-archbishop, but this time support was not forthcoming. Von Schönenberg did have some misgivings about the validity of the witchcraft accusations, but he was a weak and physically feeble ruler with little energy to resist popular pressure.[160] Moreover,

---

[152] Voltmer, "Zwischen Herrschaftskrise, Wirtschaftsdepression und Jesuitenpropaganda," 81–84.
[153] Dillinger, *Böse Leute*, 242–45; Voltmer, "Demonology and Anti-Demonology," 150; Voltmer, "Germany's First 'Superhunt'?," 232.
[154] Dillinger, *Böse Leute*, 119–33; Zenz, *Ein Opfer des Hexenwahns*, 20–23; Biesel, "Les descriptions du sabbat," 189–95.
[155] Dillinger, *Böse Leute*, 123–30, 223–29; Zenz, *Ein Opfer des Hexenwahns*, 22–23; Biesel, "Les descriptions du sabbat," 189–95.
[156] Dillinger, *Böse Leute*, 127.
[157] Dillinger, 117–18; Voltmer, "Zwischen Herrschaftskrise, Wirtschaftsdepression und Jesuitenpropaganda," 100.
[158] Franz, "Hexenprozesse in Der Stadt Trier," 342; Dillinger, *Böse Leute*, 157.
[159] Dillinger, *Böse Leute*, 247–48; Voltmer, "Zwischen Herrschaftskrise, Wirtschaftsdepression und Jesuitenpropaganda," 80.
[160] Dillinger, *Böse Leute*, 260–64; Rummel, "Phasen Und Träger Kurtrierischer Und Sponheimischer Hexenvervolgungen," 286.

the confessions of the boys made him concerned about his own personal safety.[161] Hence, on 4 July 1588, he ordered an investigation into the Flade case.[162] The new suspect responded vehemently, doing everything in his power to turn the tide rising against him. Flade wrote Von Schönenberg a letter in which he pleaded his innocence, and professed to be a good Catholic. He mobilized friends, who argued that Flade could not possibly be a witch as he had initiated and supervised witch trials himself. Yet, the number of accusations against Flade continued to grow, and at some point he made a fateful mistake: he tried to flee, not just once but twice.[163] His attempts were thwarted and two mayors of Trier, Nikolaus Fiedler and Johann von Kesten, ordered him to stay in the city. From then on his house was guarded day and night. Flade again beseeched the prince-archbishop to let him go, promising to spend the rest of his life in a convent, and to donate all his money to the electoral state. Unfortunately for Flade, Von Schönenberg interpreted his offer as an implicit confession of guilt. On 23 March 1589 he had his former ally imprisoned in the town hall, and Flade was subjected to torture.[164]

Soon Flade admitted that avarice, greediness, scientific curiosity, and "lust of the flesh" had made him the devil's prey.[165] He had been seduced by a demon in female form, and had then partaken in the various crimes that he was accused of. He had served the devil, forsaken God, attended the dances, and helped destroy harvests – in his basement he had kept a jar full of snails to harm crops. The death verdict was inescapable. On 18 September 1589 Flade was first strangled, and then burned in public in full view of almost the entire city population.[166] It would not be the last sensational burning to be seen in Trier, as the attack on the city elite did not stop with Flade. In his confessions, the former town bailiff had accused other highly placed individuals, including the two mayors who had supervised his arrest, Fiedler and Von Kesten.[167] Their burnings followed on later occasions. Within a few years a significant number of the Trier elite had been executed, both women and men, including councilors, aldermen, and some clerics.[168] The carnage did not follow the lines of the older conflict between the city and the electoral state, as the killing now happened quite randomly.[169] The total number of people executed in the city was not excessive, since they numbered only a few dozen. However, what was unparalleled was

---

[161] Franz, "Hexenprozesse in Der Stadt Trier," 339.
[162] Zenz, *Ein Opfer des Hexenwahns*, 20–24; Voltmer, "Zwischen Herrschaftskrise, Wirtschaftsdepression und Jesuitenpropaganda," 77–97.
[163] Zenz, *Ein Opfer des Hexenwahns*, 25–28; Dillinger, "Flade, Dietrich (1534-1589)."
[164] Zenz, *Ein Opfer des Hexenwahns*, 29–35.
[165] Voltmer, "Germany's First 'Superhunt'?," 255."geilheit deß fleischs"; Dillinger, *Böse Leute*, 113, 120, 200; Zenz, *Ein Opfer des Hexenwahns*, 37–53.
[166] Zenz, *Ein Opfer des Hexenwahns*, 53–55.
[167] Franz, "Hexenprozesse in Der Stadt Trier," 345; Voltmer, "Zwischen Herrschaftskrise, Wirtschaftsdepression und Jesuitenpropaganda," 84–86.
[168] Zenz, *Die Taten der Trierer*, VII:13; Behringer, *Witches and Witch-Hunts*, 97.
[169] Voltmer, "Die hexenverfolgungen im Raum Trier," 721; Franz, "Hexenprozesse in Der Stadt Trier," 339.

their social profile. While a majority of the victims were female, rich men had become a new category to suffer disproportionally from persecution.[170]

The persecutions of the Trier region
That so many accusations had come from the surrounding countryside was not accidental, as the region as a whole teemed with witch trials.[171] These had been gradually building up in the 1580s, but from 1587 things started to get completely out of hand. Especially in the territories of the electoral state, as well as in neighboring principalities like Luxemburg and Sponheim, witch-hunting reached unprecedented levels. The region was characterized by traditions of self-government by the populace, and persecutions were mostly driven forward by initiatives from those social classes.[172] When the anger against witches came to a head, communal village meetings decided to form ad hoc witch-hunt committees, so called *Hexenauschüsse*, which then instigated persecutions on a semi-democratic basis. The circumstances in which the *Auschüsse* arose were often tumultuous.[173] Participants showed their determination against the present evil through a vivid symbolic ritualism. Oaths were taken under the linden tree in the village square, or knives were stabbed into a table to be grabbed by all members as proof of unconditional allegiance. Official authorities were pressured not to intervene, and many contemporary observers noticed that the atmosphere resembled a popular revolt.[174]

Through the condonement, or partial cooperation, of the government, the *Hexenauschüsse* turned into merciless killing machines. Whenever they received names of alleged witches, investigations often resulted in execution. Resistance could be interpreted as an indication of witchcraft, offering grounds for additional arrests.[175] Confessions of the executed, as well as the names of accomplices they had mentioned, were read aloud in plain language during well-attended witch burnings.[176] Obviously, this created new streams of rumors, new accusations, and new arrests. A contemporary observed that the mere mention of a possible suspect was the beginning of "agitation, conflict, quarrel, wrangle, scolding and smearing" within their community.[177] Gerhard Schormann has argued that the public appeal of these burnings

---

[170] Dillinger, *Böse Leute*, 97–102, 206; Behringer, *Witches and Witch-Hunts*, 97; Voltmer, "Die hexenverfolgungen im Raum Trier," 721–22.
[171] Voltmer, "Gott ist tot, und der Teufel jetzt Meister!"; Rummel, "Phasen Und Träger Kurtrierischer Und Sponheimischer Hexenvervolgungen," 284; Rummel, *Bauern, Herren und Hexen*.
[172] Dillinger, "The Political Aspects of the German Witch Hunts," 68–72; Briggs, "Witchcraft and the Local Communities," 204; Dillinger, *Böse Leute*, 305–57; Rummel, "Phasen Und Träger Kurtrierischer Und Sponheimischer Hexenvervolgungen," 283; Voltmer, "Gott ist tot, und der Teufel jetzt Meister!"
[173] Rummel, "Das 'ungestüme Umherlaufen der Untertanen'.," 151; Rummel, *Bauern, Herren und Hexen*, 38–39.
[174] Rummel, "So mögte auch eine darzu kommen, so mich belädiget," 212; Rummel, "Phasen Und Träger Kurtrierischer Und Sponheimischer Hexenvervolgungen," 283.
[175] Voltmer, "Die hexenverfolgungen im Raum Trier," 742.
[176] Schormann, *Hexenprozesse in Deutschland*, 32–33; Rummel, *Bauern, Herren und Hexen*, 110.
[177] Quoted in: Voltmer, "Gott ist tot, und der Teufel jetzt Meisterl," 195."unruh, zweispalt, hader, zanck, schelten [und] schmehlen."

"was ideal for the further spread of the witchcraft doctrine."[178] Around 1590, hundreds of people were burned in the electoral state alone, and their social profile was similar to those persecuted in the city. Women were still overrepresented, but around thirty percent of the victims was now male, and elites were not spared.[179]

The most ruthless hunt of the region, though, did not happen within the confines of the electoral state. It was in the territory of the imperial abbey of St Maximin, located close to Trier, that a hunt unfolded, worse than anything Europe had seen so far.[180] Typically, involvement in persecution started after members of a community had been mentioned as sabbath accomplices elsewhere. In 1586, St Maximin received accusations from Saarburg against one of its female subjects, and the woman was arrested, tortured, she confessed, and was burned. The trial did not trigger further persecutions, as the convict did not provide names of companions.[181] However, in 1587 a new accusation, originating from the nearby town of Wiltingen, set in motion a different train of events. The trial against a new female suspect resulted in testimonies against ten accomplices, and a chain of accusations was set in motion.[182] Like the surrounding region in that year, St Maximin's population had become highly sensitized to witchcraft, so a *Hexenauschuss* was installed that proceeded zealously. Investigators believed themselves to be in a life-or-death struggle with the diabolical sect, and showed a marked interest in sabbath attendance. A preserved notebook from one of the judges, Claudius Musiel, provides insight into the dynamics of the hunt. The names of the interrogated were listed carefully alongside the accomplices whom they had mentioned, often numbering around twenty, but in some cases leading up to about sixty accusations.[183] A boy named Hans Jakob Meisenbein operated as "star witness", and altogether accused around one hundred and fifty people during the four years of his imprisonment.[184] The hunt lasted from 1587 to 1596, leading to the deaths of four to five hundred people.[185] This constituted one-fifth of the population of the imperial abbey, and the social profile of the victims was comparable to that of the electoral state. Complete families were wiped out, and some villages of the territory were largely eradicated.[186]

The persecutions of the Trier region reached their zenith around 1590. In that year the prince-archbishop organized a procession against the evils of "war, revolt, and diabolism", and people were urged to safeguard themselves against the devil's tricks.[187] However, in the next

---

[178] Schormann, *Hexenprozesse in Deutschland*, 33."die für die Verbreitung der Hexenlehre geradezu ideal war."
[179] Franz, "Hexenprozesse in Der Stadt Trier," 343; Voltmer, "Die hexenverfolgungen im Raum Trier," 739–40; Dillinger, *Böse Leute*, 100.
[180] Voltmer and Weisenstein, *Das Hexenregister des Claudius Musiel*; Voltmer, "Die hexenverfolgungen im Raum Trier," 731–32.
[181] Voltmer and Weisenstein, *Das Hexenregister des Claudius Musiel*, 33–36.
[182] Voltmer and Weisenstein, 37–82.
[183] Voltmer and Weisenstein, *Das Hexenregister des Claudius Musiel*; Behringer, *Witches and Witch-Hunts*, 97.
[184] Voltmer, 'Jesuiten und Kinderhexen', 218; Dillinger, *Böse Leute*, 254.
[185] Behringer, *Witches and Witch-Hunts*, 97; Voltmer and Weisenstein, *Das Hexenregister des Claudius Musiel*, 31.
[186] Voltmer, "Gott ist tot, und der Teufel jetzt Meister!," 197–210, 223.
[187] Voltmer, "Krieg, uffrohr und teufelgespenst," 31."krieg, uffrohr und teufelsgespenß"; Dillinger, *Böse Leute*, 177; Voltmer, "Zwischen Herrschaftskrise, Wirtschaftsdepression und Jesuitenpropaganda," 94–95.

year things gradually began to de-escalate. Complaints about miscarriages of justice were more vocal, and questions regarding payment for the trials became a source of conflict.[188] Von Schönenberg implemented a new law condemning the proceedings as disorderly and prejudiced.[189] Persecution was to be taken out of the hands of communal bodies, and placed under the strict control of the official government. Confession statements of the convicted were no longer to be read aloud in public, but kept secret. The new law evidently shows an awareness that things had gotten out of control, and that the position of the authorities themselves was in peril. Yet, while the effects of the law were soon noticeable, trials in the electoral state still lingered on for some time, only coming to a halt around 1596.[190]

That the new law should not be interpreted as a rejection of witch persecution as such, also becomes apparent in a conflict between two of Trier's major clerics.[191] One of the key people involved in the trials was Trier's suffragan Bishop Peter Binsfeld. In 1589 he published his treatise on witchcraft, the *Tractatus de confessionibus maleficorum et sagarum* (Treatise on Confessions of Sorcerers and Witches). The book was an ardent plea for more witch-hunting, mirroring many of Binsfeld's own recent experiences.[192] Among other things, he stressed the need to question suspects about accomplices, and considered a few accusations sufficient for arrest. One of Binsfeld's colleagues in Trier, however, the Dutch-German cleric Cornelius Loos, soon prepared a rebuttal.[193] This member of the Trier theological faculty levelled a head-on attack on the whole system of witch-hunting, claiming that it led to killing of the innocent. Binsfeld responded vehemently, and with government support he ensured that Loos was imprisoned. In the presence of a papal representative, Loos, in 1593, was forced to recant his arguments. His book remained unpublished.

News spreading far and wide
In retrospect, the city of Trier, the electoral state, and the abbey of St Maximin do not seem to have done themselves a great favor with these trials. On the contrary; while some people may have benefited financially, these communities were gripped by horrendous fears, their social bonds were unraveled, economic activity was destroyed, numerous lives were annihilated, and tax payers were wiped out.[194] One of the reasons for the trial slowdown after 1591 was that

---

[188] Dillinger, *Böse Leute*, 248, 332; Rummel, *Bauern, Herren und Hexen*, 35.
[189] Rummel, "Das 'ungestüme Umherlaufen der Untertanen'.," 146; Rummel, *Bauern, Herren und Hexen*, 41–42; Dillinger, *Böse Leute*, 84–86, 438; Behringer, *Hexen und Hexenprozesse in Deutschland*, 226–28.
[190] Voltmer, "Die hexenverfolgungen im Raum Trier," 726–32; Rummel, "Phasen Und Träger Kurtrierischer Und Sponheimischer Hexenvervolgungen," 267, 272–73.
[191] Dillinger, *Böse Leute*, 367; Voltmer, "Demonology and Anti-Demonology"; Voltmer, "Zwischen Herrschaftskrise, Wirtschaftsdepression und Jesuitenpropaganda," 94–97.
[192] Binsfeld, *Tractat Von Bekantnuß der Zauberer unnd Hexen*; Dillinger, *Böse Leute*, 225, 260; Voltmer, "Zwischen Herrschaftskrise, Wirtschaftsdepression und Jesuitenpropaganda," 90–92.
[193] Voltmer, "Zwischen Herrschaftskrise, Wirtschaftsdepression und Jesuitenpropaganda," 94–95; Voltmer, "Demonology and Anti-Demonology."
[194] Voltmer, "Gott ist tot, und der Teufel jetzt Meister!"; Dillinger, *Böse Leute*.

people had become physically as well as emotionally exhausted.[195] By giving in to popular demands for persecution, the authorities had also imperiled their own positions, and endangered precarious balances between jurisdictions – a disagreement about a trial between Trier and Cologne at some point nearly triggered military confrontation.[196] What is more, the city's reputation was severely damaged.[197] Trier became known as a contemporary Sodom. Protestants seized the opportunity to discredit this overly Catholic city; whether they liked witch-hunting or not, their judgments tended to be equally damning. In the eyes of witch-hunting's opponents, this carnage of the innocent illustrated Catholic brutality.[198] Supporters of witch trials on the other hand accepted the guilt of convicts, but highlighted how Catholics were unusually susceptible to Satan's schemes.[199] In a reference to Trier from 1605, the protestant preacher David Meder stated that "as experience testifies, far more of these people [witches] can be found in popery than in places where the bright light of the gospel shines."[200] In the early seventeenth century, Trier's city chronicler Johann Linden looked back in anguish at what had happened. "A plague or a cruel enemy could hardly have ravaged the region more excessively than this boundless inquisition and persecution" he lamented. In some areas, Linden observed, there were not even enough people left to cultivate the land.[201] The city chronicler appears not to have been the only one in the region to have realized that things had gone astray.[202] While the Trier region still experienced some smaller trials, it would never let things get out of hand this terribly again.[203]

While the extraordinary course of the trials seems to have hindered further persecution in the region itself, consequences elsewhere were different. First, there were the immediate spillover effects in other principalities.[204] Trier's trials had been sparked by accusations from other places, but it soon became an inflammatory hotbed for new indictments itself. Names provided by Trier's persecutors helped initiate trials in places like Sponheim, the Eifel region, and in areas around the Moselle and the Rhine. Second, information about what happened spread

---

[195] Voltmer, "Die hexenverfolgungen im Raum Trier," 731–32; Rummel, "Phasen Und Träger Kurtrierischer Und Sponheimischer Hexenvervolgungen," 273–74.
[196] Dillinger, Böse Leute, 377.
[197] Dillinger, 360–63.
[198] Voltmer, "Hexenbrenner Und Hexenbischöfe," 185; Rummel, "Phasen Und Träger Kurtrierischer Und Sponheimischer Hexenvervolgungen," 264; Voltmer, "Germany's First 'Superhunt'?," 247–49; Schmidt, Glaube und Skepsis, 73, 264–65.
[199] Rummel, "Phasen Und Träger Kurtrierischer Und Sponheimischer Hexenvervolgungen," 264; Voltmer, "Hört an neu schrecklich abentheuer / von den unholden ungeheuer," 153.
[200] Meder, Acht Hexenpredigten, 38."die Erfahrung bezeuget, das im Babstumb dieser Leute viel mehr gefunden werden, als an denen orten, da das helle liecht des Evangelij scheinet."
[201] Zenz, Die Taten der Trierer, VII:14."Kaum schlimmer kann die Pest oder ein überaus grausamer Feind im Trierer Land gewütet haben, als diese Art einer maßloser Inquisition und Verfolgung."
[202] Voltmer, "Die hexenverfolgungen im Raum Trier," 744.
[203] Rummel, "Phasen Und Träger Kurtrierischer Und Sponheimischer Hexenvervolgungen," 273–82.
[204] Dillinger, Böse Leute, 240, 369–70; Monter, "Witch Trials in Continental Europe 1560-1660," 23; Rummel, "Phasen Und Träger Kurtrierischer Und Sponheimischer Hexenvervolgungen," 269–71; Voltmer, "Herren und Hexen," 43–44.

throughout Germany and beyond.²⁰⁵ As we saw, Trier was an important center, and its trials, of course, had been sensational. A teacher of the Duke of Bavaria's son happened to be in Trier around the time, and after his return reported that "what we hear about these pernicious witches in that region borders on the unbelievable. Everywhere in the area one can see almost more stakes of burned witches than green trees, but like the Hydra only more witches seem to be growing back."²⁰⁶ An official from Hessen who resided in the electoral state informed his landgrave about "wondrous" events there. The confessions of witches had uncovered dances with "many hundreds of sorcerers", and the witches had even penetrated the prince-archbishop's sleeping room to poison him.²⁰⁷ In 1590 a newssheet printed in Ulm provided an overview of Germany's current trials, and devoted much attention to the vast number of executions in the electoral state. In one village, "so many women had been burned that only two very pious ones remained."²⁰⁸ Probably most important of all was Binsfeld's treatise. Soon translated into German, it instantly became a standard reference and witch-hunters' manual.²⁰⁹

In combination with other factors like the unusual climatic and economic hardship, the Trier hunts helped trigger an unprecedented wave of witch-hunts sweeping Germany in the years around 1590.²¹⁰ When cataloguing them, the Ulm newssheet admitted that there were actually so many trials that one could make a whole book out of it.²¹¹ One of the mechanisms causing the trials' simultaneity was sabbath accusations spreading from territory to territory.²¹² But there was also another mechanism: when communities learned about witch-hunts nearby this often activated older suspicions against individuals in their midst, followed by calls for their persecution.²¹³ To many contemporaries, the flood of trials provided evidence that alarmists like Bodin and Binsfeld had been right. This helped bring witchcraft to people's awareness as a threat that required direct and rigorous measures.²¹⁴ Cumulative notions of witchcraft also seem to have penetrated deeper layers of the population. A witness in Augsburg for instance testified before court that she had "never believed that such people existed, but only saw it now, after it

---

²⁰⁵ Dillinger, *Böse Leute*, 359–60; Behringer, *Hexenverfolgung in Bayern*, 128–29; Voltmer, "Gott ist tot, und der Teufel jetzt Meister!," 187; Decker, "Die Hexenverfolgungen im Herzogtum Westfalen," 344; Rummel, "Phasen Und Träger Kurtrierischer Und Sponheimischer Hexenvervolgungen," 261; Rummel, *Bauern, Herren und Hexen*, 294; Behringer, "Das 'Reichskhündig Exempel' von Trier"; Eyzinger, *Relationis historicae continvatio*.
²⁰⁶ Dillinger, *Böse Leute*, 360."Was wir hier von dem äußerst verderblichen Hexenvolk vernehmen, grenzt ans Unglaubliche. Überall in der Umgegend sieht man fast mehr Brandpfähle von verbrannten Hexen als grüne Bäume, so wachsen der Hydra gleich immer mehr Hexen nach."
²⁰⁷ Voltmer, "Germany's First 'Superhunt'?," 234-5."wunderberliche", "vielhundert zeubern."
²⁰⁸ Behringer, *Hexen und Hexenprozesse in Deutschland*, 221."so viel Weiber verbrannt worden, das nit mehr als zwo, so fromb gewesen, uberbliben sein."
²⁰⁹ Dillinger, *Böse Leute*, 374–75; Behringer, *Hexenverfolgung in Bayern*, 148–50; Voltmer, "Herren und Hexen," 43–44; Durrant, *Witchcraft, Gender, and Society in Early Modern Germany*, 36; Schulte, *Hexenmeister*, 140; Behringer, "Das 'Reichskhündig Exempel' von Trier," 440.
²¹⁰ Behringer, *Hexen und Hexenprozesse in Deutschland*, 180–84; Behringer, *Hexenverfolgung in Bayern*, 122–223.
²¹¹ Behringer, *Hexen und Hexenprozesse in Deutschland*, 222.
²¹² Behringer, *Hexenverfolgung in Bayern*, 133.
²¹³ Rummel, *Bauern, Herren und Hexen*, 26–27, 317; Behringer, *Hexenverfolgung in Bayern*, 154, 169.
²¹⁴ Dillinger, *Böse Leute*, 243, 359–60; Behringer, *Hexenverfolgung in Bayern*, 145, 224; Labouvie, *Zauberei und Hexenwerk*, 115.

had become so very loud and clear."[215] Historians today mostly rely on written documents, but Edward Bever reminds us of all the stories about witchcraft that must have been "transmitted across the countryside during work breaks and business socializing, over dinner tables in towns and taverns, and during the evening discussion and storytelling that spread news and ideas from household to household in the countryside."[216]

Changing concepts of witchcraft
The importance of the Trier trials lay not only in the way they enhanced the fear of witchcraft; they also stimulated some vital shifts in what witchcraft was supposed to look like. One of the hunt's striking features, as we saw, was its size. Trier came to stand for a new and dramatic type of persecution that did not kill dozens, but hundreds.[217] One of today's key experts, the German historian Rita Voltmer, cautions us that this notion of a "super-hunt" in Trier was to a certain extent a contemporary construct.[218] Reports at the time often lost sight of distinctions between the city of Trier, the electoral state, and St Maximin, and merged and inflated them into one huge event. David Meder in 1605 for instance spoke of Trier's 7,500 executions.[219] Yet, as Voltmer admits, the real number of executions was still unprecedented, and boosted the idea of witches forming large and growing networks.[220] The trend is distinctly noticeable in visual representations of the sabbath.[221] As mentioned above, sabbath crowds were already getting bigger, but in 1594 a newssheet printed in Erfurt portrayed a "Trierer Hexentanzplatz" (Trier's dancing square of witches) as an event with many dozens of visitors. It was the most elaborate sabbath depiction so far.

It is important to notice that the growing focus on witches meeting each other at elaborate sabbaths was not solely linked to Trier. Trial records from Rostock 1584 already spoke of six hundred attendants.[222] A persecution starting in Lutheran Osnabrück in 1583 led to an exceptional number of killings, as within half a year 121 women had been burned there, and by 1592 the death count reached 180.[223] A newssheet printed in Jena in 1588 reported the striking course of events, adding that witches were meeting on the Blocksberg in Saxony, where no less than 8,000 witches had assembled.[224] The new focus on the sabbath was also noticeable in other countries.[225] Before 1587, Europe's most prestigious court, the Parliament of Paris, questioned

---

[215] Behringer, *Hexenverfolgung in Bayern*, 224."hiervor nie geglaubt, das solche leuth seyen, biß sy yetzt erst sehe, daß es also alutt und offenbar werde."
[216] Bever, *The Realities of Witchcraft*, 70.
[217] Dillinger, *Böse Leute*, 359–60; Behringer, "Das 'Reichskhündig Exempel' von Trier," 437–39.
[218] Voltmer, "Germany's First 'Superhunt'?"
[219] Meder, *Acht Hexenpredigten*, 38; Voltmer, "Germany's First 'Superhunt'?," 248.
[220] Voltmer, "Gott ist tot, und der Teufel jetzt Meister!," 190; Voltmer, "Germany's First 'Superhunt'?," 242–43.
[221] Voltmer, "Hört an neu schrecklich abentheuer / von den unholden ungeheuer"; Goodare, *The European Witch-Hunt*, 74; Voltmer, "Germany's First 'Superhunt'?," 248–49, 253.
[222] Moeller, *Dass Willkür über Recht ginge*, 320.
[223] Rügge, *Die Hexenverfolgung in der Stadt Osnabrück*, 21–38.
[224] Rügge, 103–5.
[225] Monter, "Witch Trials in Continental Europe 1560-1660," 7–10; Goodare, *The European Witch-Hunt*, 73–76.

over half of the people about the sabbath before they were executed as witches. After 1587, such questions occurred in nearly ninety per cent of cases. William Monter comments: "the importance of the sabbat increased sharply at the village level in both central France and western Germany precisely when witch trials began to multiply around the end of the sixteenth century."[226] The growing attention is also perceptible in the many demonological works that appeared around the time. Nicolas Rémy gave the sabbath extensive consideration in his *Daemonolatreiae* from 1595, and Martin Delrio in 1600 was the first to present the sabbath as a highly elaborate black mass.[227] It was about to set a new standard.

Another key shift that Trier helped engender was an expansion of the witch stereotype.[228] Previous ideas about witches being normally old and poor women unraveled. The newssheet about the events in Osnabrück had already stressed that in the pitch-dark night "young and old, tall and short [...] both rich and poor" had assembled to prepare magical attacks.[229] Trier went even further, and brought to attention witches who were male, rich and powerful. It was especially this cultural 'mutation' that struck contemporaries as noteworthy.[230] When the jurist and philologist Franciscus Modius consulted St Maximin's book collection in the late 1580s, he wrote in his diary about the extraordinary number of witch burnings there, also mentioning the city of Trier, "where an extremely learned Doctor Flade was arrested, bearer of an excellent name, who had presided over the city in the archbishop's name."[231] Likewise, a report on Trier in a Dutch newssheet printed in Antwerp mentioned the burning of a "powerful and rich man, named Flade".[232] In 1590 a *Fuggerzeitung* – an influential German news report – stressed that the Trier hunt "spared no one, neither the rich nor the poor", and the Erfurt newssheet highlighted the presence of rich witches both in word and image.[233] Demonologists did not fail to notice. Binsfeld remarked that people of "high standing" could be witches too, and Delrio in 1600 referred to the Flade case explicitly.[234]

Through Trier, the concept of witchcraft attached itself to anti-elitist sentiments, thereby enlarging the potential scope of persecution. The effects already became apparent during the

---

[226] Monter, "Witch Trials in Continental Europe 1560-1660," 10.
[227] Rémy, *Demonolatry*, 47–65; Behringer, *Hexen und Hexenprozesse in Deutschland*, 184; Rio and Maxwell-Stuart, *Investigations into Magic*, 83–98.
[228] Behringer, "Das 'Reichskhündig Exempel' von Trier," 436; Behringer, *Hexen und Hexenprozesse in Deutschland*, 181; Dillinger, *Böse Leute*, 225; Voltmer, "Germany's First 'Superhunt'?," 251.
[229] Rügge, *Die Hexenverfolgung in der Stadt Osnabrück*, 33, 104."baid Jung, alt, groß und klain [...] baids reich und arm."
[230] Behringer, "Kinderhexenprozesse," 34; Rummel, "Phasen Und Träger Kurtrierischer Und Sponheimischer Hexenvervolgungen," 261; Zenz, *Die Taten der Trierer*, VII:13; Dillinger, *Böse Leute*, 225; Eyzinger, *Relationis historicae continvatio*, 90.
[231] Rummel, "Phasen Und Träger Kurtrierischer Und Sponheimischer Hexenvervolgungen," 266."wurde in der Stadt selbst ein äußerst gelehrter Doktor Flade verhaftet, Träger eines hervorragendes Namens, der schon oft der Stadt im Namen des Erzbischofs vorgestanden hatte."
[232] *Warachtighe ende verschrickelycke beschryuinge van vele toouenaers ende toouenerssen*"een grootmachtich ende rijck man, genaempt Flade."
[233] Behringer, "Das 'Reichskhündig Exempel' von Trier," 443."Und hierin Niemand verschonet, der Reichen sowohl, Alß der Armen"; Voltmer, "Hört an neu schrecklich abentheuer / von den unholden ungeheuer," 124.
[234] Binsfeld, *Tractat Von Bekantnuß der Zauberer unnd Hexen*, 84."höheren ansehens"; Dillinger, *Böse Leute*, 225–26.

wave of 1590.[235] Within the heated popular mood of the time, an alleged governmental protection of rich witches was considered one of the worst forms of corruption.[236] Such sentiments could be hazardous for authorities to ignore, so wealthy individuals were burned in more places. Some of the unusual sabbath notions of the Trier region, about rich witches being privileged over poor ones, can also be found in later trials.[237] Early seventeenth-century testimonies from Lorraine, for instance, provided confessions from a poor witch about sabbaths where "the richest and most important were normally seated at the table, and the poorest like her kept right at a distance and rejected."[238]

Of similar importance was the role played by children. As observed above, child witches had already appeared as potential witnesses before the mid-1580s. But the events in the Trier region helped turn the child-witch into a major topic in witchcraft theory, as well as in actual trials.[239] Peter Binsfeld addressed the subject on various occasions in his book, for instance when he said that witches could be "men and women, boys and girls".[240] Since children were also taken to sabbath, he thought them invaluable informants about the people present there.[241] The suffragan bishop even went as far as to advocate torture to extract their confessions.[242] Again, the effects of Trier were already noticeable during the persecutory wave of around 1590.[243] In neighboring Dietz a child was brought to court whose self-accusations might well have been ignored just a few years earlier.[244] In the southern German town of Bobingen, voluntary confessions of a fourteen year old boy triggered the arrest of forty-five people, of whom at least twenty-seven were burned.[245] The impact was lasting. Martin Delrio adopted stories about the witch-boys from Trier in his *Disquisitiones*, and child witches also figured prominently in the works of Nicolas Rémy (1595), Henri Boguet (1602) and Pierre de Lancre (1612).[246] As late as 1625, Bamberg's preacher Friedrich Förner still referred to the role of the witch children in Trier; an important detail considering the role that children would play in the subsequent hunt in his own town.[247]

---

[235] Behringer, *Hexenverfolgung in Bayern*, 202–4; Haas, *Hexen und Herrschaftspolitik*, 87, 113–14.
[236] Dillinger, *Böse Leute*, 328–29, 350.; Behringer, *Hexenverfolgung in Bayern*, 410.
[237] Pohl, *Zauberglaube und Hexenangst im Kurfürstentum Mainz*, 229–30, 263; Briggs, *The Witches of Lorraine*, 139.
[238] Briggs, *The Witches of Lorraine*, 139.
[239] Dillinger, *Kinder im Hexenprozess*, 104–6; Behringer and Opitz-Belakhal, "Hexenkinder - Kinderbanden - Straßenkinder," 22–23; Voltmer, "Jesuiten und Kinderhexen," 203–4, 218–32; Dillinger, *Böse Leute*, 253–54.
[240] Binsfeld, *Tractat Von Bekantnuß der Zauberer unnd Hexen*, 60."männer, weiber, knäblein und mägdlein."
[241] Binsfeld, 110–11.
[242] Behringer, "Kinderhexenprozesse," 35.
[243] Behringer, *Hexenverfolgung in Bayern*, 133.
[244] Dillinger, *Böse Leute*, 254.
[245] Behringer, "Kinderhexenprozesse," 41.
[246] Behringer and Opitz-Belakhal, "Hexenkinder - Kinderbanden - Straßenkinder," 23–29; Voltmer, "Jesuiten und Kinderhexen," 221–22; Walinski-Kiehl, "The Devil's Children," 173–74; Rio and Maxwell-Stuart, *Investigations into Magic*, 269.
[247] Förner, *Dämonenglaube und Zauberei im Jahre 1625*, 632–33.

The increased focus on children has attracted the attention of many historians today.[248] What exactly made children so very vulnerable in this regard? Undoubtedly, they were easier to influence, and had fewer inhibitions about providing imaginative testimonies. In contrast to adults, they probably did not fully grasp the possible consequences of their words, let alone understand how these might be turned against themselves. Given the power of childhood dreams and fantasies, it is also conceivable that they often believed what they confessed. Moreover, children perhaps enjoyed the sudden power and attention they got. Either way, the impact on further witch-hunts is indisputable. Dillinger describes children as "door openers", who often provided the first essential confessions.[249] Through the enhanced focus on child witches, the cumulative concept of witchcraft by the late sixteenth century thus came to include yet another incendiary element.

There is still another impact of the Trier persecutions often highlighted by historians.[250] Until the late 1580s German witch trials had especially been a pursuit in Lutheran areas. Wiesensteig, Rostock, and Osnabrück are cases in point. Protestant scholars were also the ones who debated the matter most fervently. Catholic Germany had remained somewhat less interested, although both proponents and opponents could be found in their ranks. Yet, the years around 1590 marked a shift. Protestant authors' negative response to the Trier hunt seems to have given witch-hunting a bad, that is to say Catholic, reputation. While there was still much Protestant support, criticisms continued to be vented loudly and clearly. In Catholic Germany, on the other hand, the witchcraft doctrine by 1590 had become an orthodoxy that was dangerous to contest in public. The treatise of Binsfeld, as well as the official condemnation of Loos, made a profound impression on contemporaries.[251] The Bavarian government for instance officially spoke out against skeptics like Weyer and others. The dogmatization removed a crucial hurdle for the further spread of trials in Catholic Germany, which would indeed experience an unprecedented surge in subsequent decades.

In sum, Trier was of pivotal relevance.[252] Rita Voltmer calls it "an unprecedented but exemplary witch-hunt." [253] Johannes Dillinger writes that "electoral Trier became the superregional paradigm of a new type of persecution." [254] Wolfgang Behringer: "the Trier persecutions were of decisive importance because the previous pattern of witch-hunting broke

---

[248] Bever, *The Realities of Witchcraft*, 106–18; Goodare, *The European Witch-Hunt*, 292–95; Dillinger, *Kinder im Hexenprozess*; Behringer, "Kinderhexenprozesse"; Behringer and Opitz-Belakhal, "Hexenkinder - Kinderbanden - Straßenkinder"; Voltmer, "Jesuiten und Kinderhexen"; Walinski-Kiehl, "The Devil's Children."
[249] Dillinger, *Kinder im Hexenprozess*, 255."Türöffner."
[250] Behringer, *Hexenverfolgung in Bayern*, 229; Behringer, *Hexen und Hexenprozesse in Deutschland*, 182–84; Behringer, "Das 'Reichskhündig Exempel' von Trier," 437–38.
[251] Behringer, *Hexenverfolgung in Bayern*, 258.
[252] Behringer, *Witches and Witch-Hunts*, 97; Robisheaux, "The German Witch Trials," 182–83; Voltmer, "Zwischen Herrschaftskrise, Wirtschaftsdepression und Jesuitenpropaganda," 107.
[253] Voltmer, "Gott ist tot, und der Teufel jetzt Meister!," 186."einer beispiellosen, aber beispielgebenden Hexenjagd."
[254] Dillinger, *Böse Leute*, 359."Kurtrier wurde zum überregional beachteten Paradigma eines neuen Verfolgungstyps."

down."[255] With its new focus on large sabbaths, rich witches, male witches, and child witches, the events of the Trier region gave the concept of witchcraft a new "virulence". What is again relevant from our Darwinian perspective, is that the events giving rise to these shifts were hardly preconceived. After the first accusations arose in 1582, it took a long time before the trials got going in earnest. That they finally took off at all, was crucially related to a rich mixture of quite coincidental occurrences, like exceedingly bad weather, heightened popular aggression, the weakness of Von Schönenberg's rulership, the unusual boys' confessions in Jesuit colleges, and specific local beliefs about witches being numerous, and in quite some cases, rich and corrupt.

It is tempting to assume that such spectacular events must have been designed and created by some primal movers, or architects, operating behind the scenes; think of Tridentine Catholicism, Von Schönenberg, Binsfeld, or the Jesuits. Yet, as many experts have stressed, this is not so much what happened.[256] Binsfeld's treatise, for instance, was only a report of, and a response to, events that were already unfolding. Dillinger argues that these persecutions developed a momentum of their own, in which "trials themselves aroused more fear of witches."[257] Günther Franz states that "the wave of trials was neither a conspiracy, nor a manufacture."[258] The same applies to the wave of persecution sweeping Germany around 1590.[259] In a passage quoted earlier (section 5.3) Wolfgang Behringer argued that its many trials took people by surprise, not resulting from any planning or coordination.

Yet again, while the *causes* of the extraordinary scale of the Trier hunts were quite accidental, things look less fortuitous when we consider their *effects*. Like the Wiesensteig trials it was hardly by accident that this set of persecutions gained so much traction. Imagine a scenario in which people in the Trier region had held some different ideas about witchcraft, for instance, that sabbaths are small, that witches are poor and female, that testimonies from children are irrelevant, and that accusations require high standards of proof. In all likelihood, the trials would have remained modest, and would not have become newsworthy. Consequently, its underlying ideas would not have spread much. But that is not what happened. The Trier persecutions contained variants that made them huge, and that was precisely what caused the sensation. Due to this widescale attention, some of the insidious cultural variants underlying the trials managed to lodge themselves into many more brains, inciting similar events elsewhere. The proposed Darwinian mechanism is visible again: quite coincidental new cultural variants are preserved because of non-accidental effects on their own continuation. What also bears upon the proposed Darwinian scenario is that the Trier persecutions were a nightmare for the communities involved. It was hardly the people of the Trier region, or their societies, who benefited. Any approach searching for the "functions" or "adaptations" of the trials may thus seem misguided. But when

---

[255] Behringer, *Witches and Witch-Hunts*, 97.
[256] Dillinger, *Böse Leute*, 240–44; Behringer, *Hexen und Hexenprozesse in Deutschland*, 184; Briggs, *Witches & Neighbours*, 347.
[257] Dillinger, *Böse Leute*, 240."Die Hexenverfolgungen selbst erregten Hexenangst."
[258] Franz, "Hexenprozesse in Der Stadt Trier," 349."Die Prozeßwelle war keine Verschwörung oder Inszenierung."
[259] Behringer, *Hexen und Hexenprozesse in Deutschland*, 184.

we look at the matter from the reproductive interests of the witch-hunting phenomenon *itself*, the Trier hunt suddenly appears like a prodigious "mutation".

Still, the concept of witchcraft had not yet evolved into its most inflammatory form. Beliefs and practices regarding witch-hunting were still not yet fully adapted to create the kind of persecutions that occurred in Bamberg 1626-1632, and other places around that time. What was lacking was their efficient judicial machinery, their more professionalized set of persecutors, and the even higher number of victims. Some crucial transformations to witch-hunting were still to come. To understand what changed in intermittent decades, we now move to yet another place; the small southern German town of Ellwangen. Here, an unfortunate event during a church service in 1611 was about to unleash one of Germany's most terrifying witch-hunts.

6.3 Ellwangen 1611

In Spring 1611, churchgoers in the town of Ellwangen celebrated the Easter Service. Its elaborate religious ritual normally provided a sense of unity and belonging. But this time an eerie incident provoked a venomous stream of rumors, which triggered a chain of events that eventually brought the town's social fabric to breaking point. A seventy-year-old woman from the nearby village of Rindelbach, Barbara Rüfin, was observed to take the consecrated host out of her mouth just after receiving it from the priest.[260] The pastor noticed the uncanny act and instantly washed his hands to cleanse them of his physical contact with her. Some churchgoers noticed the incident, and were appalled. Did Rüfin's action not suggest a disdain for the body of Christ? After the service the story went from mouth to mouth, and added to it was something else known about Rüfin: in her village she had a reputation for witchcraft. It was said that she used salves to kill livestock. Somewhat earlier, the city had already learned about a sensational case of demonic possession in nearby Rosenberg, bringing people to a state of vigilance about Satan's lingering attacks. So, was this incident of the Easter Service not an indication that Ellwangen now also had a devil's ally in its midst?

Ellwangen's authorities learned about the rumors, and found them sufficient grounds for an investigation.[261] Several people from Rüfin's local community were heard, and the inquiry laid bare the fact that Rüfin's reputation for witchcraft went back a few decades. One alleged but crucial incident had occurred many years before, concerning one of Rüfin's neighbors, Holhansen. He had suspected her of bewitching his cattle, and at some point consulted a local fortune teller, Birren Ketterin. Holhansen told the investigators that Ketterin had revealed to him that his cattle had indeed been bewitched, and that the culprit would expose herself by walking into his house to ask for three things. And who then showed up at his house, to ask for a shawl, a butter box, and a cradle? Barbara Rüfin![262] It was further found that not only villagers scorned

---

[260] Mährle, "O wehe der armen seelen," 377–80; Midelfort, *Witch Hunting in Southwestern Germany*, 101.
[261] Mährle, "O wehe der armen seelen," 377–80.
[262] Midelfort, *Witch Hunting in Southwestern Germany*, 101–2.

the seventy-year-old woman for witchcraft, but even some members of her own family. Her husband was alleged to have called her a witch who should give herself up to the authorities. Rüfin had an especially troubled relationship with her son. His choice of marriage had displeased her, since she considered his wife not good enough for him. This generated a long-lasting conflict, in which the son called his mother a witch "more than 100 times", and he even suspected her of trying to poison him by putting quicksilver in his soup.[263] On top of that, a search of Rüfin's house revealed mixtures that had the semblance of witch potions.

The investigation into the Rüfin case came at an unfortunate time for Ellwangen. The small town was the capital of a minor *Fürstpropstei* (prince-provostry), which had been under a lot of stress for some decades. The many crises of the late sixteenth and early seventeenth centuries had made themselves felt in the form of strange weather, ruined harvests, agricultural shortages, economic decline, and price inflation.[264] People as well as livestock were undernourished, and epidemics had caused many deaths. Some of the diseases were unfamiliar to people, making them seem mysterious and suspicious. Moreover, in religious and political matters Ellwangen was a spearhead of Tridentine reform.[265] Protestant peasants had temporarily overtaken the city in 1525, but after Catholicism was restored, the prince-provosts implemented strident policies of confessionalization. Jesuits gained influence, and Petrus Canisius regularly attended the town to rouse the flock. By 1603 a new prince-provost was installed, Johann Christoph von Westerstetten, who had been educated by the Jesuits and aimed to bring the population even more thoroughly within the mold of Tridentine Catholicism.[266] His activities often went along with paranoia about laymen or clerics who sabotaged the holy policies.

Typically, Ellwangen had not escaped the wave of trials around 1590.[267] Cumulative notions about flight, sabbath meetings, and the *crimen exceptum* had played their part at the time, and it was an accusation by a nineteen-year-old man against his mother that provoked snowballing accusations. It led to the execution of around twenty people within four months. The hunt had been quite traditional in its almost exclusive targeting of women, but it also showed some typical traits of the 1590 wave: it was organized in quite an ad hoc manner, starting with arrests of people at the lower level of society, but then moving up the social ladder – both rich and poor were killed. The persecutions attracted some attention elsewhere, for example, in the newssheets from Ulm and Antwerp.[268] However, due to its quite 'normal' character, this set of trials failed to receive much consideration, and thus lacked transregional importance.[269]

---

[263] Midelfort, 101. "mer als 100 mal."
[264] Midelfort, 98–100; Mährle, "O wehe der armen seelen," 342–45.
[265] Pfeifer, *Ellwangen*, 39–50; Mährle, "O wehe der armen seelen," 345–48.
[266] Durrant, *Witchcraft, Gender, and Society in Early Modern Germany*, 13; Pfeifer, *Ellwangen*, 46–50; Mährle, "O wehe der armen seelen," 369–75.
[267] Mährle, "Fürstpropstei Ellwangen," 2004, 378–80; Mährle, "O wehe der armen seelen," 354–68.
[268] *Warachtighe ende verschrickelycke beschryuinge van vele toouenaers ende toouenerssen.*
[269] Mährle, "O wehe der armen seelen," 368.

The persecution starting in 1611 was different, although this was not apparent from the beginning. The inquiry into the Rüfin case lingered on for some time, as the investigators showed a certain degree of indecision.[270] What initially dampened persecutory zeal was that not all witness statements from Rindelbach reinforced the charges. Some of the people heard stated that there was nothing serious going on with Rüfin, even the son of Holhansen. Rüfin's husband stated that he had only called his wife a witch when he was angry, and had not genuinely meant a word of what he said. Bursting into tears he begged the investigators not to harm his wife. Barbara Rüfin herself also vehemently denied all charges, professing that she did not have the slightest idea of how to bewitch cattle. She also provided an explanation for the incident during the Easter service: due to her age she had trouble swallowing, so she had taken the host out of her mouth to put it in more deeply with her fingers. Rüfin said she knew that this was not the proper way, and that she planned to express her regrets to the pastor.

Despite such uncertainties, the investigators decided to subject Rüfin to torture.[271] From 20 April onwards she was stretched twice a day for fifteen minutes. It did not immediately bring about a confession, as the seventy-year-old woman endured the sessions admirably. Yet, after a few days she could no longer bear the torments, and broke down emotionally. Rüfin provided a full elaborate confession: she had been seduced by a demon, made the pact, performed harmful magic, and attended the sabbath. As soon as the torture stopped she recanted her confessions, but once the painful questioning resumed she again confessed. After many more sessions the investigators observed that Rüfin had become "completely confused".[272] This did not prevent them from taking her testimonies in dead earnest. After all, how could she confess such terrifying details about witchcraft, if she had not actually committed the crimes? That Rüfin may have learned these notions of witchcraft from others, and that painful questioning forced her to make things up, does not seem to have crossed the persecutors' minds. On 16 May Barbara Rüfin was executed with a sword, and then burned at the stake. All her belongings fell into the hands of the Ellwangen government.

A hunt unfolds

Due to her alleged sabbath attendance Rüfin was also forced to name companions, and mentioned a few names from Rindelbach. This set the typical witch-hunting dynamic in motion, as new arrests, new torture sessions, and new names of alleged sabbath accomplices soon followed.[273] Initially this mostly concerned people from Rindelbach, but then names from Ellwangen appeared. In the case of the Trier trials, it had taken a long time before things became earnest, and proceedings had remained quite ad hoc in their implementation. The Ellwangen persecution too was hesitant for a short while, but then proceeded with more thoroughness and

---

[270] Mährle, 379–81; Midelfort, *Witch Hunting in Southwestern Germany*, 102–3.
[271] Mährle, "O wehe der armen seelen," 380–81; Midelfort, *Witch Hunting in Southwestern Germany*, 102–3.
[272] Midelfort, *Witch Hunting in Southwestern Germany*, 103.
[273] Mährle, "O wehe der armen seelen," 381–82; Midelfort, *Witch Hunting in Southwestern Germany*, 103–5.

discipline. By the end of May, the prince-provost Von Westerstetten had installed a professionalized *Hexen Deputation*, a witches' deputation, mostly consisting of people from his own entourage and that of the Jesuits. With full government support, the committee was allowed to advance under its own terms, making some pivotal innovations to the practice of witch-hunting.[274] Soon after Rüfin's trial they dispensed with witness reports and a search for circumstantial evidence. Instead, they went straight to enforcing confessions through torture, and used standardized questionnaires to inquire more efficiently about key cumulative notions. First, suspects were asked about initiation into witchcraft, then about harmful magic, then about sabbath attendance, and finally about sabbath accomplices. Suspects were not allowed to mention names of people who were already arrested or executed, and three new denunciations against individuals were considered sufficient grounds for arrest.

The unusual judicial machinery employed in Ellwangen was not wholly new. Its use was preceded in some respects by a witch-hunt from 1603 to 1606 in the prince-abbey of Fulda in central Germany. Around that same time, rampant witch-hunting occurred in the many scattered areas of the nearby electoral state of Mainz, and these trials resembled the ones in Trier. Its persecutions were organized in an improvised and fragmented manner, with local village committees being the key driving force. Overall, an estimated 650 people were killed.[275] Yet, in 1603 in Fulda, the prince-abbot Balthasar von Dernbach did something special by giving full authority over the persecutions to an ally of his, Balthasar Nuss. This judge, who had murdered a priest in his youth, sidestepped local courts and even the central government. In cooperation with just a few professional colleagues he pursued the trials under his own conditions. Within three years an estimated 276 people were burned.[276] The example gained traction in Ellwangen, where the local *Hexen Deputation* was about to take things even further.

Anyone who fell into their hands was almost certainly doomed – there was not a single release.[277] Withstanding torture was pointless, as there was no end to the agonies. A man named Georg Mair, for instance, endured twenty-four sessions, still refused to confess, but eventually died in custody. A few people managed to escape, but most others confessed and provided names of accomplices, soon followed by their burning. The efficiency of proceedings was unusual, as the time between arrest and execution only lasted around two weeks. In the summer of 1611, there was a burning of around ten people every two or three weeks, slowing down a bit to around five to eight people each time later that year. As Erik Midelfort put it, this was a "runaway hunt".[278] In that year alone 126 people were killed, to be followed by at least 143 burnings in

---

[274] Mährle, "O wehe der armen seelen," 381–90, 399–404; Midelfort, *Witch Hunting in Southwestern Germany*, 103–7; Behringer, *Witches and Witch-Hunts*, 113.
[275] Pohl, *Zauberglaube und Hexenangst im Kurfürstentum Mainz*; Robisheaux, "The German Witch Trials," 186; Behringer, *Witches and Witch-Hunts*, 108, 113.
[276] Robisheaux, "The German Witch Trials," 186; Behringer, *Witches and Witch-Hunts*, 110–13; Jäger, …… *das recht und überaus grosse sengen undt brennen* …; Rowlands, "Nuss, Balthasar (1545-1618)."
[277] Mährle, "O wehe der armen seelen," 415–18, 413–18; Midelfort, *Witch Hunting in Southwestern Germany*, 104–12.
[278] Midelfort, *Witch Hunting in Southwestern Germany*, 100.

1612.[279] Like so many trials of the period, the arrests soon fanned out over different segments of society. Women were still overrepresented, but about thirty percent were men, and nearly all social categories were hit.[280] Especially musicians and bakers appear to have been targeted disproportionately, and like the Trier trials there were also burnings of clerics. Three priests confessed to have baptized children in the devil's name for many years, which apparently explained why Ellwangen had so many witches.[281]

The *Hexen Deputation* presented its efforts as a holy pursuit against an acute and present evil, but judicial abuses were rampant.[282] Some suspects were raped in prison, and one guard offered advice on how to escape torture to a woman suspected of witchcraft, asking for her jewelry and other goods in return. Possessions of witches were confiscated, and in some cases the suspects' properties were already inventoried before they had made a first confession. Such blatant miscarriages of justice, in combination with the swelling number of victims, stimulated increased resistance in the city.[283] Rumors spread about many of the incarcerated being innocent. However, one of those most insidious traits of the witch-hunting phenomenon also made itself felt, as criticisms were interpreted as indications of guilt. At some point, one of Ellwangen's judges was horrified to see his wife convicted, but his protest soon ended in his own arrest and execution. Others faced a similar fate.

On 11 July 1613, a sensational event occurred that seemed to prove the persecutors right.[284] A sixteen-year-old girl named Maria Ostertegin voluntarily handed herself in at the city gate, declaring herself a witch. As her story went, she had been lured into witchcraft as a child by a friend named Margarethe Roßnagel, who by then was already burned. Since that point, Maria claimed, she had subjected herself to diabolical intercourse, harmful magic, and sabbath attendance. By now she could no longer endure the snares of her personal demon, and demanded her own incarceration. Without use of torture Ostertegin mentioned thirty accomplices by name, and on 21 August she was killed by sword. As a reward for her voluntary confession, the authorities granted her a proper burial in the churchyard. There are no indications that the girl was mentally impaired, raising the question of why she provoked her own death. Johannes Dillinger speculates that it might have been an early modern variant of today's "suicide by cop", where people seek death through violent encounters with the police.[285] Whatever the causes of her remarkable act may have been, to contemporaries it looked impressive. The Jesuit Johann Finck noted:

---

[279] Mährle, "O wehe der armen seelen," 382.
[280] Pfeifer, *Ellwangen*, 50–52; Mährle, "O wehe der armen seelen," 404–13.
[281] Midelfort, *Witch Hunting in Southwestern Germany*, 105.
[282] Mährle, "O wehe der armen seelen," 392–99; Midelfort, *Witch Hunting in Southwestern Germany*, 107–8.
[283] Mährle, "O wehe der armen seelen," 413–27; Midelfort, *Witch Hunting in Southwestern Germany*, 109–10.
[284] Dillinger, *Kinder im Hexenprozess*, 123–34; Dillinger, "Hexen-Eltern," 244–46; Mährle, "O wehe der armen seelen," 430–31; Midelfort, *Witch Hunting in Southwestern Germany*, 108.
[285] Dillinger, *Kinder im Hexenprozess*, 131–34.

God has provided us special comfort through a sixteen year-old girl, who was killed last month along with six others. She could no longer bear the devil's pursuits, so she turned herself in voluntarily. In tears she declared that she would rather die at the stake than suffer the devil's tyranny any longer. While standing, she received her deathblow.[286]

She was not the only underaged person to provide a confession.[287] Already in 1611, voluntary testimonies of a seven-year-old girl had prompted a chain of accusations. This girl *does* seem to have suffered from mental disabilities, and she was probably unaware that telling an eighteen-year-old girl from her village about her own parents being witches would result in both of her parents being burned, along with fifteen other people.

As in many other cases, the Ellwangen trials spilled over into other territories. The proceedings against Barbara Rüfin had already produced a name from nearby Zöbingen, bringing about a small chain of accusations there that led to a few deaths.[288] Later on, the *Hexen Deputation* aided nearby territories by assembling a book that listed sabbath accomplices from elsewhere alphabetically by the town in which they lived. Once handed over, these names led to trials in places like Ellingen, Dinkelsbühl, Aalen, and once again Zöbingen.[289] Consequences were particularly dire in Schwäbisch Gmünd, where it helped trigger a hunt that probably killed around fifty people.[290] Meanwhile, the persecution in Ellwangen slowed down a bit in 1613, partly due to the departure of its zealous prince-provost Von Westerstetten, and his succession by the more lenient Johann Christoph von Freyberg-Eisenberg.[291] Still, persecution remained intense, and since Ellwangen enjoyed much judicial and political independence from external control, it could proceed much as it liked. When trials finally came to an end in 1618, the overall death toll had reached an estimated 430 people.[292]

A broader impact
Like other huge hunts, the events attracted much attention elsewhere. Some commentators expressed admiration, like the renowned Jesuit philologist Jacob Gretser, who dedicated a book to Von Westerstetten.[293] "The more hidden, the more perniciously and dangerously this evil spreads" he wrote about witchcraft. In his view, Von Westerstetten was "kindled by divine zeal

---

[286] Duhr, *Geschichte der Jesuiten in den Ländern Deutscher Zunge*, 2:1:489."Gott hat uns besonders getröstet durch ein Mädchen von 16 Jahre, das im vorigen Monat mit sechs andern hingerichtet wurde. Es konnte die Nachstellungen des Teufels nicht länger ertragen und stellte sich freiwillig zur Haft; unter Tränen erklärte es, lieber Tod und Brandpfahl als noch länger die Tyrannei des Teufels ertragen zu wollen. Stehend empfing es den Todesstreich."
[287] Walinski-Kiehl, "The Devil's Children," 181; Mährle, "O wehe der armen seelen," 390–92; Midelfort, *Witch Hunting in Southwestern Germany*, 109.
[288] Haas, *Hexen und Herrschaftspolitik*, 125–26.
[289] Haas, 125–26; Mährle, "O wehe der armen seelen," 431–34; Mährle, "Fürstpropstei Ellwangen," 1994, 174.
[290] Midelfort, *Witch Hunting in Southwestern Germany*, 112–20; Graf, "Reichstadt Schwäbisch Gmünd."
[291] Mährle, "O wehe der armen seelen," 382, 428.
[292] Robisheaux, "The German Witch Trials," 187; Mährle, "O wehe der armen seelen," 382, 427–31.
[293] Behringer, *Hexenverfolgung in Bayern*, 241; Durrant, *Witchcraft, Gender, and Society in Early Modern Germany*, 42.

and love for the welfare of his subjects", and steadfastly exercised the power of divine justice.[294] A newssheet printed in Nurnberg in 1615 similarly praised Ellwangen's "venerable prince". Witch-hunts had often been criticized for a leniency towards the rich, but the newssheet applauded how Ellwangen proceeded without consideration of person. It executed both "rich and poor, simple and dignified, men as well as women."[295] The pamphlet further reveled in what it saw as the laudable punishment of the three witch-priests: first, incisions were made in their right hands, tonsured scalps, and foreheads. Then, salt and vinegar were rubbed into the wounds, their fingernails pulled out, and they were stripped of religious clothing. So, by the time of the burning all traces of priestly dignity had been removed.

There were also misgivings about proceedings in Ellwangen. Many towns in its vicinity, like Limpurg, Nördlingen, Bopfingen and Schwäbisch Hall, did not follow up on the accusations that were provided to them against their subjects.[296] The government of the electoral state of Pfalz even offered protection to a baker who escaped the clutches of the *Hexen Deputation*.[297] In 1618 the neighboring territory of Oettingen went so far as to officially accuse Ellwangen of judicial misconduct.[298] Wolfgang Mährle, the historian who researched the Ellwangen hunt most extensively, says that it "broke a wall of silence."[299] One of Oettingen's charges was that the *Fürstpropstei* had used confiscations of the executed to enrich itself. Ellwangen responded derisively, dismissing all accusations.[300] After all, its persecutions had solely been directed at protecting its subjects against the dangers of witchcraft, and reconverting the seduced in order to save their souls. It was acknowledged that properties of the executed were confiscated, but this happened to compensate for the harm they had done, while the money was spent on pious causes. Ellwangen also referred to the voluntary confessions – greatly exaggerating their number – as forceful proof of a conspiracy.

By the time of this exchange the hunt was already drawing to a close. The vehemence of Ellwangen's response may well have been, as Erik Midelfort nicely put it, "the kind of passionate self-defense that springs from glimmers of self-doubt."[301] What seems to have brought the Ellwangen trials down was the incredible damage they were causing. In 1613 the Jesuit Johann Finck already fearfully wondered: "where this matter will lead us or what end it might have, I do not know." He predicted that "this hideous evil has become so rampant, and has infected so

---

[294] Behringer, *Hexen und Hexenprozesse in Deutschland*, 243."Je verborgener, um so verderblicher und gefährlicher schleicht dieses Übel [...] von göttlichem Eifer und von der Liebe zu dem Wohl Ihrer Untertanen entflammt."
[295] *Zwo Hexenzeitung, Die Erste, Von Dreyen Hexen Pfaffen, Und Einem Organisten Zu Ellwang [...] Die Ander: Von Einer Unholdin Oder Hexen [...]*"hochwürdige Fürst", "arm und reicht, geringe und stattliche, so woll Manns als Weibspersohnen."
[296] Mährle, "O wehe der armen seelen," 434.
[297] Schmidt, *Glaube und Skepsis*, 362–63; Mährle, "O wehe der armen seelen," 418–19.
[298] Haas, *Hexen und Herrschaftspolitik*, 121–26; Mährle, "O wehe der armen seelen," 425–27; Midelfort, *Witch Hunting in Southwestern Germany*, 110–11.
[299] Mährle, "O wehe der armen seelen," 427."eine Mauer des Schweigens."
[300] Mährle, "Fürstpropstei Ellwangen," 1994, 173–74; Mährle, "O wehe der armen seelen," 425–27; Midelfort, *Witch Hunting in Southwestern Germany*, 110–11.
[301] Midelfort, *Witch Hunting in Southwestern Germany*, 112.

many like a plague, that if the magistrate will continue to exercise its power along this path, the whole city will languish in misery."[302] By 1618 the city was languishing in misery indeed.[303] The hunt had destroyed much of the city's social fabric, and the grief it had caused was overwhelming. Significant parts of the population were annihilated, and social life had become unpredictable. Properties and houses were abandoned, contracts had been broken, civic debts had soured, and guild and civil offices were left vacant. The care of the many orphans left behind was a pressing problem. To its dismay, Ellwangen also noticed that people were avoiding the town, and that parents were less inclined to send their children to school in such a notorious place. Like the Trier region in the 1590s, the damage seems to have engendered a certain awareness that things had gone too far. If the city was to survive, this hunt had to stop. And so it did. Later on, in the persecutory wave of the late 1620s, the *Fürstpropstei* still experienced some trials, but avoided any snowballing. Ellwangen seems to have learned a lesson.[304]

Witch-hunts of the late 1610s
Yet, the effects of the Ellwangen hunt on other places were quite different. While Ellwangen itself was careful not to foster its new way of witch-hunting, the model found fertile grounds elsewhere.[305] Wolfgang Mährle maintains that it created a "new persecutory paradigm", characterized by a more assertive top-down initiative, a more professionalized investigation, and a more lethally efficient bureaucracy.[306] Behringer argues that it helped bring about "a new type of persecution" that "gained momentum within weeks, and led to the burning of hundreds of witches within a few months."[307] Its potential for transplantation, for instance, became apparent in the southern German prince-bishopric of Eichstätt.[308] Von Westerstetten left Ellwangen to take a position as prince-bishop there, and he brought the new model of witch-hunting with him. When accusations against witches occurred in the near vicinity of the town in 1617, it initiated a hunt much along Ellwangen's lines: it was aggressively implemented from above by professional persecutors, who enjoyed the support of highest government. Its focus on women was quite traditional – they constituted an estimated eighty-eight percent of victims – but like in Ellwangen, the heart of society was attacked.[309] It was the households of brewers, butchers, innkeepers, cobblers, smiths, and tailors that were hit, as well as almost all families of the local elite. At least

---

[302] Duhr, *Geschichte der Jesuiten in den Ländern Deutscher Zunge*, 2:1:489."Wohin diese Sache noch führen wird oder welches Ende sie haben wird, sehe ich nicht, da dieses abscheuliche Übel so überhand genommen und wie eine Pest so viele angesteckt hat, daß nach Jahren, wenn der Magistrat mit der Ausübung seines Amtes fortfährt, die Stadt elend veröden wird."
[303] Lorenz, "Verfolgungsgebiete im deutschen Südwesten," 145; Mährle, "O wehe der armen seelen," 375–76, 434–38; Midelfort, *Witch Hunting in Southwestern Germany*, 111–12.
[304] Mährle, "O wehe der armen seelen," 448.
[305] Robisheaux, "The German Witch Trials," 186; Schwerhoff, "Hexenverfolgungen in der frühneizeitlichen Germania Sacra," 18; Behringer, *Hexenverfolgung in Bayern*, 237–40; Walinski-Kiehl, "Witch-Hunting and State Building," 256; Voltmer, "Hexenbrenner Und Hexenbischöfe," 202; Mährle, "O wehe der armen seelen," 438–40.
[306] Mährle, "O wehe der armen seelen," 438."eines neuen Verfolgungsparadigmas."
[307] Behringer, *Witches and Witch-Hunts*, 112–13.
[308] Durrant, *Witchcraft, Gender, and Society in Early Modern Germany*; Behringer, *Witches and Witch-Hunts*, 112.
[309] Durrant, *Witchcraft, Gender, and Society in Early Modern Germany*, xxii.

around two hundred, but perhaps even up to seven hundred people were executed.[310] In his thorough research of the trials, the British historian Jonathan Durrant concludes that they were hardly related to weather disasters, conflicts within the Eichstätt community, or rival political factions. It was mostly a product of top-down Counter Reformation zeal, of which the fight against ubiquitous diabolical sin was characteristic.[311]

The Ellwangen hunt had started at a moment of relative peace in witch-hunting history, but the Eichstätt trials were part of a larger flood.[312] In the electoral state of Mainz things re-escalated between 1616 and 1618, and an estimated 361 people were killed.[313] 1616 was also the year when the first large Bamberg hunt began, killing around two hundred people (see section 4.4). Around the same time, trials in the neighboring Franconian prince-bishopric of Würzburg produced an even higher number of three hundred estimated deaths.[314] Wolfgang Mährle has argued that the persecutory authorities of these Franconian trials "drew their inspiration from the Ellwangen example from the beginning, both in their organization, as well as in the legal implementation of proceedings."[315] It has been retorted that Mährle's claims lack conclusive evidence, but the Franconian hunts have eerie similarities to the Ellwangen model. It is telling that Friedrich Förner, the charismatic suffragan bishop of Bamberg, dedicated his witchcraft sermons to Von Westerstetten.[316]

The wave of trials of the late 1620s

The trials of the late 1610s had largely waned by the early 1620s, only to be superseded by a more lethal wave beginning around 1626.[317] By that time, the Ellwangen model was widely emulated. Popular pressure for witch-hunting remained paramount as an initial trigger for persecution. But as soon as authorities became involved, it was professional awe-inspiring *Hexenkommissare* who took control. Armed with extraordinary legal powers they pushed persecutions towards an unprecedented scale. Questionnaires were standardized, torture was relentless, and escape was nearly impossible. Also typical of this wave, as noted in contemporary reports, was its even higher involvement of children, and an enhanced attack on men and

---

[310] Behringer, *Hexenverfolgung in Bayern*, 238; Durrant, *Witchcraft, Gender, and Society in Early Modern Germany*, 20, 32, 82; Behringer, "Westerstetten, Johann Christoph von (1563-1637)."
[311] Durrant, *Witchcraft, Gender, and Society in Early Modern Germany*.
[312] Schwerhoff, "Hexenverfolgungen in der frühneizeitlichen Germania Sacra," 18; Behringer, *Hexenverfolgung in Bayern*, 235–38, 307–8.
[313] Robisheaux, "The German Witch Trials," 187.
[314] Robisheaux, 187.
[315] Mährle, "O wehe der armen seelen," 439."Die dortigen prozeßführenden Instanzen orientierten sich von Beginn an an den Ellwanger Verfolgungsmustern. Dies galt sowohl in Hinblick auf die organisatorische als auch auf die juristische Durchführung der Verfahren."
[316] Schwerhoff, "Hexenverfolgungen in der frühneizeitlichen Germania Sacra," 18; Walinski-Kiehl, "Witch-Hunting and State Building," 256; Voltmer, "Hexenbrenner Und Hexenbischöfe," 217; Förner, *Dämonenglaube und Zauberei im Jahre 1625*, 1–2.
[317] Robisheaux, "The German Witch Trials," 187–88; Behringer, *Witches and Witch-Hunts*, 108–20; Behringer, *Hexen und Hexenprozesse in Deutschland*, 186–90, 250–67.

elites.[318] Especially in ecclesiastical territories – where a relative judicial independence coincided with vigorous Tridentine Catholicism – the new model blossomed.[319] The Bamberg hunt of 1626-1632 offers a prime example. It not only outdid Ellwangen in the way it gained momentum, but also in the eventual death toll. As mentioned earlier, the simultaneous persecution in Würzburg killed around a thousand people.[320] Exemplifying the state of panic there, its prince-bishop Philip Adolf von Ehrenberg warned that because of its many witches God was about to scorch Würzburg with sulfur, fire, war, hunger and disease, just as he had done with Sodom and Gomorrah. Notable was Würzburg's unusually high number of child witches executed, and its bloodbath amongst clerics – forty-three canons and vicars were burned. "Würzburgisch Werk" (Würzburg work) became an expression throughout Germany for unrelenting persecution.

Electoral Mainz also experienced renewed trials, leading to an estimated 768 people being burned.[321] Runaway hunts swept parts of southern Germany, in places like Mergentheim, Ortenau, Baden-Baden, Oberkirch, and Offenbach.[322] In some cases even the families of the people who had instigated or perpetrated the trials in the first place were hit. Yet, it was the electoral state of Cologne, to the northwest, that would experience what Behringer calls "the most terrible witch-hunt in the German parts of the Holy Roman Empire."[323] Throughout its scattered territories around two thousand people were burned within a few years.[324] A past interpretation presumed that this hunt was a top-down "war against the witches", but recent research indicates that it was more of a complex mixture of bottom-up and top-down initiatives.[325] Economic hardship, weather disasters, and many accusations from children stimulated strong popular demands for witch-hunting. A subsequent interaction with professionalized witch commissions, condoned by high government, eventually led to the excessive brutality characteristic of these trials. Our focus on Catholic areas should not let us forget the Protestants. They were no longer in the vanguard, but still, during these decades, principalities like Mecklenburg, Pomerania, and Sachsen-Coburg, experienced persecutions that altogether killed thousands of people. They also show similar patterns, with broader segments of society targeted.[326]

---

[318] Midelfort, *Witch Hunting in Southwestern Germany*, 179; Schulte, *Hexenmeister*, 92; *Zwo Warhafftige, und doch Männiglich zuvor bekante Newe Zeitung*.; *Ein Warhafftige und gründtliche Beschreibung, Auß demm Bistumm Würtz- und Bamberg*.
[319] Dillinger, "The Political Aspects of the German Witch Hunts," 68; Rummel, "Das 'ungestüme Umherlaufen der Untertanen'.," 149.
[320] Walinski-Kiehl, "The Devil's Children," 175–77; Behringer, *Hexen und Hexenprozesse in Deutschland*, 252–58, 265; Rowlands, "Würzburg, Prince-Bishopric Of."
[321] Robisheaux, "The German Witch Trials," 187; Pohl, *Zauberglaube und Hexenangst im Kurfürstentum Mainz*.
[322] Midelfort, *Witch Hunting in Southwestern Germany*, 121–54.
[323] Behringer, *Witches and Witch-Hunts*, 115.
[324] Behringer, 113–17; Decker, "Die Hexenverfolgungen im Herzogtum Westfalen"; Grawlich, "Der Hexenkommisar Heinrich von Schultheiß."
[325] Schormann, *Der Krieg gegen die Hexen*; Becker, "Hexenverfolgung in Kurköln"; Grawlich, "Der Hexenkommisar Heinrich von Schultheiß," 316–17.
[326] Rummel and Voltmer, *Hexen und Hexenverfolgung*, 117–19; Moeller, "Es ist überaus gerechtes Gesetz, dass die Zauberinnen getötet werden"; Moeller, *Dass Willkür über Recht ginge*.

Considering the early seventeenth century, it is noticeable that the Ellwangen hunt constitutes a critical moment in a broader trend towards the rationalization of witch-hunting. The tendency is discernible in the electoral state of Mainz. In his research on the territory, Herbert Pohl observed that in the late sixteenth century arrests depended upon a mix of evidence: accusations, house warrants, witness statements, and investigations into people's reputations. Questionings tended to be somewhat improvised and open ended. But by the late 1620s, the mere mention of somebody as a sabbath accomplice was sufficient grounds for arrest, and examinations focused more efficiently on the enforcement of cumulative confessions.[327] Pohl writes: "the range of what was considered orthodox in witchcraft theory was still wide in the sixteenth century, and only experienced a certain fixation after the emergence of the new interrogatory practices of the seventeenth century, which in certain ways also expanded popular beliefs in witches."[328] The confiscation of witches' property was also rationalized, and especially the execution of rich people created possibilities for further persecution.[329] A typical example was the town of Dieburg, where between 1626 and 1630 half the city council was burned. The Austrian historian Andreas Müller found a similar trend when using digital tools to compare trial records from Rostock in 1584 with records from Hainburg between 1617 and 1618.[330] In his diagrams Müller gave main cumulative elements specific colors, and early records show a rather disorganized picture, with still quite some attention devoted to non-cumulative ideas, such as aspects of popular magic. The seventeenth-century records, on the other hand, display more orderly patterns and a more exclusive focus on cumulative notions.

The early seventeenth century was marked by the continuation of another trend: both in textual and visual representations, sabbaths became more crowded. In 1612 the French judge Pierre de Lancre published his *Tableau de l'inconstance des mauvais anges et démons* (Description of the Inconstancy of Evil Angels and Demons), which even surpassed Delrio in the extravagance of its sabbath descriptions.[331] A next version also included a baroque picture by the Polish-born artist Jan Ziarnko, showing more than fifty witches assembled.[332] By 1620, a widely reproduced German picture named "Zauberey" (Sorcery), went as far as to present the sabbath as a mass event with hundreds of visitors.[333] In our earlier discussion of the Bamberg hunt of 1626-1632 it was mentioned that the interrogator Ernst Vasoldt extracted 126 names of sabbath companions from one single suspect. In the early 1560s that would have been a highly

---

[327] Pohl, *Zauberglaube und Hexenangst im Kurfürstentum Mainz*, 170–76, 295.
[328] Pohl, 295."Die Bandbreite dessen, was im Hexenglauben als orthodox galt, war zumindest im 16. Jahrhundert noch groß und erfuhr erst durch das Aufkommen der neuen Interrogatorien im 17. Jahrhundert eine gewisse Fixierung, die in manchen Details durchaus auch eine Erweiterung des volkstümlichen Hexenglaubens mit sich brachte".
[329] Pohl, 227–30.
[330] Müller, "Elaborated Concepts of Witchcraft?"
[331] Lancre, *On the Inconstancy of Witches*.
[332] Krause, *Witchcraft, Demonology, and Confession in Early Modern France*, 98–99.
[333] Voltmer, "Herren und Hexen," 15.

implausible thing for an investigator to do. In the 1590s it was already somewhat more conceivable, but by the 1620s it had become quite obvious.[334]

It is also figures like Ernst Vasoldt who can help us understand how those German trials of the 1610s and 1620s became so big. The professionalization of witch persecution increasingly required professional persecutors. Some people became specialists, moving through Germany to offer their services in various *Hexen Kommissionen*.[335] After his dismissal from Bamberg, Ernst Vasoldt for instance found employment in the witch-hunt of Mergentheim.[336] Obviously, such experts also transmitted practical knowledge about how to proceed. It is also worth further reflecting on the significance of children. In Ellwangen their role happened to be quite limited, but by the 1620s there were hardly any runaway panics that were not initiated or enhanced by child confessions.[337] Adding to the gruesomeness, alleged child witches were increasingly executed.[338] By now children also took center stage in witchcraft theory, and a German pamphlet from 1626 was fully devoted to the subject.[339] The author expressed his dismay and amazement about the unprecedented numbers of child-witches. Why was God allowing this? "I admit, that this is a very difficult question", he acknowledged, presuming that the answer especially lay in the bad influence of parents.[340] It was their impious behavior, or conversion into witchcraft, that drove so many children into Satan's arms. Did many Biblical passages not indicate that God punishes children for the sins of their parents?

In his 1972 masterpiece on witch-hunting in southwestern Germany, Erik Midelfort contemplated on the extraordinary scale of the late 1620s trials. "The reason witch hunting developed to such extreme dimensions during this period has always been unclear" he remarked.[341] Obviously, the many disasters, like epidemics, warfare, failed harvests, and economic ruin, played their part. Yet, he noted that other periods faced similar challenges. After the 1620s things even aggravated, but witch-hunting in the 1630s and 1640s in fact began to decline. Hence, environmental disasters alone cannot do the job of explaining the events. So, Midelfort proposed looking elsewhere too:

> At least one element is missing if we consider merely the superstitious witchcraft beliefs of a region and the catalytic disasters that may have triggered panic. That element is mood – the mood of villagers, townspeople, lawyers, governors, and judges. Mood is not easily measurable; yet it clearly depends on more than superstition (or enlightenment)

---

[334] Goodare, *The European Witch-Hunt*, 236–38.
[335] Durrant, *Witchcraft, Gender, and Society in Early Modern Germany*, 10–14; Rummel and Voltmer, *Hexen und Hexenverfolgung*, 110–12.
[336] Midelfort, *Witch Hunting in Southwestern Germany*, 145.
[337] Behringer, *Witches and Witch-Hunts*, 142; Midelfort, *Witch Hunting in Southwestern Germany*, 140–41, 179; Walinski-Kiehl, "The Devil's Children," 173.
[338] Behringer, "Kinderhexenprozesse," 37.
[339] *Newer Tractat von der Verführten Kinder Zauberey*.
[340] *Newer Tractat von der Verführten Kinder Zauberey*, 3."Ich bekenne, das dieses ein sehr schwere Frag seye."
[341] Midelfort, *Witch Hunting in Southwestern Germany*, 124.

and hardship (or physical well-being). Mood is affected by national or even international surges of feeling, by experience, by local history.[342]

To understand the "mood" at that instance of the Thirty Years' War, Midelfort thought of the despair amongst Protestants, and the religious euphoria amongst Catholics.[343] There is much to say for this argument, but one crucial element still seems missing: the cumulative concept of witchcraft's adaptedness at that particular moment in time. By the late 1620s the doctrine was more predisposed than ever before to triggering runaway panics that could kill hundreds of people. Through the enhanced focus on huge sabbaths, child witnesses, professionalized investigations, and standardized questionnaires, concepts of witchcraft had evolved in ways that boosted the reproduction of witch-hunting. The general "mood" and environmental hardship still remain an essential part of the picture, but what we need to add here is the cumulative concept's ability to *exploit* such conditions.

The origin of this "design" is not to be found in grand intentional strategies or central preparation. The hunts of Wiesensteig, Trier, and Ellwangen became unusually big due to a rich blend of incidents, contingent conditions, and specific ideas about witchcraft, coming together at a specific place and moment in time. Yet, the new local cultural variants then turned into a transregional standard precisely because of their ability to create large persecution. The big hunts were the ones to have the most cultural "offspring". So, there was an exchange between what people believed about witchcraft, how this affected trials, and vice versa. Beliefs and practices mutually enforced each other. Importantly, the persecutions did not grow large because the communities or actors involved really benefited. Ellwangen further illustrates how witch-hunting could damage the communities giving rise to it. But again, when considering the reproductive interests of the witch-hunting phenomenon *itself*, Ellwangen looks like yet another lucky "mutation".

Some essential elements of the proposed Darwinian scenario are still missing, though. Until now, our focus has been mostly on new ideas and practices that *enhanced* the spread of trials. But as I have argued, a Darwinian model requires another side to that coin. The cumulative preservation of accidentally adaptive variants can only produce adaptations if those variants appeared within oceans of competitors that failed to survive as successfully. We could think of ideas about witchcraft that hindered the continuation of persecution, or that were just too insignificant to reproduce. Moreover, attention so far has mostly focused on elements of the early modern context that boosted trials, like weather disasters, anxieties over Anabaptists, sentiments against corrupt elites, or the zealotry of the Counter Reformation. However, a Darwinian model not only presumes forces that augment the survival of certain variants, but also forces that hinder it. It was said above there is no such thing as a cultural free lunch. If a cultural

---

[342] Midelfort, 124.
[343] Midelfort, 124–25.

phenomenon is to survive, it continually has to contest with other forms of culture for human attention. So, was the early modern environment indeed also a bit like a hostile jungle for the witch-hunting phenomenon? Did enemies lurk in the dark, waiting to pounce? It is this proposed cultural 'struggle for life' that will now be explored in further detail.

6.4 Culture's struggle for life

An illustrated *Flugblatt* in 1555 reported an alarming case of witchcraft in Derenburg, a town in central Germany.[344] "A terrifying story", ran the headline of an account of what had happened to three female witches and two men in October that year.[345] The newssheet began with some conventional warnings about the devil's hatred of humankind, women as his "weak tool", and the imminent last judgement that was making Satan furious.[346] The report then moved to the case itself, and an interesting storyline unfolds. Two witches named Gröbische and Gißlersche, of whom the former had already been involved in diabolical intercourse for many years, were burned on the first of October. However, when the fire of Gröbische's stake was ignited, Satan came down from the air and took her away before everyone's eyes. Two days later the witches returned to Gißlersche's place, where they violently ejected her husband from the house. A neighbor, who was alerted by all the noise, saw the witches dancing around a fire in the house, with Gißlersche's husband lying dead on the ground. A visual illustration on the *Flugblatt* depicted the events in gruesome detail. The newssheet also reported that on the fifteenth of October a third witch named Serckschen was put to the stake, among other things for burying a toad under the threshold of a house. This magical act had lamed a man and killed his cattle. Readers were reminded that the devil was still alive and well, and that everyone duly needed to seek the protection of the Lord.

    This newssheet about the case of Derenburg was typical for its time: it highlights witchcraft as a feminine crime, and its overall description is rather unelaborate. The sexual diabolical pact and harmful magic are present, but the sabbath and nightly flight remain unmentioned. What makes this newssheet remarkable, though, are some of the strange additions, like the devil saving a witch from the stake, the witches' return, the killing of the husband afterwards, and the dance around the fire. What we see here is four unusual cultural variants about witchcraft, or "mutations", that appeared in public discourse at an auspicious moment in the history of witch-hunting. The details made the story sensational, and contained much that the mid-sixteenth century German public was craving, things supernatural, dangerous, and diabolical. No wonder that a publisher was happy to print it, and that the report reached an audience as far away as Zurich, where Johann Jacob Wick included it in his news collection.[347]

---

[344] Zika, *The Appearance of Witchcraft*, 180–82; Warfield, "Witchcraft Illustrated," 467–69.
[345] Zika, *The Appearance of Witchcraft*, 180."Ein erschröckliche geschicht."
[346] Zika, 180-1."schwecheren werckzeug."
[347] Wick, *Die Wickiana*, 79–80.

Hence, these four variants had ample opportunity to become standard notions of the witchcraft mythology.

However, none of them was a reproductive success. In contrast to notions like nightly flight, large sabbaths, or the child witch, these "mutations" hardly survived. If we contemplate their features, this may not entirely come as a surprise. Take the example of the devil saving a witch from the fire while many people were watching. One problem of this variant was that it was probably too vulnerable to refutation. The diabolical witchcraft mythology faced continuous skepticism, and people who had attended a burning where such supernatural rescues allegedly occurred, might well retort that they had not seen it happen. It is probably not by accident that those supernatural events that *did* become common tropes, like flights, sabbaths, or magic, were normally thought to occur in secret. Their allegedly clandestine character circumvented the problem of refutation, as these acts were safe from empirical control. Another problem of the diabolical rescue was that it made witch-hunting futile. What is the point of a witch trial if Satan saves his witches just before they get burned? The idea of witches returning afterwards and killing a person, was even more hazardous in that regard. For the reproduction of witch-hunting, it was essential that people believed that it reduced the danger – not that it enhanced it. The variant about the witches dancing around a fire in a house may not have been a hindrance, but it probably suffered from another problem: it did not significantly help the reproduction of trials either. The variant appears too trivial to have survived the cultural "struggle for life" amongst witch beliefs, losing out to competitors that were more conducive to further persecution.

If the Darwinian model proposed here is warranted, such "failed" cultural variants must have been ubiquitous. The cultural "lucky mistakes" that became common tropes must have stood out against a continuing flood of variants that fell into obscurity.[348] As mentioned previously, research into this topic has hardly been undertaken yet. Witchcraft experts every now and then refer to strange notions about witchcraft, like "an odd tale", "an unusual picture", "a highly uncommon element", an "odd statement", or a "quite original" notion.[349] Especially Robin Briggs highlights the enormous variation in concepts of witchcraft.[350] However, what has not been undertaken so far is systematic empirical research into what such "unfit" variants looked like. How did they appear? Why were they unsuccessful? How many of them were there? Something else that has not been addressed is their potential theoretical significance: such variants may well have been essential ingredients of an evolutionary process that created the socio-cultural "design" of the cumulative concept of witchcraft. We here see how the theory of Darwinian cultural evolution can generate both new empirical questions and theoretical insights.

---

[348] Henrich, *The Secret of Our Success*, 34.
[349] Richard Kieckhefer, "The First Wave of Trials," 174–75; Briggs, *The Witches of Lorraine*, 141; Dillinger, *Kinder im Hexenprozess*, 129."ein äußerst unübliches Element" ; Briggs, *The Witches of Lorraine*, 144; Schmidt, *Glaube und Skepsis*, 44."recht originell."
[350] Briggs, "Many Reasons Why"; Briggs, *Witches & Neighbours*.

If just a few sentences in one newssheet already provide us with four failed variants, we can safely assume that further empirical research into trial records, scholarly works, pamphlets, chronicles, sermons, or visual representations, would deliver innumerable further examples. The empirical question thus lays bare an almost endless research agenda, requiring more work than any scholar could perform in a lifetime. Importantly, the failed variants that can still be retrieved by historians only represent a small percentage of all the variants that once appeared. Many witchcraft notions that were discussed in local taverns, during sermons, in sessions of torture, or at the village square, will not have made it into any document. The variants that *were* written down or printed may have disappeared because the documents were lost. For instance, when the Wiesensteig trial records vanished, they probably took unique cultural variants with them. In what follows, I discuss some examples of relatively unsuccessful witchcraft notions, but I do so with the full understanding that most likely they only represent the tip of the iceberg of all variants that once saw some light.

Visible supernatural events
Examples of supernatural events during witch burnings form one interesting category. As it turns out, the Derenberg *Flugblatt* is not the only source to mention a case. Take an extensive newssheet about a burning in Dillingen, October 1579.[351] It recounts how a witch was brought to the stake and threatened to set the executioner on fire. The executioner was not impressed, but when the witch was about to burst into flames two ravens appeared, "and in front of many people (it was a great number of them that were watching) they took her away in the air."[352] Subsequently, the executioner's clothes caught fire, and he died cruelly. A newssheet from 1588 on the persecution in Osnabruck contains another account.[353] When many witches were about to be burned, the devil appeared to take four of them with him. When the executioner ignited the fire, an awful wind suddenly arose, threatening to douse the fire. Many onlookers were terrified, and the executioner feared for his own safety. Nevertheless, he was able to maintain the fire so that the other witches received their well-deserved punishment. Dreytwein's chronicle contains another case.[354] During one of the witch burnings in Wiesensteig 1562, twenty witches were burned while more than three thousand people watched. Then, sensationally, an angel of God descended against a red sky, urging people to stay faithful to God to avoid punishment. The witches boldly responded that Satan's kingdom was better than God's kingdom, and the angel subsequently disappeared.

In the news collection of Jacob Wick we can find other examples of unusual supernatural events. During a trial in 1568, seven witches were executed in the Swiss town of Erlach, of whom one was a young woman who confessed and repented profoundly. When she was convicted in

---
[351] Kuntzen, *Newe Zeitung von einer Erschrecklichen That*.
[352] Kuntzen "und vor allem Volck (welcher eine grosse Summa gewesen sind, die da zu schaweten[in den lüfften weggeführet."
[353] Rügge, *Die Hexenverfolgung in der Stadt Osnabrück*, 105.
[354] Dreytwein, *Esslingische Chronik*, 245–46; Waite, *Eradicating the Devil's Minions*, 150.

court, "a smell spread through the whole courtroom that was so very penetrating that all judges and all others had to pinch their noses. People thought that Satan had left the smell behind, because he was unsure about his possession of the girl's soul."[355] Another report tells of a case in Luzern 1570, in which an imprisoned witch had already confessed to several crimes. When investigators reentered her cell to extract more confessions, they "found nothing but her skin, that was bloated like a bladder. They saw neither bones nor flesh", so the devil had apparently taken her interior and soul away.[356] As mentioned above, nightly flights and sabbaths were normally thought to happen in secret, but there were occasional deviations from this pattern. We already discussed Jacquier's fifteenth-century account about wayfarers who came across an assembly at night. Similarly, investigations in the Saar region produced a story about a twenty-year-old farmhand who went to sleep in his master's barn, but when waking up after his first sleep noticed that the barn was full of light.[357] The witches were having their dance there. In the Malleus Maleficarum it is maintained that the common people often sighted witches flying, like the shepherds who saw a sorceress from Waldshut fly on a demon, just after the witch and the demon had stirred up a hailstorm.[358]

While the occurrence of observable supernatural events seems to have been somewhat of a trope, none of these specific variants became common elements of witchcraft narratives. Like the rescue in Derenberg, this was probably due to the fact that these variants were vulnerable to refutation. In the case of the sudden wind in Osnabruck, or the sudden smell in Erlach, we cannot rule out that it really happened, since sudden winds and smells can have natural causes. However, these variants still seem "unfit" for robust survival because their real occurrence at that specific stage of a witch trial must have been very rare at best. The Dillingen and Osnabruck variants about the witches being saved, or the Dillingen addition about the executioner's burning, suffer from the same problem we encountered earlier in the Derenburg case: they discouraged further hunting. The sudden smell at Erlach, or the Wiesensteig angel appearing against a red sky, may also have been too insignificant in their effects on trials to reproduce any further. As argued above, the secrecy of many of the witches' acts was one of the cumulative concept's most ingenious traits. Yet, what these stories indicate is that the supporters of witch-hunting were not necessarily the ones who deliberately designed the concept that way. In fact, *they* continually introduced stories about visible supernatural events. More plausibly, it was a hidden selective process that weeded such unhelpful variants out, thus creating a more unfalsifiable concept of witchcraft.

---

[355] Wick, *Die Wickiana*, 161."ist ein söllicher böser gstank in allem ring worden, das die richter und yederman, so herumb gestanden, die nasen verhaben müssen, und geachtet, der sathan habe disen gstank hinder im gelassen, da er an dess meytlis seel verzwyflet".
[356] Wick, 179-80."haben sy nütt da gfunden, dan alleyn die hutt von iren, die ist zerblanet gwäsen als ein grose blateren; sunst habend sy weder fleisch noch beyn gsähen."
[357] Labouvie, *Zauberei und Hexenwerk*, 228.
[358] Institoris, *The Hammer of Witches*, 292.

Interestingly, even the relatively well-organized and successful persecution of Ellwangen produced a variant with much potential for undermining further hunting. During the middle years of the persecution, the trial records began to report some unusual witches' confessions. The records recount that witches were not really killed during their burning.[359] Afterwards they still appeared at the sabbaths, and lived on in a diabolical palace, a sort of witches' heaven, where they enjoyed a pleasant afterlife and continued their diabolical activities. One record noted: "nothing will happen to anybody, even when one is decapitated. It is merely an illusion, and afterwards all come together again."[360] Wolfgang Mährle and Johannes Dillinger noticed that these confessions threatened to make persecution a farce: witch-hunting would neither save people from the witches' crimes, nor ensure the witches' divine salvation. No wonder that this belief, unlike so many of Ellwangen's other variants, became an evolutionary dead-end.

Sabbath variations

Notions about witchcraft that survived were likewise characterized by continuing variations, of which some had a better chance of survival than others. There was a lot of variation regarding the objects that witches were alleged to fly on: amongst the common people there were for instance alleged sightings of flying cats and dragons.[361] Regarding witches' meetings we saw that small sabbaths lost ground to large sabbaths, due to the latter's effect of creating larger hunts. But there were also stranger deviations.[362] Take a claim from a fifteenth-century Arras treatise about witches' assemblies being held "on the same night in various forests and places."[363] This notion of sabbaths moving from place to place within one night did not take hold, which might be related to the fact that it added nothing to the sabbath's essential implication of witches knowing each other – the variant was simply superfluous. An idea that occurred occasionally, was that assemblies were set in a strange blue light.[364] Kieckhefer maintains that in an age without artificial lighting it conveyed "a powerful sense of the supernatural and in this case demonic." But he is probably also right to render it an "apparently inconsequential detail".[365] Interrogations in Lorraine produced some variants that were even hazardous for witch-hunting itself. A female suspect narrated that while at a sabbath, she could see another sabbath nearby.[366] This idea may have hindered the number of identifiable accomplices, as it reduced the number of witches present at one single sabbath. Another confession said that witches did not appear in their

---

[359] Dillinger, "Hexen-Eltern," 244–45; Dillinger, *Kinder im Hexenprozess*, 129–31; Mährle, "O wehe der armen seelen," 435.
[360] Dillinger, "Hexen-Eltern," 245."es geschehe keiner Nichts, Wann man schon die Köpf Abschlag. Seie nur ein Blenntnus dann sy kommen Alle sambt wider zu Ihnen".
[361] Goodare, "Witches' Flight in Scottish Demonology," 161; Blécourt, "The Flying Witch"; Schmidt, *Glaube und Skepsis*, 388; Groß, *Hexerei in Minden*, 280–81.
[362] Labouvie, *Zauberei und Hexenwerk*, 228–49; Briggs, *The Witches of Lorraine*, 137–46.
[363] Anonymous of Arras, "A History of the State, Case, and Condition of the Waldensian Heretics," 47.
[364] Kieckhefer, "Mythologies of Witchcraft in the Fifteenth Century," 91; Dillinger, *Böse Leute*, 135.
[365] Kieckhefer, "Mythologies of Witchcraft in the Fifteenth Century," 91.
[366] Briggs, *The Witches of Lorraine*, 141.

normal bodies, but as cats.[367] This "mutation" had the potential of undermining the reproductive mechanism of the sabbath altogether, as witches could no longer identify each other.

There were also many variants regarding what happened at witches' meetings. Some sources describe the devil in a surprisingly subservient role.[368] A newssheet printed in Cologne 1596 tells of a conflict between witches and devils at an assembly on the Lüneburg Heath.[369] The witches wanted some money back from Lucifer, and they beat demons so hard that the spirits fled. Many witches then flew to hell, where they scolded the devil for not paying them. Lucifer gave in, and a dragon appeared who brought the witches their treasures. The witches then entered a mutual fight over their new possessions. A trial record from Rostock 1584 tells a strange story about the devil being immersed in a pot to create a magical potion. A witch confessed that "she bathed Satan on a Thursday in the devil's name and he was as small as a child and she had filled the water from the bowl beside the stream and heated it up in a small pot."[370] What may have hindered the survival of these two narratives is the rather unimposing picture that they presented of Satan. The idea of the devil presiding over the sabbath on a throne, for instance, seemed better adapted to how people at the time normally thought of Christendom's arch-enemy.

Other variations describe how certain women chaired the sabbaths, in some cases being the devil in disguise.[371] Several early Italian accounts maintained that the witches' assembly was presided over by Oriente, a woman who instructed witches on healing and other matters. A confession in southern Tirol in 1506 produced a story about an ugly woman named Jostin, who was elected "queen of the land of angels", wearing a golden robe and a multicolored crown.[372] An allegation in German Bodenheim in 1618, on the other hand, concerned a male suspect who led the sabbath as king of the witches.[373] Unfamiliar motifs also appeared regarding what was being venerated. An early alpine account discussed witches adoring a statue of Jupiter, and the newssheet from Erfurt 1594 shows witches dancing around a column with a toad sitting at the top.[374] Toads were also the topic of some odd accounts in the Basque country. There was nothing strange about toads attending sabbaths as such, as they were considered filthy, diabolical animals.[375] But some reports stressed how witches were maltreating them in order to extract poisons. "They take the skin of the toads, which they bite into with their teeth, and the toads protect themselves as best they can with their feet and scratch them on the face hideously", De

---

[367] Briggs, 144.
[368] Moeller, *Dass Willkür über Recht ginge*, 321–22.
[369] *Zwo erschreckliche und unerhörte Geschicht*.
[370] Müller, "Elaborated Concepts of Witchcraft?," 15.
[371] Kieckhefer, "Mythologies of Witchcraft in the Fifteenth Century," 97; Schmidt, *Glaube und Skepsis*, 28; Moeller, *Dass Willkür über Recht ginge*, 320.
[372] Behringer, *Hexen und Hexenprozesse in Deutschland*, 111-2."Köningin von Engelland."
[373] Schmidt, *Glaube und Skepsis*, 373.
[374] Ostorero, *Le diable au sabbat*, 7–8; Voltmer, "Hört an neu schrecklich abentheuer / von den unholden ungeheuer", 132, 151.
[375] Wilson, *The Magical Universe*, 417–18; Voltmer, "Hört an neu schrecklich abentheuer / von den unholden ungeheuer," 155; Labouvie, *Zauberei und Hexenwerk*, 216.

Lancre recounts.[376] Another Bask description mentions how toads were whipped with switches and pressed on the ground with a foot to make them spew.[377] In today's world, such reports might infuriate animal rights' activists, but it was not the kind of thing that would put the early moderns into action. Unlike ideas about devil worship, or weather magic, the maltreatment of toads did not become a central motif.

In his account of the variety of sabbath notions in Lorraine, Robin Briggs draws an interesting parallel with the process of natural selection in biology. When persecutors questioned their suspects about the sabbath, the suspects sometimes added unusual individual elements. The persecutors mostly cared about names of the other witches that they had seen there, but suspects often provided more information than they were asked for. Briggs subsequently writes about the Lorraine sabbaths: "Over nearly a century the accounts do not change in any obvious way; there is no sign of any evolution in popular beliefs about the sabbath. Petty deviations from the norm were themselves normal, but unlike genetic mutations did not generate distinct new strains."[378] The similarities to natural selection may be more striking than is acknowledged here though, because most genetic mutations do not lead to new strains either. Only a small percentage does, as the overwhelming majority of genetic mutations fall into evolutionary oblivion.

Initiation and harmful magic
Initiation into witchcraft was also a topic of continuing variation. There was much diversity as to what the devil wore when he appeared to people, which names he used to introduce himself, and which un-human traits betrayed his real identity.[379] But there were also variants that strongly diverged from the common narratives. A news report about the persecution of Geneva in 1571 tells a story of a servant who rode a carriage through a forest, and happened to come across a witches' synagogue there. A demon named Moreth then brought him to the devil, who sat on a chair, and before Satan the servant was initiated into the sect.[380] The *Malleus Maleficarum* provides a confession of a young woman in the German town of Breisach who was seduced into witchcraft by her aunt in the following manner:

> One day she had to go upstairs with her aunt and enter a room at her command. There, she saw fifteen young men in green-colored garments after the fashion in which knights go about, and the aunt said to her, "Well, then! From among these young men, I will hand over to you the one that you want, and he will take you as his bride." When the young

---
[376] Lancre, *On the Inconstancy of Witches*, 403.
[377] Henningsen, *The Salazar Documents*, 116.
[378] Briggs, *Witches & Neighbours*, 39.
[379] Pohl, *Zauberglaube und Hexenangst im Kurfürstentum Mainz*, 352–59, 286; Roper, *Witch Craze*, 82–103; Hille, *Der Teufelspakt in frühneuzeitlichen Verhörprotokollen*, 52–251.
[380] Wick, *Die Wickiana*, 196–98.

woman said that she did not wish to have any of them, she was badly wounded and eventually gave in.[381]

In comparison with the idea of initiation into witchcraft through diabolical intercourse, these variants look rather meagre. The Geneva variant seems just too boring, and the Breisach variant contains trivial and relatively arbitrary details – why upstairs, why fifteen, and why green clothes? The notion of a forced initiation also makes witchcraft less punishable, since becoming a witch through coercion meant that it was not a person's own decision. The idea of female diabolical intercourse was more shocking and perverse, and better adapted to key obsessions of the age, like diabolical evil and uncontrollable female sexuality. An aspect of the Breisach story that was more common, though, was that witches introduced other witches into witchcraft. It has remained a significant competitor to the idea of initiation through diabolical contact.[382] This may not be a coincidence, because the variant has two important implications that are helpful for witch-hunting's reproduction: if one has found one witch, there might well be others, and witches should be stopped from introducing even more people. A fifteenth-century judge from Arras wrote that "Witches should not be exiled as a punishment, because they will simply go away and then return to their congregations, and what's worse, infect others." [383] These competing tropes about initiation could also coalesce, as happened in a 1589 story about a woman in Gernsheim.[384] A witchcraft treatise narrated how the woman walked in a field and complained about her poverty to a female companion. The other woman then enticed her into witchcraft by promising endless cheese and butter, and a demon appeared to solidify the pact.

Importantly, it was in the cumulative concept's best reproductive interests to retain a certain diversity and malleability, especially when it concerned harmful magic. The concept was not restricted to just a few magical acts, like weather making or bewitching of livestock. This open-endedness ensured that almost any unusual misfortune could provoke new trials. Rita Voltmer writes that "the belief in witches adapted to regional conditions: while witches near the coasts allegedly caused storms to sink ships, the ones in wine-growing areas like the Saar, Franconia, and the Moselle region, froze the vines."[385] This is not to say that *all* magical acts were helpful, as a charge from Württemberg against the town of Bretten may illustrate. As we saw earlier, the skeptic Johann Weyer ironically wondered why witches were not being used in military conflicts, but in fact that was exactly what the Württembergers in 1504 accused their

---

[381] Institoris, *The Hammer of Witches*, 283–84.
[382] See, for instance: Kieckhefer, *Hazards of the Dark Arts*, 38–41; Voltmer, "Preaching on Witccraft?," 206; Briggs, *The Witches of Lorraine*, 305; Wick, *Die Wickiana*, 161; Rublack, *The Astronomer & the Witch*, 158–61; Dillinger, *Böse Leute*, 116.
[383] Anonymous of Arras, "A History of the State, Case, and Condition of the Waldensian Heretics," 29.
[384] Frisium, *Deß Teuffels Nebelkappen*.
[385] Voltmer, "Herren und Hexen," 14."Der Hexenglaube passte sich den regionalen Gegebenheiten an: Während die Hexen an den Küsten angeblich Stürme hervorriefen, um Schiffe zu versenken, ließen sie in den Weinbaugebieten an Mosel und Saar oder in Franken die Reben durch Fröste erfrieren".

opponents of.[386] The Bretteners were alleged to have used witches to cause a storm that damaged the Württemberg army. This variant did not survive well, and the German historian Hans Jürgen Schmidt provides a plausible explanation: "the idea of using witches for a community was completely nonsensical because witchcraft was characterized precisely by the fact that it was directed against the community. Why should witches help a city where they were burned?"[387]

As explained above, the cultural Darwinian "struggle for life" should not only be interpreted as competition between various ideas and practices regarding witchcraft. There was also the competition coming from other forms of culture. This reminds us of the struggle that all biological phenomena face. Take a monkey species that lives in a rainforest. Many things in its environment enhance its survival, like mutual cooperation, beneficent microbes, ripe fruits, and trees to hide in. But if we want to understand why not all trees are teeming with monkeys, we also need to address environmental threats and pushbacks, like competition for food with other organisms, or predators and pathogens that may thrive at the monkeys' expense. Along similar lines, we may wonder why witch trials did not reproduce themselves even better, killing many more people in the process. The demonologist Henri Boguet in 1602 wrote that there were "witches by the thousands everywhere, multiplying upon the earth even as worms in the garden."[388] Such claims provided potential sustenance for an almost endless number of trials. Briggs observes that "Witchcraft appears so wonderfully functional and central to early modern Europe that is it the relative moderation and brevity of the persecutions which needs explaining."[389] Fortunately, historians have reflected on the topic a lot, and many of their answers can be integrated into a Darwinian framework.

Misfortune: competing explanations
A precondition for the spread of the witch-hunt system was that misfortune was interpreted as a result of witchcraft. However, alternative explanations acted as dangerous competitors.[390] A crucial one was divine punishment.[391] In our discussion of Wiesensteig we already met the Lutheran preachers Matthaeus Alber and Wilhelm Bidenbach, who claimed that people had only themselves to blame for the hailstorm; it was their *own* sins which had provoked God's fatherly reprimand. After all, had people not been swearing, disregarding the poor, and sinning with wine? No wonder God destroyed the vineyards. By rejecting the possibility of weather magic, and attributing the hailstorm exclusively to God, these Württemberg preachers stood in an old and

---

[386] Schmidt, *Glaube und Skepsis*, 44.
[387] Schmidt, 44."Die Vorstellung eines Einsatzes von Hexen für ein Gemeinwesen war auch deshalb völlig widersinnig, weil sich Hexerei ja gerade dadurch auszeichnete, daß sie sich gegen das Gemeinwesen richtete. Warum sollten die Unholden einer Stadt helfen, in der sie verbrannt wurden?".
[388] Levack, *The Witch-Hunt in Early Modern Europe*, 22.
[389] Briggs, "Many Reasons Why," 56; For similar viewpoints, see: Clark, "Witchcraft and Magic in Early Modern Culture," 120; Goodare, *The European Witch-Hunt*, 317.
[390] Behringer, *Witches and Witch-Hunts*, 7; Schmidt, *Glaube und Skepsis*, 157.
[391] Midelfort, *Witch Hunting in Southwestern Germany*, 34–66; Behringer, *Witches and Witch-Hunts*, 88–89; Waite, *Eradicating the Devil's Minions*, 25; Ahrent-Schulte, "Lauter falscher Wahn und starke Einbildung," 89.

well-established intellectual tradition, which nicely dovetailed with one of the main theological tenets of Christianity: the omnipotence of God.[392] The belief that God and the devil were equal opponents was regarded as a dualistic heresy, and Alber and Bidenbach tried to frame witch beliefs as such. Anyone who thought that power over the weather lay in the hands of the devil or witches did not believe "in an almighty God, but in a half-mighty God."[393]

However, for the witchcraft doctrine this theological obstacle was not insurmountable. A viable counter-strategy was not to contest the omnipotence of God – that would have been a heresy indeed – but to frame witchcraft as a tool of God's punishment.[394] It was acknowledged that human sin was ubiquitous, but that was precisely why God had given the devil permission to use witches as a harmful instrument. This explanatory model was rather complex, and, arguably, counter-intuitive. But after 1560 it gained ground at the expense of explaining misfortune as solely and directly resulting from divine punitive intervention. Wolfgang Behringer argues that the disasters of the "iron century" put the latter model under pressure. Ecological and socio-economic pressures were becoming so dramatic, and appeared so inexplicable, that solely referring to the traditional explanation of direct divine punishment no longer seemed sufficient.[395] For the broader populace it was also more appealing to externalize the blame, and to lash out against other individuals, than to solely blame oneself. Nevertheless, despite losing ground, the providentialist explanation of direct divine punishment remained a formidable challenge for the witch-hunting phenomenon. Even during its peak period around 1600, many theologians in Württemberg continued to uphold the older tradition, which seems to have played a part in the relatively low number of burnings there.[396] But also in many other places in Europe this explanatory model continued to be a hindrance.[397] For instance, after the frost in Franconia in May 1626 a priest in the Bambergian town of Scheßlitz interpreted it as "a great divine punishment" rather than an act of witchcraft.[398]

Then there was a second dangerous competitor to witchcraft as an explanatory model. Like people today, early modern Europeans could interpret misfortunes like hailstorms, illnesses, or loss of livestock, as merely incidental or natural events. Throughout world history there have been societies in which the notion of purely natural causes to misfortune seems to have been entirely alien, but early modern Christian Europe did not belong to that category.[399] At a theological level the idea of natural causes did not necessarily compete with divine intervention.

---

[392] Midelfort, *Witch Hunting in Southwestern Germany*, 35–56.
[393] Alberum and Bidenbach, *Ein Summa etlicher Predigten von Hagel und Unholden* "der glaubt nicht an den Allmechtigen, sonder an ein Halbmechtigen Gott."
[394] Duni, "Doubting Witchcraft," 214; Meder, *Acht Hexenpredigten*, 91; Bodin, *De la démonomanie des sorciers*, 270.
[395] Behringer, "Climatic Change and Witch-Hunting," 337; Weik, *Hexenwerk oder Gottes Zorn?*, 46.
[396] Midelfort, *Witch Hunting in Southwestern Germany*, 45; Rublack, *The Astronomer & the Witch*, 79.
[397] Zeck, *Im Rauch gehn Himmel geschüggt*, 131; Schmidt, *Glaube und Skepsis*, 81; Ahrent-Schulte, "Lauter falscher Wahn und starke Einbildung."
[398] Jung, "Die Bamberger Hexenverfolgungen," 73-4."die große göttliche Strafe."
[399] Wilson, *The Magical Universe*, 311; Behringer, *Witches and Witch-Hunts*, 23–25; Walz, *Hexenglaube und magische Kommunikation im Dorf der frühen Neuzeit*, 22; Levack, *The Witch-Hunt in Early Modern Europe*, 238.

In a sermon from 1602, the Lutheran German preacher Johann Georg Sigwart, for instance, accepted natural causes, but hastened to add they were only secondary to the primal cause of God's judgment: "Any Christian with a certain knowledge, or any reasonable person for that matter" would understand this.[400] Sigwart presented natural causes as just God's way of achieving his ends. Nevertheless, during the entire period of witch-hunting, natural causes often operated as a somewhat separate explanatory model. It posed a direct threat to the witchcraft doctrine, amongst both the educated and the wider populace.[401]

Johannes Nider had already identified the danger in his *Formicarius*. His fifteenth-century dialogues staged a character named "the lazy one", who wanted to be informed about witchcraft, as "some people either deny it entirely, or solely explain it out of natural causes, or think it happened only partially."[402] And indeed, critics of witch-hunting often resorted to this explanatory model.[403] When in 1620 an old woman named Katharina Kepler was subjected to a witch trial in Leonberg, southwestern Germany, she had the good fortune of being defended by her astutely intelligent son, Johannes Kepler. In his successful defense, this central figure of the scientific revolution stressed that his mother's superstitious accuser had mistaken the natural causes of her misfortune for an act of witchcraft.[404] A striking example of an uneducated person making a similar point stems from a late sixteenth-century record from the Dutch Peel region. A daughter of a woman who was convicted for witchcraft remembered a past event involving the death of a horse, whose stomach later turned out to be full of worms: "At the time nobody spoke of sorcery. Now people would say that it results from witchcraft, but I don't believe a thing of it. Not that I have much understanding of such matters, but if I may be so bold to say something about it: the illness and death of cattle, that's just nature."[405] Even a witch-hunter as ferocious as Friedrich Förner from Bamberg betrayed a belief in natural causes when arguing that sorceresses could not heal people. Sometimes it *looked* as if they made a person recover, he said, but this was merely due to coincidence.[406]

Kepler was not the only one to render certain witchcraft beliefs superstitious. However, this does not imply that the domain of superstition, as certain contemporaries as well as people today might call it, was a safe haven for the witchcraft doctrine. Here other competitors reared

---

[400] Sigwart, *Ein Predigt Vom Reiffen und Gefröst*, 3-4."Es soll aber ein Christ (als der ettwas mehr wissen muß, dann sonst ein vernünfftiger Mensch)".
[401] See, for instance: Witekind, *Christlich Bedencken und Erinnerung von Zauberey*, 111.
[402] Nider, "Formicarius," 149."Je demande à être informé complétement sur ces pratiques parce que certaines personnes ou bien les nient toutes, ou bien les expliquent seulement par des causes naturelles, ou bien ne les admettent qu'en partie."
[403] See, for instance: Ahrent-Schulte, "Lauter falscher Wahn und starke Einbildung," 90; Gareis, "Kinder in Hexenverfolgungen des französischen und spanischen Baskenlandes," 93; Henningsen, *The Salazar Documents*, 11; Spee von Langenfeld, *Cautio criminalis*, 218.
[404] Rublack, *The Astronomer & the Witch*, 9, 248.
[405] Otten, *Duivelskwartier*, 187."Toen had niemand het over toverij. Nu zouden ze zeggen dat zulke dingen allemaal het gevolg zijn van toveren, maar daar geloof ik niets van. Niet dat ik er verstand van heb, maar als ik zo vrij mag zijn er iets over te zeggen: ziekte en dood van vee, dat is gewoon de natuur."
[406] Förner, *Dämonenglaube und Zauberei im Jahre 1625*, 128.

their heads. One alternative explanation for misfortune was provided by astrology.[407] The age-old belief that the position of the planets, the Sun, and the Moon affected events on Earth was common in this period. Proponents often saw astrology as an explanation for natural causation, and it competed with witchcraft beliefs for precisely that reason. For instance, after the Franconian hunts of the late 1620s, the physician Cornelius Pleier wrote that "if the witches are alleged to have caused the thunderstorm and the frost, then why were astrologers already able long before to predict their occurrence out of merely natural causes?"[408] Further competition was to be found at the level of "superstitious" beliefs of a more popular and folkloric kind.[409] The fact that Celtic areas of the British Isles experienced relatively few trials has been linked to pervasive beliefs in fairies as agents of misfortune.[410] "Fairy belief and witch belief were, in this respect, mutually exclusive alternatives", Julian Goodare observes.[411]

Witchcraft: competing responses

As soon as competing explanations for misfortune had been shaken off, the witch-hunting phenomenon found other challenges in its path. Even if people saw witchcraft as the cause of their troubles, this did not automatically imply that their answer lay in persecution. People might for instance resort to beneficent magic. In her study on Rothenburg ob der Tauber, a German town that witnessed only few trials, Alison Rowlands observed that "as long as the system of beneficent magic retained its resilience, there was less reason for people to look to the law as a response to suspected witches."[412] In Weingarten, a renowned center for pilgrimage in southern Germany, one could buy amulets, crosses and medallions that allegedly protected against weather magic. This circumstance seems to have dampened the persecutory fervor there.[413] An increasing repression of beneficent magic from the fifteenth century onwards seems to have created more room for witch trials, but still, it remained a tough contestant for witch persecution.[414] Johannes Dillinger says that "both systems existed next to each other and experienced simultaneous surges, but competed at the same time."[415]

Then there was the possibility of deciding not to punish witches at all, but to bring them to remorse and repentance, so to regain them for the faith.[416] One of Catholic Germany's most

---

[407] Sigwart, *Ein Predigt Vom Reiffen und Gefröst*, 3; Midelfort, *Witch Hunting in Southwestern Germany*, 34–35; Wilson, *The Magical Universe*, 312–15; Dillinger, "Friedrich Spee und Adam Tanner," 37; Thomas, *Religion and the Decline of Magic*, 756–57.
[408] Pleier, *Malleus Judicum*, 9."wann die Hexen solches Gewitter, und Frost verursacht unnd zuwegen gebracht hetten, wie haben es dann die Astrologi auch in vorhergegangem Jahren, lang zuvorn fein eygentlich auß lauter natürlichen Ursachen prognoticirn können?".
[409] Briggs, *Witches & Neighbours*, 179; Goodare, *The European Witch-Hunt*, 130–33.
[410] Hutton, *The Witch*, 215–42; Goodare, *The European Witch-Hunt*, 130–33.
[411] Goodare, *The European Witch-Hunt*, 130.
[412] Rowlands, *Witchcraft Narratives in Germany*, 75.
[413] Dillinger, *Böse Leute*, 161–68.
[414] Thomas, *Religion and the Decline of Magic*, 593–98; Dillinger, *Böse Leute*, 178–82.
[415] Dillinger, *Böse Leute*, 179."Beide systemen bestanden nebeneinander und erlebten gemeinsam Konjunkturen, konkurrierten aber auch".
[416] Behringer, *Witches and Witch-Hunts*, 4; Dillinger, *Böse Leute*, 411; Dillinger, "Hexen-Eltern," 250–55.

influential theologians of the early seventeenth century, the Jesuit Adam Tanner, argued that the fight against Satan was not to be conducted by the burning of witches.[417] Tanner accepted that witches existed, but thought that persecution was a hazardous affair that too easily led to the deaths of the innocent. So, he proposed to win the witches back for God, and eventually it was up to God to judge them. At the village level there were also alternative ways of dealing with alleged witches. Accusations could be a threat to the social stability of a community, and all sorts of rituals existed for avoiding social escalation.[418] Friends and kinsfolk would try to bring about a reconciliation between quarreling individuals. Only when such normal procedures had failed, would the appeal to the forces of law become a more conceivable next step.

Even if people were convinced of the guilt of a specific witch, and favored legal punishment, they could still decide not to undertake any action because of the personal risks it might entail for them. Initiating a trial against someone was a way of making dangerous enemies, amongst both the accused and their allies. If a trial resulted in an acquittal, the accuser was sure to have a vengeful opponent living nearby.[419] Authorities could also respond harshly to what they saw as cases of defamation – think of the accuser in Esslingen who had his tongue cut off.[420] Hence, few people dared to initiate a trial without broad support.[421] In addition, there seems to have been a certain awareness that witch persecution could create unpredictable dynamics that could spiral out of control to the detriment of friends, family, or even oneself. Legal persecutors potentially also suffered the consequences. They too, could end up at the stake, as happened to Flade, or otherwise be punished for their miscarriages of justice.[422] In 1601, the parliament of Paris sentenced an executioner from Rocroi to lifelong labor on the galleys because of gross abuses during trials.[423] An investigation by Bavarian authorities in 1612 lay bare that a judge in Wemding had forged data and tortured and killed people without sufficient legal basis. He was sentenced to death.[424]

If the support for witch persecution within the populace was explicit and substantial, accusations might still lead nowhere if authorities refused to proceed. Research into witch persecution long focused on places where trials became big, but over the past decades there has been more attention paid to places where they remained small or absent.[425] Alison Rowlands' thoughtful study on Rothenburg ob der Tauber is a case in point.[426] Many accusations from below

---

[417] Behringer, *Hexenverfolgung in Bayern*, 332; Dillinger, "Friedrich Spee und Adam Tanner," 48–52.
[418] Goodare, *The European Witch-Hunt*, 92–114; Briggs, *The Witches of Lorraine*, 172; Rowlands, *Witchcraft Narratives in Germany*, 38.
[419] Briggs, *The Witches of Lorraine*, 383.
[420] Walz, *Hexenglaube und magische Kommunikation im Dorf der frühen Neuzeit*, 515; Rowlands, *Witchcraft Narratives in Germany*, 29–30.
[421] Briggs, *The Witches of Lorraine*, 176–78.
[422] Rummel and Voltmer, *Hexen und Hexenverfolgung*, 103, 112.
[423] Behringer, *Witches and Witch-Hunts*, 182.
[424] Behringer, *Hexenverfolgung in Bayern*, 303–5.
[425] Midelfort, "Witch Craze?"; Schmidt, *Glaube und Skepsis*.
[426] Rowlands, *Witchcraft Narratives in Germany*.

could well have triggered panics there, like a woman who mentioned twenty-two names of sabbath accomplices.[427] Nevertheless, doubts about the trustworthiness of accusations, risks of harming the innocent, as well as fears of the social havoc and damage that trials might cause, made councilors end such dynamics quickly. The authorities seem to have realized that mass trials were "inimical to one of their main political priorities: the maintenance of social stability and harmony in the city and its hinterland."[428] As mentioned above, the Bavarian government at some point explicitly spoke out against witchcraft skepticism, but even here people at many levels continually obstructed witch trials.[429] The Duke of Bavaria, Maximilian I, was uncertain about the matter, so proponents as well as opponents constantly tried to win him over to their side, with the latter achieving some degree of success.

If authorities did decide to try witchcraft suspects, the further reproduction of trials met new hindrances. One of the most acute threats was decently conducted judicial procedures.[430] Take the illustrious city of Venice. That the Venetian Republic failed to become a hotspot of witch burnings was not due to the absence of legal proceedings there; it was just that judges weighed the evidence carefully, and normally rendered allegations unproven.[431] Another major problem was the financial costs involved.[432] The initial religious fervor and communal solidarity of a hunt could begin to wane as soon as the bills piled up, with nobody being interested in paying them. In many cases there was simply not enough money or prison capacity to warrant continued persecution. In Bamberg, the possessions of executed rich witches provided funding for the new witch prison, but many principalities lacked such resources. In 1626 the German Catholic preacher Johann Wetzel groaned that if people would refrain from buying unnecessary dogs and horses, birds and stoves, palaces and houses, there would be enough money left finally to bring witchcraft to an end.[433] But this was not a price that everyone was willing to pay.

As soon as the killing of alleged witches began, the victims themselves normally also resisted.[434] This does not necessarily imply that these people were opposed to witch trials as such, but obviously they were unlikely to favor their own execution. This resulted in tenacious refusals to confess, the mobilization of allies, escapes from prisons, or appeals to higher courts – the persecutions that were discussed above provide ample examples. Opposition could even extend to the executions themselves. During a burning in German Werdenfels, some women at the stake yelled to the audience: "fellow pious women, flee over the mountains, for whoever falls into the

---

[427] Rowlands, 56–57.
[428] Rowlands, 25.
[429] Behringer, *Hexenverfolgung in Bayern*, 122–331.
[430] Haas, *Hexen und Herrschaftspolitik*, 73–77.
[431] Monter, "Urban Witchcraft on the Margins of the Empire," 215–16; Seitz, *Witchcraft and Inquisition in Early Modern Venice*.
[432] Rummel, *Bauern, Herren und Hexen*, 193–202, 218; Dillinger, *Böse Leute*, 347; Labouvie, *Zauberei und Hexenwerk*, 127; Goodare, *The European Witch-Hunt*, 234; Briggs, "Many Reasons Why," 55–60.
[433] Behringer, *Hexen und Hexenprozesse in Deutschland*, 260.
[434] Behringer, *Hexenverfolgung in Bayern*, 206–9; Briggs, *The Witches of Lorraine*, 162–63; Sharpe, *Witchcraft in Early Modern England*, 45.

hands of the tormentors faces severe torture and must die."[435] In 1609, persecutors in the French Labourd region had great difficulties maintaining public order during a burning.[436] An angry populace threatened the convicted witches on their way to the stake, trying to make them take back the forced accusations that they had levelled against others.

Further reproductive hazards
A hindrance that is so very obvious that it might easily escape our attention took the form of all the other things people could do with their time. Julian Goodare observes that "People in early modern Europe had lives to get on with, and they did not usually regard dealing with the witchcraft threat as the most important thing in their lives."[437] One such alternative activity was other forms of persecution. Witch trials, as was discussed earlier, were a product and a beneficiary of the broader persecutory machinery of Christian Europe. But there are indications that forms of persecution not only enhanced each other, but also competed.[438] Luther focused on what he called the heresy of spiritual sorcery, at the expense of the heresy of witchcraft. Cornelius Loos warned that witch trials were a distraction from the more urgent threat of Protestantism.[439] Some historians argue that the decline of trials against Waldensians in the fifteenth century, or against Anabaptists in the second half of the sixteenth century, created more room for witch-hunting. As a nuance to that, we might note that Robin Briggs cautions us not to think too strongly in such terms, in the sense that societies somehow *need* certain scapegoats to harass.[440] The chronological gaps between various persecutions were often too long and imprecise for such a theory to take hold.

Other distractions also posed a threat to witchcraft. Warfare and popular revolt were much higher on the authorities' list of concerns. Robin Briggs: "The rulers had far stronger motives for responding to these direct challenges than to the obscure personal grievances of peasants against neighbours whom they blamed for what outsiders must have regarded as the trivial misfortunes of village life."[441] Especially during outbreaks of war, civic attention and budgets for witch-hunting were likely to be adjusted to this immediate and more obvious danger.[442] We also need to think of all the other things that people could do with their lives, like working for their daily bread, visiting taverns, regular church attendance, or generally following the news. That Eichstätt did not experience significant witch-hunting in the years prior to Von

---

[435] Behringer, *Hexenverfolgung in Bayern*, 207-8. "Ihr frommen Weiber, fliegt über die Berge; denn wer von euch dem Züchtiger in die Hände fällt und an die strenge marter kommet, der muß sterben!"
[436] Goodare, *The European Witch-Hunt*, 220; Gareis, "Kinder in Hexenverfolgungen des französischen und spanischen Baskenlandes," 103–4.
[437] Goodare, *The European Witch-Hunt*, 259.
[438] Trevor-Roper, *The European Witch-Craze*, 35–37; Waite, *Eradicating the Devil's Minions*, 63–65, 113, 187; Goodare, *The European Witch-Hunt*, 158, 170.
[439] Eerden, "Cornelius Loos und die 'magia falsa,'" 156–60.
[440] Briggs, *Witches & Neighbours*, 404.
[441] Briggs, 405–6.
[442] Briggs, 342.

Westerstetten's appointment, was probably related to his predecessor being more interested in things like gardening and humanism.[443] Typically, in 1589 the Duke of Bavaria learned that the councilors of Ingolstadt simply had "not much appetite" for a persecution.[444] Proponents of witch-hunting often presented themselves as Cassandras to whom only limited numbers of people were listening, and they did have a point there.[445]

Lastly, we must not underestimate the corroding effect of skepticism.[446] People today often find it extraordinary what Europeans at the time believed about witchcraft, but contemporaries could express similar amazement.[447] Especially the extravagant notions about sabbaths, flights and metamorphosis were often considered contrary to nature and ridiculous. In a critique of witch-hunting named *Christliche Erinnerung* (Christian Reminder), the Lutheran theologian Johann Meyfart stated that even a child or a court jester would be ashamed of telling such things. "Where is reason? Where is people's sense?", he wondered.[448] In a critique from 1585, a Calvinist professor from Heidelberg, Hermann Witekind, poked fun at the idea of witches slipping "through openings through which one could not even stick a finger. Anyone who believes that, can also believe that fire is cold or that ice is warm."[449] Advocates of witch-hunting were well aware of such skepticism and anticipated the critiques.[450] The Lutheran preacher David Meder wrote that witchcraft was "terrifying to speak about and to hear of, and that it may appear unbelievable to many."[451] Nicolas Rémy at some point argued that witches retain a certain coldness after their contact with demons, and added that this was not at all a "ridiculous or absurd belief".[452] Still, the defense of witchcraft theory could damage one's reputation. Jean Bodin's intellectual stature was already recognized at the time, but, interestingly, his career never developed beyond a middle-ranking position at a provincial subalternate court. Amongst other factors, it may have been related to misgivings about his uncompromising views on witchcraft.[453] Petrus Caninius was at some point transferred to a post in a Swiss provincial backwater, plausibly because his superiors found him too fanatical.[454]

Now that we have learned about the many hurdles to reproduction that witch beliefs and trials encountered, it is all the more obvious why witch-hunting did not, in Julian Goodare's words,

---

[443] Durrant, *Witchcraft, Gender, and Society in Early Modern Germany*, 10–13.
[444] Behringer, *Hexenverfolgung in Bayern*, 214."nit vil Lust."
[445] Briggs, *Witches & Neighbours*, 400.
[446] Behringer, *Witches and Witch-Hunts*, 165.
[447] Behringer, *Hexenverfolgung in Bayern*, 212–13; Weyer, *Witches, Devils, and Doctors in the Renaissance*; Duni, "Doubting Witchcraft," 224–25; Schmidt, *Glaube und Skepsis*, 308; Henningsen, *The Salazar Documents*, 404; Scot, *The Discoverie of Witchcraft*, 18–19.
[448] Meyfart, *Christliche Erinnerung*, 160-1."wo ist Verstand? Wo ist Vernunft?"
[449] Witekind, *Christlich Bedencken und Erinnerung von Zauberey*, 135."daß sie durch ein löchlin geschlupffet sein, dadurch einer kaum ein finger steche. Wer solches glaubet, der kann auch glauben das feuer kalt sei, und Eys warm."
[450] See, for instance: Mirandola, *La sorcière*, 130–31; Rémy, *Demonolatry*, 74.
[451] Meder, *Acht Hexenpredigten*, 50."Es ist erschrecklich zureden und zuhören, unnd kömpt vielen ungleublich für".
[452] Rémy, *Demonolatry*, 11.
[453] Behringer, *Witches and Witch-Hunts*, 181–82; Krause, Martin, and MacPhail, "Introduction," 14–16, 44.
[454] Behringer, "Canisius, St. Peter (1521-1597)."

"hurtle onwards until it had engulfed everyone in its path."[455] Early modern Europe was a competitive cultural jungle, with reproductive threats and hazards looming all around. But that may leave us in even more awe of how ingeniously the cumulative concept spread. By inflating people's fears, and by efficiently evading its counter forces, witchcraft concepts and trials still succeeded in killing tens of thousands of people. The key argument here is that these ingenious traits did not necessarily result from the shrewdness of the actors involved. Rather, a blind selective process amongst cultural variants regarding witchcraft did much of the heavy lifting. Cultural "mutations" that accidentally enhanced persecutions, gradually accumulated into this well-adapted cultural phenomenon. Moreover, it did not primarily evolve to fulfill people's interests, as witch-hunting was often detrimental to those interests. Mostly, it adapted for the benefit of its *own* "selfish" reproduction.

Or did it? The preceding sections mostly focused on findings that confirm this interpretation, like the unplanned character of many persecutions, as well as their deleterious effects on the societies and people involved. But has the possibility of shrewd human agents operating behind the scenes not been dismissed too quickly? Has the conclusion that societies or actors mostly suffered from trials not been drawn too easily and complacently? Earlier on, it was said that some German historians have not given up on the idea of witch persecutions fulfilling hidden goals or purposes. To them, the conclusions drawn here would surely look short-sighted. Their arguments were not developed in response to this Darwinian model, as the model is new. But as we shall see, their viewpoints are still of direct relevance to it. The interpretations of these historians are more well thought-out than earlier arguments about hidden uses, so we shall also see that they pose a challenge to the model.

---

[455] Goodare, *The European Witch-Hunt*, 317.

Chapter 7: Reflections

7.1 Multifunctional instrumentalization?

In his critique of witch-hunting Cornelius Loos professed that trials had brought about "a new form of alchemy, in which gold and silver are made out of blood."[1] So, an important motivation behind it all was the pursuit of money. Loos was not the only contemporary to express such suspicions. Johann Linden – Trier's city chronicler mentioned earlier – lamented that the Trier persecutions had been supported by "many officials, who hoped to gain money and wealth from the burnings." Aldermen, hangmen, judges, notaries, scribes, and innkeepers had enriched themselves, and the executioner even "rode on a magnificent horse through the streets, dressed in gold and silver like a courtier, while his wife competed with noblewomen in the luxury of her clothing."[2] In his attack on witch-hunting from 1631, Friedrich Spee spoke of an "unholy addiction to money", and recounted how it was "discussed everywhere by many that the quickest and most convenient way of getting rich was through the burning of witches."[3] In 1645, the Count Palatine was confronted with exorbitant bills of witch-hunt committees, and he complained about people who seemed "more concerned with wages and excessive eating and drinking than with the eradication of the hideous vice of witchcraft."[4]

In earlier sections we saw that many historians over the past decades have played down alleged ulterior motives behind witch-hunts. The pursuit of money is amongst the motivations that they dismiss most eagerly, like Julian Goodare, who renders it "probably a modern fantasy." He explains: "The idea of witch-hunting for money is attractive because it attributes to the witch-hunters a motive that is readily understood in the modern world."[5] The line of reasoning has become pervasive: witch-hunting seems so very bizarre to an audience today that we presume that it must have been about something else. So, we impose our own "enlightened" frameworks upon the early modern period. If only we were to take the subjective, meaningful, and magical worldview of the historical actors seriously, we would learn that there is no need to invoke mundane considerations, including financial ones. However, if this is so, what to make of the quotes of Loos, Linden, Spee and the count? Apparently, it made perfect sense within their early modern frameworks to assume that witch-hunts were used for material goals. So why should historians today be disallowed to consider this kind of motive?

---

[1] Quoted in: Eerden, "Cornelius Loos und die 'magia falsa,'" 139."nova alchimia ex humano sanguine aurum et argentum elici"; Voltmer, "Von der besonderen Alchimie, aus Menschenblut Gold zu machen," 130.
[2] Zenz, *Die Taten der Trierer*, VII:13-4."viele Amtspersonen, die sich aus den Verbrennungen dieser Art Gold und Reichtum erhofften", "Der Scharfrichter ritt auf einem edlen Pferd einher wie ein vornehmer Hofmann, in Gold und Silber gekleidet. Sein Weib wetteiferte im Kleiderluxus mit den Adligen".
[3] Spee, *Cautio criminalis oder rechtliches Bedenken wegen der Hexenprozesse*, 296, 257."Die heillose Geldsucht", "allerhandt reden darvon, und dörffen sagen, daß kein besser bequemlichers, und sicheres Mittel seye Reich zu werden, alß vom Brandtgeldt."
[4] Rummel, "Das 'ungestüme Umherlaufen der Untertanen'.," 158."als seye es diesen leuten mehr umb den lohn und übermeßiges essen und trincken alß umb außröttung des abscheuwlichen lasters der hexerey zu thun".
[5] Goodare, *The European Witch-Hunt*, 385.

Such comments on witch persecution made by contemporaries are eagerly brought forward by several German historians who have misgivings about the trope of witch-hunting as an end in itself.[6] In their view, the idea of trials fulfilling hidden functions, or of their being used for hidden purposes, has been dismissed too radically, and they use contemporary comments to support that.[7] Take for instance a merchant from Cologne, Hermann von Weinsberg, who in 1589 expressed misgivings about the existence of witches and the validity of trials: "One could not get rid of old women and despised people more quickly than in this way."[8] In a study on trials in Mecklenburg, Katrin Moeller learned that many charges were dismissed because the accusers were already suspected of hatred, envy and vengefulness.[9] Or take the comment from a cleric in Saarland that seems similar to modern psychology. In a visitation protocol from 1580 he wrote that "whenever these people suffer from a certain shortage, or whatever else repulsive might have happened to them or their children, they will blame it on the witches, which easily puts the heaviest suspicions on people."[10]

The German historians who refer to such observations acknowledge the value of their colleagues' careful interpretation of subjective intentions.[11] By taking people's magical fears and beliefs seriously, we better understand what happened. But it is precisely by interpreting the sources carefully, they argue, that we can learn that not everything at the time was perceived as magical.[12] Early modern people knew that money could buy them things, they too wanted to get rid of enemies, they too were eager to advance socially, and rulers liked power, then as now. One does not need an enlightenment to recognize that. Accordingly, both proponents and opponents of witch-hunting already understood that accusations and trials could be used, and were used, for such ends. Supporters did not profess their ulterior motives in print, because that would have subverted their strategy. But if we look at circumstantial evidence, and the comments of contemporary critics, it becomes apparent that official motivations were not the whole story. Witch-hunting, as Walter Rummel puts it, had an "inherent suitability for the pursuit of personal interests."[13] Rita Voltmer states that it was often less about the honor of God or the protection

---

[6] Rummel, "Das 'ungestüme Umherlaufen der Untertanen'.," 156–58; Rummel, "So mögte auch eine darzu kommen, so mich beläidiget," 214–16; Voltmer, "Von der besonderen Alchimie, aus Menschenblut Gold zu machen"; Voltmer, "Hexenverfolgung und Herrschaftspraxis," 8; Rummel, "So mögte auch eine darzu kommen, so mich beläidiget," 207.
[7] Rummel and Voltmer, *Hexen und Hexenverfolgung*, 99; Voltmer, "Die hexenverfolgungen im Raum Trier," 741–45; Moeller, *Dass Willkür über Recht ginge*, 251–52; Rummel, "Das 'ungestüme Umherlaufen der Untertanen'.," 154, 161.
[8] Rummel, "Das 'ungestüme Umherlaufen der Untertanen'.," 154."Man kann der alter weiber und verhaster leut nit balder quidt werden, dan auf solche weis und maneir."
[9] Moeller, *Dass Willkür über Recht ginge*, 296.
[10] Quoted in: Labouvie, *Zauberei und Hexenwerk*, 205."Ist bei dieser gemeind ein mangel gespürt worden, das sie alles, was inen, iren Kindern und noch widerwergs begegnet, den Zauberern zumeßen, und die personen leichtlich in beschwerlichen Verdacht ziehen".
[11] Groß, *Hexerei in Minden*, 22–23; Schmidt, "Ein Politisches Ausrottungsprogramm?," 147.
[12] Voltmer, "Die politischen Funktionen der frühneuzeitlichen Hexenverfolgungen," 96–98.
[13] Rummel, "Das 'ungestüme Umherlaufen der Untertanen'.," 159."innewohnende Eignung zum Instrument der Verfolgung eigener Interessen."

of the community, than about "power, greed, bribery, envy, and revenge."[14] By attributing such motivations to early modern actors we do not move further away from their framework, but only get closer to it.

This is not to say that these historians return to the kind of grand, sweeping explanations that finally aim to crack the nut. In contrast to authors like Hansen, Harris, or Muchembled, they do not postulate an international campaign with just one or a few underlying goals in mind. "Anyone with a certain understanding of the early modern era sees that such a broad and secret conspiracy behind persecutions would have been impossible to organize and implement at the governmental level", Jürgen Michael Schmidt argues.[15] Neither do these historians presume that witch-hunts were normally conducted in a consciously cynical manner, although such cases can surely be found.[16] What they also admit is that accusations sometimes escalated into panics that became largely dysfunctional for all and everyone.[17] But overall, they see such dysfunctionality as the exception, since belief in witches normally amalgamated with concrete and opportunistic purposes. Pious religiosity and worldly functionality did not exclude each other. Mundane uses can be found at all levels, by all participants, and at all stages of trials. "Allegations of witchcraft, and even more so the resulting persecutions, could be used and instrumentalized, socially as well as politically, for a wide variety of purposes", Rummel and Voltmer contend.[18] So instead of resorting to a monocausal, or monofunctional explanation, these experts see witch-hunting as something thoroughly multifunctional.[19]

Early multifunctionalism
This notion of multifunctional instrumentalization emerged around 1990, and its early versions were close to old-school functionalism. It can be found in studies by Eva Labouvie on Saarland and by Rainer Walz on Lippe.[20] Particularly Walz was well-versed in social theory, and aimed to move away from subjective meaning towards objective function.[21] He used Durkheim as a key source of inspiration, and adopted Merton's notion of "latent functions", presuming that

---

[14] Voltmer, "Von der besonderen Alchimie, aus Menschenblut Gold zu machen," 131."Machtstreben, Habgier, Bestechlichkeit, Neid und Rachsucht."
[15] Schmidt, "Ein Politisches Ausrottungsprogramm?," 147."Wer die frühe Neuzeit nur ein wenig kennt, weiß vielmehr auch, daß solch ein globale und geheime Verschwörung der Verfolger damals organisatorisch schon auf der Herrschaftsebene völlig unmöglich zu realisieren gewesen wäre."
[16] Rummel and Voltmer, *Hexen und Hexenverfolgung*, 98; Voltmer, "Von der besonderen Alchimie, aus Menschenblut Gold zu machen," 131; Voltmer, *Hexen. Wissen was stimmt*, 83–84; Rummel, "Vom Umgang mit Hexen und Hexerei," 100; Schmidt, "Ein Politisches Ausrottungsprogramm?," 148.
[17] Walz, *Hexenglaube und magische Kommunikation im Dorf der frühen Neuzeit*, 52, 64, 515; Voltmer, "Von der besonderen Alchimie, aus Menschenblut Gold zu machen," 132; Voltmer, *Hexen. Wissen was stimmt*, 83–84, 88.
[18] Rummel and Voltmer, *Hexen und Hexenverfolgung*, 96."Hexereivorwürfe und erst recht die resultierenden Prozesse ließen sich daher gesellschaftlich und politisch für die unterschiedlichsten Zwecke nutzen und instrumentalisieren".
[19] Labouvie, *Zauberei und Hexenwerk*, 11; Voltmer, *Hexen. Wissen was stimmt*, 64; Rummel, "Vom Umgang mit Hexen und Hexerei," 95–97.
[20] Labouvie, *Zauberei und Hexenwerk*; Walz, *Hexenglaube und magische Kommunikation im Dorf der frühen Neuzeit*; Walz, "Kinder in Hexenprozessen"; Walz, "Der unreine und der schuldige Sündenbock."
[21] Walz, *Hexenglaube und magische Kommunikation im Dorf der frühen Neuzeit*, 1.

functions are "normally unconscious."[22] Witch-hunting, from this angle, is explained as offering a release from social tensions, the control over deviant groups, and the disciplining of eccentric behavior. It was a "safety valve", or an "important glue", that served to repair holes in the social fabric and to maintain social order.[23] Yet, Walz's and Labouvie's studies also show differences with the Durkheimian model. Walz additionally drew inspiration from an abstract and rather impenetrable postwar German form of functionalism, developed by the sociologist Niklas Luhmann.[24] In a typically functionalist manner, Luhmann stressed that social systems possess traits that cannot be reduced to traits or decisions of individuals.[25] He even ascribed certain abilities of decision-making to systems. Luhmann especially focused on the diversification of social systems, distinguishing various sub-systems like religion, politics, science, and economics. Building on these insights, Walz argued that early modern European society was a highly diversified system. Hence, "if one assumes that potentially every important subsystem could make a contribution to the spread of persecutions, it implies that an approach that is limited to a few causes, or that is even monocausal, becomes problematic."[26]

This observation helped spark Walz's notion of multifunctionalism. He attributed persecutions to a wide range of actors and groups, and the functions that accusations and trials fulfilled are claimed to have been potentially different in each instance. In Walz's, but also in Labouvie's studies, we find an eclectic mix of alleged underlying goals and purposes. Nearly all known answers to the *cui bono* question make their appearance.[27] Apart from Durkheimian functionalism, inspiration is drawn from the rich wells of what I described as the second and third main perspectives in the *cui bono* question, namely power structures and individual needs (see section 2.5). Walz and Labouvie propose that rulers used witch trials to enhance their power and discipline the population, that accusers wanted to get rid of enemies, that persecutory staff increased their incomes, and that at a general psychological level witch beliefs offered an explanation of otherwise contingent events, as well as the opportunity to blame others for mistakes that people had made themselves.

This continuation, or revival, of functionalist thinking in witchcraft scholarship in the 1990s is somewhat surprising, considering functionalism's unfashionable status at the time. For authors like Dillinger and Behringer it was quite easy to dismiss this partly neo-Durkheimian approach. They just needed to refer to the dysfunctional consequences of many trials, as well

---

[22] Walz, 24, 39."im Regelfall unbewußt."
[23] Labouvie, *Zauberei und Hexenwerk*, 208, 217."ein Ventil", "lücken"; Walz, "Der unreine und der schuldige Sündenbock," 199."ein wichtiges Bindemittel."
[24] Walz, *Hexenglaube und magische Kommunikation im Dorf der frühen Neuzeit*, 41–43, 54.
[25] Luhmann, *Die Gesellschaft der Gesellschaft*; Wallace and Wolf, *Contemporary Sociological Theory*, 62.
[26] Walz, *Hexenglaube und magische Kommunikation im Dorf der frühen Neuzeit*, 42."Geht man außerdem davon aus, daß theoretisch jedes wichtige Subsystem Beiträge zur Ausbreitung der Verfolgungen leisten konnte, so wird eine sich auf wenige Ursachen beschränkende oder gar monokausale Betrachtungsweise problematisch".
[27] Walz, *Hexenglaube und magische Kommunikation im Dorf der frühen Neuzeit*; Labouvie, *Zauberei und Hexenwerk*.

to Walz's neglect of subjective meaning and experience.[28] The approaches of Walz and Labouvie do indeed suffer from functionalism's lack of clarity on how subjective meaning and the origin of functions are connected. Labouvie does not address the issue, and while Walz discusses it to some extent, his account remains too unclear to be considered an explanatory model. At some points Walz makes comments that are similar to the proposals made in this dissertation. He describes functions as "the complex result of a social evolution", and refers to the work on cultural evolution by Donald Campbell.[29] In one quote he sounds markedly Darwinian when stating that "the persecutions owe their expansion to contingent initial 'successes', and the easy transferability to different conditions and structures elsewhere in Europe."[30] However, Walz also shows himself to be an old-school static functionalist when disconnecting functions from any account of their historical origin: "The separation of the trials' origins and functions is a precondition for any analysis."[31] Accordingly, Walz provides no concrete and detailed scenario of how the alleged latent functions of trials came about.

Current multifunctionalism

That the notion of "latent functions" is seen as problematic has been noted by more recent supporters of the idea of multifunctional instrumentalization.[32] While acknowledging their debts to Walz, authors like Voltmer, Rummel, and Barbara Groß, place the emphasis on competent actors as the driving force behind beliefs and persecutions. In a theoretically astute study on witchcraft in Minden, Groß is primarily interested in the "social practice" and the "social situations in which contemporary actors resorted to the option of 'witchcraft accusation' or 'witch trial', and the logic of action that they followed."[33] These historians argue that in local circumstances, witch-hunting could be an attractive course of action due to a combination of religious, political, social, and economic factors.[34] Mundane motivations played their part at both conscious and subconscious levels, and Groß links the approach to the sociology of Pierre Bourdieu. Action is "pre-structured by largely unconscious, incorporated perception, thought and action schemes, that serve the actor's orientation within their social world."[35]

---

[28] Behringer, "Hexenprozess Und Modernisierung," 330; Behringer, *Witches and Witch-Hunts*, 25; Dillinger, "Hexenverfolgungen in der Grafschaft Hohenberg," 29; Dillinger, *Böse Leute*, 197.
[29] Walz, "Der unreine und der schuldige Sündenbock," 198."das komplexe Resultat einer sozialen Evolution"; Walz, *Hexenglaube und magische Kommunikation im Dorf der frühen Neuzeit*, 1, 52.
[30] Walz, *Hexenglaube und magische Kommunikation im Dorf der frühen Neuzeit*, 41."so verdanken die Verfolgungen ihre Ausbreitung womöglich eher kontingenten Anfangs-„Erfolgen" und der leichten Übertragbarkeit auf ganz verschiedene Verhältnisse als irgendwelchen in ganz Europa vorhandenen Strukturen".
[31] Walz, 39-40."Die Trennung von Genese und Funktionen der Verfolgungen ist deswegen ein erfordernis jeder Analyse."
[32] Voltmer, "Die politischen Funktionen der frühneuzeitlichen Hexenverfolgungen," 94–96; Groß, *Hexerei in Minden*, 24–34.
[33] Groß, *Hexerei in Minden*, 24, 26."sozialen Praxis", "den sozialen Situationen, denen die zeitgenössischen Akteur auf die Handlungsoption „Hexereiverdächtigung" bzw. „Hexenprozess" zurückgriffen, und der Handlungslogik, der sie dabei folgten".
[34] Rummel and Voltmer, *Hexen und Hexenverfolgung*, 98–99.
[35] Groß, *Hexerei in Minden*, 27-8."Handeln also, das vorstrukturiert ist durch weitgehend unbewusste, inkorporierte Wahrnehmungs- Denk- Handlungsschemata, die den Akteuren zur Orientierung innerhalb ihrer sozialen Welt."

We should interpret this approach not only as a critique of old-school functionalism, but also as one of the "genuine belief historians" and their accounts of "witch panics" that took everyone by surprise. In contrast to the latter, these authors stress that trials were normally created and fostered by individuals who weighed their options, and (sub)consciously knew what they were doing.[36] The Durkheimian focus is largely abandoned, as these historians accept that the social fabric was often damaged.[37] However, the other two angles on the *cui bono* question – power perspectives and individual needs – are developed in all the more detail. There is a focus on "concrete people with concrete goals", who "always tried to take advantage of opportunities to improve their situation."[38] Witchcraft accusations and trials are especially thought to have been used to defame and exterminate opponents, as witch-hunting surpassed all previous methods of resolving long-standing conflicts.[39]

Rummel and Voltmer distinguish three main categories of instrumentalization. The first concerns "social use", in the form of bottom-up activism of the populace.[40] Especially Rummel has examined this dimension in studies on *Hexenausschüsse* in the Trier and Moselle region. He argues that for ordinary people witch-hunting could be an attractive tool to get rid of certain neighbors, or to be used as a weapon against higher classes. For members of *Hexenausschüsse* the persecutions offered a "new means of attack", "a compensation for social inferiority", and "an extraordinary seizure of power beyond their traditional means of influence."[41] Take a witch-hunt in the town of Cochem in the 1590s[42]. Under the disguise of a witch trial Rummel discerns a peasant and artisan revolt against the ruling elite of merchants. A *Hexenausschuss* installed itself in the town hall, and helped create an atmosphere of pogrom-like attacks on women from the establishment. In what was a dramatic loss of their honor, these women were publicly scolded for witchcraft, and had their veils torn from their heads. Later on, witch-hunters entered their houses, and dragged these women by their hair through the streets to the castle, where they were horribly tortured. The openly proclaimed Christian motivations could not conceal that these subjects were socially motivated to overturn traditional relations of power.

---

[36] Rummel and Voltmer, *Hexen und Hexenverfolgung*, 98; Voltmer, *Hexen. Wissen was stimmt*, 85; Voltmer, "Herren und Hexen," 13, 133; Groß, *Hexerei in Minden*; Rummel, "Vom Umgang mit Hexen und Hexerei," 80.
[37] Voltmer, "Von der besonderen Alchimie, aus Menschenblut Gold zu machen," 132–34; Voltmer, "Gott ist tot, und der Teufel jetzt Meister!," 194–96, 223.
[38] Voltmer, *Hexen. Wissen was stimmt*, 85."konkrete Menschen mit konkreten Absichten"; Rummel, "Vom Umgang mit Hexen und Hexerei," 80."immer auch um das Ausnutzen von Gelegenheiten zur Verbesserung ihrer Situation bemüht."
[39] Rummel, "Vom Umgang mit Hexen und Hexerei," 103; Groß, *Hexerei in Minden*, 266–67.
[40] Rummel and Voltmer, *Hexen und Hexenverfolgung*, 99-105."soziale Nutzung"; Rummel, "Das 'ungestüme Umherlaufen der Untertanen'."; Rummel, *Bauern, Herren und Hexen*.
[41] Rummel, "Das 'ungestüme Umherlaufen der Untertanen'.," 154."neue Angriffsmöglichkeiten"; Rummel, "So mögte auch eine darzu kommen, so mich belädiget," 223."Kompensation von sozialer Unterlegenheit"; Rummel and Voltmer, *Hexen und Hexenverfolgung*, 102."außerordentlicher Machtentfaltung jenseits der traditionellen Einflussmöglichkeiten" .
[42] Rummel, "Das 'ungestüme Umherlaufen der Untertanen'.," 152–54; Rummel, "Vom Umgang mit Hexen und Hexerei," 97.

The second category, especially prominent in Rita Voltmer's work, concerns the top-down, "stately-political use" of witch-hunting by rulers.[43] Amongst the alleged underlying purposes of witch-hunting are the disciplining of the population, the destruction of political rivals, and the "demonstration of power" as compensation for internal and external weaknesses.[44] Witch trials in politically turbulent areas were used to strengthen judicial-political claims through the creation of judicial precedents. So, when the populace called for witch-hunting, rulers often calculated whether or not to use this powerful symbolic tool for their own political ends.

A third category that Rummel and Voltmer refer to is what they call "use by specialists".[45] Particularly the late sixteenth- and early-seventeenth-century persecutions offered professional opportunities. For many witch-hunters it was a "career-strategic stroke of luck", that offered new work, new income, extensive dining at other people's costs, and the conviviality of a common mission.[46] This is also why trials increasingly targeted the rich: their money could ensure further income.[47] Moreover, the dynamics of persecution could give these professionals sudden and sensational power. The multifunctional approach pays little attention to the oppression of women as an underlying aim, but Rummel and Voltmer still stress that women could be targeted strategically because of their weaker position in society.[48] For instance, an attack on the wives of rich men could be a means of taking revenge on husbands who were more difficult to touch by law.

The earlier discussions of several German persecutions mostly focused on genuine panic and belief. But their events also offer room for instrumentalist interpretations. Dietrich Flade looks like the preeminent person people might want to get rid of, if only because they owed him debts.[49] The anti-elitist sentiments of the Trier trials remind us of Rummel's "compensation for social inferiority." Voltmer also stresses the role of the Jesuits in Trier, and how they may well have staged and manipulated the boys' confessions to enhance their own role in the fight against heretics. As she acknowledges, this was not a secret master plan in which boys were deliberately used as a fifth column, but she still assumes that some of her colleagues speak too naively of the "voluntary" child confessions.[50] Neither should we think too idealistically about Binsfeld's anti-witchcraft treatise. Like other demonologists, Voltmer thinks that he too chose this trendy topic

---

[43] Rummel and Voltmer, *Hexen und Hexenverfolgung*, 105-10."herrschaftlich-politische Nutzung"; Voltmer, "Hexenverfolgung und Herrschaftspraxis"; Voltmer, "Witchcraft in the City"; Voltmer, "Herren und Hexen"; Groß, *Hexerei in Minden*, 33–34, 336–52.
[44] Voltmer, "Herren und Hexen," 12."Machtdemonstration."
[45] Rummel and Voltmer, *Hexen und Hexenverfolgung*, 110–13"Nutzung von Hexenverfolgungen durch Spezialisten"; Rummel, *Bauern, Herren und Hexen*, 157–92.
[46] Rummel, "So mögte auch eine darzu kommen, so mich belädiget," 218."ein berufsstrategischer Glücksfall."
[47] Rummel, *Bauern, Herren und Hexen*, 315–17.
[48] Rummel and Voltmer, *Hexen und Hexenverfolgung*, 97.
[49] Voltmer, "Zwischen Herrschaftskrise, Wirtschaftsdepression und Jesuitenpropaganda," 86.
[50] Voltmer, "Jesuiten und Kinderhexen," 208, 214–17, 230."freiwilligen"; Voltmer, "Zwischen Herrschaftskrise, Wirtschaftsdepression und Jesuitenpropaganda," 77.

to ensure himself of a broader audience, and to enhance his own intellectual reputation and career.[51]

As a showcase of "stately-political use", Rita Voltmer highlights the hunt of St. Maximin, the imperial abbey close to Trier.[52] Again, Voltmer accepts that all layers of the population could be afraid of witches. Yet, while the abbot was probably also "filled with fear", she thinks that the hunt "was more important for him as a means of securing his rulership."[53] Internally, trials were used to discipline the population – especially defiant tenants and deceitful landlords – as well as to demonstrate "governmental qualities like peace-keeping and protection."[54] Externally, the imperial abbey was entangled in conflicts over judicial and political sovereignty, and witch trials were a means of signifying and solidifying its autonomy. Voltmer argues that it is not by accident that St Maximin's trial records have been preserved carefully, because authorities hoped to use them on later occasions as proof of their rule's legality. She additionally highlights that one of the key persecutors, Claudius Musiel, enlarged his lands at the expense of executed landowners. This reveals "the banality of evil".[55]

Or take the Bamberg hunt. When discussing "use by specialists", Rummel and Voltmer mention Ernst Vasoldt as an obvious example.[56] Voltmer thinks that the huge persecutions of the prince-bishoprics also fulfilled other purposes, like "the disciplining of the villages of their rural hinterlands as well as the urban elite, who showed resistance to the witch-hunting campaign." Overall, these trials could serve "an elite disciplinary program all too effectively."[57] Other authors similarly interpret the attack on Bamberg's urban elite as the elimination of a rival political faction.[58] Chancellor Georg Haan was a particularly attractive target due to envy and resentment regarding his position, the wealth that could be used as income, and of course there was his earlier resistance to persecution. Britta Gehm, who studied the Bamberg hunt in most detail, shows little interest in instrumentalization, but when discussing the trial of Haan she notices that his torture was continued even after he had made confessions that legitimated a death sentence. "One cannot help but get the impression that the investigators and torturers enjoyed seeing this once high-standing and powerful man on the floor", she speculates.[59] The hunt of Ellwangen has not received attention from the instrumentalists, and the two most extensive studies on the topic

---

[51] Voltmer, "Von der besonderen Alchimie, aus Menschenblut Gold zu machen," 132, 138; Voltmer and Weisenstein, *Das Hexenregister des Claudius Musiel*; Voltmer, "Claudius Musiel oder die Karriere eines Hexenrichters"; Voltmer, "Monopole, Ausschüsse, Formalparteien."
[52] Voltmer, "Von der besonderen Alchimie, aus Menschenblut Gold zu machen," 135–37.
[53] Voltmer, 136."von Hexenangst erfüllt", "wichtiger waren sie für ihn wohl als Mittel der Herrschaftssicherung."
[54] Voltmer, "Die politischen Funktionen der frühneuzeitlichen Hexenverfolgungen," 98."obrigkeitliche Qualitäten wie Friedensicherung, Schutz und Schirm."
[55] Voltmer, "Claudius Musiel oder die Karriere eines Hexenrichters," 254."Banalität des Bösen."
[56] Rummel and Voltmer, *Hexen und Hexenverfolgung*, 111.
[57] Voltmer, "Witchcraft in the City," 167.
[58] Flurschütz da Cruz, *Hexenbrenner, Seelenretter*, 49; Knefelkamp, "Von der Ketzerei zur Hexerei," 30–31; Renczes, *Wie löscht man eine Familie aus?*, 3–4, 147.
[59] Gehm, *Die Hexenverfolgung im Hochstift Bamberg*, 136."Man kann sich des Eindrucks nicht erwehren, daß die Kommissare und Folterknechte es genossen, diesen ehemals hochstehenden und mächtigen Mann am Boden zu sehen."

by Erik Midelfort and Wolfgang Mährle instead focus on genuine panic and dysfunctional consequences, while financial motivations are largely dismissed.[60] But in a later publication Mährle seems to have been affected by the instrumentalist school. He says that the momentum of the persecution was "largely based on material interests" and "very quickly became a career instrument for the councilors."[61]

This model of multifunctional use should be taken more seriously than earlier attempts to uncover hidden aims, like the theories of Hansen, Harris, Muchembled, or the feminists. For the idiographic historians who stress genuine belief, it was relatively easy to dismiss those older models. All they needed to do was highlight the diversity and complexity of the phenomena. However, such objections are less effective against the German model of multifunctional instrumentalization. By presuming that accusations and trials fulfilled a different set of purposes in each instance, this model also has an idiographic twist. Moreover, Harris and some feminist authors hardly studied original historical documents, but the instrumentalists are as familiar with archival sources as any historian can hope to be. Notably, the instrumentalists also use some of the rhetorical weapons of the "genuine belief historians" against their trope of witch-hunting as an end in itself. By resorting to a "generalized" and "omnipresent, all-explanatory fear of witches", it is those "genuine belief historians" who are indicted for presenting a one-dimensional explanation.[62] The instrumentalists claim that *their* approach is the richer and more multifaceted one.

The debate with its critics
Not everyone is convinced, though. In what is almost exclusively a debate in German, some "genuine belief historians" have responded.[63] Importantly, nobody has ever argued that accusations and trials were *never* used for hidden goals. Dillinger for instance accepts that Claudius Musiel in St. Maximin gained more land through trials, and Briggs considers the option of people being "sincere, however self-interested." Wolfgang Behringer offers some room for ulterior motives like revenge, political factionalism, money, or common dining.[64] The "genuine belief historians" likewise accept that trials were often connected to other conflicts. Yet, what some of the historians find problematic about the instrumentalist interpretation is that it takes things very far and underestimates the power of belief. While accepting that other interests played a role, Gerd Schwerhoff finds the term "instrumentalization" too much of a modern figure

---

[60] Midelfort, *Witch Hunting in Southwestern Germany*, 98–112; Mährle, "O wehe der armen seelen."
[61] Mährle, "Fürstpropstei Ellwangen," 2004, 382, 384."die maßgeblich in materiellen Interessen begründet lag", "sehr rasch zu einem Karriereinstrument für die deputierten Hofräte."
[62] Moeller, *Dass Willkür über Recht ginge*, 467."pauschale"; Voltmer, "Die politischen Funktionen der frühneuzeitlichen Hexenverfolgungen," 98."omnipresenten, alles erklärenden Hexenfurcht"; Rummel, "Vom Umgang mit Hexen und Hexerei," 224.
[63] Dillinger, *Böse Leute*; Tschaikner, "Nutzung oder Instrumentalisierung?"; Haas, *Hexen und Herrschaftspolitik*; Zeck, *Im Rauch gehn Himmel geschüggt*.
[64] Dillinger, *Böse Leute*, 212, 219, 229–30, 316–17, 444; Briggs, *The Witches of Lorraine*, 374; Behringer, *Hexenverfolgung in Bayern*, 135–36, 304; Behringer, *Witches and Witch-Hunts*, 25, 97, 229–30.

of thought, as it suggests that belief was used as a pretext.[65] The most outspoken critic is Johannes Dillinger, and his key problem is evidence.[66] Because how does one *prove* that witch trials were used for an ulterior purpose? He writes:

> The only unquestionable piece of evidence for the instrumentalization hypothesis would consist of a statement by an accuser showing his true colors. However, this would come down to an open admission of judicial abuse, which would not be in the accuser's interests, and will thus not be found in the sources.[67]

The instrumentalists postulate a hidden agenda, which, by its very nature, cannot be proven in that way precisely because it was hidden. But according to Dillinger this creates a "methodologically inadmissible circular argument."[68] The attribution of hidden motives requires an enormous burden of proof, and Dillinger contends that the instrumentalists fail to deliver – he for instance denies that financial gain was of much importance in Trier.[69] True, critics of trials sometimes explicitly suspected accusers and persecutors of mundane purposes, but Dillinger interprets that as a means of defense and polemics, and not as a key to better understanding the phenomenon.[70]

In addition, he argues that the instrumentalist model appears superfluous.[71] In his own "evil people paradigm" (see 5.4) the connection of witchcraft accusations to other conflicts is understood as an expression of genuine belief: witches were a part of people's perceived reality, and also of a social reality in which discernibly evil individuals seemed likely suspects. Dillinger further keeps stressing the supremacy of belief by highlighting how actions at all stages of witch trials, from shaving suspects and changing their clothing, to their torture and burning, stood in a magical light.[72] Or think of the population of Elz, which in 1589 threatened to their ruler to leave the town themselves if he would not persecute witches. "That people even considered such a step shows that they felt existentially threatened", he notes, illustrating how belief could override people's normal calculations.[73] So, with Ockham's razor, Dillinger thinks we can remove instrumentalism from our explanatory accounts. Several other German historians make similar

---

[65] Schwerhoff, "Hexerei, Geslecht und Regionalgeschichte."
[66] Dillinger, *Böse Leute*, 38, 229–33, 444; Dillinger, "Richter als Angeklagte," 167–69.
[67] Dillinger, *Hexen und Magie*, 2018, 127."Zweifelsfrei beweisen ließe sich eine Instrumentalisierung nur durch eine Selbstaussage des Klägers. Sich zu einem Justizmissbrauch zu bekennen, lag natürlich nicht im Interesse des Anklägers, so dass solche Selbstaussagen in den Quellen nicht vorliegen können" .
[68] Dillinger, *Böse Leute*, 230."Ein methodisch unzulässiger Zirkelschluß."
[69] Dillinger, 341.
[70] Dillinger, 230.
[71] Dillinger, *Hexen und Magie*, 2018, 127; Dillinger, *Böse Leute*, 355, 444.
[72] Dillinger, "Das magische Gericht"; Dillinger, "The Political Aspects of the German Witch Hunts," 67.
[73] Dillinger, *Böse Leute*, 241."Daß man an einen solchen Schritt überhaupt dachte, zeugt davon, das viele sich existentiell bedroht glaubten".

arguments, like Norbert Jung, who believes that Friedrich Förner would have "given his last shirt" for his witchcraft convictions.[74]

In turn, the instrumentalists regard such interpretations as expressions of gullibility. Historians today should question the rhetoric and self-legitimizations of witch-hunt proponents, not take them at face value. If Dillinger dismisses contemporary suspicions about instrumentalization as mere defense and polemics, then why are we not allowed to treat the legitimizations of trials as mere defense and polemics?[75] In Jürgen Michael Schmidt's view, there is more of a level playing field:

> In almost all cases there is a lack of irrefutable evidence for a genuine belief in witchcraft on account of persecutors, the witnesses or judges. Their statements might also be strategic. If we are unable to retrieve the truth, this applies to both sides: the statements of the victims and their defenders should be weighed equally to those of the persecutors.[76]

These differences of opinion are not always as significant as they may first appear. Both sides accept that there was genuine belief, that instrumentalization was possible, and that witchcraft accusations and other conflicts were interrelated. Eventually, it is a question about where to put the emphasis. The lack of self-reflexive comments and autobiographical records of witch-hunters also makes historical analysis difficult.[77] "Whole conferences have become ensnarled in this complex question of individual motive (conscious? unconscious?) and social or political function", Erik Midelfort comments.[78] It has brought the debate to somewhat of a stalemate, and some historians move towards an agnostic position.[79] Writing about the arrest of the Haan family in Bamberg, Günther Dippold comments that:

> In this example we may recognize the limits of our understanding. Was the fate of Haan and his family a coldly calculated judicial murder, or was it sincerely believed that a person who that stridently opposed witch-hunting had to be in league with the devil? In any case,

---

[74] Jung, "Die Bamberger Hexenverfolgungen," 84."wohl sein letztes Hemd gegeben."
[75] Rowlands and Voltmer, "The Persecution of Witches and the Practice of Lordship," 22; Rummel and Voltmer, *Hexen und Hexenverfolgung*, 99; Voltmer, "Hexenverfolgung und Herrschaftspraxis," 9; Schmidt, "Ein Politisches Ausrottungsprogramm?," 149.
[76] Schmidt, "Ein Politisches Ausrottungsprogramm?," 149."Schließlich fehlen fast immer auch die unumstößlichen Beweise für den festen Hexenglauben der Ankläger, der Zeugen und Richter. Auch deren Glaubenspostulate könnten nur Strategien sein. Wenn man die Wahrheit nicht zu ergründen vermag, gilt das für beide Seiten: Die Aussagen der Opfer und ihrer Verteidiger müssen dann mit denen der Verfolger gleich gewichtet werden."
[77] Briggs, *Witches & Neighbours*, 196; Voltmer, "Hexenbrenner Und Hexenbischöfe," 240; Moeller, *Dass Willkür über Recht ginge*, 479; Lehmann and Ulbricht, "Motive und Argumente von Gegnern der Hexenverfolgung von Weyer bis Spee," 10.
[78] Midelfort, "Witch Craze?," 19.
[79] Walinski-Kiehl, "Witch-Hunting and State Building," 256; Dippold, "Die 'Hexenpolitik' Der Bamberg Fürstbischöfe," 57.

it is not even said that the individuals who aimed to destroy the Haan family all thought the same.[80]

This debate over an alleged instrumentalization is mostly a debate amongst historians, but obviously it has broader interdisciplinary ramifications. The instrumentalist's claims about human behavior and culture do not look far-fetched from an interdisciplinary point of view. Barbara Groß has justifiably linked the approach to Pierre Bourdieu, who also argued that people continually defend their hierarchical position, or try to improve it, with symbolic culture being a key weapon on the battlefield. Much of it also happens at tacit or subconscious levels. But there are more approaches that resemble the instrumentalist account. Psychologists and cognitive scientists make use of the concept of "motivated reasoning".[81] It assumes that behavior can be driven by genuine intentions at a conscious level, but that such intentions are crucially influenced by hidden emotions and desires that make us believe what we *want* to believe. So, witch-hunt proponents may well have meant what they said, but they meant it precisely *because* it served their interests.

Recently, the French cognitive scientist Hugo Mercier used evolutionary psychology to draw similar conclusions.[82] Mercier maintains that evolution has designed our brains to be naturally vigilant, protecting us against ideas that would harm our own interests. Many seemingly senseless acts – apparently motivated by supernatural belief systems – in Mercier's view result from more convenient "down-to-earth considerations."[83] Amongst his examples is witch-hunting, and he argues that behind the disguise of witchcraft beliefs "the usual self-interested motives rear their ugly heads."[84] Mercier mostly focuses on witch persecution as a means to get rid of undesired individuals, and he renders the content of beliefs as of only marginal importance. "Those who can make you believe absurdities can make you commit atrocities", Voltaire once proclaimed. Mercier turns this on its head: "it is wanting to commit atrocities that makes you believe absurdities."[85] Mercier's account of witchcraft is superficial, but he would probably consider as confirmation the detailed studies of the German instrumentalists.

Implications for the Darwinian model
What bearing does the model of multifunctional instrumentalization have on the Darwinian scenario presented in this dissertation? Not everything that these historians bring forward

---

[80] Dippold, "Die 'Hexenpolitik' Der Bamberg Fürstbischöfe," 57."An diesem Beispiel erkennen wir die Grenzen unserer Erkenntnismöglichkeit. War, was mit Haan und seiner Familie geschah, ein kühl kalkulierter Justizmord oder herrschte die Überlegung vor, dass jemand, der so vehement gegen Hexenprozesse kämpfe, doch selbst mit dem Satan im Bunde stehen müsste? Dabei ist ohnehin nicht gesagt, dass alle, die sich um die Vernichtung Haans bemühten, das Gleiche dachten".
[81] Kunda, "The Case for Motivated Reasoning."; Lodge and Taber, "Three Steps towards a Theory of Motivated Political Reasoning"; Norman, *Mental Immunity*, 219.
[82] Mercier, *Not Born Yesterday*.
[83] Mercier, 120.
[84] Mercier, 189.
[85] Mercier, 202.

necessarily conflicts with it. Rainer Walz's claims about evolutionary processes and latent functions, as we saw, are vaguely similar to the idea of a Darwinian socio-cultural "design without designer". The idea of multifunctionalism also dovetails with a previous argument about Darwinian cultural evolution being a process in which cultural variants may survive due to a different set of selection pressures in each instance. Both approaches thus integrate the advantages of eclecticism. Neither has it been said that blind evolution and (sub)conscious human design exclude each other as explanatory models of how cultural adaptations arise. Still, if all the claims of the instrumentalists are warranted, the proposals made here would lose much of their potential.

The more explanatory room there is for competent agents who (sub)consciously knew what they were doing, the less room is left for blind evolution as a force of socio-cultural design. But especially in regard to the *cui bono* question the instrumentalists have reached quite different conclusions. Markedly, Rainer Walz again occasionally said things that come close to the proposals made here. For instance when he analyzes witchcraft accusations as being "autocatalytic", with rumors triggering ever more rumors, or when he says that trials of child witches "show that witch-hunts were to a large extent subject to a semantic self-enforcing mechanism, which almost seems to have imposed itself on those involved, entangling them ever more deeply into the system of belief."[86] But overall, the multifunctional instrumentalists assume that at nearly all stages of trials beneficiaries were involved, in the form of social systems or of human actors. So, while none of the proposed hidden functions or aims can explain witch-hunting on its own, it is argued that we get much closer to a sufficient explanation when we throw them all together. This interpretation conflicts with the idea of witch beliefs and trials spreading at the expense of their human hosts, as well as of their societies. It would make any "selfish meme" explanation largely redundant.

However, the instrumentalist approach is not without problems. These historians do not respond convincingly to all arguments of the "genuine belief historians". If the people accountable for witch-hunts in most cases (sub)consciously knew what they were doing, how to explain the haphazard and unpredictable course of so many trials? Why were initiators of persecution so often harmed themselves? This still suggests genuine and escalating panics, without anyone being in control, rather than people shrewdly pursuing their hidden goals. The idea of multifunctional instrumentalization also raises the question of why hunts were not even *more* common. For Rita Voltmer, the absence of trials is also instrumentalization, because people weighed their chances and concluded that it would best suit their interests *not* to persecute.[87] But if accusations and persecutions were indeed a wonderfully effective means of achieving

---

[86] Walz, "Der unreine und der schuldige Sündenbock," 197."autokatalytischen"; Walz, *Hexenglaube und magische Kommunikation im Dorf der frühen Neuzeit*, 47; Walz, "Kinder in Hexenprozessen," 231."Sie zeigen vielmehr, daß es sich bei den Hexenverfolgungen in hohen Maße um einen in sich selbst zurücklaufenden semantischen Mechanismus handelte, der den beteiligten ein Verhalten fast aufzwang, das sie tiefer in dieses Glaubenssystem verstrickte".
[87] Voltmer, "Hexenverfolgung und Herrschaftspraxis," 17; Voltmer, "Herren und Hexen," 40.

hidden ends, we might expect them to have been more frequent. What also strengthens the case of genuine belief is the correlation (see chapter 6) between the precise content of beliefs, and the way trials unfolded. Convictions about sabbaths, child witches, or rich witches were not only relevant at the margins, but absolutely essential. The specificity of witch beliefs still offers the most plausible explanation for the specificity of trials, while factors like greed, envy, or power play still appear somewhat too general and universal.

A closer look at the case studies reveals further problems, as some examples from Voltmer's work may illustrate. How strong is her evidence that persecutors in St. Maximin used trials for hidden purposes? In one publication she says that trial records "prove" that the disciplining of defiant subjects was an underlying aim. But this statement contains no reference, and in none of Voltmer's publications have I encountered the exact quotes that warrant such a strong conclusion.[88] Her claim that persecutors cared about safeguarding the principality's judicial rights looks plausible, but does that also prove that this was a hidden aim? The causal connection might have been different: persecutors cared deeply about eradicating witchcraft, and were thus extra determined to solidify the legal powers that made it possible. Overall, killing four to five hundred people – one-fifth of the abbey's own population – looks like a bizarrely lopsided way of safeguarding judicial rights. Even if we add things like the legitimization of power, or the use by specialists, it all still looks strangely out of proportion. However, if we assume that both the people and the authorities genuinely believed themselves to be involved in an apocalyptic life-or-death struggle with a sect of Satan-worshipping witches living in their midst, the scale of the persecution finally looks more plausible.

Bamberg offers another example. Voltmer's claim that hunts in the prince-bishoprics could serve "an elite disciplinary program all too effectively" appears strange, considering all the damage trials caused there.[89] We saw that the prince-bishop and his clique even had to flee Bamberg because there was no money left for defense against an approaching army. Elsewhere, Voltmer refers to Reutlingen as an instrumentalist case in point. This southern German town experienced long trial-free periods, punctuated by a few middle-sized persecutions. According to Voltmer, "recent research has found a ready explanation": generations of rulers used the trials to establish their power, and persecution was thus "characterized by the influence of personal interests to gain a successful political career."[90] Voltmer's reference is a study by Thomas Fritz, but in fact, Fritz offers a largely different account.[91] He assumes "a tremendous impact of witch belief" and a populace that recurrently demanded persecution.[92] When new and inexperienced authorities took their position, they condoned trials in a state of self-doubt and undecidedness. When the establishment then found out what incredible damage it all caused, they stopped

---

[88] Voltmer, "Von der besonderen Alchimie, aus Menschenblut Gold zu machen," 136."beweisen."
[89] Voltmer, "Witchcraft in the City," 167–68.
[90] Voltmer, 162.
[91] Fritz, "Hexenverfolgungen in der Reichsstadt Reutlingen."
[92] Fritz, 206."ungeheure Durchschlagkraft der Hexenglaube."

persecution. So, it was "through the experience and all the harm that they became smarter, never to allow trials again."[93] Only a few decades later, when this experience was forgotten, the mechanism started all over again.

Another case is Rottweil, where trials especially targeted the poor, like vagrants and beggars. Rita Voltmer: "Obviously, this policy followed the general aims of early modern city government: to purify the city from vagrants, to discipline the poor, to demonstrate power both in the territory and in the inner city and thus, to create an omnipresent authoritative urban regime."[94] Her reference is a study by Mario Zeck, but again her source says something else. Zeck explicitly dismisses an instrumentalist interpretation, as he thinks that it "completely underestimates" the power of belief.[95] Instead, his argument is fully in line with Dillinger's "evil people-paradigm". On another occasion Voltmer mentions Oettingen as a case of stately-political use, and here Alexandra Haas is the source.[96] But like Zeck, Haas rejects instrumentalism, as she finds ideological and moral motivations more plausible. Haas acknowledges that rulers sometimes gained money or territory after a trial, but sees this as a consequence rather than a cause; rulers wanted compensation for their expenses.[97] Another of Voltmer's references – Günther Jerouschek's study on Esslingen – also has its limitations. Some of his passages run parallel to Voltmer's ideas about "political trials", but Jerouschek concludes that we should take the persecutor's word for it, and he is explicitly skeptical about instrumentalization.[98]

So, overall, while much of what the instrumentalists bring forward does not sound implausible, Dillinger is right to address problems regarding evidence. The response about the level playing field is not wholly convincing either. Witch-hunt proponents consistently said that they acted in order to eradicate witchcraft. Hence, when historians postulate this motivation they can be confident that they are not making it up. But regarding the alleged instrumentalist motivations one cannot be so sure of that. When the poor were targeted, one might presume that people wanted to get rid of the poor. When the rich were targeted one might presume that people wanted to get rid of the rich. When the middle classes were targeted one might presume that rulers wanted to discipline the population and show them their power. One can always think of some instrumentalist goal, no matter what a persecution looked like. But when explanations are that flexible, and not necessarily substantiated by quotes from the sources, it becomes easy to make mistakes. It also gives the idea of multifunctional instrumentalization a ring of unfalsifiability. What findings would *disconfirm* their model?

Then there is the problem of the "design" to the cumulative concept of witchcraft. The instrumentalists also express some degree of admiration for how ingeniously the concept was

---

[93] Fritz, 302."durch die Erfahrung und den Schaden klüger geworden, nie wieder Prozesse zulassen."
[94] Voltmer, "Witchcraft in the City," 163–64.
[95] Zeck, *Im Rauch gehn Himmel geschüggt*, 70-3."völlig unterschätzt."
[96] Voltmer, "Herren und Hexen," 38–39.
[97] Haas, *Hexen und Herrschaftspolitik*, 98–99, 111, 218.
[98] Voltmer, "Witchcraft in the City," 162–63; Jerousscheck, *Die Hexen und ihr Prozess*.

adapted to serve its alleged many purposes.[99] "Since witchcraft accusations could be expanded flexibly to all sorts of new situations, they were an attractive tool for resolving a wide range of interpersonal conflicts", Katrin Moeller argues.[100] Walz notes how it helped "designating private enemies as public enemies", and Rummel emphasizes the beliefs' elasticity, which created an "almost inexhaustible potential for applying it to practically every person, every behavior and every problem."[101] The notion of a "crimen obscurum" further evaded the need for controllable proof. But the question staring us in the face again is: how did the concept develop these capacities? Most instrumentalists highlight competent actors who knew what they were doing, but were these actors also competent enough to design the concept that cleverly? At some point Voltmer states that persecutors deliberately kept definitions of heresy vague, so that they could instrumentalize it open-endedly.[102] But for the rest, the instrumentalists, except Walz on some occasions, leave the issue unaddressed.

This makes the problem we posed earlier even more urgent. Did actors understand what historians understand today, namely how beliefs about witchcraft reputations, sabbaths, flights, torture, rich witches, and child witches enhanced the reproduction of trials? From the perspective of the instrumentalists, we might expect witch-hunt proponents to have understood this, and to have elaborated upon such notions for that reason. Also, we might assume that they (sub)consciously grasped how these beliefs served their hidden interests. From the perspective of blind evolution, on the other hand, we might expect that the actors were not necessarily cognizant of the beliefs' enhancing effects on trials. But as the instrumentalists rightly point out, we should not only look at the narratives of proponents, as they may have misled their audiences about their true aims. We also need to look at contemporary critics. Did they understand how cumulative notions enhanced the spread of persecutions? And do their comments indicate, as the instrumentalists argue, that witch-hunts were substantially used for ulterior motives? We shall now delve more deeply into what primary sources may reveal on such matters.

7.2 What proponents said

If anyone fits Rummel's and Voltmer's category of a witch-hunt specialist who deliberately enhanced persecution it was Heinrich Kramer, key author of the *Malleus Maleficarum*. This Dominican cleric had already made a career in inquisition, and his personality matched his profession – Kramer was hard-working, belligerent, self-righteous, and not afraid of making

---

[99] Groß, *Hexerei in Minden*, 330; Rummel, "Das 'ungestüme Umherlaufen der Untertanen'.," 152; Rummel, "Vom Umgang mit Hexen und Hexerei," 208.
[100] Moeller, "Es ist überaus gerechtes Gesetz, dass die Zauberinnen getötet werden," 102."Weil die Hexenbeschuldigungen so flexibel au immer neue Situationen ausgeweitet werden konnten, wurden sie attraktive für die Lösung verschiedenster zwischenmenschlicher Konfliktlagen".
[101] Walz, "Der unreine und der schuldige Sündenbock," 195."den zunächst privaten Feind leicht zum öffentlichen Feind stempeln zu können"; Rummel, "So mögte auch eine darzu kommen, so mich belädiget," 225."Gerade weil dem Hexenglauben ein fast unerschöpfliches Potential zur Anwendung auf Praktisch jede Person, jedes Verhalten und jedes Problem".
[102] Rummel and Voltmer, *Hexen und Hexenverfolgung*, 14.

enemies.[103] So, it was hardly surprising that the topic of diabolical witchcraft attracted his attention when trials resurged in the 1480s. Kramer began preaching against witches in Ravensburg, which helped initiate a persecution there that killed eight women. Later on, he repeated his efforts in Innsbruck, again stimulating a climate of accusations against several women, and he also made preparations for new persecutions. However, this time authorities thwarted his attempts: Kramer was ordered to leave the city, and the bishop of Innsbruck wrote to a friend that the inquisitor had "clearly demonstrated his foolishness" by presuming "much that had not been proved."[104] This failure only made Kramer more determined, and retreating to Cologne he vindictively wrote his *Malleus maleficarum*. With the academic and inquisitor Jacob Sprenger as co-author he urged the world to eradicate diabolical witches, whose numbers were alleged to have grown enormously.

The authors assumed that the apocalypse was imminent, so the work was written in haste.[105] It is presumably one of the reasons why the book is neither very well-structured nor well written. Still, it became quite a bestseller by the standards of the time, and did have some of the desired effects of putting witchcraft on the agenda as a central issue in the struggle between Satan and humankind.[106] Historical scholars today also note that the book combined some ideas about witchcraft in a way that made the concept more inflammatory.[107] Previously, the diabolical witches' identity had remained quite abstract, but the *Malleus* linked it more effectively to people who were well-known at a popular level: village witches. It was probably Kramer's own persecutory experience that made him focus on women who were locally known for witchcraft, and since such women could readily be found throughout Europe it created much potential for further trials. The book also tapped more thoroughly into misogynous stereotypes, and offered helpful guidance on how to persecute: Kramer and Sprenger recognized the importance of torture to extract confessions, and, knowing how unpopular clerical inquisitors could be, they advocated persecution by secular authorities.[108] From our theoretical perspective, this does not look much like a blind evolutionary process silently doing its adaptive work. In Kramer we find a flesh and blood human actor, with particular aims and interests, who deliberately broadcasted witchcraft notions to encourage others to follow his persecutory enterprise.

But was the book really that shrewdly designed? Until 1560 witch-hunting did not grow much, and a closer look at the *Malleus'* content suggests that this content was a part of the problem. One of the notions most conducive to witch-hunting's spread, as we saw, was the

---

[103] Institoris, *The Hammer of Witches*; Herzig, "The Bestselling Demonologist"; Broedel, *The "Malleus Maleficarum" and the Construction of Witchcraft*, 12–17; Behringer and Jerouscheck, "'Das unheilvollste Buch der Weltliteratur'?"
[104] Broedel, *The "Malleus Maleficarum" and the Construction of Witchcraft*, 17.
[105] Behringer and Jerouscheck, "'Das unheilvollste Buch der Weltliteratur'?," 68.
[106] Broedel, *The "Malleus Maleficarum" and the Construction of Witchcraft*, 19.
[107] Goodare, *The European Witch-Hunt*, 49–52; Herzig, "Flies, Heretics, and the Gendering of Witchcraft"; Herzig, "The Bestselling Demonologist"; Broedel, *The "Malleus Maleficarum" and the Construction of Witchcraft*, 59–60, 100–101.
[108] Behringer, *Witches and Witch-Hunts*, 73–74.

witches' sabbath. The idea was already circulating at the time, and one of the *Malleus'* sources was Nider's *Formicarius*, which devoted quite some attention to the sabbath.[109] It plausibly would have helped Kramer's and Sprenger's efforts to discuss this incendiary notion in detail. But strikingly the *Malleus* hardly mentioned the notion. This omission has attracted the attention of historians. "It is interesting to note that, in spite of its enduring authority (…) the *Malleus* did not mention one of the very important and most lethal aspects of the witch image, namely her propensity to fly to and celebrate orgies at the witches' sabbath", Gerhild Williams remarks.[110] This is putting it too strongly, as the book does mention flight on several occasions, and passingly refers to witches' meetings a few times.[111] Nevertheless, in comparison with many previous and successive works, the sabbath received remarkably little attention. So why this relative absence of a notion that would have served the authors' hunt-enhancing purposes so effectively?

Explanations for the omission have been sought in several directions. The American historian Hans Peter Broedel argues that "calculated reservations" were in play.[112] Western Alpine ideas about witches' gatherings included both men and women with divergent social profiles, while Kramer and Sprenger wanted to focus almost exclusively on poor women. Allegedly, this made the sabbath unhelpful for their argument. Robin Briggs thinks that "the rigid scholastic format of the work somehow prevents them putting any emphasis on this", while Julian Goodare maintains that the omission was in fact not "a weakness in the argument, but (…) arguably a strength" as it cleared the ground for a more thorough focus on village witchcraft.[113] Christopher Mackay argues that the sabbath was "simply not relevant to the purpose of the Malleus", which was to provide a general handbook on the reality of witchcraft and how to eradicate it.[114] So, according to some of these views we might reconsider the relative omission as an intentional, or a functional trait of the work.

Such interpretations can be questioned, though. The book was lengthy, containing hundreds of pages, so why did that not leave some room for discussing the sabbath next to other topics? It is also unclear why ideas about sabbaths and female village witches should be mutually exclusive. Kramer and Sprenger could also have chosen to discuss nightly gatherings full of village witches. Moreover, if the authors had calculated reasons for not making the sabbath a part of their witch image, why did they still casually refer to it on some occasions? Closer analysis shows that they mentioned witches' meetings when they were actually making a point about something else.[115] In a discussion on witches' cannibalism of babies, for instance, they recount a case in Italian Como where a certain man had lost a child from its crib, and "went in search of it, and when he saw a gathering of women at night time, he observed that the baby was being killed and

---

[109] Institoris, *The Hammer of Witches*, 16.
[110] Williams, "Demonologies," 74.
[111] See, for instance: Institoris, *The Hammer of Witches*, 282–84, 298–99, 283–84, 294.
[112] Broedel, *The "Malleus Maleficarum" and the Construction of Witchcraft*, 130; Broedel, "Fifteenth-Century Witch Beliefs," 46.
[113] Briggs, *Witches & Neighbours*, 34; Goodare, *The European Witch-Hunt*, 50.
[114] Institoris, *The Hammer of Witches*, 283.
[115] Institoris, 283–84.

eaten while liquor was being consumed."[116] Another passage discusses how witches learn their sorcery, adding that:

> The method of learning this art was (...) that the sorcerers came to a certain gathering and by their work they saw the demon as if real in the assumed image of a human, and to him the disciple was obliged to give his word about renouncing Christianity, never worshipping the Eucharist and treading on the Cross when he could do so secretly.[117]

Elsewhere they mention how witches "inflicted epilepsy (the falling disease) on certain people with eggs that had been buried with corpses, [who were] especially interred members of their sect."[118] The fact that the *Malleus* still contains such casual references to witches meeting each other collectively, suggests that they had no deliberate reasons for playing this notion down. So, the question still stands: why did the *Malleus* not discuss witches' assemblies as a prominent topic in its own right?

Perhaps we should consider a more parsimonious and straightforward explanation here: the sabbath was not neglected for deliberate reasons, but just because the authors did not recognize its potential for boosting witch trials. Considering the late medieval German context, this is not implausible. We have already learned that the sabbath notion did not connect well with indigenous ideas about witchcraft, so it was quite obvious for Kramer and Sprenger to think of witches as acting alone or in small numbers. Other clues from the book further indicate that they did not see the potential of chains of accusations. In addition to the sparse references to meetings, the book occasionally argues that witches lure other women into witchcraft, which further shows that Kramer and Sprenger did not reject the idea of witches knowing each other.[119] However, the authors hardly capitalized on this notion for persecutory purposes. Only a few sentences passingly note that witches can denounce other witches.[120] While a long section on torture demonstrates recognition of its potential for extracting confessions, the section fails to connect torture to making suspects name accomplices.[121] One passage in this section that *does* discuss how witches knowing each other might aid persecution only offers the less auspicious advice of putting accomplices in the same cell, so that spies standing outside those cells can overhear them to learn what crimes they committed.[122] So, the authors of the *Malleus* plausibly neglected some of the best recipes for making witch-hunting prosper, simply because they did not understand those recipes.

---

[116] Institoris, 212.
[117] Institoris, 283.
[118] Institoris, 360.
[119] Broedel, The "Malleus Maleficarum" and the Construction of Witchcraft, 30; See, for instance: Institoris, The Hammer of Witches, 275, 278–81, 312.
[120] Institoris, The Hammer of Witches, 511, 577.
[121] Institoris, 541–58.
[122] Institoris, 558.

This apparent lack of comprehension of how essential cumulative notions could operate in combination does not seem to have been exceptional. Section 6.1 discussed how early ideas about witchcraft often remained patchy in comparison with the period after 1560. Like many others, Nider failed to connect sabbaths to flights, and the Strasbourg preacher Geiler von Kaysersberg was ambiguous about flights and sabbaths, and did not think of witchcraft in terms of a collective super crime. The mere fact that it took so long to combine various notions of witchcraft into the more robust and "virulent" concepts of the late sixteenth century, indicates that early proponents did not recognize how to arrange things more effectively. Someone who did combine some of the more inflammatory elements was the Italian count Gianfrancesco Pico della Mirandola.[123] After being involved in a persecution in his own principality, in 1523 he published a dialogue on witchcraft which mentioned both harmful magic, flights, torture, and even referred to a sabbath as "a very big multitude".[124] Yet, whether this also implies much understanding of how those insights could trigger a big hunt is questionable. The dialogue was called *Strix, sive de lucificatione daemonum* (The Witch, or on the Deceptions of Demons), and its structure and content suggest that the main purpose was to show that evil demons had been deceiving and tricking people since the beginning of antiquity, through oracles, images and calumnies.[125] Enhancing witch-hunting does not seem to have been the book's essential aim, since it did not provide much guidance on how to persecute, unlike the *Malleus*.[126]

From 1560 to the Trier trials

What about the period from 1560 onwards? Notions about sabbaths, flights, rich witches, or child witches began more effectively to stimulate trials, so we might expect more explicit wisdom on how to get trials going. But did proponents in this period indeed offer such insight? An influential text in the revival of witchcraft literature was Lambert Daneau's *Les sorciers* from 1574.[127] His dialogue was written in plain and accessible language, and discusses notions that influenced the rise of witch-hunting. Daneau repeatedly stressed that flights and sabbaths were real events, noting that witches could also be found equally amongst scholars, people of high standing, and the young.[128] He further warns about harmful magic, and a remark about a hunt in Savoy that killed eighty people in a single village shows his interest in large persecutions.[129] Yet again, we should not automatically interpret this as proof for an understanding of how such notions could be put to use to advance witch trials. The tract offered little practical instruction, and still failed to capitalize on essential incendiary elements. Daneau said nothing about using torture to extract names of accomplices, and neither did he discuss the potential of young witnesses. Moreover, in

---

[123] Mirandola, *La sorcière*; Stephens, "The Skeptical Tradition," 114–16; Behringer, "Walter Stephens. Demon Lovers," 89–94.
[124] Mirandola, *La sorcière*, 200. "Une trés grande multitude."
[125] Mirandola, 217–18.
[126] Stephens, *Demon Lovers*, 94.
[127] Daneau, *Les Sorciers*.
[128] Daneau, 5, 48–49, 51–52, 74, 78–79, 85–90.
[129] Daneau, 7.

so far as he offered concrete advice it was not always practical. For instance, he recommended giving suspects some freedom, so that judges could regularly check on them by surprise, so as to catch them in the act of talking to demons.[130]

The lack of proof for such understanding is not the same as proving that understanding was absent. Perhaps Daneau did comprehend how the sabbath notion generated chains of accusations, but he just did not mention it. However, that a mere discussion of witches' meetings does not imply such comprehension can be illustrated through the trial records from Rostock in 1584.[131] The documents of this German city routinely referred to sabbaths on the Blocksberg that were attended by three hundred witches, who feasted, dined, danced, and interacted with demons. At first sight this might suggest that persecutors cunningly knew how to instrumentalize the sabbath notion for furthering trials – they possibly focused on this notion in order to enhance persecution. But closer scrutiny, as performed by Andreas Müller, suggests otherwise. Müller observed that sabbath notions played no further role in the interrogations whatsoever. Investigators thought of harmful magic as being inflicted by solitary witches, and in some cases by small collectives. Müller's interpretation:

> This conflicting result shows that the witches' Sabbat is an artificial and isolated element within the documents. Here it seems highly plausible that a person with demonological knowledge or ideas must have influenced the trial and must have contributed this elaborated element of learned witchcraft belief in the otherwise individual and non-collective witchcraft imagination of Rostock.[132]

That early modern sources do not necessarily provide clues for a lack of understanding is shown by the most important witchcraft treatise from this period, Jean Bodin's *De la démonomanie des sorciers* from 1580.[133] People like Kramer, Pico, or Daneau failed to connect certain dots regarding how ideas about witchcraft could be put into action, but Bodin's book articulates that remarkably well. The French thinker repeatedly stressed the reality of sabbaths, as well as of flights over long distances to get there. He also went into quite some detail about what happened at assemblies, and emphasized an attendance by countless witches.[134] Bodin also coupled such notions to promising persecutory practices. For instance, he repeatedly underlined that witches knowing each other from sabbaths offered the opportunity of finding innumerable accomplices through painful questioning: "they can mention great numbers of the people whom they both know, and saw at the sabbath, by first name and surname."[135] In addition, Bodin

---

[130] Daneau, 113.
[131] Müller, "Elaborated Concepts of Witchcraft?"
[132] Müller, 11–12.
[133] Bodin, *De la démonomanie des sorciers*.
[134] See, for instance: Bodin, 60–62, 72–73, 223–34.
[135] Bodin, 358, 376, 384, 355."Et en nomma grand nombre par nom et surnom qu'il cognoissoit, et quant aux autres qu'il avoit veu aux Sabaths."

highlighted the importance of treating witchcraft as a *crimen exceptum*, arguing that witches "need not be arrested according to the law."[136]

Bodin also had insightful things to say about another promising investigatory opening, the child witches.[137] Regarding the enhancement of witch-hunting his argument did contain a weakness: Bodin almost exclusively focused on the daughters of witches, largely leaving out boys and children without witch parents. This limited his argument's persecutory potential. But Bodin's discussion of *how* those daughters could be used in trials shows much cunning. Girl witches, he argued, are taken to sabbaths, and "being of a tender age they can be persuaded more easily" to tell us about "the names of the persons there, the time of occurrence, the place they travelled to, and what they did there."[138] Bodin warned that girl witches could be afraid of making confessions before several investigators, so here he recommended to make them feel more comfortable by letting them speak to one investigator only, while the others should listen secretly behind a tapestry to write the child's admissions down.[139] His book is full of such manifest shrewd advice on how to stimulate trials. Regarding local reputations for witchcraft, he noted that "concerning the question of witches, common gossip is nearly infallible."[140] He also ensured that the holiness of persecution protected witch-hunters against magical harm.[141] Only the potential of flight and rich witches may not have been entirely on his radar. Bodin did not explicitly address the idea that flight implies that witches could know other witches who lived at larger distances, offering authorities the opportunity to provide their names to other authorities. And while noting that people of high standing could be witches too, he did not explicitly translate this insight into much persecutory guidance.[142]

In sum, somewhat anachronistically we might say that Bodin had much sociological and psychological insight into the workings of witch-hunting. He intelligently knew what buttons to push. I earlier posed the question whether proponents understood what historians understand today, namely how ideas about sabbaths, flights, torture, witchcraft reputations, rich witches, and child witches enhanced the reproduction of trials. In the case of Bodin it seems that we can answer this question – with flight and rich witches being a possible exception – with a clear yes. Bodin's level of comprehension is noteworthy, especially because he was not professionally involved in witch trials himself.[143] He studied demonological literature, consulted jurists about their experience, and gained information from confessions in a nearby trial of a woman who was alleged to have been introduced to witchcraft by her mother. In combination with his unusual

---

[136] Bodin, 376. "qu'il ne faut pas s'arrester aux regles de droict."
[137] Bodin, 262, 358–59, 375, 396, 428.
[138] Bodin, 358-9. "en l'aage tendre elles seront aysees à persuader", "elles nommerent les personnes, le temps, le lieu d'aller aux assemblees, et ce qu'on y faict."
[139] Bodin, 359.
[140] Bodin, 394. "quand il est question des Sorciers, le bruict commun est presque infallible."
[141] Bodin, 317.
[142] Opitz-Belakhal, "Der Magistrat als Hexenjäger," 48; see, for instance: Bodin, *De la démonomanie des sorciers*, 242.
[143] Krause, "The Will to Know and the Unknowable," 122; Krause, Martin, and MacPhail, "Introduction"; Krause, *Witchcraft, Demonology, and Confession in Early Modern France*, 1–7.

intelligence – Bodin was also one of the sharpest minds of his age on other topics – his knowledge and experience endowed him with an unusual level of insight. Yet, whatever the causes of his comprehension were, it does not offer support for the Darwinian scenario. Bodin did not "design" major ideas about witchcraft, as those ideas were already evolving before him. But his *Démonomanie* provides a compelling case of someone who understood how certain witchcraft notions boosted trials, and who shrewdly propagated those notions with that in mind.

Bodin's book spread far and wide, so we might presume that his insights became common currency. However, other key sources provide a mixed picture. Take Peter Binsfeld's *Tractatus* from 1589.[144] Written while the hunts of the region were in full swing, this book by the suffragan bishop of Trier in many ways reflected the innovations of those hunts. Binsfeld referred to children and people of "high standing" as possible witches, and highlighted gatherings, flight, and misogynous stereotypes, and he explicitly affirmed that torture should be used to question suspects about sabbath accomplices. "The sorcerers tell us about the deeds of their companions, which they saw happening at specific times and places while they were present there themselves", he writes.[145] A striking feature of the book, however, is that Binsfeld did not address one of the outstanding traits of the Trier hunts, namely their size. One passage tells of a suspect "mentioning one, two or more" companions, but there is no information about sabbaths or chains of accusations being large.[146] That a person who was directly involved in the trials omitted this prodigious cultural "mutation" suggests that neither he, nor possibly others, saw the potential of what was occurring right before their eyes. In the wave of trials that subsequently swept Germany we can find a similarly notable oversight in the newssheet from Ulm, mentioned earlier.[147] Its author encouraged witch-hunting, and gave due attention to the size of the persecutions in Trier and other places. But what he missed was what was making those trials so big: the author said nothing about (large) witches' gatherings.

There is yet another important topic concerning the level of understanding during the Trier hunts: that these persecutions spread from place to place was crucially impacted by the belief that witches could know other witches over long distances. So, we might expect persecutors to have been well aware of the importance of the notion of flight, which stimulated this "infectious" effect. But sources suggest otherwise. In his study of trial records from the region, Johannes Dillinger observed that interrogators were not particularly interested in flight.[148] In fact, they mostly discussed the topic in relation to something else that had their attention, the social status of witches. Did witches fly on simple tools, or on luxury goods, like beautiful horses and carriages? Binsfeld explicitly recounted that witches could fly over long

---

[144] Binsfeld, *Tractat Von Bekantnuß der Zauberer unnd Hexen*.
[145] Binsfeld, 123."die Zauberer besagen thaten ihrer Gesellen und Lastersgenossen, die sie auff bescheidenen plätzen, zeit und weise gesehen haben, bey welchen sie gegenwertig gewesen".
[146] Binsfeld, 88."hat zweene, order zwo, oder auch mehr besagt."
[147] Behringer, *Hexen und Hexenprozesse in Deutschland*, 218–23.
[148] Dillinger, *Böse Leute*, 120.

distances very quickly, but interestingly he also said that witches returned from sabbaths on foot.[149] So Binsfeld here mentioned a detail that threatened to undermine the reproductive advantage of the flight belief. Overall, this suggests that flight did not have its incendiary effects because involved actors understood its potential. More likely, the concept worked silently and unintentionally, due to blind evolution.

The perception of flight in the Trier trials does not seem to have been unique. In trial records from Lorraine, Robin Briggs similarly observed that flight was not seen to enable sabbaths, or long distance contacts.[150] Interrogators discussed the topic for other reasons, for instance to stress the abnormality of the whole affair. Also, when the sabbath was thought to take place close by, witches were still often presumed to fly there, and in many cases to return on foot. As Julian Goodare generalizes: "Witches' flight occurred in confessions, not because the interrogators wanted to explain large gatherings at long distances, but because flight was itself an important ingredient in witchcraft beliefs."[151] What the theory of Darwinian cultural evolution can teach us here is that the notion of flight could still serve a function of enabling beliefs in large gatherings and long distance contacts, even if the persecutors involved did not think of it in those terms themselves.

The peak period

What about the general understanding of the dynamics of witch-hunting in the period after Trier, when trials grew even bigger? This was the time when sabbath notions became most elaborate, with demonologists painting assemblies in full color and detail, and persecutions being pursued more effectively than ever before. In the case of Henri Boguet, who hunted witches in the Franche-Comté around 1600, one can indeed find quite a lot of insights. He spoke of an "infinity of witches", he repeatedly stressed that suspects should be asked for accomplices, and he linked flight to sabbath attendance.[152] Furthermore, Boguet devoted much attention to child witches, for example when describing how "by means of a child an infinite number of witches was discovered."[153] In his view, these children also deserved the death penalty, as their role in trials was "a secret judgement of god."[154]

Still, other key sources provide indications that the proponents' shrewd understanding was not necessarily at the root of witch-hunting's success around this time. Take Nicolas Rémy's *Daemonolatreiae* (1595).[155] The Lorraine inquisitor displayed much interest in the children of witch parents, including boys, also being witches.[156] The latter detail created more persecutory

---

[149] Binsfeld, *Tractat Von Bekantnuß der Zauberer unnd Hexen*, 59–61, 97, 123.
[150] Briggs, "Many Reasons Why," 60; Briggs, *Witches & Neighbours*, 40.
[151] Goodare, *The European Witch-Hunt*, 136–37.
[152] Boguet, *Discours exécrable des sorciers*, 24–25, 67–68, 334–35, 439–43, 447."une infinité de Sorciers."
[153] Boguet, 13."par le moyen d'un enfant l'on a decouvert une infinité de Sorciers."
[154] Boguet, 12, 442."secret jugement de dieu."
[155] Rémy, *Demonolatry*.
[156] Rémy, 85, 92–98.

potential than Bodin's book. Yet, what Rémy failed to address was how to use children in trials. What interested him most about the topic was the moral question of whether child witches deserved harsh punishment, which he answered affirmatively. Rémy also lengthily discussed sabbaths, which he claimed were "attended by great numbers."[157] But interestingly, he added an odd detail. The book repeatedly stated that witches cover their faces there, to prevent recognition and accusation by their companions: "They never assemble together without being masked, or with their faces blacked and often (…) covered with a flour sieve."[158] This observation shows that Rémy saw how sabbath recognition could create chains of accusations, because that was exactly what the alleged witches were trying to prevent. But remarkably, Rémy only discussed this insight in combination with the notion of face-covering, which simultaneously had the potential of undermining the reproductive dynamics of the sabbath belief entirely.

This variant did not come out of nowhere. It has been found by historians in various trial records. In Schwaben, for instance, rich witches were alleged to appear masked at the sabbath, and in Saarland suspects claimed this more generally, or stated that it was too dark to recognize companions.[159] During interrogations in Rémy's own Lorraine, suspects similarly recounted that witches covered their faces, and also that it was too dark to make things out properly.[160] Judges wanted the accused to tell them about whom and what they had seen there, so these confessions hindered their efforts.[161] Robin Briggs argues that this was also precisely what the interrogated were after: "There is a strong impression that the confessions were shaped to emphasize the lack of true involvement on the part of their makers, while the vague descriptions made it easier to evade demands to identify accomplices."[162] Briggs thinks that this "must surely have been a deliberate choice."[163] So if true, this narrative implies that the variant of face-covering appeared with the intent of impeding persecution.

If witch-hunting's proponents understood the reproductive dynamics of the sabbath notion, we might expect them to remove this dangerously unhelpful variant immediately, or at least to advise interrogators not to be misled by such dodging. But that is not what happened. Briggs found that while judges sometimes instigated additional torture, they tended to accept these evasions quite readily.[164] Rémy adopted the notion in his book on several occasions, and Martin Delrio also recounted that witches tried to avoid recognition by appearing at the sabbath "with their face covered by a mask, a linen cloth, or some other veil or facial representation."[165] Like Bodin's book, Delrio's *Disquisitiones* was shrewdly written, effectively connecting cumulative

---

[157] Rémy, 47–65.
[158] Rémy, 48, 61–63.
[159] Dillinger, *Böse Leute*, 206; Labouvie, *Zauberei und Hexenwerk*, 120.
[160] Briggs, *The Witches of Lorraine*, 137, 147, 178; Briggs, *Witches & Neighbours*, 47.
[161] Goodare, *The European Witch-Hunt*, 236.
[162] Briggs, *The Witches of Lorraine*, 137.
[163] Briggs, 178.
[164] Briggs, 178.
[165] Rio and Maxwell-Stuart, *Investigations into Magic*, 93, 97.

beliefs to investigatory techniques. For instance, he postulated that judges would sin gravely if they did not question suspects about accomplices, and he delved into the potential of torture and common gossip.[166] But that only makes it all the more striking that Delrio included face masking as a potentially undermining variant, without instruction on how to defuse it. In some ways the variant fitted nicely into demonological theory – it was a common trope that the devil and his witches tried to conceal their activities.[167] Stuart Clark highlights that the diabolical was associated with lying, illusion, falseness, and a world turned upside down, which made masks a plausible element. Yet, for the reproduction of the witch-hunting phenomenon, the adoption of this variant by several of its proponents was a marked act of "unintelligent design" that had the potential of hindering its further spread. That the variant did not gain more prominence, was plausibly due to the hidden selective process weeding it out again.

There are further indications that proponents in the heyday of trials were not fully aware of how things worked. Regarding the Ellwangen-hunt we already encountered the peculiar confessions about a diabolical palace where executed witches lived on to continue their activities.[168] Here once more a variant popped up with a potential to undermine witch-hunting, so we might expect investigators to remove it quickly. But in fact, they duly recorded the variant in trial records, and even allowed it to gain traction in confessions. This suggests that not the persecutors, but the blind Darwinian process once again silently did the eliminative work. Another interesting case is Pierre de Lancre's *Tableau de l'inconstance des mauvais anges at demons* (Picture of the Inconstancy of Evil Angels and Demons).[169] It was published in 1612, after De Lancre had supervised a large hunt in the Labourd region. The judge presented the sabbath in full baroque blossom, full of pomp and spectacle, innumerable attendants, lots of children, sexual feasting, devil worshipping, and demons joining in. So, if anyone should have comprehended how such notions were to be put into persecutory action, it was De Lancre. But unlike the works of Kramer, Bodin or Binsfeld, he hardly offered instruction on how to persecute. The book gives the impression that De Lancre eagerly wanted to tell the world about everything that he believed to have uncovered about this sensational conspiracy, rather than to connect the dots on how to create further persecution.

Or take Friedrich Förner, the preacher from Bamberg who incited the population against witches, prior to the persecution of 1626-1632. Historians have stressed his inflammatory impact there.[170] William Bradford Smith argues that such personalities could play "a vital role in the instigation and expansion of the trials", and he sees Förner as "the principal architect of the witch

---

[166] Machielsen, *Martin Delrio*, 282–83.
[167] Clark, *Thinking with Demons*, 22–23. This interpretation was also suggested to me by Robin Briggs in personal correspondence.
[168] Dillinger, "Hexen-Eltern," 244–45; Dillinger, *Kinder im Hexenprozess*, 129–31; Mährle, "O wehe der armen seelen," 435.
[169] Lancre, *On the Inconstancy of Witches*.
[170] Gehm, *Die Hexenverfolgung im Hochstift Bamberg*; Behringer, *Witches and Witch-Hunts*, 112–13.

hunts in Bamberg" who more than any other single individual must bear the onus.[171] Behringer describes the preacher as the "spiritus rector" of these trials, and generally argues that the great persecutions of this period, unlike the sixteenth-century ones, were "pre-planned ever more perfectly, and carried out ever more skillfully."[172] Förner was part of the German witch-hunting networks of his time, and well versed in demonology. So, we might expect him to know the tips and tricks of how to rouse persecution. But did the sermons of this "architect" indeed provide a blueprint, or a design, of what was about to happen? Did Förner particularly focus on the notions that would make the Bamberg hunt so huge, like sabbaths, flights, weather magic, child witches and rich witches?

The striking fact is that he did not.[173] His sermons movingly aimed to scare people with warnings about the snares of the devil and the dangers of witchcraft, but weather magic, flight, and rich witches were hardly, or not addressed. There are some passages on child witches, for instance when Förner warns against the sin of curiosity, and when he discusses the witch children of Trier.[174] But considering the importance of child accusations at this historical juncture, the attention he paid to this issue was limited. More amazingly, the sabbath is almost entirely ignored. Like the *Malleus*, Förner only passingly refers to it a few times when he is actually making a point about something else.[175] For example, he briefly noted that even when witches are not involved in killing livestock or necromancy, "they are still allied with the devil, and normally attend the meeting of poisoners to participate in what happens there."[176] In his discussion of the child witches of Trier he also casually mentioned that they attended witches' dances.[177] But the sabbath is not addressed as a topic in its own right. What Förner especially focused on instead, was the danger of consulting village witches. The suffragan bishop mentioned that people visited such cunning women for medical cures, or soothsaying, and he endlessly warned that this meant invoking the diabolical. People should *exclusively* seek the protection of the holy church and its sacraments. Arguably, this rhetorical focus looks quite a lot like instrumentalization, with Förner exploiting the witch image to solidify his own church's spiritual power at the expense of those women. But importantly, the defamation of cunning women played no major role in the subsequent hunt. That a well-connected person like Förner seems to have had so little understanding of what was making witch-hunting big, thus indicates that the Bamberg hunt was even less intentionally designed than is currently presumed. This finding strengthens the alternative Darwinian scenario.

---

[171] Bradford Smith, *Reformation and the German Territorial State*, 183; Bradford Smith, "The Persecution of Witches," 53; Bradford Smith, "Friedrich Förner."
[172] Behringer is quoted in: Bradford Smith, *Reformation and the German Territorial State*, 183; Behringer, *Hexenverfolgung in Bayern*, 136."Die großen Verfolgungen wurden immer Perfekter vorgeplant und routinierter durchgeführt".
[173] Förner, *Dämonenglaube und Zauberei im Jahre 1625*.
[174] Förner, 248, 632–33.
[175] Förner, 98, 208, 282.
[176] Förner, 98."so sind sie dennoch mit dem Teufel verbündet, nehmen gewöhnlich an den Zusammenkünften der Giftmischerinnen teil und tun üblicherweise das, was dort geschieht".
[177] Förner, 632–33.

Another important source from the time is Heinrich von Schultheis's *Eine Ausführliche Instruction* (An Extensive Instruction) from 1634. This Westphalian witch commissioner had been involved in the horrific hunts of the electoral state of Cologne, and his book offered guidance for inquisitors.[178] The work was written in the form of a dialogue between a doctor – Schultheis himself – and a somewhat skeptical higher official. In comparison to Förner, Rémy or De Lancre, the work shows a lot of insight into the workings of the super-hunts of the time. Schultheis addressed the importance of common gossip, he encouraged anonymous accusations, and disallowed suspects a proper defense. The role of torture was fully on his radar too. He emphasized its indispensability to rolling up the secret network, and offered concrete advice on *how* to torture. He also addressed the broad social profile of witches. Admittedly, Schultheis mentions the notion of rich witches only sparsely, but at some point he does state that demons at the witches' assembly deliberate with high officials.[179] Shrewdly, in another instance he also stressed that convicted witches must bear the costs of their own burnings.[180] The doctor in the dialogue further speaks positively of Würzburg, where many clerics, including Jesuits, were recently burned. Apparent piety can be a cover for treachery, he argues, and did Jesus himself not count a traitor amongst his twelve disciples?[181] Moreover, child witches are mentioned repeatedly.[182] "Children tend to tell us the truth", Schultheis says, and since the crime of witchcraft is so very secret, legal restrictions on the use of child witnesses should be abolished.[183]

In addition, Schultheis delved into the persecutory importance of the sabbath.[184] The doctor remarks that "witches are taken through the air, over houses and towns, towards the dance", and he endlessly stresses what this implies: that inquisitors should press suspects about whom they had seen there.[185] In two exemplary interrogations included in the book, Schultheis sets the example himself.[186] In a first intimidating questioning, a suspect named Gretha is confronted with her bad reputation, the accusations against her, as well as apparent inconsistencies in her declarations. Gretha initially refuses to plead guilty, exclaiming that she had rather never been born. But torture makes her confess to being a witch, and to have magically harmed others. The questioning then moves to the sabbath. "How many of you came together there?", the doctor inquires.[187] When she gives a number of fifty, the doctor is not satisfied yet, so he asks her whether there were actually less, or more. Gretha now admits that there were in fact two or three hundred witches present. The doctor forces her to mention

---

[178] Schultheis, *Eine Außführliche Instruction*; Decker, "Die Hexenverfolgungen im Herzogtum Westfalen," 361–65; Grawlich, "Der Hexenkommisar Heinrich von Schultheiß."
[179] Schultheis, *Eine Außführliche Instruction*, 299, 335–36, 348–50.
[180] Schultheis, 467.
[181] Schultheis, 308, 491.
[182] Schultheis, 2, 71, 79, 136, 140–41, 295, 305–6, 337–38.
[183] Schultheis, 330."daß die Kinder pflegen die warheit zusagen."
[184] Schultheis, 30–31, 91, 149, 269, 301, 320, 328.
[185] Schultheis, 112."das die Zauber durch Lufft uber Häuser und Stätte zum Tanz geführt werden."
[186] Schultheis, 185–253, 280–82.
[187] Schultheis, 208."Wie viel seyn ewerer wol, die darhin beysammen kommen."

names, also suggesting that she denounce people from other places. When she does not answer quickly enough, he threatens her with eternal damnation. As he explains to her: for a witch, there is no better way of showing faith and love for Jesus Christ than through naming accomplices. It would not only save her soul, but potentially also the souls of the people she named.

It is a common thread throughout the book: investigatory techniques serve the fight against the devil, and aid the higher glory of God. This is also why the names of accomplices mentioned must be correct, as God would not allow the devil to make it seem as if innocent people attend the sabbath.[188] Accordingly, Schultheis presents painful questioning as a means to break the devil's power over his subjects. Torturing the accused is not an injustice; it is way of doing suspects a favor. Any hindrance on the path towards confessions – like the accused retracting statements when torture is over – is then interpreted as a diabolical attempt to thwart their return to God. "Gretha, I beg you, don't be deceived by the devil any longer, heaven pity, he has deceived you for far too long, so tell me who taught you witchcraft", the doctor at some point exclaims to her.[189] Eventually, Gretha also sees how the devil had entrapped her, and expresses her gratitude: "Let our Lord Jesus Christ reward you my dearest Mister doctor, for keeping your best interests at heart for a poor sinner like me."[190] So all's well that ends well, and after her burning Gretha is expected to meet her eternal bliss.

Considering the methods of interrogation that Schultheis presents, we can hardly be surprised that witch-hunters like him were able to create the super-hunts of this time. But when looking more carefully, his work also betrays apparent limitations to the level of insight. The extraction of names of accomplices who attended crowded sabbaths, as we saw, is a focal point of the book. But astoundingly, in the exemplary interrogations this leads to only very few denunciations. The questioning of Gretha eventually delivers a mere three names, and the second questioning of a man named Thonnis does not exceed that. This tiny number also satisfies the doctor. So. intriguingly, the book did not finish off the incendiary potential of large sabbaths, which indicates that Schultheis did not grasp how this notion triggered large chains of accusations. There is also a notable omission in his discussion of child witches. We saw that modern historians observed that children often triggered trials through voluntary confessions – an insight that also dawned on Bodin. Schultheis, however, appears to have missed it. In one story, for instance, he describes how three boys searched for birds' nests, with one of them, Luscus, trying to invoke the devil to find more.[191] This upsets one of the other boys, and an ensuing panic in their community leads to witchcraft accusations against Luscus. Yet, while childhood fantasy and rashness thus play a role in the story, Schultheis recounts that Luscus confessed *after* being tortured. The book elsewhere also argues that children confess more easily

---

[188] Schultheis, 5, 13–15, 27.
[189] Schultheis, 191-2."Gretha ich bitte dich, lasse dich durch den Teuffel nicht länger betriegen, er hat Gott erbarms dich viel zulange betrogen, sag mir doch wer hat dich gelehrt."
[190] Schultheis, 206."De Herr Jesus Christus lohn es euch Lieber H. Doctor, das ihrs mit mir armen Sünderinnen so wol meinet."
[191] Schultheis, 98–101.

when tortured, because "a young person has more subtle, warmer and livelier blood than an old."[192] Schultheis thus emphasized a certain vulnerability of children. But what he failed to address was that children are also likely to make *voluntary* confessions, and how to exploit that in trials.

This bears upon the broader question to what extent the role of children was instigated by knowledgeable persecutors who understood their usefulness. Behringer thinks that the child accusations occurred "mostly undesired and unplanned, and were often inexplicable."[193] Rita Voltmer, as mentioned, finds such interpretations too naïve and presumes a more deliberate use of children.[194] Rainer Walz thinks the same, arguing that children provided a key tool, used in a consciously Machiavellian manner, "for the damaging or destruction of opponents."[195] Yet, Voltmer and Walz do not substantiate such claims about a shrewd understanding with clear evidence from the sources. My own findings are ambiguous. Bodin understood a lot, and Boguet apparently as well, but the texts of authors like Rémy, Förner, and to some extent Schultheiss, appear less insightful. The German pamphlet from 1626 that was entirely devoted to the topic of child witches (see 6.3) also failed to mention how children could be used in trials. The author was primarily interested in the shocking question of why so many children were seduced by the devil.[196] Importantly, within the Darwinian framework there is no longer a *need* to invoke shrewd actors if we want to explain how children came to play their incendiary role.

The question of how witch trials increasingly focused on the rich is also rife with interpretative problems. If proponents failed to address the topic this does not automatically imply that they were incognizant of how an attack on the rich served the attention for, and funding of, witch persecution. Perhaps Förner and Schultheis deliberately wanted to steer trials in that direction, but did not, or only sparsely, discussed the topic in order not to provoke the rich and powerful. Yet, we should certainly consider more non-intentional scenarios here. Erik Midelfort proposed that the increased targeting of the rich was just a by-product of something else: "One would expect persons under torture to agree most easily on the notorious, the eccentric, or the wealthy, since they were the best known persons in town."[197] This would also explain the disproportionate targeting of midwives and innkeepers. Another option might be that the people interrogated chose to mention members of the ruling classes out of revenge.[198] In Nördlingen in 1594 a rich woman was accused and burned whose husband played a major role in the persecution there as mayor. "People wanted to harm those responsible for judicial

---

[192] Schultheis, 305.
[193] Behringer, "Kinderhexenprozesse," 43. Zahlreiche Einzelbeispiele zeigen, daß "meistens ungeplant und unerwünscht, oft auch ganz unerklärlich waren."
[194] Voltmer, "Jesuiten und Kinderhexen," 208, 214–17, 230."freiwilligen"; Voltmer, "Zwischen Herrschaftskrise, Wirtschaftsdepression und Jesuitenpropaganda," 77.
[195] Walz, "Kinder in Hexenprozessen," 217–20.
[196] *Newer Tractat von der Verführten Kinder Zauberey*.
[197] Midelfort, *Witch Hunting in Southwestern Germany*, 172; Walinski-Kiehl, "La chasse aux sorcières et le sabbat des sorcières dans les évêchés de Bamberg et Würzburg," 220; Dillinger, "Richter als Angeklagte," 137.
[198] Behringer, *Witches and Witch-Hunts*, 158; Haas, *Hexen und Herrschaftspolitik*, 87, 113–19.

procedures", Alexandra Haas explains.[199] These suggestions do not appear implausible and can be integrated into a Darwinian model. The cultural adaptation would then look as follows: the focus on rich witches had the effect of larger, and more spectacular trials, which in its turn enhanced the focus on rich witches. What would give the adaptation a Darwinian twist is that the initial cultural variants leading to this focus occurred due to other factors (the ones mentioned above) than persecutors who understood these enhancing effects. In that regard, the variants' occurrence may have been a chance hit.

Implications for the Darwinian model
This brings us back to the matter of how to examine the proposed Darwinian model. Concerning the evolution of the sabbath as a cultural adaptation I formulated four hypotheses (see 5.5) that we can now consider anew. The first hypothesis – *many cultural variants regarding witchcraft appeared, most of which did not reproduce well* – had not yet been examined by witchcraft scholarship as such, and section 6.4 presented many clues for its validity. The second hypothesis – *the belief in the witches' sabbath had the effect of triggering larger and more spectacular persecutions* – was already well established, and especially sections 6.1-6.3 further substantiated it. The third hypothesis – *this effect contributed to the survival of the belief in the witches' sabbath itself* – was already addressed to some degree, and sections 6.1-6.3 examined it more closely, offering much confirmation. The fourth hypothesis – *this enhancing effect was neither intended nor recognized as such by the actors involved; it was a chance hit* – had not yet been examined at all. Especially this section is making a first attempt, and the findings are multifaceted. There are clues for understanding, especially in Bodin, which suggests that this cultural adaptation partially evolved due to involved actors who understood its underlying mechanism. But I also presented many clues for significant limitations to the apparent understanding by proponents, especially regarding the enhancing effect of large sabbaths. We cannot rule out that proponents had more understanding at subconscious levels, but as long as that does not manifest itself in the sources it remains unprovable. Hence, intentional design does not, by a long stretch, appear sufficient an explanation for this cultural adaptation. Darwinian selection comes forward as the indispensable complementary model. This also goes for other aspects of the cumulative concept of witchcraft, especially flight. Further research is required, though.

Apart from the question of what proponents did or did not understand, there is the issue of an alleged instrumentalization of trials for ulterior purposes. Do the texts of proponents provide clues in that regard? A key claim of the German instrumentalists is that earthly purposes were perfectly conceivable at the time. The sources studied indeed offer proof for that. First of all, there is the widely held idea that people became witches to achieve earthly ends. One of the earliest treatises on the topic already said that it was on the promise of revenge that the devil

---

[199] Haas, *Hexen und Herrschaftspolitik*, 114.

made people enter his society.²⁰⁰ Much later, David Meder warned that "a Christian should have no vindictive heart", as it would make him or her vulnerable to this crime.²⁰¹ Overall, witches were thought to be resentful people. Rémy maintained that "it is the way of nearly all witches now to take offence at the very slightest provocation, to spirit forth their resentment with the greatest acrimony."²⁰² Other mundane motivations were also thought to play a role.²⁰³ What lured people in, Bodin said, was Satan's false promise to "give wealth to the poor, pleasure to the afflicted, power to the weak, beauty to the ugly, knowledge to the ignorant, honor to the despised, and the favor of the great."²⁰⁴

More importantly, proponents observed that witchcraft *accusations* could be used for ulterior ends. In fact, it was something they continually warned against. Delrio prescribed that only trustworthy people should be accepted as witnesses, who had no anger, rancor or hatred against the people denounced.²⁰⁵ Others, like Bodin and Schultheis, expressed similar caution.²⁰⁶ Typically, judicial rules in the electoral state of Cologne from 1607 stated that accusations should be accepted not "from enemies or light-minded people, but from impartial, honest people."²⁰⁷ Throughout the era it was routine practice in trials to make witnesses swear an oath not to abuse procedures.²⁰⁸ That the possibility of abuse was conceivable at the time also becomes apparent in a self-defense of the Dutch-German pastor Franciscus Agricola. In 1597 he published a book on why witchcraft was the worst sin on earth, and ensured his readers that he had not written it "out of hatred for any human being."²⁰⁹ It was solely the honor of God, his compassion for the thousands of seduced souls, and his desire to end this terrifying crime that motivated him. Overall, proponents presented themselves as reasonable and ethical people, who wanted evidence to be weighed carefully, and who cared about not putting the innocent at risk.²¹⁰ It is better to let ten guilty witches go, than to harm a single innocent person, Delrio and Schultheis proclaimed.²¹¹ The latter also made clear that his daunting task of saving the witches' souls had rapidly made his hair turn grey.²¹²

---

²⁰⁰ Anonymous, "Errores gazariorum," 297.
²⁰¹ Meder, *Acht Hexenpredigten*, 40.
²⁰² Rémy, *Demonolatry*, 123.
²⁰³ Daneau, *Les Sorciers*, 51; Bodin, *De la démonomanie des sorciers*, 270–71, 303.
²⁰⁴ Bodin, *De la démonomanie des sorciers*, 305."donne richesses aux pauvres, plaisir aux affligez, puissance aux foibles, beauté aux laides, scavoir aux ignorants, honneaur aux mesprizes, et la favaur des grands."
²⁰⁵ Machielsen, *Martin Delrio*, 282–83; Rio and Maxwell-Stuart, *Investigations into Magic*, 195.
²⁰⁶ Bodin, *De la démonomanie des sorciers*, 394; Decker, "Die Hexenverfolgungen im Herzogtum Westfalen," 364; Schultheis, *Eine Außführliche Instruction*, 10, 143–48, 152–53.
²⁰⁷ Behringer, *Hexen und Hexenprozesse in Deutschland*, 239."nicht von fianden oder lichtfertigen lheuten, sondern von unpartheyschen redtlichen personsn" .
²⁰⁸ Behringer, 216, 227; Rublack, *The Astronomer & the Witch*, 216; Rummel, "So mögte auch eine darzu kommen, so mich belädiget," 205; Moeller, *Dass Willkür über Recht ginge*, 71.
²⁰⁹ Agricola, "Gründtlicher Bericht," Vorred 1."nicht ausz hasz einiger menschlicher Personen."
²¹⁰ See, for instance: Rio and Maxwell-Stuart, *Investigations into Magic*, 199–201, 215–16; Schultheis, *Eine Außführliche Instruction*, 102, 108–9, 121.
²¹¹ Machielsen, *Martin Delrio*, 283; Schultheis, *Eine Außführliche Instruction*, iv.
²¹² Schultheis, *Eine Außführliche Instruction*, 445.

What to make of such comments? That witch-hunt proponents so often stressed earthly motivations for becoming a witch, in the eyes of Rummel and Voltmer, betrays something about these proponents themselves – this was a case of psychological projection. "Not the alleged witches used the help of the devil to gain certain advantages; it was their accusers and persecutors who used the charge of witchcraft to gain social, economic, and/or political rewards."[213] The pious self-representations of proponents are also seen in a rather cynical light.[214] Rummel: "Of course there were strategies of legitimization, in which interest-based actions were camouflaged and concealed under apparently genuine motives."[215] But such virtuous talk was, in his view, a way of ideologically sanctioning the hidden benefits.[216] That sources show that instrumentalization of accusations and trials by proponents was perfectly conceivable offers some support for this scenario. Delrio's and Schultheis's words of caution might also be taken with a pinch of salt, as their proposals were in the end blatantly incautious, even by the standards of the time. Yet, we should still be careful here. Ulterior motives were thinkable, but does that also make them plausible?

Take Jean Bodin, our best example of a knowledgeable agent. As we saw, he was not involved in trials himself, and his anti-witchcraft fanaticism seems to have hindered his career. That makes it rather difficult to say what his ulterior motives might have been. Virginia Krause – a key Bodin expert – identifies different dimensions to his zeal.[217] She depicts Bodin as a man with deeply held religious convictions, who thought that an angel literally accompanied him, and communicated with him through a system of signs. Bodin had visions and dreams in which he believed to hear the voice of God and to receive his instructions. The French thinker considered himself a prophet in the tradition of the Hebrew prophets, so plausibly it is also in this light that he saw his own writing on witchcraft. "The *Démonomanie* was not the result of a strictly reasonable enterprise: it was perhaps first and foremost the fruit of Bodin's religious vocation and mystical experiences – his own deeply rooted conviction that he had privileged access to the spirit world", Krause writes.[218] Of course, one could argue that this was an indirect way of enhancing his own self-importance, but even then it is not the kind of ulterior motivation that the instrumentalists tend to think of. Profound genuine belief takes central stage here.

In the case of an inquisitor like Schultheis there are more indications for instrumentalization. Rita Voltmer claims that he probably made financial gains, and that his function as witch commissioner played a role in his ennoblement. "He made a social, if not financial, profit from such activities", she writes.[219] Tanja Grawlich says that the sparsity of

---

[213] Rummel and Voltmer, *Hexen und Hexenverfolgung*, 98.
[214] Voltmer, "Von der besonderen Alchimie, aus Menschenblut Gold zu machen," 131.
[215] Rummel, "So mögte auch eine darzu kommen, so mich belädiget," 206."Natürlich spielen dabei Strategien der Legitimation, der Verbrämung und Vermischung interessenbezogenen Handelns mit Überzeugungen eine wichtige Rolle."
[216] Rummel, 207.
[217] Krause, "The Will to Know and the Unknowable."
[218] Krause, 126.
[219] Voltmer, "Schultheiss, Heinrich von (ca 1580-ca 1646)."

sources makes it impossible to determine whether he enriched himself, but she certainly thinks it conceivable, as other commissioners in the region did make gains.[220] Yet, even in this case we should be careful.[221] The allegation lacks proof, and Schultheis's activities and devotion still seem extreme, even with the prospect of gaining such earthly advantages. So, why not presume that his avowed purposes were genuine? Maybe he really feared the consequences of not acting against witches, and he honestly thought himself to be saving witches' souls. And perhaps the stress of this grim task really did turn his hair gray. Schultheis's claim that torturing suspects was a way of doing them a favor may appear cynical. But such convictions were consistently expressed by proponents, and within the contemporary system of witch beliefs they did have a certain logical force.[222] Take Rémy, who said that "the divine Shepherd in His ineffable goodness and mercy often calls back to the fold the sheep that have been led away by the wolf, and again feeds them on His celestial pastures."[223] Rémy presented his own efforts in this light. Moreover, seen from the reproductive interests of the witch-hunting phenomenon itself, this belief may strike us as yet another of the phenomenon's ingenious "tricks" to motivate people, and thereby to further its own "selfish" spread.

Fortunately, our empirical options are not exhausted yet. What makes the current debate on instrumentalization so difficult, is that proponents of trials possibly concealed their real motivations. But as we saw, the contemporary opponents of trials were probably less secretive in that regard. The German instrumentalists are right to point to them as an invaluable source of information. These critics in quite a few cases had an advantage that historians never have: They personally knew the actors responsible for persecution. They saw them, spoke with them, listened to them, and observed how they operated in the context of a hunt. So, what were those critics' views on this matter? Did they claim that trials were used successfully for ulterior aims? Or did they assume that genuine belief had a profound impact, with consequences harmful even to actors responsible for witch-hunting? And to what extent did the critics recognize that notions like the sabbath, flight or the child witch engendered trials? We shall now have a look at early modern opponents of witch persecution.

7.3 What opponents said

When the Württemberg preachers Matthaeus Alber and Wilhelm Bidenbach in 1562 responded to the new surge of witch trials, they warned about the false and groundless talk of witches "that arose from malice and resentment and is enhanced and strengthened by all too eager credence, and which may overcome even the most innocent of one's adversaries through cunning and

---

[220] Grawlich, "Der Hexenkommisar Heinrich von Schultheiß," 318–20.
[221] Decker, "Der Hexen-Richter Dr. Heinrich von Schultheiß," 1054–55.
[222] See, for instance: Haas, *Hexen und Herrschaftspolitik*, 100–102; Bodin, *De la démonomanie des sorciers*, 254.
[223] Rémy, *Demonolatry*, 162.

deceit."²²⁴ These Lutheran pastors were far from unique in pointing out malevolent motives behind the trials.²²⁵ In 1635 Johann Meyfart identified malice, hatred, envy and resentment as key causes.²²⁶ Motives like these, he argued, created an atmosphere in which misfortune was easily interpreted as the result of witchcraft. Meyfart vividly described what such gossip could sound like: "He became rich very soon, so he's a witch. That young lady is beautiful, so that's why she's a witch. That man gives a lot of alms, so he's a witch, and she has good harvests, so that's why she's a witch."²²⁷ A few years earlier Friedrich Spee had observed that such sentiments were especially prominent in his German fatherland. The Jesuit priest argued that people in other countries could endure it when certain people became rich, but in Germany "there were others, who had not been as lucky, who would put their heads together, and pretend that this could only have happened because of witchcraft."²²⁸ Germans had more difficulties in accepting other people's happiness, so that was why these lands were so unusually ravaged by witch trials.

In section 7.1 various passages gleaned from the sources already indicated that contemporary critics suspected witch-hunt proponents of harboring ulterior motives. Many more examples can be added to the list. In an area bordering on the Palatine, the princedom of Mainz initiated a witch persecution that killed many serfs there. The Palatine objected, explicitly accusing Mainz of a political campaign: the serfs tended to side with the Palatine, so the underlying motive for their extermination seemed obvious.²²⁹ In a report on witch-hunts in the Basque country, the Spanish Jesuit Hernando de Solarte in 1611 recounted the story of a boy who had told him that three women summoned him to accuse another woman of luring him into witchcraft. Also, they instructed the boy which sabbath companions he should mention by name. In return, the women promised him four *reales*, a shirt and other goods. "Their real motive for bribing the boy was their personal hatred of these people", De Solarte explained.²³⁰ Allegedly, the women had made similar requests to other boys. Friedrich Spee spoke about a case of a city official who was blamed for misconduct, but then diverted attention to his accusers by initiating charges of witchcraft against them. "What easier way these days to take revenge", he commented.²³¹ Spee further mentioned "greedy and vicious judges" who were after the money of the people they convicted, while Johann Weyer spoke of "bloodthirsty judges".²³² Johann

---

²²⁴ Alberum and Bidenbach, *Ein Summa etlicher Predigten von Hagel und Unholden*"die aus boßheit und misgunst, jiren Anfang gewinnet, und durch gern glauben zunimpt und gesterckt würdt, wölches auch dem allerunschuldigsten durch list unnd trug seiner ungünstigen Widersächer widerfaren mag".
²²⁵ see, for example: Hocker, *Der Teufel selbst*, 296; Henningsen, *The Salazar Documents*, 156, 448; Schmidt, *Glaube und Skepsis*, 66–67.
²²⁶ Meyfart, *Christliche Erinnerung*, 98, 186–90.
²²⁷ Meyfart, 187."Dieser is bald reich worden, drumb ist er ein Trutner. Diese Jungfrau ist schön, darumb ist sie ein Trutnerin. Dieser gibt viel Allmosen, drumb ist er ein Trutner, diese bauet ihre Felder glücklichen, darumd ist sie eine Trutnerin" .
²²⁸ Spee, *Cautio Criminalis*, 3."da seind stracks andere, welchen das Glück so wohl nicht auffsitzen will, daher stecken sie die Köpfe zusammen, und haltens darvor, daß diß nicht ohne Zauberey hergehen könne."
²²⁹ Schmidt, *Glaube und Skepsis*, 327–28; Schmidt, "Ein Politisches Ausrottungsprogramm?"
²³⁰ Henningsen, *The Salazar Documents*, 154.
²³¹ Spee, *Cautio Criminalis*, 129."Wie wolte sich einer heut zu Tage besser rechen können."
²³² Spee, 10, 36, 300."Geitzige und boshafftige"; Weyer, *Witches, Devils, and Doctors in the Renaissance*, 550.

Meyfart described interrogators as people who will "seize with both hands any opportunity to put aside the law, in order to condemn and condemn, and to burn and burn at their own holy convenience. Isn't that evil?"[233] Persecutors in Ellwangen, Eichstätt, Bavaria and Cologne had to defend themselves against charges of financial abuse, and as Cornelius Loos said about the witch-hunt system: "Isn't it obvious how writers and judges try to strengthen and defend the machinery; all of them, when they describe vacuous confessions"?[234]

Keith Thomas regarded situations where charity was refused as breeding grounds for accusations of witchcraft. But his naturalistic outlook was already anticipated in 1584 by the English country squire Reginald Scot.[235] In his skeptical book *The Discoverie of Witchcraft* Scot described how suspicions arose against alleged witches who were "old, lame, bleare-eied, pale, fowle, and full of wrinkles, poore, sullen, superstitious".[236] Such women, he argued, could barely survive, so they went from door to door to ask for alms. After being rejected, the women sometimes went away cursing. When misfortune then befell the people who had been cursed, they easily misinterpreted their bad luck affair as the result of witchcraft. Moreover, anyone who suggests that the interpretation of witch-hunting as a means to oppress and stereotype women is an entirely anachronistic theory should take note of what the German preacher C. Beerman said in his Easter sermon of 1593:

> That we have so many witch burnings these days is not least due to innumerable authors who write so very dreadfully of women, and condemn virtually all of them for their evil, poisonous and diabolical nature, but subsequently pride themselves that incomparably more women are burned as witches than men, who are by nature better, and not so poisonous, cunning and devious. The public, which listens to such talk, then says: justice is being done, as these women are infernal and treacherous like the devils.[237]

Knowledgeable critics
It transpires that contemporary critics understood much of how witch-hunting worked. Historians today stress that the notion of a *crimen exceptum* allowed the relentless use of torture,

---

[233] Meyfart, *Christliche Erinnerung*, 204."greiffen darnach mit beyden Händen, verdammen und verdammen, verbrennen und verbrennen nach ihrem heiligen belieben. Ist daß nicht Bösheit?"
[234] Durrant, *Witchcraft, Gender, and Society in Early Modern Germany*, 41; Behringer, *Hexenverfolgung in Bayern*, 303–5; Midelfort, *Witch Hunting in Southwestern Germany*, 110–11; Eerden, "Cornelius Loos und die 'magia falsa,'" 150."Man sieht doch, wie die Schriftsteller und die Richter sich bemühen, die Maschinerie zu stärken und zu verteidigen; jene, wenn sie die inhaltsleeren Geständnisse beschreiben."
[235] Scot, *The Discoverie of Witchcraft*; Almond, "Doubt and Demonology."
[236] Scot, *The Discoverie of Witchcraft*, 4–5.
[237] Schwerhoff, "Hexerei, Geslecht und Regionalgeschichte," 330."Daß man in jetzig Zeit so viele Hexen verbrennt, kommt nit zum wenigst mit daher, daß unzählig viel Scribenten so unfähig von den Weibern schreiben und sie schier alle insgemein für bös, giftig und von teuflischer Natur ausschreien, und rühmen sich dann wohl, daß ungleich mehr Weiber als Unholde und Zäuberische verbrennt würden dann Männer, so von Natur besser seien und nit so giftig, listig und verschlagen. Wodurch denn das Volk, das auf solch Scribenten hört, wider die Weiber erbößt wird, und wenn sie verbrennt werden, sagen: ihnen geschicht recht, sie sind höllisch und tückisch gleich den Teufeln."

which then stimulated false confessions. But innumerable contemporaries recognized this too. The point was made by people who had to undergo this horrific ordeal. We already encountered the mayor of Bamberg Johannes Junius, who wrote that "whoever comes into the witch prison must become a witch or be tortured until he invents something out of his head." A secret letter, smuggled out of a prison in Nördlingen in 1590, makes a similar point. "Oh you, my chosen sweetheart", a woman named Rebecca Lemp wrote to her husband, "they have tortured me, although I'm as innocent as God in heaven."[238] Lemp beseeched him to send her something with which she could kill herself, as she feared that torture would destroy her body and make her confess to things perilous to her soul. Likewise, trial records from Lorraine recounted the story of Barbelline Chaperey, who said "that she had confessed more than she had committed or done, but this was because she was under torture."[239]

Printed critiques also made the point in great color and detail.[240] Many authors dwelt upon the horrors of the torture chambers, identifying them as a cause for witch-hunting going awry, killing so many innocent people. Johann Weyer described his encounter with a woman who had showed him her legs, "which had been severely maimed by the cruelty of the torments that she had endured on an earlier occasion when she had been tortured while under suspicion for the same sort of crime. Boiling oil was poured upon her legs so that a false confession might be wrung from her."[241] Somewhat earlier a jurist in Schleswig stated that "also the innocent, due to the pain, are forced to lie."[242] The Spanish inquisitor Alonso de Salazar critically examined early seventeenth-century hunts in the Basque country, and recounted how the trustworthiness of witnesses was "weakened by the force, inducement and sinister methods used to extort their declarations."[243] Johan van Heemskerck, a Dutch lawyer and poet who commented on the German hunts, said that potentially everyone had to fear for his life there. "The only reason why we have not all been found guilty of witchcraft (...) is that we have not all ended up on the rack."[244]

In his extensive critique of the witch trials, *Von Zauberern, Hexen und Unholden* (On Magicians, Witches and Sorcerers), the German jurist Johann Gödelmann in 1592 explicitly targeted Bodin's notion of the *crimen exceptum* as a source of false testimonies.[245] This professor from Rostock argued that witchcraft verdicts should always be based on material proof or eyewitness accounts. This, of course, made the alleged crime of witchcraft almost impossible to

---

[238] Grasmück, Lorenz, and Schmidt, *Hexen Und Hexenverfolgung Im Deutschen Südwesten*, 188."O Du mein auserwehlter schaz", "man hat mich gemartet, - ich bin so vnschuldig als Got im Himel."
[239] Briggs, *The Witches of Lorraine*, 43.
[240] see, for instance: Dillinger, *Böse Leute*, 366; Behringer, *Witches and Witch-Hunts*, 159; Meyfart, *Christliche Erinnerung*; Witekind, *Christlich Bedencken und Erinnerung von Zauberey*, 165–66; Scot, *The Discoverie of Witchcraft*, 21–22, 28.
[241] Weyer, *Witches, Devils, and Doctors in the Renaissance*, 524.
[242] Behringer, *Hexen und Hexenprozesse in Deutschland*, 127."Auch Unschuldige zwingt der Schmerz zu lügen."
[243] Henningsen, *The Salazar Documents*, 319–20.
[244] Heemskerck, *Batavische Arcadia*, 65-76."d'eenige reden waerom wy niet alle Toovenaers bevonden werden (...) om dat wy niet alle daer over op de pijn-banck gheraken."
[245] Gödelmann, *Von Zäuberern, Hexen und Unholden*; Behringer, *Witches and Witch-Hunts*, 173, 176.

prove. But that Gödelmann chose precisely this line of attack suggests that he understood where witch-hunting could be crucially tackled. Friedrich Spee's *Cautio criminalis* from 1631 also made torture a key target.[246] Spee acknowledged that some robust people might endure torture, and that the practice sometimes produced genuine confessions. But overall, he thought it a source of innumerable lies, and noted that not only the judges, inquisitors and commissioners, but also the assistant torturers had studied the art of interrogation, and could apply it with much agility.[247]

What was also understood was the chain mechanism, with alleged witches naming ever more companions.[248] Alber and Bidenbach observed how through confessions extracted by torture, certain women "not only falsely doom themselves but also others."[249] An aristocratic judge from Bavaria in 1590 observed that the process of a person naming other people potentially went on until the judges and executioners became too tired, and the costs too excessive, for trials to continue.[250] Or take Johann Meyfart's vivid description of witch-hunting's propensity for escalation: "Once a witchcraft trial has started, it has a tendency of not coming to a halt, but to move quickly from person to person, from sex to sex, from village to village, from town to town. Monthly, weekly, daily, hourly the number of indicated witches multiplies."[251] The more alleged witches one kills, the more alleged witches one gets, critics remarked.[252] Friedrich Spee described how at some point in a German town he met a man with a long grey beard, who had become disillusioned about witch-hunting.[253] The man had been involved in trials himself and observed how interrogators discarded all rules of proper judicial conduct. They suggested specific names to the interrogated, and then continued the torture until suspects identified sabbath accomplices under those very names. With a heavy sigh the man told Spee how his conscience at some point could no longer bear the strain of what happened before his eyes. He no longer wanted anything to do with it.

What is more, some authors explicitly identified the notion of the sabbath as an underlying cause. In his reflections on the mechanism of suspects naming accomplices, a Lutheran theologian from Lemgo, Jodocus Hocker, in 1568 said that "on what else is this most of the time based, but those fantastical dances, of which they [the suspects] recount, to the greater honor and glory of themselves, that they saw at those dances the wives of the mayor, the

---

[246] See, for instance: Spee, *Cautio Criminalis*, 25, 60–61, 67–70, 93–101, 183,.
[247] Spee, 70.
[248] Behringer, *Hexenverfolgung in Bayern*, 246.
[249] Alberum and Bidenbach, *Ein Summa etlicher Predigten von Hagel und Unholden* "Und auff sich selbst und anderen falschlich verjähen."
[250] Behringer, *Hexenverfolgung in Bayern*, 160–61.
[251] Meyfart, *Christliche Erinnerung*, 68."Wenn der Gerichtslauff oder Proceß in Hexereysachen einmal angefangen, pfleget er niemals still zu stehen, sondern eylet geschwinde von Personen zu Personen, von Geslechten zu Geslechten, von Dörffern zu Dörffern, von Städten zu Städten. Monatlich, wochentlich, täglich, stündlich wird die Zahl der angegebenen Truten vermehret."
[252] Witekind, *Christlich Bedencken und Erinnerung von Zauberey*, 136, 212.
[253] Spee, *Cautio Criminalis*, 67–68.

councilor, and the pious citizen."[254] In an attack on witch-hunting from 1585, the *Christlich bedencken und erinnerung von Zaubery* (Christian Thoughts and Recollections Concerning Witchcraft), the Calvinist professor Hermann Witekind made a similar observation. When discussing the idea of witches knowing each other from the dances, he noted that as a result of this assumption, "many an innocent woman, through malicious talk and slander, has been killed."[255] Johann Meyfart explained how "bloodthirsty and greedy judges" were eager to use a combination of torture and leading questioning to make suspects mention the names they wanted to hear.[256] Interrogators for instance asked suspects about sabbaths in the following manner: "weren't clerics, priests, preachers, monks, councilors, craftsmen, citizens and peasants present there?"[257] Inquisitors would then not stop their efforts until suspects had mentioned such people by name. Hence, Meyfart presumed that sabbath accusations were used to catch a wide variety of people, including those from higher classes.

Other contemporary insights about the workings of witch-hunting similarly preceded modern insights. Cornelius Loos pointed to long winter evenings, where peasants sat around the stove, telling each other fantastical stories. In such tales he recognized a crucial ingredient of subsequent witchcraft concepts.[258] Meyfart was aware of how official accusations arose from common gossip: "If one blows the trumpet, it resonates through the entire forest: if one accuses Anna, it resounds through the whole village, hamlet or town."[259] As soon as persecutions got going, as Spee observed, everyone avoided responsibility for what was happening. The princes said that it was the business of the civil servants and councilors, but those councilors said that they were just following orders. "Isn't that (Lord have mercy) an amusing thing?"[260] Spee furthermore addressed how the public reading of confessions during executions caused the spread of certain ideas and names. This would help explain why accusations and confessions about witchcraft could be quite similar: various people had heard the same things during those readings.[261]

Contemporary critics observed that the witchcraft doctrine was a hermetically sealed system, in which everything counted as a confirmation of witchcraft. Weyer spoke of "an inextricable labyrinth from which no way of escape, no end, can be seen."[262] Sharp-minded as usual, Spee commented that if suspects had lived indecent lives this was considered evidence for

---

[254] Hocker, *Der Teufel selbst*, 297."worauff beruhet doch solch ihr angeben die moisten zeit anders, denn auff dem fantastischen dantzen, sprechen darzu offt, zu ihrer selbst beschönung, sie haben die Burgermeisterschen, des Rhatshernn, des fromen Bürgers Weib dar, und dar mit im dantze gesehen."
[255] Witekind, *Christlich Bedencken und Erinnerung von Zauberey*, 136."dadurch manch unschuldig Weib in böß geschrey und umb ihr leben kompt."
[256] Meyfart, *Christliche Erinnerung*, 151."blutdürstige geldhungerige Richter."
[257] Meyfart, 151."Es waren zugegen Geistliche, Priester, Prediger, Mönchen, Ratsherren, Handwercker, Bürger, Bauren?"
[258] Eerden, "Cornelius Loos und die 'magia falsa,'" 150; Eerden, "Der Teufelspakt bei Petrus Binsfeld und Cornelius Loos," 61.
[259] Meyfart, *Christliche Erinnerung*, 190."Bleset einer das Horn, erschalt in den gantzen Walt: beschuldiget einer die Anna, es erschallet durch das gantze Dorff, Flecken und Stadt."
[260] Spee, *Cautio Criminalis*, 17-8."Ist das nicht (Gott erbarms) ein lustig Sache?"
[261] Spee, 98–101.
[262] Weyer, *Witches, Devils, and Doctors in the Renaissance*, 522.

their evil nature. But if they had lived seemingly decent lives this was also considered evidence, as it showed their dishonesty. If suspects reacted to accusations with fear, that demonstrated a guilty conscience. But if they did not react with fear, it demonstrated how the devil was strengthening them emotionally.[263] Regarding torture Spee wrote that:

> Titia will either confess under torture or will not confess, but whatever happens she will be a witch. If she confesses, she is a witch because she has said it herself. But if she does not confess, she is still a witch, because how otherwise could she endure the gruesome pain and torture? Whether she confesses or not, she is and remains a witch. The judges already knew that in advance, and were able to prove (whenever they wanted) that Titia was a witch.[264]

Spee further comprehended another essential mechanism: people were afraid to criticize trials due to the risk of self-incrimination – no wonder Spee published his *Cautio criminalis* anonymously.[265]

In sum, such findings from contemporary critics' texts provide confirmation for what the German instrumentalists maintain. In such early-modern discourse it was already assumed that witchcraft accusations and trials were used for a wide variety of ulterior social, political, and financial purposes. The discourse does not definitely *prove* that multifunctional instrumentalization was real, since the critics of witchcraft might have been dishonest, merely rhetorical, or possibly too cynical in misjudging the motivations of contemporaries. Still, the fact that instrumentalization was so clearly conceivable makes it more likely that there were indeed people involved who used trials to their own hidden benefit. Dillinger dismisses such contemporary suspicions as mere defense and polemics, but why not assume that the critics genuinely meant what they said? Moreover, that contemporary opponents apparently understood many aspects of how witch-hunting functioned, might also be interpreted as confirmation of the instrumentalist model. As such, it does not *prove* that the persecutors themselves possessed the same insights; perhaps critics saw things that persecutors failed to see. But what it does reveal is that certain insights were available at the time, making it more likely that proponents shared such awareness. Perhaps some witch-hunters even deliberately presented themselves as more ignorant than they actually were, because – being aware of what their critics said – they did not want to give the impression of shrewdly designing and instrumentalizing witch-hunts for their own purposes. So, importantly, these empirical findings

---

[263] Spee, *Cautio Criminalis*, 308–9.
[264] Spee, 88-9. "Titia wird entweder auff der Folter bekennen, oder wird nicht bekennen, es falle nun wie es wolle, so ist sie ein hexin: Bekennet sie, so ist sie ein Hexe, weil sie es selbst bekent hat, bekennet sie aber nicht, so ist sie dennoch eine Hexe, weil sie so grewliche Marter und Pein außgestanden hat. Mag sie deswegen bekennen oder nicht bekennen, so ist und bleibt sie dennoch ein Zaubersche. Weill dann diese Richter vorhin schon wusten, und es (wann sie nur wolten) beweissen könten, daß Titia ein Zaubersche war."
[265] Spee, 121, 128.

do not offer support for the proposed Darwinian scenario. The quotes mentioned do not point in the direction of incognizant actors who were subjected to the trickery of a culturally evolved "design without designer" that spread at the expense of its human hosts.

Limitations to critics' understanding
However, this is also the moment to begin stressing aspects of early-modern critics' discourse that actually support the Darwinian scenario. So far, I've highlighted comments showing how contemporary opponents apparently comprehended certain aspects of witch-hunting. Yet, there also seem to be limitations to their levels of understanding. One is the issue of how the notion of flight contributed to the persecutions' spread. Critics repeatedly contested their contemporaries' claims about witches' flight, and often linked this notion to belief in sabbath attendance. But what is not identified explicitly – at least not in the sources consulted for this thesis – is how the notion of flight enabled sabbaths, as well as chains of accusations over longer distances. Then there is the impact of child accusations. In none of the consulted texts was this analyzed in much detail – Bodin's sharp insights on the topic were neither adopted nor contested. The bishop of Pamplona did remark about the witch panic in the Basque country that "while there may be some element of truth in it, much is fiction, delusion and calumny which has been caused by the children and ignorant people who talked about these matters and have picked up the terms from what they have heard and from the news."[266] As we saw, Hernando de Solarte spoke briefly on the topic, and Salazar touched on children when stating that they possibly confessed in imitation of others.[267] Meyfart passingly noted that we could neither build on, nor trust, child confessions.[268] But for the rest, the topic appears remarkably absent. Even Spee, who wrote his book at a time when child accusations played a major role, did not delve into the subject.

As I pointed out earlier, critics of witch-hunting seem to have had a better understanding of the mechanism of sabbath accusations. But there are also indications to the contrary. Alber and Bidenbach did not address the sabbath at all, even though the notion played a crucial role in nearby Wiesensteig. Johann Weyer did discuss and contest the notion, but he failed to highlight how it created chains of accusations. In one instance where he referred to this connection, he did so in quite an intriguing manner. Weyer approvingly quoted the Italian physician Girolamo Cardano, who argued that sabbaths are completely fraudulent, because otherwise, "one of them [the suspects] could expose a hundred of others or even more, if as many were present (...). But they accuse only those who are known to them by sight or by rumor."[269] This passage suggests an insight into the sabbath's potential for creating large chains of accusations. But remarkably, Cardano and Weyer apparently argued that persecutors were *not* aware of that, as they did *not* press suspects to name many accomplices. On closer scrutiny, Hocker's quote also contains a

---

[266] Henningsen, *The Salazar Documents*, 192.
[267] Henningsen, 326, 332, 414.
[268] Meyfart, *Christliche Erinnerung*, 220.
[269] Weyer, *Witches, Devils, and Doctors in the Renaissance*, 504.

notable detail: he did not think that the names of highly placed women appeared on the initiative of interrogators, but because suspects mentioned them to their own greater glory. So, this presents persecutors in a rather incognizant and passive role. Spee's *Cautio criminalis* also fails to explicitly point out that the idea of witches' gatherings triggered chains of accusations. This does not mean that he did not understand it, but I found no explicit proof of understanding.

Diabolical design
Furthermore, important observations need to be made regarding how contemporary critics mostly answered the *cui bono* question, and what they thought *primarily* drove persecutions forward. True, they often pointed towards accusers and persecutors using trials for ulterior purposes. But there was a lot more to how they thought witch trials came about, and whom they believed to benefit from them. In that respect, let us again have look at the insightful contemporary comments on how the sabbath notion created havoc. Here, for instance, is Witekind's aforementioned quote in its fuller context:

> Do these witches see each other at such dances and do they know each other? Answer: if they see someone they do not see a human or physical being, but a specter, and as a result of that, many an innocent woman, through malicious talk and slander, has been killed. And I presume that the people who pretend to know where these dances occurred, and who denounce the people allegedly present there, are people who are closely aligned to the devil, and who serve him in his deceit and murder, and who get orders and payment from him, which makes them worse and more punishable than the witches.[270]

So according to Witekind the key force behind the sabbath notion and the human misery it created, was not the persecutors, but the devil. It was *he* who created the specters, and who instigated people to make false accusations.[271] "So clever and swift is Satan", Witekind said, that he created the imagination of the witches' dance to make innocent people die.[272] The argument of this Heidelberg professor fell on fertile ground, as the town physician Cornelius Pleier later approvingly plagiarized the exact quote in his own skeptical work *Malleus judicum* (The Hammer of Judges) from 1630.[273]

We saw that Jodocus Hocker also identified the sabbath as a key factor. Yet it is important to note that the passage quoted above is followed by the next observation: "as proven above,

---

[270] Witekind, *Christlich Bedencken und Erinnerung von Zauberey*, 136."Aber man sihet, sprichstu, die Hexen in solche Täntzen, und kennt sie. Antwort: So sie jemand sihet, so sihet kein Menschlich oder leiblich wesen, sonder ein Gespenst, dadurch manch unschuldig Weib in böß geschrey und umb ihr leben kompt. Und ich achte die, so die Hexen täntze wissen zu zeigen, die Personen kennen und angeben, für solche Gesellen, die auch dem Teuffel verwandt seind, im zu seinem lügen und mordt dienen, Bestallung und Sold von im darumb haben, ja auch ärger seind und sträfflicher dann die Hexen."
[271] Witekind, 189, 236.
[272] Witekind, 256."So gescheid und geschwind ist der Sathan."
[273] Pleier, *Malleus Judicum*, 34.

these dances are nothing but diabolical specters and deception, on which no reasonable judgement can be based."[274] The proof Hocker refers to among other things contains the following:

> This is the truth: that this sly fox the devil infatuates the poor women in their sleep to the extent that he creates such imaginations and illusions in them, that they honestly think that they go to wonderful meals, music, dances, and handsome young lads, with whom they briefly have intercourse, all of which is vain fantasy, deceit and trickery.[275]

The idea of witch beliefs being a diabolical manufacture was central to Hocker's account.[276] His book was named *Der Teufel selbst* (The Devil Himself), and provided an overview of Satan's trickery. Johan Meyfart similarly saw the devil as the evil genius behind witch trials, including the sabbath notion. Satan influenced people's imaginations, so that those people believed in innocent people attending witches' dances. Nobody would thus be safe anymore.[277]

In section 5.1 I observed that critics like Weyer and Spee referred to demonic forces to explain why witch-hunts occurred. This idea of the devil using witch trials to ruin humankind could be found throughout the works of contemporary critics.[278] It was a common thread in the skeptical thinking current in Württemberg, of which Alber and Bidenbach were representatives. But the argument was also used pervasively in the Calvinist Palatine, another center of resistance and skepticism.[279] For instance, while a judicial advice from 1581 did not dismiss witch trials entirely, it did stress that sabbaths were devilish fantasies, and that judges should be careful "not to be deceived and led astray by such diabolical specters."[280] When Leonhard Schug, a theologian, reflected on the mass hunts in Trier, he highlighted that the Bible proves that the devil is a deceiver who wants innocent people harmed. That was why Satan created the sabbath illusion.[281] In its conflict with Mainz, the Palatine authorities did not solely interpret the Bodenheim persecution as a shrewd political operation. They additionally argued that alleged witches' dances were diabolical dreams, and the prince of the Palatine warned that witch trials "offered the devil an unusually fine opportunity to play, and shed innocent blood."[282]

---

[274] Hocker, *Der Teufel selbst*, 297."da es doch mit dem dantzen (wie oben erweiset/) anders nichts ist, den Teuffels Gespenst und triegerey, Darauff nimer kein vernünfftiges Urtheil mag gefellet werden."
[275] Hocker, 277."Sondern dis ist die warheit, das der listige fuchs der Teuffel, die armen Weiber im schlaff dermassen bethöret, und inen solche imagination, oder einbildung ins Hertz trucken kan, das inen selbst bedünckt, sie gehen zu herlichen Malzeiten, Music spiel, dantzen, und schönen jungen Knaben, damit sie allerley kurtzweilige beywohnung treiben, Und ist doch eitel fantasey, betrug und list".
[276] Hocker, 261–316.
[277] Meyfart, *Christliche Erinnerung*, 230–35.
[278] Clark, *Thinking with Demons*, 204–8; Duni, "Doubting Witchcraft"; Flurschütz da Cruz, *Hexenbrenner, Seelenretter*, 177; Behringer, *Hexenverfolgung in Bayern*, 277–78.
[279] Schmidt, *Glaube und Skepsis*.
[280] Schmidt, 185-93."Damit er durch solches Deuffelsgespenst nit zu Abwergk gefurth und betrogen werde."
[281] Schmidt, 264–65.
[282] Schmidt, 361."daß der Teufel sonderliche guete gelegenheit hat zu spielen, undt unchuldig bluet vergiessen zu stiefften."

Countless examples can be added. A judicial advice from Ingolstadt in 1625 recommended judicial prudence in witch trials, as the procedures easily led to whole villages or towns being burned, including the innocent. Especially chain denunciations were discouraged, since they concerned "deceptions of the devil in this very hidden crime of witchcraft, making it impossible to distinguish the guilty from the innocent."[283] Regarding flights and sabbaths, Gödelmann stated that "in my simplicity, I hold them for nothing but diabolical specters, treachery and fantasy."[284] Let us also read Weyer's statement about the labyrinth (mentioned above) in its fuller context:

> Assuredly, in matters admitting of little certitude, the less cautious would not then be slipping from one single error into a thousand ones, as though trapped in an inextricable labyrinth from which no way of escape, no end, can be seen. From long experience, that crafty old weaver knows how to weave such webs skillfully.[285]

Weyer clearly thought that not the witch-hunters had contrived the labyrinth, but Satan.

Importantly, in the early modern context there was nothing special about this line of argumentation. We already saw that interpreting witchcraft beliefs as devilish trickery was an orthodox position going back to the Middle Ages.[286] The *Canon episcopi* spoke of wicked women who were diabolically deceived, and Ulrich Molitor's late fifteenth-century critique dismissed belief in visible sabbath attendants as a diabolical imagination.[287] Erik Midelfort rightly describes Molitor's views as "not the first glimmerings of an enlightened mentality but the echoes of a well-known and respected medieval tradition."[288] Moreover, invoking the devil's forces was a more common way of explaining why humans caused each other pain and suffering. Wick's news collection contained a story about a man who came home drunk and killed his pregnant wife with a knife. The illustration shows how the devil stood smiling in the door opening to enjoy the spectacle that he had helped create.[289] The religious persecution and warfare of the sixteenth century were interpreted along similar lines.[290] Likewise, diabolical stimuli were used to explain apparent supernatural effects that did not fit into religious orthodoxy. Weyer for example argued that necromancers did not receive responses from the deceased themselves, but from demons who pretended to communicate as such.[291]

---

[283] Behringer, *Hexenverfolgung in Bayern*, 325."Täuschungen des Teufels in dem sehr verborgenen Verbrechen der Zauberei Schuldige und Unschuldigen kaum zu unterscheiden."
[284] Gödelmann, *Von Zäuberern, Hexen und Unholden*, 273."achte ich nach meiner Einfalt darfür, daß es ein lauter Teuffels Gespänst, Triegerey, und Phantasey ist."
[285] Weyer, *Witches, Devils, and Doctors in the Renaissance*, 522.
[286] Duni, "Doubting Witchcraft," 205–10.
[287] Kieckhefer, *Hazards of the Dark Arts*, 142–44.
[288] Midelfort, *Witch Hunting in Southwestern Germany*, 24.
[289] Wick, *Die Wickiana*, 66.
[290] Waite, "Sixteenth-Century Religious Reform and the Witch-Hunts," 493.
[291] Weyer, *Witches, Devils, and Doctors in the Renaissance*, 127.

The idea of the devil as the arch-contriver does not play an equally important role in all critical texts. In Spee's *Cautio criminalis* it was not a central theme. Still, Spee used the idea in various ways, for instance when he argued that people responsible for trials could be witches themselves.[292] He further depicted the devil as a "jack-of-all-trades" who can play with people's senses to the extent that those people no longer see the difference between black and white, truth and falsehood.[293] This especially enabled Satan to create imaginations in old women's minds. Spee further pointed to persecutors who were themselves eventually burned as witches, which he interpreted as a devil's way of enlarging his realm.[294] Or take Alonso de Salazar, the inquisitor from the Basque country. Overall, de Salazar's writing was calm and matter of fact, and he carefully dissected the inconsistencies and improbabilities of the witch beliefs he encountered. Regarding the more absurd elements, his tone of voice was almost ironic. But on various occasions de Salazar refers to Satan as the perfidious genius behind it all.[295] About one local panic he said that "Immediately and without any effort, the Devil leaves the village in an uproar, and those unjustly incriminated exposed to condemnation and other afflictions."[296] Elsewhere he wrote that the devil created illusions in the alleged witches' minds for the "furthering of his sinister and evil purposes."[297]

This betrays an apparent ambiguity in the skeptical argument of early-modern commentators. On the one hand these critics – especially Protestant ones – said that witch-hunt proponents overestimated Satan's power at the expense of divine power. "He cannot create even a fly", Weyer said, and regarding witches he argued that "they can do nothing beyond the innate strength of human nature, even if the demon cooperate a thousand times over."[298] Yet, as soon as it came to the devil's abilities to create illusions, the same critics magnified the devil's power, turning him into the key author of witch persecution.[299] At this point their argument once again became similar to that of witch-hunt proponents. The devil was God's minister of vengeance, his executioner. So it was with divine permission that through the devil, and then through the horrors of witch trials, humans were punished for their sins.

One implication of witch persecution as a devil's tool was that the people responsible for trials had actually allowed themselves to become his marionettes. In a message to rulers, Johann Meyfart urged them to see how Satan was "amused and exalted about your Belialian tyrannies, and cheered about your grunting, scolding and snorting, which is music to his ears."[300] As mentioned above, Friedrich Förner, a proponent of witch-hunts, argued that because the devil

---

[292] Spee, *Cautio Criminalis*, 37.
[293] Spee, 179."tausent Künstler."
[294] Spee, 26.
[295] Henningsen, *The Salazar Documents*, 351, 404.
[296] Henningsen, 280.
[297] Henningsen, 314.
[298] Weyer, *Witches, Devils, and Doctors in the Renaissance*, 85.
[299] Eerden, "Cornelius Loos und die 'magia falsa,'" 156–58.
[300] Meyfart, *Christliche Erinnerung*, 255."belüstiget und erfreuet sich an eueren Belialischen Tyrannyen, und jauchtzet euer schnarchen, schelten und schnauben, auff das es in seinen Ohren lieblich ineinander klinge."

was angered by the expulsion of Protestants, he now tried to win Catholics over by seducing people to commit the sin of witchcraft. Remarkably, Cornelius Loos, a critic, used almost exactly the same argument, but then the other way around. Loos thought that Satan was so dismayed by the fact that many Catholics had escaped the abyss of Protestantism that he now used superstitious witch belief as an alternative trap.[301] In places where Catholics had once lived in harmony, Satan incited the discord of witch trials, and the persecutors had been foolish enough to let themselves be exploited for that purpose. The imaginary danger of witchcraft distracted Catholics from real dangers, like Protestant heresies.

Satan exerted his influence by interfering in many of the trials' details. He made people spit up nails, or made them speak in strange voices, so that others would interpret that as witchcraft.[302] Gödelmann considered the water ordeal a diabolical invention.[303] Johann Meyart presented torture as Satan's shrewd creation. After all, being a master of lies the devil loved all the falsehoods that painful questioning elicited.[304] God had created the human body in all its splendor and magnificence, and wanted it to remain intact. But that made it all the more attractive for Satan to have it harmed, rejoicing in the destruction of bodies that torturing brought about. Meyfart said that interrogators had even surpassed demons in their ability to ruin the human body.[305] Another diabolical trick, as we have seen, was to make people honestly believe that they were diabolical witches. The devil had a better understanding of bodily humors than any physicist, so he could move the humors in order to alter people's state of mind.[306] Being "a subtle and devious spirit, an artist skilled through long experience", Meyfart said, Satan knew how to beguile the senses and confuse people's thoughts.[307] Demented and melancholic old women with instable minds, who lacked proper Christian faith, were particularly vulnerable.[308] During their sleep demons made them dream about dances, eating, drinking, sex with demons, and the killing of children. Also, as Gödelmann argued, when such women sat down "in a state of great sorrow and melancholia they might easily be captured by the devil's swift rhetoric."[309] Satan further had an ingenious way of making gullible women think that they performed real magic: the devil knew when divinely ordained hailstorms were on their way, so he quickly told

---

[301] Eerden, "Cornelius Loos und die 'magia falsa'"; Waite, *Eradicating the Devil's Minions*, 51; Franz, "Antonius Hovaeus, Cornelius Loos und Friedrich Spee," 127.
[302] Pleier, *Malleus Judicum*, 17–18; Weyer, *Witches, Devils, and Doctors in the Renaissance*, 290-1–301.
[303] Gödelmann, *Von Zäuberern, Hexen und Unholden*, 319–38; Levack, *The Witch-Hunt in Early Modern Europe*, 236.
[304] Meyfart, *Christliche Erinnerung*, 49–54, 98, 136–53, 166.
[305] Meyfart, 137.
[306] Hocker, *Der Teufel selbst*, 278, 294; Pleier, *Malleus Judicum*, 54; Weyer, *Witches, Devils, and Doctors in the Renaissance*, 183–88.
[307] Meyfart, *Christliche Erinnerung*, 61, 226."der Teufel ein subtiler geist ist, und verschlagener, durch lange ubung geschickter bewehrter Künstler".
[308] Witekind, *Christlich Bedencken und Erinnerung von Zauberey*, 20–22, 95.
[309] Gödelmann, *Von Zäuberern, Hexen und Unholden*, 278-9."in so grosser sorg vnd schermut sitzen, auch durch deß Teuffels geschwinde Rhetorica eingenommen werden."

these women to make a storm.[310] When the hailstorm then appeared, these women mistakenly thought that they were the ones to have magically caused it. The underlying diabolical rationale was clear: due to their genuine belief such women more easily confessed, thereby giving rise to persecution.

In consequence, contemporary critics did not necessarily consider alleged witches innocent. In a skeptical treatise from 1583, *Deß Teuffels Nebelkappen* (The Devil's Hoodwink), the author Paulus Frisius portrayed witch trials as a big mistake, built upon diabolical deception. But still, he spoke of women who themselves believed to be witches as hell whores who deserved nothing but death.[311] Hocker, Molitor, or Alber and Bidembach similarly argued that the mere attempt to be a witch already warranted the death penalty.[312] Others were more lenient.[313] Pleier maintained that a lack of proper faith did not warrant the death penalty. After all, many rulers also let Jews live in their midst, and eventually it was up to God to decide.[314] Especially Witekind showed compassion, proposing to reconvert the poor wretches.[315] He additionally argued that men should be nicer to women, as it would make them less sad and melancholic, leaving the devil fewer opportunities of playing with their minds. This all further illustrates that there was no sharp distinction between "believers" and "skeptics", and that we should instead see the comments of contemporaries as belonging to a spectrum of complex and multifaceted viewpoints.

There was still another method with which the devil was thought to play with people's minds: hallucinogens.[316] Well-versed in physics as he was Satan instructed the women on how to make potions with substances like wild celery, aconite, hemlock, soporific nightshade, and baby fat. He further told them to anoint themselves and their broomsticks. As soon as the substances then entered the bodies through their skins, or through their vaginas after they had put the broomstick between their legs, the women fell into a deep sleep full of dreams. "They then believe that they will soon fly up the chimney and roam far and wide through the air to dances, fine banquets, sexual encounters, and delightful spectacles", Weyer said.[317] That such dreaming really occurred, Pleier maintained, could be learned through experience.[318] He told a story about two imprisoned alleged witches who smeared themselves with an unguent, and then fell into a

---

[310] Alberum and Bidenbach, *Ein Summa etlicher Predigten von Hagel und Unholden*; Midelfort, *Witch Hunting in Southwestern Germany*, 45; Kieckhefer, *Hazards of the Dark Arts*, 135–36; Witekind, *Christlich Bedencken und Erinnerung von Zauberey*, 103.
[311] Frisium, *Deß Teuffels Nebelkappen*, Dritten punct."Hollhur."
[312] Alberum and Bidenbach, *Ein Summa etlicher Predigten von Hagel und Unholden*; Ahrent-Schulte, "Lauter falscher Wahn und starke Einbildung," 95; Kieckhefer, *Hazards of the Dark Arts*, 151.
[313] Weyer, *Witches, Devils, and Doctors in the Renaissance*; Eerden, "Der Teufelspakt bei Petrus Binsfeld und Cornelius Loos," 60.
[314] Pleier, *Malleus Judicum*, 57–59.
[315] Witekind, *Christlich Bedencken und Erinnerung von Zauberey*, 164, 186, 202–6, 215, 239–44.
[316] Hocker, *Der Teufel selbst*, 278; Weyer, *Witches, Devils, and Doctors in the Renaissance*, 225–26; Pleier, *Malleus Judicum*, 30–31; Heemskerck, *Batavische Arcadia*, 79–84.
[317] Weyer, *Witches, Devils, and Doctors in the Renaissance*, 225.
[318] Pleier, *Malleus Judicum*, 30–32.

deep sleep. One observer stayed awake and saw that they did not move. But when the women woke up they recalled the various places they had been to, and what they did there.

This topic of alleged drug use has intrigued many modern scholars.[319] Jules Michelet maintained that alleged witches were herb experts who provided their communities with hallucinogens, so as to help them forget their misery. It was precisely such herbal knowledge that authorities wanted to destroy. It has also been pointed out that certain nightshade plants, like black henbane, mandrake, and thorn apple were available at the time, and can indeed induce hallucinations. The German researcher Gustav Schenk smoked henbane seeds and felt himself becoming weak, having perceptions of flight and vivid scenes.[320] Edward Bever – the historian who is always eager to draw attention to realities underlying witchcraft beliefs – more recently reinvestigated the role of drugs, claiming that "It was this wild and uncontrollable power that so scared the religious and secular authorities and upright citizens."[321] Most current witchcraft experts have little time for this hallucinatory dimension, though.[322] While the use of such drugs is considered theoretically possible, and may have indeed induced specific experiences, it is thought difficult to prove and overall unlikely to have played a major role. Drugs like black henbane or thorn apple are quite poisonous, and witches' recipes of the time contained many inert ingredients like bat's blood and soot. Dillinger further states that the trials' sources hardly ever confirm that the accused had specific knowledge of medical plants and hallucinogens.

The possible use of drugs is a topic in its own right, and Bever's account may not be the last word on the matter. But what is particularly relevant here is that to early modern commentators, drugs were yet another of Satan's purported ways of creating honest belief in the suspects' minds. Present-day historians allow some room for the interrogated having had a sincere belief in their own culpability.[323] Dramatic torture sessions may have shaped false memories, or caused victims to reinterpret earlier dreams, traumas, or feelings of guilt in the light of diabolical witchcraft. However, there is a notable difference between the historians of today and early-modern witchcraft critics: the former normally treat torture as the essential cause of confessions, while the latter put more emphasis on the suspects' sincere belief, supposedly influenced by Satan.

Genuine belief and evil motivation as diabolical instruments

---

[319] van Winter, "Die giftigen Schwestern der Kartoffelplanze und ihr Verwendung im Mittelalter," 364–66; Bever, *The Realities of Witchcraft*, 129–50; Duerr, *Traumzeit*; Sebald, *Witch-Children*; Michelet, *La Sorcière*; Kühlen, *Zur Geschichte der Schmerz-Schlaf- und Betäubungsmittel*, 314–74.
[320] Bever, *The Realities of Witchcraft*, 145.
[321] Bever, 150.
[322] Voltmer, *Hexen. Wissen was stimmt*, 104–9; Goodare, *The European Witch-Hunt*, 145; Levack, *The Witch-Hunt in Early Modern Europe*, 44; Dillinger, *Hexen und Magie*, 2018, 55–56; Briggs, *Witches & Neighbours*, 56; Meurger, "Plantes à illusion."
[323] Goodare, *The European Witch-Hunt*, 210–14, 307.

Genuine belief was also often thought to motivate the actors responsible for persecution, and again the devil was potentially involved.[324] What educated contemporaries regarded as the simple-minded common rabble was said to be full of delusional and fantastical stories and beliefs.[325] Hocker warned judges never to listen to the "reckless and capricious mob", as that would offer the devil further opportunities to wreak havoc on the innocent.[326] Hernando de Solarte described how a "whole district falls prey to fear" and in one of the chief perpetrators of a hunt he saw a man who "was totally convinced". Regarding ministers of justice he noted that "if they have committed some excesses in the course of the investigation their motive was in all probability that of holy zeal."[327] As mentioned above, Spee described judges of witch trials as "greedy and vicious", but he more often thought them clumsy, careless and ignorant.[328] Spee called superstition and unreasonableness key causes of trials, and in an analysis of how suggestive questioning created apparently consistent confessions, he observed that this made judges and commissioners honestly think that they had "seized the truth with both hands."[329] Meyfart argued that Satan could even trick wise and soft-hearted people. He knew how to arouse latent evil inclinations, and in the case of witch persecutors this resulted in a diabolical frenzy.[330] These people had become so "deluded and manipulated by the devil these days that they can no longer be hired by governments."[331] So within the contemporary framework there was not necessarily a contradiction between evil ulterior motives and false beliefs manufactured by the devil. Satan used and enhanced people's evil inclinations to motivate them for witch-hunting, and so to bring about human misery.[332]

There was nothing special about De Solarte attributing "holy zeal" to persecutors, as the role of witch-hunting in a broader debate about the secular use of religion illustrates. That religion could be instrumentalized for social or political ends was at the time a widely discussed topic.[333] Such secularism especially came to be associated with the work of Niccolò Machiavelli. The position of this Italian thinker, however, outraged many contemporaries. Machiavelli disregarded the veracity of religious doctrines, and in the eyes of his opponents, that was playing with religion. After all, Christian doctrines should be endorsed not because they are useful, but because they are true. So, an accusation of Machiavellianism, or political motives, became a serious allegation in early modern discourse. The trope also entered the debate over witch trials, but importantly, it was not so much the witch-hunt supporters who were associated with

---

[324] Ahrent-Schulte, "Lauter falscher Wahn und starke Einbildung," 96.
[325] Alberum and Bidenbach, *Ein Summa etlicher Predigten von Hagel und Unholden*; Spee, *Cautio Criminalis*, 2.
[326] Hocker, *Der Teufel selbst*, 296."leichtfertigen, wankelmütigen Pöbel".
[327] Henningsen, *The Salazar Documents*, 156, 158, 168.
[328] Spee, *Cautio Criminalis*, 300.
[329] Spee, 2, 70."alß ob sie Warheit selbst mit beyden Händen ergriffen hetten."
[330] Meyfart, *Christliche Erinnerung*, 132; Lehmann, "Johann Matthäus Meyfart warnt hexenverfolgende Obrigkeiten," 227.
[331] Meyfart, *Christliche Erinnerung*, 257."seyn heutiges Tages so verschmitzet, und von dem Satan verkünsteliret, daß sie sich nicht von den Obrigkeiten bestellen lassen."
[332] Hocker, *Der Teufel selbst*, 296.
[333] Clark, "Feigned dieties, pretended conferences, imaginary apparitions."

Machiavellianism.[334] Rather, it was their opponents who were framed as "politici", as "cold political Christians" who placed earthly concerns above Christian ideals.[335] The trials' advocates on the other hand were more likely to be put in the camp of the "zelanti", the zealots, or religious fanatics, who pursued holy goals irrespective of secular consequences.[336] Over the course of the seventeenth century, witch-hunting did more often come to be associated with crude political agendas.[337] In 1671 the English author John Wagstaffe wrote about Catholic persecutors "that in seeking out Witches, in tormenting and putting them to death, they did at once gratifie, as well the ambition and usurped Power of their Lord the Pope, as their own insatiable covetousness, and thirst after other mens goods."[338] Yet, due to its late date – Wagstaffe spoke about trials that were already quite distant history – and his anti-papist agenda, we need to question whether these observations were based on accurate understanding of actual trials.

Contemporaries also had good reasons for not interpreting hunts in primarily Machiavellian terms, as they already saw how persecution often *harmed* secular interests. Social and political consequences could be dramatic, even for the people responsible for trials. Spee stressed that chains of accusations, once set in motion, became difficult to stop and eventually even killed people who took initiative in the first place.[339] "It is only when they themselves have seen and learned that they were denounced, and then imprisoned, that they finally open their eyes, and bemoan their land, but only when it is already too late."[340] Spee had little compassion though, since their own poisonous tongues had incited the troubles in the first place. Regarding authorities accountable for trials, he wrote that "through this burning they devastate their lands more than any war has ever done, and yet they achieved nothing with it, which should make us weep bloody tears."[341] Meyfart similarly noted that persecutions were detrimental to rulers' interests, warning them about the diabolical dynamics that witch trials brought about:

> You will find hatred of rabble against rabble, hatred of the rabble against the rabble. You will find the envy of the poor against the rich, of craftsmen against scholars, of house owners against officials, of the evil against the noble. You will find fury, anger and quarrel

---

[334] Clark; Behringer, *Hexenverfolgung in Bayern*, 246–60; Behringer, *Witches and Witch-Hunts*, 122, 175–77; Dillinger, "The Political Aspects of the German Witch Hunts," 76.
[335] Behringer, *Hexenverfolgung in Bayern*, 250, 251, 310."kalte und politische Christen"; Behringer, *Witches and Witch-Hunts*, 177; Clark, "Feigned dieties, pretended conferences, imaginary apparitions," 280–81.
[336] Behringer, *Hexenverfolgung in Bayern*, 249–50; Behringer, *Witches and Witch-Hunts*, 174–76.
[337] Clark, "Feigned dieties, pretended conferences, imaginary apparitions."
[338] Wagstaffe, *The Question of Witchcraft Debated*, 62.
[339] Spee, *Cautio Criminalis*, 37, 80, 98, 112–13.
[340] Spee, 98."Wann die selbe nun hernach sehen unnd vernehmen müssen, das sie auch besagt seind, unnd darauff gefangen werden, alßdann thun sie erst die Augen auff, und beweinen ihr Landt, aber zu späthe, sintemahlen je hefftiger sie vormahls gegen die Zauberschen gewesen, ja ärger hält man sie alßdann, alß welche under einem solchen Eyffer, ihre Bubenstück hatten vermänteln wollen."
[341] Spee, 7."Sie verwüsten durch diß Brennen ihre Länder mehr alß je einig Krieg gethan hat, und haben doch nichts damit außgerichtet, welches man billig mit blutigen Thränen beweinen solte."

in alleys and in streets, calumny and slander in courtyards and in castles, unrest and riot in churches and in schools.[342]

As mentioned before, contemporaries already remarked that witch trials could have an escalating dynamics, and again it was thought that the devil had a hand in that. Witekind argued that the horrifying prison conditions brought female suspects to an even worse state of confusion, making them more susceptible to the devil's pursuits.[343] Confessions thus inflated even further. Furthermore, when Satan observed that his attempts at creating witch trials were successful he doubled his efforts. On the other hand, when he noted that the burning stopped, he lost confidence that people would fall for his tricks and so he gave up.[344] Critics additionally warned that the negative consequences of persecutions extended into the afterlife.[345] Witekind urged people to listen to their hearts, and to see what irresponsible and unchristian things witch-hunts were. "Killing persons is a big thing", he said, so doing that without proper evidence was a grave sin, sure to provoke God's wrath.[346] Meyfart reminded the people responsible for trials that the end of times was near, and that their unspeakable crimes severely jeopardized their own salvation.[347] His message was clear: do not let yourself be fooled by the devil.

That both sides in the debate used remarkably similar supernatural arguments could make things puzzling for contemporaries. On both sides there were people who for instance argued that certain sabbaths and flights were real while others were imaginary.[348] Take Witekind and Pleier, who accepted that the devil transported witches through the air, but only thought it unusual.[349] Especially the idea that the devil deceived the senses could give discussions an arbitrary twist. The French literary scholar Marianne Closson remarks that "great confusion reigned: how could one know the true nature of diabolical illusion? The lack of a firm answer to this question fueled the fear of being oneself a victim of the devil's deceptions."[350] Whether people considered something real or illusory could eventually just depend on what seemed most convenient or plausible. The "trump card of demonology" is what Dillinger calls the idea of diabolical deception: it could be invoked to neutralize any ostensible phenomenon that appeared

---

[342] Meyfart, *Christliche Erinnerung*, 57."Du würdest finden Hader des Pöbels gegen dem Pöbel. Du würdest finden Neid des Armen wider den Reichen, des Handwerckers gegen den Gelehrten, des Haußgesessenen gegen die Beampten, des Slechten wider die Edlen. Du würdest finden Zorn, Zorn und Zanck in Gassen und Strassen: Affterreden und Ohrenblasen in Höffen und Schlössern, Auffblehen und Auffruhr in Kirchen und Schulen."
[343] Witekind, *Christlich Bedencken und Erinnerung von Zauberey*, 148.
[344] Witekind, 214.
[345] Hocker, *Der Teufel selbst*, 297; Pleier, *Malleus Judicum*, 61–70; Spee, *Cautio Criminalis*, 49, 89, 103.
[346] Witekind, *Christlich Bedencken und Erinnerung von Zauberey*, 251."menschen tödten ist eine grosse sach."
[347] Lehmann, "Johann Matthäus Meyfart warnt hexenverfolgende Obrigkeiten"; Meyfart, *Christliche Erinnerung*, 266.
[348] Clark, *Thinking with Demons*, 209.
[349] Witekind, *Christlich Bedencken und Erinnerung von Zauberey*, 129; Pleier, *Malleus Judicum*, 30.
[350] Closson, *L'imaginaire démoniaque en France (1550-1650)*, 32."grande confusion règne : comment savoir en effet la véritable nature de l'illusion diabolique ? L'absence de réponse ferme à cette question attise la peur d'être soi-même victime des tromperies du diable."

unfitting.³⁵¹ So, we might think of the debate as occurring between two "bodies" of thought, possessing similar "immune systems", that were both able to quickly disarm any attack.

Yet, for both camps this arbitrariness was not only a strength, but also a weakness. We saw that proponents argued that witches were seemingly in bed at night, while the real people were feasting at the sabbath. But as critics remarked: why not presume that the real people were in bed while the ones feasting were the illusory ones?³⁵² Authors like Kramer, Daneau or Rémy accepted that beliefs in flights were sometimes deceptive.³⁵³ But if this was so, critics wondered, how could they be so sure that their other claims were not deceptive?³⁵⁴ In their turn, the proponents dissected similar weaknesses in the critical arguments. Weyer, like others, poked fun at apparently crazy supernatural beliefs, like old witches being very powerful. But Bodin retorted that Weyer's own argument was full of similar supernatural occurrences.³⁵⁵ "Weyer, who wants to discuss metaphysics as a physicist, confesses in a thousand instances in his book that the demons, who are intelligent spirits, enter people's bodies."³⁵⁶ Schultheis seized the obvious opportunity of dismissing the critics as being themselves fatally deceived by Satan.³⁵⁷ Yet, despite this apparently level playing field, we may today still appreciate the moral and intellectual validity of one of the critics' key arguments: in case of uncertainty one should not burn people.

Interpretative difficulties

One difficulty in interpreting such claims about the supernatural is the extent to which people meant what they said. Stuart Clark is amongst those most determined about proponents and opponents sharing the same demonological worldview, but even Clark considers the option that Spee was merely strategic, or ironic, in stating that witch-hunters were themselves witches.³⁵⁸ Regarding De Salazar, the expert Gustav Henningsen thinks that he was not really interested in demonology, and only invoked diabolical delusions to take the witch-hunters down on their own turf.³⁵⁹ But once again we should be careful when reading things in texts that the texts themselves do not explicitly say. Take De Salazar. The expert Lu Ann Homza more recently argued that his viewpoints were entirely traditional, demonstrating obedience towards authority.³⁶⁰ De Salazar's work contains no assertions that demons do not exist, and he advocated a fierce inquisition of real heresy and apostasy. So, there are no valid reasons to assume that De Salazar was really a proto-enlightened skeptic. Religious stridency can also be found amongst other

---

³⁵¹ Dillinger, *Hexen und Magie*, 2018, 45."Joker der Dämonologie."
³⁵² Gödelmann, *Von Zäuberern, Hexen und Unholden*, 209; Witekind, *Christlich Bedencken und Erinnerung von Zauberey*, 170.
³⁵³ Daneau, *Les Sorciers*, 88–89; Rémy, *Demonolatry*, 51; Institoris, *The Hammer of Witches*, 282.
³⁵⁴ Spee, *Cautio Criminalis*, 173–88.
³⁵⁵ Bodin, *De la démonomanie des sorciers*, 473, 477.
³⁵⁶ Bodin, 473."Wier, qui veut dispúter de la Metaphysique en phisicien, confesse en mille endroits de ses livres que les Diables, qui sont formes intelligibles, entrent au corps des hommes."
³⁵⁷ Schultheis, *Eine Außführliche Instruction*, 5–6, 227–28, 458.
³⁵⁸ Clark, "Glaube und Skepsis in der deutschen Hexenliteratur," 19; Clark, *Thinking with Demons*, 207.
³⁵⁹ Henningsen, *The Salazar Documents*, 94–95.
³⁶⁰ Homza, "An Expert Lawyer and Reluctant Demonologist: Alonso de Salazar Frías, Spanish Inquisitor."

critics, like Loos and Spee, who favored the persecution of Protestants, or Witekind and Pleier, who vehemently denounced dancing as a diabolical sin.[361] We earlier learned that Bodin thought that he received help from a spirit, but interestingly, so did Weyer.[362] The latter claimed that his merchant family was protected by a spirit, who for instance made announcements when potential customers were close by. Weyer claimed to have observed one of these announcements himself. To conclude, it was quite obvious and plausible to think that demonic or angelic interferences were real. So, the burden of proof today remains on those who claim that early modern critics did not mean what they said.

All this, of course, bears upon the instrumentalization debate. On the one hand, the German instrumentalists were right to point to contemporary opponents of witchcraft who too assumed that witchcraft accusations and trials were used for various hidden ends. While these findings do not *prove* the instrumentalist interpretation, they do offer a fine indication for it. However, thorough engagement with the sources reveals that this was only a limited part of the story. Contemporary suspicions about ulterior motives then dwindle in comparison to the supernatural dimension of diabolical trickery. Much of what contemporary critics said is more in line with what the "genuine belief historians" maintain today. The people responsible for witch-hunting were not so much thought of as carefully weighing their chances on how to strategically use trials to their own hidden advantage. Already at the time they were also described as zealots, full of sincere belief, while the trials' consequences were already considered harmful, even for these people themselves. The instrumentalists are cherry-picking the sources: they do not, or hardly, address the supernatural aspects, so important to critics of the time.[363] Hence, the instrumentalist model does not sufficiently address the impact of magical and religious thought. "Disbelief in belief", is what the philosopher Maarten Boudry calls this outlook.[364] For many western scholars today, the fervent religiosity of their ancestors has become a vague and unreal memory. It makes the forces of dogma and sacred belief, and how they really motivate human behavior, an underestimated factor.

However, in a different way the early-modern critics *did* see witch-hunting as a huge case of instrumentalization. But it was not the accusers or persecutors who were primarily thought to instrumentalize witch trials. In fact, the actors in the witch-hunting events were trapped and exploited by something beyond themselves. They operated as the puppets of an invisible puppeteer, to their own detriment. Nor were these actors the ones to shrewdly think through the incendiary details that made witch persecutions so big, like torture or the sabbath. The alleged key creator and beneficiary behind witch-hunting's intelligent design was Satan. This

---

[361] Voltmer, "Demonology and Anti-Demonology," 160; Schmidt, *Glaube und Skepsis*, 234; Pleier, *Malleus Judicum*, 44, 110; Witekind, *Christlich Bedencken und Erinnerung von Zauberey*, 148.
[362] Valente, "'Against the Devil, the Sublte and Cunning Enemy,'" 104–5.
[363] For a rather one-sided view on Cornelius Loos, see for instance: Voltmer, "Demonology and Anti-Demonology," 158; Voltmer, "Von der besonderen Alchimie, aus Menschenblut Gold zu machen"; For a one-sided view on Spee, so for instance: Rummel, "So mögte auch eine darzu kommen, so mich belädiget"; Rummel, "Das 'ungestüme Umherlaufen der Untertanen'".
[364] Boudry, *Illusies voor gevorderden*, 264; Boudry and Coyne, "Disbelief in Belief."

"subtle and devious spirit", "sly fox", "crafty old weaver", and "jack-of-all-trades" manufactured and instrumentalized trials to *his* own benefit. Satan shrewdly knew how to use aspects of the environment, like people's gullibility, instable old women, hallucinogens, the potential of torture, evil inclinations, or the randomness of chain accusations, to set people against each other and to bring about humanity's ruin and damnation. So, *this* was how the critics primarily answered the *cui bono* question.

These early-modern claims are neither very much in line with the German instrumentalist model, nor with what the genuine belief historians maintain. Yet, in some striking regards they do bear an eerie resemblance to the proposals made here. In this dissertation it is likewise argued that the witch-hunt system was a design, albeit not one designed by human actors. It is furthermore assumed that there was a hidden beneficiary involved, with purposes of its own. This "agency" tricked people to make them do things that greatly harmed these people's neighbors, their communities, and in many cases even these people themselves. But the hidden "agency" was not Satan, and neither was the ruin of humankind its ultimate goal. Instead, it was the cultural phenomenon of witch-hunting that benefited, and its underlying purpose was blind reproduction. Certainly, the analyses of contemporary critics cannot *prove* that these Darwinian proposals are warranted, but they do offer a strong indication for it. Many of the empirical findings presented here are surprisingly congruent with the idea of a virus-like cultural entity that spread at the expense of its human hosts. This "viral" analogy will now be spelled out in more detail.

7.4 "Viral" hunts?

"As the Alps represented the product of tectonic activity, so too was this a region of cultural tectonics, where the interaction of cultures was reflected in this remarkable conjunction of writing".[365] This is how Richard Kieckhefer describes the appearance of the cumulative concept of witchcraft in a linguistically splintered area. He is not the only witchcraft historian to resort to a geological comparison. Jürgen Michael Schmidt notes how a fifteenth-century trial in Heidelberg turned the city into "a small epicenter with a certain power of its own", while Walter Rummel sees late sixteenth-century Trier as a "regional epicenter."[366] Robin Briggs observes that "The great majority of accusations matures slowly, by a process of accretion over time", while Katrin Moeller remarks how criticisms of trials created "processes of erosion".[367]

Comparisons are also made with other physical phenomena. "The fear of witchcraft spread like a wildfire in the whole region", Iris Gareis writes about early-seventeenth-century

---

[365] Richard Kieckhefer, "The First Wave of Trials," 168.
[366] Schmidt, *Glaube und Skepsis*, 48."kleinen Epizentrum mit einer gewissen eigenen Kraft"; Rummel, "Phasen Und Träger Kurtrierischer Und Sponheimischer Hexenvervolgungen," 288.
[367] Briggs, *The Witches of Lorraine*, 377; Moeller, *Dass Willkür über Recht ginge*, 482."Erosionsprozesse."

Basque country.[368] Rita Voltmer and Karl Weisenstein speak of a "spark" of accusations that made witch-hunting disperse from place to place.[369] Or take Johan Otten, who describes the spread of trials in the Peel region as follows: "In the Summer of 1595 the fire moved from Cranendonck via Leend-Heeze-Geldrop around the Strabrecht moor, causing heavy damage in Mierlo and Lierop, to get stuck in Asten, thinning out towards Someren".[370] Regarding people's motivations Voltmer thinks that "pious religious beliefs, profane functionality, and political calculation melted with one another", while Schmidt argues that early Alpine trials resulted from a "melting of witch trials and heresy trials".[371] Later on, in 1446, the phenomenon moved from Switzerland straight to Heidelberg "like a bolt of lightning".[372] Others look for comparisons in colder spheres. Günther Dippold remarks how through the sabbath belief one trial "could develop into a veritable avalanche of persecution."[373] Britta Gehm speaks of a "snowball-like extension", and Julian Goodare refers to the witchcraft concept as "a snowball rolling downhill, gathering new layers and becoming larger".[374] Probably the most common physical comparison – also used many times here – is between the simultaneous occurrence of trials and the phenomenon of "waves".[375]

What should we make of such comparisons? Are they just stylistic metaphors without scientific import, or do they reveal deeper similarities between witch-hunting and physical nature? The question lies beyond the scope of this dissertation. Yet, one analogy that is more common than any *does* matter here: epidemic disease.[376] Already in 1650 the French scholar Gabriel Naudé said that in the fifteenth century the land of Artois had been "infected by the depraved imagination concerning the sabbath", while his compatriot Nicolas Malebranche in 1675 used witch beliefs as an example of "contagious communication and powerful imaginations."[377] This philosopher argued that people's thirst for scary stories led to the accumulation of tall tales about

---

[368] Gareis, "Kinder in Hexenverfolgungen des französischen und spanischen Baskenlandes," 107."Vielmehr verbreitete die Hexenangst wie ein Lauffeuer in der gesamten Region."
[369] Voltmer and Weisenstein, *Das Hexenregister des Claudius Musiel*, 33.
[370] Otten, *Duivelskwartier*, 12."In de zomer van 1595 trekt het vuur vanuit Cranendonck via Leend-Heeze-Geldrop met de klok mee om de Strabrechte Heide, richt zware schade aan in Mierlo en Lierop, loopt vast in Asten en kent een uitloop naar Someren".
[371] Voltmer, "Herren und Hexen," 136."Sich fromm glaubende Religiösität, profane Funktionalität und politischen Kalkül verschmolzen miteinander"; Schmidt, *Glaube und Skepsis*, 11."die Verschmelzung von Zauberei- und Ketzerprozeß.
[372] Schmidt, *Glaube und Skepsis*, 48."einem Blitzstrahl gleich."
[373] Dippold, "Hexereiprozesse Im Hochstift Bamberg," 229."konnte sich zu einer wahren Lawine der Verfolgung entwickeln."
[374] Gehm, *Die Hexenverfolgung im Hochstift Bamberg*, 230."schneeballartigen Ausweitung"; Goodare, *The European Witch-Hunt*, 66.
[375] Blauert, *Frühe Hexenverfolgungen*, 17; Behringer, *Hexenverfolgung in Bayern*, 128; Durrant, *Witchcraft, Gender, and Society in Early Modern Germany*, 4; Briggs, "Witchcraft and the Local Communities," 201.
[376] For some examples, see: Mackay, *Memoirs of Extraordinary Popular Delusions and the Madness of Crowds*, 158; Soldan and Heppe, *Geschichte der Hexenprozesse*, 4; Hansen, *Zauberwahn, Inquisition und Hexenproceß im Mittelalter*, 3; Thomas, *Religion and the Decline of Magic*, 547; Behringer, *Hexenverfolgung in Bayern*, 128; Walz, "Der unreine und der schuldige Sündenbock," 197; Hutton, *The Witch*, 41.
[377] Naudé, *Iugement de Tout Ce Qui a Esté Imprimé Contre Le Cardinal Mazarin*, 320.'le pays d'Artois fut infecté de ces imaginations dépravées touchant le sabbat"; Malebranche, *Recherche de la vérité*, I:278-338."De la communication contagieuse des imaginations fortes."

witchcraft, while the genuine belief in witches "strengthens itself" through the burnings.[378] More recently, Wolfgang Behringer observed that "The implementation of witchcraft persecutions spread contagiously, but any politically coordinated effort with that direct intent was conspicuously lacking." [379] Elsewhere he writes that Petrus Canisius, being a supporter of exorcisms and witch-hunting, "presumably infected a whole generation of young Jesuits with these ideas."[380] Voltmer speaks of lists of accomplices that could turn "endemic" trials into "epidemic" ones, and Johannes Dillinger notes that "At the end of the 1620s, as before in the 1590s, the population of the Dreiherrischen became 'infected' by the witch-hunts of the electoral state of Trier." [381] Briggs designates the kind of huge persecution that killed hundreds as "a parasitic one", and when describing how Ellwangen provided names of accomplices to other towns, Erik Midelfort notes that "In this way the germ of witch-hunting could pass from town to town very much like an epidemic."[382] The English historian Diarmaid MacCulloch explores the analogy in greatest detail:

> The chronology and geography are as episodic and developmental as the gradual spread of a slowly incubating disease. After initial symptoms in early fifteenth century Switzerland, there was a break-out of active persecutions in central Europe in the mid-sixteenth century, then occasional outbreaks in Protestant England, sometimes severe but always marginal to mainland pathology; Ireland and the Catholic Iberian peninsula remained islands of virtual immunity, and Dutch Protestants made an early recovery. The pathology intensified in central Europe, especially among Catholics; it also spread outwards to produce some intense late persecutions in Protestant Scotland from the 1590s, and the famous but short-lived and wholly isolated repetition of Protestant English paranoia in Salem, Massachusetts, in 1692, which led to nineteen deaths.[383]

Taking the similarities seriously
The similarities between pathogens and the witch-hunting phenomenon are indeed striking. Sudden outbursts of witch persecution occurred resembling the "outbreaks" of contagious disease. Through the spread of fear, and the naming of accomplices, witch trials in one place could then "infect" other places, leaving many casualties in their wake. MacCulloch is also onto something in drawing a parallel to incubation. People can carry a pathogen and infect others without outwardly showing symptoms of disease. This looks vaguely similar to the relationship between the cumulative concept of witchcraft and the practice of witch-hunting: people often

---

[378] Malebranche, *Recherche de la vérité*, I:333."cette croyance se fortifie."
[379] Behringer, "Witchcraft Studies in Austria, Germany and Switzerland," 84.
[380] Behringer, "Canisius, St. Peter (1521-1597)."
[381] Voltmer, "Herren und Hexen," 16; Dillinger, *Böse Leute*, 382."Am Ende der 1620er wie zuvor in den 1590er Jahren ließ sich die Bevölkerung des Dreiherrischen von den Hexenverfolgungen in Kurtrier sich ‚anstecken' ".
[382] Briggs, *Witches & Neighbours*, 402; Midelfort, *Witch Hunting in Southwestern Germany*, 106.
[383] MacCulloch, *Reformation*, 563.

carried the concept in their minds without directly instigating trials. For instance, when the prince-provost Von Westerstetten left Ellwangen to take a position as prince-bishop of Eichstätt, it was not immediately visible from the outside that within his brain cells resided an extremely lethal "strain" of witch beliefs that later helped trigger the hunt of Eichstätt that killed hundreds. Epidemiology is also familiar with the concept of "superspreaders"; unusually contagious people who contaminate many others. Along the lines of Behringer we might think of Petrus Canisius as a case in point. Canisius became seriously "contaminated" around 1562 – the year of the Wiesensteig hunt – and through his preaching and teaching he then "infected" innumerable others with this potentially lethal cultural "virus".

Coronaviruses are known for their little spikes, which enable them to ingeniously attach themselves to human cell receptors; the proteins on the cell's surface that function as openings.[384] Obviously, the cumulative concept of witchcraft did not literally contain spikes, but it did possess ingenious methods of attaching itself to people's thought worlds. By making a connection to deeply-rooted fears, as well as to interpersonal conflicts, the concept entered people's minds and made them see things in a different light. Unusual events became acts of witchcraft, and distrusted individuals became diabolical witches. We saw that viral and bacterial pathogens can "manipulate" or "hijack" the behavior of their carriers for the pathogen's own reproductive purposes. Think of the rabies virus, and how it turns dogs into restless wanderers with foaming mouths, eager to bite. Asking what function this behavior has for the dog will not get us anywhere. But when we ask what function it has for the rabies virus, it all makes perfect functional sense. Along similar lines we might interpret the cumulative concept of witchcraft as a cultural "virus" that entered people's minds, and "manipulated" their behavior: people started panicking, accusing others, torturing and killing suspects, and spreading accusations over long distances. The lesson of epidemiology is that asking what function it had for the actors involved does not necessarily give us more insight. But when we ask what function it had for the reproduction of the witch-hunting phenomenon itself, it all makes perfect functional sense.

This again raises the question of what to make of such comparisons, in this case between witch persecution and contagious disease. Are they merely permissible as stylistic metaphors, or do they warrant serious scientific consideration? In itself, the comparison between socio-cultural phenomena and contagious disease is an old one, and even predates the modern germ theory of disease. During the Reformation, opposing factions eagerly framed each other's religions as "plagues", and before the battle of Waterloo an English newspaper wrote that the ungodly opinions in France formed "the most deadly of all contagions, the contagion of immorality."[385] In the late nineteenth century, when the hypothesis of infectious disease turned into a scientific fact, the comparison became even more prevalent.[386] The French precursor of social psychology

---

[384] Saplakoglu, "Here's Why the New Coronavirus Is so Good at Infecting Human Cells."
[385] Schilling, *Aufbruch und Krise: Deutschland 1517-1648*, 207; Pohl, *Zauberglaube und Hexenangst im Kurfürstentum Mainz*, 19; Zamoyski, *Phantom Terror*, 95.
[386] Mercier, *Not Born Yesterday*, 96–97.

Gustave le Bon studied the behavior of mobs, and thought that their behavior could be dictated by forces outside of people's personal interests. "Within crowds, ideas, sentiments, emotions, and beliefs possess a contagious power that is as intense as the power of microbes", he wrote.[387] The Italian criminologist Scipio Sighele maintained that "moral contagion is as certain as some physical diseases", while Bronislaw Malinowski spoke of the "contagiousness of faith".[388] In popular culture, the analogy remains pervasive to this day – just think of "epidemics of violence", "computer viruses", or social media content "going viral". In academic literature the comparison also keeps popping up: meme-theorists, then, are hardly unique.[389]

Moral and theoretical complications

However, at the same time, much academic scholarship has grown skeptical of the comparison.[390] One of the reasons is moral misgivings; the analogy has proven susceptible to political and ideological abuse.[391] The Nazis were obsessed about biological comparisons, and often marked the Jews as "bacilli", "germ carriers", a "virus", or a "racial tuberculosis" that threatened the Aryan body.[392] Since it is obvious that disease should be annihilated, this dehumanizing language helped remove moral considerations, and made people more prone to committing genocide. Strikingly, the moral hazards of the pathogenic comparison also became apparent during witch-hunts. We already encountered Friedrich Förner, who described witchcraft as "a plague of the soul", and wanted to ensure that *"the healthy part will not be impaired* and *the sick cattle will not infect the entire sheepfold"*. A pastor in Osnabruck in 1594 described how "the vice of sorcery unfortunately spread like a pestilence in this community, infecting countless people."[393] A Jesuit in Westphalia in 1630 exclaimed that "due to the neighboring heretics, this land has been infected by the evil of witchcraft."[394] In addition, people expressed concerns about the "infection" of children, and David Meder recounted how it "often happened between partners, that the one infected the other."[395] Such language did not stimulate caution and mildness on the persecutors' part.[396]

---

[387] Bon, *Psychologie des foules*, 113."Dans les foules, les idées, les sentiments, les émotions, les croyances possèdent un pouvoir contagieux aussi intense que celui des microbes".
[388] Quoted in: Mercier, *Not Born Yesterday*, 96; Malinowski, *Magic, Science and Religion*, 63.
[389] See, for instance: Hatfield et al., *Emotional Contagion*; Gates, "The Epidemic of Violence against Healthcare Workers"; Christakis and Fowler, *Connected*; Gladwell, *The Tipping Point*.
[390] Warren and Power, "It's Contagious"; Mercier, *Not Born Yesterday*; Davis, "Contagion as Metaphor."
[391] Sontag, *Illness as Metaphor*.
[392] Lang, *Act and Idea in the Nazi Genocide*, 16; Lang, *Genocide*, 25; Sontag, *Illness as Metaphor*, 84–85.
[393] Rügge, *Die Hexenverfolgung in der Stadt Osnabrück*, 112."wie das Laster der Zauberey, leider, in dieser Gemeine, gleich wie ein Pestilentz weit im sich gegriffen, und so viel angesticket hatte".
[394] Decker, "Die Hexenverfolgungen im Herzogtum Westfalen," 360."Dieses Land ist wegen der benachbarten Häretiker vom Laster der Zauberei angesteckt".
[395] Roper, *Witch Craze*, 210; Midelfort, *Witch Hunting in Southwestern Germany*, 141; Meder, *Acht Hexenpredigten*, 41."als offtermals van den Eheleuten geschicht, da eins das andere anstecket."
[396] For some further examples of the comparison, see: Kieckhefer, *Hazards of the Dark Arts*, 93; Spee von Langenfeld, *Cautio criminalis*, 249; Bodin, *De la démonomanie des sorciers*, 288, 357, 404, 471; Lancre, *On the Inconstancy of Witches*, 423.

In addition to moral reservations there are scientific misgivings. The comparison is often considered a catchy but deceptive metaphor, and many of the objections raised against meme-theory are also used more generally against this idea of socio-cultural "epidemics." The differences between biological and cultural processes are thought too substantial for this analogy to take hold. Zachary Warren and Séamus Power note that "Ideas, beliefs, and behavior are normatively regulated and made up of meanings and symbols, whereas diseases are made of biological agents."[397] Microbes and viruses "cannot make meaning out of their social world the way persons do and do not negotiate and choose to participate in "contagion" the way humans do."[398] The comparison is thought to reify culture and to discharge humans from their own responsibilities. The cognitive scientist Hugo Mercier (see 7.1) additionally raises evolutionary objections: "We evolved neither to send nor to receive pathogens – indeed, a good chunk of our evolution is devoted to avoiding the effects of pathogens."[399] By contrast, we *did* evolve to receive signals from other humans, and our natural "vigilance" shields us from signals that subvert our interests.

How to respond to such objections? The many ideological mishandlings of the comparison should indeed alarm us, especially when humans rather than forms of culture are likened to pathogens. When drawing the parallel, we thus need to be on the alert for abuse. Still, moral hazards should not prevent us from further exploring the analogy. If we allow moral considerations to determine research outcomes, we succumb to the moralistic fallacy. Having said that, there might actually be good *moral* reasons for examining the parallel in more detail. If cultural phenomena really do have the ability to evolve pathogen-like traits, would it not be in our best interests to learn more about the process underlying this? Our understanding of contagious disease has saved innumerable lives. Might a better understanding of conceivably similar cultural patterns not enhance human wellbeing too? More insight into culture's ways may perhaps help us defuse some of culture's harmful tricks. Or as Ted Cloak put it: "if we *are* the slaves of some of 'our' cultural traits, isn't it time we knew it?"[400] In this light it is laudable that the philosopher Andy Norman is pioneering the science of "mental immunity" against alleged mind parasites.[401]

Regarding the scientific dimension critics are also right in calling for a certain degree of caution. Richard Dawkins observes that "the greatest advances in science have come about because some clever person spotted an analogy between a subject that was already understood, and another still mysterious subject", but he also admits that "one of the hallmarks of futile crankiness is overenthusiastic analogizing" – he learned this when reading many letters of his

---

[397] Warren and Power, "It's Contagious," 361.
[398] Warren and Power, 366.
[399] Mercier, *Not Born Yesterday*, 106.
[400] Cloak, "Is a Cultural Ethology Possible?," 178.
[401] Norman, *Mental Immunity*.

readers.[402] So, eventually it is about finding a balance between indiscriminate analogizing on the one hand, and dogmatic rejection on the other. In that light Dawkins was right to consider the pathogenic analogy as too promising to leave it aside. Of course, we should not literally describe cultural phenomena as viruses, bacteria or epidemics. Those words were developed for biological things, and the differences with cultural phenomena are innumerable. It is for this reason that, when applied to culture, such biological terms are continually put between inverted commas here. Yet, what may still be interpreted in a more literal sense, and what does not require inverted commas, are some of the similarities among the underlying processes. Alex Mesoudi justifiably states that what happens in cultural processes is not "a bit like" Darwinian selection, but to a certain extent *is* Darwinian selection.[403] The reality of the equivalence is also plausibly why the outcomes of biological and cultural processes can be markedly similar in some regards.

That analogies regarding epidemic disease can have real scientific value becomes apparent in Wolfgang Behringer's following comment: "Witch beliefs are not confined to functionally explainable features. There is a fascinating surplus of fantastical elements, fairy-like attributes, which cannot be explained by mere functionalism, such as the ability to fly through the air."[404] Behringer thought of Durkheimian functionalism here, and from that angle the belief in flight indeed appears superfluous. But this is why Daniel Dennett stressed that we need to cast our nets out widely, as functional beneficiaries can be elusive. The analogy of the "selfish" cultural "pathogen" can make us ask a new question here: how does the witch-hunting phenomenon's own virus-like reproduction benefit? From that perspective the flight belief's functionality suddenly stares us right in the face: it enhanced the sabbath notion and helped trigger chains of accusations over long distances. Importantly, analogies about cultural "pathogens" do not make meaning or symbols irrelevant, let alone imply that humans cannot make decisions. The lesson is different: human decision making is greatly impacted by the culture that we absorb, and not all functional properties of symbolic and meaningful culture were designed by human hand. Paraphrasing Clifford Geertz we might say that humans are animals suspended in webs of significance that they have not only spun themselves. To a certain extent it was blind Darwinian evolution that did the spinning. What the pathogenic analogy teaches us is that these webs are not necessarily spun to serve human interests. A key purpose involved is the "egotistical" reproduction of those webs themselves.

All this will sound alien to many humanistic scholars and social scientists. It may appear to be reification at its worst, with culture operating as an agency with interests of its own. Human culture obviously cannot exist without us, and only obtains meaning when we give it meaning. So, attributing such active properties to culture may therefore seem misguided. But here the analogy to viruses is especially enlightening, as viruses cannot exist without a host either.[405]

---

[402] Dawkins, *The Blind Watchmaker*, 195.
[403] Mesoudi, *Cultural Evolution*, 2011, viii–ix.
[404] Behringer, *Witches and Witch-Hunts*, 2.
[405] Modrow, *Viren*, 20–21; Cordingley, *Viruses*.

Cellular organisms survive due to the ability to manufacture proteins and metabolisms of their own, but viruses cannot do that. "Viruses are just matter with informational content", the virologist Michael Cordingley explains.[406] To persist, viral DNA or RNA needs to reside inside a cellular organism and use the organism's machinery for the viruses' own reproductive purposes. Cordingley: "Viruses are obligate parasites of cells, but act egotistically and without regard to the success of their host's genome: they are *egotistical, independently evolving infectious information*."[407] This is where the viral analogy is helpful: culture also consists of matter with informational content – in this case located in brains or in artefacts – which cannot persist without a population of (human) hosts. What the viral analogy shows is that none of this implies that culture cannot have "egotistical" purposes of its own. Reification means turning something abstract into something real. But culture *is* something real, so its reification does not have to be a sin. It may actually be a virtue.

Mercier's concern about human vigilance can also be overcome. He is right that our minds possess evolved mechanisms that defend our interests. Yet, though our bodies also possess evolved immune systems that defend our interests, pathogens still often make us ill – they just evolved ways of evading immune systems. So why should cultural "pathogens" not be able to evade human inborn vigilance? An underlying evolutionary parallel would be the following: for their survival human bodies need to open themselves up for food, water, air, sex, and beneficial microbes. Likewise human minds need to open themselves up for beneficial culture. But such openings come at a price, because biological or cultural "pathogens" can camouflage their real nature and use those openings to enter the body and sabotage its machinery to their own advantage.[408] A crucial trick of the cumulative concept of witchcraft was that it actually appealed to some our human vigilance for certain recurrent dangers. Take fear or anger; emotions evolved to protect humans against real threats. Yet, during a witch-hunt these defensive mental features were directed at an illusory threat, and no longer served the purposes for which they originally evolved. In this case a cultural phenomenon *exploited* those traits to its own benefit. Notably, some scholars with a cognitive orientation are also more open-minded about the idea of witch-hunting subverting people's interests.[409] Nora Parren argues that biologically adaptive cognitive traits can stimulate witch persecution, but that "the end result may actually be anti-social and have negative consequences for everyone."[410] Niek Koning says: "If the human fear reaction to signs of deceit, envy, or other people's scrutiny runs wild, the result may be paranoia." It leads to a "virulence of witch phenomena" and to systems becoming "pathological".[411]

---

[406] Cordingley, *Viruses*, 2.
[407] Cordingley, 18.
[408] Richerson and Boyd, *Not By Genes Alone*, 150; Dennett, *Breaking the Spell*, 229.
[409] Koning, "Witchcraft Beliefs and Witch Hunts"; Parren, "The (Possible) Cognitive Naturalness of Witchcraft Beliefs."
[410] Parren, "The (Possible) Cognitive Naturalness of Witchcraft Beliefs," 411.
[411] Koning, "Witchcraft Beliefs and Witch Hunts," 162, 168, 171.

Further parallels

As I said, such ideas will raise many eyebrows among historians. However, as is the case with Darwinian cultural evolution in general, it is not difficult to reconcile the pathogenic analogy with things that historians traditionally hold dear. Take historical contingencies. That a new coronavirus was able to conquer the world in 2020 was not due only to its inherent properties, but also to a stroke of luck. The strain made an early appearance in the well-connected Chinese city of Wuhan, after which people who had passed through quickly took the virus across the globe. Had the pathogen appeared in a provincial backwater, things could well have ended differently. In this light we might wonder what would have happened to the Alpine witchcraft mythology, had the great ecumenical council of 1431-1437 not occurred in its close vicinity. Without this "superspread event" of Basel, the Alpine concept might have remained stuck in its local context. In the late sixteenth century, an even more elaborate concept of witchcraft was lucky enough to trigger persecution in the well-connected and prestigious city of Trier, which greatly enhanced its spread. This illustrates how evolutionary success in a "viral" model is far from predetermined, but depends on contingent conditions.

A further parallel worth exploring are the circumstances in which epidemic diseases are liable to strike. The ravaging effects of the plague in fourteenth-century Europe – where it possibly killed up to forty percent of the population – has been linked to people's physical condition at the time.[412] After the economic boom of the high Middle Ages, the continent suffered from overpopulation, and famines of the early fourteenth century had made people weaker and more vulnerable to epidemic disease. Similarly, the Spanish flu pandemic of 1918-1920 is often linked to the malnourishment, poor hygiene, and overcrowded camps and hospitals at the end of World War I.[413] Another interesting case is cholera.[414] The bacterium was long endemic in the Indian Bay of Bengal, where it caused seasonal epidemics. But in the nineteenth century new reproductive opportunities appeared. The bacterium spreads through the fecal-oral route, and thrives especially in poor sanitary conditions. When humans drink contaminated water, it enters the body, causing heavy and potentially lethal diarrhea. Through this route the bacterium then enters the water again, to be drunk by other humans, and the cycle starts all over again. The Industrial Era, with its globalized trade and polluted slums full of malnourished people, provided ideal circumstances for the bacterium. Cholera happened to be pre-adapted to, and then further adapted to, the conditions of a new era, becoming a worldwide evolutionary success. As the historical expert Frank Snowden writes about epidemic diseases: "They exploit the features of a society that are social, economic, political, and environmental."[415]

Similarities to the spread of the witch-hunting phenomenon come to mind. Here we might think of a reproductive cycle in which beliefs caused trials and trials caused beliefs. The

---

[412] Krause and Trappe, *Die Reise unserer Gene*, 174–202; Snowden, *Epidemics and Society*, 28–82.
[413] Morens and Fauci, "The 1918 Influenza Pandemic"; Cordingley, *Viruses*, 109.
[414] Snowden, *Epidemics and Society*, 233–68; Crawford, *How Microbes Shaped Our History*, 130–38.
[415] Snowden, *Epidemics and Society*, 234.

phenomenon also revealed ingenious abilities of exploiting social, economic, political, and environmental circumstances. By 1560 witch-hunting had already existed for some time, but like cholera, it happened to be pre-adapted, and then able to further adapt itself to the conditions of a new era. The climatic disasters, economic hardship, religious fervor, apocalyptic anxieties, and politico-religious division of the decades around 1600 provided ideal conditions for this cultural "pathogen" to spread. Especially Germany, with its political fragmentation, vulnerable economies, ecclesiastical states, ardent clerics, and zealous rulers, was susceptible to "outbreaks" of witch-hunting. In that regard it is interesting to compare Germany with the neighboring protestant Dutch Republic. In the sixteenth century these lands also experienced trials, but by the early seventeenth century the Northern Netherlands made, in MacCulloch's words, "an early recovery". This premature stop seems related to the unusual prosperity of the Dutch "Golden Age".[416] The Republic became the vibrant center of an international trade network, with fairly secure food supplies, mitigated effects of ecological disasters, and rulership by a relatively rationalistic and self-confident merchant class. By the standards of the time, the Republic was also lenient towards religious pluralism. It was the type of environment in which the witch-hunting phenomenon no longer stood much chance of survival.[417]

What the comparison to viruses or bacteria can furthermore remind us of is that Dennett's *cui bono* question does not have to be addressed unequivocally. We learned that the relationship between organisms on the one hand, and the microbes or viruses residing inside them on the other, can be ambiguous. Just think again of Ed Yong's statement about "a continuum of lifestyles, between 'bad' parasites and 'good' mutualism", with allies who can disappoint us and enemies that rally to our side. Some microbes even harm and benefit their hosts at the same time. If applied to our cultural case study this would suggest that the relationship between the witch-hunting phenomenon and its human hosts may also have been ambiguous. The key focus here is on how the phenomenon harmed its human hosts, but this does not rule out that hosts in certain cases did benefit. I have already pointed out that the German instrumentalists have brought forward a relevant perspective that has some grounding in the sources, and we need to remain open-minded about cases where people did (sub)consciously use trials to their own advantage. Hence, the Darwinian approach can help us address the *cui bono* question in a multifaceted manner, integrating the strengths of other approaches, while adding a new and yet unexplored layer of explanation.

The functions that we attribute to specific elements of the witch-hunt system can also be multifaceted. The example of the elephant's trunk already showed how things in a Darwinian world can have multiple functions at the same time. Regarding the sabbath notion the focus here mostly lies with its enhancing effect on trials through the creation of chains of accusations, but

---

[416] Waardt, *Toverij en samenleving*; Levack, *The Witch-Hunt in Early Modern Europe*, 246; Goodare, *The European Witch-Hunt*, 326.
[417] Voltmer, "Witchcraft in the City," 151; Behringer, *Witches and Witch-Hunts*, 128.

we should also consider additional functions; that is, other effects that enhanced the notion's survival. In his intellectualist interpretation of witchcraft beliefs, Stuart Clark almost entirely ignores the practices of trials and reduces the demonological worldview to an internal intellectual system. However, he does make an important point about the sabbath: in this "age of cognitive extremism", where people thought in terms of binary opposites, the sabbath notion made a good fit.[418] According to Clark this was why it "was able to survive for so long as something invariant and intelligible – something eminently thinkable."[419] In a Darwinian framework we can translate this insight as the sabbath notion being well adapted to its intellectual environment. In addition, we might think of entertainment and pornography as functions.[420] The extravagant and sexually loaded sabbath descriptions of authors like Delrio and De Lancre must have been exciting to read for people at the time. For such authors, as well as for their readers, it possibly fulfilled a subconscious function of indulging in pornographic interests under the self-deceptive veneer of a pious cause. De Lancre considered what happens at the sabbath "so dirty that it is shameful to talk about", but it did not prevent him from talking about it in great color and detail.[421]

Evolutionary dilemmas

Another insightful notion from the toolkit of evolutionary biology is that of the "evolutionary trade-off". It concerns the idea that an increase in the potency of one adaptive trait causes a decrease in the potency of other adaptive traits.[422] For instance, running fast offers animals the obvious advantage of escaping predators or catching prey. But the advantages come at significant costs. Running fast demands much energy, creates risks of falls and slippages, requires longer legs that are prone to bone fractures, while enhanced maneuverability reduces physical strength.[423] Similarly, a hallmark of viruses is their replication speed, which helps them adapt quickly and evade immune systems. But what viruses gain in rapidity they lose in replication fidelity, with maladaptive mutations becoming more frequent.[424] From this angle we might also consider the evolutionary costs and benefits of certain elements of the witch-hunting phenomenon. The sabbath notion is our prime example of an adaptive trait, but we should also consider a reproductive downside here: reduced credibility. Witches' gatherings already appeared fantastical to many contemporaries, so the notion at the same time hindered witch-hunting's spread.[425] In regard to evolutionary trade-offs we might furthermore wonder why the expensive practice of burning witches at stakes did not give way to burning witches in ovens, as

---

[418] Clark, *Thinking with Demons*, 1–148.
[419] Clark, 134.
[420] Goodare, *The European Witch-Hunt*, 139; Machielsen, *Martin Delrio*, 221.
[421] Lancre, *On the Inconstancy of Witches*, 199.
[422] Flatt and Heyland, *Mechanisms of Life History Evolution*, 141–42.
[423] Wynn et al., "Running Faster Causes Disaster."
[424] Holmes, *The Evolution and Emergence of RNA Viruses*, 46–47; Cordingley, *Viruses*, 15, 84.
[425] Briggs, *Witches & Neighbours*, 34–36, 51.

happened in Zeil and some other places.⁴²⁶ Plausibly, in the economy of culture, stake burnings were worth their costs as their public display fulfilled a pivotal function of "infecting" the audience more deeply with the witchcraft doctrine.⁴²⁷

We could also think in terms of evolutionary trade-offs regarding the social categories that were targeted. After its initial phase in the Alps, witch beliefs and trials long focused especially on women, who were often relatively poor. For the reproduction of the witch-hunting phenomenon this offered the advantage of tapping into misogynous stereotypes, while people in power did not have to feel threatened about being targeted themselves. So, while witch-hunting should not be understood as "women hunting", this type of persecution of course still crucially depended on, and benefited from, its patriarchal and misogynous context. But the persecutory focus on poor women also created evolutionary disadvantages. It reduced the short-term reproductive potential, as half the population, that is men, remained largely unassailable. Confiscations provided little funding for further trials, and the witchcraft doctrine made itself vulnerable to certain criticisms: we already saw how skeptics like Weyer and Spee poked fun at witch trials often being based on confessions of women, who purportedly made credulous and unreliable witnesses.⁴²⁸ Critics also thought that it was quite absurd to think that a figure as imposing as Satan would rely on such insignificant creatures. Johann Weyer: "Who does not see that toothless old women are totally inept instruments for disturbing sky, air, clouds, and winds? Let us not, therefore, suppose that these evil spirits are so foolish and helpless as to approach these women."⁴²⁹ Moreover, if the devil was indeed able to carry witches to a sabbath, so the sixteenth-century Italian lawyer Gianfrancesco Ponzinibio wondered, "why would he do it only with a few persons, and of lowly status, as he is impartial, being the tempter of the whole world?."⁴³⁰

By the late sixteenth and early seventeenth centuries this weak spot was resolved, as almost all social groups were targeted, including rich men. Chapter six showed how this opened up new reproductive vistas for the witch-hunting phenomenon. Now tapping into anti-elitist sentiments, the number of potential victims multiplied, hunts became more sensational, and confiscations supported further trials. But in their turn these trends also had their costs. A crucial effect of indiscriminate persecution was that more groups in society began to feel threatened by trials, and to become more determined in their resistance.⁴³¹ Earlier on we learned that the persecutions of Trier and Ellwangen enhanced trials in other places, but hindered further hunting

---

[426] For other examples of "witch-ovens", see: Behringer, *Witches and Witch-Hunts*, 154; Voltmer, "Hexenbrenner Und Hexenbischöfe," 215.
[427] The importance of burnings is for instance stressed in: Schormann, *Hexenprozesse in Deutschland*, 33; Goodare, *The European Witch-Hunt*, 219.
[428] Krause, *Witchcraft, Demonology, and Confession in Early Modern France*, 126; Kieckhefer, *Hazards of the Dark Arts*, 118; Behringer, *Witches and Witch-Hunts*, 140.
[429] Weyer, *Witches, Devils, and Doctors in the Renaissance*, 563.
[430] Duni, "Law, Nature, Theology and Witchcraft in Ponzinibio's De Lamiis (1511)," 231.
[431] Midelfort, *Witch Hunting in Southwestern Germany*, 121–63, 178–92.

in Trier and Ellwangen themselves. Once people had seen with their own eyes what horror such trials caused, and learned how their own networks had been attacked, they became more hesitant about starting a witch-hunt again. Such effects were also notable after more modest panics. During the wave of around 1590, accusations in Wallerstein included the wife of the ruling count, which seems to have provoked lasting doubts about witch-hunting among its governmental dignitaries.[432] Bavaria experienced similar persecution, but the first peak there was also its only peak, as the trials' uncontrollable dynamics again stimulated misgivings within the establishment.[433] Overall, indiscriminate panics were often followed by increased caution and resistance.[434]

It is probably not by accident that in places where trials continued at a steadier pace, persecutions were also more restricted in their social profiles and less overwhelming in their scale. In a comparative study of sabbath notions in Lorraine and Trier, the German historian Elisabeth Biesel noted that Lorraine sabbaths were imagined as festival-like village events, attended by around six to thirty witches, while Trier sabbaths were more crowded and extravagant.[435] Apart from the content of Lorraine beliefs, Robin Briggs also points to Lorraine's judicial peculiarities that prevented trials from spiraling out of control.[436] They led to "a curious equilibrium", in which no mounting resistance to persecution came about, and trials eventually produced one of the highest death tolls in Europe.[437] German Rottweil shows a somewhat similar pattern. Persecution here mostly targeted the poor, and due to its protracted character it eventually amounted to an impressive 266 burnings.[438] Nearby Rottenburg provides a further interesting case. Its panics of the late sixteenth century failed to bring witch-hunting to an end, and Erik Midelfort links this to its relatively narrow range of victims: "the stereotyped identification of witches as old women suffered so little shock", he argues, that support for persecution remained substantial enough for trials to continue. Only around 1600, when high officials came under attack, did Rottenberg's witch-hunts decline.[439] In sum, in the places where they occurred, indiscriminate panics offered short-term reproductive advantages, but long-term reproductive disadvantages.

The observation that large "outbreaks" of witch-hunting provoked continued resistance has given rise to one of the most common epidemiological analogies of witchcraft historiography: immunization.[440] Wolfgang Mährle observes that after the persecution of 1611-1618 Ellwangen

---

[432] Haas, *Hexen und Herrschaftspolitik*, 87, 113–14.
[433] Behringer, *Hexenverfolgung in Bayern*.
[434] Levack, "The Decline and End of Witchcraft Prosecutions," 432; Voltmer and Eiden, "Rechtsnormen, Gerichts- Und Herrschaftspraxis Bei Hexereiverfahren in Lothringen, Luxemburg, Kurtrier Und St. Maximum Während Des 16. Und 17. Jahrhunderts"; Midelfort, *Witch Hunting in Southwestern Germany*, 121–63.
[435] Biesel, "Les descriptions du sabbat."
[436] Briggs, *The Witches of Lorraine*.
[437] Briggs, 386.
[438] Zeck, *Im Rauch gehn Himmel geschüggt*.
[439] Midelfort, *Witch Hunting in Southwestern Germany*, 90–94, 179; Goodare, *The European Witch-Hunt*, 245.
[440] Behringer, *Hexenverfolgung in Bayern*, 159.

reached a "high level of immunization", and regarding the southwestern German hunts of the late 1620s Erik Midelfort notes that the "lesson learned in those panics may have provided immunity from witch trials."[441] Joseph Klaits argues that "a frightening outbreak frequently provided immunity to witch hunting for a generation or more."[442] Epidemiologists also know that the immunity of a population can be temporary: when the immunized generation has deceased, people become vulnerable again, and diseases strike anew.[443] This recurrently happened in the history of the plague. It may remind us of what Thomas Fritz observed in Reutlingen (see 7.1): after a few generations the horrid experience of earlier hunts was forgotten, so trials occurred anew. Yet, overall "immunization" from witch-hunting often seems to have had durable effects, as panics did not frequently occur in the same place more than once or twice.[444] Wolfgang Behringer observes that local historians often note that witch persecution in their region was only an exception, making them atypical. But Behringer argues that the atypical was, in fact, typical: "As a general rule we can conclude that the burning of witches was an exception – everywhere."[445] He explains: "normally people are not interested in burning their neighbours, and governments do not wish to wipe out their tax-payers."

In section 5.5 it was stressed that this finding of panics not often occurring in the same place more than once or twice strongly argues against the witch-hunting phenomenon as a product of cultural group selection. The latter model would assume that witch beliefs and trials survived because they enhanced the functioning of socio-cultural groups. But witch trials simply did not occur frequently enough within single groups for any such selective process to take hold. That witch burnings tended to be the exception everywhere, also creates additional problems for the instrumentalization approach. If trials were indeed as multifunctional as these German historians presume, "immunizing" effects should have been unlikely. If people (sub)consciously learned how witch-hunts served their ulterior interests wonderfully well, we should expect them to become eager in re-using the tool on later occasions. But historical records overall reveal something else: many people were overtaken by the witch-hunting phenomenon, and in retrospect realized that their interests had been harmed and that something had gone awry. This provides strong clues for a "selfish meme"-like model. It seems that we are dealing here with a cultural "pathogen" that moved from place to pace, leaving many casualties and "immunized" survivors in its wake. The intriguing parallel of "immunization" may also help us address the last question posed in this dissertation: why did this well-adapted phenomenon eventually cease to exist? The final section will examine this problem in detail.

7.5 The end of witch-hunting

---

[441] Mährle, "Ellwangen - Hexenverfolgungen""hochgradige Resistenz"; Midelfort, *Witch Hunting in Southwestern Germany*, 194.
[442] Klaits, *Servants of Satan*, 171.
[443] Krause and Trappe, *Die Reise unserer Gene*, 197–200.
[444] Roper, *Witch Craze*, 11; Goodare, *The European Witch-Hunt*, 245; Behringer, *Witches and Witch-Hunts*, 148–49.
[445] Behringer, *Witches and Witch-Hunts*, 148–49.

The key question in this dissertation is why witch-hunting became so big, not why it eventually ended. Explaining its rise is also the more challenging theoretical problem: that people started doing something that harmed their interests is more puzzling than that they stopped doing it. Still, the decline of witch-hunting is an interesting topic in its own right, and may also help us further reflect on the Darwinian proposals made in this thesis. After all, if the witch-hunting phenomenon was so well adapted to enhance its own spread, why did it begin to falter after 1630, to come to a definitive end in the eighteenth century? The waning of witch beliefs and trials may also help us compare competing explanatory models. Do patterns of decline offer indications of multifunctional instrumentalization, or do they further suggest a central role for genuine belief? The end of witch-hunting has already received ample attention from historians, and we shall now see how their findings bear upon the Darwinian framework.

The most obvious direct cause of witch-hunting's decline after 1630 was a central European development external to the phenomenon itself: the Thirty Years' War.[446] We learned that its first phase presented no hindrance to witch-hunting. However, the early 1630s signified a tipping point, as the impact of the Swedish army on the Bamberg hunt already illustrated. In those years the war turned into one of the most brutal and devastating conflicts of European history.[447] Many German and foreign armies traversed the Holy Roman Empire, pillaging and brutalizing the population. Famines and epidemics raged, and the loss of people was startling. In some regions that had been rife with witch trials, like southwestern Germany, Saarland, and Lorraine, up to sixty to eighty percent of the population perished.[448] As I argued, hardship normally enhanced witch trials, but in this case the destitution was so extreme that it became a hindering factor. Most attention was diverted to warfare, and whole societal structures collapsed. It left little capacity for witch persecution. Trials had normally been triggered by apparently mysterious unfortunate events, but now the cause of people's misfortune was obvious: marauding soldiers.[449] Accusations also traditionally sprang from accreted reputations for witchcraft within communities, but the mass mortality probably erased many such social memories. Julian Goodare: "Survivors and new immigrants did not remember who had been bewitching whom, nor did they care anymore."[450]

It is important to note that there was nothing special about witch-hunting receding for a while. Earlier waves also came and went, so arguably the Thirty Years' War just enhanced a normal trend. What especially warrants attention is that trials did not return to earlier levels after the war ended in 1648.[451] There was a resurgence of persecution in the 1650s and 1660s, and some waves of trials continued to occur after that. Yet, the overall trend was unmistakably

---

[446] Pohl, *Zauberglaube und Hexenangst im Kurfürstentum Mainz*, 289; Decker, "Die Hexenverfolgungen im Herzogtum Westfalen," 335; Midelfort, *Witch Hunting in Southwestern Germany*, 75–77; Dillinger, *Hexen und Magie*, 2018, 149.
[447] Schmidt, *Die Reiter der Apokalypse*.
[448] Labouvie, *Zauberei und Hexenwerk*, 251–52; Midelfort, *Witch Hunting in Southwestern Germany*, 75.
[449] Decker, "Die Hexenverfolgungen im Herzogtum Westfalen," 335; Midelfort, *Witch Hunting in Southwestern Germany*, 75.
[450] Goodare, *The European Witch-Hunt*, 350–51.
[451] Goodare, 321.

downwards.[452] So why did new generations not adopt the phenomenon as fervently as their predecessors? One explanatory strategy of historians that we first explore is to consider broad changes to European history that were not necessarily related to the witch-hunting phenomenon, but still impacted it negatively. From a Darwinian angle we might frame that as changes to the "environment" that made witch beliefs and trials less well adapted. Another strategy is to look at *internal* mechanisms of the witch-hunting system that helped bring about its own demise. This dimension, as we shall see, again reveals intriguing parallels to the evolution of epidemic diseases.

External factors

One key environmental factor was climate. After the mid-fifteenth century average temperatures had been going down rapidly, but in the seventeenth century the trend stabilized.[453] Compared with earlier times, weather conditions remained extreme, but people had become used to them. Extreme cold and frost no longer seemed to require a special explanation, like witchcraft. The period from 1550 to 1650 had also been one of intense population pressure and contracting resources, but after 1650 those strains lessened.[454] The dramatic loss of population in the Thirty Years' War left more resources for subsequent generations, and while life remained harsh for many, socio-economic conditions did begin to improve somewhat. The earlier inflation resulting from demographic growth levelled off, and real wages rose. People began to feel slightly more secure and less at the mercy of contingent events. For the witchcraft concept these developments left fewer opportunities for stoking up hatred amongst them.

Another major development of the era was the continuing consolidation of state power and shifts in judicial practices related to that.[455] Witch panics had especially flourished in politically fragmented areas where sloppy judicial procedures were not hindered by external interference. After 1650 such conditions became more unusual. Centralized states had always been a hindering factor for witch-hunting, but in the second half of the seventeenth century they grew more powerful. Their focus on the eradication of religious deviance also lost some terrain to more secular concerns like commerce and industry.[456] State formation further encouraged more well-developed judicial procedures, and trials increasingly fell into the hands of a professionalized class of jurists who weighed evidence more carefully. Within this context torture and the death penalty grew somewhat old-fashioned.[457] Painful questioning was increasingly seen as untrustworthy because it made people confess to things that they had not done. Moreover, jurists came to focus on other forms of evidence than confessions, making torture less

---

[452] Dillinger, *Hexen und Magie*, 2018, 137–52; Behringer, *Hexen und Hexenprozesse in Deutschland*, 400–408.
[453] Matthews and Briffa, "The 'Little Ice Age,'" 21.
[454] Dillinger, *Hexen und Magie*, 2018, 148–49; Levack, *The Witch-Hunt in Early Modern Europe*, 249–51; Schilling, *Die neue Zeit*, 285–344.
[455] Dillinger, *Hexen und Magie*, 2018, 144–48; Levack, *The Witch-Hunt in Early Modern Europe*, 131–40; Schilling, *Die neue Zeit*, 345–81.
[456] Goodare, *The European Witch-Hunt*, 332–33.
[457] Goodare, 328–29.

necessary. The decline of the death penalty was related to rationalized states becoming interested in alternative punishments, like putting criminals to use in the state's galleys, colonies, or communal workhouses.

That states became more secular in their orientation, with religious zealotry giving way to raison d'état, was part of a broader shift in European religious life.[458] The trend should not be exaggerated, as religion remained pivotally important for Europe, both in people's personal lives as well as in politics. The persecution of religious deviance also remained common.[459] But the ideal of the godly state did lose some of its vigor. The horrors of religious intolerance and warfare had disillusioned many people, making them wary of religious fanaticism, and more lenient towards religious pluralism – the Dutch Republic had been ahead of its time.[460] In religious thought, the providential tradition that explained misfortune as a direct form of divine punishment also remained a competitor to witchcraft as an explanation.[461] In Württemberg, for instance, this idea gained new strength after 1630. Lutheran Germany in general experienced the rise of Pietism, a movement which placed more emphasis on God as the source of all spiritual power, while limiting the impact of the devil.

But a different competitor to witchcraft as an explanation came to pose the most lethal threat: natural causation.[462] The judicial confrontation in 1620 between the accusers of Katharina Kepler, and the defense by her son Johannes Kepler, foreshadowed a conflict of worldviews that would eventually bring witch-hunting to its knees. Kepler did not in think in terms of a ubiquitous devil in a decaying world, but was more interested in natural causes and human progress.[463] In combination with his astronomic discoveries this made him a prime representative of what historians came to call the scientific revolution. We should not overestimate the importance of this revolution for witch-hunting's decline, as trials were already on the retreat before the new science began to have much of an impact. Neither was it apparent from the beginning that the one system of thought would eventually destroy the other, as some scholars tried to combine both systems of belief. Still, the rise of the new worldview soon began to hamper witch-hunting. René Descartes did not explicitly write about witchcraft, but his rationalistic system offered little room for the interference of spiritual agencies.[464] The world was understood as an orderly, regular machine, subject to laws of nature, in which nightly flights, sabbaths, magic, or diabolical intercourse no longer fitted. When elites began to adopt such rationalized views in the

---

[458] Levack, *The Witch-Hunt in Early Modern Europe*, 245–49; Schilling, *Die neue Zeit*, 456–514; Waardt, *Toverij en samenleving*, 207; Goodare, *The European Witch-Hunt*, 329–34.
[459] Kaplan, *Divided by Faith*.
[460] Behringer, *Witches and Witch-Hunts*, 134; Goodare, *The European Witch-Hunt*, 331.
[461] Bever, "Witchcraft Prosecutions and the Decline of Magic," 276; Levack, *The Witch-Hunt in Early Modern Europe*, 247.
[462] Behringer, *Witches and Witch-Hunts*, 137; Levack, *The Witch-Hunt in Early Modern Europe*, 240–45; Goodare, *The European Witch-Hunt*, 335–42.
[463] Rublack, *The Astronomer & the Witch*; Behringer, *Witches and Witch-Hunts*, 184.
[464] Bever, "Witchcraft Prosecutions and the Decline of Magic," 241–44; Behringer, *Witches and Witch-Hunts*, 184.

seventeenth century, it made them less likely to favor supernatural explanations over natural ones.

Lastly, changes to ideas about women deserve consideration.[465] In contrast to stereotypes about sexually rapacious creatures who easily allied themselves with the devil, from the mid-seventeenth century onwards stereotypes came to focus on the alleged weakness and delicacy of females. "Women were increasingly seen as frail rather than threatening, needing protection, not control", Bernard Capp writes.[466] The humoral understanding of the human body lost ground, and women were thought of as less interested in, or even resistant to, sex. We should not be mistaken: such stereotypes also enhanced patriarchy, as it presented females as unfit to rule. But the idea of women being involved in diabolical intercourse and rampant feasting at the witches' sabbath did not connect well with these new categories.

Internal factors
In addition to certain *external* changes to the European "environment", we need to address *internal* mechanisms within the witch-hunting phenomenon. In the previous section we already encountered mechanisms of "immunization", with indiscriminate panics making people less likely to initiate further hunts. In certain ways such self-limiting effects were already present from the beginning.[467] In Arras people had become wary of witch-hunting after the panic of 1459-1460, and in her detailed study on the relative absence of persecution in Rothenburg ob der Tauber, Alison Rowlands noted that jurists wrote negatively about what happened in Wiesensteig in 1562. They interpreted the event as a warning of "the unpleasant consequences which could ensue if witchcraft cases were pursued on a dangerous, unstable basis by judicial authorities."[468] So, while the scale of the Wiesensteig hunt enhanced further persecution, it hindered it at the same time. Yet, in this period such impeding consequences did not yet compensate the enhancing ones. The wave of 1630, however, seems to have been a turning point. Julian Goodare: "The importance of the 1630 watershed should not be overstated, since both tendencies probably operated in some places both before and after that date, but there does seem to have been an overall downward trend thereafter."[469]

Bamberg was a crucial case in this shift, at least in Germany.[470] The hunt did have some enhancing effects elsewhere, as the news spread far and wide. Proponents of trials in Bavaria, for instance, heralded the persecution at Bamberg as a laudable example.[471] Yet the fact that so many higher authorities, like the *Reichshofrat,* the *Reichskammergericht,* and the Holy Roman

---

[465] Bever, *The Realities of Witchcraft,* 409; Bever, "Witchcraft Prosecutions and the Decline of Magic," 290; Capp, "Gender and Family."
[466] Capp, "Gender and Family," 45.
[467] Goodare, *The European Witch-Hunt,* 245–46.
[468] Rowlands, *Witchcraft Narratives in Germany,* 25–26.
[469] Goodare, *The European Witch-Hunt,* 260.
[470] Gehm, *Die Hexenverfolgung im Hochstift Bamberg,* 180–81, 227.
[471] Behringer, *Hexenverfolgung in Bayern,* 241.

Emperor spoke out against it, while the Bamberg government was subjected to enormous external pressure, discouraged trials elsewhere. Illustratively, the persecutors in the electoral state of Cologne were alarmed by the *Reichshofrat's* decision, becoming more hesitant in their own persecutions.[472] The scale of the Bamberg hunt was so overwhelming, its judicial procedures so irresponsible, and the carnage amongst higher classes so brutal, that it stimulated wariness about witch-hunting amongst significant parts of German establishments.

The response to Bamberg did not stand on its own. Throughout Germany, the enormity of the persecutory wave around 1630 stimulated what Erik Midelfort has called "the crisis of confidence".[473] Contemporaries, including people who had themselves stimulated persecution, widely observed that the whole system seemed to have developed a dynamics of its own which nobody could control, and which invited social chaos and anarchy.[474] Bodin had once recommended witch-hunting on the promise that it would reduce afflictions and trouble.[475] But trials hardly seemed to offer improvement to people's lives, while in fact the self-destruction of whole communities appeared imminent. Typically, in Offenburg accusations and killings had escalated, intruding into many segments of society, including the ranks of the councilor-judges. This helped bring about a shift in public opinion, with lawyers, preachers, and rulers becoming worried about public safety, and innocent people being killed.[476] Even in Würzburg the prince-bishop prohibited further trials, which seems related to accusations that targeted himself as well as his chancellor.[477] "By an agonizing process, towns and finally whole regions came to reject the procedure of torture and denunciation", Midelfort notes.[478] Importantly, in his view this new German resistance did not stem from any sort of early Enlightenment thought, and neither was it related to a decreasing belief in the devil. It was mostly the escalating *practices* of trials that made people distrustful of the whole thing.

The new scale of persecution also stimulated more well-thought-out and effective criticisms.[479] This for instance becomes apparent when we compare Johann Weyer's attack on witch-hunting from 1563 to Friedrich Spee's attack from 1631. Weyer directed much of his criticisms against the *belief* in witchcraft, but as we saw earlier this made his plea rather arbitrary; he largely used the same demonological reasoning as his opponents. How this potentially weakened his argument becomes visible in his discussion of a witchcraft case in the town of

---

[472] Gehm, *Die Hexenverfolgung im Hochstift Bamberg*, 180–81.
[473] Midelfort, *Witch Hunting in Southwestern Germany*, 121–63; Voltmer and Eiden, "Rechtsnormen, Gerichts- Und Herrschaftspraxis Bei Hexereiverfahren in Lothringen, Luxemburg, Kurtrier Und St. Maximum Während Des 16. Und 17. Jahrhunderts."
[474] Briggs, *Witches & Neighbours*, 51, 360; Dillinger, *Hexen und Magie*, 2018, 144–4; Labouvie, *Zauberei und Hexenwerk*, 195, 255.
[475] Bodin, *De la démonomanie des sorciers*, 435–36.
[476] Midelfort, *Witch Hunting in Southwestern Germany*, 126–31.
[477] Midelfort, 192.
[478] Midelfort, 191.
[479] Clark, "Glaube und Skepsis in der deutschen Hexenliteratur"; Decker, "Die Hexenverfolgungen im Herzogtum Westfalen," 365.

Elten.⁴⁸⁰ Weyer described how it was told that at a specific spot in a road chariots were often overturned and people cast from their horses. The villagers attributed the assaults to witchcraft and a woman named Sibyl Duiscops was executed for it. Assaults allegedly then ended, and villagers attributed the cessation to the execution. Weyer, however, proposed a different explanation:

> In fact, the Devil ceased voluntarily and even gladly from the harassment which he alone had brought on, so that by this cessation he might plunge men deeper into the abyss of unbelief, and so that he might render them guilty of a bloodthirsty sentence, which is what he eagerly desires, especially in the case of the innocent, since he is a murderer from the very beginning.⁴⁸¹

In retrospect we might appreciate Weyer's position from a moral point of view, but intellectually this argument was remarkably feeble. The persecutors' scenario was more plausible by the standards of the time, since it was a simpler and more parsimonious scenario that required fewer questionable assumptions. So, while Weyer's argumentation may have helped prevent witch-hunting from becoming even bigger, its arbitrary nature plausibly made it less effective than he hoped for.⁴⁸² Yet, considering the fact that attacking demonology was a non-starter, what could critics do?

Shrewdly, Friedrich Spee shifted his attention from witch beliefs to the practices of witch trials. In what Behringer calls "a Ciceronian masterpiece", Spee in the beginning of his *Cautio Criminalis* accepts that witches exist and subscribes to views of authors like Delrio, Bodin and Remy.⁴⁸³ With some false modesty he also presents as his sole aim to ensure that no innocent person will be convicted. But his subsequent attack on the procedures of witch trials becomes so very merciless and devastating that little of those procedures remains. Considering the unreliability of witchcraft allegations, Spee eventually contests that diabolical witchcraft exists at all, as it is "built upon accusations and confessions that were extracted through pain and torture."⁴⁸⁴ Stuart Clark sees Spee's argument as part of a general shift in criticism becoming increasingly focused on procedures instead of beliefs.⁴⁸⁵ "It was much more difficult for critics to distance themselves intellectually from orthodox demonology than to pick holes in particular trial procedures and investigate techniques on largely technical grounds."⁴⁸⁶ Especially torture could

---

⁴⁸⁰ Weyer, *Witches, Devils, and Doctors in the Renaissance*, 521.
⁴⁸¹ Weyer, 521.
⁴⁸² Behringer, *Witches and Witch-Hunts*, 171–72.
⁴⁸³ Behringer, 179; Spee von Langenfeld, *Cautio criminalis*, 217.
⁴⁸⁴ Spee von Langenfeld, *Cautio criminalis*, 287, 407."Besagungen und Bekantnussen, so durch Pein und Marter heraus getrieben worden, beruhet."
⁴⁸⁵ Clark, "Glaube und Skepsis in der deutschen Hexenliteratur"; Clark, *Thinking with Demons*, 208.
⁴⁸⁶ Clark, *Thinking with Demons*, 208.

be criticized in a non-arbitrary manner within the boundaries of acceptable contemporary discourse.

Clark's claim is contested by Jürgen Michael Schmidt, who argues that a critique of procedures was already part and parcel of skeptical comments from the beginning.[487] There is much to say for that, but there does seem to have been a certain shift in focus that made criticisms more effective.[488] Spee published his tract anonymously, as it was too dangerous to speak out openly about such matters in Catholic Germany, and his argument provoked vitriolic responses. But the book is widely thought to have weakened the witch-hunting phenomenon in Germany decisively.[489] A Jesuit chronicle in Paderborn – a former hotspot of trials – praised Spee as "a man distinguished by piety, science, and a nobility of birth" who expressed great pity for the unfortunate victims of the dreadful evil of witch-hunting.[490] Spee also directed much of his argument to the princes of Germany, knowing that they were the ones best able to stop it. His book indeed appears to have had some of the desired effects, making authorities less willing to allow the cycle of torture and denunciation unfold. Within a Darwinian framework we might interpret this as a case of culture-culture coevolution, in which the increased "virulence" and adaptedness of witch beliefs and trials provoked more well adapted "immunizing" responses. This does not imply that everything about this process was Darwinian – the shrewd new adaptedness of Spee's argument looks more like a product of intentional design than blind evolution.

As I said, the decline of witch trials may also help us further compare the accounts of the German instrumentalists with those of the "genuine belief historians". Notably, the instrumentalists say relatively little on the decline, which seems related to the fact that their framework does not offer a plausible scenario for it. After all, why would people stop persecuting witches if it provided them with such a wonderful multifunctional tool? It is unlikely that people after 1630 were no longer interested in money, power, envy or revenge. The instrumentalists have made some proposals, though. Moeller and Rummel separately argue that the underlying interests of witch-hunters at some point just became too obvious.[491] Many people learned to see how accusers and persecutors were tricking people, and thus no longer fell for it. But this argument raises more questions than it answers. If people increasingly understood how witchcraft accusations and trials were instrumentalized for hidden ends, then why did they not decide to use it for their *own* ends? Did people after 1630 become more morally conscious?

---

[487] Schmidt, *Glaube und Skepsis*, 220.
[488] Dillinger, *Hexen und Magie*, 2018, 145.
[489] Robisheaux, "The German Witch Trials," 190; Behringer, *Witches and Witch-Hunts*, 181; Bever, "Witchcraft Prosecutions and the Decline of Magic," 271.
[490] Behringer, *Hexen und Hexenprozesse in Deutschland*, 266. "ein durch Frömmigkeit, Wissenschaft und Adel der Geburt ausgezeichneter Mann".
[491] Rummel, "Das 'ungestüme Umherlaufen der Untertanen'.," 160–61; Rummel, "Vom Umgang mit Hexen und Hexerei," 106; Moeller, *Dass Willkür über Recht ginge*, 481.

Neither do Moeller and Rummel provide evidence that people after 1630 gained more understanding of how instrumentalization worked.

Another instrumentalist explanation for why witch-hunting ended is that it increasingly lost many of its functions, and came to affect too many groups in society too negatively.[492] Katrin Moeller writes about the late phase that "Witch persecution had long lost its function as a safety valve of social conflict, and instead became a source of conflict itself. The unravelling of former persecutory alliances thus brought trials to an end."[493] Rita Voltmer similarly argues that the mass persecutions became so obviously destructive that people came to reject them. But again, this raises more questions than it answers. If witch beliefs and trials were created by knowledgeable agents who (sub)consciously knew what they were doing – which is what instrumentalists often stress – then why did persecutions become dysfunctional in the first place? This line of argument also contradicts other instrumentalist claims. Moeller's statement about persecution becoming too conflict-ridden is surprising, as the instrumentalists normally see conflicts as a *cause* of accusations and trials. Voltmer's statement about mass persecutions being dysfunctional challenges her other claim about them serving "an elite disciplinary program all too effectively." Again, the account of the "genuine belief historians" appears more plausible. Midelfort's scenario of a "crisis of confidence" presumes that genuine belief in the guilt of convicts crucially drove persecutions forward. So, when this genuine belief began to falter, trials also faltered. In addition, the self-limiting effects of panics indicate that persecutions were often dysfunctional and had a deleterious effect on the actors involved.

Further parallels with contagious disease

These mechanisms allow us to draw further parallels with the evolution of contagious disease. Amongst epidemiologists it is well known that pathogens can limit their own reproduction by being too lethal.[494] Take Ebola, one of the deadliest diseases we know. The disease expert Johannes Krause writes that "Ebola kills extremely quickly, so the virus has very little time to jump from one infected person to another. Ebola outbreaks thus burn down rapidly, meaning that the virus does not have enough time to spread to more distant populations." This differs from the seasonal flu, of which "new forms migrate from Southeast Asia to the whole world almost every year."[495] Importantly, the killing of hosts is not what pathogens are necessarily after – their sole

---

[492] Labouvie, *Zauberei und Hexenwerk*, 265; Voltmer, *Hexen. Wissen was stimmt*, 88; Moeller, *Dass Willkür über Recht ginge*, 213; Moeller, "Es ist überaus gerechtes Gesetz, dass die Zauberinnen getötet werden," 102–7.
[493] Moeller, "Es ist überaus gerechtes Gesetz, dass die Zauberinnen getötet werden," 104."Die Hexenverfolgung hatte längst ihren Charakter als Ventil sozialer Konflikte verloren und war stattdessen selbst zum Streitpotential angewachsen. Der Zerfall der zuvor geschlossen Verfolgungsallianz führte schließlich zur Beendigung der Prozesswelle".
[494] Modrow, *Viren*, 46; Dennett, *Darwin's Dangerous Idea*, 362; Krause and Trappe, *Die Reise unserer Gene*, 176; Crawford, *How Microbes Shaped Our History*, 16, 24.
[495] Krause and Trappe, *Die Reise unserer Gene*, 176."Bekanntlich tötet Ebola äußerst schnell, dem Virus bleibt damit nur sehr wenig Zeit, von einem infizierten Menschen auf einen anderen überzuspringen. Weil Ebola-Ausbrüche schnell ausbrennen, der Virus also nicht die Zeit hat, auf weiter entfernte Populationen überzugehen, konnte es sich bei zurückliegenden Ausbrüchen in

purpose is survival.[496] That pathogens still often kill can be a by-product of disease symptoms enhancing a pathogen's spread. We saw that the cholera bacterium often causes lethal diarrhea, but the underlying rationale is not the killing, but entering the water again. Plague bacterium provokes deadly sepsis in its victims, but again the death of the host is not the aim. It happens because sepsis is related to human blood teeming with plague bacteria, so when plague sufferers are bitten by fleas the bacterium continues its reproductive cycle, and lives to see another day.[497]

Pathogens survive in a world full of evolutionary dilemmas and trade-offs.[498] When highly virulent, viruses can cause rapidly progressive disease and are more readily transmitted. So, while a reduced virulence may lengthen the life of hosts, under certain conditions it can come at the price of lower levels of replication and fewer successful transmissions. But in their turn the aggressive "hit-and-run" epidemics are at risk of overplaying their hand by being *too* deadly, and triggering more vigorous responses of immune systems.[499] After their initial successes such diseases commonly burn themselves up, and evolve into milder forms. This for instance happened to syphilis.[500] When arriving in late-fifteenth-century Europe, syphilis was an extreme killer that killed around sixteen million people within fifty years. The disease ate away parts of people's brains, with sufferers becoming insane and dying in terrifying agony. But due to self-limiting effects these strains gave way to the less fearsome ones that we know of today. So, survival is about finding an evolutionary balance. Aggressiveness especially occurs when pathogens jumped species only recently, and did not yet have the time to evolve into a more gentle evolutionary détente.[501] But there are always exceptions to this rule.[502] In 1675 the English physician Thomas Sydenham described scarlet fever as a disease that made patients feel rigors and shivers, but added that the "symptoms are however moderate".[503] By the nineteenth century, on the other hand, some strains of scarlet fever had evolved into epidemic killers that were compared even to typhus and plague.

These mechanisms loosely remind us of what happened in the evolution of witch persecution. The ultimate goal of this cultural phenomenon was not necessarily to kill people. Rather, it was self-reproduction. The cumulative concept of witchcraft constantly needed to enter new minds again, and we might interpret deadly and spectacular hunts as the concept's way of achieving that end. Yet, its reproductive "strategy" of creating indiscriminate panics also made the witch-hunting phenomenon overplay its hand. Such comparisons should not be taken too literally, considering the innumerable differences in detail. But still, the end of witch

---

der Regel nicht weit ausbreiten. Ganz anders die Grippe, von der fast jedes Jahr neue Formen von Südostasien aus in die ganze Welt wandern."
[496] Krause and Trappe, 176.
[497] Krause and Trappe, 179–81.
[498] Cordingley, *Viruses*, 195; Crawford, *How Microbes Shaped Our History*, 24.
[499] Cordingley, *Viruses*, 117–19.
[500] Krause and Trappe, *Die Reise unserer Gene*, 221; Crawford, *How Microbes Shaped Our History*, 63–67.
[501] Crawford, *How Microbes Shaped Our History*, 24; Cordingley, *Viruses*, 72–73.
[502] Cordingley, *Viruses*, 46–53.
[503] Cordingley, 47.

persecution reveals striking parallels with overly deadly pathogens burning themselves up. This observation raises a follow-up question: why did evolutionary processes in the history of witch trials create such self-limiting aspects in the first place? Why did this cultural phenomenon not "decide" to stick to a more restricted profile of victims, thus safeguarding a more durable survival, as for instance happened in Lorraine and Rottweil? Here Darwinian theory may again provide an answer: evolutionary processes do not think about the long term. Richard Dawkins: "Genes have no foresight. They do not plan ahead."[504] If a certain new variant enhances short-term reproductive success it will simply reproduce, irrespective of long-term effects. Hence, the evolutionary mechanisms that were set in motion by the hunts of Wiesensteig, Trier, Ellwangen and Bamberg could not foresee how after 1630 those same mechanisms would help put the "R-number" of this cultural "virus" below 1.0.

At the same time, we should not underestimate the capacities of this cultural "virus" to respond to challenges. When real viruses are confronted with new defenses of immune systems, they often evolve ways of evading those defenses. So, in our cultural case study we might expect processes of culture-culture coevolution, in which the witch-hunting phenomenon evolved ways of evading the new hindrances it found on its path. Due to critics like Spee, torture came to be applied less frequently in witchcraft cases, thereby removing one of witch-hunting's essential reproductive tricks. So, if the phenomenon was to survive, it needed to find a way around that. And that is exactly what happened. Witch beliefs and trials more than ever came to focus on the one category of people who often confessed without torture: children.[505] From 1630 onwards witch trials almost exclusively started with accusations from children, and also targeted them more prominently as victims. The category of rich men, on the other hand, receded. This had the downside that less funding for persecution could be harnessed, making trials smaller again. But at this historical juncture, that offered the reproductive advantage of not irritating elites too much. "The mitigation of witch trials thus simultaneously ensured their perpetuation", Wolfgang Behringer writes.[506] The tempering of witch-hunts after 1630 thus bears an intriguing resemblance to aggressive pathogens evolving into less lethal forms.

The late phase of witch-hunting also further shows mechanisms of "immunization". Notably, late trials often occurred in places that had shown restraint during the peak period from 1560 to 1630.[507] We earlier saw that Lutheran Esslingen kept its head relatively cool in 1562, but one century later it experienced a hunt that led to dozens of killings, most of whom were men.[508]

---

[504] Dawkins, *The Selfish Gene*, 22; Dennett, *Freedom Evolves*, 53.
[505] Dillinger, *Hexen und Magie*, 2018, 116–18; Behringer, "Kinderhexenprozesse," 32, 45; Behringer, *Hexenverfolgung in Bayern*, 332–99; Behringer, *Hexen und Hexenprozesse in Deutschland*, 404.
[506] Behringer, *Hexenverfolgung in Bayern*, 341."Die Entschärfung der Hexenprozesse ermöglichte deshalb gleichzeitig ihre Perpetuierung."
[507] Roper, *Witch Craze*, 133; Goodare, *The European Witch-Hunt*, 318–21; Midelfort, *Witch Hunting in Southwestern Germany*, 77; Behringer, *Hexenverfolgung in Bayern*, 336–38.
[508] Midelfort, *Witch Hunting in Southwestern Germany*, 154–57; Vöhringer-Rubröder, "Reichstadt Esslingen"; Jerouscheck, *Die Hexen und ihr Prozess*.

Other traditionally cautious towns like Rothenberg, Nurnberg, and Salzburg also only now experienced their most dramatic trials, while former hotspots like Mainz, Bamberg, and Würzburg remained largely unaffected. That the witchcraft concept still had the ability to cause much havoc is illustrated by the Lutheran town of Calw, southwestern Germany.[509] In 1683 an eleven-year-old boy accused an elderly woman of teaching him demonic witchcraft, while also naming children whom he allegedly saw at the sabbath. These children were pressed to tell what they knew, which provoked fanciful testimonies. A panic ensued, and parents guarded their children at night to prevent witches from approaching them. The town was rife with hatred and suspicion, with accusations becoming rampant. A few alleged witches were executed, and one woman was lynched by a mob. Higher authorities, however, responded differently. Calw fell under Württemberg rule, and an investigatory committee was installed that advised against further trials. In 1684 all talk about witchcraft was prohibited and a company of forty soldiers restored order.

Moeller's and Rummel's instrumentalist viewpoint might lead us to expect that an escalation was avoided because critics understood how accusers and persecutors instrumentalized the panic for their own hidden purposes. But that is not what happened. The religious and political authorities were certainly convinced of shrewd instrumentalization, but it was not the shrewdness of the accusers and persecutors that they thought to be dealing with. They interpreted the fears as genuine, and considered the panic harmful for both these people as well as the community. Still, it was thought to be the devil who cunningly benefited from all of it.[510] *He* created the dreams in children's minds and the subsequent delusions, so as to ruin the city and drive innocent people to their deaths. In response, preachers urged the populace not to fear witchcraft, but to be all the more on the alert for Satan's trickery and deception. So, even these relatively late critiques still fit nicely with the idea of the witch-hunting phenomenon being a "design" that overcame people, and spread at those people's own expense.

The pattern of late witch trials mostly occurring in regions and towns that had not been 'immunized' yet can be seen throughout the continent.[511] When west-central Europe became more resistant, witch-hunting moved towards the largely untainted outskirts of the western world. Having remained relatively unaffected so far, Poland and Hungary only experienced their historic peaks of witch-hunting in the late seventeenth and eighteenth centuries.[512] In Sweden, a wave of trials spread through many parts of the country between 1668 and 1676, killing over two hundred people.[513] Torture was rare, but children who were allegedly possessed by demons

---

[509] Midelfort, *Witch Hunting in Southwestern Germany*, 158–63; Walinski-Kiehl, "The Devil's Children," 177–78; Dillinger, *Kinder im Hexenprozess*, 117–23.
[510] Walinski-Kiehl, "The Devil's Children," 177–78; Dillinger, *Kinder im Hexenprozess*, 120–21; Midelfort, *Witch Hunting in Southwestern Germany*, 161–63.
[511] Goodare, *The European Witch-Hunt*, 318–21; Behringer, *Witches and Witch-Hunts*, 138–40, 185–90; Levack, *The Witch-Hunt in Early Modern Europe*, 207–8.
[512] Goodare, *The European Witch-Hunt*, 319.
[513] Behringer, *Witches and Witch-Hunts*, 138–39; Walinski-Kiehl, "The Devil's Children," 174.

produced elaborate confessions. They recounted stories about a mythical site called Blåkulla, where they attended a sumptuous witches' sabbath replete with dining and feasting. The children were not tried and did not have to fear punishment, which further enhanced the likelihood of denouncements. The old reproductive cycle of ideas triggering trials and trials triggering ideas still operated in this period. Due to their sensational character, news of the Swedish trials aroused international attention. The events reached a book on witchcraft published in 1681 by the English writer Joseph Glanvill, which then influenced a clergyman in New England, Cotton Mather, who helped initiate the renowned persecution of Salem in 1692.[514] In this town in colonial Massachusetts the ideal of the godly state was still vigorously pursued, and confessions by allegedly possessed children prompted a significant panic there. The use of spectral evidence, with the "specter" of witches purportedly appearing to children, resulted in numerous accusations and no less than nineteen executions.[515] Stories about Salem then reached a young girl in Scotland, who in 1696 then began to suffer from possession-like symptoms such as convulsions and torpor.[516] Here it helped initiate a set of trials resulting in seven executions.

However, such events on the fringes of the western world were amongst the last significant throes of European witch-hunting. In the eighteenth century the phenomenon still lingered on in some pockets – especially in Eastern Europe – but its end was inescapable.[517] In the context of the Enlightenment, Europe became a hostile environment. In 1612 Pierre de Lancre presaged that his witchcraft convictions would, at some point in the future, become "the most respected, as they are the most reflective of the law of God and of his Church."[518] The statement did not age well, as due to their obscure, zealous, and intolerant character, witch beliefs and trials became the ideal target for enlightened thinkers.[519] Proponents of persecution were attacked ever more openly and severely. Calls for trials remained prominent amongst peasants, but for the reproduction of witch-hunting that was perhaps more a curse than a blessing. The dismissal of witch beliefs became an elitist way of distinguishing oneself from the apparently backward populace.[520] Brian Levack: "The persistence of superstitious beliefs among the peasantry may have actually contributed, in a somewhat ironic way, to the triumph of skepticism among the elite."[521] Moreover, witch-hunting required "a mood of high seriousness", as Goodare puts in, and in that regard a lethal danger was on the rise: witch beliefs were

---

[514] Briggs, *Witches & Neighbours*, 55.
[515] Levack, *The Witch-Hunt in Early Modern Europe*, 202–3; Goodare, *The European Witch-Hunt*, 342; Behringer, *Witches and Witch-Hunts*, 145–46.
[516] Levack, *Witch-Hunting in Scotland*, 115–30; Behringer and Opitz-Belakhal, "Hexenkinder - Kinderbanden - Straßenkinder," 32.
[517] Behringer, *Witches and Witch-Hunts*, 138.
[518] Lancre, *On the Inconstancy of Witches*, 567.
[519] Dillinger, *Hexen und Magie*, 2018, 143; 185-90 Behringer, *Witches and Witch-Hunts*.
[520] Levack, *The Witch-Hunt in Early Modern Europe*, 240–45.
[521] Levack, 244.

increasingly ridiculed and satirized.[522] In mid-eighteenth century Bavaria the question of whether witchcraft existed still prompted a heated intellectual debate, in which a skeptical cleric stated before the Bavarian academy of sciences that "When reading old trial records and Delrio, this famous defender of witchcraft's existence, I could not stop myself from laughing about this hilarious flight of the witches."[523] Overall, as Stuart Clark has argued, witch beliefs lost their allies in the world of thought, just as those allies were losing theirs.[524] Country after country repealed its anti-witchcraft laws, and the phenomenon suffered a fate that it shares with almost all species of living nature: it failed to adapt to new circumstances and went extinct.[525]

Or did it? Witch trials indeed ended, but one could argue that the concept of witchcraft adapted to the new age, and is still vividly amongst us. The new evolutionary future that lay ahead already became apparent in 1697, when the French writer Charles Perrault included the witch figure in his collection of fairy tales, the *Histoires ou contes du temps passé* (Stories and Tales of Times Gone By). From that time onwards witches began to appear ever more prominently in fictional stories, often read to children.[526] Especially through the tales of the Grimm brothers and later the films of Disney, the witch turned into an iconic figure of the modern fairy tale world. Some elements of the early modern witch were preserved, like flight, cannibalism, evilness, and their normally female identity. But the new "environment" of fairy tales also produced new selection pressures. The adoration of the devil retreated, and a common new trope became the witch who lived solitarily in the forest, like the crone in the story about Hansel and Gretel. In the early modern period that variant would have been disastrous for witch-hunting's spread, hindering chains of accusations. But in the modern fairy tale environment it fitted nicely, so as to create a sense of mystery and horror that frightened children. Again, the developments are vaguely reminiscent of the evolution of pathogens. Some illnesses that once ravaged adult populations evolved into milder forms as childhood diseases.[527] So might we interpret the fairy tale witch as the cultural equivalent of a childhood disease? The question lies beyond the scope of this research. The topic here is the evolution of the witch-hunting phenomenon, and marked by that infamous trial of Anna Göldi in Glarus 1782, that phenomenon indeed went extinct. So, it is also here that our story ends.

---

[522] Goodare, *The European Witch-Hunt*, 346; Bever, "Witchcraft Prosecutions and the Decline of Magic," 281–82.
[523] Behringer, *Hexenverfolgung in Bayern*, 371-2."Ich habe mich des Lachens nicht enthalten können, als ich in dem berühmten Vertheidiger der hexerey, in dem Del Rio, oder in einem alten Hexenprocesse, die lustige Spazierfahrt der unholden gelesen habe".
[524] Clark, *Thinking with Demons*, 686.
[525] Levack, *The Witch-Hunt in Early Modern Europe*, 252–56.
[526] Goodare, *The European Witch-Hunt*, 346–47; Roper, *Witch Craze*, 251.
[527] McNeill, *Plagues and Peoples*, 50–51, 61, 117, 131, 140–41.

Conclusion

> To come very near to a true theory, and to grasp its precise application, are two very different things, as the history of science teaches us. Everything of importance has been said before by somebody who did not discover it.[1]
>
> - Alfred North Whitehead
>
> Most innovations are really just novel recombinations of existing ideas, techniques, or approaches; a tool is taken from one domain and applied in another.[2]
>
> - Joseph Henrich

If there is one theory that confirms these observations, it is Darwin's theory of evolution by natural selection. We saw that both the perceived outcomes of the evolutionary process, as well as its ingredients, had already been widely recognized before Darwin. Naturalists were perfectly aware that traits of living organisms are ingeniously adapted to environments. They also saw that organisms vary, that there is a reproduction of traits, and that most organisms quickly vanish in a relentless struggle for life. Hence, it might not be entirely surprising that it took so long before the relevance of Darwin's mechanism became widely appreciated by biologists. Was his mechanism not just a redescription of things that people knew all along, or a tautology that merely stated that what survives, survives, because it survives? However, what made Darwin's discovery of natural selection so important was not the recognition of its various ingredients; it was the understanding of the counter intuitive effect that these ingredients had *in combination*. Immanuel Kant professed that the mechanistic model of science would never explain the purposefulness of living nature. But that was exactly what Darwin did. His theory explains how a mindless and purposeless process can produce purposeful outcomes in the form of design without designer. This insight has helped unite the disciplines of the life sciences into a more consistent framework, and it set a fruitful research agenda that continues to this day.

These observations are important when assessing the future of Darwinian theory in the social sciences and the humanities. We started with Daniel Dennett's prediction of Darwinism being a "universal acid" that eats through any barrier it encounters. Old landmarks will still be recognizable, but transformed in fundamental ways. The focus here has been on qualitative history, which, so far, has hardly been affected by the universal acid's alleged transformative power. It raised my main question: can Darwinism renew qualitative history? Or does the theory

---

[1] Quoted in: Merton, *Social Theory and Social Structure*, 1.
[2] Henrich, *The WEIRDest People in the World*, 437.

face an impenetrable barrier after all, and will it fail to succeed, like so many earlier science-oriented approaches, in turning history into an integral part of the sciences? My answer has been that Darwinian theory does in fact hold the promise of revitalizing qualitative historical scholarship. This dissertation supports what many Darwinians claim today, namely that the theory can unite existing disciplines into a more consistent framework, while simultaneously producing new insights and research questions. Yet, it has also been argued that this transformative power is not so much built upon seeing things that nobody ever saw before, nor that "soft" qualitative methodologies will finally be made subservient to "hard" science. Instead, the prospects of Darwinism especially concern a recombination of ideas, tools, and empirical findings that were already available. Moreover, rather than making qualitative methodologies like hermeneutics or thick description compliant, it will give them a whole new relevance.

So how can Darwinism exactly renew the study of history? The programs of evolutionary psychology and gene-culture coevolution provide valid research agendas that shed new light on the evolved biological propensities of human behavior, and on the intriguing interactions between genes and culture. But at the same time, it has also been argued that these approaches have their limitations. Cultural phenomena possess a semi-autonomous dynamics of their own, which cannot be reduced to biological traits. Yet, through the idea of Darwinian *cultural* evolution, it is exactly the semi-autonomous "emergent" properties of culture to which Darwinism can contribute insights. Two crucial ideas took center stage in this dissertation. The first concerns the idea of a process of the selection and retention of accidentally adaptive cultural variants leading to cultural forms of "design without designer". The second idea states that those designs may be well-built to benefit no one, except the reproduction of those cultural forms themselves. Like certain "selfish" genes, or pathogens, some cultural phenomena may spread at the expense of their human hosts, as well as of their societies.

Some skeptics tend to see the new cultural Darwinism as old wine in new bottles, and indeed the upcoming field of cultural evolution makes claims that may remind us of older non-Darwinian approaches. For long, numerous social scientists and scholars of the humanities already argued that socio-cultural phenomena possess functional traits that seem unintended and unrecognized by the actors involved. Especially sociological and anthropological functionalism made it a key focus of attention, offering innumerable plausible examples. What many socio-cultural scholars also observed is that forms of culture vary, that they are reproduced, that some forms survive better than others, and that there is such a thing as unintended consequences. Yet, what had not been properly assessed so far is the counter intuitive outcome of these ingredients *in combination*. Critics of old-school functionalism righty pointed out that the movement failed to provide a credible explanation for how "latent functions" arise. Importantly, that is precisely what cultural Darwinism has to offer. Beliefs and practices may survive because of initially accidental effects that were neither intended nor recognized as such. Through the cumulative preservation of such cultural chance hits, cultural phenomena can indeed adapt to their environments outside of people's (sub)conscious awareness. This claim is neither vacuous nor tautological, as it sets a clear research agenda: can we find such hidden functions? Do certain cultural variants indeed persist because of effects that the involved actors did not perceive as such?

The question of who or what benefits from cultural phenomena also has old precedents. *Cui bono?* Who benefits? From that angle, the functionality of cultural forms has traditionally been sought in three major directions: the maintenance of social systems, the maintenance of power structures, and the fulfillments of individual needs. These approaches all have their merits, and the development of the field of cultural evolution shows that the advantages of these perspectives can potentially be integrated into a more consistent overarching Darwinian framework. The survival of a particular cultural variant can be due to multiple factors at the same time, and be different in each instance. This implies that the beneficiaries of a particular cultural form, like beliefs in the afterlife, can be multifaceted and subject to change. Where the theory of Darwinian cultural evolution has something genuinely new in store for us, is in the idea of culture reproducing "selfishly". Selfish gene theory in biology taught us that biological adaptations are best understood when we look at them from the perspective of the reproductive interests of the hereditary information – located on genes – behind those adaptations. This idea makes logical sense: genetic variants that instruct organisms to reproduce those particular variants will be most successful at exactly that. What authors like Dawkins, Dennett and Blackmore have brought forward, is that we may look at cultural information in a similar way. Cultural variants that make people spread those variants will be most successful in doing exactly that. What the comparison with harmful pathogens can further help us understand is that such reproduction may even continue when the human carriers and their societies are greatly harmed. This proposal is controversial, even within the field of cultural evolution. But again, it sets a clear research agenda: does the historical record provide examples of such phenomena?

In sum, the model of Darwinian cultural evolution does not have to throw away the strengths of older approaches. Many evolutionary theorists bring forward that human intentions remain a vitally important explanation for how socio-cultural functions arise – much culture contains forms of design *with* designers. Such directedness makes cultural evolution a less Darwinian process than the evolution of living nature. But since human (sub)conscious design seems insufficient an explanation for *all* adaptations, cultural Darwinism provides an indispensable outcome. Regarding the *cui bono* question, we saw that the theory does not remove older answers either. Rather, it arranges them into a more orderly toolkit, while adding a prodigious new tool to the set. What the cultural Darwinians have not sufficiently addressed so far, however, is the importance of qualitative historical tools. As a strongly quantitative field, current cultural evolution has little time for things like thick description, hermeneutics and *verstehen*, that is, the careful interpretation of how actors themselves perceive things, as well as the contextual meaning of symbols. This is a loss, since those tools are essentially important if we want to put the key Darwinian hypotheses to the test. The claim that actors often do not comprehend the functionality of many cultural assets requires detailed consideration of what actors did or did not understand in that regard. The hypothesis that cultural phenomena spread "selfishly" also requires careful attention to how involved actors themselves perceived the benefits of the cultural items they transmitted. Hence, the current Darwinian toolkit is badly in need of some qualitative methods. To see how this integration can be put into practice, this dissertation has delved into one case study: the European witch persecutions.

Regarding this case study, Whitehead's dictum proves applicable again. This thesis suggests that Darwinian theory can produce genuinely new insights about these infamous trials. Yet again, the newness is mostly built upon a rearrangement and recombination of insights and empirical findings that were already familiar to witchcraft scholarship – a high-quality historical field. One essential non-Darwinian insight that I made use of is that the early modern witch-hunt system has the semblance of an intelligent design. Contemporary critics of trials, like Johann Weyer, Hermann Witekind and Johann Meyfart, already made this observation, arguing that the devil was the evil genius behind it. A "subtle and devious spirit", a "sly fox", a "crafty old weaver", and a "jack-of-all-trades", the devil knew how to activate people's evil inclinations and lure them into a labyrinth of witch beliefs from which there was hardly any escape. Satan's ultimate goal was to make people suffer from the horrors of witch-hunting; innocent people were tortured and burned, while persecutors ruined their own salvation. Modern scholars obviously abandoned this diabolical interpretation, but the semblance of an intelligent design continued to attract attention. This time it was thought that the witch-hunt system contained "built-in structures" that were "fabricated", "braided", "designed", and "perfected" by the actors responsible for persecutions. Purportedly, it was the ruling classes, men, Catholic inquisitors, new city elites, or witch-hunt professionals who designed the system, so as to rob or oppress either the poor, women, the ordinary populace, the rich, or traditional peasant culture.

These commentators also had good reasons for assuming the existence of an underlying intelligent manufacture. Cumulative witchcraft beliefs, as they evolved over the course of the fifteenth to seventeenth centuries, indeed became remarkably well adapted to scaring the Europeans of the time. This was an era of widespread fears of diabolical evil, subversive anti-Christian communities, harmful magic of "village witches", uncontrollable female power and sexuality, as well as the hazards of illness and ecological disaster. Gradually, a cumulative concept of witchcraft ingeniously came to arrange these anxieties into something even more frightening. As it was told, the devil made a pact with people, women in particular, through sexual intercourse. He then formed anti-Christian communities with his witches, who met each other at perverse nightly gatherings, called witches' sabbaths, that were full of blasphemous rituals and sexual misconduct. To enable their attendance, Satan offered his witches the possibility of a nightly flight. Also, he gave them magical powers to harm ordinary Christians, for instance through causing illness, or extreme weather conditions that ruined harvests. Since these diabolical activities, as well as the identity of witches, normally remained concealed, it was difficult to find out who the witches were through ordinary investigatory means alone. So that would allow the use of torture to make people confess, and tell who else they had seen at the witches' sabbath. An additional option was to resort to the witness statements of alleged child witches, who were less hesitant in making confessions.

In combination, the elements of this "cumulative concept of witchcraft" developed a striking propensity for creating witch-hunts. If something bad happened under suspicious circumstances, like an unusual frost that ruined a harvest, people might think of diabolical witches as culprits. If one alleged witch had then been found, like a local "village witch" or a child full of fanciful testimonies, a chain of accusations could start. Torture subsequently had the potential of producing confessions about an ever widening circle of alleged sabbath accomplices. During an escalating panic the danger of witchcraft might appear even worse than anticipated. Chains of accusations could also spread over long distances, since the belief in the nightly flight implied that witches knew sabbath accomplices who lived far away. So, in combination, this amalgam of ideas had the ability of mobilizing people's deepest fears, and to create the dynamics of an intensifying and "contagious" persecution. Hence, no wonder both contemporary critics, as well as many modern observers, assumed an underlying intelligent plan.

However, over the past decades many historians like Erik Midelfort, Wolfgang Behringer, Johannes Dillinger, Robin Briggs and Julian Goodare have concluded that there do not seem to have been such shrewd designers involved. Detailed scrutiny of how concepts of witchcraft developed, and how they instigated trials, indicate a rather unplanned process. Reflections on the course of events often only occurred after the scale of new trials had become apparent. Moreover, had there been shrewd underlying designers or motivations involved, we should expect quite regular patterns of persecution, with some groups being targeted rather than others. But trials occurred quite haphazardly, while it was highly diverse who took the initiative and who became the victims. There were for instance complex interactions between rulers and popular classes, in which no party really seems to have been in charge. True, females were pointedly overrepresented amongst the victims – misogyny and the unequal power balance between the sexes were an important part of the picture. But a significant minority of victims still consisted of men, which makes oppression of women an unlikely ultimate aim. Moreover, the effects of witch-hunts were often damaging for all and everyone. Persecutions were expensive, they disrupted communities, and in quite a few cases even the people who perpetrated trials were burned as witches themselves. Many experts today thus conclude that witch-hunting was not a means to a hidden end. Driven forward by a genuine belief in the danger of witchcraft, it was mostly an end in itself. But if this is so, how did the concept of witchcraft become so well adapted to create ever new witch trials? And if the actors involved were so often harmed, why did the phenomenon spread for such a long time?

To explain this, the Darwinian theory of cultural evolution is indispensable. The hypothesis that has been developed in this thesis is as follows: many cultural variants regarding witchcraft appeared, most of which did not reproduce well. However, every now and then variants appeared, or recombined, that *accidentally* created larger, more persistent and more "infectious" witch trials. The size of those persecutions then made those variants receive wide attention, and enter many new minds. Later on, this wider dissemination produced similar persecutions in other places. So, it was through repeated rounds of selection and accumulation that the beliefs about witchcraft evolved into an ever more "virulent" concept. Whether the actors involved understood how certain ideas or practices enhanced the spread of witch-hunting, or whether they themselves or their societies benefited from it, does not necessarily matter. The "designer" may well have been the blind process of Darwinian evolution, while the key beneficiary involved was potentially the witch-hunting phenomenon itself. Some historians have already made remarks about self-enhancing interactions between what people believed about witches, how this affected trials, and vice versa. Yet, within a Darwinian framework such isolated observations can be turned into a more consistent explanation, that also lends itself to further empirical study. Did innumerable variants regarding witchcraft indeed appear, only to lose the "struggle for survival"? Did some of the crucial notions about witchcraft, like the sabbath, nightly flight and the child witch, indeed create larger witch-hunts, and then reproduce because of that effect? Did the actors who introduced and maintained those variants understand their enhancing effect, and broadcast those elements for that reason? These questions have not been properly examined yet. So, whatever one might think of cultural Darwinian theory, it at least has the ability to generate new research questions.

To examine the proposed scenario, I especially delved into German trials in the period between 1560 and 1630. This was the time and place where witch-hunting experienced its most significant growth. Mostly by examining historical studies already available, I especially looked at the persecution of Wiesensteig in 1562, the trials of the Trier region around 1590, and the Ellwangen hunt from 1611-1618. As it turned out, it was mostly due to quite accidental causes, like previous panics about anabaptists, weak rulership, or weather disasters, as well as some highly specific cultural variants, like child accusations, an attack on rich witches, or beliefs in huge sabbaths, that these hunts became unusually large. But it was precisely because of their size that those persecutions received most attention, with their cultural variants thus becoming more prevalent. What I further studied is the alleged "struggle for life" between elements of culture, and indeed I found a wide range of less successful variants. Think of notions about alleged supernatural events during witch burnings, or details about sabbaths that were too trivial and inconsequential for becoming a reproductive success. Hence, paraphrasing Darwin we might say that the cultural evolutionary process was daily and hourly scrutinizing every variation, even the slightest; rejecting that which was bad, preserving and combining all that was good; silently and insensibly working, whenever and wherever opportunity offered, at the improvement of the witchcraft concept.

Yet, a thorough engagement with primary sources, like pamphlets, sermons, treatises, chronicles and witch-hunt manuals, also shows that we should not routinely assume that involved actors were unaware of how certain aspects of witch-hunting worked. The most striking case is the witch-hunt supporter Jean Bodin. In his *Démonomanie des sorciers* from 1580 he showed much understanding of how cultural elements like the witches' sabbath, the child witch, or torture could be used in trials to enforce many confessions. He also broadcasted those notions for that reason. The work of other contemporaries – proponents and opponents of trials alike – further indicate that many functional features of the witch-hunt system were already understood at the time. Theorists of cultural evolution should thus not too quickly presuppose incognizant actors; if possible, one should always try to examine what people comprehended or not. Neither should we too easily assume that there were no human beneficiaries involved. The model of multifunctional instrumentalization, as developed by several German historians like Rita Voltmer and Walter Rummel, can be of value here. Instead of older and rather cynical approaches that postulated just one or a few underlying aims, these historians argue that witchcraft accusations and trials were instrumentalized, in each instance, for a different set of hidden purposes. Examples include getting rid of enemies, career opportunities, or the enhancement of power. They further maintain that we should not so much think of plain cynicism, but of ulterior motives amalgamating with genuine belief. This interpretation to some extent corresponds to the sources, as people at the time also presumed that such instrumentalization was possible. Proponents of trials said that it was a risk, while opponents said that it really happened. Overall, it seems far from unlikely that such underlying purposes indeed played a role, at least every now and then.

However, this research also produced many results that offer support for the idea of "blind" evolution, with the witch-hunting phenomenon spreading in a pathogen-like way. One finding is that there were notable limitations to what contemporaries seem to have understood about what made cumulative notions of witchcraft so inflammatory. The levels of comprehension of Bodin appear to have been quite unique. Other influential supporters, Kramer, Binsfeld or Förner for instance, do not seem to have grasped how the idea of large witches' sabbaths could be used to stimulate large chains of accusations. The contemporary understanding of the incendiary role of flight or of child witches also appears limited at best. So, overall, human intention and recognition seem insufficient an explanation for the adaptedness of the witch-hunting phenomenon. Darwinian selection comes forward as the indispensable additional explanation.

Moreover, the model of multifunctional instrumentalization also has its flaws. Supporters of trials consistently said that they hunted witches in order to eradicate witches. So how to prove that there were actually different motivations at play? True, critics at the time regularly said that the trials were used for ulterior purposes. But generally, those critics paid far more attention to the idea of Satan being the crucial designer and beneficiary of it all. Contemporary opponents argued that the people responsible for witch-hunts were exploited by something beyond themselves. It was Satan who operated as the invisible puppeteer, with the witch-hunters being his marionettes. Persecutors had been stupid enough to let themselves be tricked by the devil, who then made them do things that not only harmed others, but also those persecutors' own interests. While this contemporary interpretation is not in line with the German instrumentalist model, is does bear a striking semblance to the Darwinian proposal made in this dissertation. It was the most surprising empirical finding of this research: sharp-minded contemporaries also thought that the witch-hunt system tricked people, turning those people into instruments for a purpose that did not align with their own purposes. But instead of the perceived sinister agency of Satan, the proposal made here is that the "agency" of a cultural "pathogen" was involved, ingeniously adapted to survive for another day. So, it was not the devil, but the virus-like cultural phenomenon that operated as the hidden "puppeteer".

Historians have already compared witch-hunts to contagious disease innumerable times, and for good reasons. There were "outbreaks" of witch-hunting, with towns "infecting" other towns, and many casualties as a result. Yet, the comparison has only been used as a figure of speech. But why not take it more seriously? Many aspects of the witch-hunting phenomenon seemed to defy all functionalist analysis. Even after we throw together numerous known functionalist perspectives, as the German multifunctionalists did, much of the phenomenon remains mysterious. Witchcraft beliefs and trials often appear to have been *dys*functional for all and everyone, and to have contained innumerable superfluous details. Yet, as soon as we look at it from the perspective of the virus-like reproductive interests of the witch-hunting phenomenon itself, all these aspects suddenly make a lot of functional sense. The diabolical pact, the sabbath, nightly flight, harmful magic, child witches, torture, or the escalating accusations, were all wonderfully adapted to ensure witch-hunting's own "selfish" spread. The socially transmitted information that we call culture, which is physically located in human brains and artefacts, can use human carriers for its own reproductive purposes. Hence, through their apparently sincere belief in the righteousness of what they were doing, the people responsible for witch trials appear to have let themselves be overtaken by a nasty cultural "parasite".

This approach will appear outlandish to many historians. But importantly, it can be easily reconciled with key features of traditional qualitative history. Several German persecutions have been presented here in the form of a chronological story, as a narrative. Doing this was important because it helped us comprehend how witchcraft concepts developed, how trials occurred, and also how actors experienced things and then acted upon those experiences. Emile Durkheim once dismissively wrote that the historians' focus on "series of accidents" hindered scientific progress. But for this Darwinian approach such accidents and events remain crucial. It is in the innumerable small-scale and rather accidental incidences that the creative source of Darwinian cultural evolution must be sought. This further illustrates how Darwinism is both a nomothetic and idiographic theory, studying the general and the particular at the same time. Concepts of witchcraft, and the ways in which trials unfolded, were continually changing and adapting to particular circumstances, with the witch-hunting phenomenon lacking any timeless "essence". Neither does the theory imply determinism. In this dissertation I especially traced how the concept of witchcraft became so well adapted that it enabled the huge persecutions of the late 1620s, as for instance occurred in Bamberg. But nothing of that is to say that it *had* to evolve in that direction. Had the climate not deteriorated, had religious strife not been as intense, or had Germany not remained as politically fragmented, the phenomenon would probably not have grown so huge. Contingency and complexity remain essential. Yet, most importantly, the proposed Darwinian approach still requires qualitative methods. It creates a new relevance for interpreting the symbolic world that actors were living in, to re-create their thoughts in our own minds, and to carefully consider what historical sources can, or cannot, reveal to us today.

This is not an argument about an "unconditional surrender" of history to science, but about a new qualitative research agenda that lies ahead. The empirical questions regarding witch trials raised in this thesis deserve more detailed scrutiny. Can we uncover further examples of cultural variants that did not survive well? Do additional sources tell us more about what people did, or did not, comprehend about the functional features of the witch-hunt system? How did other contemporary critics, not studied here, address the question of who benefited? What is more, one essential type of source material has only been assessed here through the accounts of other historians, namely trial records. These documents are difficult to study, as they normally lie in local archives and require paleographic expertise. But surely they are bound to contain further clues regarding the key questions asked. Plausibly, they may also provide further hints on how the victims of persecutions, who were predominantly female, experienced what happened to them, and what role they played. Of course, we can only hear their voices through the writings of interrogators, but the records will still likely provide us with additional insights. What, for instance, was the role of suspects in the creation and spread of conspicuous new variants, like the idea of rich witches, or of large sabbaths?

Moreover, this qualitative Darwinian approach, and the idea of "selfish" culture, can be applied to a multitude of further case studies other than the witch-hunt. We might think of other topics of early modern history that we only touched upon, like the fanaticism of the religious wars, anti-Semitism, apocalyptic anxieties, or the self-destructiveness of certain anabaptist sects. Another obvious area of future research is non-western forms of witch-hunting. Can the viral analogy also help us better understand how those persecutions evolved? In addition, we should think of cultural phenomena in today's world. Current conspiracy theories are a plausible candidate. The QAnon conspiracy theory, for instance, effectively taps into key anxieties of our time, like pedophile networks and corrupted politicians. Or take the widespread practice of overwork. Are many people so immersed in overwork because they and their societies benefit from it? Or is this cultural practice especially well-built for self-reproduction, irrespective of its mental and social consequences, like burn-outs? And what to think of woke ideology? Does it solely serve the emancipation of disadvantaged groups, or is it also well adapted to set people against each other, and to spread through the discord and publicity that it engenders? In other words, new investigatory vistas can be opened up.

This is also where the theory carries the promise of enhancing human welfare. "If we *are* the slaves of some of 'our' cultural traits, isn't it time we knew it?", Ted Cloak rightly asked. Considering the pervasiveness of biological pathogens, it is surely worth the effort to probe whether cultural equivalents indeed exist. And if we conclude that they do exist in greater number, it would be urgently necessary to better understand their ways. Perhaps it could help us disarm some of culture's nasty tricks, of which the witch trials provide us such a horrifying example. If the study of cultural "pathogens" would emulate only a fraction of the successes in our medical fight against biological pathogens, the efforts would already be worth their weight in gold. At the same time, we must proceed carefully. Like most microorganisms, most forms of culture are probably neutral or beneficial for their human carriers. So, when adopting the selfish culture hypothesis there is a risk of becoming overly paranoid about our culture, seeing harmful cultural "pathogens" under every rock. It might make us eradicate forms of culture that actually benefit us. So, also in that regard, let us always keep the merits of other viewpoints on the *cui bono* question in mind. Hopefully, the selfish culture hypothesis will eventually sharpen our understanding of how culture works, and enable us to make better decisions on what forms of culture to remove, and what forms to cherish.

But most of all, the aim here was a scientific one. It has been argued that Darwinian theory, despite all the nuances like the importance of human intentions, indeed has features of a "universal acid" that carries the promise of revitalizing qualitative historical scholarship. Most essentially, it can help us realize that many social scientists and scholars of the humanities have overestimated human capabilities. Our socio-cultural structures and webs of meaning were not only created and spun by ourselves. To a large extent, it was blind Darwinian evolution that did the creative work. More ominously, these hidden evolutionary processes do not necessarily work out well for us. At least in some cases culture may be adapted to exploit our vulnerabilities and turn us into instruments for its own propagation. The case study of the European witch persecutions has shown how this theory provides a whole new perspective in the study of history. Experts on the witch-hunts have been looking for the beneficiaries of this horrific phenomenon in every nook and cranny, but failed to find them in substantial numbers. But apparently this was because one crucial beneficiary has been overlooked all the time: the witch-hunting phenomenon itself.

Ritchie, David G. *Darwin and Hegel and Other Philosophical Studies*. Edited by Peter P. Nicholson. Vol. 2. Collected Works of D.G. Ritchie. Bristol: Bristol Thoemmes, 1998.

———. "Social Evolution." *International Journal of Ethics* 6, no. 2 (1896): 165–81.

Ritzer, George. *Contemporary Sociological Theory and Its Classical Roots: The Basics*. 2nd ed. New York: McGraw-Hill, 2007.

———. "Sociology: A Multi Paradigm Science." *The American Sociologist* 10, no. 3 (August 1975): 156–67.

Robbins, Rossell Hope. *The Encyclopedia of Witchcraft and Demonology*. New York: Crown, 1959.

Robert Aunger. *Darwinizing Culture: The Status of Memetics as a Science*. Oxford: Oxford University Press, 2001.

Robisheaux, Thomas. "The German Witch Trials." In *Oxford Handbook of Witchcraft in Early Modern Europe and North America*, by Brian P. Levack, 179–98. Oxford: Oxford University Press, 2013.

Rogers, Deborah S., and Paul R. Ehrlich. "Natural Selection and Cultural Rates of Change" 105, no. 9 (2008): 3416–20.

Roper, Lyndal. *Witch Craze: Terror and Fantasy in Baroque Germany*. New Haven: Yale University Press, 2006.

Rorty, Richard. *Objectivity, Relativism, and Truth: Philosophical Papers*. Cambridge: Cambridge University Press, 1990.

———. *Philosophy and Social Hope*. London: Penguin Books, 1999.

Rose, Hilary, and Steven Rose. *Alas Poor Darwin: Arguments Against Evolutionary Psychology*. London: Random House, 2010.

Rose, Nikolas. "The Human Sciences in a Biological Age." *Theory, Culture & Society* 30, no. 1 (2013): 3–34.

Rose, Steven. Richard Dawkins interviews Steven Rose. Youtube, November 25, 2012. https://www.youtube.com/watch?v=QceGqKZMqIM.

———. "The Biology of the Future and the Future of Biology." In *Explanations: : Styles of Explanation in Science*, by John Cornwell, 125–43. Oxford: Oxford University Press, 2004.

Rose, Steven P. R. *Lifelines: Biology, Freedom, Determinism*. London: Vintage, 2005.

Rosenau, Pauline Marie. *Post-Modernism and the Social Sciences: Insights, Inroads, and Intrusions*. Princeton NJ: Greenwood Publishing Group, 1992.

Rosenberg, Karen R., and Wenda Trevathan. "Birth, Obstetrics and Human Evolution." *BJOG: An International Journal of Obstetrics & Gynaecology* 109, no. 11 (November 1, 2002): 1199–1206.

———. *Costly and Cute Helpless Infants and Human Evolution*. Santa Fe: University of New Mexico Press, 2016.

Rovers, Frits. *"Dan liever de lucht in!": Jan van Speijk en de Belgische Opstand*. Verloren verleden ; dl. 12. Hilversum: Verloren, 2000.

Rowlands, Alison. "Nuss, Balthasar (1545-1618)." In *Encyclopedia of Witchcraft: The Western Tradition*, III:842–43. Santa Barbara: ABC-CLIO, 2006.

———. "Witchcraft and Gender in Early Modern Europe." In *The Oxford Handbook of Witchcraft in Early Modern Europe and Colonial America*, by Levack, 449–67. Oxford: Oxford University Press, 2013.

www.ingramcontent.com/pod-product-compliance
Lightning Source LLC
LaVergne TN
LVHW011927070526
838202LV00054B/4521